barbri ®

BAR REVIEW

MPQ2

Practice Questions Volume 2

D1473506

MULTISTATE TESTING

To be used in conjunction with the Summer 2008
and Winter 2009 BAR/BRI Bar Review Courses

THOMSON
™
BAR/BRI

BAR/BRI gratefully acknowledges the assistance of the National Conference of Bar Examiners in granting permission to reprint the following released Multistate questions, which have appeared on actual Multistate Bar Examinations. Released questions copyright © 1983, 1987, 1990 by the National Conference of Bar Examiners and Educational Testing Service. All rights reserved.

MULTISTATE PRACTICE EXAM: All Questions *except* 1, 4, 5, 6, 7, 8, 9, 11, 14, 20, 21, 22, 23, 24, 26, 27, 28, 31, 32, 34, 35, 36, 37, 40, 44, 45, 48, 50, 56, 59, 61, 62, 65, 66, 67, 68, 71, 72, 76, 79, 91, 92, 93, 96, 97, 99, 100, 101, 103, 104, 105, 106, 109, 111, 112, 113, 114, 119, 120, 121, 122, 125, 126, 132, 138, 139, 140, 142, 151, 155, 156, 161, 162, 163, 164, 166, 168, 172, 173, 174, 178, 179, 180, 184, 187, 190, 192, 194, 196, 198, 199, 200

RELEASED MULTISTATE QUESTIONS: All Questions

All other questions and *all* analytical answers were prepared by BAR/BRI.

SUMMARY OF CONTENTS

HOW TO USE THE MULTISTATE TESTING BOOKS

Three books comprise BAR/BRI Multistate Testing: Practice Questions Volume 1, Practice Questions Volume 2, and the Simulated MBE Book.

The two Practice Questions books together contain over 2,000 MBE-type multiple choice questions. However, we do ***NOT*** recommend that you do all of the questions offered, ***especially at the expense of reading the outlines and working on essay questions.*** Your course will probably provide a Paced Program™ with specific assignments from these books, or you can follow the suggested approach below to focus your MBE preparation. The questions for the first two steps below are in Volume 1, which has more detailed instructions for these steps.

Step 1: Do the ***Workshop Testing Drills***, the section with the shaded margins at the front of Volume 1. After completing the questions in a subject, access the corresponding MBE Workshop Testing Drills lecture, available on DVD or in the Enrolled Student Center on the BAR/BRI website, to review the questions and learn test-taking techniques for that subject.

Step 2: Do the ***Question Sets*** arranged by subject in Volume 1. You can also do these questions using the BAR/BRI StudySmart® software—choose the Paced Program mode in the software to do the questions arranged by question set.

Step 3: Once you have had the substantive lectures on all six MBE subjects, your course will administer the ***Simulated MBE*** (in the Simulated MBE Book) under timed conditions. BAR/BRI strongly recommends that you take this exam when it is scheduled by your course. There is no substitute for experiencing the time pressures imposed by a pace of 1.8 minutes per question.

Step 4: For additional exposure to questions in a mixed subject format, you can do the two Mixed Question Sets in Volume 1, the ***Half Day Practice Exam*** in this book, and/or the ***Full Day Practice Exam*** in this book. If you can, do these questions under exam time conditions; *e.g.*, for the Half Day Exam, set aside a three-hour block of time and try to answer that set of questions within that time period. You also may wish to analyze some of the ***Released Questions*** if you are looking for additional questions to review, but remember that these older questions may not be as representative as the newer questions developed by BAR/BRI.

Step 5: ***Don't panic.*** The MBE is not an easy exam, but you can miss a lot of questions and still get a passing score. As long as you keep on a reasonable schedule and use BAR/BRI's suggested approach for working through the questions, you will be prepared for the MBE.

BAR REVIEW

*Half Day Practice Exam
and Analytical Answers*

Multistate Practice Exam

HALF DAY EXAM

Time—3 hours

You will be given three hours to work on this test. Be sure that the question numbers on your answer sheet match the question numbers in your test book. You are not to begin work until the supervisor tells you to do so.

Your score will be based on the number of questions you answer correctly. It is therefore to your advantage to try to answer as many questions as you can. Give only one answer to each question; multiple answers will not be counted. If you wish to change an answer, erase your first mark completely and mark your new choice. Use your time effectively. Do not hurry, but work steadily and as quickly as you can without sacrificing your accuracy.

YOU ARE TO INDICATE YOUR ANSWERS TO ALL QUESTIONS ON THE SEPARATE ANSWER SHEET PROVIDED.

DIRECTIONS

Each of the questions or incomplete statements in this test is followed by four suggested answers or completions. You are to choose the **best** of the stated alternatives. Answer all questions according to the generally accepted view, except where otherwise noted.

For the purpose of this test, you are to assume that Articles 1 and 2 of the Uniform Commercial Code have been adopted. You are also to assume relevant application of Article 9 of the U.C.C. concerning fixtures. The Federal Rules of Evidence are deemed to control.

The terms "Constitution," "constitutional," and "unconstitutional" refer to the federal Constitution unless indicated to the contrary.

You are also to assume that there is no applicable statute unless otherwise specified; however, survival actions and claims for wrongful death should be assumed to be available where applicable. You should assume that joint and several liability, with comparative negligence, is the relevant rule unless otherwise indicated.

DO NOT OPEN THE TEST UNTIL
YOU ARE INSTRUCTED TO DO SO.

ANSWER SHEET (HALF DAY EXAM)

1. Ⓐ Ⓑ Ⓒ Ⓓ	26. Ⓐ Ⓑ Ⓒ Ⓓ	51. Ⓐ Ⓑ Ⓒ Ⓓ	76. Ⓐ Ⓑ Ⓒ Ⓓ
2. Ⓐ Ⓑ Ⓒ Ⓓ	27. Ⓐ Ⓑ Ⓒ Ⓓ	52. Ⓐ Ⓑ Ⓒ Ⓓ	77. Ⓐ Ⓑ Ⓒ Ⓓ
3. Ⓐ Ⓑ Ⓒ Ⓓ	28. Ⓐ Ⓑ Ⓒ Ⓓ	53. Ⓐ Ⓑ Ⓒ Ⓓ	78. Ⓐ Ⓑ Ⓒ Ⓓ
4. Ⓐ Ⓑ Ⓒ Ⓓ	29. Ⓐ Ⓑ Ⓒ Ⓓ	54. Ⓐ Ⓑ Ⓒ Ⓓ	79. Ⓐ Ⓑ Ⓒ Ⓓ
5. Ⓐ Ⓑ Ⓒ Ⓓ	30. Ⓐ Ⓑ Ⓒ Ⓓ	55. Ⓐ Ⓑ Ⓒ Ⓓ	80. Ⓐ Ⓑ Ⓒ Ⓓ
6. Ⓐ Ⓑ Ⓒ Ⓓ	31. Ⓐ Ⓑ Ⓒ Ⓓ	56. Ⓐ Ⓑ Ⓒ Ⓓ	81. Ⓐ Ⓑ Ⓒ Ⓓ
7. Ⓐ Ⓑ Ⓒ Ⓓ	32. Ⓐ Ⓑ Ⓒ Ⓓ	57. Ⓐ Ⓑ Ⓒ Ⓓ	82. Ⓐ Ⓑ Ⓒ Ⓓ
8. Ⓐ Ⓑ Ⓒ Ⓓ	33. Ⓐ Ⓑ Ⓒ Ⓓ	58. Ⓐ Ⓑ Ⓒ Ⓓ	83. Ⓐ Ⓑ Ⓒ Ⓓ
9. Ⓐ Ⓑ Ⓒ Ⓓ	34. Ⓐ Ⓑ Ⓒ Ⓓ	59. Ⓐ Ⓑ Ⓒ Ⓓ	84. Ⓐ Ⓑ Ⓒ Ⓓ
10. Ⓐ Ⓑ Ⓒ Ⓓ	35. Ⓐ Ⓑ Ⓒ Ⓓ	60. Ⓐ Ⓑ Ⓒ Ⓓ	85. Ⓐ Ⓑ Ⓒ Ⓓ
11. Ⓐ Ⓑ Ⓒ Ⓓ	36. Ⓐ Ⓑ Ⓒ Ⓓ	61. Ⓐ Ⓑ Ⓒ Ⓓ	86. Ⓐ Ⓑ Ⓒ Ⓓ
12. Ⓐ Ⓑ Ⓒ Ⓓ	37. Ⓐ Ⓑ Ⓒ Ⓓ	62. Ⓐ Ⓑ Ⓒ Ⓓ	87. Ⓐ Ⓑ Ⓒ Ⓓ
13. Ⓐ Ⓑ Ⓒ Ⓓ	38. Ⓐ Ⓑ Ⓒ Ⓓ	63. Ⓐ Ⓑ Ⓒ Ⓓ	88. Ⓐ Ⓑ Ⓒ Ⓓ
14. Ⓐ Ⓑ Ⓒ Ⓓ	39. Ⓐ Ⓑ Ⓒ Ⓓ	64. Ⓐ Ⓑ Ⓒ Ⓓ	89. Ⓐ Ⓑ Ⓒ Ⓓ
15. Ⓐ Ⓑ Ⓒ Ⓓ	40. Ⓐ Ⓑ Ⓒ Ⓓ	65. Ⓐ Ⓑ Ⓒ Ⓓ	90. Ⓐ Ⓑ Ⓒ Ⓓ
16. Ⓐ Ⓑ Ⓒ Ⓓ	41. Ⓐ Ⓑ Ⓒ Ⓓ	66. Ⓐ Ⓑ Ⓒ Ⓓ	91. Ⓐ Ⓑ Ⓒ Ⓓ
17. Ⓐ Ⓑ Ⓒ Ⓓ	42. Ⓐ Ⓑ Ⓒ Ⓓ	67. Ⓐ Ⓑ Ⓒ Ⓓ	92. Ⓐ Ⓑ Ⓒ Ⓓ
18. Ⓐ Ⓑ Ⓒ Ⓓ	43. Ⓐ Ⓑ Ⓒ Ⓓ	68. Ⓐ Ⓑ Ⓒ Ⓓ	93. Ⓐ Ⓑ Ⓒ Ⓓ
19. Ⓐ Ⓑ Ⓒ Ⓓ	44. Ⓐ Ⓑ Ⓒ Ⓓ	69. Ⓐ Ⓑ Ⓒ Ⓓ	94. Ⓐ Ⓑ Ⓒ Ⓓ
20. Ⓐ Ⓑ Ⓒ Ⓓ	45. Ⓐ Ⓑ Ⓒ Ⓓ	70. Ⓐ Ⓑ Ⓒ Ⓓ	95. Ⓐ Ⓑ Ⓒ Ⓓ
21. Ⓐ Ⓑ Ⓒ Ⓓ	46. Ⓐ Ⓑ Ⓒ Ⓓ	71. Ⓐ Ⓑ Ⓒ Ⓓ	96. Ⓐ Ⓑ Ⓒ Ⓓ
22. Ⓐ Ⓑ Ⓒ Ⓓ	47. Ⓐ Ⓑ Ⓒ Ⓓ	72. Ⓐ Ⓑ Ⓒ Ⓓ	97. Ⓐ Ⓑ Ⓒ Ⓓ
23. Ⓐ Ⓑ Ⓒ Ⓓ	48. Ⓐ Ⓑ Ⓒ Ⓓ	73. Ⓐ Ⓑ Ⓒ Ⓓ	98. Ⓐ Ⓑ Ⓒ Ⓓ
24. Ⓐ Ⓑ Ⓒ Ⓓ	49. Ⓐ Ⓑ Ⓒ Ⓓ	74. Ⓐ Ⓑ Ⓒ Ⓓ	99. Ⓐ Ⓑ Ⓒ Ⓓ
25. Ⓐ Ⓑ Ⓒ Ⓓ	50. Ⓐ Ⓑ Ⓒ Ⓓ	75. Ⓐ Ⓑ Ⓒ Ⓓ	100. Ⓐ Ⓑ Ⓒ Ⓓ

Question 1

Oswald owned an old, unoccupied, and extremely run-down building in Hooverville. The walls were unstable and beginning to buckle. Oswald knew of the building's condition, but he did not want to spend the money needed to repair it and hoped that the Hooverville Redevelopment Commission would want his land to build a shopping mall.

Timmy was a driver for U-Pump-It Tanker Lines, a concern that operated tanker trucks that delivered gasoline to filling stations. U-Pump-It's rules required drivers to park only in legally designated parking areas. After completing his deliveries for the day in Hooverville, Timmy stopped for a cup of coffee. He did not want to spend time trying to find a parking place on a side street, so he parked in front of Oswald's building, which was located on a through street. The area in front of Oswald's building was clearly marked, "No Parking At Any Time." Timmy walked to the Emporium Restaurant, where he ordered coffee and the daily special.

Hooverville was located in an area subject to minor earthquake activity. Just as Timmy began his lunch, a quake jolted Hooverville. The quake was not strong enough to cause damage to structurally sound buildings, but was sufficient to cause the walls of Oswald's building to collapse. The building fell on top of the U-Pump-It truck, causing the truck to roll over on its side. Gasoline leaked from the truck and began streaming down the street. Elvira, a pedestrian walking two blocks away, lit a cigarette and casually tossed a match in the street. The stream of gasoline had just reached that street and the match caused the gasoline to ignite. The flames spread to a nearby commercial building. An explosion occurred, causing many windows in a neighboring apartment building to be blown inward. Flying glass was propelled into Bonnie's apartment. Bonnie suffered multiple cuts and a serious eye injury from the flying glass.

Bonnie brings a negligence action against U-Pump-It Tanker Lines. If the court finds in favor of U-Pump-It, it will be because:

(A) The court follows the Cardozo view regarding foreseeable plaintiffs.

(B) Timmy was acting outside the scope of his employment when Bonnie was injured.

(C) Oswald was the legal cause of Bonnie's injuries because his building was in an unreasonably dangerous condition.

(D) The company had a rule against illegal parking on streets.

Question 2

Olivia and Scarlet were roommates who both attended a prestigious fashion design school. When Olivia had received her acceptance letter from the school, she splurged and purchased a new Scandervan 2001 sewing machine for $1,000 so that she would be more than adequately equipped for her design assignments. One day when Olivia was at class, Scarlet loaned Olivia's sewing machine to Violet, whose own machine lacked the fancy options of the Scandervan 2001. Scarlet had loaned Olivia's Scandervan 2001 to other design students on several prior occasions. Unfortunately, Violet, who was not familiar with the delicate Scandervan 2001, caused extensive damage to the machine when she tried to create a cutting edge design by sewing silverware on a dress. It would cost $400 to repair the sewing machine.

If Olivia sues Scarlet for the damage Violet caused to the sewing machine, what will be the result?

(A) Olivia will recover $1,000.

(B) Olivia will recover the fair market value of the sewing machine.

(C) Olivia will recover $400.

(D) Olivia will recover nothing, because Scarlet did not damage the machine and Violet's conduct was not intentional.

GO ON TO THE NEXT PAGE

Question 3

Orbison owned Rockacre, but was badly in need of ready cash. He conveyed Rockacre to Presley, who put the deed in his guitar case and took off for a three-week tour of the Orient. Orbison knew that Presley had left town, and Orbison still found himself strapped for money. He offered to sell Rockacre to Madonna for $5,000. Although Madonna had heard Presley say he had bought Rockacre, Madonna thought $5,000 was a terrific price for the property. She paid Orbison $5,000 and received a deed from him, which she promptly recorded. Madonna subsequently conveyed Rockacre to Fats for $15,000. Fats knew nothing about Presley's deed and Fats promptly recorded the deed from Madonna. Two weeks later, upon his return from the Orient, Presley recorded his deed to Rockacre. A month after that, Fats conveyed Rockacre to Chubby for $17,000. Chubby knew that Presley held a deed to Rockacre, but paid Fats $17,000 anyway. Chubby immediately recorded and filed an appropriate action against Presley and against Fats to determine ownership of Rockacre. Assume that Rockacre is situated in a state with the following statute:

> No conveyance or mortgage of an interest in land is valid against any subsequent purchaser for value without notice thereof whose conveyance is first recorded.

The court will most likely rule that:

(A) Presley has superior rights to both Fats and Chubby.

(B) Fats has superior rights to both Presley and Chubby.

(C) Chubby has superior rights to both Presley and Fats.

(D) Chubby has superior rights to Fats, but Presley has superior rights to Chubby.

Question 4

In which of the following situations is the offered evidence most likely to be admitted?

(A) In Paula's action against David for assault, David offers the testimony of Walter, a surprise witness who, it was just discovered, witnessed the altercation between Paula and David; when questioned by the judge, David's counsel agrees to permit a continuance following Walter's testimony so that Paula will have time to prepare for cross-examination of Walter.

(B) In Peter's negligence action against Dolores arising from an accident in which a 2004 Camaro struck Peter while he crossed Main Street at a crosswalk, Peter offers the testimony of Winchell, the owner of a garage, who will state that Dolores arranged to have the brakes of the subject 2004 Camaro relined and adjusted the day after the accident; Dolores stipulated in her responsive pleadings that she was the owner of the 2004 Camaro.

(C) In Patrick's action for personal injuries against Don arising from a collision between the two while both rode in a bicycle race, Patrick offers a videotape showing a surgeon resetting his broken leg, in which it was necessary to rebreak the leg while Patrick was anesthetized.

(D) In Penelope's defamation action against Delbert, Penelope offers the testimony of Wanda, who will state that when she heard Delbert describe Penelope as "the biggest shyster in Middleville," she understood him to mean that Penelope was an incompetent lawyer; Wanda is the eleventh person Penelope has called to interpret the quoted statement.

GO ON TO THE NEXT PAGE

Question 5

Twin Falls has a city ordinance that makes it unlawful for any group of individuals or organizations in excess of 20 persons to demonstrate, march, or picket in the city's civic center without first posting a bond with the police department and receiving a permit. The permit procedure takes at least one working day, and a "parade" permit costs $10. The requirement for a license is that each demonstration in excess of 20 persons have one parade marshal for each 20 persons who must be responsible for insuring that the demonstration remains on the city sidewalks, does not block traffic, and does not become noisy or unruly. The ordinance, in addition to making a violation a misdemeanor, authorizes the police department to terminate any demonstration if "any person in the demonstration, without provocation, uses, in the presence of other persons not a party to the demonstration, annoying, disturbing, opprobrious words and abusive language in such a manner as tending to cause a breach of the peace."

YAAF (the Young Americans Against Fascism) brings suit in the state court to enjoin the city from preventing their scheduled demonstration on Memorial Day without a permit, and to enjoin the city from using this ordinance to require them to have a permit.

YAAF's strongest contention for finding the provisions of this statute unconstitutional is that:

(A) The city's civic center is a place where demonstrations of this type normally occur, and the city cannot prevent citizens from demonstrating there.

(B) There is no showing by the city that YAAF's demonstrators are likely to become disruptive or unruly.

(C) The ordinance is overbroad and unduly vague.

(D) The First and Fourteenth Amendments ensure the right of association in public places without interference.

Question 6

Carol owed June $90,000, which was due on January 1. On January 15, Carol offered to pay June $80,000 if June would agree to accept the amount in full satisfaction of the $90,000 debt. June agreed and Carol paid $80,000 to June.

If June then sues Carol for $10,000, June will:

(A) Win, because Carol had an obligation to pay $90,000 on January 1.

(B) Lose, because of June's agreement to accept $80,000.

(C) Lose, because there was an accord and satisfaction.

(D) Lose, because June agreed to the $80,000 after the January 1 due date.

Question 7

Parafun, Inc. manufactured and sold parachutes for use by sport skydivers. The corporation's product development committee selected a design for a parachute submitted by Silk, one of Parafun's three professional designers. The chute was placed on the market, with the warning, "This parachute should be discarded after 150 jumps." Parafun's market researchers had established that the usual practice among sport skydivers was to discard a parachute after 100 jumps.

After the design had been approved and the product was successfully manufactured and marketed, Silk took several of the parachutes to an independent stress analysis laboratory. The scientists tested the chutes and concluded that there was a 1% failure rate on the chutes for jumps 100 through 150, because the center of the parachute might tend to collapse because of a design defect. Silk did not report this problem to his superiors at Parafun, because he feared he would be fired.

Several months after Silk received the testing report, Airborne, a sport skydiver, used one of the chutes designed by Silk and manufactured and sold by Parafun. Airborne's use was the 115th jump for the chute. When Airborne leaped from the airplane, the chute opened properly, but halfway down, the center of the chute collapsed inward. Airborne hurtled to the ground to his death. An investigation established that Silk knew of the design defect.

If Parafun is charged with manslaughter in a common law jurisdiction, the verdict should be:

(A) Guilty, because Silk was Parafun's employee and he designed the instrumentality of death.

(B) Guilty, because Airborne died as a result of the failure of a product manufactured and sold by Parafun.

(C) Not guilty, because a corporation cannot be found guilty of manslaughter.

(D) Not guilty, because there was only a 1% chance of parachute failure.

Question 8

Just before going on an expedition to the Amazon, Farley gave his brother, Milton, a power of attorney to sell his house, which stated:

> My brother, Milton, is specifically empowered to sell and convey all, or any part, of the real property owned by me as of this date.

Several weeks later, Milton sold Farley's house to Glenda and conveyed to her a customary deed containing covenants of title. A year later, when Farley returned from the expedition, he was served with a complaint by Glenda, who was suing him for breach of covenant because it turned out that Farley's former wife owns one-half the house that Milton had sold on behalf of his brother.

In this suit, Glenda should:

(A) Prevail, because Farley, through his attorney-in-fact, Milton, had covenanted with regard to the title of the property.

(B) Prevail, if in fact Farley's former wife has filed a claim against Glenda for her interest in the house.

(C) Not prevail, unless the power to "sell and convey" is construed to include the power to execute a usual form of deed used to convey real property.

(D) Not prevail, because Farley did not make any specific covenants with regard to the sale of this house.

GO ON TO THE NEXT PAGE

Question 9

Patrice sued David on a breach of contract theory. Winston testified for Patrice. On cross-examination, which of the following questions is the trial judge most likely to rule improper?

(A) "Weren't you convicted last year of forgery?"

(B) "Isn't it true that you and Patrice have been best friends for many years?"

(C) "Isn't it true that you are known in the community as an alcoholic?"

(D) "Didn't you cheat your business partner out of a large amount of money last month?"

Question 10

Arthur's hobby was restoring classic cars, and he frequently attended shows at which people with similar interests would gather to display their handiwork, compare techniques and information, and view products of manufacturers who catered to such hobbyists. At one such show, Arthur was examining a 1947 Pontiac "Stretch" Roadster when the owner, who was standing nearby, indicated that he was trying to sell the car. Bud, who stated that he had restored the Pontiac himself, told Arthur that (I) the car was restored using nothing but genuine Pontiac parts or parts that Bud had handmade himself. He said that (II) "this is the finest restoration of a 1947 'Stretch' Roadster in the United States, and one of the two best in the world." As they were discussing price, Bud pointed out that (III) "this car has the original 'rearing horse' grille that was installed by the dealer on 1947 'Stretch' Roadsters." Arthur agreed to purchase the car for a considerable sum, and had it transported to his home. Later, he discovered that Bud had not been entirely truthful about the restoration. In his action for deceit, Arthur establishes that Bud knew, when he made statements (I), (II), and (III), above, that each was false. Assuming that all the other elements of deceit are proven, which of the three statements will support Arthur's claims?

(A) Statement (I) only.

(B) Statements (I) and (II).

(C) Statements (I) and (III).

(D) Statements (I), (II), and (III).

Question 11

Astro developed a new synthetic liquid that could safely double the output of electrical power plants. He built a manufacturing plant unlike any other in the world capable of producing this liquid. A byproduct of the production of the liquid was a hazardous chemical that was not biodegradable in the environment. Astro buried the waste chemical in a depression on his land. Before doing so, Astro secured expert opinion, based on soil analysis, that led him reasonably to believe that the earth beneath the disposal site was impermeable, and that there was no danger of contaminating the underground waters. The chemical, nonetheless, seeped through the underlying soil strata, and was carried by the flow of percolating water to a well used by Herder to water his sheep, which he raised on an adjacent property. The chemical rendered the water in the well unfit for consumption by sheep.

If Herder's sheep were harmed by drinking from the contaminated well, and Herder asserts a claim against Astro for damages to the sheep, which of the following facts, if established, would best aid Astro's case? Assume that the jurisdiction follows traditional contributory negligence rules.

(A) Many companies converted their power plants so that they could utilize the synthetic liquid developed by Astro.

(B) Herder did not do what a reasonable person would have done to prevent harm to his sheep after he learned that the well was contaminated.

(C) If he had exercised ordinary care, Herder would have discovered the contamination before his sheep were harmed.

(D) Astro's plant was in place and in operation before Herder purchased his property.

GO ON TO THE NEXT PAGE

Question 12

The legislature of the state of Westcoast enacted a statute authorizing all state agencies having legal departments or employing lawyers to subscribe to a computerized legal research service provided by LawComp, Inc. A contract was duly entered into between the state and the corporation. Before LawComp could begin installation of the necessary equipment in state offices, it was revealed that Westcoast's state university system had exhausted its budgeted resources and would not be able to operate without additional money. The legislature then repealed the statute authorizing use of the computer legal service and allocated the funds thereby released to the university.

LawComp brings an action against the state to enforce the contract. The trial court should rule that the statute repealing authorization for LawComp's services is:

(A) Invalid, because it violates the constitutional prohibition against impairment of contracts.

(B) Valid, because the legislature has constitutional power to repeal its own enactments.

(C) Invalid, because the state is equitably estopped to renounce a valid bid it has accepted.

(D) Valid, because the sovereign may not constitutionally be sued without its own consent.

Question 13

As Sandra, a newspaper reporter, was walking to her home, she saw undercover officer Cole chasing Tim. Cole yelled, "Don't let him get away. I'm a police officer and he's just mugged a man!" Sandra immediately put out her leg and tripped Tim. When Tim fell, he broke his glasses and badly gashed his cheek.

If Sandra was sued by Tim for battery, she would have:

(A) No valid defense unless she had other reasons to believe Cole was a police officer besides his statement.

(B) A valid defense if Sandra believed that Cole had grounds to arrest Tim.

(C) A valid defense if she actually witnessed the crime.

(D) No valid defense if a felony had not in fact been committed.

Question 14

The citizenry of East Rabbit's Foot had experienced a tremendous increase in the incidence of begging in the downtown area. In response, the city council enacted an ordinance that required anyone soliciting for charitable contributions of any sort in any public place to wear an identity card issued by the local police department. Identity cards could be obtained by filling out an affidavit providing identification and address information about the applicant and further affirming that the applicant was not soliciting for personal use and belonged to a recognized charitable organization.

George, a member of Airbreathers Against Tobacco ("AAT"), wishes to solicit contributions by similarly minded persons for use in his organization's campaign against public smoking. He does not want to comply with the identity card ordinance. He comes to you for legal advice and asks the advisability of challenging the ordinance in federal court.

You should inform George that the ordinance is probably:

(A) Unconstitutional, because it violates the First Amendment's prohibition of government infringement of the right of free speech.

(B) Unconstitutional, because it prevents religious organizations from obtaining contributions from their members, and thus interferes with the free exercise of religion.

(C) Constitutional, because it represents a reasonable balancing of the state's police power interest in protecting its citizens from fraud and annoyance against the right of people to seek charitable contributions.

(D) Constitutional, because preventing fraud in the solicitation for charitable contributions is a compelling interest.

Question 15

Marty was driving his auto on a public street of Duffyville on his way home from a party. His wife, Dolly, occupied the passenger seat. Two police officers, Dragby and Casey, noticed that Marty's car was weaving and generally being driven in an erratic manner. They pursued the vehicle and curbed it. When Marty emerged from the driver's seat, he was obviously inebriated, and the officers wrote out a drunk driving citation, and insisted that Marty accompany them to the station house. Marty accompanied Casey in the squad car, and Dragby drove Marty's car to the local precinct with Dolly in the passenger seat. Dolly walked into the station house with Marty.

As Marty was being booked, Dragby took a standard police search form with him and began searching the car. Beneath the passenger seat he found Dolly's purse. He opened the purse and found a plastic zip-lock bag containing a small amount of marijuana. Dolly was charged with possession of drugs. At Dolly's trial, her attorney moved to suppress the admission of the marijuana seized from Dolly's purse into evidence.

Should the court rule favorably on the motion?

(A) Yes, because when conducting a search incident to an arrest the police may not open a closed container.

(B) Yes, because the police lacked probable cause to search Dolly's purse.

(C) No, because the search was incident to the lawful arrest of Marty.

(D) No, because the marijuana was discovered during the course of a valid inventory search.

Questions 16-17 are based on the following fact situation:

Sam was a famous auto racer and builder of racing cars. He and Bob signed a contract for sale of one of Sam's hand-built race cars for $25,000, the price to be paid and the car to be delivered one week later.

The day after the contract was signed, Sam called Bob and told him that Sam's wife, Winnie, who had a half interest in the race car, would not go along with the sale at $25,000. Winnie would agree to a sale for $40,000.

16. If Winnie in fact has a half interest in the racing car:

    (A) There is no enforceable contract because the car cannot be sold unless both owners convey title.

    (B) There is an enforceable contract only if Bob was unaware of Winnie's interest when he signed with Sam.

     (C) There is an enforceable contract regardless of whether Bob was aware of Winnie's interest at the time he signed.

    (D) The contract is discharged by prospective inability of performance.

17. Assume for purposes of this question only that there was an enforceable contract between Sam and Bob. Bob fails to tender $25,000 to Sam on the date set for delivery and Sam does not deliver the car. On these facts:

    (A) Sam can recover from Bob for breach of contract.

    (B) Bob can recover from Sam for breach of contract.

    (C) Neither can recover until one of the parties tenders performance.

    (D) The contract is terminated.

Question 18

When she died, Clara left a valid holographic will that contained the following provision:

> I want my only child, Truman, to have my house when I die and to live there as long as he wants. After that, I want it to go to my grandchildren.

At the time of Clara's death, Truman was married to Dina, and they had a married son, Sam. Both Truman and Dina moved into the house, but about six months later, they separated and Dina moved out.

The following year, Truman and Sam were involved in an airplane crash in which Truman was immediately killed. Several weeks later, Sam died, leaving his young widow, Tanya. Dina brings a suit against Tanya claiming an interest in the house as Truman's widow. There is no statute in this jurisdiction that governs the issue of the right of an estranged spouse to inherit property from a decedent spouse, but if Truman is found to own property at the time of his death, it is possible that Dina could inherit one-half as his surviving spouse.

In this suit, Dina should most likely:

(A) Prevail, because Clara's will gave Truman a fee simple interest in the property.

(B) Prevail, because the devise to Clara's grandchildren in her will is invalid as it violates the Rule Against Perpetuities.

(C) Not prevail, because Sam had a vested remainder interest subject to open, which became indefeasibly vested.

(D) Not prevail, because Sam had a contingent remainder interest by reason of Clara's will, and the contingency occurred.

GO ON TO THE NEXT PAGE

Question 19

Prole was the chief operating officer of the Squidco Division of Octopus Corp., a privately held manufacturing and marketing firm. The Squidco plant was the major employer in Middletown, and Prole was a respected figure with a good reputation in the community. He served on the boards of several Middletown charities and was otherwise active in civic activities.

Prole was suddenly fired by Dante, the executive vice president of Octopus Corp., prompting rumors about the financial health of Squidco. A reporter from the Middletown *Herald* interviewed Dante, and asked Dante why Prole had been dismissed. Dante said: "Prole was fired because Prole was a bad manager and Squidco Division lost money because of Prole's stewardship." Dante's statement was printed in the Middletown *Herald*, and was picked up by business-oriented publications.

If Prole sues the Middletown *Herald* for defamation, which of the following statements with regard to damages is correct?

(A) To prevail, Prole must plead and prove pecuniary damages, such as an inability to find a position with another company.

(B) To prevail, Prole must show evidence of actual injury, such as mental distress.

(C) Damages are presumed because the written repetition of a slander is characterized as libel.

(D) Damages are presumed if Prole is not deemed to be a public figure.

Question 20

In a medical malpractice action, Dr. Zorba was called as an expert witness by the plaintiff and testified that the surgical procedure utilized by the defendant was so new and experimental as to constitute negligence under the accepted standard of practice in the relevant medical community. On cross-examination by defendant's counsel, the following occurred: Counsel: "Dr. Zorba, is *Modern Surgical Procedures* by Weston a reliable authority in your area of specialty?" Dr. Zorba: "Yes." Counsel: "Did you rely upon the treatise in reaching the conclusion that my client was negligent?" Dr. Zorba: "I did not." Defense counsel now proposes to read a passage from the treatise stating that the surgical procedure at issue is widely accepted by responsible medical practitioners. Plaintiff's counsel objects.

How should the court rule?

(A) For defendant, but it should also caution the jury that the evidence may only be considered in impeachment of Dr. Zorba.

(B) For defendant.

(C) For plaintiff, because Dr. Zorba did not rely upon the treatise in forming his expert opinion.

(D) For plaintiff, because the passage from the treatise is inadmissible hearsay.

Question 21

Congress enacted a law requiring all civil service employees to retire at age 75, except when such employees are employed by the armed services. Civil service employees of the armed services are required to retire at age 65. Portman is an employee of the Department of the Army; he is 65 years old. He files suit in the federal district court seeking a declaratory judgment that would prevent the Army from requiring him to retire before age 75.

Portman's strongest argument in support of his contention that the statute's provisions regarding civil service employees of the armed services are invalid is that this provision:

(A) Denies him the privileges and immunities of national citizenship.

(B) Denies him a property right without just compensation.

(C) Is invidious discrimination on the basis of age in violation of the Fifth Amendment.

(D) Is not within the enumerated powers of Congress under Article I, Section 8.

Question 22

Velma entered into an argument with her neighbor Diana over the height of the bushes on Velma's property. Diana claimed that the bushes were so high that when she attempted to pull out of her own driveway, she was unable to see if traffic was approaching from the south. Diana demanded that Velma cut the bushes down to half their present height. When Velma refused, Diana, in a fit of anger, slapped Velma. Velma reached into her purse, drew out a pistol, and fired a shot at Diana but missed. Just as Velma cocked the pistol to fire another shot, Diana grabbed a shovel and hit Velma over the head, killing her instantly. Diana was charged with the murder of Velma. At trial, Diana testified that she hit Velma because she believed that Velma would have shot and killed her if she did not.

If the jury believes Diana, it should find her:

(A) Guilty of murder, because she did not retreat.

(B) Guilty of murder, because she was the original aggressor in the encounter and had not withdrawn.

(C) Not guilty of murder, because Velma was the first to resort to deadly force.

(D) Not guilty of murder, because she had no opportunity to premeditate.

Question 23

Alpha gratuitously conveyed his interest in Greekacre to Beta by quitclaim deed. Beta promptly recorded. Six months later, Alpha conveyed his interest in Greekacre to Gamma for $50,000. Alpha gave Gamma a warranty deed, which Gamma promptly recorded.

As between Beta and Gamma, who has the superior right to title to Greekacre?

(A) Beta, regardless of the type of recording statute.

(B) Gamma, regardless of the type of recording statute.

(C) Beta, because she recorded prior to Gamma recording.

(D) Gamma, because he took by warranty deed rather than quitclaim deed.

Question 24

Daisy is on trial for fraud. One item of critical evidence in this trial is a check for $10,000 that purportedly was signed by her. Daisy has denied that she signed the check in question. The prosecutor calls Julius, the landlord of the apartment building in which Daisy resided for three months before her arrest. Julius intends to testify that it is Daisy's signature on the check, and he bases his opinion of the authenticity of her signature on the ground that he saw her sign the lease to his apartment.

The trial court should find this testimony:

(A) Admissible, because there was only a short period of time between when Julius saw her sign the lease and the time of trial.

(B) Admissible, because any person can testify to the authenticity of another's signature, if that witness has previously seen that person's signature.

(C) Inadmissible, because Julius has only seen the signature once and is not acting as a handwriting expert.

(D) Inadmissible, because the testimony is inherently unreliable.

Question 25

After a bomb explosion in an airport locker, Detective Jones received some information from Carlos, an informant who had given him reliable information several times in the past, that Karl was a member of a radical group that took credit for the bombing. Carlos told Jones that, three months before, he had been in Karl's apartment and on that occasion had seen what appeared to be some sticks of dynamite. Reasonably believing that Carlos's information established probable cause, Jones prepared an affidavit for a search warrant. After the warrant was issued, Jones and a group of police raided Karl's apartment. No evidence connecting Karl with the bombing was discovered, but in the search of his apartment the police discovered several grams of cocaine.

At his trial for possession of narcotics, Karl's motion to suppress the evidence would probably be:

(A) Denied, because Carlos was a reliable informant and Jones reasonably believed that Carlos's information was accurate and that the warrant was properly issued.

(B) Granted, because in fact the police did not discover any evidence linking Karl to the bombings and, therefore, the seizure of the cocaine was fruit of the poisonous tree.

(C) Granted, if the court determines that the information supplied by Carlos to Jones concerned information too remote in time to justify a claim of probable cause at the time Jones requested the search warrant.

(D) Granted, because the search warrant was not issued for the purpose of searching Karl's apartment for illegal drugs.

GO ON TO THE NEXT PAGE

Question 26

The state of Alpine has a Fair Employment Act that provides a remedy for victims of employment discrimination. The Act requires complainants to bring charges before the Alpine Fair Employment Commission within 180 days of the occurrence of alleged unlawful employment practices. The Commission then has 120 days to convene a factfinding conference to obtain evidence, ascertain the parties' positions, and explore settlement possibilities. Larson was discharged from his job with Widget Corp. purportedly because of a physical handicap unrelated to his ability to perform his job. Larson filed a timely complaint, alleging unlawful termination of employment, as required by the statute. However, through inadvertence, the Commission scheduled the factfinding conference for a date five days after expiration of the 120-day statutory period. At the conference, Widget moved that the charge be dismissed for lack of a timely conference. The Commission denied the motion. Widget petitioned the Alpine Supreme Court. The court held for Widget, stating that the failure to comply with the 120-day requirement deprived the Commission of jurisdiction to consider Larson's charge. On appeal to the United States Supreme Court, Larson argues that his right to due process will be violated if the Commission's error is allowed to extinguish his cause of action.

Which of the following best describes the viability of Larson's due process claim?

(A) The claim fails, because Larson had no protected property interest in his job.

(B) The claim fails, because the Alpine legislature, having conferred on claimants a remedy for claims of unfair employment practices, has the prerogative to establish limiting procedures for such claims.

(C) The claim succeeds, because Larson had a protected property interest in the remedy.

(D) The claim succeeds, because of the fundamental unfairness of leaving Larson without a remedy.

Question 27

Deborah was at work when her husband called her and said, "You lazy procrastinator, you were supposed to be working in the front yard this weekend while I did the backyard. Ned just tripped over those roots I told you to take out. He's really been badly hurt and I'll bet he sues us for all we're worth." Deborah then told her secretary, Walter, "Ned just got hurt because I forgot to do my yard work." On returning home, however, Deborah discovered that Ned had tripped over roots from his own tree in his own yard. Ned disagreed and sued Deborah and her husband. At trial, Ned called Walter to testify as to Deborah's statement to him.

Walter's testimony will be:

(A) Excluded, because Deborah had no first-hand information when she made her statement to Walter.

(B) Excluded, because it is inadmissible lay opinion.

(C) Admitted, because it is not hearsay.

(D) Admitted to impeach Deborah's expected testimony as to the result of her own investigation.

GO ON TO THE NEXT PAGE

Question 28

The legislature of State Red recently enacted a statute that defined first degree murder as murder with premeditation and deliberation, or a homicide in the commission of arson, rape, robbery, burglary, or kidnapping. The statute defined second degree murder as all other murder at common law.

In which of the following situations is defendant most likely to be guilty of first degree murder?

(A) Believing that his neighbor Paul had stolen his lawn mower, defendant walked over to his neighbor's house and punched him in the nose, intending to injure him. As a result of the blow, Paul fell back, hit his head, and died.

(B) After leaving a bar in a highly intoxicated state, defendant attempted to drive home. While so doing, he struck Oscar, who was legally crossing the street in a marked crosswalk. Oscar died instantly.

(C) Infuriated over having caught Mary having an affair with defendant's husband, defendant bought a shotgun and shot and killed Mary as she was leaving her house on her way to work.

(D) Immediately after being punched by Betty, defendant in a rage took a knife and stabbed and killed Betty.

Question 29

Filmont designed and constructed a playground for children. Shortly thereafter, Filmont dedicated the property to the city of Oakville, to be used as a public park. Ken, a 10-year-old resident of Oakville, was playing at the park when he fell off the monkey bars, breaking his leg. On his behalf, Ken's parents filed suit against Filmont and Oakville, on the grounds of negligence in the design of the monkey bars. At the trial, Filmont was granted a directed verdict, because Oakville now owns the park. Ken's parents appealed the granting of the directed verdict as to Filmont.

The appellate court will most likely hold that:

(A) The decision to grant the directed verdict should be upheld, because Filmont was relieved of liability when he dedicated the park to Oakville.

(B) The decision to grant the directed verdict should be upheld, because Filmont designed and constructed the park in the public interest.

(C) The decision to grant the directed verdict should be overturned if plaintiffs introduced evidence that Filmont dedicated the park to Oakville in an effort to avoid liability for the park's negligent design.

(D) The decision to grant the directed verdict should be overturned, because Filmont's liability for negligence was not affected by the dedication of the park to Oakville.

Question 30

Drew was tried for the July 21 murder of Victor. Drew called Warren to testify to an alibi. On cross-examination of Warren, the prosecutor asked, "Weren't you on the jury that acquitted Drew of another criminal charge?"

The best reason for sustaining an objection to this question is that:

(A) The question goes beyond the scope of direct examination.

(B) The probative value of the answer would be substantially outweighed by its tendency to mislead.

(C) The question is a leading question.

(D) Prior jury service in a case involving a party renders the witness incompetent.

GO ON TO THE NEXT PAGE

Questions 31-32 are based on the following fact situation:

Mary's doctor informed her that she had a rare blood disease that was almost always fatal. He further informed her that there was no treatment known to medical science for this disease. Out of desperation, Mary consulted Quack, who claimed to have a cure for the blood disease. Mary entered into an agreement with Quack under which Quack promised to treat Mary for the blood disease. However, no price was given for the treatment. After two months of treatment, Mary did not appear to have improved at all. Mary's father, Stu, went to see Quack and told Quack that if Quack would cure Mary of the blood disease, Stu would pay Quack $25,000. Four months later, after weekly sessions with Quack, Mary again went to see her doctor. This time her doctor told her that she appeared to have recovered completely from the blood disease, because all tests for the disease proved negative, and that, in his opinion, she was completely cured.

31. Assume for the purposes of this question only that Mary refused to pay Quack anything. Quack brings suit against Mary for services rendered. Quack will:

  (A) Recover whatever amount Quack shows is his normal fee for the treatment.

  (B) Recover a reasonable price for his services.

  (C) Not recover, because no price term was contained in the original contract.

  (D) Not recover, because Quack cannot prove that he was the cause of Mary's recovery.

32. Assume for the purposes of this question only that Stu refuses to pay Quack the $25,000. Quack brings suit against Stu. Quack will:

  (A) Recover nothing, because Stu's promise constituted no legal detriment to him.

  (B) Recover nothing, because Quack had a preexisting duty to Mary under their prior agreement.

  (C) Recover the reasonable value of his services, because they are less than $25,000.

  (D) Recover $25,000, because Stu was bargaining for Mary's recovery.

Question 33

The state of West Dakota has the following statute:

> No conveyance or mortgage of an interest in land is valid against any subsequent purchaser for value without notice thereof whose conveyance is first recorded.

Judy, a West Dakota resident, owned several parcels of land there, including Steppeacre. Judy conveyed Steppeacre to Keith. Keith placed the deed in a safe deposit box but did not record the instrument before departing on an extended visit to Adak, a chic resort island in the Aleutian chain. Six months after Keith departed, Judy conveyed Steppeacre to Clyde, who promptly recorded his deed. Clyde had heard from several sources that Judy had sold Steppeacre to Keith, but he was sure that Judy would not sell him property she had already sold to someone else.

Six months after Clyde took possession of Steppeacre, Keith returned from Adak, tanned and rested. When he went to visit Steppeacre he found Clyde there.

Keith now sues Clyde in ejectment. Who owns Steppeacre?

  (A) Keith, because his deed from Judy came earlier than Clyde's.

  (B) Clyde, because he recorded first.

  (C) Keith, because Clyde is not protected by the recording act.

  (D) Clyde, because his recording cured any possible defect of his knowing of the earlier sale.

GO ON TO THE NEXT PAGE

Question 34

State Blue has a statute making it a crime to operate a motor vehicle while intoxicated. State Blue has another statute providing that a blood alcohol level of .10 raises a presumption of intoxication. State Blue police spotted Billy Bob's pickup weaving from lane to lane on the highway and they stopped the truck. Billy Bob took a breathalyzer test that indicated a .12 blood alcohol level, and so Billy Bob was charged with operating a motor vehicle while intoxicated.

At trial, at the close of all the evidence, and over Billy Bob's objection, the judge instructed the jury: "If you are convinced that, at the time Billy Bob was pulled over, his blood alcohol level was .10 or greater, you must presume that he was intoxicated."

Billy Bob was convicted, and he is appealing on the ground that the judge's instruction was improper. The appellate court should:

(A) Affirm, because the judge may instruct the jury on the law, and he merely cited the state statute.

(B) Reverse and remand, because the jury should have been left to draw its own conclusion without the judge's instruction.

(C) Reverse and remand, because the presumption might lead the jury to believe that the prosecution did not have to meet its burden of proving Billy Bob guilty beyond a reasonable doubt.

(D) Reverse and remand, because the instruction was substantially more prejudicial than probative.

Question 35

Capitol City, West Carolina, has a city ordinance that prohibits the distribution of pamphlets "on public sidewalks or other public areas when foot traffic is sufficiently heavy and the manner of distribution of the pamphlets causes obstruction of the foot traffic so as to result in spillover onto public streets where vehicular traffic creates a danger to human life." The West Carolina state fair is held at fairgrounds whose entrances lie along a busy multilane street. Roger, who was distributing pamphlets advocating repeal of the federal milk price support program during Dairy Day at the state fair, attracted a crowd of about 10 farmers and children outside the fairgrounds entrance at which he stood, but most of the few fairgoers entering the fair at that late afternoon time simply ignored him. When one of the dairy farmers became irate and threatened to "knock his block off," Roger was arrested by a fair security guard and subsequently prosecuted under the city ordinance.

Which of the following statements is correct regarding the city ordinance and Roger's prosecution?

(A) The ordinance is void on its face and void as applied to Roger.

(B) The ordinance is valid on its face but void as applied to Roger.

(C) The ordinance is valid on its face and valid as applied to Roger.

(D) The ordinance is void on its face but valid as applied to Roger.

Question 36

Woody is on trial for embezzlement. He does not take the stand. Which of Woody's previous convictions is most likely to be admitted into evidence against him?

(A) A 7-year-old conviction for arson, a felony.

(B) A 12-year-old conviction for embezzlement, a felony.

(C) A 6-month-old conviction for disorderly conduct, a misdemeanor.

(D) A 2-year-old conviction for felonious sexual assault.

GO ON TO THE NEXT PAGE

Question 37

Cyrus and Myrtle are adjoining landowners. On Myrtle's property there is a natural fresh-water spring. Cyrus asked Myrtle if it would be possible to build an irrigation ditch from the spring to his property in order to provide water for his cattle. Since the spring supplied more than enough water to meet Myrtle's needs, she agreed, provided that Cyrus construct the ditch in such a manner that it would need the least maintenance possible, because Myrtle did not wish to be continually bothered by Cyrus's coming on her land. Cyrus constructed a concrete irrigation ditch from the spring to the land. The cost of construction of the ditch was $25,000. The only maintenance required on the ditch was a semiannual cleaning. Three years later, Myrtle informed Cyrus that her water needs had increased and that she could no longer allow Cyrus to take water from the spring. In addition, Myrtle did not allow Cyrus on her land to do the semian-nual cleaning, resulting in the blocking of the ditch.

Cyrus wishes to keep water flowing through the irrigation ditch to his land. Which of the following would be his strongest argument?

(A) Cyrus owns a valid easement appurtenant to Myrtle's property.

(B) Because Myrtle has allowed Cyrus to construct the irrigation ditch, Myrtle would be estopped from preventing Cyrus from coming onto her land.

(C) Cyrus, although a licensee, has expended such a substantial sum of money in con-structing the irrigation ditch that Myrtle may not terminate Cyrus's license now.

(D) Cyrus, although a licensee, may continue to enter Myrtle's property to clean and main-tain the ditch until he is able to acquire another source of water.

Question 38

Delbert had his laptop computer stolen from his office during a recent holiday weekend. He went to Alice's computer resale shop to find a replacement and saw what he mistakenly thought was his computer. He questioned Alice, who told him that someone had just sold her the computer a few days ago, but she refused to give him any information on the seller and would not let him inspect it more closely. That night, after the shop was closed, Delbert forced open the back door and took the computer. Alice's clerk, who lived in an apartment above the shop, heard someone breaking in and called the police. Delbert was apprehended a block away from the building.

If Delbert is charged with burglary in a jurisdiction retaining the common law criminal offenses, which of the following facts will be most relevant in determining his guilt or inno-cence?

(A) His mistake as to the identity of the com-puter was not reasonable.

(B) He was unaware that there was an apart-ment above the shop and did not believe that anyone lived in the building.

(C) He realized that the computer was not his before he carried it out.

(D) None of the above facts are relevant.

GO ON TO THE NEXT PAGE

Question 39

Seth owned Slateacre, a rental property in Rock City that generated steady income. After Seth's second child was born, Seth properly executed a will containing the following disposition of Slateacre: "To Truman in trust to pay the educational expenses of my children, but if any of them do not graduate from Rockville University by the age of 30, then for the benefit of Rockville University's scholarship fund for residents of Rock City." When Seth died, he had three children, all preschoolers. The jurisdiction in which the parties and property are located retains the common law Rule Against Perpetuities.

Is the gift in trust to Rockville University valid?

(A) Yes, because the gift is a valid charitable trust.

(B) Yes, because the doctrine of cy pres is applicable.

(C) No, because the gift is not for a valid charitable purpose.

(D) No, because the gift violates the Rule Against Perpetuities.

Question 40

Harriet observed an automobile accident that took place across the street from her house. She noticed at the time that the green car, which was driven by Def, did not come to a complete stop at the stop sign and entered the intersection to strike the yellow car driven by Plee after Plee's car had already entered the intersection. Plee sued Def for damages and injuries, but the trial did not take place until almost three years after the accident. Plee wanted Harriet to testify on his behalf against Def, but Harriet's recollection of the accident was very fuzzy. The night before she was scheduled to testify, Harriet consulted her diary, in which Harriet had noted that Def's car ran the stop sign and entered the intersection after Plee's car was already in the intersection. Plee's attorney called Harriet to the stand, and she testified regarding Def's failure to observe the stop sign and Def's entrance into the intersection after Plee.

On cross-examination, Def's attorney asked Harriet if she had consulted any materials to prepare for her testimony. Harriet admitted that her recollection of the accident had been fuzzy and that she had consulted her diary the night before her testimony. Def's attorney immediately moved that Harriet's testimony be stricken from the record.

The court should rule that:

(A) Harriet's testimony is admissible if, after reviewing her notes, she had an independent recollection of the event.

(B) Harriet's testimony is admissible, because the contents of her diary are protected under the work product rule.

(C) Harriet's testimony should be stricken, because her diary was not made available to the opposing party prior to trial.

(D) Harriet's testimony should be stricken, because it is not the best evidence.

Question 41

In which of the following situations is the defendant most likely to be convicted of burglary?

(A) Unreasonably mistaking Walter's briefcase for his own, Defendant removes the briefcase from Walter's office and takes it home, placing it in his hall closet.

(B) Believing that it is not illegal to take a relative's property, Defendant enters his brother's home through an unlocked door while his brother is sleeping and takes his $2,000 television set. Defendant later sells the set at a flea market.

(C) When Leon refuses to pay back the $25 he borrowed from Defendant two weeks ago, Defendant enters Leon's apartment and removes $25 from his wallet, believing that he is recouping the loan.

(D) Intending to use it for a trip to the store and then return it, Defendant takes Arthur's bicycle from Arthur's garage and rides it to the store. While there, someone else steals the bicycle and it is never returned.

Question 42

Owens owned Goldacre in fee simple. In 1985, Owens executed a deed conveying Goldacre "to Private School for the life of my wife Wilma, and then to my children, their heirs and assigns, in equal share, provided, however, that School shall use the premises for educational purposes only." School then erected a temporary building on Goldacre and conducted certain classes within the building. In 2000, one of School's former students informed the principal of School that a geological survey of the area had indicated that there were valuable minerals beneath the surface of Goldacre. School, badly in need of money, granted to Mine Co. a right to remove the minerals from a one-acre portion of Goldacre upon the payment of a percentage of the value of the minerals removed. From 2000 to 2004, Mine Co. conducted mining operations on the one-acre portion of Goldacre. School had continued to conduct classes in the temporary building located on Goldacre. In 2004, while Owens and Wilma were still alive, both of Owens's children filed suit against School and Mine Co. seeking damages for the removal of minerals since 2000, an injunction preventing further acts of removal, and all other appropriate remedies.

Which of the following would be the most likely result?

(A) School and Mine Co. should be enjoined, and damages should be recovered, but impounded for future distribution.

(B) The children should succeed, because the interest of School terminated with the first removal of minerals from Goldacre.

(C) The injunction should be granted, but damages should be denied because Owens and Wilma are not parties to the action.

(D) Damages should be awarded, but the injunction should be denied.

GO ON TO THE NEXT PAGE

Question 43

Moss, a state legislator, was the chairman of a committee that disbursed funds to schools in the state for various projects. A portion of the funds that were used were received from the federal government as part of a federal revenue sharing plan. Moss was charged with a violation of federal law when he and his committee made a $10,000 grant for textbooks to a private school for whites only. Moss's defense is that his action as chairman of this committee was in the course of his legislative duties, and thus, immune from federal interference.

The best argument that would support Moss's constitutional claim is:

(A) If the state law authorizes Moss's action, he cannot be prosecuted for violation of a federal law.

(B) The Tenth Amendment forbids the federal government from restricting the state's rights regarding the education of minor children within the state.

(C) The doctrine of federalism prevents the federal government from interfering with a member of the state's legislature in the performance of his legislative duties.

(D) As long as the private school is not a parochial school, federal law cannot limit a state's rights regarding the education of minor children within the state.

Questions 44-46 are based on the following fact situation:

Stone operated a newsstand on leased space in an office building. On March 15, Quinn purchased the office building and told Stone that he wanted to negotiate a new lease. During the negotiations, Stone and Quinn orally agreed that Stone would have the exclusive right to sell newspapers and magazines in the office building. Quinn prepared a written lease outlining the Stone-Quinn agreement, but forgot to include the agreement that Stone would have exclusive rights in the office building. Stone was given a copy of the lease to read, but Stone merely glanced over the lease because he assumed it reflected his agreement with Quinn. Stone then signed the lease, which included a merger and integration clause. On March 30, Quinn leased space to Jacobs for the establishment of a drug store to be run by Jacobs. The Quinn-Jacobs lease did not prevent Jacobs from selling newspapers or magazines. As a result of the competition, Stone lost substantial profits in his business.

44. Stone brings suit to reform the contract to reflect his exclusive right to sell newspapers and magazines in the office building. The most likely result of this suit is that:

(A) Stone will prevail.

(B) Stone will prevail only if he can prove a mutual mistake.

(C) Stone will not prevail because of the application of the parol evidence rule.

(D) Stone will not prevail because the mistake on his part was unilateral.

45. Assume for purposes of this question only that Stone's prior lease had given him the exclusive right to sell newspapers and magazines in the office building. Assume further that Stone told Quinn that he wanted the new lease to be the same as the old lease, and that Quinn had handed the new lease to Stone and represented it to be the same as the old lease, knowing that this was not true. Stone signed the lease without reading it because Quinn told him that there was no reason to read the new lease. If Stone sues Quinn, Stone could obtain:

(A) Rescission.

(B) Reformation.

(C) Novation.

(D) Repudiation.

GO ON TO THE NEXT PAGE

46. If Stone sues Quinn for misrepresentation, any statements made by Quinn before the lease was signed:

    (A) Would be barred by the parol evidence rule.

    (B) Would not be barred by the parol evidence rule.

    (C) Would be admitted if the lease was proved to be an incomplete agreement of the parties.

    (D) Would not be admitted because they occurred prior to the signing of the lease.

Questions 47-48 are based on the following fact situation:

Walter purchased a new power boat with an inboard engine from City Marine. The boat was manufactured by Watersports, Inc. Later that summer, Walter was using his boat on the lake to tow some of his friends while they waterskied when he found himself near the end of the lake where the large dam that had formed the lake was located. Several hundred feet from the dam were large pylons bearing signs warning boaters to stay at least 50 yards away. Between the pylons and the dam, about 100 feet from the pylons, was a partially submerged chain link fence covering the underwater pipes that drew water to run the hydroelectric generating turbines.

Walter decided to show off by weaving his boat in and out of the warning pylons. As he rounded the last of them, the steering mechanism of his boat jammed, and it and Walter were propelled into the chain link fence. Tom, who was skiing behind the boat, was pulled into one of the pylons. Both Walter and Tom were severely injured. The jurisdiction follows traditional contributory negligence rules.

47. Walter brings an action for damages against City Marine on a theory of strict liability in tort. Who will prevail?

    (A) City Marine, if it properly inspected the boat before selling it to Walter.

    (B) City Marine, if Walter is found to have been negligent in weaving in and out of the pylons.

    (C) Walter, if he can show that the steering failed due to a defect present when the boat left the manufacturer.

    (D) Walter, because the steering mechanism failed while he was operating the boat.

48. If Tom brings a negligence action against Watersports, Inc., and it is found that the steering failure resulted from a manufacturing defect in the boat, will he recover for his injuries?

    (A) No, because he did not purchase the boat.

    (B) No, if Walter is found to have been negligent in weaving in and out of the pylons.

    (C) Yes, if the defect in the steering mechanism could have been discovered by Watersports, Inc. in the exercise of reasonable care.

    (D) Yes, unless the defect in the steering mechanism could have been discovered by City Marine in the exercise of reasonable care.

GO ON TO THE NEXT PAGE

Question 49

A standard commercial unit for widgets is one gross, *i.e.,* 144 widgets. Buyer ordered from Seller 50 gross of widgets at $100 per gross, with the widgets to be delivered on or before October 3. On September 15, 50 boxes arrived from Seller. Each box was labeled, "Widgets—one gross." On finding that one of the boxes contains 143 widgets, Buyer considered whether to:

I. Seek cover.

II. Immediately sue for breach.

III. Reject the entire shipment of widgets.

Which of the above can Buyer do?

(A) I. and III. only.

(B) I. and II. only.

(C) III. only.

(D) I., II., and III.

Question 50

Olman expected the value of property near Middletown to increase substantially. To buy a tract known as Blueacre, Olman secured a $10,000 mortgage on Blueacre from Exbank. After completing the purchase, Olman wished to make certain improvements on Blueacre. To finance them, Olman took out a $2,000 second mortgage on Blueacre from Wybank. Both mortgages were promptly and properly recorded. Before Olman made a payment on either mortgage, the federal government announced that it would begin storing nuclear waste products in the Middletown area. The value of property, including Blueacre, plummeted. Olman did not pay either Exbank or Wybank. Exbank brought a proper action to foreclose, notifying both Olman and Wybank. Purch bought Blueacre at the foreclosure sale for $6,000, the property's fair market value.

Assuming there are no special statutes in the jurisdiction regarding deficiency judgments, Olman owes:

(A) $5,000 to Exbank and $1,000 to Wybank.

(B) $4,000 to Exbank and $2,000 to Wybank.

(C) Nothing to Exbank and $2,000 to Wybank.

(D) $4,000 to Exbank and nothing to Wybank.

Question 51

Donald was convicted of burglary after a jury trial at which the prosecution established that Donald broke into Shelley's house at night by cutting open a window screen and climbing into a bedroom, then was frightened into leaping out the same window when Shelley, who was lying in bed in that same bedroom, produced a revolver from beneath her pillow. Donald testified in his own defense that he entered the house merely to use the telephone, and thus lacked the requisite intent for the entry to constitute burglary. The trial court, after instructing the jury on the elements of burglary, said, "If you find that by a fair preponderance of the evidence Donald has shown that he intended to use the telephone when he entered Shelley's home, then you must find him not guilty."

If Donald appeals his conviction, will he likely obtain a reversal?

(A) Yes, because the trial court's instruction permitted the jury to use the wrong standard of proof, in that they were told to find by a preponderance rather than beyond a reasonable doubt.

(B) Yes, because the trial court's instruction placed the burden of proof upon Donald.

(C) No, because any error in instructions was harmless, since it is more likely than not that the jury would have convicted him anyway.

(D) No, because the trial court is permitted to comment upon the evidence.

GO ON TO THE NEXT PAGE

Question 52

The city of West Rabbit's Foot, which lies astride a major interstate highway, recently passed a referendum declaring itself to be a "nuclear free zone." The referendum included a provision making criminal any importation of specified nuclear materials into the city limits. The law was immediately challenged in federal court by an interstate trucking firm which regularly transported prohibited nuclear materials through West Rabbit's Foot on the highway. The case ultimately reached the United States Supreme Court, which held in a 5-4 decision that the challenged ordinance was constitutional because the city had a rational basis for concluding that the citizens of West Rabbit's Foot would be safer if the prohibited materials were kept outside of town, and because the ordinance did not unduly burden interstate commerce. Many other towns and cities throughout the nation considered similar enactments after the Supreme Court decision was announced. You are a lobbyist hired by the trucking industry to persuade Congress that a federal statute prohibiting the state regulation of interstate transportation of nuclear materials must immediately be enacted. Congress member Bluster has tentatively agreed to sponsor such legislation, but wants to know whether such a federal statute would pass constitutional muster.

You should advise Bluster that the proposed statute would probably be held:

(A) Unconstitutional, since the Supreme Court has already ruled that local governments may prohibit specified nuclear materials from crossing their borders.

(B) Unconstitutional, because the disparate treatment of interstate versus intrastate carriers of nuclear materials would violate the Equal Protection Clause of the Fourteenth Amendment.

(C) Constitutional, because Congress has plenary power to regulate interstate commerce.

(D) Constitutional, because the Supremacy Clause requires that state enactments bow to conflicting federal legislation.

GO ON TO THE NEXT PAGE

Question 53

Shelley lived in a house on a large corner lot. A few hundred feet down the street was a convenience store used by many people in the neighborhood, and everyone would take a short cut across Shelley's front yard rather than staying on the sidewalk that bordered her lawn. The heavy foot traffic was starting to wear a path through her lawn, and everyone left soft drink cans and candy wrappers strewn all over her front yard. Shelley therefore decided to build a fence around her front lawn, and hired Jack, a local contractor, to do the work. The next afternoon, Jack started the job by surveying the property and digging post holes. After he had completed that task, he left to do another small job in that area, leaving behind a wheelbarrow with a shovel leaning against it. When Shelley noticed that Jack had left the wheelbarrow and shovel in her front yard, she called his office and spoke to his wife. Jack's wife said that he was on another job in the area and must have intended to pick up the wheelbarrow and shovel on his way back. Shelley said that was fine, and left to go to her weekly bridge club meeting. Later that evening, Jack, who had finished the other job, returned to his office without stopping at Shelley's house.

Eric, who owned a house down the street from Shelley, was walking to the convenience store to pick up a six-pack of beer. Because it was summer, it was still quite light, although it was 7 p.m. When he came to Shelley's house he took his usual short cut. A police car with siren wailing went by on the main street just as Eric was walking by the wheelbarrow, and as he followed the police car with his eyes, he tripped over the shovel leaning against the wheelbarrow and fell, breaking his arm.

Is Shelley liable to Eric for his broken arm and related damages?

(A) No, because she did not create the condition that harmed him.

(B) No, because the danger to which he was exposed was open and obvious.

(C) Yes, because she was aware of the condition that harmed him.

(D) Yes, because she knew that he frequently cut across her lawn on the way to the convenience store.

Question 54

Fred, a licensed real estate broker, and Tom, a homeowner, entered into a written listing agreement in which, among other things, Tom promised to pay Fred a commission of 6% of the selling price of Tom's home if Fred obtained a buyer ready, willing, and able to purchase it. Tom's home was listed in a service made available to real estate professionals, with an asking price of $80,000.

Murray, looking for a home to buy, went to Fred's real estate office and was shown Tom's home. He submitted a written offer to purchase the home for $80,000, but Tom rejected this offer by, according to its terms, not accepting it within a stated period. Tom did not want to sell to Murray because, given the amount Murray had intended to borrow, Tom would have had to take back a second mortgage for a portion of his equity, and he did not consider Murray a good credit risk.

Murray brings an action against Tom for specific performance, seeking to compel him to sell the home. What is the probable outcome of this litigation?

(A) Tom will win, because no writing or writings constitute a memorandum sufficient to satisfy the Statute of Frauds.

(B) Tom will win, because Murray's remedy at law is adequate.

(C) Murray will win, because he is a third-party beneficiary of the agreement between Tom and Fred.

(D) Murray will win, because there is a memorandum that satisfies the Statute of Frauds.

GO ON TO THE NEXT PAGE

Question 55

Both Kenton and Evan owned their own homes on large tracts of land next to each other in the country. Evan, a physics teacher at the local college, was also a model rocket enthusiast. On many occasions he would launch one of his rockets from the back area of his property, and although none of Evan's rockets ever came near Kenton's property, Kenton was understandably upset. Kenton complained to Evan several times about his hobby and the fact that Evan stored flammable fuels in his house. Once, Kenton complained to the county sheriff, whereupon Evan was charged with violating a local ordinance that prohibits the improper storage of flammable liquids on residential property. He was given a warning and told that he must have proper storage permits and facilities if he intended to keep the fuels for his model rockets on his property. Although Evan obtained the proper permits to build underground storage tanks for his fuels, he continued to store them in 55-gallon drums in a shed located on the edge of his property farthest away from Kenton.

Eventually, Kenton brought a suit based on public nuisance against Evan. If Kenton is seeking an injunction against Evan to prevent his storing flammable liquids on his property and his launching model rockets, the defense by which Evan most likely would prevail is that:

(A) He obtained a permit from the city to build storage tanks for the fuels.

(B) There is no showing that Kenton suffered any special damage.

(C) This is not a residential neighborhood.

(D) There is no specific ordinance that prohibits Evan from launching model rockets on his own property.

Question 56

Harry and Wilma were going through a divorce proceeding and were contesting the value of their house. Harry, a real estate agent familiar with property values in the area, had personally prepared an appraisal shortly before commencement of the divorce proceedings. The appraisal document stated that the house was worth $200,000. Nora, a next-door neighbor of Harry and Wilma's, had seen this appraisal document.

During settlement negotiations, Harry maintained that the house was worth $180,000. When negotiations proved to be fruitless, the parties proceeded to trial. At trial, Wilma called Nora to testify as to the value placed on the house in the appraisal document. Nora's only knowledge as to the house's value comes from having read the document. Harry's attorney objects.

May Nora testify as to the value stated in the appraisal document?

(A) Yes, because she has personal knowledge of the contents of the document.

(B) Yes, if Harry has destroyed the document.

(C) No, because the appraisal document is the best, and thus the only admissible, evidence.

(D) No, because Nora's testimony would be inadmissible hearsay.

GO ON TO THE NEXT PAGE

Question 57

During a gang shootout in City, Joe looked for Egbert among the combatants because he wanted to kill him. He spotted Ira, who resembled Egbert. Believing Ira to be Egbert, Joe shot at Ira and missed. The bullet passed through a window and killed Gladys, who was asleep on her sofa.

Joe may properly be convicted of:

I. Attempted murder of Egbert.

II. Attempted murder of Ira.

III. Murder of Gladys.

(A) I. and II. only.

(B) II. only.

(C) II. and III. only.

(D) None of the above.

Questions 58-60 are based on the following fact situation:

Justin is being tried for the murder of Harvey, which occurred during the course of the robbery of Harvey's house.

58. A witness to the robbery and murder had aided the police artist in making the composite picture by which Justin was identified. This witness disappeared before trial, and the prosecutor now wants to offer the sketch into evidence. The sketch is:

   (A) Inadmissible, under the best evidence rule.

   (B) Inadmissible, as hearsay not within any exception.

   (C) Admissible, as a record by a public employee.

   (D) Admissible, as a prior identification.

59. Justin took the stand in his own defense. His attorney asked him about the robbery and murder, and Justin denied committing the crimes. His attorney asked him what he said to the police when he was first arrested and he said, "I told them I knew nothing of the crimes because I was in Seattle at the time." This answer should be:

   (A) Stricken, because it is self-serving.

   (B) Stricken, because it is hearsay.

   (C) Admissible, because Justin can competently testify to statements he made himself.

   (D) Admissible, as a prior consistent statement.

60. On cross-examination of Justin, the prosecution asks Justin whether he was convicted of fraud within the previous year. This question is:

   (A) Improper, because fraud is not probative of a tendency to commit violence.

   (B) Improper, unless the proper foundation was laid.

   (C) Proper, because fraud is a form of stealing, and so it will tend to show that Justin could commit robbery.

   (D) Proper, because it tends to show that Justin would lie.

GO ON TO THE NEXT PAGE

Question 61

In which of the following situations is the named defendant most likely to suffer a criminal conviction that would be upheld on appeal?

(A) Byron, who admits to an undercover operative that he regularly snorted Jack Daniels whiskey until last Christmas, is prosecuted under a law effective January 1 of this year that makes it a felony for anyone to snort any alcoholic beverage.

(B) Chadwick, when asked by an off-duty police officer to sell two Super Bowl tickets for five times their face value, loudly proclaims, "I couldn't do that, stranger, because scalping is a felony in this state!" Chadwick, who is unaware that the buyer is a police officer, then whispers to the buyer, "But if you make it six times face value, you've got a deal, buddy." Also unknown to Chadwick, effective the previous week, it is no longer a criminal offense in that state to scalp tickets to sports events. Chadwick is prosecuted for attempted scalping.

(C) State law makes it a misdemeanor to place water in a container that has held chlorine bleach. Duncan, whose car has overheated in the desert, walks several miles to a deserted gas station that has running water and fills an old chlorine bleach container with water to carry back to his car. On the way back, he is picked up by the highway patrol who notice the bleach container and ask what is inside. When Duncan answers, "Water," he is arrested for violation of the misdemeanor statute.

(D) Ed, sitting at a bar whose bartender is an undercover police officer, says to the officer, "God, I'd like to kill my wife. If there was any way I thought I could do it and not get caught, I'd blow her away in a second." Ed is prosecuted for violating a statute that proscribes intent to murder.

Question 62

Congress enacted a statute, over the President's veto, that granted Congress the power to compel the President to remove United States troops from foreign territory when such troops have for 60 days been engaged in hostilities and there has been no formal declaration of war. The statute also provided that Congress may force the President to withdraw the troops before the 60 days have elapsed if Congress passes a joint resolution to that effect.

Which of the following statements best describes the likely result of judicial review of the constitutional validity of this statute?

(A) The statute is a valid exercise of Congress's authority under the war power.

(B) The statute is constitutionally suspect as an infringement on the President's exclusive power, as commander in chief, over matters relating to war.

(C) The statute is a valid exercise of Congress's foreign relations powers.

(D) The statute is constitutionally suspect, because the joint resolution is not subject to a presidential veto.

GO ON TO THE NEXT PAGE

Question 63

Due to intense foreign competition in the domestic market and other adverse economic conditions, the domestic manufacturers of horse liniment formed a trade association, the American Horse Liniment Institute ("AHLI"), whose main purpose was to lobby Congress for tariff protection and for grants-in-aid to modernize their plants, which everyone agreed were less efficient than those of their Asian and European competitors.

Congress passed legislation providing some degree of protection from foreign competition and appropriating $200 million for grants-in-aid to domestic horse liniment manufacturers. However, because of concern about inefficiencies in the industry, the legislation was amended to allow the Secretary of Commerce to deny grants to horse liniment manufacturers who failed to meet certain "management efficiency standards" outlined in the legislation.

Lum & Bagel Co., a liniment manufacturer and a member of AHLI, petitioned the Secretary of Commerce for a $15 million grant, the amount to which Lum & Bagel would be entitled under the legislation, based upon the number of its employees and plants and upon its average production of horse liniment over a 10-year period. The Secretary of Commerce refused to award funds to Lum & Bagel, because she determined that Lum & Bagel was making no attempt to improve its management efficiency. Lum & Bagel filed suit against the Secretary of Commerce, asserting that the power granted to the Secretary was unconstitutional.

Is the legislation constitutional?

(A) Yes, because the Secretary of Commerce, as a representative of the executive branch, may be granted regulatory authority.

(B) Yes, because the executive branch, represented by the Secretary of Commerce, shares power with Congress in the field of foreign commerce.

(C) No, because there was an improper delegation of legislative power.

(D) No, because the executive branch may not impound funds appropriated by Congress.

GO ON TO THE NEXT PAGE

Question 64

Strobe, the owner of Goldacre, decided to sell her property and move to another state. She told her friends to "spread the word" that she wished to sell. After one week, Strobe received in the mail a written offer, signed by Briggs, to purchase Goldacre for $50,000. The written offer was legally sufficient to form a written contract for the sale of Goldacre. Strobe called Briggs and said that the offer was acceptable, but that she did not want to sign it at that time because she wanted to "make sure the paper was legal." The next day Strobe visited her attorney, gave him the written offer from Briggs, and asked him to prepare a formal contract for the sale of Goldacre on the same terms and conditions as those in the written offer. When the attorney had finished, Strobe signed the contract prepared by her attorney and mailed it to Briggs. Later that day, before Briggs had received the contract, Norris called Strobe and offered to buy Goldacre for $60,000, which Strobe accepted immediately over the phone. Strobe called Briggs and told him that she had received a higher offer from Norris that she had accepted. Strobe then signed a written contract to sell Goldacre to Norris. When Norris received the contract he signed it and then promptly and properly recorded it, and sent Strobe the specified down payment. Briggs received the written contract from Strobe the next day. The recording statute in the jurisdiction provides:

> Any conveyance of an interest in land, other than a lease for less than one year, shall not be valid against a subsequent purchaser for value, without notice thereof, whose conveyance is first recorded.

In an appropriate action brought by Briggs against Strobe and Norris for specific performance and to quiet title, Briggs will:

(A) Win, because the written offer satisfies the Statute of Frauds.

(B) Win, because the contract of sale satisfied the Statute of Frauds.

(C) Lose, because he never entered into a binding contract with Strobe.

(D) Lose, because the recording statute protects Norris.

Questions 65-66 are based on the following fact situation:

In 1998, Jane sold Wes her resort hotel for $250,000. Wes paid $100,000 down and agreed to pay the balance in equal monthly installments over the next 15 years.

Jane's eldest son, Luke, started law school in 1999 and, because Jane wanted to help him with his educational and living expenses, she sent a letter to Wes instructing him to send Luke $500 a month from the money he owed to Jane until Jane instructed him otherwise.

Wes was unable to raise the capital he needed to expand the hotel, and in 2000 he sold the resort to Funco in exchange for Funco's agreement to assume all his obligations and to provide him with a long-term contract to be the hotel's manager. Funco agreed with these terms and assumed the contract Wes had with Jane.

In 2002, when Luke had completed law school, Jane's other son, Zack, was getting married. Jane knew Zack could not afford to buy a house so Jane told Zack that she would instruct Wes and Funco to send the full installments to Zack so he could buy a house if Zack agreed that Jane could have the funds back if she ever needed them. Zack agreed, and Jane wrote a letter to Wes informing him of this agreement and instructing him that the full payment should now go to Zack. Zack was given a copy of this letter.

In 2003, Funco wanted to get out of the resort business, and it sold the hotel and all the obligations back to Wes. About this same time, Jane promised her sister's daughter, Susan, that if she wanted to go to Europe for several months to study art, Jane would pay her expenses. Susan agreed, and Jane sent another letter to Wes telling him to send the monthly installments to Susan until Jane told him otherwise. Wes did so.

GO ON TO THE NEXT PAGE

Several months later Jane died, leaving all her cash (and the balance due on the note from Wes) to Zack.

65. Luke sued Wes, claiming he was entitled to receive $500 per month from 2002 until all sums due to Jane had been paid. How would a court hold?

(A) Judgment for Wes, because Luke was only a gratuitous assignee and had no protected rights against Wes.

(B) Judgment for Luke, because he had changed his position in reliance upon Jane's agreement.

(C) Judgment for Wes, because Jane had the right to stop making payments to Luke at anytime.

(D) Judgment for Luke, because his rights were vested when Wes was instructed to make the payments to him.

66. If Zack were to sue Funco to recover the sums paid to Susan, how would a court hold?

(A) Judgment for Zack, because he was a creditor beneficiary, had notice, and had changed his position in reliance on the contract.

(B) Judgment for Zack, because he was a donee beneficiary and had assented to the agreement.

(C) Judgment for Funco, because Zack's rights had not vested before being extinguished by the subsequent assignment.

(D) Judgment for Funco, because Zack was only an incidental beneficiary of its agreement with Wes.

Questions 67-68 are based on the following fact situation:

Leftacre and Rightacre are adjoining 50-acre parcels of land. For many years, Leftacre and Rightacre have been thriving dairy farms. In 1959, McWilliams, the owner of Rightacre, purchased Leftacre. She continued to operate both parcels as separate dairy farms. In 1979, McWilliams sold Rightacre to Stone, who promptly and properly recorded the deed. Since Rightacre had no direct access to a public road, McWilliams wrote into the deed, "Stone, his heirs and assigns shall have the right to use the existing dirt path along the eastern border of Leftacre for ingress and egress to Rightacre." The dirt path, which connected with a public road on the northern boundary of Leftacre, was wide enough for motored vehicle traffic and had been graded for that purpose. In 1994, Sandberg purchased Leftacre from McWilliams. In 2002, Stone died, leaving a will that devised all his interest in Rightacre to O'Toole.

67. For this question only, assume the following facts: In 2003, Sandberg decided to subdivide Leftacre into lots for single-family residences. Since no street in the proposed subdivision will align with the dirt path mentioned in the 1979 deed from McWilliams to Stone, O'Toole will be without ingress and/or egress to Rightacre. O'Toole instituted an appropriate action to enjoin the blocking of the dirt path. The most likely result is that judgment will be for:

(A) O'Toole, because the owner of the servient tenement cannot obstruct an express easement.

(B) O'Toole, because O'Toole has a way by necessity.

(C) Sandberg, because there has been a significant change in conditions and circumstances.

(D) Sandberg, because the appropriate remedy for O'Toole is damages, not injunction.

GO ON TO THE NEXT PAGE

68. For this question only, assume the following facts: In 2003, O'Toole decided to subdivide Rightacre into several lots for single-family residences. O'Toole notified Sandberg that he, O'Toole, will spend the money to improve the dirt path into a private driveway by paving it and doubling its width to 24 feet. He will also provide appropriate drainage for such an improved driveway by means of ditches on either side of the pavement. Sandberg had ceased using Leftacre as a dairy farm five years earlier, and it has been vacant ever since. Sandberg instituted an appropriate action for a declaratory judgment to establish that O'Toole cannot so improve the dirt path. If Sandberg prevails in such an action, it will be because:

(A) The proposed improvement exceeds the scope of an easement by necessity.

(B) The proposed improvement constitutes a burden that exceeds the scope of an express easement.

(C) The servient owner has the obligation for maintenance of an easement for right-of-way, and hence can control the nature of its improvement.

(D) The proposed subdivision so changes the nature of the use of the dominant tenement that any easement has been abandoned.

Question 69

Which of the following plaintiffs has/have standing to sue in federal court?

I. Jane Pease files suit on behalf of herself and taxpayers nationwide to challenge the federal government's spending so much money on military weaponry instead of using the funds for social programs.

II. The "Save Our Wildlife" group files suit to block further oil drilling in the nation because such drilling is contrary to the public's interest in preserving wildlife.

III. The "End Nuclear Power Now Society" files suit challenging a state law that requires disclosure of the Society's membership, alleging that the law infringes on its members' freedom of association.

IV. Luigi Vercotti files suit to challenge exclusionary zoning practices by Carson City, alleging that the challenged zoning made it too expensive for him to buy a home in Carson City.

(A) I. only.

(B) II. and III. only.

(C) III. only.

(D) III. and IV. only.

Question 70

Concerned with the rising amount of organized crime activity in this country, Congress enacts the Stop Organized Crime Act ("SOCA"), which enumerates certain activities, and states that in addition to any crimes these activities currently constitute, they will henceforth constitute the criminal act of intentional furtherance of the goals of organized crime. Among the enumerated activities is the interstate distribution of cocaine. For purposes of this question, you are to assume that the Act is constitutional and otherwise valid in all respects.

Dalton is arrested by federal agents after having driven a truck containing cocaine from Florida to Illinois, where he delivered his illicit cargo to Thomas. At trial, Dalton is convicted of interstate distribution of cocaine, as well as of a violation of SOCA.

Dalton may be sentenced:

(A) Under either statute, but not both.

(B) Under both statutes.

(C) Only under the statute that carries a lesser maximum sentence.

(D) Only under the statute that carries a greater maximum sentence.

GO ON TO THE NEXT PAGE

Question 71

Egbert has died without having executed a will, and his rather substantial estate must be distributed by the probate court. The jurisdiction's applicable statute provides that where a decedent leaves neither issue nor spouse, nor parents, his estate goes to his brothers and sisters and their descendants. Egbert was never married, had no children, and both of his parents are dead. Tamara, whose birth certificate was destroyed by fire, seeks to establish that she is the daughter of Egbert's only sibling, Ethel, now also deceased.

Tamara offers into evidence the statement in a trust instrument recorded pursuant to statute in the office of the county recorder (in which the original is kept). The instrument was executed by Egbert's father, Ethelbert, and recited that certain specified real property conveyed by Ethelbert into the trust should be held for the benefit of "my devoted son Egbert and my beloved daughter Ethel and her loving daughter Tamara." The document actually offered is an enlarged print photocopy of microfilm records, authenticated by an employee of the county.

The trial court should:

(A) Exclude the evidence, because it is not the best evidence.

(B) Exclude the evidence, because it is inadmissible hearsay not within any recognized exception.

(C) Admit the evidence, because it is a record of a document affecting an interest in property.

(D) Admit the evidence, because it constitutes a past recollection recorded.

Questions 72-73 are based on the following fact situation:

Parker was a guest at Hotel, located about 200 miles from his home. After Parker had spent two nights at Hotel, he received a call at 5 a.m. from his wife, who told him that their child had just been rushed to the hospital and was in critical condition. Parker decided to hurry home. He called the airport and reserved space on the next flight out, scheduled to leave at 6:15 a.m. Parker packed and rushed to the lobby. However, it happened that a number of guests were checking out early that morning, and thus there was a long line ahead of him and only one cashier on duty. Parker hoped that the line would move quickly, but when he heard the first guest in line arguing with Stockton, the desk clerk, over a 25¢ telephone charge, he realized that he would never make it to the airport in time if he continued to wait in line. The hotel had no express check-out service available, so he left without paying his bill and flew home.

As soon as Parker's child was out of danger, he wrote a letter to Hotel, apologizing for his swift departure and enclosing payment for two nights' lodging; he also added an extra $25 "to cover any inconvenience and billing expense" he may have caused. Meanwhile, Stockton discovered that Parker had left without paying. On Hotel's behalf, Stockton signed a complaint with the state police, charging Parker with theft of services. The police went to the appropriate magistrate, and a warrant was sworn out for Parker's arrest. The day after Parker left Hotel, Hotel received Parker's letter and payment. However, no one notified the police that Parker had paid his bill. Three days after Parker left Hotel, the state police, armed with a warrant, came to Parker's office and arrested him. Despite Parker's objections, he was taken to jail. Although he repeatedly told the police that he had paid his bill and suggested that they call Hotel, they refused to do so. After holding Parker for 18 hours, the police called Hotel. The manager told the police, "Yes, we got Parker's check two days ago, but we were too busy to call you." The police, with apologies, released Parker. Parker sued Hotel and the state police for false imprisonment.

GO ON TO THE NEXT PAGE

72. In Parker's action against Hotel, who will prevail?

    (A) Hotel, because Hotel reasonably believed that Parker stole services.

    (B) Hotel, because the police were not employees of Hotel.

    (C) Parker, because Hotel failed to promptly notify the police that Hotel had received Parker's check.

    (D) Parker, because Hotel failed to have an adequate number of cashiers on duty when Parker wanted to check out.

73. Will Parker prevail in his action against the police?

    (A) Yes, because of Parker's protestations of innocence.

    (B) Yes, because Parker had not stolen services.

    (C) No, because the police acted pursuant to a valid warrant.

    (D) No, because Hotel had reasonable grounds for signing a complaint against Parker.

Question 74

The Federal Endangered Species Act imposes criminal penalties for killing certain specified animals that have been determined by Congress to be of importance to the tourism industry in the region in which the animal is located. Among the animals protected are the Puce Bandicoots of the Great Spotted Valley area of the state of Wilderness. The state of Wilderness classifies Puce Bandicoots as varmints that may be destroyed at will by anyone with a general hunting license.

Rancher, who possesses a valid state of Wilderness general hunting license, regularly shoots and kills Puce Bandicoots that prey upon his artichoke plants.

If Rancher is prosecuted under the federal statute, and challenges the constitutionality of the law, which of the following is the **strongest** constitutional argument in support of the federal statute?

(A) The commerce power.

(B) The Necessary and Proper Clause.

(C) The police power.

(D) The power to regulate federal lands.

Question 75

Manfred recently moved from an apartment to a house with a large yard. Fortunately, Manfred worked as a checkout clerk at Gardenshop, a nursery and garden supply concern, and was eligible for a discount on a lawn mower. Lately, he had been eyeing a fancy new model of power mower, but even with his discount, it was out of reach. When Manfred's neighbors began complaining about his yard, Manfred decided that he would simply take his dream mower. Gardenshop had so many, they would never miss it, he reasoned. The next day, he took a mower from the Garden Equipment Department and hid it behind some crates on the loading dock. He planned to take the mower home with him that night because he was scheduled to close the business for that day. At the end of the day, however, Manfred became afraid that he would be caught. He returned the mower to the Garden Equipment Department and went home as usual.

Manfred has most likely committed:

(A) Larceny.

(B) Attempted larceny.

(C) Embezzlement.

(D) No crime.

GO ON TO THE NEXT PAGE

Questions 76-77 are based on the following fact situation:

Zelda, a paving contractor with an excellent reputation in the community, entered into a written contract with Norman to pave the parking lot behind his new store. The contract contained no provision regarding assignment.

A few days after they entered into the contract, Zelda realized that scheduling difficulties would make it impossible for her to complete the job in the time Norman needed to have the job done. Instead of running the risk of being in breach of contract, she assigned the job to one of her competitors, Kurt, whom she regarded as being almost as good as she, and who agreed to do the job for the contract price.

76. With regard to this assignment by Zelda, which of the following statements is true?

(A) The assignment is valid only if Norman agrees to accept performance by Kurt.

(B) Zelda breached her contract with Norman by assigning it to Kurt without his prior consent.

(C) Norman must accept performance by Kurt.

(D) The assignment is valid, even if Norman objects, as long as Zelda supervises the performance of the contract by Kurt.

77. Assume for the purposes of this question only that Kurt paved the parking lot under the contract, but Norman did not realize that Kurt was substituting for Zelda until the job was half complete. Upon learning that, Norman let Kurt complete the job. If Kurt fails to perform the job in accordance with the original terms of the agreement between Zelda and Norman, Norman:

(A) Has a cause of action only against Kurt for damages.

(B) Has a cause of action against Kurt and Zelda for damages.

(C) Has no cause of action against Kurt, because he and Kurt are not in privity of contract.

(D) Has no cause of action against Zelda, because he accepted performance from Kurt.

Question 78

Developer owned a large tract of land that she had surveyed by a licensed surveyor and then subdivided into numerous lots. At the time of the survey, the surveyor drove wooden stakes into the ground to mark the boundaries. The surveyor then made a plat of the survey and recorded the plat in the County Recorder of Deeds Office.

On June 1, Andrew purchased Lot 20 in the tract from Developer. Prior to purchase, Developer had shown Andrew the wooden stakes, and Andrew accepted such stakes as marking the boundaries of Lot 20. After taking possession of Lot 20, Andrew built a house thereon and enclosed it with a fence.

On September 5, Bruce purchased Lot 21 from Developer. Lot 21 was adjacent to Lot 20. After taking possession of Lot 21, Bruce hired a licensed surveyor to survey Lot 21. This surveyor discovered that, according to the recorded plat, Andrew's fence extended two feet onto Lot 21. Upon learning this, Bruce demanded that Andrew remove his fence. Andrew refused.

If Bruce sues Andrew, who will prevail?

(A) Andrew, because he bought his lot first.

(B) Andrew, because the surveyor's stakes are controlling.

(C) Bruce, because the recorded plat controls.

(D) Bruce, because the adverse possession period has not run.

GO ON TO THE NEXT PAGE

Question 79

During Dan's prosecution for burglary, the prosecution calls Teddy to the stand, and the following takes place: Prosecutor: "After Dan left the room, what did Roger say to you, if anything?" Previous evidence has established that Roger and Dan had agreed, prior to the time Dan left the room, to burglarize a jewelry store. Defense counsel: "Objection!" Court: "Overruled." Teddy then testifies about what Roger said.

If defense counsel wishes to complain about the court's ruling in this matter on appeal, what more should she do before the trial concludes?

(A) Nothing.

(B) Ask the court for the reasons that the objection was overruled.

(C) Restate the objection for the record, stating the grounds therefor.

(D) Request the trial court to order the prosecution to make an offer of proof.

Question 80

Davis is arrested and tried for battery. At trial, the prosecution offers evidence that shows Davis punched Verne in the stomach. In which of the following situations is Davis most likely to be not guilty of battery?

(A) Davis was heavily intoxicated and was attempting to swat at a fly when he punched Verne.

(B) Davis, who had just awakened from a deep sleep, was not fully aware of what was happening and mistakenly thought Verne was attacking him.

(C) Davis was suffering from an epileptic seizure and had no control over his motions.

(D) Davis, angered by something Verne had said, punched him in retaliation.

Question 81

Dag lost about $500 while playing poker with several persons at Vance's house. When Dag accused Vance of cheating, Vance asked him to leave. Dag became abusive and refused to leave, so Vance and a couple of other players forced him to go.

Angry and determined to get back his money, Dag went to his home and got his gun. He put his pistol into his coat pocket and headed back to Vance's house intending to shoot Vance if he did not give back the $500. But, because Vance knew that Dag had a reputation for being violent, after the altercation at the house Vance had called the police. Just as Dag was about to step onto Vance's property, the police pulled up and stopped him. They frisked him, and finding the pistol in his pocket, arrested him.

A state statute prohibits entry onto the property of another with the intent to commit violence thereon.

If charged with attempt under this statute, most likely Dag will be found:

(A) Not guilty, because this is an "attempt" statute, and there cannot be an attempt of an attempt.

(B) Not guilty, because it would be an attempt to convict a person for a guilty mind.

(C) Guilty, because Dag was trying to enter the property and he had the necessary state of mind.

(D) Guilty, because the statute was designed to protect the public from violence, and Dag is dangerous.

GO ON TO THE NEXT PAGE

Question 82

The state of Eastern Seaboard enacted a sales tax on specified items purchased within the state. The General Services Administration ("GSA") of the United States Government purchased from a dealer in Scrodtown, the largest city in Eastern Seaboard, 100 new automobiles for use by federal agencies operating within the state.

Must GSA pay the sales tax applicable to the new auto purchase?

(A) No, unless Congress has consented to such a tax.

(B) No, because the tax unfairly discriminates against interstate commerce.

(C) Yes, because the tax is nondiscriminatory.

(D) Yes, because there is a rational basis for the tax and it does not appear to be a disguised penalty.

Question 83

Lonny owned Gold Acre, a 40-acre tract of land improved with a one-story house. Lonny leased Gold Acre to Truman for a 15-year period. After five years had expired, the government condemned 15 acres of the property for road construction and allocated the compensation award to Lonny and Truman according to the respective interest so taken. It so happened, however, that Truman had used the 15 acres taken by the government to store vehicles necessary in Truman's work. Truman knew of no other place nearby where he could store the vehicles. There is no applicable statute in the jurisdiction where the property is located, nor any provision in the lease relating to the condemnation. Truman quit possession, claiming that he could no longer live in the premises if he could not park the vehicles needed in his work close to where he lived. Lonny brought suit against Truman to recover rent.

The most likely result of this suit is that Lonny will:

(A) Prevail, because the relationship of landlord and tenant was unaffected by the condemnation, thus leaving Truman still obligated to pay rent.

(B) Prevail, because of the implied warranty on the part of the tenant to return the demised premises in the same condition at the end of the term as they were at the beginning.

(C) Not prevail, because there has been a breach of the implied covenant of quiet enjoyment by Lonny's inability to provide Truman with possession of the whole of the property for the entire term.

(D) Not prevail, because there has been a frustration of purpose that excuses Truman from further performance of his contract to pay rent.

Question 84

Tyrone challenged Dennison to an automobile race from Smalltown to Littleburg, a distance of 11 miles. The only road that ran between the two cities was Highway 17, a two-lane country road. At the 7-mile mark, Tyrone attempted to pass Dennison by pulling into the lane to the left of the center line. At that moment, Pryor's car came into view, heading directly at Tyrone's vehicle. Tyrone applied his brakes and attempted to pull back into the lane to the right of the center line. In so doing, Tyrone lost control of his vehicle and collided with Pryor's car. Dennison's car, having already passed Pryor's car, was not involved in the collision. Pryor brings suit against Dennison for damages suffered in the collision.

Which of the following would be Dennison's best course of action?

(A) Seek dismissal of the claim, because Dennison did not cause Pryor's damage.

(B) Seek indemnity from Tyrone, if Pryor recovers a judgment against Dennison.

(C) Ask the court to limit his liability to one-half of Pryor's damages.

(D) Seek contribution from Tyrone, if Pryor recovers a judgment against Dennison.

GO ON TO THE NEXT PAGE

Question 85

State A, suffering from a severe loss of tax revenues due to an initiative that cut state sales taxes in half, enacted legislation that ended cost-of-living increases in all state employees' pensions.

If a state organization of employees brought suit against the appropriate state official in the federal court to reinstate the increase, the most likely result will be that:

(A) The employees' organization will prevail, because the statute violates the prohibition against the impairment of the obligations of contracts by a state.

(B) The employees' organization will prevail, if it can show that the statute violates the state's constitution.

(C) The employees' suit will be dismissed, because the Eleventh Amendment prohibits a state's citizens from suing a state official for official acts in a federal court.

(D) The employees' organization will not prevail, because the state always has the power to amend its own legislation.

Question 86

Jeff lived in Arkanzona, a state where gambling was illegal. Nevertheless, Jeff gambled on a regular basis. Unfortunately, Jeff had a string of bad luck and needed a loan. Jeff asked his friend Steve to lend him $5,000 to bet on a football game. Jeff claimed that the heavily favored Sabrebacks would lose the game because the game was fixed, and thus he could make a fortune by betting $5,000 against them. Steve, not wanting to miss out on a good deal, agreed to lend Jeff $2,500 if Jeff would bet the other $2,500 for Steve. Jeff agreed, took Steve's $5,000, and placed the bet. Jeff's tip paid off and Jeff won on 4-to-1 odds. He gave Steve his $5,000 back but refused to tender any winnings.

If Steve sues Jeff to recover the winnings due under the contract, who will prevail?

(A) Steve, because he fully performed his part of the bargain.

(B) Steve, because the court will not allow Jeff to unfairly profit from his illegal contract.

(C) Jeff, because the contract was illegal and the court will not enforce an illegal contract.

(D) Jeff, because the contract was illegal and the court will only act to put the parties in the status quo ante, and Steve already has his money back.

Question 87

Doris was at a restaurant eating lunch when she looked up and saw another woman take Doris's coat off the coat rack and walk out the door with it. Doris quickly left and followed the woman. She saw the woman enter a house where she apparently lived. Later, when Doris knew that the woman was not at home, Doris opened a window in the woman's house, climbed in, and got her coat out of the front closet. When she put the coat on, however, she noticed for the first time that in fact it was not her coat. But, because it was so cold outside, Doris decided to wear this coat home and to return it the next day. The following day Doris changed her mind and decided to keep the coat.

Doris is guilty of:

(A) Larceny.

(B) Burglary.

(C) Both larceny and burglary.

(D) Neither larceny nor burglary.

Question 88

Paula's friend Roberto told her that she could use his lakeside cabin for the weekend. Roberto gave Paula instructions on how to find his cabin, but once Paula arrived at the lake, she found that all the cabins looked very similar. Paula re-checked Roberto's instructions and then entered the cabin that she thought belonged to Roberto. In fact, the cabin belonged to Otto.

After Paula unpacked her luggage, she realized that the cabin was quite cold. Thus, she gathered some wood from the woodpile and started a fire in the fireplace. Unbeknownst to Paula, the fireplace flue was blocked and so an explosion ensued; Paula was injured by the explosion. Otto had known that the flue was blocked, but he had not gotten around to having the problem fixed.

If Paula sues Otto for her injuries, who will prevail?

(A) Paula, because Otto knew that the flue was defective.

(B) Paula, because Otto had a duty to warn of the defect.

(C) Otto, but only if he had no reason to antici-pate that anyone would be in the cabin.

(D) Otto, because he owed no duty to Paula.

Question 89

On Halloween night, Darryl, who is 12 years old, dressed up as a bandit by wearing dark clothes and a pair of panty hose over his head and went trick or treating. Darryl carried a toy gun that looked like a real firearm. Darryl's method of operation was to go up to a house and ring the bell. When the person answered, he pointed his toy gun at the person's face and said, "Your money or your life," and then shouted, "Trick or treat!" At the fifth house he went to, Darryl began his routine, but before he could say "trick or treat," Patty, the homeowner, screamed and slammed the door in Darryl's

face. Still shaken by the experience, Patty suffered a heart attack five minutes later.

Has Patty a cause of action against Darryl?

(A) Yes, for intentional infliction of emotional distress.

(B) Yes, for assault.

(C) No, because Darryl is only 12 years old.

(D) No, because Patty should have known that the gun was a toy since it was Halloween.

Question 90

The jurisdiction in which Dawn lives follows the common law Rule Against Perpetuities. If Dawn conveys her property to "Clara, her heirs and assigns, as long as the premises are used for noncommercial purposes, then to Grant, his heirs and assigns," Dawn's interest in the property, if any, is:

(A) Nothing.

(B) A reversion in fee simple absolute.

(C) A possibility of reverter.

(D) A right of entry based on a condition subsequent.

Questions 91-92 are based on the following fact situation:

The Drug Control Act is a federal law that seeks to control those substances that are dangerous to the health of the population in general. The statute provides substantial penalties for violations of the Act. The Food and Drug Administration has conducted a substantial number of tests on a new drug called Gelutan. The results of the studies show that the drug might have dangerous side effects when taken regularly, and the Food and Drug Administration now seeks to prohibit its distribution under the Drug Control Act.

GO ON TO THE NEXT PAGE

91. Drugco, a major pharmaceutical company that desires to market Gelutan, sues to have the statute declared unconstitutional. The most likely result in this suit is that the statute will be declared to be:

    (A) Constitutional, as a proper exercise of the general welfare power.

    (B) Constitutional, as a proper exercise of Congress's power to regulate interstate commerce.

    (C) Unconstitutional, because it interferes with the right of privacy of Gelutan users.

    (D) Unconstitutional, because it deprives Drugco of property without just compensation.

92. Assume for the purposes of this question only that, after further tests, Gelutan is cleared for use in a limited manner as an over-the-counter drug, but only if the drug is produced in pill form. Assume further that Congress, as an extension of the Drug Control Act, enacts an additional provision that levies a one cent per pill tax on Gelutan. This provision is:

    (A) Constitutional, under the Supremacy Clause.

    (B) Constitutional, because it is a proper exercise of congressional power to raise revenue.

    (C) Unconstitutional, because the pills are not being sold in interstate commerce.

    (D) Unconstitutional, because it interferes with state sovereignty.

Question 93

In which of the following cases would a leading question *least likely* be permitted over objection?

(A) When asked on direct examination of a disinterested witness.

(B) When asked on direct examination of a minor.

(C) When asked on cross-examination of an expert witness.

(D) When related to the name, address, or occupation of the witness.

Question 94

On November 7, Margo agreed with Oscar to paint his house for $10,000, payment to be made upon completion of the job. On November 14, while the job was still incomplete, Margo told her paint supplier, Percy, that if he would give her the paint she needed, she would have Oscar pay to him directly the $3,000 for paint that she owed him. Percy agreed, and Margo sent Oscar a letter setting forth this agreement.

On December 1, Margo had completed the job, but Oscar refused to pay Percy any money. In a suit by Percy against Oscar, what would be Oscar's best defense?

(A) Percy had already supplied the paint before the agreement, and therefore he had not relied on Oscar's promise.

(B) Percy was not an intended beneficiary of the agreement between Oscar and Margo.

(C) Margo had not painted the house in a proper, workmanlike manner.

(D) Margo attempted to assign her rights before completion and an assignment to receive money before personal services are performed is inoperable.

Question 95

Dennis got into a fight with his former roommate Tom over some money that Dennis claimed Tom owed for some long distance telephone calls. When Tom refused to pay the money, Dennis took two tickets that Tom had purchased for the All Star game, intending to give them back to Tom the day after the game. Dennis is charged with larceny.

Most likely Dennis will be found:

(A) Not guilty, because he intended to return the tickets to Tom.

(B) Not guilty, because he believed that Tom owed him money.

(C) Guilty, because he intended to deprive Tom of the value of the tickets.

(D) Guilty, because the intent to return is not a good defense.

Question 96

Seth was one of a group of persons who were engaged in a demonstration against the discriminatory practices of a private club. During the demonstration, Seth threw a bomb containing highly toxic gas through the window of the club. At the time he threw the bomb, he knew that the club's president, Larsen, was inside the building. Unknown to Seth, Carver, the club's treasurer, was also inside.

Seth is charged with attempted murder of both Larsen and Carver. At trial, Seth testified that the reason he threw the bomb was that he wanted to make sure that nobody would be able to use the club, and that he did not intend to hurt anyone.

Presuming that the jury believes Seth, he can be convicted of the attempted murder of:

(A) Larsen.

(B) Carver.

(C) Both Larsen and Carver.

(D) Neither Larsen nor Carver.

Questions 97-98 are based on the following fact situation:

Maude's will left her farm in Rural County to her two grown children, Lisa and Louis. The will stated that the farm passed to the children "jointly, as tenants in common." Lisa and Louis, having had no interest in farming, had long since moved to Paree, a large city located about 150 miles from the farm. However, after Maude's death, Louis had second thoughts about living on the farm. His children were becoming disciplinary problems in school, and remembering some of his strict but kindly teachers in the Rural County schools, he decided to move back to the farm. Thus, Louis and his family moved into Maude's home. Louis rented various parts of the land to sharecroppers. Louis regularly sent half of any profits from the farm to his sister.

97. Assume that Lisa dies, survived only by her daughter Estelle. By will Lisa left all of her property to Estelle. Louis, however, refuses to pay any of the profits of the farm to Estelle and claims an exclusive interest in the farm. If Estelle sues Louis, how will a court most likely rule?

(A) For Louis, because he actively managed the use of the farm and Lisa never showed any interest in it.

(B) For Louis, because he survived Lisa, the other joint tenant.

(C) For Louis, because the unities of time, title, and interest have been destroyed by Lisa's death.

(D) For Estelle, because she inherited her mother's interest.

GO ON TO THE NEXT PAGE

98. If Estelle sues not only for the profits from the farm but also seeks an accounting for the years that Louis had exclusive possession of the farm, how will a court most likely rule on this issue?

(A) An accounting will be granted since Louis occupied or controlled more than half of the land.

(B) An accounting will be granted since Louis ousted Lisa from possession.

(C) No accounting will be granted since Lisa had the right to use the property but chose not to do so.

(D) No accounting will be granted if Louis has held the property for the statutory period required for adverse possession.

Question 99

In July of last summer George, a grape grower, contracted with Walter's Winery to deliver "500 tons of premium quality pinot chardonnay grapes grown on my ranch Grapeacre in Grape County." The price was to be $1,000 per ton and delivery was to be on or before September 15. In August of the same year, George entered into an identical contract with Vinnie's Vintner Co. to sell 300 tons of premium quality pinot chardonnay grapes.

George completed his harvest by September 10 and had 800 tons of premium quality grapes. On September 11, an unexpected rain ruined 400 tons, and George notified Walter and Vinnie on that day that he would only be able to deliver 250 tons to Walter and 150 tons to Vinnie. On September 14, Vinnie purchased an additional 150 tons of premium quality pinot chardonnay grapes from Godfrey, one of several other available sources for premium quality pinot chardonnay grapes. These grapes along with the 150 tons from George gave Vinnie the 300 tons he needed.

On September 15, what is Walter's Winery's legal position with regard to George's failure to deliver the 500 tons of grapes required by his contract?

(A) If Walter has given George a written notice of termination, Walter will have the right to refuse to accept the 250 tons of grapes but will have no cause of action for damages against George.

(B) Even if Walter has given George a written notice of termination, Walter must accept the 250 tons of grapes and will have no cause of action for damages against George.

(C) Since Vinnie's purchase establishes that it is possible for George to perform by obtaining additional grapes from other available sources, Walter may accept the 250 tons from George and recover damages for George's failure to deliver the balance of the amount specified by the contract.

(D) Since George's contract with Walter was entered into before his contract with Vinnie, George is bound to deliver the entirety of his grape crop to Walter.

Question 100

A statute in State B stated that directors of orphanages, homes for the developmentally disabled, and similar institutions stand in loco parentis to the children under their charge. Dieter, a mentally disabled 11-year-old child, had been abandoned by his parents and lived in the Miserere Home, a State B residential facility for the developmentally disabled operated by the Sisters of Hope, a religious order. Sister Mary Smith was the director of the facility. The Miserere Home had no fence around it, because children who lived there were not considered to be dangerous. Dieter wandered away from the premises and was gone for 36 hours before he was found by the police and returned to Miserere. When Dieter was away from the facility, he beat up Paul, a five-year-old boy. Paul's parents filed suit against Sister Mary on Paul's behalf.

Assuming that no other liability statute applies, who will prevail?

(A) Paul, because under the statute Sister Mary has the responsibilities and duties of a parent.

(B) Paul, because Sister Mary is strictly liable for Dieter's acts.

(C) Sister Mary, because parents are not vicariously liable for the intentional torts of their children.

(D) Sister Mary, unless she knew that Dieter had dangerous propensities.

STOP

ANSWER KEY AND SUBJECT KEY

Answer		Subject	Answer		Subject
1.	A	Torts	51.	B	Criminal Law/Procedure
2.	B	Torts	52.	C	Constitutional Law
3.	C	Real Property	53.	B	Torts
4.	A	Evidence	54.	A	Contracts
5.	C	Constitutional Law	55.	B	Torts
6.	A	Contracts	56.	B	Evidence
7.	C	Criminal Law	57.	C	Criminal Law
8.	C	Real Property	58.	B	Evidence
9.	C	Evidence	59.	B	Evidence
10.	C	Torts	60.	D	Evidence
11.	B	Torts	61.	C	Criminal Law
12.	A	Constitutional Law	62.	D	Constitutional Law
13.	B	Torts	63.	A	Constitutional Law
14.	A	Constitutional Law	64.	D	Real Property
15.	B	Criminal Law/Procedure	65.	C	Contracts
16.	C	Contracts	66.	C	Contracts
17.	B	Contracts	67.	A	Real Property
18.	C	Real Property	68.	B	Real Property
19.	B	Torts	69.	C	Constitutional Law
20.	B	Evidence	70.	B	Criminal Law/Procedure
21.	C	Constitutional Law	71.	C	Evidence
22.	C	Criminal Law	72.	B	Torts
23.	A	Real Property	73.	C	Torts
24.	B	Evidence	74.	A	Constitutional Law
25.	A	Criminal Law/Procedure	75.	A	Criminal Law
26.	C	Constitutional Law	76.	C	Contracts
27.	C	Evidence	77.	B	Contracts
28.	C	Criminal Law	78.	B	Real Property
29.	D	Torts	79.	C	Evidence
30.	B	Evidence	80.	C	Criminal Law
31.	B	Contracts	81.	C	Criminal Law
32.	D	Contracts	82.	A	Constitutional Law
33.	C	Real Property	83.	A	Real Property
34.	C	Evidence	84.	D	Torts
35.	B	Constitutional Law	85.	A	Constitutional Law
36.	B	Evidence	86.	C	Contracts
37.	C	Real Property	87.	A	Criminal Law
38.	B	Criminal Law	88.	C	Torts
39.	A	Real Property	89.	D	Torts
40.	A	Evidence	90.	C	Real Property
41.	B	Criminal Law	91.	B	Constitutional Law
42.	A	Real Property	92.	B	Constitutional Law
43.	C	Constitutional Law	93.	A	Evidence
44.	B	Contracts	94.	C	Contracts
45.	A	Contracts	95.	C	Criminal Law
46.	B	Contracts	96.	D	Criminal Law
47.	C	Torts	97.	D	Real Property
48.	C	Torts	98.	C	Real Property
49.	C	Contracts	99.	A	Contracts/Sales
50.	B	Real Property	100.	D	Torts

Answer to Question 1

(A) If U-Pump-It prevails, it will be because the court follows the Cardozo approach to duty questions. Under Cardozo's approach in *Palsgraf v. Long Island Railroad,* a plaintiff can recover for the defendant's breach of duty only if she can establish that a reasonable person would have foreseen a risk of injury to her in the circumstances; *i.e.,* that she was located in a foreseeable zone of danger. Here, even assuming that Timmy breached a duty by parking his truck on the street, Bonnie was not within a foreseeable zone of danger and would not be able to recover damages under this view. (B) is incorrect because Timmy's stopping for a cup of coffee after making deliveries does not take him outside the scope of the employment relationship. Hence, if Timmy breached a duty to Bonnie, U-Pump-It would be vicariously liable for her injuries. (C) is incorrect because even if Oswald were a legal (proximate) cause of Bonnie's injuries, that would not preclude Timmy and U-Pump-It from being a legal cause as well. (D) is wrong because the fact that Timmy violated company rules by parking on the street would not prevent U-Pump-It from being liable for Timmy's actions, because he was still acting within the scope of his employment relationship.

Answer to Question 2

(B) Olivia will recover the fair market value of the machine because Scarlet is liable for conversion. Conversion is the intentional interference with the plaintiff's right of possession in the chattel that is serious enough to warrant that the defendant pay the full value of the chattel. Conversion will be found if the defendant was using the chattel without permission and it was accidentally damaged, as in this case. The remedy for conversion is the fair market value of the chattel at the time and place of conversion. Thus, (B) is correct and (A) is incorrect. (C) is incorrect because that would be the remedy for trespass to chattels, which is a less serious interference than conversion. Here, an unauthorized use that resulted in damages equaling almost half the chattel's original cost is too serious an interference in nature and consequences to be only trespass to chattel. (D) is incorrect because Scarlet's lending the sewing machine without permission satisfies the intent requirement. Even though the damage was accidental, Scarlet is liable for conversion.

Answer to Question 3

(C) Under a race-notice statute such as the one in this question, a subsequent purchaser is protected only if he purchases without notice of prior conveyances and records first. However, even though Madonna had notice of Presley's deed and was therefore not a bona fide purchaser, and could not have prevailed against Presley, that does not mean that a bona fide purchaser from her would not prevail against Presley. Fats was a subsequent bona fide purchaser from Madonna and recorded before Presley. Thus, Fats would prevail over Presley. Chubby, who had notice of Presley's deed when he subsequently acquired his deed from Fats, will also prevail over Presley. This is due to the "shelter doctrine," which is applied to the recording acts. Under that doctrine, once a bona fide purchaser enters the chain of events, she can subsequently deed the land to a party who had notice of the prior deed and that party is also accorded the status of a bona fide purchaser. Thus, once Fats, a bona fide purchaser, enters the picture and gets the protection of the act, he can sell to Chubby, who gets the protection of the act even though he purchased with notice. Chubby comes under the shelter doctrine. The theory behind the shelter doctrine is that it extends full protection to bona fide purchasers in that it does not limit their ability to market the property. Otherwise, if they could not sell to parties with notice, their ability to market the property would be impaired. The exception to the shelter doctrine is that it does not apply to the first purchaser with notice—Madonna. Thus, if Fats had subsequently sold to Madonna, she would not have been accorded the status of a bona fide purchaser. The reason for the exception is obvious—to discourage fraud. Note also that because Chubby has a deed from Fats, he prevails over Fats. Therefore, (A), (B), and (D) are all incorrect.

Answer to Question 4

(A) The testimony of a surprise witness is not inadmissible if the party against whom the testimony is offered is granted a continuance to prepare for cross-examination. Therefore, the evidence in (A) will likely be admitted. The evidence in (B) is less likely to be admitted because it is of a subsequent remedial measure which is generally inadmissible and cannot be justified in this case as showing ownership when the defendant has conclusively admitted such ownership. (C) is wrong because most likely the judge will find that the probative force of the evidence is substantially outweighed by its prejudicial effect. (D) is not the best answer. While the evidence offered in (D) is clearly relevant, an acceptable reason for excluding the evidence would be that its probative value is substantially outweighed by needless presentation of cumulative evidence. It is possible that the evidence in (D) would be admitted, but it is not as likely to be admitted as the evidence in (A).

Answer to Question 5

(C) Although the First and Fourteenth Amendments severely limit the states' right to regulate public speech, reasonable regulations based on time, place, and manner are constitutionally permissible. (D) is thus wrong. (A) is wrong because the fact that the civic center is a place normally used for demonstrations of this type does not bar the city from restricting the demonstration; that is exactly why the city sought to impose certain limitations on these demonstrations. (B) is also incorrect, because a municipality does have the limited right to place certain limitations on a citizen's right of free speech in these circumstances, even when there is absolutely no reason to believe that the demonstration will be anything but peaceful and quiet. However, any such regulation by the city cannot be substantially overbroad (e.g., censor protected speech) or vague (i.e., be so unclear as to what is prohibited that a demonstrator is required to censor himself). The statute's provisions for terminating a parade and arresting demonstrators are too overbroad and vague to meet any legitimate state purpose. Absent any court decisions that have limited construction of the regulation so as to remove the threat to constitutionally protected expression, the statute's imprecise terms could be applied to protected speech and do not provide persons with reasonable notice as to what speech is prohibited.

Answer to Question 6

(A) June will win because consideration generally is required for modification of a contract, and Carol's preexisting debt cannot serve as valid consideration. Consideration generally is necessary to modify a contract. Payment of a smaller sum than due will not be sufficient consideration for a promise by a creditor to discharge a debt unless the consideration is in some way new or different (e.g., payment before maturity or to one other than the creditor) or the amount of debt is subject to an honest dispute (and so the parties are giving up the right to litigate the amount, which is consideration sufficient to support a modification in and of itself). Here, nothing indicates that Carol gave anything new or different in exchange for the lower payment. Moreover, the amount was not in dispute. Therefore, there is no consideration supporting the modification, so the modification is unenforceable. (Note that even if the money was owed on a contract under the U.C.C., which permits modification without consideration, the modification still would be unenforceable because the modification must still have a good faith purpose and nothing in the facts indicates that the modification was made in good faith.) (B) is incorrect because the agreement was not supported by consideration. As discussed above, consideration is required to support Carol and June's agreement. Payment by Carol of a smaller sum than due is not sufficient consideration. Therefore, June is not bound by the agreement, and she may recover the $10,000. (C) is incorrect because accord and satisfaction require that the amount of the debt be in *dispute*. A contract may be discharged by an accord (an agreement, supported by consideration, to accept some other performance in lieu of the performance required under the existing contract) and satisfaction (the performance of the accord agreement). A partial payment of an original debt will suffice for an accord and satisfaction where there is a "bona fide dispute" as to the claim. However, because the amount of Carol's debt was not in dispute, her payment of $80,000 was not valid consideration for an accord agreement. Therefore, Carol's original debt has not been discharged by an accord and satisfaction, and June may recover the $10,000. (D) is incorrect because it is irrelevant. A contract can be modified before or after the date of performance if the modification is supported by consideration. As discussed above, Carol's payment of a preexisting debt is not valid consideration for the new agreement. Therefore, June is entitled to the $10,000 owed from the original contract, even though she agreed after the due date to settle for $80,000.

Answer to Question 7

(C) Parafun will not be guilty of *manslaughter* because at common law a corporation is not responsible for the criminal acts of its employees. Common law took the position that since the corporation had no mind, it could not form the mens rea necessary for a traditional crime, and since the corporation could not be imprisoned, there was no criminal liability imposed on the corporation for the common law crimes committed by its agents. While the common law rule has been changed by statute in many jurisdictions, the question does not indicate the existence of such a statute. Absent a statute, Parafun will not be guilty of manslaughter. (A) is wrong because, as stated above, at common law a corporation would not be liable for a common law crime. In addition, at common law an employer is not responsible for the unauthorized criminal conduct of his employees. (B) is wrong. Even if criminal liability could be imposed on Parafun for the crimes of Silk, there would have to be a showing that Silk was at least *reckless* in causing the death. (B) seems to impose liability on Parafun without regard to the mental state of Silk. (D) is wrong. The fact that there was only a 1% chance of parachute failure would be a factor for the jury to consider in deciding whether a person acted "recklessly"; it would not as a matter of law negate criminal liability.

Answer to Question 8

(C) There are many types of deeds that can be used to convey real property, some of which contain no covenants at all, such as quitclaim deeds. Thus, if Farley can show that the power of attorney did not include the power to convey a deed containing covenants, Glenda would not prevail. Thus, (A) is wrong. (D) is incorrect because although Farley did not make any specific covenants, Milton did. Farley will be held to those covenants if it is found that the power of attorney was intended to grant Milton the power to convey a deed containing covenants. (B) is incorrect because Glenda could have a claim for breach of the covenant of title and right to convey even if Farley's former wife did not bring a claim against her. The fact that she may have to defend such a suit is sufficient breach to entitle Glenda to institute an action.

Answer to Question 9

(C) This answer can best be understood by examining the permissible questions first. (A) asks about a prior conviction for forgery. Under Federal Rule 609, prior convictions of crimes requiring proof or admission of an act of dishonesty or false statement may be inquired into if they are less than 10 years old. This crime is one of dishonesty and is not too old; therefore, the question is proper. (B) is also a proper question. It goes to bias, which is always a permissible line of inquiry. (D) relates to prior bad acts for which there is no conviction. Federal Rule 608(b) permits cross-examination concerning prior bad acts if, in the discretion of the court, they are probative of truthfulness. Cheating a business partner is dishonest, and Winston is a witness not a party; therefore, this question is proper. That leaves alternative (C). If the ability to observe, relate, or recall were at issue, then this question could be a permissible line of inquiry, especially since Winston is not a party and is not likely to be prejudiced by the question. On the other hand, the probative value of the other questions is obvious. Since the other questions are all obviously right, this is the one most likely to be ruled improper.

Answer to Question 10

(C) Arthur's statements (I) and (III) were false representations of material facts and therefore actionable. To establish a prima facie case of intentional misrepresentation (deceit), a plaintiff must establish (i) a misrepresentation made by the defendant, (ii) scienter, (iii) an intent to induce plaintiff's reliance on the misrepresentation, (iv) causation (*i.e.,* actual reliance), (v) justifiable reliance, and (vi) damages. Usually, there is a requirement that the false representation be of a material past or present fact; whether the restoration was accomplished with genuine or hand-made parts as in statement (I), or whether it contained original equipment as in statement (III), are statements of fact that would be very material to a potential buyer of classic cars. Hence, assuming that all the other elements of deceit are proved, both of these statements can be the basis of Arthur's claim. Statement (II), on the other hand, will not support Arthur's misrepresentation claim because he cannot show justifiable reliance on the statement. As a general matter, reliance on false statements of opinion, value, or quality will be viewed as unjustified. Bud's claims that this is the "finest" restoration and "one of the two best" are statements of opinion as to quality. An exception to this rule might apply if Arthur were purchasing the car to enter into competition, or if Bud had superior knowledge of the subject matter, but here there is no indication what Arthur's plans are, and Arthur's experience with classic cars would make his reliance on Bud's opinion unjustified. Thus, (C) is correct; only statements (I) and (III) will support Arthur's claims.

Answer to Question 11

(B) Under the "avoidable consequences" rule, a plaintiff has a duty to mitigate damages to avoid further injuries from the defendant's conduct. Since Herder's property was damaged in this situation, Herder's claim would be based on strict liability. As such, simple contributory negligence would not be a good defense in jurisdictions following traditional contributory negligence rules. (C) is therefore incorrect. But if the plaintiff discovers the existence of the danger and fails to act reasonably to prevent further harm from occurring, the defendant would have a good defense. (A) is incorrect because there is no balancing of utility and risk where ultrahazardous activities are involved. (D) is incorrect because Herder would have had to have known of and appreciated the risk involved when he purchased the property to constitute assumption of the risk. Thus, (B) is the only correct answer.

Answer to Question 12

(A) As a general rule, a state may not retroactively alter a contract to which it is a party. While that prohibition is not absolute, legislation that reduces the contractual burdens on the state will be strictly scrutinized. Here, the legislature is simply making a choice about how to distribute resources to meet competing needs, and the impairment will be stricken. A state may repeal its own enactments, but may not do so when repeal violates a constitutional prohibition. Thus, (B) is incorrect. Sovereign immunity is not a constitutional doctrine, nor is equitable estoppel, except as subsumed in the Due Process Clause in a manner not as directly applicable under these circumstances as the impairment of contracts doctrine. Therefore, (C) and (D) are incorrect.

Answer to Question 13

(B) Sandra, acting at Cole's direction, has the same privilege as Cole to make a felony arrest if there are reasonable grounds for doing so. The fact that Cole announced himself as a police officer, and that as a newspaper reporter, Sandra may have been familiar with police techniques, tends to show that her mistake, if any, would probably be reasonable. (A) is wrong; this is a misstatement of law. Since the facts indicate that Cole was a police officer, the reasonableness of her belief is irrelevant. (C) is wrong; Sandra need not have been a witness to make an arrest for a felony. (D) is wrong; this would deny Sandra the benefit of Cole's privilege to make an arrest if he has reasonable grounds to believe that a felony has been committed. In a case such as this, the citizen is privileged to the same extent as an officer.

Answer to Question 14

(A) The ordinance is probably unconstitutional because it violates free speech rights under the First Amendment. The Supreme Court has held that a charitable appeal for funds involves a variety of speech interests protected by the First Amendment. In one case, an ordinance that prohibited door-to-door solicitation by organizations that did not use at least 75% of their receipts for charitable purposes was struck down by the Court. The present ordinance would probably run afoul of the same rule, since in effect it prohibits all charitable solicitation absent relatively burdensome compliance with its registration provisions. The ordinance is also vulnerable because it limits the right of solicitation to those who belong to "a recognized charitable organization." (B), while a correct statement of law, does not apply in these circumstances. The question is directed toward the challenge George would mount, not one that a religious organization might pursue. (C) is incorrect. Since the First Amendment rights at issue here are fundamental, a "reasonable balance" is not enough; the government ordinance is a direct, content-based regulation, and will be subjected to strict scrutiny. (D) is incorrect because even if the prevention of fraud is a compelling state interest, the statute is not narrowly tailored to achieve that interest, which is required under the strict scrutiny standard.

Answer to Question 15

(B) The motion to suppress the evidence will be granted because the police did not have probable cause to search the car. When the police place the driver of an automobile under arrest, there are a number of alternatives with respect to a search of the car: (i) Regardless of the crime for which the defendant is arrested, the police can search the entire passenger area of the car as a search incident to an arrest. However, the search incident to an arrest must be conducted at the time of the arrest. (ii) If the police have probable cause to search the car—*i.e.*, reasonable grounds for believing that a legitimate item of seizure is in the car—a search of the entire car can be made without a warrant. The search based on probable cause can be made at the time of the arrest or at a later time. (iii) If the police take the car under their control for an administrative reason (such as to get the car off the highway), they can "inventory" the items in the car under certain circumstances. In this question, the search of the car at the police station would have been valid *if* the police had probable cause to search the car. The question does not provide any facts that could form the basis for probable cause to search. Thus, the motion to suppress will be granted because of the lack of probable cause. (A) is wrong for two reasons: The search could not be justified as a search incident to an arrest since the arrest had been completed. Also, when conducting a valid search incident to an arrest, the police *may* open up a closed container within the arrestee's "wingspan." (C) is wrong because, as stated, a search incident to an arrest must occur at the time of the arrest. (D) is wrong. The police can conduct an administrative inventory if the car has been impounded by the police, and the police are, in fact, conducting an inventory of the items in the car. In this question, the car had not been impounded by the police, nor would it need to be since Dolly could drive it home. Also, it is clear from the facts that a traditional search was taking place.

Answer to Question 16

(C) Sam's unconditional promise to sell created a contract even if Bob knew of Winnie's interest. When a promise is unconditional, the failure to perform according to its terms is a breach of contract. By not making his promise conditional on Winnie's consent to convey her interest, Sam impliedly undertook to obtain her consent. Therefore, the contract is enforceable. (Note that this does not necessarily mean that Bob will be able to get the car; he may have to settle for damages because of Winnie's interest.) (A) is incorrect although partially true. It is true that Sam cannot sell Winnie's half of the car without her consent; however, that does not make the contract here unenforceable. As stated above, by making his promise unconditional, Sam undertook a duty to obtain Winnie's consent to sell the car. His failure to do so is a breach of contract, but a breach does not negate a contract; it merely gives the nonbreaching party a right to certain remedies. Therefore, the contract is enforceable, even if Winnie refuses to sell her interest. (B) is incorrect because Bob's knowledge of Winnie's interest is irrelevant to the issue of the contract's enforceability. As discussed above, Sam's unconditional promise implied that Sam would obtain Winnie's consent to convey her interest in the car. Therefore, the contract is enforceable regardless of whether Bob was aware of Winnie's interest at the time he signed. (D) is incorrect because "prospective inability" is not a ground for discharge. Prospective failure of consideration occurs when a party has reasonable grounds to believe that the other party will be unable or unwilling to perform when due. The prospective inability of performance does not discharge the contract; rather, it allows the innocent party to suspend further performance until he receives adequate assurances that performance will be forthcoming. Therefore, the contract between Sam and Bob is not discharged because of prospective inability of performance.

Answer to Question 17

(B) Bob can recover from Sam because Sam's statement to Bob that Winnie would not go along with the sale should reasonably be interpreted as a repudiation. Anticipatory repudiation occurs where a promisor, prior to the time set for performance, unequivocally indicates that he cannot or will not perform when the time comes. Anticipatory repudiation gives the nonrepudiator the option of suspending his performance and waiting to sue until the performance date, or to sue immediately. Here, Sam unequivocally stated that he could not deliver the car for $25,000 because of Winnie's refusal to convey her interest. This repudiation excused Bob's tender on the date set for delivery, and gave rise to an immediate action for damages. (A) is incorrect because Bob's duty to tender $25,000 on the date set for delivery was excused by Sam's repudiation. As discussed above, Sam's statement that Winnie would not agree to a $25,000 sale was an anticipatory breach. Therefore, Bob's duty to tender the $25,000 was excused, leaving Sam without a cause of action for breach. (C) is incorrect because Sam's repudiation the day after the contract was signed gave rise to an *immediate* action for damages. As discussed above, Sam's statement about Winnie's refusal to sell for under $40,000 was an anticipatory repudiation. This repudiation excused Bob's duty to tender the $25,000 and gave him the right to immediate recovery from Sam for breach of contract. (D) is incorrect because the contract was not terminated. As discussed above, Sam's statement about Winnie's unwillingness to sell the car for $25,000 was an anticipatory breach.

This repudiation excused Bob's duty to tender the $25,000 and gave rise to an immediate action for damages. Therefore, Bob's failure to tender the $25,000, which he no longer had a duty to do, did not terminate the contract.

Answer to Question 18

(C) It seems clear that Clara intended her grandchildren to inherit the property at some time, and that the only thing she desired was that Truman be able to live there as long as he wanted. Since Truman could conceivably live there all his life, this devise would be deemed a life estate in Truman, with a vested remainder in Sam. Sam's interest would, however, be subject to open (partial defeasance) since it was possible that Truman could have other children. At Truman's death, Sam's interest became indefeasibly vested. (A) is incorrect because the language of the will clearly does not express an intent that Truman take a fee simple absolute. (B) is incorrect because however many children Truman may have, his life would be the measuring life, and the grandchildren would inherit upon his death. Thus, this would not violate the Rule Against Perpetuities. (D) is wrong because Sam's interest was vested on his birth. It is true that it was subject to open and the time of possession was contingent on Truman's decision to live in the house, but Sam's basic remainder interest was always vested.

Answer to Question 19

(B) To prevail, Prole must show evidence of actual injury. When a defamatory statement involves a matter of public concern, the plaintiff must provide competent evidence of actual injury (*i.e.*, presumed damages are not permitted absent a showing of knowledge of falsity or reckless disregard of truth). Actual injury is not limited to out-of-pocket loss; it may include impairment of reputation, personal humiliation, and mental anguish. Here, the reasons for the firing of the chief operating officer of a town's largest employer, and the financial health of that employer, are matters of public concern for the readership of the Middletown *Herald*. Hence, Prole will have to prove actual injury to prevail. (A) is incorrect because pecuniary damages are not necessary in libel cases. If not for the fact that a matter of public concern was involved, damages would be presumed. (C) is wrong even though it is a true statement. The common law rule of presumed damages is supplanted by the constitutional rules because a matter of public concern is involved. (D) is wrong because even if Prole is not a public figure, the article involved a matter of public concern, so damages will not be presumed.

Answer to Question 20

(B) The court should rule for the defendant and allow the treatise to be read and considered by the jury as substantive evidence. Although the treatise constitutes hearsay because it is an out-of-court statement offered to prove the truth of the matter asserted (that the surgical procedure was accepted), it falls within one of the exceptions to the hearsay rule. Under Federal Rule 803(18), information in treatises can be read into evidence if the treatise is: (i) relied upon by the expert or is called to his attention during cross-examination, and (ii) is established as reliable by the witness, another expert, or judicial notice. The treatise itself is not admitted into evidence, but rather the relevant section is read in. Thus, (B) is correct and (D) is incorrect. (A) is incorrect because the Federal Rules allow such evidence to be used substantively and do not limit the information to impeachment, as a number of state courts do. (C) is incorrect because the information in a learned treatise is admissible as long as it is established to be reliable; however, if the opposing party did rely on the treatise, the offering party need not otherwise establish reliability.

Answer to Question 21

(C) The strongest possible argument here is (C) because equal protection claims are made against the federal government pursuant to the Fifth Amendment's Due Process Clause. The Supreme Court has held that this provision implicitly includes a requirement for equal protection. Although Portman has little chance of prevailing because only a rational basis test is used for age discrimination claims, this answer is the only possible basis for challenging the law. (A) is wrong because both constitutional provisions referring to privileges and immunities apply to *state* government conduct and are never used against the federal government. The Fourteenth Amendment provides that no state shall deny any citizen the privileges or immunities of national citizenship. Article IV provides that no state shall deny citizens of other states the privileges and immunities it accords its own citizens. (B) is wrong because a "just compensation" claim will only provide him compensation for his loss of property. Even if his job is considered to be a property right, the just compensation claim would not provide him the relief he wants, which is reinstatement in his job. (D) is wrong because even though there is no express provision in Article I, Section 8, concerning this legislation, it certainly is within congressional powers.

Answer to Question 22

(C) The jury should find Diana not guilty of murder. Even though Diana was the initial aggressor, she reacquired her right to self-defense because Velma responded to Diana's use of nondeadly force with deadly force without giving Diana a chance to withdraw. (B) is therefore incorrect. (A) is incorrect because the majority of jurisdictions do not require a party to retreat. Furthermore, even in those jurisdictions that follow the retreat rule, a person is not required to retreat unless she can do so with complete safety. (D) is incorrect because a defendant can be guilty of murder even if she did not premeditate.

Answer to Question 23

(A) Because Beta recorded prior to the subsequent conveyance, Beta has the superior right to title regardless of the type of recording statute. A conveyance that is recorded can never be divested by a subsequent conveyance through operation of the recording statutes. By recording, the grantee gives constructive (or "record") notice to everyone. Hence, proper recording prevents anyone from becoming a subsequent BFP. Since Alpha's conveyance to Beta was recorded at the time of Alpha's conveyance to Gamma, Gamma cannot prevail. Gamma will clearly lose under a pure race statute because Beta recorded first. Gamma will also lose under notice and race-notice statutes because the conveyance to Beta was recorded at the time of the conveyance to Gamma. Gamma, therefore, had record notice and cannot claim the protection that these types of statutes provide for subsequent purchasers for value who take *without* notice. Thus, (A) is correct and (B) is incorrect. The fact that Beta is merely a donee rather than a bona fide purchaser does not mean that her recording has no effect. It is only the *subsequent* taker who has to be a BFP rather than a donee to utilize the recording statute. The prior grantee, regardless of her status, protects her interest by recording because it prevents anyone from becoming a subsequent BFP. (C) is incorrect because, as noted above, Beta will prevail under any type of recording act, but not necessarily because she recorded prior to Gamma's recording. If the jurisdiction has a notice statute, whether Beta recorded prior to Gamma's recording is irrelevant. Rather, it is the fact that Beta recorded prior to Gamma's *purchase* that gives Beta superior title in a notice jurisdiction, because Gamma would have record notice of the conveyance and thus would not qualify as a bona fide purchaser. (D) is incorrect because the quitclaim/warranty deed distinction does not affect who has title to Greekacre; that status merely affects the parties' respective causes of action and ability to recover against Alpha.

Answer to Question 24

(B)   Any person can testify to the authenticity of another's signature as long as that witness has seen the person's signature and can express an opinion regarding its authenticity. There is no requirement that the witness have seen the signature recently, and thus (A) is not the best answer, even though the length of time since the witness last saw the signature in question may go to the weight that should be given the witness's testimony. Nor is it decisive that the witness testifying regarding the signature has only seen it once. Under this circumstance, the witness's testimony may lack reliability, but that is a fact for defense counsel to bring out. Thus, (C) is incorrect. The testimony is of sufficient reliability to permit its admission. Thus, (D) is wrong.

Answer to Question 25

(A)   In order to issue a valid search warrant, the magistrate must determine that there exists reasonable grounds to believe that a legitimate item of seizure is located at the place to be searched, *i.e.*, "probable cause to search." However, a finding that the warrant was invalid because it was not supported by probable cause will not entitle a defendant to exclude the evidence obtained under the warrant if the police reasonably relied on the warrant's facial validity. Hence, (A) is correct. (B) and (D) are wrong because once the police are in the defendant's apartment with a facially valid search warrant, it is immaterial that they are unable to find the items for which the search warrant was issued, and if in their legal search they turn up other contraband, evidence of this discovery is admissible. (C) is incorrect. It is true that the length of time between the time an informant observed some facts and the time this information is given to the police is important, because the greater the time, the less chance that the facts still remain the same and, therefore, there is less probable cause to believe that the designated items are still in the place where the informant says they are. However, as discussed above, a determination that probable cause is absent will not necessarily require that the evidence be excluded.

Answer to Question 26

(C)   Larson has more than an abstract interest in redressing his grievance. His right to redress, guaranteed by the state through its statutory enactment, is itself a property right. Although the legislature may elect not to confer a property interest, it may not constitutionally authorize the deprivation of such an interest, once conferred, without appropriate procedural safeguards. [Logan v. Zimmerman Brush (1982)] Thus, the state statute cannot be applied so as to deprive Larson of his property interest in using the statutory procedure for possible redress of unfair employment practices without at least affording him an opportunity for an appropriate hearing. It follows that (A) and (B) are incorrect, both because they state the wrong result and because they misstate the applicable rules. As indicated, Larson has a property interest and thus (A) is wrong. (B), in turn, describes a valid general rule but does not describe this case. The state can enact specific procedures, expect Larson to follow them, and bar the claim if he fails to do so. That is, however, not what happened here. Rather, the state itself failed to act in a timely manner, and the statutory time limit operated indiscriminately to extinguish Larson's claim. Finally, (D) is incorrect because it is too general. What happened to Larson was "unfair" because it deprived him of a property right, not because the state is required to provide any remedy, or a specific remedy.

Answer to Question 27

(C)   This question involves an admission—*i.e.,* a statement by a party (Deborah) being offered against her. An admission is ***not considered a hearsay statement***. [Fed. R. Evid. 801(d)(2)] Thus, (C) appears to be correct—that Walter's testimony about Deborah's statement will be admitted because it is not hearsay. (C) is not an ideal answer, though, because it is so incomplete. The fact that an item of evidence is nonhearsay does not automatically render it admissible. For example, if nonhearsay evidence is irrelevant, it would not be admissible. Thus, deciding whether (C) is the *best* answer requires a thorough assessment of the alternatives. (D) can be quickly discarded as incorrect. Impeachment evidence is not admissible until *after* the witness to be impeached has testified. It would be improper to admit Walter's testimony for the purpose of impeaching Deborah's *expected* testimony as to the result of her own investigation of the accident. (A) is tempting, but it is also incorrect. Normally, an out-of-court statement of a declarant, like the in-court testimony of a witness, is admissible only if it was made *with personal knowledge*. This requirement, however, does not apply to admissions. Thus, although Deborah's statement ("Ned just got hurt because I forgot to do my yard work") was made without personal knowledge, it will be admissible. As a party, Deborah will have ample opportunity to explain why she made the statement even though she lacked personal knowledge about the accident that injured Ned. The persuasiveness of her explanation will determine whether the jury takes her admission seriously. (B) is also incorrect. The common law requirement that lay witnesses were not permitted to give opinions, but only allowed to state facts, has been rejected in favor of a *helpfulness standard*. For example, Rule 701 allows lay witnesses to give testimony in opinion form as long as it is helpful to a clear understanding of the testimony or the determination of a fact in issue. Similarly, an admission is not rendered inadmissible merely because it is in opinion form. For example, a party's statement that "I was negligent" or "It was all my fault" will be admitted into evidence as an admission. Therefore, although (C) is not an ideal answer, it is basically correct, and (A), (B), and (D) are clearly incorrect.

Answer to Question 28

(C)   This question requires analysis of each of the fact patterns. (A) would not be first degree murder. There was no premeditated and deliberate killing, and battery is not one of the listed crimes. Common law murder does include the situation where the actor, with the intent to cause serious bodily harm, causes the death of another person, but that would be second degree murder under the State Red statute. (B) would not be first degree murder. Here again there was no premeditated and deliberate killing and DWI is not one of the crimes listed. Common law murder does include the fact situation where the actor causes death under circumstances demonstrating an extreme indifference to the value of human life, but that would be second degree murder under the statute. (D) would not be first degree murder. Killings that take place during the heat of passion after sufficient provocation are manslaughter at common law and would not be considered a premeditated and deliberate killing under the statute. Being assaulted by another would be sufficient provocation. (C) would probably be considered first degree murder. There was premeditation and deliberation. Finding one's spouse in a sex act with another is considered sufficient provocation and, if the killing had occurred immediately (no cooling off period) while the defendant was in a rage, the crime would have been manslaughter. In (C), however, the killing did not take place immediately—the defendant purchased a gun. (C) might be debatable but it is clearly the fact situation that is most likely to be first degree murder.

Answer to Question 29

(D)   The trial court's decision should be overturned. The prevailing rule is that in performing services of designing and constructing improvements on property eventually deeded to the city, a developer must accept responsibility for prededication negligence. Hence, the trier of fact should be permitted to consider evidence of Filmont's negligence. To hold otherwise would allow the developer to avoid liability merely by dedicating the grounds to a city. Thus, (A) and (B) are incorrect. (C) is incorrect because presenting evidence of a bad motive on Filmont's part is not necessary to find him liable.

Answer to Question 30

(B) This question raises several different issues: competency of witnesses, use of leading questions on cross-examination, the proper scope of cross-examination, and the probative value/prejudicial impact balancing test. Through a process of elimination, (B) emerges as the correct answer. (D) is incorrect. Under the Federal Rules, ***virtually all*** witnesses with personal knowledge are competent to testify. [Fed. R. Evid. 601] A witness is not rendered incompetent simply by having served on a jury in a prior case involving a party to the current suit. Such prior jury service might render the witness's testimony ***unpersuasive***, but it would not make it ***inadmissible***. (C) is incorrect because ordinarily, leading questions are permitted ***on cross-examination***. [Fed. R. Evid. 611(c)] The prosecutor's question is a leading question, but that is perfectly permissible, especially in a case like this, where the alibi witness, Warren, is not "friendly" toward the prosecution. (A) is incorrect because cross-examination is generally limited in scope to the subject matter of the direct examination ***and matters affecting the credibility of the witness*** [Fed. R. Evid. 611(b)], and the prosecutor's question is, in a roundabout way, an attempt to impeach Warren's credibility. The implication behind the question is that if Warren had served on a jury that acquitted Drew of another criminal charge, Warren would be inclined to think Drew innocent of the pending charge. Alternatively, the implication behind the question could be that Warren is the kind of person who is "soft on crime" and for that reason is not a credible witness. In either event, since the question is an attempt to impeach Warren's testimony, it is within the proper scope of cross-examination. This leaves (B) as the remaining correct answer. (B) is not unquestionably correct, because the probative value/prejudicial impact balancing test found in Rule 403 is weighted heavily toward admission of evidence. For evidence to be excluded under this balancing test, its probative value must be substantially outweighed by its prejudicial impact. Nevertheless, in this case, a plausible reason for sustaining an objection to the prosecutor's question is that the probative value of the answer would be substantially outweighed by its tendency to mislead. The question and answer would inevitably let the jury know that Drew had been previously charged with a crime. This information could be highly prejudicial to his defense. Since the question and answer have little probative value (the negative inferences pertaining to Warren's credibility being very weak), it is reasonable to sustain an objection to the question on the basis that its probative value is substantially outweighed by its prejudicial impact.

Answer to Question 31

(B) Quack will be able to recover a reasonable price for his services. While the parties failed to agree on a material term, most courts today will imply reasonable terms if they are consistent with the parties' intent as otherwise expressed. Terms that can be supplied by a reasonableness standard include a price term for the performance of services. Unless the parties have shown at the time of contracting that they do not want a contract until they agree on a price, a reasonable price will be implied. (A) is wrong because Quack's fee is not necessarily reasonable although the court will take into account Quack's normal fee when it determines the reasonable fee. (C) is wrong because it fails to take into account that a court will imply a reasonable price term. (D) is wrong because it is irrelevant. In contract, a party need not prove that the "performing" party actually caused the performance. Mary received the performance she bargained for here—a cure.

Answer to Question 32

(D) Since there was consideration for Stu's promise, his promise is enforceable and Quack has a right to recover $25,000. (A) is wrong because a promise to pay $25,000 is a legal detriment. (B) is wrong because the preexisting duty rule does not apply since Stu was looking for additional consideration from Quack: Under the Quack-Mary contract, Quack agreed only to *treat* Mary; under the Quack-Stu contract, Quack would be paid only if he *cured* Mary. Moreover, it is not clear that Quack was under a duty to continue treating Mary when Stu approached Quack. (C) is incorrect because a court will not change the price agreed upon by the parties just because one party agreed to pay more than the reasonable value of the consideration that he was to receive. Furthermore, the facts do not establish that the value of Quack's services was in fact less than $25,000.

Answer to Question 33

(C) In a race-notice jurisdiction such as West Dakota, a subsequent purchaser must have taken *without notice* of the earlier sale and must have been the first to record. Otherwise the recording act will not apply. Clyde was indeed the first to record, but he took with notice that the property had been sold before. It does not matter how the subsequent purchaser learns of the earlier sale; if that person knows about it, he loses. Since the recording act does not apply to protect Clyde, the common law rule of first-in-time, first-in-right gives title to Keith. Thus, (C) is correct, and (B) is wrong. (A) is not as good an answer as (C) because if the recording act did apply, Keith's receiving a deed before Clyde would not give him superior rights to Steppeacre. (D) is wrong because recording does not cure the problem of Clyde taking with notice.

Answer to Question 34

(C) When the existence of a presumed fact is submitted to the jury in a criminal case, the judge must instruct the jury that it *may* regard the basic facts as sufficient evidence of the presumed fact, but that it is not *required* by law to do so. If, as here, the presumed fact (intoxication) is an element of the offense, its existence must be proved beyond a reasonable doubt. Thus, the judge should have instructed the jury that it may regard a blood alcohol concentration of .10 or more as sufficient evidence of intoxication, not that it must do so. The instruction appears to relieve the prosecution of its burden of proving intoxication beyond a reasonable doubt. It follows that (A) is incorrect. (B) is incorrect because a jury should be instructed on the applicable law—*e.g.*, permissible inferences as to intoxication. (D) is incorrect because an instruction is supposed to inform the jury of the law, not be probative. The term "probative" applies to relevance of evidence, not jury instructions.

Answer to Question 35

(B) Substantially overbroad or vague statutes regulating First Amendment rights are void on their face, and persons may not be prosecuted for their violation even if their conduct might otherwise be subject to valid regulation. Conversely, statutes that reasonably regulate the time, place, and manner of speech in public forums may be unconstitutional if applied in situations where the First Amendment activity is unreasonably infringed. Here, the statute is a valid time, place, and manner restriction because it is content neutral, it is narrowly tailored to serve a significant government interest, and it leaves open alternative channels of communication. However, it is being applied to circumstances that do not provide any reasonable basis for regulation of the speech. Thus, (B) is correct: while Roger's conduct can be regulated, it is the threat by the farmer that triggers Roger's arrest, not his violation of the statute. (A) and (D) are incorrect since the statute itself is valid on its face. (C) is incorrect, in turn, because it wrongly asserts that Roger may be prosecuted under these circumstances.

Answer to Question 36

(B) Since Woody did not take the stand, this evidence is not being offered for impeachment and, thus, the 10-year time limit does not apply. Evidence of other crimes is admissible against an accused in a criminal case if it is relevant to some issue other than the defendant's character or disposition to commit the crime charged. Where, as here, the crime charged is embezzlement, evidence that the defendant committed embezzlement before might be admissible to establish fraudulent intent. The crimes in (A), (C), and (D) are not relevant to any issue other than character and propensity to commit a crime; therefore, they are inadmissible. The fact that (A) and (D) are felonies would be important only if this were impeachment evidence, which it is not.

Answer to Question 37

(C) The original grant by Myrtle to Cyrus was a license, which is a personal privilege to go upon the land belonging to the licensor. When Cyrus expended a substantial sum of money in reliance on the license, the license became irrevocable under the doctrine of estoppel. (A) is wrong because Myrtle was estopped from terminating the license, not just from preventing Cyrus from coming onto her land. (D) is wrong because the duration of the irrevocable license is based on what the parties contemplated would be the duration when the oral license was granted and the facts do not indicate that they intended it to exist until Cyrus acquired another source of water. (B) is wrong because the estoppel is based not on the mere construction of the ditch but the expenditure of a substantial sum of money in reliance on the license. Therefore, (C) is a better answer than (B).

Answer to Question 38

(B) It will be most relevant to determining Delbert's guilt or innocence if he was unaware that the building he broke into was a dwelling. An element of the crime of common law burglary is that the breaking and entering be of the dwelling of another; hence, awareness of the building's use as a dwelling is a component of the mens rea for the crime. Delbert's ignorance or mistake regarding the building's use as a dwelling may negate the mens rea for that element of the crime of burglary. (A) is incorrect because it is not necessary that Delbert's mistake as to the identity of the computer be reasonable. Ignorance or mistake as to a matter of fact will affect guilt only if it shows that the defendant did not have the state of mind required for the crime. While courts have required that a mistake offered to negate the existence of a general intent be reasonable, *any* mistake of fact, reasonable or unreasonable, is a defense to a specific intent crime. Here, burglary requires the specific intent to commit a felony inside the dwelling at the time of entry. Delbert may not have had the intent to commit a felony if he believed that he was just retrieving his own computer that had been stolen. If so, the fact that his belief was unreasonable is irrelevant; it still negates the specific intent to commit a felony. (C) is incorrect because his realization that the computer was not his after he had broken into the shop is not relevant for purposes of burglary (although he may have committed larceny under those circumstances). The intent to commit a felony must have existed at the time of entry. If the intent is formed after the entry is completed, burglary is not committed. (D) is wrong because, as discussed above, Delbert's ignorance of the building's status as a dwelling may be a defense.

Answer to Question 39

(A) The gift in trust to Rockville University is a valid charitable trust. To be valid, a charitable trust must have an indefinite group of beneficiaries. The beneficiaries must be reasonably numerous and not individually identified. The trust may be for the benefit of an established charity or for a group of persons, as long as it is for a charitable purpose. Here, a trust for the benefit of a university to pay for the educational expenses of residents of a city qualifies as a charitable trust. Thus, (A) is correct and (C) is incorrect. (B) is incorrect because the doctrine of cy pres applies only when the purposes of a charitable trust are impossible to fulfill, are illegal, or have been completely fulfilled, allowing a court to redirect the trust to a different purpose that is as near as may be to the settlor's original intent. Here, because the trust purposes can be fulfilled, the doctrine does not apply. (D) is incorrect because the gift to Rockville University is certain to vest within the perpetuities period. The Rule Against Perpetuities applies to the equitable future interests of the beneficiaries in a private trust just as it does to legal future interests. Seth's three children are lives in being at the time the trust becomes effective, which is Seth's death. The executory interest in trust held by Rockville University is certain to either take effect or fail during those lives in being.

Answer to Question 40

(A) This question involves testimony by a witness, Harriet, whose recollection has been refreshed by reference to a document (her diary). Under the Federal Rules, any materials can be used to refresh one's recollection, and the Rules do not prohibit the use of such materials before trial. Thus, (A) is correct. (B) can quickly be discarded as incorrect. The contents of Harriet's diary are not remotely protected under the work product rule. The work product rule involves a product, such as a document, *prepared in anticipation of litigation or preparation for trial*, by or on behalf of *a party*. Harriet is not a party, and her diary was not prepared in anticipation of litigation or preparation for trial. It is, presumably, merely a collection of private thoughts transcribed for Harriet's personal edification. (D) is also incorrect. The best evidence rule does not literally require a party to produce the best evidence possible to prove a point. Rather, it requires the production of the original document *when attempting to prove the contents of a document*. [Fed. R. Evid. 1002] Although Harriet used a document to refresh her recollection and enable her to testify, her testimony concerned the details of an auto accident, *not the contents of the document*. Since Harriet was testifying about an event, as opposed to the contents of her diary, her testimony was proper, notwithstanding the failure to produce the diary. (C) is a tempting answer, but ultimately incorrect. If a witness's recollection has been refreshed prior to trial by reference to a document, the court has discretion to require that the document be disclosed to the opposing party. [Fed. R. Evid. 612] The court is not *required* to order disclosure. In this case, there is no indication that the court ordered disclosure of the diary or that Plee failed to comply with an order to produce the diary. All that is known is that, upon learning through cross-examination of Harriet that she had consulted her diary the night before, Def's attorney immediately moved that Harriet's testimony be stricken from the record. Since there is nothing improper about a witness's refreshing her recollection prior to trial, Def's motion should be denied and Harriet's testimony should remain on the record.

Answer to Question 41

(B) Burglary requires a breaking and entry of a dwelling of another at nighttime with the intent to commit a felony therein. Here, Defendant entered his brother's home at night with intent to take the television. A mistake as to application of the criminal law does not excuse a violation of that law. In (A), the defendant would not be guilty of burglary. There is no indication of a breaking and entering, the office would probably not be a dwelling, and, most important, defendant's belief that he owned the briefcase would negate the intent to commit a larceny or other felony. In (C), the defendant would probably not be guilty of burglary. At common law, an honest belief that you were entitled to take the property of another as repayment for a debt negated the intent necessary for larceny. In (D), the defendant would not be guilty of burglary. The garage would probably not be a dwelling and, most important, the defendant did not have the "intent to permanently deprive" necessary for larceny.

Answer to Question 42

(A) Both damages and an injunction would be in order. School has a life estate *pur autre vie* while Owens's children have a vested remainder subject to open. Absent an "open mine" in existence at the creation of the life estate and remainder, a life tenant cannot extract minerals from the land because it depletes the corpus and constitutes waste. Thus, the remainderman could recover damages and obtain an injunction for the unlawful waste. (B) is wrong since School's action did not terminate its interest. School's interest is not a defeasible one at all since the language that purports to restrict its use to educational purposes is only precatory and provides for no termination or forfeiture if School fails to comply. (C) is wrong because it is entirely unnecessary for Owens and Wilma to be parties since neither of them has any interest in the land. (D) is wrong because the injury to the land is permanent and therefore should be prevented by an injunction.

Answer to Question 43

(C) The general principles of intergovernmental immunity prevent federal interference with state governmental functions. Though there is not a great deal of bite left in the Tenth Amendment under current case law, particularly with regard to congressional conditions on expenditures of federal money, this is still the best argument presented. (B) is not the best answer because it goes too far; the doctrine of federalism relates to the *functions* of state government, not to all the *actions* of the state government. Clearly, the federal government could prevent the state from exercising its power in such a manner as to deprive its citizens of their federal rights, including those rights with regard to public education. (A) is obviously wrong, because the doctrine of federal preemption prevents the states from interfering with the effect and purposes of federal law. (D) is wrong because it is too narrow. Aside from the problem of separation of church and state, there are many reasons why the federal government could limit a state's rights in this area.

Answer to Question 44

(B) Stone is likely to prevail only if he can prove a mutual mistake. A contract can be reformed to reflect the original intent of the parties where there has been a mutual mistake in the integration. The plaintiff's negligence is not a bar to reformation. Here, both parties were unaware that the written contract did not reflect their agreement. (A) is not as good an answer as (B) because it fails to mention the mutual mistake element. (C) is wrong because the parol evidence rule does not apply in an action for reformation; if it did, contracts could rarely be reformed. (D) is wrong because the mistake here was not unilateral. Both parties believed that the written lease contained the exclusivity provision.

Answer to Question 45

(A) Stone can obtain rescission in equity without waiting to be sued on the contract. The grounds for rescission would be the intentional misrepresentation by Quinn that the second agreement was the same as the first. (B) is incorrect because reformation requires that the agreement not reflect the intention of the parties. Here, there was never any intent on the part of Quinn to agree to the terms of the old agreement. (C) would not apply to this fact situation—a novation substitutes another party for one of the original parties to the contract. (D) is incorrect because, as noted above, Stone need not repudiate the contract and wait to be sued for breach. He may immediately file an action in equity to obtain rescission.

Answer to Question 46

(B) Statements made by Quinn before the lease was signed would not be barred by the parol evidence rule. This rule provides that a writing that constitutes a complete and final expression of the bargain may not be varied by prior written or oral statements or contemporaneous oral statements. However, the parol evidence rule does not bar prior statements when the cause of action is for misrepresentation, which is attacking the validity of the agreement. Thus, (A) and (D) are wrong. While (C) is true, it is not as good an answer as (B) because the statements could be admitted even if the lease was not proved to be an incomplete agreement.

Answer to Question 47

(C) To recover on a theory of strict tort liability, Walter must show that his injuries were caused by an unreasonably dangerous defect in the boat that existed when the boat left City Marine's control; (C) is the only alternative that reflects this requirement. A prima facie case in products liability based on strict tort liability consists of: (i) a strict duty owed by a commercial supplier; (ii) breach of that duty; (iii) actual and proximate cause; and (iv) damages. Examples of commercial suppliers include manufacturers, retailers, wholesalers, and assemblers. Breach of duty is established by proving that the product is in a defective condition unreasonably dangerous to users. A plaintiff need not prove that the defendant was at fault in selling or producing a dangerous product. To prove actual cause, a plaintiff must trace the harm suffered to a defect in the product that existed when the product left the defendant's control. Here, if the steering failed due to a defect present when the boat left the manufacturer, that defect must also have been present when Walter bought the boat from City Marine, the retailer. This defect rendered the boat unreasonably dangerous to users such as Walter. By selling the boat in such condition, City Marine breached its strict duty, and this breach actually and proximately caused Walter to incur severe personal injuries. Thus, given the additional fact in (C), Walter will prevail. (A) is incorrect because any inspection of the boat by City Marine prior to sale would be relevant to a *negligence* action, but not to one based on strict liability. Even if City Marine had conducted a reasonable inspection of the boat, strict liability will still lie if the boat left City Marine's control with a defect that rendered it unreasonably dangerous. (B) is incorrect because ordinary contributory negligence is not a defense in strict liability actions in jurisdictions that retain traditional contributory negligence rules. To the extent that Walter is "misusing" the boat by weaving in and out of the pylons, it is a reasonably foreseeable misuse that the commercial supplier must take into account. To avail itself of Walter's conduct as a defense, City Marine must show that Walter voluntarily and unreasonably encountered a known risk. The facts herein do not indicate any such knowing assumption by Walter of the risk of harm from the defective steering mechanism. (D) is incorrect because it does not establish the causation element. City Marine's strict tort liability depends on whether the steering mechanism failed because of a defect present at the time it sold the boat to Walter. If the boat was not defective at the time of sale, or if any defect that was present had nothing to do with the failure of the steering mechanism, City Marine will not be liable for a subsequent failure of the steering mechanism from some other cause.

Answer to Question 48

(C) Watersports, Inc. will be liable for negligence if it should have discovered the defect in the steering mechanism. To establish a prima facie case for negligence in a products liability case, plaintiff must show the existence of a legal duty owed by the defendant to that particular plaintiff, breach of that duty, actual and proximate cause, and damages. To prove breach of duty, plaintiff must show (i) negligent conduct by the defendant leading to (ii) the supplying of a defective product by the defendant. The call of the question indicates that Watersports, Inc. supplied a defective product. If the defect could have been discovered by Watersports, Inc. in the exercise of reasonable care, it was negligent in not discovering the defect and preventing the boat from being sold. Choice (A), which addresses the duty element, is incorrect because a manufacturer of boats such as Watersports, Inc. is a "commercial supplier" owing a duty of due care to any foreseeable plaintiff. Although Tom did not purchase the boat (and so was not in privity with Watersports, Inc.), he was a friend of the owner of the boat and was using it when he was injured; he is therefore a foreseeable plaintiff. (B) is incorrect because Walter's negligence would be imputed to Tom only where he and Walter stand in such a relationship to each other (*e.g.,* an employer-employee relationship) that the courts would find it proper to charge Tom with Walter's negligence (such that Tom would be vicariously liable for Walter's negligent conduct if a third party had sued Tom). Here, the facts do not indicate any relationship that would warrant imputing Walter's negligence to Tom. Choice (D), which addresses the causation element, is incorrect because an intermediary's negligent failure to discover a defect is foreseeable negligence and therefore ***not*** a superseding cause. Watersports, Inc., the defendant whose original negligence created the defect, will still be liable.

Answer to Question 49

(C) Under the "perfect tender rule," Buyer may reject the entire shipment (III.). This power to reject is tempered by the U.C.C.'s provisions allowing Seller to "cure" defects. Although "cure" is not mentioned as an option, (C) remains a better answer than the others because I. and II. are not permissible options for the buyer at this time. With regard to I., the contract's delivery date has not yet arrived and Seller must be given an opportunity to "cure" before the Buyer seeks "cover." II. is not an option because the delivery date has not yet arrived and there is no reason to anticipate that Seller will not make good before the date in question. There is no breach until the delivery date, and an anticipatory breach situation does not exist. Hence, (A), (B), and (D) are incorrect.

Answer to Question 50

(B) Absent any anti-deficiency statutes, Olman remains personally liable to pay for any shortfall arising from the foreclosure sale. Proceeds from the sale are used to satisfy the senior interests first. Hence, all of the proceeds ($6,000) went to Exbank. Thus, Olman must pay the balance still due Exbank ($4,000) and the entire amount of the Wybank mortgage ($2,000), which is terminated by the foreclosure of the senior mortgage. (A) is wrong because foreclosure sales are not allotted proportionally between senior and junior interests. (C) is wrong because foreclosure does not extinguish the underlying debt. (D) is wrong because Wybank's mortgage does not remain on the land after foreclosure of the senior mortgage; hence, Olman is liable for that debt as well.

Answer to Question 51

(B) Burglary is the breaking and entering of the dwelling house of another in the nighttime with the intent to commit a felony inside the house. The prosecution must prove every element of the offense, including intent, beyond a reasonable doubt. Since the trial court's instructions placed the burden of proving lack of intent on Donald, they were in error. Thus, (B) is correct, and (D) is incorrect. (A) is incorrect because it focuses on the standard of proof, when the burden of proof is the issue. (C) is incorrect because it is impossible to make the harmless error analysis without knowing more about the state of the evidence, and the test for constitutional error is "harmless beyond a reasonable doubt," not by a preponderance, as suggested by the answer.

Answer to Question 52

(C) Congress's power over interstate commerce is broad, and the federal statute is clearly authorized by that power. The Court's 5-4 decision has no bearing here, since it was simply explaining what the standard was in the absence of any express congressional action. (A) is wrong because the fact that a state regulation does not burden interstate commerce in the absence of federal regulation does not preclude the federal government from subsequently enacting conflicting regulations which void the state law. (B) is wrong because the Fourteenth Amendment does not bind the federal government, and because a regulation of interstate commerce would rarely be classified as violating equal protection as to intrastate commerce. (D) is not the best answer because the Supremacy Clause alone does not speak to the validity of a federal statute, merely to its precedence over conflicting state enactments. The Supremacy Clause would operate, accordingly, only *after* the new statute is enacted, and would render the West Rabbit Foot ordinance invalid.

Answer to Question 53

(B) Eric cannot recover because the cause of his injury was not a highly dangerous concealed artificial condition. Generally, the owner or occupier of land does not owe a duty to an ordinary trespasser to warn of dangerous conditions on the land or to make the land safe. Where the trespasser is an anticipated trespasser—*i.e.,* where the landowner knows that people habitually intrude upon a particular part of her land—a duty to warn of or make safe highly dangerous concealed artificial conditions known to the landowner arises. However, there is no duty to warn of conditions so apparent that the trespasser should be able to discover them himself. Here, even though Eric qualifies as an anticipated trespasser, the wheelbarrow and shovel were neither concealed nor highly dangerous. Thus, (B) is correct. (A) is incorrect because it would be irrelevant whether the landowner created the artificial condition if she were otherwise liable because she allowed the condition to remain on her land. (C) is incorrect because mere knowledge of the dangerous condition does not impose a duty to warn. (D) is incorrect because, as stated above, Shelley had no duty to warn of obvious artificial conditions.

Answer to Question 54

(A) Murray cannot obtain specific performance against Tom because the absence of a written memorandum signed by Tom and containing the essential terms of an agreement between Murray and Tom means that there is no enforceable contract. To obtain specific performance, there must be an enforceable contract between the parties. Pursuant to the Statute of Frauds, a contract for the sale of land is not enforceable unless it is evidenced by a writing signed by the party sought to be bound. In addition to this signature, the writing should contain a recital of consideration, the terms and conditions of the agreement, the identity of the party sought to be charged, and an identification of the contractual subject matter. Murray is attempting to obtain specific performance of a contract to purchase Tom's house. Thus, Murray must show the existence of a contract through a writing sufficient to satisfy the Statute of Frauds. The only writings mentioned in the facts are Murray's written offer to purchase the house and the real estate listing agreement between Tom and Fred. The latter reflects only an agreement between Tom and Fred as to the terms of Fred's services as a broker in connection with the sale of Tom's house. This in no way constitutes written evidence of an agreement between Tom and Murray. Murray's written offer was never signed by Tom and was, in fact, rejected by Tom in a manner consistent with its terms. Thus, this writing does not memorialize an agreement between Tom and Murray for the sale of Tom's house; no agreement was ever reached. Therefore, there is no enforceable contract that can be the subject of specific performance. (D) is incorrect because, as explained above, there is no memorandum signed by Tom that lists the essential terms of an agreement between Tom and

Murray. In fact, there was never any such agreement, much less a writing reflecting its terms. (B) is incorrect because a purchaser of land is almost always deemed to have an inadequate remedy at law. Each parcel of land is always considered unique; *i.e.,* unlike any other that could be purchased with the same sum of money. Thus, if Murray did have a cause of action against Tom, he would not have an adequate remedy at law. (C) is incorrect because the facts do not indicate that Fred and Tom intended that Murray or any other third person benefit by their agreement. Application of the factors that courts use to determine whether a third party is an intended beneficiary who can enforce a contract between the contracting parties or an incidental beneficiary who has no rights under the contract indicates that Murray is not an intended beneficiary. The agreement did not: (i) expressly designate a third party; (ii) indicate that performance was to be made directly to a third party; or (iii) state that a third party had any rights under the contract. Also, there is no relationship between Murray and either Tom or Fred from which it could be inferred that either Tom or Fred wished to make the agreement for Murray's benefit. Thus, Murray is not an intended beneficiary of the agreement between Tom and Fred and cannot recover on that agreement.

Answer to Question 55

(B) A public nuisance exists when a property owner is using his property in such a manner that it creates an unreasonable risk to the public in general. The owner need not be violating a specific statute in order to be a public nuisance; hence, (D) is incorrect. Nor is it determinative that the owner has a permit to engage in the activity if the owner's use otherwise constitutes a public nuisance. (Albeit, in many cases it would be hard to show a public nuisance if the owner did have a permit to use his property in a certain manner. But the facts of this case show that Evan had not complied with the provisions of the permit.) Evan would be correct in arguing that it is not a nuisance per se in storing the flammable liquids on his property since this is not a residential neighborhood; however, (C) is not the best answer because it still could be shown that under this particular situation it was a nuisance. Nevertheless, it is generally the duty of the local district attorney to bring actions to enjoin public nuisances, and private citizens will generally have no standing to bring such suit unless the private citizen can show that he suffers some special injury in addition to that sustained by the general public. The facts in this case fail to show such special injury, so (B) would be Evan's best defense.

Answer to Question 56

(B) Under the best evidence rule, in proving the terms of a writing, where the terms are material, the original writing must be produced. Secondary evidence of the writing, such as oral testimony regarding the writing's contents, is permitted only after it has been shown that the original is unavailable for some reason other than serious misconduct of the proponent. Here, the value of the house is of major importance, and the contents of the document are closely related to this central issue. Consequently, Nora, whose only knowledge of this significant litigated issue comes from having read the document, is precluded from testifying as to the contents of the document unless the unavailability of the writing is established. Destruction of the original without fault of the party offering the secondary evidence constitutes a satisfactory explanation for nonproduction of the original and justifies the admissibility of secondary evidence. Thus, (B) is a better answer than (C). (A) is incorrect because personal knowledge of the contents does not in and of itself justify admissibility of the testimony. (D) is incorrect because the appraisal document, personally prepared by Harry, constitutes an admission by a party-opponent; *i.e.,* a prior acknowledgment by a party of one of the relevant facts. Under the Federal Rules, such statements are nonhearsay.

Answer to Question 57

(C) Joe's actions with respect to Egbert never rose to the level of attempt under either the traditional "proximity test" or the modern Model Penal Code test; here, there is no evidence that Egbert was even present. Thus, I. is incorrect, and so (A) is incorrect. Even though Joe thought Ira was Egbert, he intended to kill the person at whom he aimed (Ira). His actions with regard to Ira fulfill the test for attempt under every approach. Therefore, Joe could be convicted of the attempted murder of Ira, and II. is correct. Furthermore, Joe's intent to kill Ira is transferred to Gladys, making Joe guilty of murder. Thus, III. is correct. Therefore, choice (C) is correct, and (B) and (D) are incorrect.

Answer to Question 58

(B) Under Rule 801 of the Federal Rules, prior identification can be admissible and the sketch could be deemed a prior identification. However, to be admissible, the witness must be there to testify at trial and be subject to cross-examination. The witness in this case is unavailable; hence, this exception does not apply. (D) is therefore incorrect. (A) applies to documentary evidence and has no relevance to this question. (C) is likewise not applicable, because this exception applies only to information within the *personal knowledge* of the public employee. In this case the public employee gained the knowledge from the hearsay statement of an absent witness.

Answer to Question 59

(B) Prior consistent statements are admissible to rebut a charge that the witness is lying or exaggerating because of some motive; however, since the facts in this question do not indicate that such a charge has been made against Justin, the statement is no more than hearsay. Hence, (D) is wrong. (C) is wrong because an out-of-court statement made by a witness is hearsay without regard to who made the statement. (A) is wrong because all evidence given by a witness in his own defense should be self-serving. This may go to the weight of the evidence, but it has nothing to do with its admissibility.

Answer to Question 60

(D) Justin has taken the stand in his own defense, and therefore the prosecutor can attack his credibility as a witness. Under Federal Rule 609, evidence of conviction of a crime requiring proof of an act of dishonesty or false statement can always be used to attack a witness's character for truthfulness. (A) is incorrect because even if fraud were probative of the tendency to commit violence, evidence of other crimes is not admissible to prove that a person has a propensity to commit criminal acts. (C) is incorrect for the same reason. (B) is incorrect because no foundation is needed to show a prior conviction for impeachment purposes.

Answer to Question 61

(C) Conviction of the defendant in (A) would violate the constitutional proscription against ex post facto laws. (B) is an example of attempting, with criminal intent, to do an act which is not itself a crime. (D) is an example of a person prosecuted for guilty thoughts, which is unconstitutional. The defendant in (C) could be found guilty under either of two theories. The statute could be interpreted as a strict liability statute. Under that interpretation, the defendant would be guilty because he engaged in the prohibited behavior. Alternatively, the statute could be interpreted as requiring a mens rea. Under that interpretation, he could be guilty upon a determination that he intentionally put water in a container that had held chlorine bleach.

Answer to Question 62

(D) Action having the purpose and effect of altering the legal rights, duties, and relations of persons, including executive branch officials, must be subjected to the possibility of presidential veto.

[Immigration & Naturalization Service v. Chadha (1983)] Although the President (or his predecessor) had the opportunity to veto the statute, the adoption of a joint resolution that shortens the time that the President may use the troops would have the purpose and effect of altering the rights and duties of the President, which accrue to him by virtue of his rather extensive military powers, and would not be subject to a presidential veto. For this reason the statutory provision may be an unconstitutional legislative veto of executive action. It follows that (A) and (C) are therefore incorrect. (B) is incorrect because the President does not have *exclusive* power over matters relating to war. Such power is shared with Congress.

Answer to Question 63

(A) Congress may delegate many of its powers to executive agencies, provided adequate standards are established to govern exercise of the delegated power. The power was properly delegated to the Secretary of Commerce because the statute "outlines" the "management efficiency standards" to be followed. (B) is incorrect because Congress has sole authority over foreign commerce; the authority is not shared with the executive branch. (C) is incorrect because the delegation is proper if adequate standards are established; as determined above, there are adequate standards here. (D) is incorrect because there is no executive impoundment here, merely a refusal to grant funds based upon standards established by Congress. Such standards are proper where, as here, Congress acts pursuant to its spending power and the standards are specified in advance.

Answer to Question 64

(D) Norris paid a fair price for Goldacre and had no knowledge of Briggs's claim to Goldacre at the time he purchased the property. He would thus qualify as a bona fide purchaser for value and, since he was the first to record, he would have priority over Briggs. (A) and (B) are incorrect because the recording act determines priority among purchasers of property while the Statute of Frauds deals only with the validity of an individual contract. (C) is incorrect because Strobe's signing the contract, which contained the same terms and conditions as Briggs's offer, constituted an acceptance, which became effective upon dispatch under the "mailbox rule" of contract law.

Answer to Question 65

(C) Wes will prevail because Luke was a gratuitous assignee of the contract between Wes and Jane, and Jane had expressly reserved the right to stop the payments at any time, which she did by making a subsequent assignment of the right to Zack. (A) is wrong because Luke had rights under the contract that he could enforce against Wes until Jane revoked the assignment. (B) is wrong because the facts do not show a change in position in reliance upon Jane's actions. (D) is wrong because Luke's right to receive the funds was limited to the period in which Jane told Wes to send the funds.

Answer to Question 66

(C) Jane had reserved the right to reassign the proceeds at any time, and had assigned them to Susan before she died. Zack's initial interest in the proceeds was subject to Jane's right to revoke by a subsequent assignment, which Zack had acknowledged. During the time Funco sold back the hotel and obligations to Wes, the proceeds were assigned to Susan; therefore, Zack's rights were not vested. (A) and (B) are wrong because there was no vesting when Funco was an obligor. Zack was not a third-party beneficiary of the original agreement between Jane and Wes; he was a subsequent assignee of Jane's rights. While he may have been a third-party beneficiary of the agreement between Wes and Funco, he did not assent to it or change his position in reliance on it; hence, his rights did not vest. (D) is wrong because the contract between Funco and Wes expressly required Funco to assume Wes's obligations. Zack was an intended beneficiary of that agreement, but his rights did not vest before they were extinguished by the subsequent assignment.

Answer to Question 67

(A)   The language in the deed from McWilliams to Stone creates an express easement with Leftacre as the servient estate and Rightacre as the dominant estate. As such, Sandberg has no right to obstruct O'Toole's use of the easement. (B) is incorrect because O'Toole has an express easement, not an easement by necessity. While it is true that, in the absence of an express easement, Stone may have had a claim of an easement by necessity, an easement by necessity will not be implied when an express easement is provided. (C) is incorrect because a change in conditions and/or circumstances will not terminate an express easement. (D) is incorrect because injunctive relief is possible where a property right is involved.

Answer to Question 68

(B)   The grant was for use of a dirt path, not for a 24-foot-wide paved road, and a court could easily find this burden excessive. (A) is incorrect because the easement involved is an express easement, not an easement by necessity. (C) is an incorrect statement of law; the owner of a servient estate does not have the obligation to maintain an easement and cannot unilaterally control the nature of its improvement. (D) is incorrect because a surcharging of the easement does not terminate it; it merely gives the owner of the servient estate the right to stop the additional use.

Answer to Question 69

(C)   The only plaintiff who would have standing is the Society. The Society has standing because the statute causes injury to the Society itself. Disclosure of membership would affect the ability of the Society to keep and obtain members in violation of the First Amendment. Thus, it has standing to sue. I. is wrong because taxpayers have no standing to challenge federal expenditures unless the taxpayer alleges that the challenged measure was enacted under Congress's taxing and spending powers and that it exceeds a specific constitutional limitation on those powers. Here, the taxpayer made no such allegations and probably could not show that the spending violated a specific constitutional limitation. Thus, (A) is incorrect. (B) is wrong because standing cannot be based on a claim to the public at large; the group must allege some specific injury to itself or its members. IV. is wrong because general financial inability to buy is not sufficient injury; the plaintiff must show that absent the zoning, there would be a substantial probability that he could buy a home. (D) is therefore incorrect.

Answer to Question 70

(B)   Double jeopardy does not prohibit the imposition of cumulative sentences for two or more statutorily defined offenses specifically intended by the legislature to carry separate punishments, even though constituting the "same" crime under the *Blockburger* test (*i.e.*, each offense does not require proof of some additional fact that the other does not) when the punishments are imposed at a single trial. Absent a clear intention, it is presumed that multiple punishments are not intended for offenses constituting the same crime under *Blockburger*. Here, it is clear that Congress, in enacting SOCA, intended that certain offenses, such as interstate distribution of cocaine, be subject to separate punishments. (B) is the only alternative that expresses the view that Dalton may be sentenced under both statutes. Thus, it is the correct answer, and (A), (C), and (D) are incorrect.

Answer to Question 71

(C) Statements in a document affecting an interest in property are admissible, pursuant to Federal Rule 803(15), if they are relevant to the purpose of the document. Thus, (B) is incorrect. (A) is incorrect because properly authenticated copies of recorded writings may be used in lieu of originals. [Fed. R. Evid. 902(4)] (D) is incorrect because the trust instrument cannot qualify as a recorded recollection; there is no witness testifying that he made or adopted the writing while the events were fresh in his mind and he has no present recollection.

Answer to Question 72

(B) Hotel will prevail because the swearing out of a complaint that was proper at the time may not serve as a basis for a false imprisonment action despite the failure to cancel the complaint (although in some circumstances such swearing out may give rise to an action for malicious prosecution). Thus, (C) is incorrect. (A) is incorrect because the reasonableness of Hotel's belief that Parker stole services is irrelevant. Even if Hotel's belief was unreasonable, it does not establish the intent required for false imprisonment. (D) is wrong because the absence of an adequate number of cashiers is not an act confining one within fixed boundaries, as required for false imprisonment.

Answer to Question 73

(C) It is a defense to false imprisonment that the police acted under a *valid* arrest warrant. The warrant was valid here, and that should serve as a complete defense. Mere statements by a defendant that he is innocent do not compel the police to follow the defendant's suggestions. It follows that (A) is incorrect. (B) is incorrect because the police acted under a valid warrant and are not charged with knowing whether Parker actually committed the crime with which he was charged. (D) is incorrect because the reasonableness of Hotel's actions will not affect the liability of the police. Even if Hotel did not have reasonable grounds for signing the complaint, the police will not be liable because they acted pursuant to a valid warrant.

Answer to Question 74

(A) Congress has the power, under the Commerce Clause, to regulate any activity that, taken cumulatively, has substantial economic or commercial effect on interstate commerce. Although there are limits on the power of Congress to regulate commerce, in only a few cases has the Court invalidated a federal law as exceeding the scope of Congress's commerce power. Since Congress has concluded that the animal is important to the region's tourism industry, and given the comparative weakness of the other answers, (A) is the strongest argument. (B) is incorrect because the Necessary and Proper Clause must be linked with another constitutional power of Congress. Here it is presented by itself, not in connection with another power, and thus it is incorrect. (C) is incorrect because there is no federal police power. (D) is wrong. The facts of this question do not offer any facts suggesting that the animals are on federal lands. Thus, the power to regulate federal lands is irrelevant.

Answer to Question 75

(A) Larceny is the taking and asportation of the personal property of another by trespass and with the intent to permanently deprive the person of his interest in the property. Here, the moving of the mower to the loading dock constituted the taking and carrying away. Since Manfred did not have express or implied permission to move merchandise in this way, it was trespassory. Clearly, he intended to permanently deprive Gardenshop of its interest in the mower. Thus, the larceny was complete when Manfred moved the mower to the loading dock, and (B) and (D) are therefore incorrect. (C) is incorrect because to be guilty of embezzlement, Manfred would have had to have been in possession of the mower when he converted it. Since Manfred did not have especially broad power over the mower and it was not given to him by a third party, he merely had custody, not possession, of the mower.

Answer to Question 76

(C) Norman must accept Kurt's performance. The assignment by Zelda of the contract involved a delegation of her duties to Kurt. While generally all contractual duties may be delegated to a third person, duties involving personal judgment and skill may not be delegated. However, a contract for paving generally would not be regarded as involving a personal subject matter; hence, Zelda could delegate the duties to another competent contractor without Norman's consent and Norman must accept performance. Thus, (A) and (B) are wrong. (D) is a misstatement of law; Zelda need not supervise. Norman may sue Zelda if Kurt fails to perform under the contract.

Answer to Question 77

(B) The delegator remains personally liable for performance of the agreement even though the delegatee is performing the contract. Hence, (A) is incorrect. (C) is incorrect because although Norman and Kurt are not in privity of contract, Norman is a third-party beneficiary of the agreement between Kurt and Zelda. When there is a delegation of duties, both the delegator and the delegatee are liable for performance of the agreement. (D) is wrong because if the services to be performed are not personal, the obligee has no choice but to accept performance, and it would be unfair that if by accepting performance, the obligee waives his rights as against the delegator.

Answer to Question 78

(B) The plat is only intended to be a representation of the actual survey as made upon the land itself. The plat is in the nature of a certified copy of an instrument that will be controlled by the original. Where a survey as made and marked upon the ground conflicts with the plat, the survey prevails. Thus, Andrew had a right to rely on the surveyor's stakes as establishing the boundaries of Lot 20. Thus, (B) is correct, and (C) is incorrect. (A) is incorrect because priority in purchase would not entitle Andrew to take land that was not part of Lot 20. (D) is incorrect because, while it is true that the adverse possession period has not run, Andrew need not rely on adverse possession to prevail.

Answer to Question 79

(C) The record on appeal must show that a specific objection was made and that the challenged evidence was inadmissible on that ground, before the trial court's action can be considered error. (A) is wrong because the defense counsel's objection did not state specific grounds for the objection; counsel merely said, "objection." (B) is wrong; the court is never required to state the reason for overruling an objection. (D) makes no sense at all. The objection was overruled and the evidence was received. "Offers of proof" are sometimes made when evidence is held inadmissible.

Answer to Question 80

(C) Battery is a general intent crime that can be established with a mental state of recklessness. In addition, all crimes require a voluntary act on the part of the actor. The epileptic seizure would negate both the voluntary act and the culpable mental state. In (A), the defendant would probably be guilty of battery. Intoxication is not a defense to a general intent crime, and the defendant's behavior would probably be classified as reckless. In (B), the defendant *might* be found guilty of battery. If Davis reasonably believed he was under attack, he would be justified in punching Verne; it would be a jury question as to whether his belief was reasonable. While under the facts of (B) it is possible that Davis would be not guilty, it is not as good an answer as (C), where it is clear there would be no criminal liability. In (D), the defendant would be guilty of battery. The facts do not justify a self-defense claim.

Answer to Question 81

(C) An attempt requires both a specific intent to commit the crime and an overt act in furtherance of that intent. Since Dag intended to enter Vance's property and was apprehended just before doing so, both requirements for attempt can be established. (A) is incorrect because Dag is not being charged with the attempt to commit violence, but with the attempt to enter onto the property. (B) is also wrong because clearly it is Dag's actions that are prohibited and not just the state of his mind. (D) is a poor answer because Dag cannot be convicted unless it is proved that he committed the offense with which he has been charged, and this answer does not require that the elements of the crime be proved.

Answer to Question 82

(A) As a direct tax upon the federal government, the sales tax is invalid unless Congress has consented to such a tax. (B) is wrong because the tax is on all autos purchased in the state, regardless of their source, and thus, there is no burden on interstate commerce. (C) is wrong because direct state taxation of the federal government is invalid whether or not discriminatory, absent the consent of Congress. (D) is wrong because, as stated, unless Congress consents, a direct tax on the federal government is invalid. Thus, the fact that there is a rational basis and that the tax is not a penalty does not matter: the question is one of the *power* to tax, not whether the tax itself is appropriate.

Answer to Question 83

(A) In a partial condemnation case, the landlord-tenant relationship continues, as does the tenant's obligation to pay the entire rent for the remaining lease term. (B) is wrong because, while the tenant generally is obligated to return the premises in the same condition as when received, that obligation would not be considered breached by the actions of a third party such as the government. (C) is wrong because the covenant of quiet enjoyment can be breached only by actions of the landlord and not those of a third party, such as the government. (D) is wrong because the law of landlord and tenant traditionally refuses to recognize frustration of purpose as grounds for termination of a lease.

Answer to Question 84

(D) Tyrone and Dennison are joint tortfeasors who are each jointly and severally liable for Pryor's injuries. As such, either may be sued for the entire amount of damages suffered. (C) is therefore incorrect. However, if Dennison is found to be liable to Pryor, he may seek contribution from Tyrone to force Tyrone to pay a portion of the recovery. He would have no right to indemnity because he is actively negligent in causing Pryor's injuries. (B) is therefore incorrect. (A) is incorrect because Dennison was a substantial factor in causing Pryor's injuries.

Answer to Question 85

(A) The Constitution prohibits the impairment of contractual obligations by a state except in certain narrow circumstances. The sort of "emergency" normally required for such state action is arguably present here, given the loss in tax revenues. But it is unlikely that the state would prevail since the termination of annual cost-of-living adjustments is permanent, and appears to be the sort of self-interest driven choice to reduce the state's contractual burdens that the Court has found suspect in comparable cases. (B) is wrong because federal courts do not have the jurisdiction to decide questions regarding an individual state's own constitution. (C) is wrong because the Eleventh Amendment does not bar suits against state officials unless retroactive relief is sought. (D) is wrong because although a state may amend its own statutes, it cannot do so in such a manner as to violate constitutional prohibitions.

Answer to Question 86

(C) The general rule is that a court will not enforce a contract if its subject matter or consideration is illegal; the court will leave the parties as it finds them. Here, the subject matter of the contract, placing gambling bets, is illegal in the state. Thus, (A) is wrong because Steve's performance is irrelevant. (B) is wrong because the court will refuse to help either party to an illegal contract, even where one party has gained unfairly. (D) is wrong because the court will not put the parties back into the position they were in prior to entering into the contract, but rather will leave them where they stand.

Answer to Question 87

(A) When Doris took the coat, knowing it was not her own, she committed a trespassory taking. However, she was not then guilty of larceny because she did not have an intent to "steal" the coat (*i.e.*, to permanently deprive the owner of the coat). However, under the continuing trespass doctrine, her possession continued to be trespassory, and when she later formed the intent to steal, her actions became larceny. Therefore, (D) is incorrect. Doris is not guilty of common law burglary. Her entry was effected shortly after lunchtime; *i.e.*, during the day, and burglary requires a nighttime entry. Also, Doris did not intend to commit a felony when she entered the house, since she believed the coat was her own. Thus, (B) and (C) are also incorrect.

Answer to Question 88

(C) Paula was a trespasser in Otto's cabin because she entered the cabin without permission or privilege. A landowner generally owes no duty to an undiscovered trespasser. However, if a landowner discovers or should anticipate the presence of a trespasser, he must exercise ordinary care to warn the trespasser of or to make safe concealed, unsafe, artificial conditions known to the landowner that involve a risk of death or serious bodily harm. Here, it is true that Otto owed no duty to Paula. However, had he known of or had reason to anticipate the presence of someone in the cabin, he would have owed a duty to warn of or to make safe the fireplace. Thus, (C) is a better answer than (D). (A) is wrong because Otto's knowledge of the defect is important only if he owed a duty to Paula, which he did not. (B) is wrong because, as stated, he had no duty to warn Paula because he did not know of her presence.

Answer to Question 89

(D) The reasonableness of Patty's apprehension of immediate harmful or offensive contact is determined by the reasonable person standard. Thus, although it may be a close question here because of Darryl's appearance and the authentic appearance of the gun, the fact that four other home-owners had not been frightened by Darryl's routine indicates that a reasonable person would have recognized that this was just a youngster engaging in traditional Halloween activity. Since all of the other choices are clearly wrong, (D) is the best option. (B) is wrong because if Patty's apprehension of immediate harm was unreasonable, Patty does not have a no cause of action for assault. Furthermore, Darryl did not have the requisite intent for assault. While he may have intended to momentarily startle the person answering the door, he did not intend to cause apprehension of immediate harmful or offensive contact. (A) is wrong because Patty does not have a cause of action for intentional infliction of emotional distress; dressing up as a bandit and carrying a toy gun while trick or treating is not extreme and outrageous conduct so as to transcend all bounds of decency. (C) is wrong because minors may be liable for their intentional torts.

Answer to Question 90

(C) Grant's interest would be void under the Rule Against Perpetuities since his interest could (and most likely would) vest more than 21 years after a life in being. Hence, the instrument would be read as if the executory interest to Grant did not exist. Clara's interest is a fee simple determinable; thus, the grantor, Dawn, retains a possibility of reverter. (A) is therefore incorrect. (B) is incorrect because a possibility of reverter rather than a reversion arises upon a conveyance of a fee simple determinable. (D) is incorrect because the estate created was a fee simple determinable, not a fee simple subject to a condition subsequent. Moreover, rights of entry must be expressly raised in the conveyance.

Answer to Question 91

(B) Since Congress's power to regulate interstate commerce is plenary, Congress has the right to prohibit completely the transportation of "harmful" substances in the channels of commerce. Congress could also otherwise regulate the manufacture and use of harmful drugs as part of its regulation of commerce. (A) is wrong because this Act has nothing to do with Congress's right to expend federal tax revenues, and the general welfare power has to do with Congress's spending power. (C) is incorrect because the constitutional right of privacy does not include the right to ingest harmful drugs. (D) is incorrect because this Act is a restriction on property use that is considered harmful to the public health and welfare; consequently, it is considered regulation and not a taking within the meaning of the Fifth Amendment, and no compensation would be required.

Answer to Question 92

(B) A tax, even though enacted for a regulatory rather than a revenue-raising purpose, can be upheld as a "necessary and proper" exercise of Congress's power to tax under Article I, Section 8, Clause 1. This will be especially true if the revenues derived from the measure are used to cover the expenses associated with the federal regulatory scheme. Since the question does not involve the attempted exercise of a state's sovereignty, there is no issue of the Supremacy Clause, and (A) is wrong. (C) is incorrect because Congress has broad power to regulate commerce, and the sale of the drug could probably be said to have a substantial economic effect on interstate commerce even if it was not actually being sold in interstate commerce. (D) is wrong because the states do not have the exclusive right to tax within their boundaries.

Answer to Question 93

(A) Leading questions are allowed on the direct examination of a "hostile" witness. There is no rule that allows leading questions on the direct examination of a "disinterested" witness. A leading question is normally permitted on cross-examination whether the witness is a layperson or an expert. (C) is, therefore, wrong. (B) is wrong because leading questions may be asked of very young or very old witnesses at the discretion of the court. (D) is wrong because a leading question may be asked of any witness on preliminary matters not in dispute.

Answer to Question 94

(C) Margo assigned part of her claim against Oscar to Percy, and, as a general rule, the assignee is subject to the same defenses that the obligor has against the assignor. If Margo, the assignor, had not done the work properly, Oscar would have a defense against her, hence he can use this defense against Percy. (A) is immaterial, because this is not a third-party beneficiary agreement, but an assignment of the right to receive money. Thus, (B) must also be ruled out. (D) is wrong because an assignment of a future claim is not inoperable.

Answer to Question 95

(C) The only value his tickets will have to anyone is if they are used for admission to the All-Star game. Consequently, since Dennis did not intend to return the tickets to Tom until after the game, Dennis intended to permanently deprive Tom of the value of the tickets and most likely would be found guilty of larceny. (A) is not a correct answer because, although the intent to return the tickets may be a valid defense in some situations, in this situation Tom would have been permanently deprived of their value when they were returned, and therefore Dennis's intention would not be a valid defense. (B) is a tempting answer, but it is not the most likely. There are no facts that indicate the relative value of the tickets to the money that Dennis claims Tom owes him. (D) is not the most likely answer, because the intent to return may be a valid defense in some instances.

Answer to Question 96

(D) Seth *cannot* be convicted of the attempted murder of either Larsen or Carver. Attempted murder is a specific intent crime. Although it is true that a defendant can be found guilty of murder when his actions demonstrate a very high degree of recklessness, if the charge is *attempted* murder, it must be shown that the defendant committed an act with the *intention* of killing someone. If the jury believed that Seth had no intention of killing either Larsen or Carver, he cannot be convicted of attempted murder of either. Thus, (D) is correct, and (A), (B), and (C) are wrong.

Answer to Question 97

(D) Although the language in Maude's will uses the word "jointly," the grant also states "as tenants in common." Since no right of survivorship is mentioned, the court will most likely find that this language establishes a tenancy in common, rather than a joint tenancy. Lisa can pass her interest in the property by will, and thus Estelle now holds the property as a tenant in common with Louis. (A) is wrong; Louis's management of the use of the farm does not entitle him to an exclusive interest in it. (B) is wrong because the interest created by Maude's will was a tenancy in common, not a joint tenancy. (C) is wrong because the unities only apply to a joint tenancy.

Answer to Question 98

(C) Louis had the right to possess and enjoy the whole of the farm subject to the equal right of Lisa to do the same. The fact that Lisa chose not to exercise her right does not make Louis's possession wrongful. Therefore, an accounting is not warranted here. (A) is wrong because, as stated,

Louis may enjoy the whole of the property. (B) is wrong; there is nothing in the facts to indicate an ouster. (D) is wrong because Louis cannot take by adverse possession unless there has been an ouster; his possession was not hostile to Lisa's interest.

Answer to Question 99

(A) This is a question requiring precise knowledge of the U.C.C. The problem is governed by U.C.C. sections 2-615 and 2-616. A crop failure resulting from an unexpected cause excuses a farmer's obligation to deliver the full amount as long as he makes a fair and reasonable allocation among his buyers. George has done this by allocating pro rata between Walter and Vinnie. Nevertheless, under U.C.C. section 2-616 the buyer may either accept the proposed modification or terminate the contract. Thus, (B) is wrong. (C) is wrong because even though alternative sources are available, George is not obligated to use them because the contract was tied to a designated parcel of land—"my [George's] ranch." (D) is wrong because it is contrary to the provision of U.C.C. section 2-615, which permits the farmer to make an allocation.

Answer to Question 100

(D) Parents are not vicariously liable at common law for the intentional torts of their children (although many states have imposed limited liability for certain conduct by statute). However, a parent (or anyone else having care or custody of a child) can be held liable for injuries caused by the child where the parent herself was negligent. For example, the parent may be liable for failing to exercise reasonable care to protect against the child's known dangerous tendencies. Here, pursuant to statute, Sister Mary stood in loco parentis to Dieter. Thus, Sister Mary could be held liable if she knew that Dieter had dangerous propensities, and failed to take appropriate measures (*e.g.*, keeping a closer watch on Dieter). Sister Mary then would be liable for her own negligence, not vicariously liable for Dieter's intentional tort. (D) is the only alternative that mentions the important factor of Sister Mary's knowledge regarding Dieter's dangerous propensities. (A) is incorrect because it ignores the fact that Sister Mary's liability depends upon her knowledge of any dangerous propensities on the part of Dieter. (B) is incorrect because neither raising children generally nor operating a home for developmentally disabled children are abnormally dangerous activities giving rise to strict liability. (C) is incorrect because it assumes that Sister Mary's liability, if any, will be based on vicarious liability.

BAR REVIEW

Multistate Practice Exam

A.M. EXAM

Time—3 hours

You will be given three hours to work on this test. Be sure that the question numbers on your answer sheet match the question numbers in your test book. You are not to begin work until the supervisor tells you to do so.

Your score will be based on the number of questions you answer correctly. It is therefore to your advantage to try to answer as many questions as you can. Give only one answer to each question; multiple answers will not be counted. If you wish to change an answer, erase your first mark completely and mark your new choice. Use your time effectively. Do not hurry, but work steadily and as quickly as you can without sacrificing your accuracy.

YOU ARE TO INDICATE YOUR ANSWERS TO ALL QUESTIONS ON THE SEPARATE ANSWER SHEET PROVIDED.

DIRECTIONS

Each of the questions or incomplete statements in this test is followed by four suggested answers or completions. You are to choose the *best* of the stated alternatives. Answer all questions according to the generally accepted view, except where otherwise noted.

For the purpose of this test, you are to assume that Articles 1 and 2 of the Uniform Commercial Code have been adopted. You are also to assume relevant application of Article 9 of the U.C.C. concerning fixtures. The Federal Rules of Evidence are deemed to control.

The terms "Constitution," "constitutional," and "unconstitutional" refer to the federal Constitution unless indicated to the contrary.

You are also to assume that there is no applicable statute unless otherwise specified; however, survival actions and claims for wrongful death should be assumed to be available where applicable. You should assume that joint and several liability, with comparative negligence, is the relevant rule unless otherwise indicated.

DO NOT OPEN THE TEST UNTIL
YOU ARE INSTRUCTED TO DO SO.

ANSWER SHEET (A.M. EXAM)

1. Ⓐ Ⓑ Ⓒ Ⓓ	26. Ⓐ Ⓑ Ⓒ Ⓓ	51. Ⓐ Ⓑ Ⓒ Ⓓ	76. Ⓐ Ⓑ Ⓒ Ⓓ
2. Ⓐ Ⓑ Ⓒ Ⓓ	27. Ⓐ Ⓑ Ⓒ Ⓓ	52. Ⓐ Ⓑ Ⓒ Ⓓ	77. Ⓐ Ⓑ Ⓒ Ⓓ
3. Ⓐ Ⓑ Ⓒ Ⓓ	28. Ⓐ Ⓑ Ⓒ Ⓓ	53. Ⓐ Ⓑ Ⓒ Ⓓ	78. Ⓐ Ⓑ Ⓒ Ⓓ
4. Ⓐ Ⓑ Ⓒ Ⓓ	29. Ⓐ Ⓑ Ⓒ Ⓓ	54. Ⓐ Ⓑ Ⓒ Ⓓ	79. Ⓐ Ⓑ Ⓒ Ⓓ
5. Ⓐ Ⓑ Ⓒ Ⓓ	30. Ⓐ Ⓑ Ⓒ Ⓓ	55. Ⓐ Ⓑ Ⓒ Ⓓ	80. Ⓐ Ⓑ Ⓒ Ⓓ
6. Ⓐ Ⓑ Ⓒ Ⓓ	31. Ⓐ Ⓑ Ⓒ Ⓓ	56. Ⓐ Ⓑ Ⓒ Ⓓ	81. Ⓐ Ⓑ Ⓒ Ⓓ
7. Ⓐ Ⓑ Ⓒ Ⓓ	32. Ⓐ Ⓑ Ⓒ Ⓓ	57. Ⓐ Ⓑ Ⓒ Ⓓ	82. Ⓐ Ⓑ Ⓒ Ⓓ
8. Ⓐ Ⓑ Ⓒ Ⓓ	33. Ⓐ Ⓑ Ⓒ Ⓓ	58. Ⓐ Ⓑ Ⓒ Ⓓ	83. Ⓐ Ⓑ Ⓒ Ⓓ
9. Ⓐ Ⓑ Ⓒ Ⓓ	34. Ⓐ Ⓑ Ⓒ Ⓓ	59. Ⓐ Ⓑ Ⓒ Ⓓ	84. Ⓐ Ⓑ Ⓒ Ⓓ
10. Ⓐ Ⓑ Ⓒ Ⓓ	35. Ⓐ Ⓑ Ⓒ Ⓓ	60. Ⓐ Ⓑ Ⓒ Ⓓ	85. Ⓐ Ⓑ Ⓒ Ⓓ
11. Ⓐ Ⓑ Ⓒ Ⓓ	36. Ⓐ Ⓑ Ⓒ Ⓓ	61. Ⓐ Ⓑ Ⓒ Ⓓ	86. Ⓐ Ⓑ Ⓒ Ⓓ
12. Ⓐ Ⓑ Ⓒ Ⓓ	37. Ⓐ Ⓑ Ⓒ Ⓓ	62. Ⓐ Ⓑ Ⓒ Ⓓ	87. Ⓐ Ⓑ Ⓒ Ⓓ
13. Ⓐ Ⓑ Ⓒ Ⓓ	38. Ⓐ Ⓑ Ⓒ Ⓓ	63. Ⓐ Ⓑ Ⓒ Ⓓ	88. Ⓐ Ⓑ Ⓒ Ⓓ
14. Ⓐ Ⓑ Ⓒ Ⓓ	39. Ⓐ Ⓑ Ⓒ Ⓓ	64. Ⓐ Ⓑ Ⓒ Ⓓ	89. Ⓐ Ⓑ Ⓒ Ⓓ
15. Ⓐ Ⓑ Ⓒ Ⓓ	40. Ⓐ Ⓑ Ⓒ Ⓓ	65. Ⓐ Ⓑ Ⓒ Ⓓ	90. Ⓐ Ⓑ Ⓒ Ⓓ
16. Ⓐ Ⓑ Ⓒ Ⓓ	41. Ⓐ Ⓑ Ⓒ Ⓓ	66. Ⓐ Ⓑ Ⓒ Ⓓ	91. Ⓐ Ⓑ Ⓒ Ⓓ
17. Ⓐ Ⓑ Ⓒ Ⓓ	42. Ⓐ Ⓑ Ⓒ Ⓓ	67. Ⓐ Ⓑ Ⓒ Ⓓ	92. Ⓐ Ⓑ Ⓒ Ⓓ
18. Ⓐ Ⓑ Ⓒ Ⓓ	43. Ⓐ Ⓑ Ⓒ Ⓓ	68. Ⓐ Ⓑ Ⓒ Ⓓ	93. Ⓐ Ⓑ Ⓒ Ⓓ
19. Ⓐ Ⓑ Ⓒ Ⓓ	44. Ⓐ Ⓑ Ⓒ Ⓓ	69. Ⓐ Ⓑ Ⓒ Ⓓ	94. Ⓐ Ⓑ Ⓒ Ⓓ
20. Ⓐ Ⓑ Ⓒ Ⓓ	45. Ⓐ Ⓑ Ⓒ Ⓓ	70. Ⓐ Ⓑ Ⓒ Ⓓ	95. Ⓐ Ⓑ Ⓒ Ⓓ
21. Ⓐ Ⓑ Ⓒ Ⓓ	46. Ⓐ Ⓑ Ⓒ Ⓓ	71. Ⓐ Ⓑ Ⓒ Ⓓ	96. Ⓐ Ⓑ Ⓒ Ⓓ
22. Ⓐ Ⓑ Ⓒ Ⓓ	47. Ⓐ Ⓑ Ⓒ Ⓓ	72. Ⓐ Ⓑ Ⓒ Ⓓ	97. Ⓐ Ⓑ Ⓒ Ⓓ
23. Ⓐ Ⓑ Ⓒ Ⓓ	48. Ⓐ Ⓑ Ⓒ Ⓓ	73. Ⓐ Ⓑ Ⓒ Ⓓ	98. Ⓐ Ⓑ Ⓒ Ⓓ
24. Ⓐ Ⓑ Ⓒ Ⓓ	49. Ⓐ Ⓑ Ⓒ Ⓓ	74. Ⓐ Ⓑ Ⓒ Ⓓ	99. Ⓐ Ⓑ Ⓒ Ⓓ
25. Ⓐ Ⓑ Ⓒ Ⓓ	50. Ⓐ Ⓑ Ⓒ Ⓓ	75. Ⓐ Ⓑ Ⓒ Ⓓ	100. Ⓐ Ⓑ Ⓒ Ⓓ

Question 1

Dennis robbed a bank and fled in a getaway car driven by an accomplice, not realizing that one of the bundles of money he took had the serial numbers recorded and had a tiny tracking device attached to the wrapper. The bank contacted its security consultant, who obtained portable tracking equipment and was able to trace the bundle of money to Dennis's house. The police were notified and they arrived at Dennis's house a few hours after the robbery. They knocked on the door and announced their presence, and saw someone matching the description of the robber in the hallway. They entered and arrested the suspect, Dennis, and then conducted a protective sweep of the house for the accomplice, who they believed had a gun. They did not find him, but while checking a closet they discovered several of the bundles of money from the bank and a gun Dennis had used in the robbery. The police also discovered two clear plastic bags of what appeared to be marijuana sitting on top of a dresser. They seized the money, the gun, and the two bags; later testing confirmed that the substance in the bags was marijuana.

Dennis was charged with the bank robbery and with possession of the marijuana. At a preliminary hearing, he moves to suppress introduction of the money, gun, and marijuana.

The court should:

(A) Grant the motion as to the marijuana but not as to the money or the gun because the money and gun were found as a result of the protective sweep for Dennis's accomplice.

(B) Grant the motion as to the money and the gun but not as to the marijuana because the bags containing the marijuana were clearly visible on the dresser during the search.

(C) Grant the motion as to all of the evidence seized.

(D) Deny the motion as to all of the evidence seized.

Questions 2-3 are based on the following fact situation:

In a writing signed by both parties, Paul Plannah, a renowned architect, agreed for a fee of $25,000 to design and supervise construction of a new house for Phoebe Threedee, a famous sculptor, the fee to be paid upon completion of the house. Plannah and Threedee got along poorly and, when the design plans were about two-thirds complete, they had a heated argument over the proper location of a marble staircase. Hoping to avoid such encounters, Plannah, without Threedee's knowledge, assigned to Donna Drafty, a newly licensed architect practicing solo, "all of my rights and duties under my design and construction-supervision contract with Threedee." Drafty expressly promised Plannah to carry out the work to the best of Drafty's ability.

2. For this question only, assume that Threedee, on learning of the assignment, refused to allow Drafty to proceed as architect and brought an action against Plannah to compel him to resume and complete performance of the contract.

Is Threedee entitled to such relief?

(A) Yes, because Plannah's services under the contract are unique.

(B) Yes, because Plannah has personally completed two-thirds of the design work.

(C) No, because the Plannah-Threedee contract is one for personal services by Plannah.

(D) No, because Plannah effectively delegated his remaining duties under the Plannah-Threedee contract to Drafty.

GO ON TO THE NEXT PAGE

3. For this question only, assume that Three-dee allowed Drafty to proceed with the design work, but that Drafty, without legal excuse, abandoned the project shortly after construction began.

Which of the following legal conclusions are correct?

I. Plannah is liable to Threedee for legal damages, if any, caused by Drafty's default.

II. Drafty is liable to Threedee for legal damages, if any, caused by Drafty's default.

III. Threedee is indebted to Drafty, on a divisible contract theory, for a pro-rated portion of the agreed $25,000 architect's fee promised to Plannah.

(A) I. and II. only.

(B) I. and III. only.

(C) II. and III. only.

(D) I., II., and III.

Question 4

Demand Delivery Company employed several messengers to deliver packages by car to nearby towns. The company also allowed some employees to use company cars for personal use from time to time. Because her car was in the repair shop, Eileen had borrowed a Demand car for the weekend and was using it to do some grocery shopping. Because she was glancing at a newspaper on the seat next to her, she did not notice the traffic light at the upcoming intersection change to red. She proceeded into the intersection, crossing the path of a rented van driven by Billy. Billy swerved to avoid Eileen and struck a lightpost and several parked cars, severely damaging the van. At the time of the accident, Billy was exceeding the posted speed limit; he would have been able to avoid hitting the lightpost and the cars had he been going the proper speed. Precision Leasing, which rented the van to Billy, brings a lawsuit against Eileen and Demand. The jurisdiction retains traditional contributory negligence rules.

Will Precision be able to recover any damages from Demand?

(A) Yes, if Demand was aware that Eileen had a poor driving record.

(B) No, because Billy exceeded the posted speed limit.

(C) Yes, unless Billy had the last clear chance to avoid the accident.

(D) No, because Eileen was not acting within the scope of her employment when the accident occurred.

Question 5

Percy was shopping in ValuMart, a large department store. ValuMart was remodeling its menswear department and had hired Contractor to do the work. Cora, a carpenter employed by Contractor, was working on the ValuMart job. When Cora left ValuMart to take her lunch break, she left a carpenter's level projecting out into one of the aisles. Before Cora returned from lunch, Percy came down that aisle and tripped over the level. Percy fell and struck his head on the sharp corner of a display case. Percy required hospitalization and sued ValuMart for his injuries.

Will Percy prevail in his suit against ValuMart?

(A) Yes, because Contractor's employee left the level in the aisle.

(B) Yes, if ValuMart's employees had a reasonable time to discover the level before Percy fell.

(C) No, because ValuMart's employees did not leave the level in the aisle.

(D) No, if ValuMart's employees were unaware that the level was in the aisle.

Questions 6-7 are based on the following fact situation:

In the recently enacted Fair Opportunity Act, the United States Congress provided, among other things, that an employer whose products are in any way used by or sold to the federal government must meet certain very specific standards for integration of its workforce and affirmative action programs. Both civil and criminal penalties are established for violation of the Act, and it permits private civil suits for injunctive relief or for damages to enforce its provisions.

The city of Davis, California also enacted a jobs opportunity ordinance effective the same year, requiring that any employer doing business with the city have a workforce consonant with the ethnic and gender composition of the population of the city. The local ordinance permits employers to apply for exemptions from its requirements if they can demonstrate that the pool of potential qualified employees has a different mix of ethnicity or gender than the general population. The population of Davis is approximately 55% female and 45% male, 75% white, 10% Asian, 7% black, 7% Hispanic, and 1% other ethnic backgrounds.

Watson Janitorial Service, a private employer located in the city of Davis, does contract cleaning and maintenance for both the local United States Department of Agriculture office and for the City Jail. Its workforce is 95% male, 55% black, 40% Hispanic, and 5% other ethnic backgrounds. The city of Davis notified the company that it would either have to bring its workforce into compliance with the local job opportunity ordinance or its contract with the City Jail would be terminated. The United States Department of Justice has notified Watson Janitorial that it meets the guidelines of the Fair Opportunity Act, and that the contract with the Department of Agriculture is not in jeopardy.

6. Watson Janitorial brings an action in state court to enjoin enforcement of the Davis ordinance. It argues that the local rule is invalid since it conflicts with the federal statute by creating more stringent standards. The trial court should rule:

(A) There is no conflict, since Congress intended only that the Fair Opportunity Act apply to employers who dealt exclusively with the federal government.

(B) There is no conflict, since Davis is permitted to impose more strict requirements to a local problem than those established by the federal government.

(C) The federal act preempts the local ordinance and thus the latter cannot be enforced.

(D) The federal act preempts the local ordinance only insofar as it attempts to regulate employers who do business with the federal government, so the ordinance may not be enforced only as to Watson Janitorial, but is otherwise valid.

7. Assume for the purposes of this question only that the United States Department of Agriculture notifies Watson Janitorial that its workforce is in violation of the Fair Opportunity Act and that a referral will be made to the Department of Justice for prosecution unless the federal standards are met within six months. If Watson challenges the validity of the federal statute in court, what is the government's best response to the argument that Congress has exceeded its legitimate powers?

GO ON TO THE NEXT PAGE

I. The act is a valid enforcement of the Due Process Clause of the Fifth Amendment.

II. The act is a valid exercise of the commerce power.

III. The act is a valid exercise of the Enabling Clause of the Thirteenth Amendment.

IV. The act is a valid exercise of the federal police power.

(A) I. and III. only.

(B) II. and III. only.

(C) I. and III. only.

(D) II. and IV. only.

Question 8

Amp, an electrical contractor, sued Short, a homeowner. Amp alleged that Short refused to pay for extensive wiring repairs performed on Short's home by Wilson, an employee of Amp. Amp called Wilson to the stand as a witness. Wilson, under oath, testified that he did not perform any work at Short's home. Wilson also denied writing a letter to Lee telling Lee that Wilson was going to do electrical work on Short's house. Without releasing Wilson as a witness, Amp offers in evidence the letter written by Wilson to Lee.

If Wilson's letter to Lee is properly authenticated, the trial court should:

(A) Admit the letter for impeachment purposes only.

(B) Admit the letter as both substantive and impeachment evidence.

(C) Exclude the letter because a party may not impeach his own witness.

(D) Exclude the letter because it is inadmissible hearsay.

Question 9

In which of the following situations is Defendant most likely to be *not guilty* of the charge made?

(A) Believing that state law made it a crime to purchase Valium without a prescription, Defendant purchased without a prescription a certain quantity of Valium. Unknown to Defendant, the state legislature had repealed the statute, and Valium could be legally purchased without a prescription. Defendant is charged with attempting to purchase Valium without a prescription.

(B) While in the course of a fight, Defendant, intending to kill Stan, ran up and stabbed Stan from behind. Unknown to Defendant, Stan had been stabbed through the chest only seconds before by another participant in the fight, killing him instantly. Defendant is charged with attempted murder.

(C) Defendant misrepresented his identity to a garage in order to take possession of an automobile that had been left with the garage for repairs earlier that week. The owner of the garage was not deceived and refused to turn over possession. Defendant is charged with attempting to obtain property by false pretenses.

(D) Police arrested Robber as he was leaving a house where he had stolen a good deal of property. As part of a plea-bargain arrangement, Robber took the property to Defendant and offered to sell it. Defendant, believing the property to be stolen, purchased it. Defendant is charged with attempting to receive stolen property.

GO ON TO THE NEXT PAGE

Question 10

The city of Newtown adopted an ordinance providing that street demonstrations involving more than 15 persons may not be held in commercial areas during "rush" hours. "Exceptions" may be made to the prohibition "upon 24-hour advance application to and approval by the police department." The ordinance also imposes sanctions on any person "who shall, without provocation, use to or of another, and in his presence, opprobrious words or abusive language tending to cause a breach of the peace." No court has of yet interpreted the ordinance.

Which of the following is the strongest argument for the unconstitutionality of both parts of the ordinance on their faces?

(A) No type of prior restraint may be imposed on speech in public places.

(B) Laws, regulating by their terms expressive conduct or speech, may not be overbroad or unduly vague.

(C) The determination as to whether public gatherings may be lawfully held cannot be vested in the police.

(D) The right of association in public places without interference is ensured by the First and Fourteenth Amendments.

Question 11

Truffle agreed in writing to lease a restaurant site in a newly constructed mall from Lentil, the owner of the property. The term of the tenancy was two years, and rent was payable in monthly installments at the beginning of each month. At the end of the second year, there had been no discussions between Truffle and Lentil regarding renewal or termination. Truffle did not vacate the premises at the end of the term; instead, she sent a check for the next month's rent to Lentil. Lentil cashed the check after the term had expired but informed Truffle that his acceptance of the check did not mean that he was going to renew the lease or let Truffle stay. At the end of that month, Lentil seeks advice on whether he can evict Truffle.

How should Lentil be advised to proceed?

(A) Lentil must give Truffle a full 30 days' notice before beginning eviction proceedings because a month-to-month periodic tenancy has been created.

(B) Lentil may begin eviction proceedings as soon as the additional month has expired.

(C) Lentil may not evict Truffle for 11 months and must give six months' notice before beginning eviction proceedings because a year-to-year periodic tenancy has been created.

(D) Lentil may not evict Truffle for 11 months but need not give any notice prior to eviction because a tenancy for years for a term of one year has been created.

Question 12

Dirk broke into Vera's house one night. As he started to stuff silverware into a sack, he was surprised by Vera, who had arrived home earlier than usual. Dirk struck Vera on the head with a candlestick and tied her up. He finished filling his sack and left.

The police discovered Vera several hours later and rushed her to the hospital. Dirk was apprehended by the police early the following morning with the loot still in his possession. He was taken to police headquarters, given *Miranda* warnings, and asked if he wished to make a statement about the prior evening's events. The police did not mention that Vera had been seriously injured and was in the hospital. Dirk said he understood his rights and was willing to talk. He then admitted that he committed the burglary of Vera's house. The following day, Vera died from injuries caused by the blow to her head.

If, at Dirk's trial for murder, Dirk moves to prevent introduction of the confession into evidence, his motion should most probably be:

(A) Denied, because failure of the police to advise Dirk of Vera's condition was harmless error since felony murder does not require intent to kill or injure.

(B) Denied, because Dirk's waiver of his rights did not depend upon the nature of the charges that were later filed against him.

(C) Granted, because Dirk could not make a knowing and intelligent waiver unless he had information concerning Vera's condition.

(D) Granted, because the use of a confession to burglary in a prosecution for murder violates due process where the police withheld information about the potential seriousness of the offense.

Question 13

West, a witness in a contract case, testified on direct examination that four people attended a meeting. When asked to identify them, she gave the names of three, but despite trying was unable to remember the name of the fourth person.

The attorney who called her as a witness seeks to show her his handwritten notes of the part of his pretrial interview with her in which she provided all four names.

The trial court is likely to consider the showing of the notes taken as:

(A) A proper attempt to introduce recorded recollection.

(B) A proper attempt to refresh West's recollection.

(C) An improper attempt to lead the witness.

(D) An improper attempt to support West's credibility.

GO ON TO THE NEXT PAGE

Question 14

Buyer, a retail seller of lawn and garden equipment, entered into a written contract with Seller, a manufacturer of wheelbarrows. The terms of the contract call for Seller to deliver 100 fifteen-pound capacity, red wheelbarrows to Buyer by March 1. On February 28, Buyer received from Seller 90 fifteen-pound capacity, red wheelbarrows and 10 twenty-pound capacity, red wheelbarrows. A letter accompanying the shipment stated, "We no longer make fifteen-pound capacity wheelbarrows. We are sending the last 90 we have in stock along with 10 twenty-pound capacity wheelbarrows. The twenty-pound capacity were sent as an accommodation to you." Which of the following correctly states the rights of Buyer?

I.   Buyer can reject the entire shipment.

II.   Buyer can accept the 90 conforming wheelbarrows, reject the 10 nonconforming wheelbarrows, and sue Seller for damages.

III. Buyer can accept the entire shipment and sue Seller for damages.

(A) Only I. and II. are correct.

(B) Only I. is correct.

(C) I., II., and III. are correct.

(D) Only II. is correct.

Question 15

The German-made Doppelpferd, featuring sleek styling and remarkable fuel efficiency, is the most popular automobile in the United States. Its United States sales are booming, and the average retail markup in such sales is 30%. Hardsell Motors, Inc., a franchised Doppelpferd dealer in the United States, contracted with Shift to sell him a new Doppelpferd for $9,000 cash, the sale to be consummated after delivery to Hardsell of the car, which Hardsell ordered from the manufacturer specifically for Shift. The signed retail contractual document was a form drafted by Hardsell's lawyer, and Shift did not question or object to any of its terms, including the price inserted by Hardsell. When the car arrived from Germany, Shift repudiated the contract. Hardsell at once sold the car for $9,000 cash to Karbuff, for whom Hardsell had also ordered from the manufacturer a Doppelpferd identical to Shift's.

In an action against Shift for breach of contract, Hardsell will probably recover:

(A) $9,000 minus what it cost Hardsell to purchase the car from the manufacturer.

(B) $9,000 minus the wholesale price of an identical Doppelpferd in the local wholesale market among dealers.

(C) Nominal damages only because Hardsell resold the car to Karbuff without lowering the retail price.

(D) Nothing, because the parties' agreement was an adhesion contract and therefore unconscionable.

GO ON TO THE NEXT PAGE

Question 16

Pike sued Digger, the contractor who constructed Pike's house, for breach of warranty of habitability. At trial, in cross-examination of Pike, Digger's attorney asked whether Pike had sued another contractor 30 years earlier, claiming similar defects in another house built for Pike. The question was not objected to and Pike answered that she had had some "water problems" with the first house she ever purchased, but no suit was filed.

Digger then called Wirth, the contractor of 30 years earlier, to testify that Pike had brought suit against Wirth for defects in the earlier house, many of which were like those now claimed to be found in the home Digger built, but that the case was settled without trial.

The trial court should rule Wirth's offered testimony:

(A) Admissible as proper impeachment since Pike will have an opportunity to deny or explain Wirth's statement.

(B) Admissible, because Pike failed to object to Digger's questions on cross-examination relative to the prior suit.

(C) Inadmissible, because the best evidence of the former suit is the court record.

(D) Inadmissible, because its probative value is substantially outweighed by the danger that it will confuse the issues and waste time.

Questions 17-18 are based on the following fact situation:

Hammond decided to kill his wife by poisoning her. He asked his friend, Jordan, a pharmacist, to obtain some curare, a deadly poison, and to give it to him without recording the transaction. Because Jordan suspected Hammond's motive, she supplied Hammond with a small quantity of Marvane, an antibiotic, instead of curare. Marvane is harmless if administered in small quantities, except for the less than 1% of the population who are allergic to the drug.

Hammond injected his wife with the Marvane while she slept. She was allergic to the drug and died from the injection. Jordan was distraught and confessed the entire affair to the police, explaining that she had failed to report Hammond's conduct to the authorities because she feared that it would end their friendship if she did.

17. Jordan is an accomplice to:

(A) Murder.

(B) Manslaughter.

(C) Criminally negligent homicide.

(D) No degree of criminal homicide.

18. In a common law jurisdiction, Hammond is guilty of:

(A) Murder only.

(B) Murder and conspiracy.

(C) Attempted murder only.

(D) Attempted murder and conspiracy.

GO ON TO THE NEXT PAGE

Question 19

Abco developed a new drug, ZB, for treatment of Wegener's disease. Abco extensively tested ZB for several years on animals and human volunteers and had observed no undesirable side effects. The Federal Drug Administration ("FDA") then approved ZB for sale as a prescription drug.

Five other drug companies, each acting independently, developed drugs identical to ZB. Each of these drugs was also approved by the FDA for sale as a prescription drug. True Blue Drug, a wholesaler, bought identically shaped pills from all six of the manufacturers and sold the pills to drugstores as Wegener's X.

This drug had a long-delayed side effect. Sons of male users of Wegener's X are sterile. One such son, Crane, brought an action against Abco for his damages. Abco, through True Blue Drug, supplied about 10% of the Wegener's X sold in the state where Crane lived. It is not possible to establish which of the five companies supplied the particular pills that Crane's father took.

If Crane asserts a claim against Abco based on strict liability in tort, which of the following will be a decisive question in determining whether Crane will prevail?

(A) Does the res ipsa loquitur doctrine apply?

(B) Can liability be imposed on Abco without proof that Abco knew that the drug had an undesirable side effect?

(C) Is Abco relieved of liability by the FDA approval of the drug?

(D) Can liability be imposed on Abco without showing that its pills were used by Crane's father?

Questions 20-21 are based on the following fact situation:

Lightpost, Inc., the owner of a retail outlet mall, leased one of its retail units to Shirts by Sam ("Shirts"), a chain selling casual apparel, for a period of five years. The lease agreement provided that Shirts would pay to Lightpost, as additional rent, a share of maintenance costs for the construction and upkeep of the parking lots and other common areas in the mall, and Lightpost would be responsible for maintaining these areas. The maintenance fee was calculated based on total square footage of each unit and amounted to $1,000 a month for the unit leased by Shirts. The agreement also permitted assignments and subleases. For four years, Shirts operated its apparel store and paid all rent and maintenance fees. At the end of the fourth year, Shirts properly assigned the lease to Shoes by Sheila ("Shoes"), a discount shoe outlet.

20. Assume for purposes of this question only that, at the time it assigned the lease, Shirts owed $3,000 in maintenance fees for the last three months of its occupancy, and that Shoes paid its rent but did not pay any maintenance fees to Lightpost for the first six months. Shoes then abandoned the property. Lightpost made reasonable efforts during the last six months of the term to relet the unit but was unable to do so. After applying the security deposit to satisfy the balance of the rent, Lightpost wishes to collect the unpaid maintenance fees during the last 15 months of the lease, totaling $15,000. Who is liable for those fees and in what amount?

(A) Shirts and Shoes are jointly and severally liable for the $15,000 in fees.

(B) Shirts is solely liable for $3,000 in fees, and Shirts and Shoes are jointly and severally liable for $12,000 in fees.

(C) Shirts is solely liable for $3,000 in fees, Shoes is solely liable for $6,000 in fees, and Shirts and Shoes are jointly and severally liable for $6,000 in fees.

(D) Shirts is solely liable for $3,000 in fees, and Shoes is solely liable for $12,000 in fees.

GO ON TO THE NEXT PAGE

21. Assume for purposes of this question only that, shortly after Shirts assigned the lease to Shoes, Lightpost sold the mall to Lakeview, Ltd. Lakeview took subject to all of the leases, including Shoes's lease, but did not assume any of Lightpost's obligations under it. Five months after the sale, a contractor originally hired by Lightpost who was reconstructing the parking lot in front of Shoes's store walked off the job because he had not received any progress payments from either Lightpost or Lakeview during the past five months. After notifying Lightpost and Lakeview and receiving no response, Shoes agreed to pay the contractor $20,000 up front to finish the job so that the store would have parking for the holiday shopping season. Shoes then withheld its rent payment of $2,000 for that month and brought an action against Lightpost and Lakeview to recover the balance of the payment to the contractor. Shoes had paid its maintenance fees in advance for the rest of its term.

Are either Lightpost or Lakeview liable to Shoes?

(A) Neither Lakeview nor Lightpost is liable to Shoes because Shoes is in breach of its covenant to pay rent.

(B) Lightpost is liable to Shoes, but Lakeview is not, because Lakeview did not assume Lightpost's obligations.

(C) Lakeview is liable to Shoes, but Lightpost is not, because the sale by Lightpost to Lakeview severed any privity of estate between Lightpost and Shoes.

(D) Both Lakeview and Lightpost are liable to Shoes because the maintenance duties constitute an independent covenant that is part of the lease and that runs with land.

Question 22

To secure an express lane on the information superhighway, the federal government contracted with a number of communications utilities to install fiberoptic communication lines between major federal offices across the country. The utilities, which maintained ownership of the lines, contracted with the federal government to install the lines on a "cost plus fixed fee" basis, whereby all installation costs would be reimbursed by the government. One such line was installed in State Yellow's capital city, Plains, where the Department of the Interior maintained its western regional office. State Yellow imposes a tax on the installation of all communication lines in the state, including fiberoptic cable lines. It seeks to impose the tax on the line running to the federal office.

Will the state be permitted to impose the tax?

(A) Yes, because the tax is indirect and nondiscriminatory.

(B) Yes, because the tax is a valid exercise of state power under the Tenth Amendment.

(C) No, because the tax burdens the activities of the federal government.

(D) No, because the activity taxed involves interstate commerce.

GO ON TO THE NEXT PAGE

Question 23

In an action by Patrick against David, one of the issues is whether David is a licensed psychotherapist. Normally, the names of all licensed psychotherapists are registered with the office of the State Department of Professional Registrations. Patrick wishes to introduce a certified document, signed by the chief registrar of the Department, stating that an examination of the Department's rolls does not disclose David's name.

Should the document be admitted?

(A) Yes, because a statement of absence from public record is admissible.

(B) Yes, but only if the chief registrar is unavailable.

(C) No, because the document is hearsay not within an exception.

(D) No, because the document is not self-authenticating.

Question 24

Westside Shopping Center contracted with Bill's Security Service to provide nighttime monitoring of mall property. Bill had heard about a store in another part of the country that used poisonous snakes as deterrents to burglars. Bill was something of an amateur herpetologist, and so, without the manager's permission, he began placing several of his pet rattlesnakes in the shopping center at night and posting signs at night saying, "Beware of poisonous snakes."

The shopping center was conducting a contest to attract shoppers in which a compact car was filled with jelly beans, and the contestant who came nearest to guessing the number of beans would win the car. John, a graduate student at the local liberal arts college, decided to break into the shopping center, take a sample of the jelly beans in a given volume of the car's interior, then, using the manufacturer's figures for interior volume, calculate the number of beans in the car. Sunday morning at 5 a.m., John used a crowbar to lever open a glass entryway and tiptoed toward the contest car. As he was carefully opening a vent window to take his sample of jelly beans, one of Bill's rattlers that had been lying under the car bit John on the ankle. Bill came running upon hearing John's screams and applied snakebite treatment. John was hospitalized for two weeks and had to miss a semester of school as a result of the snakebite.

If John brings an action against the shopping center, will he likely recover?

(A) No, because he was a trespasser on shopping center property.

(B) No, because he was guilty of breaking and entering.

(C) Yes, because the use of poisonous snakes for security amounted to unreasonable force.

(D) Yes, if he had not seen the signs warning of the poisonous snakes.

GO ON TO THE NEXT PAGE

Question 25

On a wholly random basis, a state agency has given a few probationary employees who were not rehired at the end of their probationary period a statement of reasons and an opportunity for a hearing; but the agency has very rarely done so. No statute or rule of the agency required such a statement of reasons or a hearing.

The employment of Masters, a probationary employee, was terminated without a statement of reasons or an opportunity for a hearing. The agency did not even consider whether it should give him either.

A suit by Masters requesting a statement of reasons and a hearing will probably be:

(A) Successful, on the grounds that failure to give Masters reasons and an opportunity for a hearing constituted a bill of attainder.

(B) Successful, on the grounds that an agency's inconsistent practices, even if unintentional, deny adversely affected persons the equal protection of the laws.

(C) Unsuccessful, because Masters does not have a right to be rehired that is protected by procedural due process.

(D) Unsuccessful, because the conditions of state employment are matters reserved to the states by the Tenth Amendment.

Question 26

Marvin Manufacturing Company was in the business of making copper tubing. Golde Industries telephoned Marvin's sales department and placed an order for 10,000 linear feet of copper tubing at a sale price of $2 per foot. The tubing was to be used in the production of a custom order for one of Golde's customers. Marvin installed special equipment for the manufacture of the tubing to Golde's specifications and had completed a portion of the order when Golde again telephoned the sales department. This time, however, Golde canceled its order, saying it no longer had need of the tubing because its

customer had been declared bankrupt, and refused to pay for the order.

If Marvin sues for breach, it will:

(A) Win, because the contract is fully enforceable.

(B) Win, because the contract is enforceable to the extent of the portion of the order completed.

(C) Lose, because a contract for the sale of goods over $500 must be in writing.

(D) Lose, because the parol evidence rule would preclude testimony about the initial telephone call.

Question 27

Police investigating a homicide had probable cause to believe that Drake had committed it. They then learned from a reliable informant that, a short while ago, Drake had gone to Trent's house to obtain a false driver's license from Trent, a convicted forger. Believing that Drake might still be there, the police, without obtaining a warrant, went to Trent's house. They entered the house and found Drake hiding in the basement. He was arrested and given his *Miranda* warnings. At the police station, he confessed to the homicide.

At a preliminary hearing, Drake's attorney contends that the confession should be suppressed on Fourth Amendment grounds.

Is the court likely to agree?

(A) Yes, because the police did not have a search warrant to enter Trent's house and there were no exigent circumstances.

(B) Yes, because the police did not have an arrest warrant for Drake and there were no exigent circumstances.

(C) No, because a reliable informant told police that Drake was in Trent's house.

(D) No, because the police had probable cause to arrest Drake.

GO ON TO THE NEXT PAGE

Question 28

All of the deeds for the lots in the 5100 block of Elm Street contained a restrictive covenant requiring that all houses built on the lots be set back a minimum of 50 feet from the sidewalk. Local zoning regulations required that all homes in the area of the 5100 block of Elm Street be set back a minimum of 35 feet from the sidewalk. Dampier purchased a lot on the 5100 block of Elm Street on which it would be possible to build a home with a 50-foot setback. However, the lot was of an unusual shape, and Dampier applied to the city zoning commission asking for a variance allowing him to build a house set back 30 feet from the sidewalk. In his petition, Dampier cited the unusual shape of the lot and asserted that it would cause hardship for him to build in compliance with the 35-foot setback required by the zoning regulations. The zoning commission granted Dampier the variance. Nora, whose home was located at 5130 Elm Street, noticed surveyors putting up ropes 30 feet from the sidewalk on Dampier's lot, and she discovered that Dampier planned to build a home with only a 30-foot setback.

Nora seeks to enforce the restrictive covenant and brings suit to enjoin Dampier from building a residence with a setback of less than 50 feet. Who will prevail?

(A) Dampier, because zoning regulations take precedence over restrictive covenants as a matter of public policy.

(B) Dampier, because equity will not impose a hardship.

(C) Nora, because Dampier will be unjustly enriched if he is permitted to build a 30-foot setback.

(D) Nora, because a zoning variance does not affect the enforcement of a restrictive covenant.

Questions 29-30 are based on the following fact situation:

On January 1, Awl and Howser agreed in writing that Awl would build a house on Howser's lot according to Howser's plans and specifications for $60,000, the work to commence on April 1. Howser agreed to make an initial payment of $10,000 on April 1, and to pay the balance upon completion of the work.

On February 1, Awl notified Howser that he (Awl) would lose money on the job at that price, and would not proceed with the work unless Howser would agree to increase the price to $90,000. Howser thereupon, without notifying Awl, agreed in writing with Gutter for Gutter, commencing April 1, to build the house for $75,000, which was the fair market cost of the work to be done.

On April 1, both Awl and Gutter showed up at the building site to begin work, Awl telling Howser that he had decided to "take the loss" and would build the house for $60,000 as originally agreed. Howser dismissed Awl and allowed Gutter to begin work on the house.

29. In a contract action by Awl against Howser, which of the following would the court decide under the prevailing American view?

(A) Howser will win because Awl in legal effect committed a total breach of contract.

(B) Howser will win because Gutter's contract price was $15,000 lower than the $90,000 demanded by Awl on February 1.

(C) Awl will win because Howser did not tell him before April 1 about the contract with Gutter.

(D) Awl will win because he attempted to perform the contract as originally agreed.

GO ON TO THE NEXT PAGE

30. For this question only, assume that Awl is liable to Howser for breach of contract and also assume the following additional facts: Gutter finished the house on schedule and then showed Howser that he (Gutter) had spent $85,000 on the job. Howser thereupon paid Gutter the full balance of their contract price plus an additional $10,000, so that Gutter would not lose money.

In a contract action by Howser against Awl, Howser will recover:

(A) The difference between the fair market value of the completed house and Awl's original contract price.

(B) $30,000, the difference between Awl's original contract price and the amount Awl demanded on February 1.

(C) $25,000, the difference between Awl's original contract price and the total amount Howser paid Gutter for building the house.

(D) $15,000, the difference between Awl's original contract price and Gutter's contract price.

Question 31

Benjamin, a foreign correspondent, wished to purchase Whiteacre. Smith, the owner of Whiteacre, was not yet sure he wished to sell the property. He was waiting to see if his bid on another parcel was going to be accepted. Before Smith could make up his mind, Benjamin was assigned to cover an ethnic conflict in eastern Europe that was escalating into a war. Prior to his departure, Benjamin gave his attorney, Lenora, $100,000 and his power of attorney. He instructed Lenora that, should Whiteacre be put up for sale, she was authorized to: offer up to $100,000 for it, enter into a binding contract to purchase it on Benjamin's behalf, and if he did not return in time, she was authorized to close on the property. In early January, Smith put Whiteacre on the market. Lenora offered $75,000 for it, which Smith readily accepted. On January

15, Lenora, on Benjamin's behalf, entered into a written contract to purchase Whiteacre for $75,000. Closing was set for February 15. During this time, Lenora heard nothing from Benjamin. When he had not returned by the date of closing, Lenora attended the closing and tendered the $75,000. Smith tendered a deed made out to Benjamin as the grantee.

On February 20, news was received that Benjamin had been killed by a stray bullet on January 14. Benjamin's will left his entire estate to his niece, Nellie. In the meantime, Smith has had someone offer him $150,000 for Whiteacre. Having heard of Benjamin's death, Smith believes the conveyance to Benjamin is invalid. Smith brings a suit to quiet title to Whiteacre.

The court will most likely find that the owner of Whiteacre is:

(A) Nellie, because Lenora held the deed on constructive trust for Benjamin's estate.

(B) Nellie, because of the operation of the doctrine of equitable conversion.

(C) Smith, because a deed to a nonexistent person is void and conveys no title.

(D) Smith, because the risk of loss is on the buyer.

GO ON TO THE NEXT PAGE

Question 32

Patricia sued Doris for injuries suffered when her car collided in an intersection with one driven by Doris. At trial, Patricia testified that she had had the right-of-way over Doris to enter the intersection. Doris did not cross-examine. Patricia then called Wendy to testify that, shortly after the collision, as she pulled Patricia from the car, Wendy heard Patricia say, "I think I'm dying! Didn't the other driver see I had the right-of-way?" Wendy's testimony was admitted over defense counsel's objections. On appeal from a verdict for Patricia, Doris challenges the admission of Wendy's testimony.

Should the trial court's ruling be upheld?

(A) Yes, because Patricia's statement was made under belief of impending death.

(B) Yes, because Patricia's statement was an excited utterance.

(C) No, because Patricia's credibility had not been attacked.

(D) No, because Patricia's belief that she had the right-of-way had already been established without contradiction.

Question 33

There is high and persistent unemployment in the industrialized state of Green. Its legislature therefore enacted a statute requiring every business with annual sales in Green of over $1 million to purchase each year goods and/or services in Green equal in value to at least half of its sales in Green.

Which of the following parties most clearly has standing to contest the constitutionality of this statute of Green in federal court?

(A) A business in another state that supplies from that other state 95% of the goods and services bought by a corporation that has annual sales in Green of $20 million.

(B) A corporation selling $300,000 worth of goods in Green but presently purchasing only $10,000 in goods and services in Green.

(C) The governor of an adjacent state on behalf of the state and its residents.

(D) The owner of high-grade, secured bonds issued by a corporation with sales in Green of $10 million that currently purchases only $1 million in goods and services in Green.

Questions 34-35 are based on the following fact situation:

Jaywalking (crossing a street outside of a crosswalk or not at an intersection) is punishable by a fine in Metropolis. Bert, who had lived in Metropolis all of his 67 years, was out window-shopping with his wife, Ruth, also 67, when he saw a friend across the street at a diner they both frequented. Telling Ruth that he would be right back, he saw that there were no cars nearby and so strode briskly across the street in the middle of the block. As he reached the other sidewalk, a police officer who had been checking parked cars for parking violations stepped up to Bert and said, "Hold it buddy, let's see your driver's license," and then reached for her citation book. Bert, a city dweller from birth, had always walked or used public transportation, had never learned to drive, and did not have a driver's license. When he told the officer that he did not have a driver's license, she said, "All right, I'm taking you in," and seized his wrist, twisting it up and behind him in a personnel control lock. A black belt in judo, Bert easily slipped the officer's grasp. "You asked for it," she then growled, and pulled her baton from her belt. When she attempted to strike Bert, he moved swiftly to the side, chopped at her arm, and caused the baton to fall from her grasp to the pavement. At that point two other officers arrived on the scene and arrested Bert. Ruth watched the entire episode from across the street and became greatly distressed.

GO ON TO THE NEXT PAGE

34. Bert brings an action against the first officer for battery. What will be the probable outcome of this litigation?

    (A) He will lose, because he struck the officer.

    (B) He will lose, because the offense was committed in the officer's presence.

    (C) He will win, unless he is found guilty of jaywalking.

    (D) He will win, because the officer was not privileged to arrest him.

35. Ruth also sues the officer, alleging intentional infliction of emotional distress. Will she recover?

    (A) No, unless the officer knew that Ruth and Bert were husband and wife.

    (B) No, if the officer did not know that Ruth was watching from across the street.

    (C) Yes, because the officer's conduct regarding Bert was extreme and outrageous.

    (D) Yes, because the officer's conduct caused Ruth to be severely emotionally disturbed.

Questions 36-37 are based on the following fact situation:

One night after work, Dunken stopped in at a bar next to his place of employment to have a few drinks before heading home. While there, he became intoxicated. Upon leaving the bar, Dunken decided that he would drive home rather than walk. Dunken went next door to a used car lot to take a car to drive home. However, Dunken discovered that there were no keys in any of the cars. He then broke into the main office of the used car lot where he surmised correctly that the keys would be kept. As he left the office with keys to one of the cars, Dunken saw a security guard coming toward him. Dunken pushed the guard to the side as he ran past. The guard fell back, hit his head on the pavement, and died. Dunken then climbed into the car and drove away. On his way home, he was so intoxicated that he missed his exit. Making an illegal u-turn to go back, he struck a car legally parked on the side of the road, killing its occupant. Relevant statutes extend burglary to include buildings not used as a dwelling. First degree murder is defined as "the premeditated and intentional killing of another or a killing during commission of a rape, robbery, burglary, or arson." Second degree murder is defined as all murders that are not first degree murder.

36. If Dunken is charged with first degree murder for the death of the security guard, the court should charge the jury on the issue of the defense of intoxication that:

    (A) Voluntary intoxication is no defense to the crime of first degree murder as defined by the statute.

    (B) Voluntary intoxication is a defense to the crime of first degree murder if Dunken would not have killed the security guard but for the intoxication.

    (C) Voluntary intoxication is a defense to the crime of first degree murder if it prevented Dunken from forming the intent to commit a burglary.

    (D) Voluntary intoxication is a defense to first degree murder if it prevented Dunken from forming the intent to kill the security guard.

37. If Dunken is charged with homicide for the death of the occupant of the parked car, the most serious crime for which Dunken can be convicted is:

(A) First degree murder.

(B) Second degree murder.

(C) Involuntary manslaughter based on criminal negligence.

(D) Involuntary manslaughter based on unlawful conduct.

Question 38

The High National Grasslands is owned by the United States and is located in the center of a large western state. Acting pursuant to a federal statute authorizing such action, the United States Bureau of Land Management leased the grazing rights in the High National Grasslands to ranchers located nearby. Grazingland Company owns a vast amount of rangeland adjacent to the High National Grasslands and leases its land for livestock grazing purposes to the same ranchers, but at prices higher than those charged by the Bureau. Grazingland Company sued the Bureau in an appropriate federal district court to restrain the Bureau from competing with that company by leasing the High National Grasslands.

Which of the following constitutional provisions may most easily and directly be used to justify the federal statute authorizing this leasing program of the Bureau of Land Management?

(A) The General Welfare Clause of Article I, Section 8.

(B) The Federal Property Clause of Article IV, Section 3.

(C) The Commerce Clause of Article I, Section 8.

(D) The Supremacy Clause of Article VI.

Question 39

In Peck's antitrust suit against manufacturers of insulation, Peck's interrogatories asked for information concerning total sales of insulation by each of the defendant manufacturers in a particular year. The defendants replied to the interrogatories by referring Peck to the *Insulation Manufacturer's Annual Journal* for the information.

If, at trial, Peck offers the annual as evidence of the sales volume, this evidence is:

(A) Admissible, as an adoptive admission of the defendants.

(B) Admissible, as a business record.

(C) Inadmissible, as hearsay not within any exception.

(D) Inadmissible, as lacking sufficient authentication.

GO ON TO THE NEXT PAGE

Question 40

Farmer's Garden Foods ("FGF") was a manufacturer of quality red cheese made from imported yaks' milk. In a written agreement between FGF and Gourmet Mart ("GM"), a retail seller of fine quality foods, FGF agreed to "sell all output of FGF red cheese to GM," and GM agreed to "sell FGF red cheese exclusively." The agreement went on to state that GM would pay $150 for each 10-wheel container of red cheese ordered from FGF.

Under the above facts, what are the relative obligations of the parties?

(A) FGF has to sell all of its output to GM; GM has to buy all of FGF's output.

(B) FGF has to sell all of its output to GM; GM has to sell exclusively FGF red cheese.

(C) FGF has to sell all of its output to GM; GM has to sell exclusively FGF red cheese but it does not have to buy any.

(D) FGF has to sell all of its output to GM; GM has to buy all of FGF's output and has to sell exclusively FGF red cheese.

Question 41

Constance owned Greenacre in fee simple. She executed two instruments in the proper form of deeds. The first instrument purported to convey an undivided one-half interest in Greenacre to Henry and his wife, Audrey, as joint tenants with right of survivorship. The second instrument purported to convey an undivided one-half interest in Greenacre to Susan, the only child of Henry. Susan was 13 years old at the time. The common law joint tenancy is unmodified by statute.

No actual consideration was paid for the deeds. Constance handed the two deeds to Henry. Henry promptly and properly recorded the deed to himself and Audrey and put the deed to his daughter, Susan, in a safe-deposit box without recording it.

The same year, Henry, Audrey, and Susan were on a vacation when the plane in which they were flying went down, and all three were killed simultaneously. Henry, Audrey, and Susan died intestate. The applicable statute in the jurisdictions provides that "when title to property on its devolution depends on priority of death and there is insufficient evidence that the persons have died otherwise than simultaneously, the property of each person shall be disposed of as if he had survived." An appropriate action was instituted by the heirs of Henry, Audrey, and Susan. Constance, who is not an heir of any of the deceased, was a party to the action.

The court should determine that title to Greenacre is:

(A) Entirely in Constance.

(B) One-half in the heirs of Henry and one-half in the heirs of Audrey.

(C) One-half in Constance, one-quarter in the heirs of Henry, and one-quarter in the heirs of Audrey.

(D) One-half in the heirs of Susan, one-quarter in the heirs of Henry, and one-quarter in the heirs of Audrey.

GO ON TO THE NEXT PAGE

Question 42

Argus Corporation is privately owned and incorporated in the state of Kiowa. It contracted with the United States to construct a dam across the Big Sandy River in the state of Arapahoe. The state of Arapahoe imposed a gross receipts tax on all business conducted within the state. Arapahoe sued Argus Corporation to collect that tax on the receipts Argus received under this federal contract. No federal statutes or administrative rules are applicable, and the contract between the United States and the Argus Corporation does not mention state taxation.

The court should hold the state tax, as applied here, to be:

(A) Constitutional, because a state has exclusive jurisdiction over all commercial transactions executed wholly within its borders.

(B) Constitutional, because private contractors performing work under a federal contract are not immune in these circumstances from nondiscriminatory state taxation.

(C) Unconstitutional, because it violates the Supremacy Clause.

(D) Unconstitutional, because it imposes an undue burden on interstate commerce.

Question 43

Able, an attorney, sued Clinton, a client, for his fee, based on an agreed hourly rate. Clinton subpoenaed the attorney's time records for the days on which he purported to have worked for Clinton to show that Able had billed an impossible number of hours to Clinton and others on those days. Clinton's subpoena provided that any information concerning the matters handled for other clients be deleted or masked. Able moved to quash the subpoena on the ground of attorney-client privilege.

The subpoena should be:

(A) Upheld, because the information about hours billed is not within the privilege.

(B) Upheld, because an attorney has no right to invoke his client's privilege without instructions from the client.

(C) Quashed, because an attorney is entitled to a right of privacy for the work product in his files.

(D) Quashed, because no permission was obtained from the other clients to divulge information from their files.

Questions 44-45 are based on the following fact situation:

Torgeson, a prosperous widower, owned Fruitacre, a large tract of land located near Sunbelt City. Fruitacre was primarily used for extensive citrus orchards, but Torgeson was sure that rapidly growing Sunbelt City would expand toward Fruitacre, and that Fruitacre would be a prime tract for a residential subdivision within 20 years. Torgeson wanted to see his three grandchildren, Hubert (age 22), Dubert (age 17), and Luberta (age 15), benefit from the large price that he was sure Fruitacre would bring, but he was also concerned that the grandchildren be of sufficient maturity. Torgeson suggested to his only child, Diana, that he give her a life interest in Fruitacre, and that Diana's children take Fruitacre upon her death. Diana told Torgeson that she did not need the income from Fruitacre and would prefer that Torgeson give the land directly to Hubert, Dubert, and Luberta. Torgeson arrived at what he felt was a reasonable compromise, using his good friend, Fran (age 55), as the person to whom he conveyed the land. Torgeson's conveyance read, in pertinent part, as follows: "I convey Fruitacre to Fran for life, remainder to all of my grandchildren who ever attain the age of 25, and if none of them attains such age, to the Sisters of Charity."

GO ON TO THE NEXT PAGE

44. The grandchildren's interest can best be described as:

(A) A contingent remainder.

(B) A vested remainder.

(C) An executory interest.

(D) Nothing.

45. The Sisters of Charity's interest can best be described as:

(A) A contingent remainder.

(B) A vested remainder subject to total divestment.

(C) An executory interest.

(D) Nothing.

Questions 46-47 are based on the following fact situation:

Until 1954, the state of New Atlantic required segregation in all public and private schools, but all public schools are now desegregated. Other state laws, enacted before 1954 and continuing to the present, provide for free distribution of the same textbooks on secular subjects to students in all public and private schools. In addition, the state accredits schools and certifies teachers.

Little White School House, a private school that offers elementary and secondary education in the state, denies admission to all non-Caucasians. Stone School is a private school that offers religious instruction.

46. Which of the following is the strongest argument *against* the constitutionality of free distribution of textbooks to the students at the Little White School House?

(A) No legitimate educational function is served by the free distribution of textbooks.

(B) The state may not in any way aid private schools.

(C) The Constitution forbids private bias of any kind.

(D) Segregation is furthered by the distribution of textbooks to these students.

47. Which of the following is the strongest argument *in favor of* the constitutionality of free distribution of textbooks to the students at Stone School?

(A) Private religious schools, like public nonsectarian schools, fulfill an important educational function.

(B) Religious instruction in private schools is not constitutionally objectionable.

(C) The purpose and effect of the free distribution of these textbooks is secular and does not entangle church and state.

(D) The Free Exercise Clause requires identical treatment by the state of students in public and private schools.

GO ON TO THE NEXT PAGE

Question 48

Edgar was employed as an electrician by Edgewater Electric Services. Edgewater had contracts with a number of large office and condominium buildings to provide emergency electrical services and repairs at any hour of the day or night. Edgewater also advertised in the telephone "yellow pages": "If it's an electrical emergency, call Edgewater Electric Services—night or day." Although Edgar usually worked from 8 a.m. to 4 p.m. at Edgewater, the nature of Edgewater's emergency services required Edgar to be "on call" 24 hours a day. Therefore, Edgewater required Edgar to drive his company van to his home each night, so he would be in a position to speed off to an emergency with all of his tools and equipment at hand. One afternoon, Edgar left the Edgewater Electric offices at 4 p.m. as usual. However, when he left the main highway, he did not turn left toward his home but instead turned right toward the supermarket a few blocks away to pick up some items for dinner. While leaving the supermarket parking lot, Edgar drove negligently and struck Parka, a pedestrian. Parka suffered serious injuries and required several operations and a lengthy hospital stay. Parka filed suit against Edgewater for $100,000.

Is Parka likely to recover from Edgewater?

(A) Yes, because Edgar's trip to the market was only a slight deviation from the direct route to his home.

(B) Yes, but only if Edgewater knew that Edgar had proclivities to drive negligently.

(C) No, because turning in the opposite direction from his home constituted a "frolic" by Edgar.

(D) No, because an employer is not liable for the torts of an employee traveling to and from work.

Question 49

Smythe was charged with the murder of his wife. In his defense, he testified that, at the time he killed her, he believed that his wife was planning to destroy the world by detonating a massive explosive device that she had developed and built in the basement of their home. He further testified that he had tried many times to dissuade his wife from her plan and had tried to destroy devices that she stored in the basement. She had, he testified, foiled his efforts by, on two occasions, signing papers for his hospitalization, which lasted for a brief period each time. He said that he had concluded that the only way to prevent her scheme was to kill her and that he had become so obsessed with the importance of doing so that he could think of nothing else. One day when he saw her open the door to the basement, he lunged at her and pushed her down the steps to her death.

The best defense raised by Smythe's testimony is:

(A) Lack of the requisite mental element.

(B) Lack of the requisite act element.

(C) Insanity.

(D) Belief that the situation justified his actions.

GO ON TO THE NEXT PAGE

Question 50

Scholastica, the Academic Dean at Woodbine College, was well liked and considered a competent scholar and a fine teacher. However, six months after her appointment as Dean, Scholastica received a certified letter from Rector, the Provost of Woodbine College, summarily dismissing her. No reasons were given in the letter for Scholastica's dismissal. Scholastica had her lawyer, Loretta, contact Rector to discover the basis of her dismissal, if possible. Two days later, Loretta received a letter from Rector stating, in relevant part, "Scholastica was dismissed from her employment at Woodbine College because I received an anonymous telephone call informing me that Scholastica was involved in selling drugs to students. One can't be too careful about these things in this day and age." Rector had, in fact, received such a phone call, but the basis of the statement was untrue, because Scholastica had never even used illegal drugs, much less sold them.

If Scholastica files suit against Rector for libel:

(A) Scholastica will win, if Rector should have verified the anonymous statement before repeating it to Loretta.

(B) Scholastica will lose, because by having her attorney ask the reason for the dismissal, Scholastica impliedly consented to the statement in the letter.

(C) Rector will win, because Rector was merely repeating the defamatory communication of another.

(D) Rector will lose, because Scholastica was not dealing in drugs.

Question 51

Rose was convicted in federal court of possession of one kilogram of heroin with intent to distribute. She was sentenced to a prison term. Subsequently, Rose was indicted by a federal grand jury for conspiracy to distribute the same kilogram of heroin. She moved to dismiss the indictment.

Her motion should be:

(A) Denied, because the Double Jeopardy Clause does not apply when the second prosecution is for violation of a separate statute.

(B) Denied, because each prosecution requires proof of an element that the other does not.

(C) Granted, because the Double Jeopardy Clause protects her against a second prosecution for the same criminal conduct.

(D) Granted, because the Due Process Clause protects her against double punishment for the same criminal conduct.

Questions 52-53 are based on the following fact situation:

Three states, East Winnetka, Midland, and West Hampton, are located next to one another in that order. The states of East Winnetka and West Hampton permit the hunting and trapping of snipe, but the state of Midland strictly forbids it in order to protect snipe, a rare species of animal, from extinction. The state of Midland has a state statute that provides, "Possession of snipe traps is prohibited. Any game warden finding a snipe trap within the state shall seize and destroy it." Snipe traps cost about $15 each.

GO ON TO THE NEXT PAGE

Prentis is a resident of West Hampton and an ardent snipe trapper. She drove her car to East Winnetka to purchase a new improved snipe trap from a manufacturer there. In the course of her trip back across Midland with the trap in her car, Prentis stopped in a Midland state park to camp for a few nights. While she was in that park, a Midland game warden saw the trap, which was visible on the front seat of her car. The warden seized the trap and destroyed it in accordance with the Midland statute after Prentis admitted that the seized item was a prohibited snipe trap. No federal statutes or federal administrative regulations apply.

52. For this question only, assume that Prentis demonstrates that common carriers are permitted to transport snipe traps as cargo across Midland for delivery to another state and that, in practice, the Midland statute is enforced only against private individuals transporting those traps in private vehicles. If Prentis challenges the application of the Midland statute to her on the basis only of a denial of equal protection, this application of the statute will probably be found:

(A) Constitutional, because the traps constitute contraband in which Prentis could have no protected property interest.

(B) Constitutional, because there is a rational basis for differentiating between the possession of snipe traps as interstate cargo by common carriers and the possession of snipe traps by private individuals.

(C) Unconstitutional, because the state cannot demonstrate a compelling public purpose for making this differentiation between common carriers and such private individuals.

(D) Unconstitutional, because interstate travel is a fundamental right that may not be burdened by state law.

53. For this question only, assume that a valid federal administrative rule, adopted under a federal consumer product safety act, regulates the design of snipe traps. The rule was issued to prevent traps from causing injury to human beings, *e.g.*, by pinching fingers while persons were setting the traps. No other federal law applies. Which of the following best states the effect of the federal rule on the Midland state statute?

(A) The federal rule preempts the Midland state statute, because the federal rule regulates the same subject matter— snipe traps.

(B) The federal rule preempts the Midland state statute, because the federal rule does not contain affirmative authorization for continued state regulation.

(C) The federal rule does not preempt the Midland state statute, because the Midland state statute regulates wild animals, a field of exclusive state power.

(D) The federal rule does not preempt the Midland state statute, because the purposes of the federal rule and the Midland state statute are different.

Question 54

Dryden is tried on a charge of driving while intoxicated. When Dryden was booked at the police station, a videotape was made that showed him unsteady, abusive, and speaking in a slurred manner. If the prosecutor lays a foundation properly identifying the tape, should the court admit it in evidence and permit it to be shown to the jury?

(A) Yes, because it is an admission.

(B) Yes, because its value is not substantially outweighed by unfair prejudice.

(C) No, because the privilege against self-incrimination is applicable.

(D) No, because specific instances of conduct cannot be proved by extrinsic evidence.

GO ON TO THE NEXT PAGE

Question 55

Simmons and Boyd entered into a written contract for the sale and purchase of Wideacre. The contract provided that "Simmons agrees to convey a good and marketable title to Boyd 60 days from the date of this contract." The purchase price was stated as $60,000.

At the time set for closing, Simmons tendered a deed in the form agreed to in the contract. Boyd's examination of the record prior to the date of closing had disclosed, however, that the owner of record was not Simmons, but Olson. Further investigation by Boyd revealed that, notwithstanding the state of the record, Simmons had been in what Boyd concedes is adverse possession for 15 years. The period of time to acquire title by adverse possession in the jurisdiction is 10 years. Boyd refuses to pay the purchase price or to take possession "because of the inability of Simmons to transfer a marketable title."

In an appropriate action by Simmons against Boyd for specific performance, Simmons will:

(A) Prevail, because he has obtained a "good and marketable title" by adverse possession.

(B) Prevail, because Simmons's action for specific performance is an action in rem even though Olson is not a party.

(C) Not prevail, because Boyd cannot be required to buy a lawsuit even if the probability is great that Boyd would prevail against Olson.

(D) Not prevail, because Simmons's failure to disclose his lack of record title constitutes fraud.

Question 56

Jane, an architectural historian, bought a house in 1979 from William. She paid him $50,000 in cash, and the balance of the $150,000 sale price came from the proceeds of a mortgage she took out with State National Bank. The mortgage was recorded.

In 1987, Jane borrowed $5,000 from the Home Finance Company, using her house as security. Home Finance recorded its mortgage on the property.

In 1996, Jane had an architect friend design an addition to her house. She borrowed $40,000 from Property Equity Lenders, Inc. to pay for this construction. Property Equity did not record the mortgage Jane gave it to secure this debt.

In 2003, Jane lost her job and was unable to make payments on some of her obligations. She made the payments on the State National mortgage, but was unable to make any payments on either the Home Finance or Property Equity Lenders mortgages. Home Finance filed foreclosure of its mortgage.

At the foreclosure sale, Susan bought the property. After acquiring the property at the sale, what is Susan's obligation toward the holders of the other two mortgages, State National Bank and Property Equity Lenders, Inc.?

(A) She takes the property subject to both mortgages.

(B) She takes the property subject to neither mortgage.

(C) She takes the property subject to Property Equity Lenders's mortgage, but not subject to State National Bank's mortgage.

(D) She takes the property subject to State National Bank's mortgage, but not subject to Property Equity Lenders's mortgage.

GO ON TO THE NEXT PAGE

Questions 57-58 are based on the following fact situation:

Alpha and Beta made a written contract pursuant to which Alpha promised to convey a specified apartment house to Beta in return for Beta's promise (1) to convey a 100-acre farm to Alpha and (2) to pay Alpha $1,000 in cash six months after the exchange of the apartment house and the farm. The contract contained the following provision: "It is understood and agreed that Beta's obligation to pay the $1,000 six months after the exchange of the apartment house and the farm shall be voided if Alpha has not, within three months after the aforesaid exchange, removed the existing shed in the parking area in the rear of the said apartment house."

57. Which of the following statements concerning the order of performances is *least* accurate?

   (A) Alpha's tendering of good title to the apartment house is a condition precedent to Beta's duty to convey good title to the farm.

   (B) Beta's tendering of good title to the farm is a condition precedent to Alpha's duty to convey good title to the apartment house.

   (C) Beta's tendering of good title to the farm is a condition subsequent to Alpha's duty to convey good title to the apartment house.

   (D) Alpha's tendering of good title to the apartment house and Beta's tendering of good title to the farm are concurrent conditions.

58. Alpha's removal of the shed from the parking area of the apartment house is:

   (A) A condition subsequent in form but precedent in substance to Beta's duty to pay the $1,000.

   (B) A condition precedent in form but subsequent in substance to Beta's duty to pay the $1,000.

   (C) A condition subsequent to Beta's duty to pay the $1,000.

   (D) Not a condition, either precedent or subsequent, to Beta's duty to pay the $1,000.

GO ON TO THE NEXT PAGE

Question 59

Cantebury Trails operated a fleet of touring buses. It owned its own garage for repairing and maintaining its fleet. Behind this garage was a large vacant lot in which Cantebury Trails stored old, discarded, and wrecked buses, which it salvaged for parts or sold for scrap. This area was fenced in by a five-foot-high chain link fence, but Cantebury was aware that children from the neighborhood would climb the fence and play among the junked buses. Consequently, Cantebury Trails would have one of its employees walk through the storage area sometime during the day to chase away any children who may have scaled the fence.

One Saturday afternoon, when Cantebury Trails' garage had closed for the weekend, a group of children climbed over the storage area's fence to play army among the junked buses. One of the children, Donny (who had been chased away from the lot before and who also had been warned by his parents not to play in these buses), was trying to climb on the roof of one of the old buses, when he slipped on the front bumper of the bus and his arm broke through the front windshield. As a result of this accident, Donny severed the tendon and nerves in his right arm, leaving it permanently disabled.

Through an appropriate guardian, Donny brought suit against Cantebury Trails for his injury.

Which of the following, if established, would most aid Donny in showing that Cantebury Trails breached a duty owing to him?

(A) It would have been economically feasible to remove the windows from all the abandoned buses.

(B) This area would be classified more as a residential neighborhood than an industrial area.

(C) Cantebury Trails could have eliminated the risk of injury without unduly interfering with its normal operations.

(D) Cantebury Trails improperly maintained the fence that surrounded the lot with the discarded and abandoned buses.

Question 60

Cars driven by Pugh and Davidson collided, and Davidson was charged with driving while intoxicated in connection with the accident. She pleaded guilty and was merely fined, although, under the statute, the court could have sentenced her to two years in prison.

Thereafter, Pugh, alleging that Davidson's intoxication had caused the collision, sued Davidson for damages. At trial, Pugh offers the properly authenticated record of Davidson's conviction.

The record should be:

(A) Admitted as proof of Davidson's character.

(B) Admitted as proof of Davidson's intoxication.

(C) Excluded, because the conviction was not the result of a trial.

(D) Excluded, because it is hearsay not within any exception.

GO ON TO THE NEXT PAGE

Question 61

In which of the following situations is Defendant *least likely* to be guilty of burglary in a jurisdiction that has extended burglary to buildings other than dwellings but otherwise retains the common law requirements?

(A) Defendant posed as a member of a cleaning crew so that a security guard would give him access to a department store after it was closed for the night, and then hid in a storage closet until the cleaning crew left. He then stole a quantity of jewelry from several jewelry cases, and forced open a loading dock door to escape from the building.

(B) Defendant, intending to steal money and valuables from a house he believed was unoccupied for the evening, pushed open a mail slot and reached his hand in to try to unlock the front door. The owners' dog bit Defendant's hand and he immediately pulled it out and fled.

(C) Defendant was owed $500 by Victor, his bookie. While Victor was out of town one night, Defendant went to Victor's house to get his money, because he knew that Victor had $500 in cash in a desk drawer and the debt was long overdue. Defendant opened an unlocked window and entered the house. He could not find the cash, so he decided to take a painting that he knew was worth substantially more than $500. He later sold it for $1,000 and kept the proceeds.

(D) Defendant, a security officer in a housing project, saw Von, who was wanted on a warrant for drug dealing, through a window of an apartment one evening. He fired his gun at Von from the sidewalk, intending to injure him, although Defendant knew that he was not legally authorized to use deadly force in that situation. The bullet went through the window and missed Von, lodging in a wall behind him.

Question 62

In a contract action between Ted and Violet, brought in federal court on the basis of diversity jurisdiction, the major issue is the value of Greenacre. Ted's attorney calls Realtor to the stand and qualifies her as an expert on property valuation. Since Realtor had not personally inspected the property, Ted's attorney was prepared to ask Realtor a hypothetical question based on evidence adduced at the trial. However, the trial had already dragged on longer than expected, and to save time, Ted's attorney merely asks Realtor, "In your expert opinion, how much is Greenacre worth?" Violet's attorney objects.

The objection should be:

(A) Sustained, because an expert may not render an opinion on an ultimate issue.

(B) Sustained, because an expert must disclose the basis for her opinion.

(C) Overruled, because qualification as an expert creates a presumption of a proper basis for the opinion.

(D) Overruled, because Violet is entitled to immediate cross-examination of Realtor.

GO ON TO THE NEXT PAGE

Question 63

Talbot and Rogers, as lessees, signed a valid lease for a house. Lane, the landlord, duly executed the lease and delivered possession of the premises to the lessees.

During the term of the lease, Rogers verbally invited Andrews to share the house with the lessees. Andrews agreed to pay part of the rent to Lane, who did not object to this arrangement, despite a provision in the lease that provided that "any assignment, subletting or transfer of any rights under this lease without the express written consent of the landlord is strictly prohibited, null and void." Talbot objected to Andrews's moving in, even if Andrews were to pay a part of the rent.

When Andrews moved in, Talbot brought an appropriate action against Lane, Rogers, and Andrews for a declaratory judgment that Rogers had no right to assign. Rogers's defense was that he and Talbot were tenants in common of a term for years, and that he, Rogers, had a right to assign a fractional interest in his undivided one-half interest.

In this action, Talbot will:

(A) Prevail, because a co-tenant has no right to assign all or any part of a leasehold without the consent of all interested parties.

(B) Prevail, because the lease provision prohibits assignment.

(C) Not prevail, because he is not the beneficiary of the nonassignment provision in the lease.

(D) Not prevail, because his claim amounts to a void restraint on alienation.

Question 64

John Smith has denied his purported signature on a letter that has become critical in a breach of contract suit between Smith and Miller. At trial, Miller's counsel calls Alice, a teacher, who testifies that she taught John Smith mathematics in school 10 years earlier, knows his signature, and proposes to testify that the signature to the letter is that of John Smith. Smith's counsel objects.

The trial judge should:

(A) Sustain the objection on the ground that identification of handwriting requires expert testimony and the teacher does not, per se, qualify as an expert.

(B) Sustain the objection on the ground that the best evidence of Smith's handwriting would be testimony by a person who had examined his writing more recently than 10 years ago.

(C) Overrule the objection on the ground that a schoolteacher qualifies as an expert witness for the purpose of identifying handwriting.

(D) Overrule the objection on the ground that a layman may identify handwriting if he has seen the person in question write, and has an opinion concerning the writing in question.

GO ON TO THE NEXT PAGE

Question 65

Harold and Wanda, once married to each other, had gone through a bitter divorce. The divorce decree awarded custody of the couple's four-year-old son Jake to Wanda, with Harold receiving visitation rights. On the first opportunity that Harold had to take Jake for the weekend, Harold disappeared with Jake. Wanda was greatly distressed and called Harold's parents, Grandmaw and Grandpaw, on a weekly basis, always asking if they knew anything about the whereabouts of Harold and Jake. Grandmaw and Grandpaw knew quite well where Harold and Jake were, and they often sent money to help support Harold while he was on the run. However, they always insisted that they knew nothing about the child. Four years after Jake was abducted, the police arrested Harold and returned Jake to his mother.

Wanda files an action against Grandmaw and Grandpaw alleging infliction of emotional distress. Will Wanda prevail?

(A) Yes, because Grandmaw and Grandpaw acted in deliberate disregard of a high probability that their actions would cause Wanda to suffer emotional distress.

(B) Yes, but only if Grandmaw and Grandpaw actually knew that their actions would cause Wanda to suffer emotional distress.

(C) No, unless Wanda can prove that she suffered physical harm.

(D) No, because Wanda never was in a zone of danger.

Question 66

Fritz was appointed as an administrative judge to review claims against the federal government made by Indians under the congressional statute, the Indian Claims Arbitration Act of 1957. For 20 years Fritz heard, reviewed, and arbitrated disputed claims made against the government by various Indian tribes and their citizens. When Fritz found a claim to be valid, he would make a recommendation to the Bureau of Indian Claims that the claim be paid. If Fritz found the claims to be without merit, or if the Bureau decided against his recommendation, the claimant would have the right to bring suit in a federal court. Last year, a presidential commission recommended the abolition of the Bureau of Indian Claims as a cost-cutting measure. The commission reasoned that whatever increase there may be in litigation in the federal court would be balanced by the decrease in claims because individual Indians would not have the money to retain a lawyer to pursue the claims. Congress acted on this recommendation and repealed the Act. Fritz was offered a position as an attorney in the Department of Transportation, but he turned it down and brought suit against the government.

What is the likely result of this suit?

(A) Fritz prevails, because it violates the doctrine of separation of powers for the executive branch to interfere with a congressional act by recommending its repeal.

(B) Fritz prevails, because it violates the Constitution to terminate the tenure of a federal judge during good behavior.

(C) The government prevails, because it established Fritz's position and it can terminate it at will.

(D) The government prevails, because Fritz had no judicial discretion or powers in his position with the Bureau.

GO ON TO THE NEXT PAGE

Question 67

Barbara Bates, a resident of the city of Middletown, belonged to a rather extreme political group that advocated the overthrow of the United States government. Among Bates's grievances against current government was a belief that young people were being brainwashed by public school curricula. To end this practice, Bates decided to run for the local school board in the next general election so that she will have a voice in future curricula decisions. Middletown's election laws required all candidates for the school board to sign a loyalty oath and file it with the town clerk in order to have their names placed on the ballot for the next school board election. When Bates arrived at the clerk's office to file her candidacy, she was informed of the loyalty oath requirement and was shown the oath. Bates read the oath and objected to the requirement that she sign it.

Which of the following statements is correct as to whether Middletown may constitutionally require Bates to sign the oath in order to have her name placed on the ballot?

(A) The loyalty oath requirement is valid if the candidate must merely affirm that she does not advocate the violent overthrow of the state or federal governments.

(B) The loyalty oath requirement is valid if the candidate must merely affirm that she will oppose the violent overthrow of the state or federal governments.

(C) The loyalty requirement is valid if the candidate must merely affirm that she has never been a member of any organization dedicated to the violent overthrow of the state or federal governments.

(D) No oath is constitutionally permissible as a condition for ballot qualification.

Question 68

The state of Florissippi prohibits publication of the identity of victims of sexual crimes, but allows trials of such cases to be televised, as long as the victim's face is blocked out. Recently, Billy K. Callahan, the nephew of a United States Senator, was accused of raping a woman at his family's estate in Florissippi. Because of the notoriety of the Callahan family, the press was eager to enlighten the public as to all aspects of the Callahan case. Edward R. Burro, a reporter for a metropolitan newspaper published in Florissippi, discovered the name of Billy's victim from a police report that inadvertently included the victim's name and published the victim's identity in the next edition of the paper. Burro and the paper were fined $2,500 for violating the statute.

If Burro and the paper challenge the fine, the court should rule:

(A) For the state, because it has a compelling interest in protecting the privacy of its citizens.

(B) For the state, because inclusion of the victim's identity in the police report was inadvertent.

(C) For Burro and the paper, because the state does not have a compelling interest in prohibiting the dissemination of the lawfully obtained information here.

(D) For Burro and the paper, because the First Amendment allows the press to print any information that it legally obtains.

GO ON TO THE NEXT PAGE

Questions 69-70 are based on the following fact situation:

Eureka, Inc., inventor of the LBVC, a laser-beam vegetable chopper, ran a television ad that described the chopper and said, "The LBVC is yours for only $49.99 if you send your check or money order to Box 007, Greenville. Not available in stores." Gourmet, who owned a retail specialty shop, wrote Eureka, "What's your best, firm price for two dozen LBVCs?" Eureka sent a written reply that said in its entirety, "We quote you for prompt acceptance $39.99 per unit for 24 LBVCs." Gourmet subsequently mailed a check to Eureka in the appropriate amount, with a memo enclosed saying, "I accept your offer for 24 LBVCs."

69.   A contract would arise from these communications only if:

   (A)   Both parties were merchants.

   (B)   Eureka had at least 24 LBVCs in stock when Gourmet's check and memo were received.

   (C)   Gourmet's check and memo were mailed within three months after his receipt of Eureka's letter.

   (D)   Gourmet's check and memo were mailed within a reasonable time after his receipt of Eureka's letter.

70.   For this question only, assume the following facts: Eureka shipped 24 LBVCs to Gourmet after receiving his check and memo, and with the shipment sent Gourmet an invoice that conspicuously stated, among other things, the following lawful provision: "These items shall not be offered for resale at retail." Gourmet received and read, but disregarded, the invoice restriction and displayed the 24 LBVCs for resale. Eureka has a cause of action against Gourmet for breach of contract only if:

   (A)   Eureka, as inventor of the LBVC, was *not* a merchant.

   (B)   The invoice restriction was a material alteration of preexisting terms.

   (C)   Eureka's written reply that quoted $39.99 per LBVC, but did not contain a restriction on retail sales, was *not* an offer that Gourmet accepted by ordering 24 LBVCs.

   (D)   Gourmet was consciously aware when taking delivery of the goods that the television ad had said, "Not available in stores."

GO ON TO THE NEXT PAGE

Question 71

The state of Meddle's legislature enacted a law totally revising the tax structure. While the legislation purported to abolish the unpopular "inheritance" tax, which was modeled on the federal gift and inheritance tax laws, it in fact amounted to a massive tax increase, because all inherited money now qualified as "income" and became subject to the state's high income tax. Because of the negative political consequences of voting for a tax increase, the legislators who drew up the bill made it exceedingly complicated and difficult for laypersons, or even trained professionals, to comprehend. Since tax forms were not to be mailed out until after the November elections, enough votes were found to pass the new tax law. One provision of the law stated: "Any person who knowingly fails to declare any monies received during a tax year in excess of $500 that should have been declared under the Meddle Revenue Code shall be guilty of a Class 4 felony and be subject to incarceration in the state penitentiary for a period not to exceed 367 days and/or be subject to appropriate fines as listed in Schedule S of section 32.666 of the Meddle Statutes Annotated."

During the course of the first tax year in which the new tax law was in effect, Donna inherited $3,500 from her Uncle Enos. When Donna received her tax forms, she was rather confused because of all the complicated computation schedules and fine print. The State Department of Revenue had planned to include a supplemental booklet explaining the new law along with the tax forms. However, a computer glitch caused the booklet not to be included in the mailings to the "panhandle" area of the state, where Donna lived. Donna called Lem, her attorney, and asked him if the inherited money needed to be included on her income tax return. Lem assured her that the income tax applied only to earned income, interest, and dividends. Donna also called the regional branch of the State Department of Revenue. The telephone operator transferred her call to Michael, who was a law student at South Meddle University and a part-time intern in the revenue department. His work in the revenue department dealt mostly with state sales and use taxes, but he had recently completed law school courses on federal income and gift and estate taxes. Michael told Donna that inherited funds were not "income" for purposes of the income tax. Donna filed her state income tax return, but did not declare the $3,500 inherited from Enos.

If Donna is subsequently charged with a Class 4 felony pursuant to the statute quoted above, which of the following represents Donna's best defense?

(A) Donna's mistake regarding the law's coverage negates the state of mind required by the statute.

(B) Donna never received a booklet explaining the law from the Department of Revenue.

(C) Donna relied on Michael's advice.

(D) Donna relied on Lem's advice.

GO ON TO THE NEXT PAGE

Question 72

Sassoon, whose deer hunting forays had been unsuccessful for the past four years running, resolved that this season he would get a deer. Sassoon constructed a hunting outfit which made him appear, from the waist up, to be a sixteen-point buck. Below the waist he wore camouflage pants and hiking boots. Opening day, he stationed himself in the midst of a thicket in what was reputedly the most heavily populated deer area in the state, doused himself with the odor of a doe in estrus, and awaited his prey.

Meanwhile, O'Shaunessy was also happily embarking upon opening day activities. After consuming several Bloody Marys and cans of beer while he waited for the deer to come to him in the field, he was barely able to distinguish flora from fauna. O'Shaunessy caught sight of Sassoon as the former staggered along a game trail. O'Shaunessy took one look at the rack (antlers) on the papier mache deerhead, and let loose with his rifle. One of the bullets grazed Sassoon's head, knocking him unconscious.

The jurisdiction in which Sassoon and O'Shaunessy hunt and live retains traditional contributory negligence. In an action by Sassoon for personal injuries against O'Shaunessy, what is the probable outcome of the litigation?

(A) O'Shaunessy will win, because he did not have the requisite intent to justify imposing liability.

(B) O'Shaunessy will win, if he can prove that he did not have the last clear chance to avoid injuring Sassoon.

(C) Sassoon will win, if he can establish that O'Shaunessy's act of hunting while intoxicated was willful and wanton.

(D) Sassoon will win, because he can show that O'Shaunessy was negligent in hunting while intoxicated.

Question 73

A state statute provides that persons moving into a community to attend a college on a full-time basis may not vote in any elections for local or state officials that are held in that community. Instead, the statute provides that for voting purposes all such persons shall retain their residence in the community from which they came. In that state the age of majority is 18.

Which of the following is the strongest argument to demonstrate the unconstitutionality of this state statute?

(A) A state does not have an interest that is sufficiently compelling to justify the exclusion from voting of an entire class of persons.

(B) There are less restrictive means by which the state could assure that only actual residents of a community vote in its elections.

(C) Most persons moving to a community to attend college full-time are likely to have attained the age of majority under the laws of this state.

(D) On its face this statute impermissibly discriminates against interstate commerce.

Questions 74-75 are based on the following fact situation:

Seller and Buyer executed an agreement for the sale of real property.

74. Assume for this question only that Seller dies before closing and his will leaves his personal property to Perry and his real property to Rose. There being no breach of the agreement by either party, which of the following is correct?

GO ON TO THE NEXT PAGE

(A) Death, an eventuality for which the parties could have provided, terminates the agreement if they did not so provide.

(B) Rose is entitled to the proceeds of the sale when it closes, because the doctrine of equitable conversion does not apply to these circumstances.

(C) Perry is entitled to the proceeds of the sale when it closes.

(D) Title was rendered unmarketable by Seller's death.

75. Assume for this question only that Buyer dies before closing, there being no breach of the agreement by either party. Which of the following is appropriate in most jurisdictions?

(A) Buyer's heir may specifically enforce the agreement.

(B) Seller has the right to return the down payment and cancel the contract.

(C) Death terminates the agreement.

(D) Any title acquired would be unmarketable by reason of Buyer's death.

Question 76

At trial of Pendergast's battery action against Dellacourt, arising from an incident in which Dellacourt allegedly bit off Pendergast's ear, Winchester testified that he was taking a short-cut through an urban alley one morning and heard someone cry "Help!" Rushing around the corner of a building, Winchester saw Pendergast lying on the sidewalk in a pool of blood, with his left ear missing. Dellacourt, who was standing nearby, turned quickly and made a move as if to approach Winchester, and so Winchester ran down the sidewalk away from Dellacourt to summon the police.

The following exchange then occurred during cross-examination of Winchester by Dellacourt's counsel. D: "You didn't actually see my client bite off the plaintiff's ear, did you, Mr. Winchester?" W: "No." D: "For all you know, my client could have been an innocent bystander like yourself, but one who didn't run away but stayed to offer assistance." W: "I ran away because I was afraid of the defendant and because I wanted to call the police." D: "For all we know you might have been running out of that alley because you had just committed a crime yourself, Mr. Winchester." W: "Look, Dellacourt is the one who bit off the ear, not me!" D: "If you arrived on the scene after the alleged ear biting, how can you possibly know my client is the one who bit off the plaintiff's ear?" W: "Because I read in the newspaper the next day that an eyewitness to the entire event told police that he saw Dellacourt spit the ear out after I left." Dellacourt then moved to have Winchester's last remark stricken from the record.

If the trial court denies Dellacourt's motion, that ruling is most strongly supported by which of the following?

(A) The report of the eyewitness was an excited utterance.

(B) The report of the eyewitness was a statement of recent perception.

(C) The error in admitting the statement could not be cured by an appropriate jury instruction.

(D) The remark was invited by the cross-examiner's questions.

Questions 77-78 are based on the following fact situation:

Cycle Company manufactured a bicycle that it sold to Bike Shop, a retail bicycle dealer, which in turn sold it to Roth. Shortly thereafter, while Roth was riding the bicycle along a city street, he saw a traffic light facing him turn from green to amber. He sped up, hoping to cross the intersection before the light turned red. However, Roth quickly realized that he could not do so and applied the brake, which failed. To avoid the traffic that was then crossing in front of him, Roth turned sharply to his right and onto the sidewalk, where he struck Perez, a pedestrian. Both Perez and Roth sustained injuries. Assume that the jurisdiction follows traditional contributory negligence rules.

77. If Roth asserts a claim against Bike Shop based on strict liability in tort, will Roth prevail?

 (A) Yes, if the brake failed because of a defect present when the bicycle left the factory of Cycle Company.

 (B) Yes, because the brake failed while Roth was riding the bicycle.

 (C) No, if Roth contributed to his own injury by speeding up.

 (D) No, if Bike Shop carefully inspected the bicycle before selling it.

78. If Perez asserts a claim based on negligence against Cycle Company, and if it is found that the brake failure resulted from a manufacturing defect in the bicycle, will Perez prevail?

 (A) Yes, because Cycle Company placed a defective bicycle into the stream of commerce.

 (B) Yes, if the defect could have been discovered through the exercise of reasonable care by Cycle Company.

 (C) No, because Perez was not a purchaser of the bicycle.

 (D) No, if Roth was negligent in turning onto the sidewalk.

Question 79

While hiking through an area that had been recently devastated by a fire, Hiker discovered a sign that stated: "Now entering State Wilderness Area." Thinking that the sign would make a nice decoration, Hiker took the sign home with him. He was arrested and charged with violating the state statute that provides, "Any person who appropriates to his own use property owned by the state shall be guilty of a crime and shall be punished by a fine of not more than $5,000 or by imprisonment for not more than two years or by both such fine and imprisonment." At trial, Hiker admitted taking the sign, but claims that he believed the sign had been abandoned since the area had recently been devastated by a fire. In fact the sign had not been abandoned.

Hiker will most likely be found:

(A) Guilty, because this is a strict liability offense.

(B) Guilty, because intent is not placed in issue by this statute.

(C) Not guilty, unless the jury finds that the state had taken adequate steps to inform the public that the sign had not been abandoned.

(D) Not guilty, if the jury finds Hiker honestly believed the sign had been abandoned.

GO ON TO THE NEXT PAGE

Question 80

While crossing Spruce Street, Pesko was hit by a car that she did not see. Pesko sued Dorry for her injuries.

At trial, Pesko calls Williams, a police officer, to testify that, 10 minutes after the accident, a driver stopped him and said, "Officer, a few minutes ago I saw a hit-and-run accident on Spruce Street involving a blue convertible, which I followed to the drive-in restaurant at Oak and Third," and that a few seconds later Williams saw Dorry sitting alone in a blue convertible in the drive-in restaurant's parking lot.

Williams's testimony about the driver's statement should be:

(A) Admitted as a statement of recent perception.

(B) Admitted as a present sense impression.

(C) Excluded, because it is hearsay not within any exception.

(D) Excluded, because it is more prejudicial than probative.

Questions 81-83 are based on the following fact situation:

A written contract was entered into between Bouquet, a financier-investor, and Vintage Corporation, a winery and grape-grower. The contract provided that Bouquet would invest $1 million in Vintage for its capital expansion and, in return, that Vintage, from grapes grown in its famous vineyards, would produce and market at least 500,000 bottles of wine each year for five years under the label "Premium Vintage-Bouquet."

The contract included provisions that the parties would share equally the profits and losses from the venture and that, if feasible, the wine would be distributed by Vintage only through Claret, a wholesale distributor of fine wines. Neither Bouquet nor Vintage had previously dealt with Claret. Claret learned of the contract two days later from reading a trade newspaper. In reliance thereon, he immediately hired an additional sales executive and contracted for enlargement of his wine storage and display facility.

81. If Vintage refuses to distribute the wine through Claret and Claret then sues Vintage for breach of contract, is it likely that Claret will prevail?

(A) Yes, because Vintage's performance was to run to Claret rather than to Bouquet.

(B) Yes, because Bouquet and Vintage could reasonably foresee that Claret would change his position in reliance on the contract.

(C) No, because Bouquet and Vintage did not expressly agree that Claret would have enforceable rights under their contract.

(D) No, because Bouquet and Vintage, having no apparent motive to benefit Claret, appeared in making the contract to have been protecting or serving only their own interests.

GO ON TO THE NEXT PAGE

82. For this question only, assume the following facts. Amicusbank lent Bouquet $200,000 and Bouquet executed a written instrument providing that Amicusbank "is entitled to collect the debt from my share of the profits, if any, under the Vintage-Bouquet contract." Amicusbank gave prompt notice of this transaction to Vintage.

If Vintage thereafter refuses to account for any profits to Amicusbank and Amicusbank sues Vintage for Bouquet's share of profits then realized, Vintage's strongest argument in defense is that:

(A) The Bouquet-Vintage contract did not expressly authorize an assignment of rights.

(B) Bouquet and Vintage are partners, not simply debtor and creditor.

(C) Amicusbank is not an assignee of Bouquet's rights under the Bouquet-Vintage contract.

(D) Amicusbank is not an intended third-party beneficiary of the Bouquet-Vintage contract.

83. For this question only, assume the following facts. Soon after making its contract with Bouquet, Vintage, without Bouquet's knowledge or assent, sold its vineyards but not its winery to Agribiz, a large agricultural corporation. Under the terms of this sale, Agribiz agreed to sell to Vintage all grapes grown on the land for five years. Agribiz's employees have no experience in wine-grape production, and Agribiz has no reputation in the wine industry as a grape producer or otherwise. The Bouquet-Vintage contract was silent on the matter of Vintage's selling any or all of its business assets.

If Bouquet seeks an appropriate judicial remedy against Vintage for entering into the Vintage-Agribiz transaction, is Bouquet likely to prevail?

(A) Yes, because the Vintage-Agribiz transaction created a significant risk of diminishing the profits in which Bouquet would share under his contract with Vintage.

(B) Yes, because the Bouquet-Vintage contract did not contain a provision authorizing a delegation of Vintage's duties.

(C) No, because Vintage remains in a position to perform under the Bouquet-Vintage contract.

(D) No, because Vintage, as a corporation, must necessarily perform its contracts by delegating duties to individuals.

Question 84

Miller applied to the state liquor board for transfer of the license of Miller's Bar and Grill to a new site. The board held a hearing on the application.

At that hearing, Hammond appeared without being subpoenaed and stated that Miller had underworld connections. Although Hammond did not know this information to be true, he had heard rumors about Miller's character and had noticed several underworld figures going in and out of Miller's Bar and Grill. In fact, Miller had no underworld connections.

In a claim against Hammond based on defamation, Miller will:

(A) Not recover if Hammond reasonably believed his statement to be true.

(B) Not recover if the board granted Miller's application.

(C) Recover, because Hammond's statement was false.

(D) Recover, because Hammond appeared before the board voluntarily.

Question 85

Arthur and Celia, brother and sister, both of legal age, inherited Goodacre, their childhood home, from their father. They thereby became tenants in common.

Goodacre had never been used as anything except a residence. Arthur had been residing on Goodacre with his father at the time his father died. Celia had been residing in a distant city. After their father's funeral, Arthur continued to live on Goodacre, but Celia returned to her own residence.

There was no discussion between Arthur and Celia concerning their common ownership, nor had there ever been any administration of their father's estate. Arthur paid all taxes, insurance, and other carrying charges on Goodacre. He paid no rent or other compensation to Celia, nor did Celia request any such payment.

Thirty years later, a series of disputes arose between Arthur and Celia for the first time concerning their respective rights to Goodacre. The jurisdiction where the land is located recognizes the usual common law types of co-tenancies, and there is no applicable legislation on the subject.

If Arthur claims the entire title to Goodacre in fee simple and brings an action against Celia to quiet title in himself, and if the state where the land is located has an ordinary 20-year adverse possession statute, the decision should be for:

(A) Arthur, because during the past 30 years Arthur has exercised the type of occupancy ordinarily considered sufficient to satisfy the adverse possession requirements.

(B) Arthur, because the acts of the parties indicate Celia's intention to renounce her right to inheritance.

(C) Celia, because there is no evidence that Arthur has performed sufficient acts to constitute her ouster.

(D) Celia, because one co-tenant cannot acquire title by adverse possession against another.

Question 86

David is being tried in federal court for criminal conspiracy with John to violate federal narcotics law. At trial, the prosecutor calls David's new wife, Wanda, and asks her to testify about a meeting between David and John that she observed before she married David.

Which of the following is the most accurate statement of the applicable rule concerning whether Wanda may testify?

(A) The choice is Wanda's.

(B) The choice is David's.

(C) Wanda is permitted to testify only if both Wanda and David agree.

(D) Wanda is compelled to testify even if both Wanda and David object.

Question 87

Dillon held up a gasoline station. During the robbery he shot and killed a customer who attempted to apprehend him. Dillon was prosecuted for premeditated murder and convicted. Thereafter, he was indicted for armed robbery of the station. Before the trial, his attorney moved to dismiss the indictment on the ground that further proceedings were unconstitutional because of Dillon's prior conviction.

The motion to dismiss should be:

(A) Granted, because once Dillon was convicted on any of the charges arising out of the robbery, the prosecution was constitutionally estopped from proceeding against Dillon on any charge stemming from the same transaction.

(B) Granted, because the Double Jeopardy Clause prohibits a subsequent trial on what is essentially a lesser included offense.

(C) Denied, because there is no constitutional requirement that all known charges against Dillon be brought in the same prosecution.

(D) Denied, because estoppel does not apply when the defendant is charged with violating two different statutes.

Question 88

An appropriations act passed by Congress over the President's veto directs that $1 billion "shall be spent" by the federal government for the development of a new military weapons system, which is available only from the Arms Corporation. On the order of the President, the Secretary of Defense refuses to authorize a contract for purchase of the weapons system. The Arms Corporation sues the Secretary of Defense, alleging an unlawful withholding of these federal funds.

The strongest constitutional argument for the Arms Corporation is that:

(A) Passage of an appropriation over a veto makes the spending mandatory.

(B) Congress's power to appropriate funds includes the power to require that the funds will be spent as directed.

(C) The President's independent constitutional powers do not specifically refer to spending.

(D) The President's power to withhold such funds is limited to cases where foreign affairs are directly involved.

Question 89

Potts, a building contractor, sued Dennis for failure to pay on a small cost-plus construction contract. At trial, Potts, who personally supervised all of the work, seeks to testify to what he remembers about the amount of pipe used, the number of workers used on the job, and the number of hours spent grading.

Dennis objects on the ground that Potts had routinely recorded these facts in notebooks which are in Potts's possession.

Potts's testimony is:

(A) Admissible as a report of regularly conducted business activity.

(B) Admissible as based on firsthand knowledge.

(C) Inadmissible, because it violates the best evidence rule.

(D) Inadmissible, because a summary of writings cannot be made unless the originals are available for examination.

GO ON TO THE NEXT PAGE

Question 90

A grand jury was investigating a bank robbery. The only information known to the prosecutor was a rumor that Taylor might have been involved. The grand jury subpoenaed Taylor. He refused to answer questions about the robbery and was granted use immunity. He then testified that he and Simmons had robbed the bank. The grand jury indicted both Taylor and Simmons for the bank robbery. The prosecutor permitted Simmons to enter a plea to a lesser offense in exchange for Simmons's agreement to testify against Taylor. The prosecutor had no evidence as to the identity of the robbers except the testimony of Simmons and Taylor.

At Taylor's trial, his objection to Simmons's being permitted to testify should be:

(A) Sustained, because the prosecutor may not bargain away the rights of one co-defendant in a deal with another.

(B) Sustained, because Simmons's testimony was acquired as a result of Taylor's grand jury testimony.

(C) Overruled, because the police suspected Taylor even before he testified in the grand jury hearing.

(D) Overruled, because a witness cannot be precluded from testifying if his testimony is given voluntarily.

Questions 91-93 are based on the following fact situation:

Dino purchased a new Belchfire automobile from Dealer. Within a few days of the purchase, Dino returned the car to Dealer for repairs. Dino complained, "There's something wrong with the brakes. The car keeps pulling to the left whenever I apply them." Dealer's mechanic readjusted the brakes but did not detect any other problem with the brake system. Dealer's mechanic told Dino, "You shouldn't have any more problems with those brakes. However, if the same problem does occur, don't panic. The car may pull to the left, but the brakes will still work, allowing you to stop the car."

Dino drove the car home. It worked fine for two days, but then the brakes started pulling to the left again. As Dino was driving the car back to Dealer's shop for further repair, he saw Pedestrian crossing the street. Dino pressed his foot down on the brake pedal, but the master cylinder failed, and the car would not stop. Dino's car struck Pedestrian, injuring him.

91. If Pedestrian sues Dino for his injuries:

(A) Pedestrian will prevail, because Dino knew that there was a problem with his brakes.

(B) Pedestrian will prevail, because drivers have a duty to maintain their vehicles in safe working order.

(C) Dino will prevail, because he had no reason to know that his brakes would not stop the car.

(D) Dino will prevail, because he diligently had his brakes repaired.

92. If Pedestrian sues Belchfire Motors, the manufacturer of Dino's car, on a theory of strict liability for his injuries:

(A) Pedestrian will prevail, because manufacturers are strictly liable for accidents that result from defects in their products.

(B) Pedestrian will prevail, if the master cylinder was defective when the vehicle left Belchfire's control.

(C) Belchfire will prevail, because Dealer's mechanic readjusted the brakes.

(D) Belchfire will prevail, unless the car model had a history of brake defects.

93. If Pedestrian brings a negligence action against Dealer for his injuries:

(A) Pedestrian will prevail, if the car was sold by Dealer with an unreasonably dangerous defect.

(B) Pedestrian will prevail, because Dealer's mechanic did not discover the defective cylinder.

(C) Dealer will prevail, unless the defect should have been discovered when the mechanic inspected the car.

(D) Dealer will prevail, unless Belchfire was negligent in designing or manu-facturing the master cylinder.

Question 94

Fernwood Realty Company developed a residential development, known as the Fernwood Development, which included single-family dwellings, town houses, and high-rise apartments for a total of 25,000 dwelling units. Included in the deed to each unit was a covenant under which the grantee and the grantee's "heirs and assigns" agreed to purchase electrical power only from a plant Fernwood promised to build and maintain within the development. Fernwood constructed the plant and the necessary power lines. The plant did not supply power outside the development. An appropriate and fair formula was used to determine price.

After constructing and selling 12,500 of the units, Fernwood sold its interest in the develop-ment to Gaint Realty Investors. Gaint operated the power plant and constructed and sold the remaining 12,500 units. Each conveyance from Gaint contained the same covenant relating to electrical power that Fernwood had included in the 12,500 conveyances it had made.

Page bought a dwelling unit from Olm, who had purchased it from Fernwood. Subsequently, Page, whose lot was along the boundary of the Fernwood development, ceased buying electrical power from Gaint and began purchasing power from General Power Company, which provided such service in the area surrounding the Fernwood development. Both General Power and Gaint have governmental authorization to provide electrical services to the area. Gaint instituted an appropriate action against Page to enjoin her from obtaining electrical power from General Power.

If judgment is for Page, it most likely will be because:

(A) The covenant does not touch and concern the land.

(B) The mixture of types of residential units is viewed as preventing one common devel-opment scheme.

(C) The covenant is a restraint on alienation.

(D) There is no privity of estate between Page and Gaint.

Question 95

Amy Docent, a state college instructor, was discharged because of her refusal to comply with a state statute requiring public employees to swear or affirm that they will (1) "uphold and defend" the state and federal constitutions, and (2) "oppose the overthrow" of the state or federal governments "by force, violence, or by any improper method." The statute had previously been held constitutional by the state supreme court. Docent filed a complaint in federal district court alleging the unconstitutionality of the statute and seeking an injunction and damages.

Which of the following is the state's strongest argument for sustaining the validity of the statute?

(A) Government employment is a privilege, not a right.

(B) The oath as a whole is only a commitment to abide by constitutional processes.

(C) The First and Fourteenth Amendments permit a state to fix the conditions of state employment.

(D) The state has a compelling need to keep disloyal persons out of governmental positions of trust.

Question 96

Charlie entered into a contract with Computer Barn to purchase three MBI computers for $4,500 for use in his business office. However, when the computers arrived at his office, Charlie saw that they were Kumquat computers. Because he was short of computers, Charlie asked his secretaries to use the Kumquats. One week later, however, his secretaries complained about the Kumquats, and therefore Charlie wrote to Computer Barn: "I'm rejecting the three Kumquats that you sent to me. Please return my $4,500." Computer Barn refused to do so.

The legal effect of Charlie's retention and use of the Kumquats for one week before notifying Computer Barn was:

(A) An acceptance of the three Kumquats, because Charlie was aware that the computers were not MBIs.

(B) An acceptance of the three Kumquats if Charlie's use thereof was more than reasonably required to test whether the Kumquats were acceptable substitutes for the MBIs.

(C) Not an acceptance, because the Kumquats were nonconforming.

(D) A waiver of any claim for damage against Computer Barn on account of nondelivery of the MBIs.

GO ON TO THE NEXT PAGE

Question 97

Flipper was a wholesale distributor of pinball machines and other mechanical and electronic games. Flipper's headquarters were in Azura, the largest city in the state of Blue, but Flipper's business served the entire state. There were no plants manufacturing the types of machines that Flipper sold within a thousand miles of Blue, and certain very popular machines were in scarce supply. Arcade owned and operated two video game arcades in Slate, the third-largest city in Blue. Arcade also sold and leased machines to taverns and convenience stores in the Slate area.

On August 3, Flipper sent a letter to Arcade, which Arcade received on August 5. The letter stated, in relevant part: "I now have in stock those 20 electronic poker games that you wanted for your business. I can guarantee delivery until September 2 at $2,000 per machine."

On August 16, Flipper sold the 20 electronic poker games to Tilt at a price of $2,300 per machine. On August 17, Flipper telegrammed Arcade: "Am revoking offer regarding poker machines; have already sold same at higher price." Arcade received the telegram the same day.

During the month of August, the Blue legislature was in special session, mainly to deal with a budget crisis in public schools throughout the state. However, certain other legislation was also debated during the special session. The special session passed a bill declaring the sale of electronic gambling machines to be illegal in the state of Blue. The definition of electronic gambling machines included the poker machines distributed by Flipper. The governor signed the bill into law on August 28, and it became effective immediately.

On August 30, Arcade wired Flipper: "Accept your offer to sell me 20 poker games at $2,000 per machine." Flipper received the telegram the same day.

If Flipper is not obliged to sell Arcade 20 electronic poker machines at $2,000 each, it will be because:

(A) Flipper had already sold the machines at a higher price.

(B) The state law banning the sale of such machines operated to revoke the offer.

(C) Flipper revoked his offer before Arcade accepted.

(D) The state law banning the sale of such machines renders the performance of Flipper's duties impossible.

GO ON TO THE NEXT PAGE

Question 98

Acting on an anonymous telephone call, police went to Desmond's apartment, knocked on the door, and demanded to search it for narcotics. When Desmond refused, the police forced the door open and placed him under arrest. As they were removing him from the apartment, Desmond offered to give the officers "valuable information" in exchange for his release. Before he could say anything else, Desmond was given *Miranda* warnings by the police. Thereafter, he told the police that he had stored some heroin in his friend's apartment and that he and his friend had been going to sell it. The heroin was recovered, and Desmond was prosecuted for conspiracy to sell narcotics and for possession of narcotics. At his trial, Desmond moved to suppress his statements.

Which of the following is Desmond's best argument in support of the motion to suppress?

(A) Desmond is entitled to know the identity of his accuser, and the state cannot supply this information.

(B) The police should have given Desmond *Miranda* warnings prior to entry into the apartment, and the warnings were ineffectual once Desmond offered to give the police information.

(C) Desmond was intimidated by the forced entry into the apartment, and since the statements were involuntary and coerced, their use against him would violate due process of law.

(D) The statements were fruits of an unlawful arrest, and though the *Miranda* warnings may have been sufficient to protect his right against self-incrimination, they were not sufficient to purge the taint of the illegal arrest.

Question 99

Supermedia, a television station, was conducting a "person on the street" interview segment live for its evening "magazine" show and asking citizens of the community what they thought were the biggest problems facing the city. When the interviewer stopped Don and asked him the question, he replied, "Corruption in city government, particularly the mayor."

William, mayor of the city, has now brought an action for defamation against Don. At trial, William has produced testimony as to his honesty and good character.

Which of the following evidence could Don properly adduce at trial as part of his defense?

I. The fact that William was convicted two years ago of taking a bribe to award a city contract for solid waste disposal.

II. The testimony of Harold, a local newspaper editor, that William is known throughout the state as a corrupt politician.

III. The testimony of Allen, a former campaign manager of William's, that William was corrupt.

(A) I. only.

(B) I. and II. only.

(C) I. and III. only.

(D) I., II., and III.

GO ON TO THE NEXT PAGE

Question 100

Purr entered into a written contract to buy Oldacre from Venn at a price of $160,000. At the time the contract was entered into, Purr gave Venn a cashier's check for $10,000, representing Purr's "earnest money." According to procedures provided for by state law, the contract was promptly and properly recorded in the office of the county's Recorder of Deeds. The closing date was set for April 29.

On April 17, Purr's attorney conducted a title search, during which the lawyer discovered that Venn's distant cousin, Kuzz, had a legitimate claim to a 1/10 undivided interest in Oldacre, based upon some confusing language in the will of Venn's grandfather, from whom Venn inherited Oldacre. On April 26, Purr paid Kuzz $10,000 and Kuzz gave Purr a quitclaim deed, surrendering any and all interest Kuzz had in Oldacre. Purr informed Venn of the situation and told Venn, "I'll see you at the closing." On April 29, Purr appeared at the Equity Title Company offices at the time appointed in the land-sale contract for the closing. Purr tendered a certified check to the closing officer, but Venn never appeared at the closing. Purr asked the closing officer to place the certified check in escrow and promptly sued Venn for specific performance.

Will Purr prevail in his specific performance action?

(A) Yes, if the certified check is for $150,000.

(B) Yes, if the certified check is for $140,000.

(C) No, because Purr should have informed Venn of the title defect to allow Venn to obtain marketable title, but Venn must return Purr's earnest money.

(D) No, because Purr has become a co-tenant of Venn and an action for partition rather than specific performance is appropriate.

STOP

Multistate Practice Exam

P.M. EXAM

Time—3 hours

You will be given three hours to work on this test. Be sure that the question numbers on your answer sheet match the question numbers in your test book. You are not to begin work until the supervisor tells you to do so.

Your score will be based on the number of questions you answer correctly. It is therefore to your advantage to try to answer as many questions as you can. Give only one answer to each question; multiple answers will not be counted. If you wish to change an answer, erase your first mark completely and mark your new choice. Use your time effectively. Do not hurry, but work steadily and as quickly as you can without sacrificing your accuracy.

YOU ARE TO INDICATE YOUR ANSWERS TO ALL QUESTIONS ON THE SEPARATE ANSWER SHEET PROVIDED.

DIRECTIONS

Each of the questions or incomplete statements in this test is followed by four suggested answers or completions. You are to choose the *best* of the stated alternatives. Answer all questions according to the generally accepted view, except where otherwise noted.

For the purpose of this test, you are to assume that Articles 1 and 2 of the Uniform Commercial Code have been adopted. You are also to assume relevant application of Article 9 of the U.C.C. concerning fixtures. The Federal Rules of Evidence are deemed to control.

The terms "Constitution," "constitutional," and "unconstitutional" refer to the federal Constitution unless indicated to the contrary.

You are also to assume that there is no applicable statute unless otherwise specified; however, survival actions and claims for wrongful death should be assumed to be available where applicable. You should assume that joint and several liability, with comparative negligence, is the relevant rule unless otherwise indicated.

DO NOT OPEN THE TEST UNTIL
YOU ARE INSTRUCTED TO DO SO.

ANSWER SHEET (P.M. EXAM)

101. Ⓐ Ⓑ Ⓒ Ⓓ	126. Ⓐ Ⓑ Ⓒ Ⓓ	151. Ⓐ Ⓑ Ⓒ Ⓓ	176. Ⓐ Ⓑ Ⓒ Ⓓ
102. Ⓐ Ⓑ Ⓒ Ⓓ	127. Ⓐ Ⓑ Ⓒ Ⓓ	152. Ⓐ Ⓑ Ⓒ Ⓓ	177. Ⓐ Ⓑ Ⓒ Ⓓ
103. Ⓐ Ⓑ Ⓒ Ⓓ	128. Ⓐ Ⓑ Ⓒ Ⓓ	153. Ⓐ Ⓑ Ⓒ Ⓓ	178. Ⓐ Ⓑ Ⓒ Ⓓ
104. Ⓐ Ⓑ Ⓒ Ⓓ	129. Ⓐ Ⓑ Ⓒ Ⓓ	154. Ⓐ Ⓑ Ⓒ Ⓓ	179. Ⓐ Ⓑ Ⓒ Ⓓ
105. Ⓐ Ⓑ Ⓒ Ⓓ	130. Ⓐ Ⓑ Ⓒ Ⓓ	155. Ⓐ Ⓑ Ⓒ Ⓓ	180. Ⓐ Ⓑ Ⓒ Ⓓ
106. Ⓐ Ⓑ Ⓒ Ⓓ	131. Ⓐ Ⓑ Ⓒ Ⓓ	156. Ⓐ Ⓑ Ⓒ Ⓓ	181. Ⓐ Ⓑ Ⓒ Ⓓ
107. Ⓐ Ⓑ Ⓒ Ⓓ	132. Ⓐ Ⓑ Ⓒ Ⓓ	157. Ⓐ Ⓑ Ⓒ Ⓓ	182. Ⓐ Ⓑ Ⓒ Ⓓ
108. Ⓐ Ⓑ Ⓒ Ⓓ	133. Ⓐ Ⓑ Ⓒ Ⓓ	158. Ⓐ Ⓑ Ⓒ Ⓓ	183. Ⓐ Ⓑ Ⓒ Ⓓ
109. Ⓐ Ⓑ Ⓒ Ⓓ	134. Ⓐ Ⓑ Ⓒ Ⓓ	159. Ⓐ Ⓑ Ⓒ Ⓓ	184. Ⓐ Ⓑ Ⓒ Ⓓ
110. Ⓐ Ⓑ Ⓒ Ⓓ	135. Ⓐ Ⓑ Ⓒ Ⓓ	160. Ⓐ Ⓑ Ⓒ Ⓓ	185. Ⓐ Ⓑ Ⓒ Ⓓ
111. Ⓐ Ⓑ Ⓒ Ⓓ	136. Ⓐ Ⓑ Ⓒ Ⓓ	161. Ⓐ Ⓑ Ⓒ Ⓓ	186. Ⓐ Ⓑ Ⓒ Ⓓ
112. Ⓐ Ⓑ Ⓒ Ⓓ	137. Ⓐ Ⓑ Ⓒ Ⓓ	162. Ⓐ Ⓑ Ⓒ Ⓓ	187. Ⓐ Ⓑ Ⓒ Ⓓ
113. Ⓐ Ⓑ Ⓒ Ⓓ	138. Ⓐ Ⓑ Ⓒ Ⓓ	163. Ⓐ Ⓑ Ⓒ Ⓓ	188. Ⓐ Ⓑ Ⓒ Ⓓ
114. Ⓐ Ⓑ Ⓒ Ⓓ	139. Ⓐ Ⓑ Ⓒ Ⓓ	164. Ⓐ Ⓑ Ⓒ Ⓓ	189. Ⓐ Ⓑ Ⓒ Ⓓ
115. Ⓐ Ⓑ Ⓒ Ⓓ	140. Ⓐ Ⓑ Ⓒ Ⓓ	165. Ⓐ Ⓑ Ⓒ Ⓓ	190. Ⓐ Ⓑ Ⓒ Ⓓ
116. Ⓐ Ⓑ Ⓒ Ⓓ	141. Ⓐ Ⓑ Ⓒ Ⓓ	166. Ⓐ Ⓑ Ⓒ Ⓓ	191. Ⓐ Ⓑ Ⓒ Ⓓ
117. Ⓐ Ⓑ Ⓒ Ⓓ	142. Ⓐ Ⓑ Ⓒ Ⓓ	167. Ⓐ Ⓑ Ⓒ Ⓓ	192. Ⓐ Ⓑ Ⓒ Ⓓ
118. Ⓐ Ⓑ Ⓒ Ⓓ	143. Ⓐ Ⓑ Ⓒ Ⓓ	168. Ⓐ Ⓑ Ⓒ Ⓓ	193. Ⓐ Ⓑ Ⓒ Ⓓ
119. Ⓐ Ⓑ Ⓒ Ⓓ	144. Ⓐ Ⓑ Ⓒ Ⓓ	169. Ⓐ Ⓑ Ⓒ Ⓓ	194. Ⓐ Ⓑ Ⓒ Ⓓ
120. Ⓐ Ⓑ Ⓒ Ⓓ	145. Ⓐ Ⓑ Ⓒ Ⓓ	170. Ⓐ Ⓑ Ⓒ Ⓓ	195. Ⓐ Ⓑ Ⓒ Ⓓ
121. Ⓐ Ⓑ Ⓒ Ⓓ	146. Ⓐ Ⓑ Ⓒ Ⓓ	171. Ⓐ Ⓑ Ⓒ Ⓓ	196. Ⓐ Ⓑ Ⓒ Ⓓ
122. Ⓐ Ⓑ Ⓒ Ⓓ	147. Ⓐ Ⓑ Ⓒ Ⓓ	172. Ⓐ Ⓑ Ⓒ Ⓓ	197. Ⓐ Ⓑ Ⓒ Ⓓ
123. Ⓐ Ⓑ Ⓒ Ⓓ	148. Ⓐ Ⓑ Ⓒ Ⓓ	173. Ⓐ Ⓑ Ⓒ Ⓓ	198. Ⓐ Ⓑ Ⓒ Ⓓ
124. Ⓐ Ⓑ Ⓒ Ⓓ	149. Ⓐ Ⓑ Ⓒ Ⓓ	174. Ⓐ Ⓑ Ⓒ Ⓓ	199. Ⓐ Ⓑ Ⓒ Ⓓ
125. Ⓐ Ⓑ Ⓒ Ⓓ	150. Ⓐ Ⓑ Ⓒ Ⓓ	175. Ⓐ Ⓑ Ⓒ Ⓓ	200. Ⓐ Ⓑ Ⓒ Ⓓ

Question 101

Egbert, who was sent to prison for nine years for car theft, vowed to get even with Charles, the prosecutor at his trial. While in prison, Egbert was told by another prisoner, Duane, that when Charles was in private practice as a criminal defense attorney, he had represented Duane in a drug charge. Duane claimed that because he did not have the cash to pay Charles his fees, he offered to pay his fees with five ounces of cocaine, and Charles accepted.

Although Egbert had no independent reason to believe that what Duane said was true, when he got out of prison he learned that Charles was running for District Attorney. Egbert went to one of the local papers and sold them the story for $1,000. In the article that resulted, Egbert was quoted as saying "I only hope that Charles suffers like I had to suffer for the last nine years."

Although the allegation was false, Charles withdrew from the race as a result of the article.

In a suit by Charles against Egbert for defamation, the probable result would be:

(A) Charles prevails because Egbert acted with deliberate malice towards Charles.

(B) Charles prevails if Egbert should have known that the story was false.

(C) Egbert prevails because the story was a matter of public concern.

(D) Egbert prevails if he honestly believed the truth of the assertion made by Duane.

Question 102

A statute in a jurisdiction makes it a crime to sell ammunition to a minor (defined as a person under the age of 18). The courts have interpreted this statute as creating a strict liability offense that does not require knowledge of the age of the purchaser and as creating vicarious liability. Duncan, who was 16 years old, but looked four or five years older, entered a store owned by Mathews and asked a clerk for a box of .22 caliber shells. Mathews had instructed her employees not to sell ammunition to minors. The clerk asked Duncan his age. Duncan said he was 20. The clerk then placed a box of shells on the counter and asked, "Anything else?" Duncan said that was all he wanted but then discovered he did not have enough money to pay for the shells, so the clerk put the box back onto the shelf.

If Mathews, the owner of the store, is charged with attempting to violate the statute, her best argument would be that:

(A) It was impossible for the sale to have occurred.

(B) She had strictly instructed her employees not to sell ammunition to minors.

(C) Duncan lied about his age.

(D) The clerk did not have the mental state needed for attempt.

GO ON TO THE NEXT PAGE

Question 103

Technix, Inc. produces the most up-to-date, high-speed mainframe computers on the market, and Cruncher Corporation is on the cutting edge of data storage technology. Technix and Cruncher contracted to purchase/sell a "Yellow Giant" computer. The written contract stated that Cruncher would purchase "one Technix 'Yellow Giant' computer at a price of $175,000." At the time, the going price for Yellow Giant computers was $150,000. When Technix delivered a Yellow Giant on the specified date, Cruncher refused to accept delivery and refused to pay. Technix sued Cruncher for breach, claiming that its expensive computers were manufactured to order and so it was forced to dispose of the Yellow Giant at a price far below fair market value. In defending the suit, Cruncher's president wishes to testify that Cruncher rejected the Yellow Giant because both parties knew that Cruncher really wanted a "Purple Giant," a machine much faster than the Yellow Giant, but which the parties agreed would be called in the contract a "Yellow Giant" to keep competitors in the dark as to Cruncher's new capabilities, and that the parties had executed contracts in the past that had specified a less powerful computer than the model that was actually delivered.

Should the testimony of Cruncher's president be admitted?

(A) Yes, because Cruncher is entitled to reformation of the contract.

(B) Yes, because the president's testimony would explain the meaning of a disputed contract term.

(C) No, because the parol evidence rule applies and the president's testimony contradicts a term in the written contract.

(D) No, because the Statute of Frauds applies, since the contract is for a large amount of money.

Questions 104-105 are based on the following fact situation:

The state of Floribama has recently had a problem with people dealing in, and with, its booming garment industry. The use of independent contractors by major garment makers, most of whom were headquartered out of state, had led to the hiring of illegal aliens to work under conditions reminiscent of 19th century sweatshops.

The legislature of Floribama enacted a statute to remedy the situation and to protect its citizens against the problems in the future. The statute provides:

I. That all garment makers must be licensed by the state attorney general.

II. That all subcontractors (defined separately in the statute) must be separately licensed by the attorney general and must have been a citizen of the United States for five years and a resident of Floribama for one year.

104. The requirement that garment makers be licensed by the attorney general is:

(A) Constitutional, because it is within the proper scope of the exercise of the police powers of the state.

(B) Constitutional, because the attorney general is designated as the proper person to enforce the law.

(C) Unconstitutional, as a burden on interstate commerce.

(D) Unconstitutional, as a violation of the Privileges and Immunities Clause of Article IV.

GO ON TO THE NEXT PAGE

105. The second clause of the legislation concerning subcontractors is subject to a constitutional challenge based on:

(A)   The Equal Protection Clause of the Fourteenth Amendment.

(B)   The Privileges and Immunities Clause of the Fourteenth Amendment.

(C)   The Due Process Clause of the Fifth Amendment.

(D)   The Tenth Amendment reserved powers of the state.

Question 106

Proctor sued Dahl for injuries received in an automobile accident. Wandrus was the only neutral eyewitness to the accident, and the lawyers for Proctor and Dahl mutually agreed on a time and place to depose Wandrus. The attorneys and Wandrus appeared as scheduled, but the court reporter who had been ordered for the occasion failed to show up. Because rearranging the deposition would be time-consuming and difficult, the attorneys decided to go ahead with the deposition. Wandrus was not required to give oath or affirmation prior to his testimony, but neither attorney had any reason to believe that Wandrus had any motivation to lie. During the deposition, the attorneys tape recorded their questions and Wandrus's responses. Each attorney received a copy of the tape of the deposition. Wandrus suffered a heart attack and died two months after the deposition. Shortly thereafter, the case came to trial.

Assuming proper notice is given, what evidence of Wandrus's deposition is admissible at trial?

(A)   An authenticated copy of the tape of the deposition only.

(B)   The testimony of the lawyers who conducted the deposition regarding Wandrus's statement only.

(C)   Either an authenticated copy of the tape or the testimony of the lawyers is admissible.

(D)   Neither a copy of the tape nor the testimony of the lawyers is admissible.

Question 107

Taylor and Scott, an unmarried couple, purchased a condominium as tenants in common and lived in the condominium for three years. Subsequently, they made an oral agreement that, on the death of either of them, the survivor would own the entire condominium, and, as a result, they decided they did not need wills.

Two years later, Taylor and Scott were involved in the same automobile accident. Taylor was killed immediately. Scott died one week later. Both died intestate. Taylor's sole heir is his brother, Mark. Scott's sole heir is her mother, Martha. Mark claimed one-half of the condominium, and Martha claimed all of it. The jurisdiction has no applicable statute except for the Statute of Frauds; nor does it recognize common law marriages.

In an appropriate action by Martha claiming the entire ownership of the condominium, the court will find that:

(A)   Martha owns the entire interest because Taylor and Scott did not make wills in reliance upon their oral agreement.

(B)   Martha owns the entire interest because she is entitled to reformation of the deed to reflect the oral agreement.

(C)   Mark and Martha each own an undivided one-half interest because Taylor and Scott each died as the result of the same accident.

(D)   Mark and Martha each own an undivided one-half interest because the Statute of Frauds applies.

GO ON TO THE NEXT PAGE

Question 108

A state statute provides that only citizens of the United States may be employed by that state. In an action brought in a federal court, a resident alien who was prevented from obtaining state employment as a garbage collector solely because of his alien status challenged the statute's constitutionality as applied to his circumstances.

Which of the following statements concerning the burden of persuasion applicable to this suit is correct?

(A) The alien must demonstrate that there is no rational relationship between the citizenship requirement and any legitimate state interest.

(B) The alien must demonstrate that the citizenship requirement is not necessary to advance an important state interest.

(C) The state must demonstrate that there is a rational relationship between the citizenship requirement and a legitimate state interest.

(D) The state must demonstrate that the citizenship requirement is necessary to advance a compelling state interest.

Question 109

Owner owned a piece of property located on the corner of a busy intersection. People walking past the intersection would often cut across Owner's property rather than walk along the sidewalk. Owner erected a sign asking people not to cut across his property, as it was ruining his lawn, but this did not stop the practice. Owner had captured a young bobcat several months earlier and had decided to keep him as a pet. In an effort to stop people from cutting across his yard, Owner erected a large sign which read, "Beware of Bobcat." Knowing that a bobcat attacks using its claws, he took it to Vet to have its claws removed. Vet failed to remove all of the bobcat's claws. Owner was not aware that Vet had not removed all of the bobcat's claws. Owner kept the bobcat on a leash in the front yard. The leash was long enough to allow the bobcat access to most of Owner's property; however, the bobcat could not reach the sidewalk which ran adjacent to Owner's property. The next day, Tina was walking home from the market. When she came to the intersection, she cut across Owner's property rather than staying on the sidewalk. The bobcat charged at Tina and slashed her legs severely with its one remaining claw.

If Tina brings suit against Owner for her injuries caused by the bobcat, Tina will:

(A) Recover, because the bobcat was not a domesticated animal.

(B) Recover, unless Tina was aware of the sign on Owner's property.

(C) Not recover, because Tina was a trespasser.

(D) Not recover, because Vet was the cause of the injury.

GO ON TO THE NEXT PAGE

Question 110

Pullen used aluminum brackets in her business. On the telephone listed as hers in the telephone book, Pullen received a call in which the caller said, "This is John Denison of Denison Hardware Company. We have a special on aluminum brackets this week at 30% off." Pullen ordered brackets from the caller. When the brackets were never delivered, Pullen sued Denison for breach of contract.

At trial, Denison, who denies having made the telephone call, objects to Pullen's testimony concerning it. When asked, Pullen testifies that, aside from the telephone call, she had never heard Denison speak until she met him in the judge's chambers before the trial and that, in her opinion, the voice on the telephone was Denison's.

The strongest argument for admission of Pullen's testimony concerning the telephone call is that:

(A) The call related to business reasonably transacted over the telephone.

(B) The call was received at a number assigned to Pullen by the telephone company.

(C) After hearing Denison speak in chambers, Pullen recognized Denison's voice as that of the person on the telephone.

(D) Self-identification is sufficient authentication of a telephone call.

Question 111

Drake owned a small warehouse that he leased to Teague, who used it as a storage and distribution center for fresh cut flowers being shipped to area florists. Drake wanted to put Teague out of business so that he could lease the warehouse to someone else at a higher rent. He entered the warehouse one night using a master key, and turned off the cooling system to destroy the flowers. To ensure that all of Teague's inventory would be destroyed, he also deployed several kerosene space heaters. While he was filling one, a small amount of kerosene spilled and was ignited by an ash from his cigarette. Although the fire that started was small at first, Drake panicked when he saw the flames and ran out of the building. The fire eventually spread to the walls of the building and heavily damaged it before being extinguished by firefighters.

If Drake is charged with arson, can he be found guilty?

(A) Yes, because Drake caused the fire during the commission of a malicious felony.

(B) Yes, because Drake did nothing when the kerosene caught on fire.

(C) No, because Drake did not intend to set the building on fire.

(D) No, because Drake cannot be liable for arson of a building that he owned.

GO ON TO THE NEXT PAGE

Question 112

Dietz and Atkins worked together as pickpockets. Dietz approached Verner from the front to distract him, holding a small camera and asking him to take a picture, while Atkins came up from behind with a knife to slice open Verner's back pocket of his pants and remove his wallet. Verner was drunk and believed Dietz had a gun and was trying to rob him, but was unaware of Atkins behind him. Verner reached into his back pocket to hand over his wallet and was cut by Atkins's knife as it was slicing through his pocket. The wallet dropped to the ground as Verner clutched his hand. Atkins picked it up and Dietz and Atkins fled while Verner knelt on the ground in pain. Dietz was apprehended shortly thereafter and charged with robbery.

Should Dietz be found guilty?

(A) Yes, because Atkins obtained the property by means of force.

(B) Yes, because Verner believed that Dietz would shoot him if he did not give up his wallet.

(C) No, because neither Dietz nor Atkins intended to use force against Verner to obtain the property.

(D) No, because Verner's belief that Dietz was robbing him was unreasonable.

Question 113

Professor Peterson, an expert on American Colonial and Revolutionary History, conducted full-day tours through the historic sites of Philadelphia every Wednesday and Thursday through the summer months. Peterson's fee for his services was $105, which did not include the entrance fees for several of the historical sites. Other persons and organizations conducted various American history tours through the city for somewhat less than Peterson, but Peterson's tour was generally rated the best by the leading tourist guidebooks because Peterson personally conducted the tours and shared his encyclopedic knowledge of American history and the city of Philadelphia.

David had recently moved to Philadelphia, and all of his co-workers praised Professor Peterson's tour, but David was not inclined to pay $105 for a tour of the historical sites of his new city. Therefore, David took a day off one Thursday and "hung around" the Liberty Bell monument, where Peterson's tour started. That day Peterson was conducting 27 persons on the tour. Most of the participants had paid in advance, but Peterson was holding up a sign with information about the tour and handing out brochures, one of which David took. Peterson accepted a few additional participants who signed up on the spot, but David was not among them. All day long, David hung around at the fringe of this group, paying the entrance fees separately but following the group through the different historical sites. However, he always positioned himself close enough to Peterson's group so that he could hear virtually every word of Peterson's lecture, although David did not ask Peterson any questions. David signed his name and address on the register at Independence Hall. Peterson noted this and took down the information. Two days after the tour concluded, David received a bill from Peterson in the amount of $105.

David will most likely be required to pay Peterson:

(A) $105, because that is the contract price for the tour.

(B) $105, because the amount of the contract was less than $500, making the Statute of Frauds inapplicable.

(C) $105, if that is a reasonable fee for the lectures based on Peterson's expertise.

(D) Nothing, because the historical sites were open to the public and David paid his own way.

GO ON TO THE NEXT PAGE

Question 114

In compliance with a federal statute requiring buildings to be made accessible to persons with disabilities, Walter installed wheelchair ramps at both entrances to his office building located on Blackacre, which he had owned for many years. One year later, Walter entered into a contract with Barbara to sell Blackacre, including the office building. After having the property surveyed, Barbara notified Walter that she was not going to complete the sale because the wheelchair ramp on the south side of the building extended over the property line and into the adjoining parcel of Whiteacre, making the title unmarketable. Walter insisted that Barbara proceed with the sale, and brought an action to compel her performance.

If the court were to find that title is marketable, it will be because:

(A) The wheelchair ramp is required by federal law.

(B) Walter currently owns Whiteacre and acquired Whiteacre and Blackacre as part of a larger parcel.

(C) The wheelchair ramp extends only 10 inches over the property line.

(D) The contract between Walter and Barbara requires Walter to convey only a quitclaim deed.

Question 115

An ordinance of City makes it unlawful to park a motor vehicle on a City street within 10 feet of a fire hydrant. At 1:55 p.m., Parker, realizing he must be in Bank before it closed at 2 p.m. and finding no other space available, parked his automobile in front of a fire hydrant on a City street. Parker then hurried into the bank, leaving his aged neighbor, Ned, as a passenger in the rear seat of the car. About five minutes later, and while Parker was still in Bank, Driver was driving down the street. Driver swerved to avoid what he mistakenly thought was a hole in the street and sideswiped

Parker's car. Parker's car was turned over on top of the hydrant, breaking the hydrant and causing a small flood of water. Parker's car was severely damaged and Ned was badly injured. There is no applicable guest statute and the jurisdiction follows traditional contributory negligence rules.

If Ned asserts a claim against Parker, the most likely result is that Ned will:

(A) Recover, because Parker's action was negligence per se.

(B) Recover, because Parker's action was a continuing wrong that contributed to Ned's injuries.

(C) Not recover, because a reasonably prudent person could not foresee injury to Ned as a result of Parker's action.

(D) Not recover, because a violation of a city ordinance does not give rise to a civil cause of action.

Questions 116-118 are based on the following fact situation:

On May 1, Ohner telegraphed Byer, "Will sell you any or all of the lots in Grove subdivision at $5,000 each. Details follow in letter." The letter contained all the necessary details concerning terms of payment, insurance, mortgages, etc., and provided, "This offer remains open until June 1." On May 2, after he had received the telegram but before he had received the letter, Byer telegraphed Ohner, "Accept your offer with respect to lot 101." Both parties knew that there were 50 lots in the Grove subdivision and that they were numbered 101 through 150.

GO ON TO THE NEXT PAGE

116. For this question only, assume that Ohner and Byer were bound by a contract for the sale of lot 101 for $5,000, that on May 3 Ohner telephoned Byer and stated that because he had just discovered that a shopping center was going to be erected adjacent to the Grove subdivision, he would "need to have $6,000 for each of the lots including lot 101," that Byer thereupon agreed to pay him $6,000 for lot 101, and that on May 6, Byer telegraphed, "Accept your offer with respect to the rest of the lots." Assuming that two contracts were formed and that there is no controlling statute, Byer will most likely be required to pay:

(A) Only $5,000 for each of the 50 lots.

(B) Only $5,000 for lot 101, but $6,000 for the remaining 49 lots.

(C) $6,000 for each of the 50 lots.

(D) $6,000 for lot 101, but only $5,000 for the remaining 49 lots.

117. For this question only, assume that on May 5, Ohner telephoned Byer stating that he had sold lots 102 through 150 to someone else on May 4, and that Byer thereafter telegraphed Ohner, "Will take the rest of the lots." Assume further that there is no controlling statute. In an action by Byer against Ohner for breach of contract, Byer will probably:

(A) Succeed, because Ohner had promised him that the offer would remain open until June 1.

(B) Succeed, because Ohner's attempted revocation was by telephone.

(C) Not succeed, because Byer's power of acceptance was terminated by Ohner's sale of the lots to another party.

(D) Not succeed, because Byer's power of acceptance was terminated by effective revocation.

118. For this question only, assume that on May 6, Byer telegraphed Ohner, "Will take the rest of the lots," and that on May 8, Ohner discovered that he did not have good title to the remaining lots. Which of the following would provide the best legal support to Ohner's contention that he was not liable for breach of contract as to the remaining 49 lots?

(A) Impossibility of performance.

(B) Unilateral mistake as to basic assumption.

(C) Termination of the offer by Byer's having first contracted to buy lot 101.

(D) Excuse by failure of an implied condition precedent.

GO ON TO THE NEXT PAGE

Question 119

Ford defeated Hudson in a close election to determine the president of the State Carpenters' Union. Shortly after the election, Hudson discovered that Ford had been a member of the Communist Party 15 years ago. The United States has a statute that prohibits a member of the Communist Party from serving as an officer of a labor union. Hudson revealed this information to the executive board of the Carpenters' Union, which declared Ford's election as president invalid. Ford brings suit in federal court challenging the constitutionality of the United States statute.

The court will most likely hold the statute to be:

(A) Constitutional, because the statute bears directly on the internal security of the United States.

(B) Constitutional, if the government can show a rational basis for the adoption of the statute.

(C) Unconstitutional, because the federal government may never discriminate among persons on the basis of political affiliation.

(D) Unconstitutional, as a bill of attainder.

Question 120

Peters sued Dietrich, claiming that they had entered into an oral agreement whereby Dietrich agreed to hire Peters as Chief Engineer of Dietrich Products and Peters agreed to take the job at a specified salary, and that Dietrich had subsequently breached their employment contract by refusing to hire Peters. At the trial of Peters's suit, Dietrich took the stand and denied having any contract with Peters for employment or otherwise. In response, Peters offers into evidence a properly authenticated phone message to Dietrich's wife, Wanda, that Dietrich had left with the switchboard operator at her office. The message stated, "I know you won't be happy, but I've offered Peters the Chief Engineer position and he's accepted." Dietrich's attorney objects.

The phone message should be ruled:

(A) Admissible, because it is the statement of a party-opponent.

(B) Admissible, if it is a recent perception.

(C) Inadmissible, because it is a privileged communication between husband and wife.

(D) Inadmissible, because it is hearsay not within any recognized exception to the hearsay rule.

GO ON TO THE NEXT PAGE

Questions 121-122 are based on the following fact situation:

Husband and Wife were going through a nasty divorce. Wife hired Patrick, a retired detective, to spy on Husband. Patrick followed Husband to Hotel, where he saw Husband meet a woman and go into her hotel room. Patrick checked into the adjoining room, placed an electronic listening device on the wall, and listened to the activities of Husband and the woman in the next room. While Patrick was listening, a burglar broke into Patrick's room and hit Patrick over the head with a blackjack. As a result, Patrick was hospitalized. A state statute makes adultery a crime.

121. If Patrick sues Hotel for his injuries:

(A) Patrick will prevail if Hotel's management had reason to believe the hotel room locks were inadequate.

(B) Patrick will prevail, because innkeepers owe their guests a very high degree of care.

(C) Hotel will prevail, because the burglar was a superseding intervening cause.

(D) Hotel will prevail if it was in compliance with a state statute setting minimum standards for hotel room locks.

122. If Husband sues Patrick for invasion of privacy:

(A) Husband will win, because he had an expectation of privacy in the woman's hotel room.

(B) Husband will win, unless Patrick's electronic eavesdropping was legal.

(C) Husband will lose, because adultery is illegal.

(D) Husband will lose if Patrick published nothing about Husband's activities.

Question 123

In 1975, Hubert Green executed his will which in pertinent part provided, "I hereby give, devise, and bequeath Greenvale to my surviving widow for life, remainder to such of my children as shall live to attain the age of 30 years, but if any child dies under the age of 30 years survived by a child or children, such child or children shall take and receive the share which his, her, or their parent would have received had such parent lived to attain the age of 30 years."

At the date of writing his will, Green was married to Susan, and they had two children, Allan and Beth. Susan died in 1980 and Hubert married Waverly in 1982. At his death in 1990, Green was survived by his wife, Waverly, and three children, Allan, Beth, and Carter. Carter, who was born in 1984, was his child by Waverly.

In a jurisdiction that recognizes the common law Rule Against Perpetuities unmodified by statute, the result of the application of the Rule is that the:

(A) Remainder to the children and to the grandchildren is void because Green could have subsequently married a person who was unborn at the time Green executed his will.

(B) Remainder to the children is valid, but the substitutionary gift to the grandchildren is void because Green could have subsequently married a person who was unborn at the time Green executed his will.

(C) Gift in remainder to Allan and Beth or their children is valid, but the gift to Carter or his children is void.

(D) Remainder to the children and the substitutionary gift to the grandchildren are valid.

GO ON TO THE NEXT PAGE

Question 124

Downs was indicted in state court for bribing a public official. During the course of the investigation, police had demanded and received from Downs's bank the records of Downs's checking account for the preceding two years. The records contained incriminating evidence.

On the basis of a claim of violation of his constitutional rights, Downs moves to prevent the introduction of the records in evidence. His motion should be:

(A) Granted, because a search warrant should have been secured for seizure of the records.

(B) Granted, because the records covered such an extensive period of time that their seizure unreasonably invaded Downs's right of privacy.

(C) Denied, because the potential destructibility of the records, coupled with the public interest in proper enforcement of the criminal laws, created an exigent situation justifying the seizure.

(D) Denied, because the records were business records of the bank in which Downs had no legitimate expectation of privacy.

Question 125

After a bitter custody battle, the court dissolving Mary and Jason's marriage ordered that Mary had sole custody of their three-year-old son, Mark. Jason was allowed to have Mark for visitation purposes for two weeks every summer, one weekend per month, and Christmas or Thanksgiving during alternate years. During the first summer visitation period, Jason took Mark to stay with Jason's parents (Mark's grandparents). When the two-week period ended, both Jason and Mark disappeared from sight. Under an assumed name, Jason leased a poultry farm 15 miles from his parents' home and kept Mark there. Mark enjoyed living on the farm and really enjoyed helping collect eggs and doing other activities with his dad.

Mary was distraught and frantic when Jason failed to return Mark. She tried to find Jason but was unable to learn of his whereabouts. Two years after Mark and Jason's disappearance, one of Jason's neighbors saw a program about missing children on television. The neighbor saw Mark's picture and notified local police. Mark and Mary were quickly reunited.

If Mary files suit on Mark's behalf seeking damages from Jason for false imprisonment, who will prevail?

(A) Mark, because Jason did not have legal custody of Mark.

(B) Mark, because Jason deprived Mark of his mother's care for two years.

(C) Jason, because Mark did not realize he was confined.

(D) Jason, because Mark enjoyed living on the farm.

GO ON TO THE NEXT PAGE

Question 126

Drake was arrested and charged with the battery of Burns. At trial, Drake testified that he struck Burns only in self-defense because Burns had threatened to kill him. Drake further testified without objection that he had told Crane, the arresting officer, that he had acted in self-defense. In rebuttal, the prosecutor called Crane to testify that Drake made no such statement to him.

Officer Crane's testimony is:

(A) Admissible, as an admission by silence of a party-opponent.

(B) Admissible, because it contradicts Drake's assertion.

(C) Inadmissible, because it is extrinsic evidence on a collateral matter.

(D) Inadmissible, because Drake had a constitutional right to remain silent.

Question 127

A federal statute set up a program of dental education. The statute provided that the Secretary of Health and Human Services "shall, on a current basis, spend all of the money appropriated for this purpose" and "shall distribute the appropriated funds" by a specified formula to state health departments that agree to participate in the program. In the current year Congress appropriated $100 million for expenditure on this program.

To ensure a budget surplus in the current fiscal year, the President issued an executive order directing the various Cabinet Secretaries to cut expenditures in this year by 10% in all categories. He also ordered certain programs to be cut more drastically because he believed that "they are not as important to the general welfare as other programs." The President identified the dental education program as such a program and ordered it to be cut by 50%. Assume that no other federal statutes are relevant.

To satisfy constitutional requirements, how much money must the Secretary of Health and Human Services distribute for the dental education program this year?

(A) $50 million, because the President could reasonably determine that this program is not as important to the general welfare as other programs.

(B) $50 million, because as chief executive the President has the constitutional authority to control the actions of all of his subordinates by executive order.

(C) $90 million, because any more drastic cut for the program would be a denial of equal protection to beneficiaries of this program as compared to beneficiaries of other programs.

(D) $100 million, because the President may not unilaterally suspend the effect of a valid federal statute imposing a duty to spend appropriated monies.

Question 128

Four years ago, Owen held Blackacre, a tract of land, in fee simple absolute. In that year he executed and delivered to Price a quitclaim deed which purported to release and quitclaim to Price all of the right, title, and interest of Owen in Blackacre. Price accepted the quitclaim and placed the deed in his safe deposit box.

Owen was indebted to Crider in the amount of $35,000. In September of the current year, Owen executed and delivered to Crider a warranty deed, purporting to convey the fee simple to Blackacre, in exchange for a full release of the debt he owed to Crider. Crider immediately recorded his deed.

In December, Price caused his quitclaim deed to Blackacre to be recorded and notified Crider that he (Price) claimed title.

Assume that there is no evidence of occupancy of Blackacre and assume, further, that the jurisdiction where Blackacre is situated has a recording statute which required good faith and value as elements of the junior claimant's priority. Which of the following is the best comment concerning the conflicting claims of Price and Crider?

(A) Price cannot succeed, because the quitclaim deed through which he claims prevents him from being bona fide (in good faith).

(B) The outcome will turn on the view taken as to whether Crider paid value within the meaning of the statute requiring this element.

(C) The outcome will turn on whether Price paid value (a fact not given in the statement).

(D) Price's failure to record until December of the current year estops him from asserting title against Crider.

Question 129

Brown contended that Green owed him $6,000. Green denied that he owed Brown anything. Tired of the dispute, Green eventually signed a promissory note by which he promised to pay Brown $5,000 in settlement of their dispute.

In an action by Brown against Green on the promissory note, which of the following, if true, would afford Green the best defense?

(A) Although Brown honestly believed that $6,000 was owed by Green, Green knew that it was not owed.

(B) Although Brown knew that the debt was not owed, Green honestly was in doubt whether it was owed.

(C) The original claim was based on an oral agreement, which the Statute of Frauds required to be in writing.

(D) The original claim was an action on a contract, which was barred by the applicable statute of limitations.

Question 130

Ellis, an electrical engineer, designed an electronic game known as Zappo. Ellis entered into a licensing agreement with Toyco under which Toyco agreed to manufacture Zappo according to Ellis's specifications and to market it and pay a royalty to Ellis.

Carla, whose parents had purchased a Zappo game for her, was injured while playing with the game. Carla recovered a judgment against Toyco on the basis of a finding that the Zappo game was defective because of Ellis's improper design.

In a claim for indemnity against Ellis, will Toyco prevail?

(A) Yes, because as between Ellis and Toyco, Ellis was responsible for the design of Zappo.

(B) Yes, because Toyco and Ellis were joint tortfeasors.

(C) No, because Toyco, as the manufacturer, was strictly liable to Carla.

(D) No, if Toyco, by a reasonable inspection, could have discovered the defect in the design of Zappo.

GO ON TO THE NEXT PAGE

Question 131

Defendant was charged with murder. His principal defense was that he had killed in hot blood and should be guilty only of manslaughter. The judge instructed the jury that the state must prove guilt beyond a reasonable doubt, that the killing was presumed to be murder, and that the charge could be reduced to manslaughter, and Defendant accordingly found guilty of this lesser offense, if Defendant showed by a fair preponderance of the evidence that the killing was committed in the heat of passion on sudden provocation. Defendant was convicted of murder. On appeal, he seeks a new trial and claims error in the judge's instructions to the jury.

Defendant's conviction will most probably be:

(A) Affirmed, because the judge carefully advised the jury of the state's obligation to prove guilt beyond a reasonable doubt.

(B) Affirmed, because Defendant's burden to show hot blood was not one of ultimate persuasion but only one of producing evidence to rebut a legitimate presumption.

(C) Reversed, because the instruction put a burden on Defendant that denied him due process of law.

(D) Reversed, because presumptions have a highly prejudicial effect and thus cannot be used on behalf of the state in a criminal case.

Question 132

While on walking patrol in a commercial district in the early evening, Officer Murdoch noticed that a light was on in Walker's Machine Shop. Curious about what was going on inside, the officer tried to look through the window of the shop, but it had been painted on the inside so that only a strip about three inches at the top, eight feet above street level, was still transparent. Officer Murdoch quietly brought two trash cans from a neighboring business over to the window, stood on them and saw, through the strip of unpainted window, that the shop owner's son Tommy was inside with a friend, sucking white powder into his nose through a rolled up tube of paper from off a small mirror. Recognizing from his experience and training that Tommy was snorting cocaine, Officer Murdoch knocked at the front door to the shop, and Tommy let him in. Murdoch immediately arrested Tommy and his friend. In the back room of the shop through whose window he had peered, Murdoch found and seized several grams of cocaine, a razor blade, and a mirror.

In Tommy's subsequent prosecution for possession of cocaine, Tommy seeks to bar introduction of the cocaine, mirror, and razor blade into evidence. His motion will probably be:

(A) Granted, because Officer Murdoch could not have known that Tommy was snorting cocaine absent a chemical test of the substance being snorted.

(B) Granted, because Officer Murdoch violated Tommy's reasonable expectation of privacy.

(C) Denied, because the search was incident to a valid arrest.

(D) Denied, because Tommy consented to Officer Murdoch's entry into the shop.

GO ON TO THE NEXT PAGE

Question 133

Parmott sued Dexter in an automobile collision case. At trial, Parmott wishes to show by extrinsic evidence that Wade, Dexter's primary witness, is Dexter's partner in a gambling operation.

This evidence is:

(A) Admissible as evidence of Wade's character.

(B) Admissible as evidence of Wade's possible bias in favor of Dexter.

(C) Inadmissible, because criminal conduct can be shown only by admission or record of conviction.

(D) Inadmissible, because bias must be shown on cross-examination and not by extrinsic evidence.

Questions 134-136 are based on the following fact situation:

Farquart had made a legally binding promise to furnish his son Junior and Junior's fiancee a house on their wedding day, planned for June 10 of the following year. Pursuant to that promise, Farquart telephoned his old contractor-friend Sawtooth and made the following oral agreement—each making full and accurate written notes thereof:

> Sawtooth was to cut 30 trees into fireplace logs from a specified portion of a certain one-acre plot owned by Farquart, and Farquart was to pay therefor $20 per tree. Sawtooth agreed further to build a house on the plot conforming to the specifications of Plan OP5 published by Builders, Inc. for a construction price of $18,000. Farquart agreed to make payments of $2,000 on the first of every month for nine months beginning August 1 upon monthly presentation of a certificate by Builders, Inc. that the specifications of Plan OP5 were being met.

Sawtooth delivered the cut logs to Farquart in July, when he also began building the house. Farquart made three $2,000 payments for the work done in July, August, and September, without requiring a certificate. Sawtooth worked through October, but no work was done from November 1 to the end of February because of bad weather; and Farquart made no payments during that period. Sawtooth did not object. On March 1, Sawtooth demanded payment of $2,000; but Farquart refused on the grounds that no construction work had been done for four months and Builders had issued no certificate. Sawtooth thereupon abandoned work and repudiated the agreement.

134. Assuming that Sawtooth committed a total breach on March 1, what would be the probable measure of Farquart's damages in an action against Sawtooth for breach of contract?

(A) Restitution of the three monthly installments paid in August, September, and October.

(B) What it would cost to get the house completed by another contractor, minus installments not yet paid to Sawtooth.

(C) The difference between the market value of the partly built house, as of the time of Sawtooth's breach, and the market value of the house if completed according to specifications.

(D) In addition to other legally allowable damages, an allowance for Farquart's mental distress if the house cannot be completed in time for Junior's wedding on June 10.

GO ON TO THE NEXT PAGE

135. Assuming that Sawtooth committed a total breach on March 1, and assuming further that he was aware when the agreement was made of the purpose for which Farquart wanted the completed house, which of the following, if true, would best support Farquart's claim for consequential damages on account of delay beyond June 10 in getting the house finished?

(A) Junior and his bride, married on June 10, would have to pay storage charges on their wedding gifts and new furniture until the house could be completed.

(B) Junior's fiancee jilted Junior on June 10 and ran off with another man who had a new house.

(C) Farquart was put to additional expense in providing Junior and his bride, married on June 10, with temporary housing.

(D) On June 10, Farquart paid a $5,000 judgment obtained against him in a suit filed March 15 by an adjoining landowner on account of Farquart's negligent excavation, including blasting, in an attempt to finish the house himself after Sawtooth's repudiation.

136. What was the probable legal effect of the following?

I. Sawtooth's failure to object to Farquart's making no payments on November 1, December 1, January 1, and February 1.

II. Farquart's making payments in August through October without requiring a certificate from Builders.

(A) Estoppel-type waiver as to both I. and II.

(B) Waiver of delay in payment as to I. and revocable waiver as to II.

(C) Mutual rescission of the contract by I. combined with II.

(D) Discharge of Farquart's duty to make the four payments as to I. and estoppel-type waiver as to II.

Question 137

Rogers gave Mitchell a power of attorney containing the following provision:

> My attorney, Mitchell, is specifically authorized to sell and convey any part or all of my real property.

Mitchell conveyed part of Rogers's land to Stone by deed in the customary form containing covenants of title. Stone sues Rogers for breach of a covenant.

The outcome of Stone's suit will be governed by whether:

(A) Deeds without covenants are effective to convey realty.

(B) The jurisdiction views the covenants as personal or running with the land.

(C) Stone is a bona fide purchaser.

(D) The power to "sell and convey" is construed to include the power to execute the usual form of deed used to convey realty.

GO ON TO THE NEXT PAGE

Question 138

Responding to an open bid solicitation from the procurement office of the Defense Department, Midwest Technologies submitted a bid for the development of a new flame-resistant fabric. Upon review of the bids, Midwest was notified that it was the low bidder; however, its bid for the contract was denied because of its failure to meet guidelines on minority representation that the procurement office imposed on firms contracting with the Defense Department. Several months later, the project was rebid. Although Midwest did not participate, company officials later learned that the contract had been awarded to another regional company, Great Plains Technologies, after the procurement office waived its minority representation guidelines for that project. Midwest filed an action in federal district court seeking only to enjoin performance of the contract.

The court should:

(A) Dismiss the action, because Midwest cannot show a relationship between the procurement office's award of the contract and any injury that it may be claiming.

(B) Dismiss the action, because the federal government may enter into contracts under whatever conditions it chooses.

(C) Decide the case on the merits, because the procurement office must show that its waiver of the minority representation guidelines was necessary to further a compelling government interest.

(D) Decide the case on the merits, because Midwest can claim that the unequal treatment of the two bidders violated its rights under the Due Process Clause of the Fifth Amendment.

Question 139

Phyllis was crossing the street at a crosswalk, but did not look both ways. As she walked, Phyllis was hit by a car driven by Brett, and immediately afterwards, she was struck by a car driven by Andrew. As a result of these collisions with the cars, Phyllis suffered severe injuries. Although it was impossible to determine which portion of Phyllis's injuries was caused by Andrew and which by Brett, at the trial of Phyllis's suit, the jury determined that Andrew was 20% negligent, that Brett was 40% negligent, and that Phyllis was 40% negligent. It was further determined that Phyllis had suffered $100,000 in damages. Phyllis had already received $10,000 from her group medical insurance plan. Andrew had a $500,000 auto liability insurance policy, and Brett is now insolvent.

In a pure comparative negligence jurisdiction, how much will Phyllis recover in damages from Andrew?

(A) $90,000.

(B) $60,000.

(C) $50,000.

(D) $20,000.

GO ON TO THE NEXT PAGE

Question 140

Ben contracted to buy Woodacre, a parcel of land, from Owen, with deed to be delivered and money paid on August 1. Ben planned to build a high-rise building on Woodacre. Ben had visually inspected the land, but did not take any special notice of the fact that a stream flowed up to the eastern property line of Woodacre and reappeared just beyond the western property line. In fact, there was a conduit under the surface of Woodacre through which the waters of the stream were diverted. On July 28, one of Ben's friends mentioned the existence of the conduit to Ben. Ben was amazed, and when Owen tendered a deed to Woodacre on August 1, Ben refused to accept it, stating, "I wouldn't have tried to buy Woodacre if I'd known about that conduit."

Owen files suit, demanding performance by Ben or damages for breach. Who should prevail?

(A) Owen, because Ben had ample opportunity to discover the existence of the conduit before he agreed to buy Woodacre.

(B) Owen, because the purpose for which Ben intended to use Woodacre is irrelevant.

(C) Ben, because Owen had a duty to provide a marketable title.

(D) Ben, because of the doctrine of frustration of purpose.

Question 141

Donaldson broke into Professor Ruiz's office to look at examination questions. The questions were locked in a drawer, and Donaldson could not find them. Donaldson believed that looking at examination questions was a crime, but in this belief he was mistaken.

Charged with burglary, Donaldson should be:

(A) Acquitted, because he did not complete the crime and he has not been charged with attempt.

(B) Acquitted, because what he intended to do when he broke in was not a crime.

(C) Convicted, because he had the necessary mental state and committed the act of breaking and entering.

(D) Convicted, because factual impossibility is not a defense.

Question 142

Nolan was negligently driving down the road, not paying attention to where he was going. Because of this, he hit and seriously injured Sue, who was lawfully crossing the street. The accident was witnessed by Martha, who suffered extreme emotional distress that physically affected her nervous system.

Martha brings suit against Nolan for negligent infliction of emotional distress in a jurisdiction that has not adopted the "foreseeability" test for this tort.

The most likely result of the suit will be that:

(A) Martha will win, because she witnessed Sue being seriously injured by Nolan.

(B) Martha will win, because severe shock to the nervous system constitutes a physical injury.

(C) Martha will lose, unless she was crossing the street with Sue.

(D) Martha will lose, unless she was a close relative of Sue.

GO ON TO THE NEXT PAGE

Question 143

An issue in Parker's action against Daves for causing Parker's back injury was whether Parker's condition had resulted principally from a similar occurrence five years before, with which Daves had no connection.

Parker called Watts, his treating physician, who offered to testify that when she saw Parker after the latest occurrence, Parker told her that before the accident he had been working full-time, without pain or limitation of motion, in a job that involved lifting heavy boxes.

Watts's testimony should be:

(A) Admitted, because it is a statement of Parker's then-existing physical condition.

(B) Admitted, because it is a statement made for purposes of medical diagnosis or treatment.

(C) Excluded, because it is hearsay not within any exception.

(D) Excluded, because Parker is available as a witness.

Question 144

A state statute requires the permanent removal from parental custody of any child who has suffered "child abuse." That term is defined to include "corporal punishment of any sort."

Zeller very gently spanks his six-year-old son on the buttocks whenever he believes that spanking is necessary to enforce discipline on him. Such a spanking occurs no more than once a month and has never physically harmed the child.

The state files suit under the statute to terminate Zeller's parental rights solely because of these spankings. Zeller defends only on the ground that the statute in question is unconstitutional as applied to his admitted conduct. In light of the nature of the rights involved, which of the following is the most probable burden of persuasion on this constitutional issue?

(A) The state has the burden of persuading the court that the application of this statute to Zeller is necessary to vindicate a compelling state interest.

(B) The state has the burden of persuading the court that the application of this statute to Zeller is rationally related to a legitimate state interest.

(C) Zeller has the burden of persuading the court that the application of this statute to him is not necessary to vindicate an important state interest.

(D) Zeller has the burden of persuading the court that the application of this statute to him is not rationally related to a legitimate state interest.

Questions 145-146 are based on the following fact situation:

Dunbar and Balcom went into a drugstore, where Dunbar reached into the cash register and took out $200. Stone, the owner of the store, came out of a back room, saw what had happened, and told Dunbar to put the money back. Balcom then took a revolver from under his coat and shot and killed Stone.

Dunbar claims that Stone owed her $200 and that she went to the drugstore to try to collect the debt. She said that she asked Balcom to come along just in case Stone made trouble but that she did not plan on using any force and did not know that Balcom was armed.

GO ON TO THE NEXT PAGE

145. If Dunbar is prosecuted for murder on the basis of felony murder and the jury believes her claim, she should be found:

   (A) Guilty, because her companion, Balcom, committed a homicide in the course of a felony.

   (B) Guilty, because her taking Balcom with her to the store created the risk of death that occurred during the commission of a felony.

   (C) Not guilty, because she did not know that Balcom was armed and thus did not have the required mental state for felony murder.

   (D) Not guilty, because she believed she was entitled to the money and thus did not intend to steal.

146. If Dunbar is prosecuted for murder on the basis of being an accessory to Balcom in committing a murder and the jury believes her claim, she should be found:

   (A) Guilty, because in firing the shot Balcom was trying to help her.

   (B) Guilty, because she and Balcom were acting in concert in a dangerous undertaking.

   (C) Not guilty, because she had no idea that Balcom was armed and she did not plan to use force.

   (D) Not guilty, because she was exercising self-help and did not intend to steal.

Question 147

Duncan was charged with aggravated assault. At trial Duncan did not testify; however, he sought to offer opinion evidence of his good character for truth and veracity.

This testimony should be:

   (A) Admitted, because a criminal defendant is entitled to offer evidence of his good character.

   (B) Admitted, because a party's credibility is necessarily in issue.

   (C) Excluded, because evidence of character is not admissible to prove conduct in conformity therewith.

   (D) Excluded, because it is evidence of a trait not pertinent to the case.

Question 148

Otto conveyed Goldacre to "Andy, his heirs and assigns, but if Andy dies and is not survived by children by his present wife, Jane, then to Bob and his heirs and assigns." Shortly after taking possession, Andy discovered rich metal deposits on the land, opened a mining operation, and removed and sold a considerable quantity of valuable ore without giving Bob any notice of his action. Andy has no children. Andy, Jane, and Bob are all still living. Bob brought an action in equity for an accounting of the value of the ore removed and for an injunction against further removal.

If the decision is for Andy, it will be because:

   (A) Bob has no interest in Goldacre.

   (B) The right to take minerals is an incident of a defeasible fee simple.

   (C) The right to take minerals is an incident of the right to possession.

   (D) There was no showing that Andy acted in bad faith.

GO ON TO THE NEXT PAGE

Question 149

After being notified by Dr. Josephs that Nurse Norris's employment with his office was terminated, Norris applied for a position with Hospital. In her application, Norris listed her former employment with Josephs. Josephs, in response to a telephone inquiry from Hospital, stated that "Norris lacked professional competence." Although Josephs believed that to be a fair assessment of Norris, his adverse rating was based on one episode of malpractice for which he blamed Norris but which in fact was chargeable to another doctor. Because of Josephs's adverse comment on her qualifications, Norris was not employed by Hospital.

If Norris asserts a claim based on defamation against Josephs, will Norris prevail?

(A) Yes, because Josephs was mistaken in the facts on which he based his opinion of Norris's competence.

(B) Yes, because Josephs's statement reflected adversely on Norris's professional competence.

(C) No, if Norris authorized Hospital to make inquiry of her former employer.

(D) No, if Josephs had reasonable grounds for his belief that Norris was not competent.

Question 150

A 10-lot subdivision was approved by the proper governmental authority. The authority's action was pursuant to a map filed by Diaz, which included an undesignated parcel in addition to the 10 numbered lots. The shape of the undesignated parcel is different and somewhat larger than any one of the numbered lots. Subdivision building restrictions were imposed on "all the lots shown on said map."

Diaz contracts to sell the unnumbered lot, described by metes and bounds, to Butts. Is title to the parcel marketable?

(A) Yes, because the undesignated parcel is not a lot to which the subdivision building restrictions apply.

(B) Yes, because the undesignated parcel is not part of the subdivision.

(C) No, because the undesignated parcel has never been approved by the proper governmental authority.

(D) No, because the map leaves it uncertain whether the unnumbered lot is subject to the building restrictions.

Question 151

On March 15, Venus Viniferous entered into a written agreement with Tipple Winery that provided that Venus would sell 1,600 tons of tokay grapes to Tipple for $750 per ton, delivery to be no later than November 1 of the same year. By November 1, Venus had delivered only 700 tons of grapes, and had informed Tipple by telegram that she had used the remainder of her crop in the production of her own boutique winery's latest release, Tokay With Me wine cooler. Tipple purchased an additional 900 tons of tokay grapes from other growers at the then-prevailing market price of $800 per ton. Venus has submitted an invoice to the marketing department of Tipple for $525,000. The head of marketing has come to you, Tipple's legal officer, for advice on how to respond to this billing.

Ignoring incidental costs of cover, you should advise her to:

(A) Pay the $525,000, since by accepting delivery of the 700 tons of grapes Tipple waived an objection to Venus's breach.

(B) Pay Venus the market value of her 700 tons of grapes as of November 1, less the cost of cover for the remaining 900 tons.

(C) Pay Venus $480,000, representing the contract price for the grapes she delivered less the cost of cover for the remaining 900 tons.

(D) Pay Venus nothing, since she will be unable to enforce any claim for payment in court.

GO ON TO THE NEXT PAGE

Question 152

Dray was prosecuted for bank robbery. At trial, the bank teller, Wall, was unable to identify Dray, now bearded, as the bank robber. The prosecutor then showed Wall a group of photographs, and Wall testified that she had previously told the prosecutor that the middle picture (concededly a picture of Dray before he grew a beard) was a picture of the bank robber.

Wall's testimony is:

(A) Inadmissible, because it is hearsay not within any exception.

(B) Inadmissible, because it is a violation of Dray's right of confrontation.

(C) Admissible as prior identification by the witness.

(D) Admissible as past recollection recorded.

Questions 153-154 are based on the following fact situation:

Barnes had been a beekeeper for many years, making a modest living selling honey in the area surrounding his farm. When he became aware of a sudden demand for beeswax for use in the manufacture of candles and certain types of exotic soaps sold in specialty shops, he built a plant to manufacture these items. The candle and soap business developed so rapidly that Barnes found it profitable to sell his bee farm to Stevens for $50,000. The sale contract provided that "Barnes reserves the right to purchase all of the beeswax produced by Stevens during the next five years at the current market price at time of delivery, delivery and payment to be made at weekly intervals, and Stevens agrees to supply in any event a minimum of 100 pounds of beeswax per month during that period." When the sale was closed, Barnes's lawyer handed Stevens's lawyer a letter stating: "This is to notify you that I will take all of your beeswax production until further notice."

For one year, Stevens delivered to Barnes and Barnes paid for all of the beeswax produced by Stevens. During that year, Stevens, who was an expert beekeeper, increased his beeswax production by 100% by increasing the number and productivity of the bees. Stevens then proposed to Barnes that, since he had doubled production, it would only be fair that he supply Barnes with half of his new total, but in any event a minimum of 100 pounds per month, leaving Stevens free to sell the remainder of the wax at higher prices for new uses being made of beeswax. Barnes, in a signed writing, agreed to the proposal by Stevens for the remaining period of the original contract. During the following year, Stevens delivered to Barnes, and Barnes paid for, one-half of all of the beeswax produced by Stevens.

As the first year of the new contract ended, Stevens was stung by a bee and, due to an allergy, became so seriously and permanently ill and impaired as to be unable to attend to the bees. From that time on he never made another delivery to Barnes.

153. The modification between Barnes and Stevens reducing the contractual amounts by 50% was:

(A) Enforceable in all respects.

(B) Enforceable only to the extent of beeswax tendered by Stevens.

(C) Unenforceable, because there was no consideration for Barnes's promise to take only one-half of the production.

(D) Unenforceable, because of the indefiniteness as to the quantity of the goods.

154. Assuming that contractual obligations existed between Barnes and Stevens, Stevens's refusal to perform was:

(A) Justifiable, because he had not promised to produce any beeswax.

(B) Justifiable, because his performance was excused because of his permanent disability.

(C) Justifiable only if he gave Barnes reasonable notice so that Barnes could buy beeswax elsewhere.

(D) Not justifiable and constituted a breach of contract.

Question 155

A statute in the state of Peridot permits the state to seize and dispose of real property that was used to commit or facilitate the commission of a felony drug offense. After Keith's arrest for selling cocaine out of his home, a felony, the state instituted an action of forfeiture against Keith's house and property. After notice to Keith and a hearing, a judge granted the order and the state seized the property. Six months later, after the time for any appeals had expired, the property was sold at a public auction to a third party. It was only when the third party brought an action to quiet title that Northwest Bank, the holder of a properly recorded mortgage on Keith's property, learned of the forfeiture. Because the bank's mortgage payments were automatically deducted from an account Keith had under a different name, no one at the bank was aware that the property had been seized. The only notice provided to parties other than Keith was a public notice published for three weeks in a general circulation newspaper. The bank defends the quiet title action on the ground that it did not receive the notice required under the United States Constitution to protect its interest in the property.

If the court rules that Northwest Bank's rights under the Due Process Clause of the Fourteenth Amendment were violated by the state's seizure of the property, it will be because:

(A) In any judicial proceeding affecting rights to real property, a claimant is required to provide notice and an evidentiary hearing to all parties with a legal interest in the property before taking actions affecting their rights.

(B) The government itself was the party that seized the property, rather than a private party using governmental processes.

(C) The notice was not adequate under the circumstances to apprise a party with a properly recorded legal interest in the property.

(D) The jurisdiction treats the mortgagee as having title to the property rather than merely a lien.

GO ON TO THE NEXT PAGE

Question 156

Darren's car was stopped by Officer Jones for a minor traffic violation. The officer recognized Darren as a suspect in a multimillion-dollar bank fraud scheme that had just been discovered by the authorities. She placed Darren under arrest and gave him *Miranda* warnings. She then asked for permission to search the trunk of the car. Darren nodded and unlocked the trunk. Officer Jones searched the trunk and discovered a bag containing what appeared to be cocaine in a compartment in the trunk. When later tests determined that it was cocaine, the authorities added a charge of transporting illegal narcotics to Darren's indictment. At a preliminary hearing, Darren moved to have evidence of the cocaine excluded as the result of a search in violation of the Fourth Amendment.

Should the court grant Darren's motion?

(A) Yes, because one taken into custody cannot give valid consent to a search that would otherwise require a warrant.

(B) Yes, because the search exceeded the scope of a permissible search incident to a lawful arrest.

(C) No, if the court finds that Darren's consent was voluntary under the circumstances.

(D) No, because persons have a lesser expectation of privacy in their vehicles for purposes of the Fourth Amendment.

Question 157

In which of the following situations is Defendant most likely to be guilty of the crime charged?

(A) Without the permission of Owner, Defendant takes Owner's car with the intention of driving it three miles to a grocery store and back. Defendant is charged with larceny.

(B) Defendant gets permission to borrow Owner's car for the evening by falsely promising to return it, although he does not intend to do so. Two days later, he changes his mind and returns the car. Defendant is charged with larceny by trick.

(C) Defendant gets permission to borrow Owner's car for the evening by misrepresenting his identity and falsely claiming he has a valid driver's license. He returns the car the next day. Defendant is charged with obtaining property by false pretenses.

(D) With permission, Defendant, promising to return it by 9 p.m., borrows Owner's car. Later in the evening, Defendant decides to keep the car until the next morning and does so. Defendant is charged with embezzlement.

GO ON TO THE NEXT PAGE

Questions 158-159 are based on the following fact situation:

In a trial between Jones and Smith, an issue arose about Smith's ownership of a horse, which had caused damage to Jones's crops.

158. Jones offered to testify that he looked up Smith's telephone number in the directory, called that number, and that a voice answered, "This is Smith speaking." At this, Jones asked, "Was that your horse that tramped across my cornfield this afternoon?" The voice replied, "Yes." The judge should rule the testimony:

(A) Admissible, because the answering speaker's identification of himself, together with the usual accuracy of the telephone directory and transmission system, furnishes sufficient authentication.

(B) Admissible, because judicial notice may be taken of the accuracy of telephone directories.

(C) Inadmissible unless Jones can further testify that he was familiar with Smith's voice and that it was in fact Smith to whom he spoke.

(D) Inadmissible unless Smith has first been asked whether or not the conversation took place and has been given the opportunity to admit, deny, or explain.

159. Jones seeks to introduce in evidence a photograph of his cornfield to depict the nature and extent of the damage done. The judge should rule the photograph:

(A) Admissible if Jones testifies that it fairly and accurately portrays the condition of the cornfield after the damage was done.

(B) Admissible if Jones testifies that the photograph was taken within a week after the alleged occurrence.

(C) Inadmissible if Jones fails to call the photographer to testify concerning the circumstances under which the photograph was taken.

(D) Inadmissible if it is possible to describe the damage to the cornfield through direct oral testimony.

Question 160

Pursuant to a state statute, Clovis applied for tuition assistance to attend the Institute of Liberal Arts. He was qualified for such assistance in every way except that he was a resident alien who did not intend to become a United States citizen.

The state's restriction of such grants to United States citizens or resident aliens seeking such citizenship is probably:

(A) Valid, because aliens are not per se "a discrete and insular minority" specially protected by the Fourteenth Amendment.

(B) Valid, because the line drawn by the state for extending aid was reasonably related to a legitimate state interest.

(C) Invalid, because the justifications for this restriction are insufficient to overcome the burden imposed on a state when it uses such an alienage classification.

(D) Invalid, because the Privileges and Immunities Clause of Article IV does not permit such an arbitrary classification.

GO ON TO THE NEXT PAGE

Question 161

Dickens purchased an old house in a neighborhood undergoing gentrification. He planned to slowly fix up the house as his time and finances permitted. Dickens financed his purchase by taking out a mortgage on the property with Britannia Bank, which the bank recorded. Although the house needed a lot of work, for most purposes it was quite livable. However, the windows were very dilapidated, and it was clear that Dickens's winter heating bills would skyrocket because of the ineffective insulation provided by the windows. Therefore, Dickens purchased some custom-made windows from Fenster, a retail dealer specializing in windows, awnings, and gutters. The modern windows used three panes of glass for improved insulation and they were easily removable from the window frames to make cleaning them a less odious chore. Because Dickens had spent a lot of money on the house already, he lacked sufficient funds to pay the $3,000 Fenster wanted for a complete set of new windows. Fenster agreed to sell the windows to Dickens on an installment payment plan with the windows as security. Dickens installed the windows himself and stored the old windows in the basement of the house. Dickens made three payments to Britannia Bank on the $30,000 mortgage and he made two payments to Fenster on the windows. Dickens then lost his job and ceased making payments to Britannia Bank and Fenster. Dickens has departed to parts unknown and Fenster wishes to remove the windows from the house. Britannia Bank objects. The matter winds up in court.

How should the court rule on Fenster's request to remove the windows?

(A) Fenster may remove the windows, because the old windows are available for the bank to restore the house to its original condition.

(B) Fenster may remove the windows, because the windows are designed to be removable.

(C) Fenster may not remove the windows, because regardless of their form, windows are an integral part of the house.

(D) Fenster may not remove the windows, because the bank's lien is senior to Fenster's.

GO ON TO THE NEXT PAGE

Question 162

Phil Phossell owns Phil's Antiques, a small antique shop in an area of the country rife with Revolutionary War artifacts. On a visit to an estate sale, he purchased a 200-year-old powder horn inscribed with the name Stuart Harrison, a soldier in the Revolutionary War and a member of a family that was very prominent in the area at that time. Donna Director is the curator of the nearby Harrison Museum, which displays numerous artifacts owned by the family during that period. She approached Phil when she heard of his purchase and indicated that she wanted to acquire the powder horn for the museum. The price that she offered was slightly higher than what Phil had been planning to ask for it when he offered it for sale in his shop and was a very fair price for an item of that nature. Phil, however, refused to sell to her because he did not like the way she had done business with other antique dealers in the past. After her attempts at friendly persuasion had failed, Donna turned to threats. Saying that she had a power of attorney from the heirs of Stuart Harrison, she claimed that the law allowed her to bring a replevin action to seize it from Phil if he did not accept her offer. In fact, her statements were false and she had no power to obtain the powder horn. However, Phil believed her and grudgingly agreed to sell her the item for the price that she had offered. Several days later he learned that her statements were false and he became very distressed.

Can Phil recover damages in a misrepresentation suit against Donna?

(A) Yes, but only if Donna knew that her statements were false when she made them.

(B) No, because Phil suffered no pecuniary harm.

(C) Yes, because Phil would not have made the transaction with Donna if not for her false statements.

(D) No, because Phil had no right to rely on Donna's statements regarding the law.

Question 163

Pursuant to its power under the Commerce Clause, Congress adopted legislation requiring all employers to pay employees at least $8 per hour and prohibiting employers from requiring any employee to work more than a 12-hour day. The legislation also provided that any employee whose rights under the legislation are violated by his employer may bring a cause of action for damages against the employer in the federal district court in the district where the employee resides. The legislation defined "employer" to include "all commercial employers, all charities that compensate workers for their time, and all state and local governments."

Roy Desota worked as a paramedic for the Aridzona state police. Because of the nature of the job, Aridzona required its state police paramedics to work a 24-hour shift. They would then be off for 48 hours. Roy was unhappy with this arrangement and preferred to work a regular 10- or 12-hour day. A friend of Roy told him about the federal legislation discussed above, and Roy immediately brought an action against the state of Aridzona in federal district court.

The district court should hold:

(A) In favor of Roy, because under the Commerce Clause, Congress can create a federal court cause of action for damages against state governments.

(B) In favor of Roy, because Congress has the power to regulate the jurisdiction of the federal courts pursuant to Article III.

(C) Against Roy, because the federal legislation was not enacted pursuant to Congress's power to enforce the Fourteenth Amendment.

(D) Against Roy, because Congress has no power to remove the states' Eleventh Amendment immunity from suit in federal court.

GO ON TO THE NEXT PAGE

Question 164

Elliot was placed on trial for robbery. There was no accurate eyewitness identification of the perpetrator because the perpetrator had worn a nylon stocking over his head while committing the crime. However, certain circumstantial evidence pointed to Elliot; therefore, the prosecutor's office obtained an indictment against him. At the trial, Elliot took the stand in his own defense. He stated, "I didn't have anything to do with that robbery, but I know who did. The robber was Evans." The jury acquitted Elliot of the robbery charge.

The prosecutor became convinced that Evans had, in fact, committed the robbery in question, and successfully argued that the grand jury should indict Evans for the crime. At Evans's trial, the prosecution called Elliot to the stand, with the expectation that Elliot would incriminate Evans. Instead, to the prosecutor's surprise, Elliot testified, "Evans didn't have anything to do with that robbery, but I know who did, because I committed the robbery myself." When asked about his testimony at his own trial, Elliot refused to answer, claiming his privilege against self-incrimination. Finding her case in a shambles, the prosecutor wishes to call Janet to the stand as a witness. Janet was a juror in Elliot's robbery trial and is prepared to testify that Elliot said Evans committed the robbery.

If the defense objects, the court should rule that Janet's testimony is:

(A) Admissible to impeach Elliot's credibility, but not as substantive evidence of Evans's guilt.

(B) Admissible to impeach Elliot's credibility and as substantive evidence of Evans's guilt.

(C) Inadmissible, because former jurors are not competent to testify concerning cases upon which they served as jurors.

(D) Inadmissible, because a transcript of Elliot's testimony at his robbery trial is the best evidence.

Question 165

Davison was driving through an apartment building area plagued with an unusually high incidence of burglaries and assaults. Acting pursuant to a police department plan to combat crime by the random stopping of automobiles in the area between midnight and 6 a.m., a police officer stopped Davison and asked him for identification. As Davison handed the officer his license, the officer directed a flashlight into the automobile and saw what appeared to be the barrel of a shotgun protruding from under the front seat on the passenger side of the car. The officer ordered Davison from the car, searched him, and discovered marijuana cigarettes and a shotgun.

At Davison's trial for unlawful possession of narcotics, his motion to suppress the use of the marijuana as evidence should be:

(A) Sustained, because the marijuana was discovered as a result of the unlawful stopping of Davison's automobile.

(B) Sustained, because the use of the flashlight constituted a search of the interior of Davison's automobile without probable cause.

(C) Denied, because the officer's conduct was consistent with the established police plan.

(D) Denied, because the discovery of the gun in plain view created the reasonable suspicion necessary to justify the arrest and search of Davison.

GO ON TO THE NEXT PAGE

Question 166

Hunko, a popular professional wrestler, entered into a written agency contract with Adman, who agreed to try to get Hunko's picture on a variety of food products. Hunko promised that Adman would have the exclusive right to promote Hunko on food product lines. They agreed that Hunko would receive 70% of the proceeds and Adman would receive 30%. Adman was able to persuade the makers of "Chocolate Charms" breakfast cereal to put Hunko's picture on the cereal boxes. Shortly after Adman confirmed the Chocolate Charms deal with the cereal manufacturer, Hunko and Adman agreed orally that henceforth Hunko would receive 50% of the proceeds, including proceeds from the Chocolate Charms deal, and Adman would receive the other 50%. Hunko received a $10,000 check from Chocolate Charms, and he promptly sent Adman a check for $3,000. Adman demanded an additional $2,000, but Hunko refused to pay.

If Adman sues Hunko for the $2,000, the party likely to prevail is:

(A) Hunko, because of the parol evidence rule.

(B) Adman, because consideration is not required for a modification.

(C) Hunko, because Adman had a preexisting legal duty to secure food product promotions for Hunko.

(D) Hunko, because an exclusive contract requires that the party given the privileges of exclusivity use his best efforts.

Question 167

At a time when Ogawa held Lot 1 in the Fairoaks subdivision in fee simple, Vine executed a warranty deed that recited that Vine conveyed Lot 1, Fairoaks, to Purvis. The deed was promptly and duly recorded.

After the recording of the deed from Vine to Purvis, Ogawa conveyed Lot 1 to Vine by a warranty deed that was promptly and duly recorded. Later, Vine conveyed the property to Rand by warranty deed and the deed was promptly and duly recorded. Rand paid the fair market value of Lot 1 and had no knowledge of any claim of Purvis.

In an appropriate action, Rand and Purvis contest title to Lot 1. In this action, judgment should be for:

(A) Purvis, because Purvis's deed is senior to Rand's.

(B) Rand, because Rand paid value without notice of Purvis's claim.

(C) Purvis or Rand, depending on whether a subsequent grantee is bound, at common law, by the doctrine of estoppel by deed.

(D) Purvis or Rand, depending on whether Purvis's deed is deemed recorded in Rand's chain of title.

Question 168

Paul sued Dave for making a slanderous statement that greatly embarrassed Paul. Dave denied that he ever made such a statement. At trial, Paul called Willie to the stand, and Willie testified that he heard Dave make the statement on August 4. Dave discredited Willie, and Paul offers evidence of Willie's good reputation for truthfulness.

The rehabilitation is most likely to be permitted if the discrediting evidence by Dave was testimony that:

(A) Willie and Paul had known each other since childhood.

(B) Willie had been convicted of perjury in an unrelated case.

(C) Willie had attended a school for mentally retarded children.

(D) Willie disliked Dave.

GO ON TO THE NEXT PAGE

Questions 169-171 are based on the following fact situation:

Poe ordered some merchandise from Store. When the merchandise was delivered, Poe decided that it was not what he had ordered, and he returned it for credit. Store refused to credit Poe's account, continued to bill him, and, after 90 days, turned the account over to Kane, a bill collector, for collection.

Kane called at Poe's house at 7 p.m. on a summer evening while many of Poe's neighbors were seated on their porches. When Poe opened the door, Kane, who was standing just outside the door, raised an electrically amplified bullhorn to his mouth. In a voice that could be heard a block away, Kane called Poe a "deadbeat" and asked him when he intended to pay his bill to Store.

Poe, greatly angered, slammed the door shut. The door struck the bullhorn and jammed it forcibly against Kane's face. As a consequence, Kane lost some of his front teeth.

169. If Poe asserts a claim based on defamation against Kane, will Poe prevail?

(A) Yes, if Kane's remarks were heard by any of Poe's neighbors.

(B) Yes, because Kane's conduct was extreme and outrageous.

(C) No, unless Kane knew that Poe owed no money to Store.

(D) No, unless Poe suffered some special damage.

170. If Poe asserts a claim based on intentional infliction of emotional distress against Kane, will Poe prevail?

(A) Yes, because Kane's conduct was extreme and outrageous.

(B) Yes, because Kane was intruding on Poe's property.

(C) No, unless Poe suffered physical harm.

(D) No, if Poe still owed Store for the merchandise.

171. If Kane asserts a claim based on battery against Poe, will Kane prevail?

(A) Yes, because Poe had not first asked Kane to leave the property.

(B) Yes, if Poe knew that the door was substantially certain to strike the bullhorn.

(C) No, if Kane's conduct triggered Poe's response.

(D) No, because Kane was an intruder on Poe's property.

GO ON TO THE NEXT PAGE

Question 172

Dan beat out Rick for the starting middle linebacker position on the Central City College football team. After practice, Rick came up behind Dan and shoved him in the back. When Dan turned around, Rick punched him in the jaw, knocking out a tooth and giving him a split lip. Before Dan could retaliate, the two were quickly separated by other players. Rick taunted him, "The next time I see you I won't go so easy on you." That night Dan was at a bar frequented by the football players, some of whom were teasing him about the altercation that afternoon. Dan was enraged but did not respond. He then saw Rick enter the room but kept his back to him. Suddenly he felt someone shove him in the back. Pulling out his pocketknife, he whirled and stabbed the person behind him, believing it to be Rick. In fact, it was Tom, who was intoxicated and had stumbled and fallen into Dan. The knife severed a major artery, and Tom died on the way to the hospital.

Dan is charged with murder for Tom's death. At trial, Dan's attorney requests the judge to instruct the jury on voluntary manslaughter. How should the judge respond?

(A) Agree to give the instruction if Dan presents evidence that he honestly believed in the need to use deadly force in self-defense, even though his belief was unreasonable.

(B) Agree to give the instruction because the jury may consider the altercation earlier in the day together with the shove at the bar.

(C) Refuse to give the instruction because Tom was an innocent victim of Dan's mistake.

(D) Refuse to give the instruction because, regardless of Dan's mistake, a shove is an inadequate provocation as a matter of law.

Question 173

When the latest generation of interactive video games reached the video arcades in State Russet, community groups and civic leaders were alarmed to discover that the most popular games among young teenagers had graphic displays of violence and sexual themes. The state legislature quickly responded to the public outcry. With the stated aim of protecting minors from the perceived evils of offensive but not necessarily obscene materials, the legislature enacted a statute banning the commercial licensing of video arcade games with a specifically defined degree of graphic violent or sexual content.

Delmar, the owner of a chain of video arcades in State Russet shopping malls, was denied licenses for a number of video games that he wanted to install at his arcades. He challenges the state's action in federal district court.

The court will probably find the State Russet statute:

(A) Constitutional, because for materials accessible to minors, the state may adopt a different standard for determining whether the material is offensive or obscene than the standard it applies for adults.

(B) Constitutional, because the statute precisely defines the type of content that is prohibited in the video games.

(C) Unconstitutional, because narrower means are available to deny minors access to the objectionable material without affecting rights of adults.

(D) Unconstitutional, because some of the banned video games may have serious literary, artistic, political, or scientific value, as determined by contemporary community standards, and thus do not fall within the definition of obscenity.

GO ON TO THE NEXT PAGE

Question 174

Dent and Wren were playing golf. After they had completed nine holes, Dent left to make a telephone call. When he returned, he told Wren, "My wife was just involved in an accident. She ran a red light and hit another car. I have to skip the back nine." After arriving at the scene of the accident, Dent, after talking with bystanders, determined that his wife had not driven through a red light. Notch, the driver of the other car, brought suit against Dent's wife for injuries suffered in the accident. To help establish liability, Notch seeks to have Wren testify as to Dent's statements on the golf course.

Wren's testimony is:

(A) Admissible as an admission.

(B) Admissible as a statement against interest.

(C) Inadmissible, because it is hearsay not within any recognized exception.

(D) Inadmissible, because it constitutes opinion.

Question 175

Ortega owned Blackacre in fee simple and by his will specifically devised Blackacre as follows: "To my daughter, Eugenia, her heirs and assigns, but if Eugenia dies survived by a husband, a child or children, then to Eugenia's husband during his lifetime with remainder to Eugenia's children, their heirs and assigns. Specifically provided, however, that if Eugenia dies survived by a husband and no child, Blackacre is specifically devised to my nephew, Luis, his heirs and assigns."

While Ortega's will was in probate, Luis quitclaimed all his interest in Blackacre to Eugenia's husband, Jose. Three years later Eugenia died, survived by Jose but no children. Eugenia left a will devising her interest in Blackacre to Jose. The only applicable statute provides that any interest in land is freely alienable.

Luis instituted an appropriate action against Jose to establish title to Blackacre. Judgment should be for:

(A) Luis, because his quitclaim deed did not transfer his after-acquired title.

(B) Luis, because Jose took nothing under Ortega's will.

(C) Jose, because Luis had effectively conveyed his interest to Jose.

(D) Jose, because the doctrine of after-acquired title applies to a devise by will.

Questions 176-177 are based on the following fact situation:

On June 1, Kravat, a manufacturer of men's neckties, received the following order from Clothier: "Ship 500 two-inch ties, assorted stripes, your catalogue No. V34. Delivery by July 1."

On June 1, Kravat shipped 500 three-inch ties that arrived at Clothier's place of business on June 3. Clothier immediately telegraphed Kravat: "Reject your shipment. Order was for two-inch ties." Clothier, however, did not ship the ties back to Kravat. Kravat replied by telegram: "Will deliver proper ties before July 1." Clothier received this telegram on June 4, but did not reply to it.

On June 30, Kravat tendered 500 two-inch ties in assorted stripes, designated in his catalogue as item No. V34; but Clothier refused to accept them.

176. Did Clothier properly reject the ties delivered on June 3?

(A) Yes, because the ties were nonconforming goods.

(B) Yes, because Kravat did not notify Clothier that the ties were shipped as an accommodation to Clothier.

(C) No, because Kravat could accept Clothier's offer by prompt shipment of either conforming or nonconforming goods.

(D) No, because Clothier waived his right to reject the ties by not returning them promptly to Kravat.

GO ON TO THE NEXT PAGE

177. Did Clothier properly reject the ties tendered on June 30?

    (A) Yes, because Kravat's shipping the three-inch ties on June 1 was a present breach of contract.

    (B) Yes, because Kravat's shipping the three-inch ties on June 1 was an anticipatory repudiation.

    (C) No, because Kravat cured the June 1 defective delivery by his tender of conforming goods on June 30.

    (D) No, because a contract for the sale of goods can be modified without consideration.

Question 178

Deanna was moving to Russia to work in a foreign policy institute, and was in the process of moving out of the apartment that she had shared with Vanessa, who was not in at the time. Just before leaving, Deanna collected numerous items of hers from Vanessa's room that Vanessa had borrowed, usually without permission. As she was leaving the apartment, she grabbed what she believed to be her laptop computer, which Vanessa had often borrowed to do reports for work. Because it was an older, slower machine, she planned to trade it in for a different model at a computer resale store during a stopover in London. When she arrived at the computer store she discovered that she had taken a brand new, state-of-the-art laptop that Vanessa had apparently just purchased.

Is Deanna guilty of larceny of the computer?

(A) No, because she mistakenly believed that the computer she had picked up was hers.

(B) No, if her mistake as to whose computer she had picked up was reasonable.

(C) Yes, because she intended to permanently deprive Vanessa of the computer when she took it.

(D) Yes, if she decides to keep the computer or trade it in for a different one.

Question 179

Don Dent was on trial for the murder of Michael Richards. At the trial, Dent put forth the defense of self-defense, claiming that Michael was about to kill him when he shot Michael. To help establish that he was in fear of Michael, Dent called Walter to testify. Walter will testify that he heard Sam Smith say to Dent, "Michael Richards is a mean, vicious killer; he has murdered three people in the past year."

Walter's testimony is:

(A) Admissible under the state of mind exception to the hearsay rule.

(B) Admissible nonhearsay.

(C) Inadmissible, because it is hearsay not covered by an exception.

(D) Inadmissible, because it does not help establish that Dent acted in self-defense.

GO ON TO THE NEXT PAGE

Question 180

Lordsville was a small, agricultural village with a population of 400. It was a quiet, conservative town, and 90% of the inhabitants belonged to the Lordsville Church of Jesus, a white-washed frame building located on Lordsville's main street. The Lordsville Village Council consisted of five members, all of whom were members of the Lordsville Church of Jesus. The Council unanimously appropriated $350 to pay Mower to mow the lawn of the Lordsville Church of Jesus for a year. Mower was a 15-year-old resident of Lordsville and a member of the Lordsville Church of Jesus whose father had been killed the previous year when he was struck by lightning. Curmudgeon, a Lordsville resident, lived in a tiny house and paid only $200 per year in village and county property taxes, but he was incensed that any of it should go to support what he called "a bunch of holier-than-thou, superstitious, holy-rollers." Curmudgeon filed suit in federal district court to strike down the Council's appropriation to mow the church lawn.

Should the court entertain Curmudgeon's suit?

(A) No, because Curmudgeon paid so little in taxes that his interest in the matter, if any, is too minimal.

(B) No, because taxpayers lack standing to sue over appropriations by duly constituted legislative bodies.

(C) Yes, because a taxpayer may sue under the authority of the First Amendment's Establishment Clause if a fund into which he has paid is being used for religious purposes.

(D) Yes, because taxpayers have standing to sue when questions involving constitutional rights are at issue.

Question 181

Acorp and Beeco are companies that each manufacture pesticide X. Their plants are located along the same river. During a specific 24-hour period, each plant discharged pesticide into the river. Both plants were operated negligently and such negligence caused the discharge of the pesticide into the river.

Landesmann operated a cattle ranch downstream from the plants of Acorp and Beeco. Landesmann's cattle drank from the river and were poisoned by the pesticide. The amount of the discharge from either plant alone would not have been sufficient to cause any harm to Landesmann's cattle.

If Landesmann asserts a claim against Acorp and Beeco, what, if anything, will Landesmann recover?

(A) Nothing, because neither company discharged enough pesticide to cause harm to Landesmann's cattle.

(B) Nothing, unless Landesmann can establish how much pesticide each plant discharged.

(C) One-half of Landesmann's damages from each company.

(D) The entire amount of Landesmann's damages, jointly and severally, from the two companies.

GO ON TO THE NEXT PAGE

Question 182

For a valuable consideration, Amato, the owner of Riveracre, signed and gave to Barton a duly executed instrument that provided as follows: "The grantor may or may not sell Riveracre during her lifetime, but at her death, or if she earlier decides to sell, the property will be offered to Barton at $500 per acre. Barton shall exercise this right, if at all, within 60 days of receipt of said offer to sell." Barton recorded the instrument. The instrument was not valid as a will.

Is Barton's right under the instrument valid?

(A) Yes, because the instrument is recorded.

(B) Yes, because Barton's right to purchase will vest or fail within the period prescribed by the Rule Against Perpetuities.

(C) No, because Barton's right to purchase is a restraint on the owner's power to make a testamentary disposition.

(D) No, because Barton's right to purchase is an unreasonable restraint on alienation.

Question 183

In a contract suit by Perez against Drake, each of the following is an accepted method of authenticating Drake's signature on a document offered by Perez *except*:

(A) A nonexpert who, in preparation for trial, has familiarized himself with Drake's usual signature testifies that, in his opinion, the questioned signature is genuine.

(B) The jury, without the assistance of an expert, compares the questioned signature with an admittedly authentic sample of Drake's handwriting.

(C) A witness offers proof that the signature is on a document that has been in existence for at least 20 years, that was in a place where it would likely be if it was authentic, and that has no suspicious circumstances surrounding it.

(D) A witness testifies that Drake admitted that the signature was his.

GO ON TO THE NEXT PAGE

Question 184

The industrial city of Tunbridge suffered from battles over gang turf and a rash of drive-by shootings. Most street gangs were affiliated with one of the two loose gang confederations that fought for dominance, the Assassins and the Ghouls. To "issue a warning" to the Ghouls, a carload of Assassins, armed with Uzi sub-machine guns, sped into the Ghouls' neighbor-hood. It was late at night when the car passed a corner store, around which the Ghouls were known to congregate during daylight hours. The Assassins knew that the store closed at 6 p.m. and that the Ghouls went elsewhere after night-fall. As the Assassins drove by, they sprayed the store with submachine gunfire, smashing the windows and pocking the brick exteriors. One of the bullets struck and killed Jamie, a six-year-old girl who was asleep in an apartment located on the second floor, above the corner store. A few days later, the police arrested Dennison, who admitted to being a member of the Assas-sins and to having been in the car when the Assassins shot up the store. Dennison was placed on trial for the murder of Jamie.

If Dennison takes the stand in his own de-fense, and the jury believes Dennison's testi-mony, which of the following assertions by Dennison would be his best defense to the murder charge?

(A) "I was the driver of the car and did not actually shoot into the building."

(B) "I took a lot of drugs that night, and I was so high that I don't even remember the incident; I was certainly in no condition to form an intent to kill somebody."

(C) "Another member of my gang pointed a gun at me. I was really scared that if I didn't shoot into the building I would be seriously injured or killed myself."

(D) "I believed that the building was aban-doned and had no idea that there would be people inside it."

Questions 185-186 are based on the following fact situation:

Orris had title to Brownacre in fee simple. Without Orris's knowledge, Hull entered Brown-acre in 1950 and constructed an earthen dam across a watercourse. The earthen dam trapped water that Hull used to water a herd of cattle he owned. After 12 years of possession of Brownacre, Hull gave possession of Brownacre to Burns. At the same time, Hull also purported to transfer his cattle and all his interests in the dam and water to Burns by a document that was sufficient as a bill of sale to transfer personal property but was insufficient as a deed to transfer real prop-erty.

One year later, Burns entered into a lease with Orris to lease Brownacre for a period of five years. After the end of the five-year term of the lease, Burns remained on Brownacre for an additional three years and then left Brownacre. At that time Orris conveyed Brownacre by a quitclaim deed to Powell. The period of time to acquire title by adverse possession in the juris-diction is 10 years.

185. After Orris's conveyance to Powell, title to Brownacre was in:

(A) Hull.

(B) Orris.

(C) Burns.

(D) Powell.

GO ON TO THE NEXT PAGE

186. After Orris's conveyance to Powell, title to the earthen dam was in:

(A) The person who then held title to Brownacre in fee simple.

(B) Burns, as purchaser of the dam under the bill of sale.

(C) The person who then owned the water rights as an incident thereto.

(D) Hull, as the builder of the dam.

Question 187

As part of the Domestic Security Act, Congress established a permanent commission to evaluate the security of federal government buildings located in the District of Columbia. The commission would have the authority to evaluate current security conditions, establish new security guidelines, and coordinate security procedures among various governmental agencies. The legislation provided that three members of the commission were to be appointed by the President, two members by a committee of the House of Representatives, and two members by the United States Supreme Court. The President had the authority to veto any of the selections to the commission made by the congressional committee or the Supreme Court.

If a party with the requisite standing challenges the legislation and it is found unconstitutional, it will most likely be because:

(A) The President's power to veto a particular selection made by the congressional committee constitutes an improper exercise of the veto power.

(B) The commission will be exercising administrative powers.

(C) The judiciary does not have the power to make appointments to an advisory commission.

(D) The legislation does not provide for Senate confirmation of the presidential appointees.

Question 188

Johnson and Tenniel owned Brownacre as joint tenants with the right of survivorship. Johnson executed a mortgage on Brownacre to Lowden to secure a loan. Subsequently, but before the indebtedness was paid to Lowden, Johnson died intestate with Stokes as her only heir at law. The jurisdiction in which Brownacre is located recognizes the title theory of mortgages.

In an appropriate action, the court should determine that title to Brownacre is vested:

(A) In Tenniel, with the entire interest subject to the mortgage.

(B) In Tenniel, free and clear of the mortgage.

(C) Half in Tenniel, free of the mortgage, and half in Stokes subject to the mortgage.

(D) Half in Tenniel and half in Stokes, with both subject to the mortgage.

GO ON TO THE NEXT PAGE

Question 189

In 1980 Omar, the owner in fee simple absolute, conveyed Stoneacre, a five-acre tract of land. The relevant, operative words of the deed conveyed to "Church [a duly organized religious body having power to hold property] for the life of my son, Carl, and from and after the death of my said son, Carl, to all of my grandchildren and their heirs and assigns in equal shares; provided that Church shall use the premises for church purposes only."

In an existing building on Stoneacre, Church immediately began to conduct religious services and other activities normally associated with a church.

In 1995, Church granted to Darin a right to remove sand and gravel from a one-half acre portion of Stoneacre upon the payment of royalty. Darin has regularly removed sand and gravel since 1995 and paid a royalty to Church. Church has continued to conduct religious services and other church activities on Stoneacre.

All four of the living grandchildren of Omar, joined by a guardian ad litem to represent unborn grandchildren, instituted suit against Church and Darin seeking damages for the removal of sand and gravel and an injunction preventing further acts of removal. There is no applicable statute.

Which of the following best describes the likely disposition of this lawsuit?

(A) The plaintiffs should succeed, because the interest of Church terminated with the first removal of sand and gravel.

(B) Church and Darin should be enjoined, and damages should be recovered but impounded for future distribution.

(C) The injunction should be granted, but damages should be denied, because Omar and Carl are not parties to the action.

(D) Damages should be awarded, but the injunction should be denied.

Question 190

Dolly, a middle-aged woman who loved children but had never been able to have any of her own, often gave candy and other treats to children outside the Tot Town Kindergarten and Preschool. She befriended a number of the children, but was particularly fond of four-year-old Jane, who always called her "Aunt Dolly" and greeted her with a cheerful smile. One Friday afternoon, the school bus was late and Dolly talked to Jane in front of the school. She told Jane, "Your Mommy has had to go out of town for the weekend and asked me to take care of you." Although Jane had been taught, "Never talk to strangers," she did not consider "Aunt Dolly" to be a stranger and readily believed her. Dolly took Jane home with her and proceeded to give Jane treats and toys. On Saturday Dolly took Jane to the zoo, which Jane thoroughly enjoyed. Dolly heard on the radio that a search was being conducted for Jane, whom Jane's mother had reported as missing to the police. Dolly made sure that Jane did not watch any television where Jane might see her picture on the screen. Jane had a fine weekend with Dolly, and then Dolly returned Jane to her own front porch on Monday morning. Jane had three new dresses, a stuffed animal, and other toys with her. Jane rang the doorbell shortly after Dolly drove off. Jane's mother asked Jane where she had been. Jane told her, "I was at the zoo with Aunt Dolly." A police investigation quickly located Dolly, who was placed under arrest. Assume that the jurisdiction where this occurred maintains a traditional, common law definition of criminal false imprisonment and has a typical, modern kidnapping statute.

Dolly can be properly convicted of:

(A) Kidnapping only.

(B) Either kidnapping or false imprisonment.

(C) Both kidnapping and false imprisonment.

(D) Neither kidnapping nor false imprisonment.

GO ON TO THE NEXT PAGE

Question 191

Dean, charged with murder, was present with her attorney at a preliminary examination when White, who was the defendant in a separate prosecution for concealing the body of the murder victim, testified for the prosecution against Dean. When called to testify at Dean's trial, White refused to testify, although ordered to do so.

The prosecution offers evidence of White's testimony at the preliminary examination. The evidence is:

(A) Admissible as former testimony.

(B) Admissible as past recollection recorded.

(C) Inadmissible, because it would violate White's privilege against self-incrimination.

(D) Inadmissible, because it is hearsay not within any exception.

Question 192

The town of Hometown had a municipal auditorium that all groups were permitted to use. Lately, Bhagwan Bigbucks has begun to hold recruiting seminars for his religious cult at the auditorium. Sensing the displeasure of the voting public and fearing that the auditorium would become a mecca of fringe religious groups, the Hometown Town Council adopted the following ordinance: "Effective immediately, no religious groups will be permitted to use the Municipal Auditorium for meetings, speeches, or other public gatherings."

Bigbucks, who was having great success recruiting followers in Hometown, challenged the constitutionality of the ordinance in federal court. His suit should:

(A) Fail, because the ordinance treats all religions equally.

(B) Fail, because continuing to allow religious groups to use the auditorium would violate the Establishment Clause of the First Amendment.

(C) Succeed, because "religious groups" is an unconstitutionally vague term.

(D) Succeed, unless Hometown can show that the ordinance serves a compelling government interest.

Question 193

Light Company is the sole distributor of electrical power in City. The company owns and maintains all of the electric poles and equipment in City. Light Company has complied with the National Electrical Safety Code, which establishes minimum requirements for the installation and maintenance of power poles. The Code has been approved by the federal and state governments.

Light Company has had to replace insulators on its poles repeatedly because unknown persons repeatedly shoot at and destroy them. This causes the power lines to fall to the ground. On one of these occasions, Paul, Faber's five-year-old son, wandered out of Faber's yard, intentionally touched a downed wire, and was seriously burned.

If a claim on Paul's behalf is asserted against Light Company, the probable result is that Paul will:

(A) Recover if Light Company could have taken reasonable steps to prevent the lines from falling when the insulators were destroyed.

(B) Recover, because a supplier of electricity is strictly liable in tort.

(C) Not recover unless Light Company failed to exercise reasonable care to stop the destruction of the insulators.

(D) Not recover, because the destruction of the insulators was intentional.

GO ON TO THE NEXT PAGE

Question 194

Ash held good record title to Whiteacre. Ash conveyed Whiteacre to Bay for $90,000. Bay never recorded her deed. A year after Ash conveyed Whiteacre to Bay, Ash drew up a deed for conveyance of Whiteacre and gave it to Cedar as a gift. Cedar knew nothing of the prior conveyance to Bay, and Cedar recorded his deed. A year later, Cedar sold Whiteacre to Date via an installment land sale contract. The full purchase price was $100,000, and Date made his first installment payment of $40,000 to Cedar. Date received a deed from Cedar and promptly and properly recorded it. According to the terms of the installment agreement, Date was to make two further payments of $30,000 each. The first of these payments was due a year after the closing date and the second payment a year after that. Bay learned from a friend about Cedar's conveyance of Whiteacre to Date. Bay files suit against Date, seeking to oust Date from Whiteacre and to quiet title in Bay. The recording statute in State White, where Whiteacre is located and where all the parties reside, reads in relevant part: "No conveyance shall be good against a subsequent purchaser for value, without notice, unless it be recorded."

The court considers the following possible orders regarding ownership of Whiteacre:

I. Award Date a 40% share of Whiteacre as a tenant in common with Bay.

II. Grant Whiteacre to Bay, but order Bay to pay Date $40,000.

III. Grant Whiteacre to Date, but order Date to pay Bay the remaining $60,000 in payments.

IV. Grant Whiteacre solely to Date, based upon the recording statute, without any compensation to Bay.

V. Grant Whiteacre solely to Bay without any compensation to Date because Date purchased from a donee.

Which of the judicial orders would it be appropriate for the court to make?

(A) I. or II. only.

(B) III. or IV. only.

(C) V. only.

(D) I., II., or III. only.

Question 195

According to a statute of the state of Kiowa, a candidate for state office may have his name placed on the official election ballot only if he files with the appropriate state official a petition containing a specified number of voter signatures. Roderick failed to get his name placed on the state ballot as an independent candidate for governor because he failed to file a petition with the number of voter signatures required by state statute. In a suit against the appropriate state officials in federal district court, Roderick sought an injunction against the petition signature requirement on the ground that it was unconstitutional.

Which of the following, if established, constitutes the strongest argument for Roderick?

(A) Compliance with the petition signature requirement is burdensome.

(B) The objectives of the statute could be satisfactorily achieved by less burdensome means.

(C) Because of the petition signature requirement, very few independent candidates have ever succeeded in getting on the ballot.

(D) The motivation for the statute was a desire to keep candidates off the ballot if they did not have strong support among voters.

GO ON TO THE NEXT PAGE

Question 196

Acting on a hunch, Officer Blue went to Mildred's apartment, broke in, and searched it. Officer Blue found exactly what she was looking for under Mildred's bed: a red velvet sack filled with jewels. The attached note read, "Millie, here are the goods from the Winthrop heist. Johnny." It was well known in the community that Mildred's boyfriend was a jewel thief named Johnny Lightfingers. Officer Blue also knew that the Winthrop estate had been burglarized three days ago.

Just as Officer Blue finished reading the note, Mildred returned. Officer Blue immediately placed Mildred under arrest as an accessory to the Winthrop burglary. Based on the evidence obtained from Mildred's apartment, a search warrant was issued for Johnny's apartment. The search yielded burglar tools and more jewels from the Winthrop estate. Johnny was immediately arrested and charged with the Winthrop burglary.

At Johnny's trial for the Winthrop burglary, Johnny's attorney files a motion to suppress the evidence consisting of the bag of jewels and note, the tools, and the jewels from Johnny's apartment. The court should:

(A) Grant the motion as to the bag of jewels and note, but deny it as to the evidence found in Johnny's apartment.

(B) Grant the motion, because all of this evidence is fruit of the poisonous tree.

(C) Deny the motion, because the police would have caught Johnny with the goods eventually.

(D) Deny the motion, because the police had a warrant to search Johnny's apartment.

Question 197

Astin left her car at Garrison's Garage to have repair work done. After completing the repairs, Garrison took the car out for a test drive and was involved in an accident that caused damages to Placek.

A statute imposes liability on the owner of an automobile for injuries to a third party that are caused by the negligence of any person driving the automobile with the owner's consent. The statute applies to situations of this kind, even if the owner did not specifically authorize the mechanic to test-drive the car.

Placek sued Astin and Garrison jointly for damages arising from the accident. In that action, Astin cross-claims to recover from Garrison the amount of any payment Astin may be required to make to Placek. The trier of fact has determined that the accident was caused solely by negligent driving on Garrison's part, and that Placek's damages were $100,000.

In this action, the proper outcome will be that:

(A) Placek should have judgment for $50,000 each against Astin and Garrison; Astin should recover nothing from Garrison.

(B) Placek should have judgment for $100,000 against Garrison only.

(C) Placek should have judgment for $100,000 against Astin and Garrison jointly, and Astin should have judgment against Garrison for 50% of any amount collected from Astin by Placek.

(D) Placek should have judgment for $100,000 against Astin and Garrison jointly, and Astin should have judgment against Garrison for any amount collected from Astin by Placek.

GO ON TO THE NEXT PAGE

Questions 198-199 are based on the following fact situation:

Although by all appearances Herb and Edna, an elderly couple, were destitute, they had, in fact, substantial cash in the bank. Their new neighbors, the Smiths, feeling sorry for them on Thanksgiving, bought a month's supply of food and gave it to Herb and Edna. Later, Edna confided in the Smiths that she and Herb had money and told them that, because they had been so kind, she was leaving them money in her will. All of Herb's and Edna's bank accounts were held in joint tenancy. When Edna died, at the Smiths' request Herb gave the Smiths the following signed instrument: "In consideration of my wife's promise to the Smiths, and their agreement not to sue her estate, I agree to pay them the sum of $5,000." When Herb died of a heart attack several days later, the Smiths asked the administrator of his estate to pay them the $5,000. The administrator refused on the ground that there was no consideration for the agreement.

198. Besides the consideration stated in Herb's written instrument, what other fact would strengthen the Smiths' claim?

   (A) They would have never given the food if they had known Herb and Edna had money.

   (B) They believed they could sue Edna's estate.

   (C) The majority of the funds in the bank were left to Edna by her parents.

   (D) Edna's promise to them was in writing.

199. On which of the following theories would it be most likely that the Smiths would recover?

   (A) Herb's written instrument was a binding unilateral contract.

   (B) Herb's acceptance of the food was fraudulent.

   (C) Herb is bound by promissory estoppel.

   (D) Herb and the Smiths entered into a valid compromise.

Question 200

Vincent was engaged in a telephone conversation with Walter. At one point in the conversation, Vincent said to Walter, "There's my doorbell. Hold the line a minute while I go see who it is." Two minutes later Vincent returned to the phone. He told Walter, "Dornbach is here. I'll have to hang up. Talk to you later." The next morning, Vincent's housekeeper found him dead and obviously the victim of foul play. Dornbach was arrested and charged with Vincent's murder.

The prosecution seeks to have Walter testify at Dornbach's trial as to Walter's telephone conversation with Vincent. The prosecution's attempt is met by an objection from the defense.

How should the court rule on Walter's testimony?

   (A) Admissible, as a present sense impression.

   (B) Admissible, as evidence of the victim's state of mind.

   (C) Admissible, as a prior identification.

   (D) Inadmissible, as hearsay not within any recognized exception to the hearsay rule.

STOP

ANSWER KEY AND SUBJECT/TOPIC KEY

	Answer	Subject Matter
1.	C	Criminal Law/Procedure—search and seizure
2.	C	Contracts—specific performance
3.	A	Contracts—assignment and delegation
4.	A	Torts—vicarious liability
5.	A	Torts—duty of owners and occupiers of land
6.	B	Constitutional Law—preemption
7.	B	Constitutional Law—legislative power
8.	B	Evidence—impeachment
9.	A	Criminal Law—attempt/impossibility
10.	B	Constitutional Law—freedom of expression
11.	B	Real Property—landlord-tenant
12.	B	Criminal Law/Procedure—*Miranda* rights
13.	B	Evidence—refreshing recollection
14.	C	Contracts/Sales—buyer's remedies
15.	A	Contracts/Sales—measure of damages
16.	D	Evidence—probative value/impeachment
17.	D	Criminal Law—parties to crime
18.	A	Criminal Law—conspiracy/homicide
19.	D	Torts—proof of fault/products liability
20.	B	Real Property—assignment of leasehold interest
21.	D	Real Property—transfer of leased property
22.	A	Constitutional Law—intergovernmental immunity
23.	A	Evidence—hearsay
24.	A	Torts—duty of owners and occupiers of land
25.	C	Constitutional Law—procedural due process
26.	A	Contracts/Sales—Statute of Frauds
27.	D	Criminal Law/Procedure—warrantless arrest
28.	D	Real Property—equitable servitude
29.	A	Contracts—excuse of condition/anticipatory repudiation
30.	D	Contracts—measure of damages
31.	C	Real Property—delivery of deeds
32.	B	Evidence—hearsay exceptions
33.	A	Constitutional Law—standing
34.	D	Torts—battery/privilege of arrest
35.	B	Torts—intentional infliction of emotional distress
36.	C	Criminal Law—murder/intoxication
37.	B	Criminal Law—murder/intoxication
38.	B	Constitutional Law—legislative powers
39.	A	Evidence—admissions of party-opponent
40.	C	Contracts—consideration/requirements contract
41.	D	Real Property—tenancy in common
42.	B	Constitutional Law—intergovernmental immunities
43.	A	Evidence—attorney-client privilege
44.	D	Real Property—Rule Against Perpetuities
45.	D	Real Property—Rule Against Perpetuities

46.	D	Constitutional Law—Equal Protection Clause
47.	C	Constitutional Law—Establishment Clause
48.	A	Torts—vicarious liability
49.	C	Criminal Law—insanity
50.	B	Torts—defamation
51.	B	Criminal Law/Procedure—double jeopardy
52.	B	Constitutional Law—equal protection
53.	D	Constitutional Law—preemption
54.	B	Evidence—probative value
55.	C	Real Property—marketable title
56.	D	Real Property—priority of mortgages
57.	C	Contracts—conditions
58.	A	Contracts—conditions
59.	C	Torts—duty of owners and occupiers of land
60.	B	Evidence—public records exception to hearsay rule
61.	C	Criminal Law—burglary
62.	D	Evidence—expert testimony
63.	C	Real Property—assignments and subletting
64.	D	Evidence—lay opinions
65.	A	Torts—intentional infliction of emotional distress
66.	D	Constitutional Law—judicial power
67.	B	Constitutional Law—freedom of belief
68.	C	Constitutional Law—freedom of the press
69.	D	Contracts/Sales—offer and acceptance
70.	C	Contracts/Sales—"battle of the forms"
71.	B	Criminal Law—state of mind
72.	C	Torts—contributory negligence
73.	B	Constitutional Law—regulation of voting rights
74.	C	Real Property—equitable conversion
75.	A	Real Property—equitable conversion
76.	D	Evidence—scope of cross-examination
77.	A	Torts—strict products liability
78.	B	Torts—products liability based on negligence
79.	D	Criminal Law—larceny
80.	C	Evidence—hearsay
81.	D	Contracts—third-party beneficiaries
82.	C	Contracts—assignment of rights
83.	A	Contracts—delegation of duties
84.	A	Torts—defamation
85.	C	Real Property—adverse possession
86.	A	Evidence—husband-wife privilege
87.	C	Criminal Law/Procedure—double jeopardy
88.	B	Constitutional Law—separation of powers
89.	B	Evidence—personal knowledge requirement
90.	B	Criminal Law/Procedure—immunized testimony
91.	C	Torts—duty of care
92.	B	Torts—strict products liability
93.	C	Torts—negligence
94.	A	Real Property—equitable servitude
95.	B	Constitutional Law—freedom of expression

96.	B	Contracts/Sales—acceptance
97.	B	Contracts—offer and acceptance
98.	D	Criminal Law/Procedure—exclusionary rule
99.	D	Evidence—character evidence
100.	B	Real Property—marketable title/specific performance
101.	D	Torts—defamation
102.	D	Criminal Law—attempt
103.	B	Contracts/Sales—parol evidence rule
104.	A	Constitutional Law—state regulation of commerce
105.	A	Constitutional Law—Equal Protection Clause
106.	C	Evidence—hearsay rule
107.	D	Real Property—Statute of Frauds
108.	D	Constitutional Law—equal protection
109.	C	Torts—strict liability
110.	C	Evidence—lay opinions
111.	B	Criminal Law—arson
112.	A	Criminal Law—robbery
113.	A	Contracts—implied-in-fact contract
114.	B	Real Property—easements/marketable title
115.	C	Torts—proximate cause
116.	B	Contracts—consideration
117.	D	Contracts—offer and acceptance
118.	C	Contracts—offer and acceptance
119.	D	Constitutional Law—individual rights
120.	A	Evidence—privileged communications/admissions
121.	A	Torts—duty of innkeepers
122.	A	Torts—invasion of privacy
123.	D	Real Property—Rule Against Perpetuities
124.	D	Criminal Law/Procedure—search and seizure
125.	B	Torts—false imprisonment
126.	C	Evidence—impeachment
127.	D	Constitutional Law—executive power
128.	B	Real Property—recording
129.	B	Contracts—mistake
130.	A	Torts—indemnity
131.	C	Criminal Law/Procedure—burden of proof
132.	B	Criminal Law/Procedure—search and seizure
133.	B	Evidence—impeachment/bias
134.	B	Contracts—measure of damages
135.	C	Contracts—consequential damages
136.	B	Contracts—discharge of duties
137.	D	Real Property—covenants for title
138.	A	Constitutional Law—standing
139.	B	Torts—comparative negligence
140.	A	Real Property—marketable title
141.	B	Criminal Law—burglary/impossibility
142.	C	Torts—negligent infliction of emotional distress
143.	B	Evidence—hearsay rule
144.	A	Constitutional Law—fundamental rights
145.	D	Criminal Law—felony murder

146.	C	Criminal Law—parties to crime
147.	D	Evidence—character evidence
148.	B	Real Property—executory interests
149.	D	Torts—defamation
150.	D	Real Property—marketable title
151.	C	Contracts/Sales—buyer's remedies
152.	C	Evidence—prior identification by witness
153.	A	Contracts/Sales—consideration
154.	D	Contracts—impossibility
155.	C	Constitutional Law—procedural due process
156.	C	Criminal Law/Procedure—consent to search
157.	B	Criminal Law—larceny
158.	A	Evidence—authentication
159.	A	Evidence—authentication
160.	C	Constitutional Law—equal protection
161.	D	Real Property—fixtures
162.	B	Torts—misrepresentation
163.	C	Constitutional Law—judicial power
164.	B	Evidence—impeachment
165.	A	Criminal Law/Procedure—search and seizure
166.	C	Contracts—consideration/preexisting duty rule
167.	D	Real Property—conveyancing
168.	B	Evidence—rehabilitation of impeached witness
169.	D	Torts—defamation
170.	A	Torts—intentional infliction of mental distress
171.	B	Torts—battery
172.	B	Criminal Law—manslaughter
173.	C	Constitutional Law—obscenity/overbreadth
174.	C	Evidence—hearsay/admission of party opponent
175.	C	Real Property—transfer of executory interest
176.	A	Contracts/Sales—rejection of nonconforming goods
177.	C	Contracts/Sales—remedies for breach
178.	A	Criminal Law—larceny
179.	B	Evidence—hearsay/relevance
180.	C	Constitutional Law—taxpayer standing/Establishment Clause
181.	D	Torts—causation/joint and several liability
182.	B	Real Property—right of first refusal
183.	A	Evidence—authentication
184.	D	Criminal Law—homicide/malice aforethought
185.	A	Real Property—adverse possession
186.	A	Real Property—fixtures
187.	B	Constitutional Law—separation of powers
188.	C	Real Property—mortgage of joint tenancy
189.	B	Real Property—life estates
190.	B	Criminal Law—kidnapping
191.	A	Evidence—former testimony
192.	D	Constitutional Law—Equal Protection Clause/freedom of speech
193.	A	Torts—proximate cause
194.	D	Real Property—conveyancing/recording
195.	B	Constitutional Law—ballot restrictions

196.	D	Criminal Law/Procedure—search and seizure
197.	D	Torts—indemnity
198.	B	Contracts—consideration
199.	D	Contracts—consideration
200.	A	Evidence—hearsay/present sense impression

MULTISTATE PRACTICE EXAM ANALYTICAL ANSWERS

Answer to Question 1

(C) The court should suppress all of the evidence because it was the fruit of an unlawful arrest. As a general rule, the police must have an arrest warrant to effect an arrest of an individual in his own home. There is no general "emergency" exception to the warrant requirement. While police officers in hot pursuit of a fleeing felon or trying to prevent the destruction of evidence may sometimes make a warrantless search and seizure, the burden is on the government to show that one of those exceptions applies. Here, the police did not arrive at Dennis's house in hot pursuit of Dennis, and there was no indication that Dennis might be destroying the money or other evidence; *i.e.,* there were no circumstances precluding them from keeping the house under surveillance while they obtained a warrant. Hence, the arrest was illegal. Because an arrest constitutes a seizure under the Fourth Amendment, the exclusionary rule applies, and evidence that is the fruit of the unlawful arrest may not be used against the defendant at trial. Here, all of the evidence was seized without a warrant and none of the other exceptions to the warrant requirement are applicable. While the protective sweep that turned up the money and gun probably would have been within the bounds of a search incident to an arrest because the police had reason to believe an armed accomplice was present, the illegality of the arrest makes the search unlawful. Similarly, while the bags of marijuana were discovered in plain view, the police have to be legitimately on the premises for that exception to apply. Thus, (C) is correct; (A), (B), and (D) are incorrect.

Answer to Question 2

(C) Threedee cannot compel Plannah to resume performance. Contracts for personal services are not subject to specific performance notwithstanding the fact that damages might be inadequate or difficult to assess or the services to be performed are unique. The courts reason that specific performance of personal service contracts is tantamount to involuntary servitude and would present enforcement problems. At most, Threedee would be able to obtain an injunction to prevent Plannah from working on another project at the times Plannah agreed to work for Threedee. Thus, (C) is correct and (A) is incorrect. (B) is incorrect because it is irrelevant. Whether specific performance is available at all generally depends on whether the subject matter is unique, but even a contract for unique services cannot be enforced by specific performance. The fact that a party has begun performance is irrelevant. (D) is incorrect because duties involving personal skill and judgment may not be delegated absent consent by the obligee (Threedee). Plannah did not have Threedee's consent and so there was no valid delegation.

Answer to Question 3

(A) Conclusions I. and II. are correct, and III. is incorrect. I. is correct because when contractual duties are delegated, the delegator remains liable on the contract, even if the delegate assumes the duties. The result might be different if the obligee expressly consented to the delegation of duties and released the original obligee (a novation), but that did not happen here. Here, Threedee allowed Drafty to proceed with the design work, but that does not, without more, constitute a novation. II. is also correct. The liability of a delegate turns on whether there has been a mere "delegation" or delegation plus an "assumption of duty." Here the delegate, Drafty, "assumed the duties" by making a promise to perform supported by consideration (*i.e.,* the right to collect Plannah's fees). Thus, the non-delegating party (Threedee) can sue for nonperformance. III. is incorrect because the facts do not describe a "divisible" contract. The rule of divisibility allows a party who has performed one of the units of a divisible contract to claim the agreed upon fee for that unit even though he fails to perform the other units. The three requirements are: (i) performance of each party is divided into two or more parts under the contract; (ii) the number of parts due from each is the same; and (iii) the performance of each part by one party is agreed upon as the corresponding part (quid pro quo) from the other party. [Restatement (Second) of Contracts §266] Here the facts establish none of the three requirements. Hence, Threedee is not indebted to Drafty on this theory. Based on the above, (A) is correct, and (B), (C), and (D) are incorrect.

Answer to Question 4

(A) Demand will be liable if it entrusted its car to Eileen knowing that she had a poor driving record. In the absence of negligence on Demand's part, it will not be liable for Eileen's negligent driving either as Eileen's employer or as the owner of the automobile she was driving. An employer will be vicariously liable for tortious acts committed by its employee only if the tortious acts occur within the scope of the employment relationship. While Eileen was using Demand's car, she was not conducting any business for Demand. Her use of the car to go grocery shopping was a personal errand outside the scope of her employment for which Demand is not vicariously liable. Demand is also not vicariously liable for permitting Eileen to drive its car—the general rule in most jurisdictions is that an automobile owner is not vicariously liable for the tortious conduct of another driving the owner's automobile. However, the owner may be liable for its own negligence in entrusting the car to a particular driver. If Eileen had a poor driving record and Demand was aware of this fact, its furnishing Eileen with a car constituted a breach of its duty to other drivers. This breach was an actual and proximate cause of the damage to Precision's van, making Demand liable to Precision for damages. (B) is incorrect. Even though Billy's violation of the posted speed limit probably constituted contributory negligence, it will not be imputed to Precision. Just as an automobile owner generally would not be vicariously liable for the driver's negligence, a driver's *contributory* negligence will not be imputed to the automobile owner who is suing the other driver. Since there is no indication that Precision was itself negligent in leasing the van to Billy, Billy's conduct in exceeding the speed limit will not prevent Precision from recovering. (C) is incorrect because the fact that Billy had the last opportunity to avoid the accident is irrelevant to Precision's right to recover from Demand. The doctrine of last clear chance does not apply because it is essentially *plaintiff's rebuttal* against the defense of contributory negligence; it would not be raised by Demand as a defense (*i.e.,* if Demand asserted that Billy was contributorily negligent, Precision could rebut by asserting that *Eileen* had the last clear chance to avoid the accident). (D) is wrong because the fact that Eileen was on personal business only establishes that Demand is not vicariously liable in its status as Eileen's employer. It could be liable for its own negligence if it furnished her with a car knowing that she had a poor driving record.

Answer to Question 5

(A) Percy will prevail because the employee of the contractor hired by ValuMart left the level in the aisle. The general rule that a principal will not be vicariously liable for the acts of its independent contractor agent is subject to several broad exceptions, including one for duties that are nondelegable because of public policy considerations. One of these duties is the duty of a business to keep its premises safe for customers. Hence, a business would be liable for the negligence of an employee of an independent contractor to the same extent as for the negligence of its own employee. Here, Cora was employed by Contractor, which was hired by ValuMart. Cora breached the duty owed to business invitees such as Percy by leaving the level projecting out into one of the aisles. Percy was injured as a result, so he will prevail in a suit against ValuMart. (B) is incorrect. As part of the duty owed to business invitees, ValuMart employees have a duty to make reasonable inspections of their premises to discover unsafe conditions (such as if a customer had spilled something slippery in an aisle). However, even if they did not have a reasonable time to discover the level, ValuMart is liable because it is responsible for Cora's conduct. (C) is wrong because, as discussed above, ValuMart is liable under these circumstances for the conduct of its independent contractor's employee. (D) is wrong because ValuMart is liable regardless of the knowledge of its employees.

Answer to Question 6

(B) If the federal legislation does not address the issue of preemption, and a problem is uniquely local, the local government is permitted to enact rules more strict than the federal standards. The Court has made it clear that for preemption, either the federal statute must *expressly* preempt state measures, or its preemptive force must be clear by either "occupying the field" or posing a conflict that makes compliance with both measures impossible. Since the facts do not indicate that the federal measure expressly preempts state regulation, and since neither of the implied preemption conditions are met, (B) is the correct answer and (C) and (D) are incorrect. (A) misstates the facts.

Answer to Question 7

(B) Congress has addressed the problem of racial discrimination primarily under the commerce power, but the Thirteenth Amendment does contain an enabling clause that would authorize this type of statute because it is not limited to governmental action. [*See* Patterson v. McLean Credit Union (1989)] While the Due Process Clause of the Fifth Amendment has been applied to the federal government in the same way that the Equal Protection Clause of the Fourteenth Amendment has been applied to states in racial segregation cases, Watson Janitorial is not a government agency and therefore the Fifth Amendment argument would not be very effective, since it is not the government itself that is being accused of discrimination. Thus, (A) and (C) do not offer the best response, since option I. presents a weak case. (D) is incorrect because option IV. misstates the law: there is no general federal police power.

Answer to Question 8

(B) The letter is admissible as substantive evidence as well as for impeachment purposes. For the purpose of impeaching the credibility of a witness, a party may show that the witness has, on another occasion, made statements that are inconsistent with some material part of his present testimony. This may be done by first cross-examining the witness as to the prior inconsistent statement that he has made. If the witness denies having made the statement or fails to remember it, the making of the statement may be proved by extrinsic evidence. A proper foundation must be laid by giving the witness an opportunity to explain or deny the statement, and it must be relevant to some issue in the case. Here, Wilson has denied on cross-examination that he wrote the letter to Lee. Amp can then impeach Wilson by offering the letter into evidence. Because Wilson has not been released as a witness, he will have an opportunity to explain or deny the statement, and it is relevant to whether any work was done at Short's home. Because prior inconsistent statements are generally hearsay, they often are admissible only for purposes of impeachment. In this case, however, the statement is admissible as substantive evidence because it falls within an exception to the hearsay rule. Under Rule 803(3), a statement of a declarant's then existing state of mind is admissible as a basis for a circumstantial inference that the declarant acted in accordance with his state of mind. [*See also* Mutual Life Insurance Co. v. Hillmon] Wilson's statement that he was going to do electrical work on Short's house is admissible as circumstantial evidence tending to show that he followed through with his plans and did the electrical work, which is what the statement is being offered to establish. In this case, therefore, the letter should be admissible as both substantive and impeachment evidence, making (B) correct and (A) incorrect. (C) is incorrect because the Federal Rules provide that the credibility of a witness may be attacked by any party, including the party calling him. [Fed. R. Evid. 607] (D) is incorrect. The letter is hearsay because it is being offered to prove the truth of the matter asserted—that Wilson was going to do electrical work on Short's house—as a basis for inferring that Wilson did do the work. However, as discussed above, it falls within the "present state of mind" exception to the hearsay rule.

Answer to Question 9

(A) To prove an attempt, the government must establish that the defendant had a specific intent to commit the crime and committed an act beyond mere preparation for the offense. There can be no attempt, however, if there is no crime on the books to cover either the defendant's behavior or his intended behavior. This is known as the doctrine of legal impossibility. In (A), the defendant could not be found guilty of attempting to purchase Valium without a prescription because it was not illegal to purchase Valium without a prescription. In (B), (C), and (D), the defendant could be held for attempt. In each fact situation, the defendant acted with the specific intent to commit the crime. In (B), the death of the intended victim made it impossible to commit the homicide. In (C), the refusal of the garage owner to be deceived made it impossible to commit false pretenses. In (D), the fact that the property no longer had "stolen" status made it impossible to commit the crime of receiving stolen property. The mistake as to the attendant circumstances in (B) and (D) and the inability to complete the crime in (C) all constitute factual impossibility, which is not a defense to attempt.

Answer to Question 10

(B) A regulation will not be upheld if it is overbroad (i.e., if it prohibits substantially more speech than is necessary). If a regulation punishes a substantial amount of protected speech, judged in relation to the regulation's plainly legitimate sweep, the regulation is facially invalid unless a court has limited construction of the regulation so as to remove the threat to constitutionally protected expression. If a criminal law or regulation fails to give persons reasonable notice of what is prohibited, it may violate the Due Process Clause on vagueness grounds. This principle is applied somewhat strictly when First Amendment activity is involved in order to avoid the chilling effect a vague law might have on speech (i.e., if it is unclear what speech is regulated, people might refrain from speech that is permissible for fear that they will be violating the law). The ordinance at issue here is overbroad in banning all street demonstrations of more than 15 people in commercial areas during rush hour. This regulation bans far more speech than is necessary. This regulation is also unduly vague because "rush" hours is apparently not defined in the ordinance. The section of the ordinance referring to certain types of prohibited language is also so vague as to be facially invalid. (A) is incorrect because prior restraints may be imposed on speech in public places if such restraints are granted under narrowly and clearly defined standards. (C) is incorrect because the police have powers to prevent breaches of the peace. (D) is incorrect since the state may interfere with the right of association, where, for example, there is an imminent danger to public health and welfare.

Answer to Question 11

(B) Lentil may begin eviction proceedings at any time. When a tenant continues in possession after the termination of her right to possession, the landlord has two choices of action: he may treat the hold-over tenant as a trespasser and evict her under an unlawful detainer statute, or he may, in his sole discretion, bind the tenant to a new periodic tenancy, in which case the terms and conditions of the expired tenancy apply to the new tenancy. Here, while Lentil accepted the check sent by Truffle, he informed Truffle that he was not electing to bind her to a new tenancy. Lentil may keep the check because he is entitled to rent for the month that Truffle was a hold-over tenant, but at the end of that month he has the right to evict Truffle because no periodic tenancy was created and Truffle's right to possession has terminated. (A) is incorrect because Lentil did not elect to create a periodic tenancy. Furthermore, had he done so, the tenancy would have been a year-to-year tenancy rather than a month-to-month tenancy because it is a commercial lease for more than one year, rather than a residential lease. (C) is incorrect because, as discussed above, Lentil did not elect to create a periodic tenancy when Truffle held over. (D) is incorrect because no tenancy for years is created when a tenant holds over. If the landlord elects to bind the tenant to a new tenancy, it will be a periodic tenancy, regardless of whether the original tenancy was a tenancy for years.

Answer to Question 12

(B) Dirk's motion should be denied because his waiver of his *Miranda* rights was valid. Even though the prosecution must show, by a preponderance of the evidence, that a defendant's waiver of his *Miranda* rights was knowing, voluntary, and intelligent, the suspect need not have been informed of all subjects of an interrogation to effect a valid waiver. The police were not required to tell Dirk of Vera's condition. (A) is incorrect because no error was involved. (C) is incorrect for the reasons described in the analysis of option (A), *i.e.,* the police need not inform the subject of all aspects of the interrogation for the waiver to be considered valid. (D) is incorrect because due process requires only that confessions be voluntary, *i.e.,* not the product of official compulsion. Withholding information about the potential seriousness of the offense does not violate due process.

Answer to Question 13

(B) Showing West the notes is a proper attempt to refresh her recollection. A witness may use any writing or thing for the purpose of refreshing her present recollection. This is known as "present recollection revived." Under most circumstances she may not read from the writing while she actually testifies because the writing is neither authenticated nor in evidence. Here, the writing was shown to her solely to refresh her recollection and is, therefore, proper. (A) is incorrect because it describes "past recollection recorded," which is a hearsay exception [Fed. R. Evid. 803(5)] allowing the writing itself to be introduced into evidence if a proper foundation is laid for its admissibility. Here there is no attempt to enter the notes into evidence. (C) is incorrect because what the attorney is asking to do does not constitute a traditional "leading question," which generally calls for a "yes" or "no" answer or is framed to suggest the desired answer. Furthermore, the ordinary rules on leading questions may be waived when the witness needs help to respond because of loss of memory. (D) is incorrect because aiding a witness's present recollection has nothing to do with bolstering the witness's credibility (which generally may not be done until the witness has been impeached).

Answer to Question 14

(C) I. is correct. Buyer has a contract for 100 wheelbarrows; she is not required to accept anything less. II. is also correct. Buyer can accept if she wants less than the full order and hold Seller responsible for damages. III. is also correct. Under the U.C.C., if a valid contract existed, Buyer can accept the entire shipment and sue Seller for damages. If there had been no prior contract and Seller had attempted to accept by shipment, shipment of the "accommodation" units would be a counteroffer and if Buyer accepted them, she could not sue for damages. However, here there was a prior written contract. Thus, since all the statements are correct, (C) is the correct pick, and (A), (B), and (D) are wrong.

Answer to Question 15

(A) Hardsell can collect his lost profits, *i.e.,* the difference between the contract price ($9,000) and what Hardsell paid to purchase the car from the manufacturer. In a contract for the sale of goods, a seller can collect his lost profits when the buyer breaches if the seller cannot be made whole by a subsequent sale of the item contracted for. This occurs where the seller has an unlimited supply of the goods and demand is limited (*e.g.,* a car dealership), because in such a situation, the seller would have been able to sell to the subsequent purchaser anyway. This is known as a lost volume situation, and in such a situation, the U.C.C. allows the seller to sue for his lost profits. Generally, lost profit is measured by the difference between the cost of goods and the contract price, less the seller's saved expenses. (B) is incorrect because it uses the wrong measure for lost profits. The cost of a similar car in the local wholesale market is irrelevant since Hardsell did not purchase the car on the wholesale market, but rather purchased the car from the manufacturer. Hardsell's actual price will be used to determine his lost profit. (C) is incorrect because although Hardsell resold the car, the resale has not made him whole since he could have sold a car to Karbuff anyway. Thus, the resale does not put Hardsell in as good a position as he would have been had Shift performed (the goal of contract remedies). Thus, Hardsell will be allowed to recover his lost profits, as explained above. (D) is incorrect because contracts of adhesion are not unconscionable per se, and there is nothing in the facts to indicate a degree of unconscionability that would render the contract voidable at buyer's option.

Answer to Question 16

(D)   The trial court should rule Wirth's testimony inadmissible because its probative value is substantially outweighed by the danger that it will confuse the issues and waste time. Where a witness makes a statement not directly relevant to the issues in the case, the rule against impeachment (other than by cross-examination) on a collateral matter applies to bar the opponent from proving the statement untrue either by extrinsic contradictory facts or by a prior inconsistent statement. The purpose of the rule is to avoid the possibility of unfair surprise, confusion of issues, and undue consumption of time. An issue is considered collateral if it would not be admissible other than to contradict the testimony. Evidence that a person has previously filed similar claims is generally inadmissible to show the invalidity of the present claim. At best, this evidence shows the plaintiff's tendency toward litigation. Unless there is evidence that the previous claim was false, the probative value of such evidence is deemed outweighed by the risk of confusion of the issues. Since the prior suit would not be the subject of proof independent of impeachment, it is a collateral matter, and extrinsic evidence, such as Wirth's testimony, is inadmissible. (A) is wrong because the testimony is not proper impeachment and is inadmissible. Furthermore, this choice states the foundational requirement for introducing a prior inconsistent statement. This is not a prior inconsistent statement and, if the testimony were admissible, the opportunity to explain or deny would not be required. (B) is wrong because the failure to object merely meant that Pike's answer to the question was admitted into evidence; it does not change the fact that the matter is collateral. Since it is a collateral matter, extrinsic evidence will not be permitted. (C) is wrong for two reasons. First, the suit is a fact that exists independently of the court record, and thus, the best evidence rule would not apply. Furthermore, as stated above, extrinsic evidence of any kind is not admissible on a collateral matter; Digger is limited to cross-examination for impeachment in these circumstances.

Answer to Question 17

(D)   Jordan is not an accomplice to criminal homicide because intent is required to invoke accomplice liability. To be convicted as an accomplice, a person must have given aid, counsel, or encouragement with the intent that an offense be committed or, in some cases, with knowledge that he was contributing to the commission of a crime. Jordan supplied the apparently benign antibiotic to prevent the possible commission of a crime of homicide rather than to aid or abet the commission of such crime by Hammond. Jordan lacked intent to commit any of the homicide crimes. (A) is incorrect because murder is the unlawful killing of a human being with malice aforethought and

Jordan lacked any of the states of mind required to establish malice. (B) is incorrect because voluntary manslaughter involves a killing after adequate provocation, and "unlawful act" involuntary manslaughter requires a killing in the course of a felony or a malum in se misdemeanor. None of these situations is present here. (C) is incorrect because criminal negligence requires negligence of a greater degree than the "reasonable person" standard for torts. Jordan did not reach this degree of negligence by supplying Hammond with the usually harmless antibiotic.

Answer to Question 18

(A) Hammond is guilty of murder only. Murder requires a killing of a human being with malice aforethought. Hammond planned to kill his wife and proceeded to do so. It is irrelevant that he killed her by injecting her with a drug that is normally harmless rather than with the poison he thought he was injecting. Ignorance or mistake as to a matter of fact will affect criminal guilt only if the defendant did not have the state of mind required for the crime. (B) is incorrect because no legal conspiracy existed. The common law elements of conspiracy are: (i) an agreement between two or more persons, (ii) an intent to enter into an agreement, and (iii) an intent to achieve the objective of the agreement. By this definition, Jordan was not a co-conspirator, and therefore Hammond is not guilty of common law conspiracy because he did not have an agreement with another guilty party. (C) is incorrect because, for reasons given above, Hammond's mistake of fact regarding the substance he was injecting into his wife does not reduce murder to attempted murder. (D) is incorrect for reasons given in the analysis of options (B) and (C).

Answer to Question 19

(D) The decisive question in this case involves establishing causation in a strict products liability action. A cause of action based on strict liability for products requires: (i) strict duty owed by a commercial supplier; (ii) breach of that duty; (iii) actual and proximate cause; and (iv) damages for a prima facie case. Option (D) goes to the question of actual causation (*i.e.,* whether Abco was the cause-in-fact of Crane's injuries), which is an essential element in strict liability cases. The issue here is whether the court will apply an "enterprise liability" theory (which has been done in negligence cases). In these cases, courts use an alternative causes approach, which shifts the burden of proof to each of the several defendants to establish that its negligence was not the actual cause of plaintiff's injury. (A) is incorrect because res ipsa loquitur, which allows the trier of fact to infer a breach of duty on the part of the defendant, is only applicable in negligence cases. (B) is incorrect because in strict liability cases the supplier can be held liable even if it was unaware of the harm the product could cause. (C) is incorrect because FDA approval would not affect Abco's liability in a strict liability action.

Answer to Question 20

(B) Shirts is liable for the total amount on privity of contract grounds, and Shoes is liable for $12,000 on privity of estate grounds. When a leasehold interest is assigned, the assignor and the landlord are no longer in privity of estate; the assignee is now in privity of estate with the landlord. Hence, each is liable to the other on all covenants in the lease that "run with the land." Here, the agreement to pay a maintenance fee for upkeep of the common areas of the mall is a covenant that runs with the land because it burdens the tenant and benefits the landlord with respect to their interests in the property (*i.e.,* it "touches and concerns" the land). Shoes is therefore liable for the maintenance fees for the 12-month term of its tenancy. However, since Shoes was not in privity of estate prior to the assignment, it is not liable for the $3,000 in maintenance fees that Shirts owed; thus, (A) is incorrect. (C) and (D) are incorrect because Shirts continues to be liable for the maintenance fees after the assignment. While the original tenant is no longer in privity of estate with the landlord after assignment, the tenant can still be held liable on its original contractual obligation in the lease, *i.e.*, on privity of contract. This allows the landlord to sue the original tenant where the assignee has disappeared, is judgment-proof, etc. Here, Shirts is liable for the period Shoes occupied the property as well as the period the property was abandoned. Thus, Lightpost has the choice of suing either Shirts (under privity of contract) or Shoes (under privity of estate) for the $12,000 in maintenance fees, as provided in choice (B).

Answer to Question 21

(D) Both Lakeview and Lightpost are liable to Shoes. A landlord's assignment of the rents and reversion interest, such as through a sale of the property, is subject to the same rules as a tenant's assignment of the leasehold interest. The assignee is liable to the tenants for performance of all covenants made by the original landlord in the lease, provided that those covenants touch and concern the land. The burdens of those covenants run with the landlord's estate and become the burdens of the new landlord. The original landlord also remains liable (on privity of contract grounds) on all covenants that he made in the lease. Here, the duty to maintain the parking lot touches and concerns the land because it benefits the tenant and burdens the landlord with respect to their interests in the property. Thus, regardless of who hired the contractor, Lakeview had a duty to ensure that the contractor completed the work, and is liable to Shoes for the costs Shoes incurred to have the work completed. (B) is incorrect because the fact that Lakeview did not contractually assume Lightpost's obligations does not alter its liability to Shoes under privity of estate principles. Had Lakeview contractually assumed the obligations, Shoes could have also proceeded against Lakeview on a contractual basis as a third-party beneficiary of the assumption agreement. Even without the assumption, Lakeview is liable to Shoes on privity of estate grounds. (C) is wrong because the fact that privity of estate between Lightpost and Shoes was severed by the sale does not alter Lightpost's privity of contract obligations. Because Lightpost made a covenant in the lease to maintain the parking lot, he is contractually obligated to fulfill that covenant regardless of the sale of the property to Lakeview. (A) is incorrect because the failure of Shoes to pay rent does not excuse the prior breach of the covenant to maintain the parking lot. As a general rule, covenants in a lease are independent of each other. Thus, if one party breaches a covenant, the other party can recover damages, but must still perform his promises under the lease. Absent application of constructive eviction, an implied warranty of habitability, or some other statutory provision, Shoes may not have had authority to withhold rent despite the breach of the maintenance covenant, and Lakeview may now have the option to terminate the lease as a result. Even if that were the case, however, both landlords would remain liable to Shoes for the damages incurred from the breach of the maintenance agreement while the lease was in force.

Answer to Question 22

(A) The state may impose a tax on the fiberoptic line. A state tax levied directly against the property or operation of the federal government without the consent of Congress is invalid. However, nondiscriminatory, indirect taxes on the federal government or its property are permissible if they do not unreasonably burden the federal government. Because this tax is not levied directly against the government but rather against the provider of a service that the government is obtaining, and is levied on all communications lines in the state, the tax is valid. The fact that the economic burden of the tax will ultimately be borne by the government under the "cost plus" contract does not invalidate the tax. (B) is wrong because the Tenth Amendment provides that powers not delegated to the United States, nor prohibited to the states, are reserved to the states. This limits Congress's power to regulate the states but does not serve as an independent grant of power to the states. Both the federal government and the state government have the power to tax, but the federal law is supreme in this area. (C) is incorrect because not every state tax that burdens the federal government is invalid. A nondiscriminatory tax on a service provided to the federal government by a private entity does not appear to be an unreasonable burden on the operation of the federal government. (D) is wrong because the fact that interstate commerce is involved does not invalidate the tax. Power over commerce is concurrent, belonging to both the states and the federal government. While federal law is supreme in the area of interstate commerce, state legislation that affects interstate commerce is not automatically invalidated.

Answer to Question 23

(A)   The document should be admitted. Related to the exception to the hearsay rule for public records and other official writings, Federal Rule of Evidence 803(10) provides that evidence in the form of a certification or testimony from the custodian of public records that she has diligently searched and failed to find a record is admissible to prove that a matter was not recorded, or, inferentially, that a matter did not occur. Here, David's status as a licensed psychotherapist would normally be revealed in the records of the department. The document here at issue is admissible, under the foregoing hearsay exception, as a means of proving that David is in fact not licensed. (B) is incorrect because this hearsay exception does not require unavailability of the declarant. (C) is incorrect because, as explained above, the statement of absence from public record forms an *exception* to the hearsay rule. (D) is incorrect because a public document that has been signed and certified is self-authenticating under Rule 902; hence, no testimonial sponsorship for the document is required.

Answer to Question 24

(A)   John's status as a trespasser on shopping center property precludes his recovery against the shopping center. This question does not identify the basis for John's action against the shopping center; therefore, you have to consider all of the shopping center's potential grounds for liability. Because Bill's Security Service is an independent contractor, something more than simple vicarious liability is needed to make the shopping center liable for Bill's torts. And because the shopping center did not authorize the use of snakes to guard the stores, it is not liable for an intentional tort, even though the use of poisonous snakes would otherwise be unreasonable force in defense of property. Another potential basis for liability is the shopping center's status as owner or occupier of the property. The general rule is that a landowner owes no duty to a trespasser whose presence is undiscovered to warn of or make safe concealed dangerous conditions or dangerous activities on the land. However, trespassers who are discovered or whom the landowners should anticipate because they habitually and routinely enter the land are owed a higher duty. The landowner will be liable for concealed, dangerous, artificial conditions known to the landowner and negligently conducted active operations, including those of third persons of whom the landowner has the ability and authority to control. Here, John was neither discovered nor anticipated. No one actually noticed him before his injury, and nothing in the facts indicates that people habitually broke into the mall—the mere fact that the shopping center had a security guard is not sufficient to make someone breaking in an anticipated trespasser. Thus, even if the shopping center should have supervised Bill more closely, it owed no duty to John because he was a trespasser. (B) is incorrect because the fact that John was guilty of breaking and entering is irrelevant. Had John been a discovered or anticipated trespasser, the shopping center might be liable to John for, *e.g.*, negligent supervision of the security service, even though John broke into the building. (C) is incorrect because the shopping center did not authorize use of the poisonous snakes. If it had, (C) would be correct because a landowner may only use reasonable force to defend his property, and may not use indirect force that will cause death or serious bodily harm, such as a spring gun or deadly animal, when he could not use such force directly, such as here. (D) is incorrect because it is irrelevant. Undiscovered trespassers need not be warned of the dangers on the land; the landowner owes no duty to them.

Answer to Question 25

(C) Masters's suit will be unsuccessful because he has no right to a hearing here since he has no life, liberty, or property interest at stake. The Due Process Clause requires a hearing only when a life, liberty, or property interest is at stake. Masters clearly is not at risk of losing his life or liberty, and the Supreme Court has made clear that neither is a property interest involved here. To have a property interest in continued government employment, there must be a statute, regulation, contract right, or clear policy that the employee can be dismissed only for cause. Absent such a right to employment, the employee is an at-will employee and may be terminated without a hearing. Here, there was no law, contract, or policy giving Masters a right to a job absent cause for firing him. Therefore, no hearing was required. (A) is incorrect because bills of attainder involve criminal or otherwise punitive measures inflicted without judicial trial. Nothing here indicates that Masters is being punished; rather he is not being retained as an employee. (B) is incorrect because while the Equal Protection Clause prohibits government from discriminating between similarly situated persons unreasonably, where, as here, no fundamental right or suspect or quasi-suspect right is involved, the discriminatory government action will be upheld as long as it is rational. The random hearing policy here could be rational (*e.g.*, it might provide a sufficient sample to ensure that probationary employees are not being terminated for improper reasons); thus, it will be upheld. (D) is incorrect because it is too broad. Not every aspect of state government employment is protected by the Tenth Amendment. [*See, e.g.*, Garcia v. San Antonio Metropolitan Transit Authority (1985)]

Answer to Question 26

(A) Marvin will win because the contract is fully enforceable under the U.C.C. Tubing is a good, and so Article 2 of the U.C.C. applies. The contract is for the sale of goods over $500 (10,000 linear feet at $2/foot); so ordinarily section 2-201 would require a writing. However, section 2-201(3) provides that a writing is not required where the contract is for "specially manufactured" goods not suitable for resale in the ordinary course of the seller's business and the seller has made a substantial beginning of their manufacture or commitments for their procurement. Because the tubing is a custom order of unique specifications and Marvin has begun manufacture, this exception to the U.C.C. Statute of Frauds applies. (B) is incorrect because the contract is fully enforceable. While Marvin is required to mitigate damages, it is entitled to the full range of contract remedies to put it in the position it would have been in had Golde not breached (*i.e.*, benefit of the bargain damages on the entire contract). (C) is incorrect because while it is true that a contract for the sale of goods over $500 must ordinarily be evidenced by a signed writing, the "specially manufactured goods" exception (*see* above) applies here. (D) is incorrect because the parol evidence rule bars admissibility of evidence that varies an integrated writing; here, there is no writing at all.

Answer to Question 27

(D) The court is not likely to agree to suppress the confession for two reasons: Drake probably has no standing to raise a violation of Trent's Fourth Amendment rights, and even if he did, the confession would not be excluded because it was not the fruit of the Fourth Amendment violation. Under the Fourth Amendment, the police generally can arrest, without a warrant, anyone that they have reasonable grounds to believe has committed a felony. There are two exceptions, however, when a warrant is required: Absent exigent circumstances, the Fourth Amendment requires the police to have a warrant to arrest a person in his own home or to search the premises of a third person for an arrestee. Here, the police had probable cause to arrest Drake and the arrest did not occur in Drake's home. Although the arrest did take place in Trent's home and the police did not obtain a warrant to search Trent's home, this will not help Drake because the warrant requirement for a third person's premises is intended to protect the third person's expectation of privacy; while the search may have violated Trent's Fourth Amendment rights, Trent is not being charged with an offense. The Supreme Court has held that a person can have evidence excluded on Fourth Amendment grounds only if that person's Fourth Amendment rights were violated; a person has no standing to raise a violation of another's Fourth Amendment rights. A person has standing to object to the search of a place only if the person has an ownership or possessory interest in the place searched or is an overnight guest in the place searched. Here, the police entered Trent's home, and the facts indicate that Drake was there only to obtain a forged license. Thus, Drake probably has no standing to raise the Fourth Amendment violation. Furthermore, even if he had standing, his confession could still be used against him. While the exclusionary rule generally provides that evidence obtained or derived from exploitation of illegally obtained evidence must be excluded, the Supreme Court has held that where the police have probable cause to arrest a defendant and improperly arrest him in his home without a warrant, a confession made by the defendant at the police station is admissible because it is not the fruit of the unlawful arrest (since the police could have lawfully arrested the defendant the moment he stepped outside of the house). [New York v. Harris (1990)] Here, even if the arrest were unlawful because of the absence of a warrant, the police had probable cause to arrest Drake and so could have waited until he left Trent's house. Hence, the confession at the police station was not a fruit of the unlawful arrest and should not be suppressed. (A) is wrong because, as discussed above, it is unlikely that Drake can establish that the warrantless entry by itself was a violation of his own reasonable expectation of privacy. (B) is incorrect because the absence of an arrest warrant, even if it would have made the arrest unlawful under the circumstances, would not require suppressing the confession. As discussed above, the confession was not the fruit of the unlawful arrest because the police had probable cause to arrest Drake as soon as he left the house. (C) is wrong because it is irrelevant. The fact that a reliable informant gave them Drake's location, even assuming that it would have helped establish probable cause for searching there, does not excuse the requirement that a magistrate make an independent evaluation of probable cause before issuing a warrant.

Answer to Question 28

(D) Nora will be able to enforce the restrictive covenant as an equitable servitude. Zoning regulations and restrictive covenants in private deeds are completely separate concepts. Both must be complied with, and neither provides any excuse for violating the other. Thus, a variance from the government regulation does not prevent enforcement of the private covenant. The court will enforce the covenant as an equitable servitude because Nora is seeking an injunction. An equitable servitude is a covenant that, regardless of whether it runs with the land at law, equity will enforce against the assignees of the burdened land who have notice of the covenant. Here, all of the deeds contained the restrictive covenant. There is no indication that Dampier did not have notice of the restriction, and it is both possible and reasonable for him to comply with the restriction at this stage. Privity of estate is not required because the majority of courts enforce the servitude as an equitable interest in the land itself. Hence, Nora will obtain the injunction. (A) is incorrect because, as noted above, zoning regulations and covenants in deeds are completely separate; thus, the zoning regulation would not take precedence over the covenant. The only time a zoning regulation might prevent enforcement of such a covenant is where enforcement would result in a zoning violation (e.g., covenant calls for single family residential housing only, while the land is zoned strictly commercial). (B) is an incorrect statement of law. Equity will impose a hardship, although it will try to balance the hardships between the parties. Here, the hardship on Dampier is not unreasonable because it is possible for him to build a house that complies with the setback restriction and he has not yet dug the foundation for the house he was planning. (C) is incorrect because nothing in the facts indicates that Dampier will be unjustly enriched by building his home in violation of the covenant; *e.g.,* there is no indication that his home or property will be worth more simply because it has a 30-foot setback rather than a 50-foot setback.

Answer to Question 29

(A) Howser will win because Awl's notice constituted an anticipatory repudiation, which can be treated as an immediate and total breach of contract. If a contract is executory on both sides and one party *unequivocally* notifies the other party that he will not perform when his duty is due, the nonrepudiating party has the option of treating the repudiation as an immediate and total breach and suing for damages. Although the repudiator can retract the repudiation, this must be done before the nonrepudiating party relies on the repudiation. Here, the contract was wholly executory (since neither party had performed) when Awl said that he would not perform at the agreed price. Since Awl's statement was unequivocal, it constitutes an anticipatory repudiation. Thus, Howser was free to find someone to substitute for Awl. Since Howser did find a substitute, he relied on the repudiation and so Awl's attempted revocation was invalid. (B) is incorrect because the difference in price between Awl's demand and Gutter's price is irrelevant. Under the common law, Awl had a contractual duty to perform at the price he agreed to, and his statement that he would not do so constituted an anticipatory repudiation regardless of the price Awl was attempting to obtain. (C) is incorrect because Howser had no duty to inform Awl of the contract with Gutter. The repudiating party is the wrongful party in an anticipatory repudiation situation, and so the law does not impose a duty of notification on the nonrepudiator. If the repudiator suffers harm by his repudiation, it is his own fault. (D) is incorrect because, as stated above, a repudiator can revoke the repudiation only if the non-repudiating party has not relied on the repudiation. Here, Howser had relied (by hiring Gutter). Thus, it is too late for Awl to revoke the repudiation.

Answer to Question 30

(D) Howser can recover $15,000, the difference between Awl's contract price and the contract price of the substitute performance. In construction contract cases where the builder breaches, the proper measure of damages is the difference between the cost of obtaining substitute perfor-mance (*i.e.,* the cost of completion) and the contract price. Here, while Howser actually paid $25,000 more than Awl's contract price to have the house built, he was obligated to pay only $15,000 more since Gutter had a legal duty to build the house for his contract price and no more. Howser will not be able to recover the $10,000 difference because he has a duty to mitigate damages, and paying more than he was actually obligated to pay breaches the duty. (A) and (B) are incorrect because they do not apply the proper measure of damages formula. (C) is incorrect because the "cost of completion" does not include the additional $10,000 Howser gave Gutter to save Gutter from having performed the job at a loss. As explained above, Howser was not re-quired to pay Gutter the $10,000 to complete the house and Howser's paying the extra amount breaches his duty to mitigate damages. Thus, Howser cannot recover the extra $10,000.

Answer to Question 31

(C) Smith owns Whiteacre because a deed to a nonexistent person is void and conveys no title. Because Benjamin was dead when the deed was delivered, the deed passed nothing and was a nullity. Note that Smith will be required to return the $75,000 to Benjamin's estate to avoid unjust enrichment. (A) is wrong because title never passed from Smith. Furthermore, even if it had, it would not have passed even bare legal title to Lenora since she was not a grantee and Smith did not intend to pass title to her. (B) is wrong because Benjamin was killed before the contract was formed. Had he been alive at that time, the contract would have been valid and executory on his death. If a buyer dies after the contract for sale was entered into but before it has been completed, his heirs or devisees can demand a conveyance of the land at the closing. Since Benjamin was dead when the contract was entered into, however, Lenora's agency was no longer valid and there was no contract. (D) is wrong because the term "risk of loss" refers to risk of the property's being destroyed after the contract is signed but before closing. Here, the property was not destroyed. Moreover, there was no valid contract since Benjamin died before the contract was signed. Therefore, the risk of loss is irrelevant.

Answer to Question 32

(B)   The testimony was properly admitted under the excited utterance exception to the hearsay rule. Statements made under the stress of some exciting event and relating to that event are admissible as an exception to the hearsay rule. (A) is incorrect because the Federal Rules require the maker of a dying declaration to be unavailable for the declaration to be admissible. (C) is incorrect; even though the statement bolsters the credibility of Patricia, it still qualifies as an exception to the hearsay rule and is admissible substantive evidence. (D) is incorrect because it is up to the broad discretion of the trial judge under Federal Rule 403 whether to exclude relevant evidence based on needless presentation of cumulative evidence. There is nothing to indicate that admission of the testimony constituted an abuse of discretion.

Answer to Question 33

(A)   The party in choice (A) is the only one which clearly meets the "injury in fact" requirement for standing. The plaintiff should "have such a personal stake in the outcome of the controversy as to ensure the concrete adversariness that sharpens the presentation of issues." The business will be clearly injured if its customer is required to drastically reduce purchases to comply with the State Green statute. In addition, the fact that the proposed plaintiff is not a citizen of State Green indicates the interstate impact of the State Green legislation. (B) is incorrect, because the corporation's sales are not large enough to fall within the ambit of the State Green statute, so no injury in fact has been suffered. (C) is incorrect because the general rule is that a plaintiff must have standing in his own right, he cannot assert the rights of another to obtain standing, and nothing here indicates that the governor has a concrete stake here. (D) is incorrect because the potential plaintiff's claim is far too tenuous. While the corporation whose bonds the potential plaintiff owns will be subject to the law, it is not likely that the potential plaintiff will suffer any injury since he has no interest in the corporation's profitability (a bondholder does not share in a corporation's profits, but is only entitled to repayment, and since the owner's bonds here are secured, his investment is protected no matter what happens to the corporation).

Answer to Question 34

(D)   Bert will win because the officer was not privileged to arrest Bert. A police officer is privileged to make an arrest without a warrant for a felony or for a breach of the peace committed in her presence, but not for a misdemeanor not involving a breach of the peace. If the arrest is privileged, the officer may use only that degree of force necessary to effect the arrest, but never deadly force. Here, Bert's offense of jaywalking was a misdemeanor that did not involve a breach of the peace, so the officer did not have a privilege of arrest and committed a battery by grabbing Bert. (A) is incorrect because the fact that Bert struck the officer after she came at him with a baton would not affect her liability for the initial battery. (B) is incorrect because an ordinary misdemeanor cannot be the basis of an arrest even if it is committed in the presence of the officer; it must also constitute a breach of the peace. (C) is incorrect because it is irrelevant whether Bert will be found guilty of jaywalking—the officer was not privileged to arrest Bert for it.

Answer to Question 35

(B) If the officer was unaware that Ruth was watching, the officer could not have the requisite intent to inflict emotional distress. For intentional infliction of emotional distress based on conduct directed at a third person, recovery is ordinarily limited to plaintiffs who are not only present at the time, but are known by the defendant to be present, so that the mental distress is likely to have been anticipated by the defendant. (A) is not as good an answer, because even if the officer knew the precise relationship between Ruth and Bert, the essential fact of the officer's knowledge of Ruth's presence is not established. (C) and (D) state elements of the tort, but are meaningless without the necessary intent towards Ruth.

Answer to Question 36

(C) The court should instruct the jury that Dunken is not liable for first degree murder if he did not form the intent to commit the crime of burglary, because a defense to the underlying felony precludes a conviction for felony murder. Voluntary intoxication is a defense to specific intent crimes, such as burglary, if it prevents the defendant from formulating the requisite intent. In the absence of Dunken's liability for burglary, he cannot be convicted of first degree murder based on the facts presented here. (A) is incorrect because voluntary intoxication may be a defense to first degree murder under the circumstances here. (B) is an incorrect statement of law; the intoxication must negate a specific intent for the underlying felony for it to serve as a defense. (D) is incorrect; while premeditated murder is a specific intent crime for which voluntary intoxication may be a defense, nothing in the facts suggests that the charge is based on premeditation. Here, the first degree murder charge is based on commission of a burglary.

Answer to Question 37

(B) The most serious crime for which Dunken can be convicted is second degree murder, because voluntary intoxication is not a defense to that crime. Under the statute, second degree murder encompasses all murders committed with "malice aforethought." Voluntary intoxication is not a defense to crimes requiring malice, including murder based on malice aforethought. Malice aforethought includes acting with reckless indifference to an unjustifiably high risk to human life (*i.e.,* an abandoned and malignant heart), and the jury could find that his reckless driving while intoxicated satisfies that standard. (A) is wrong because, regardless of Dunken's intoxication, there is no evidence that Dunken premeditated the victim's killing or was committing one of the enumerated felonies at the time of the victim's death. (C) and (D) are wrong because, while the jury could find Dunken guilty of only involuntary manslaughter based on criminal negligence or unlawful conduct, it could instead find that he was acting with reckless indifference to human life, which would result in a conviction for the more serious offense of second degree murder.

Answer to Question 38

(B) The property power of Article IV, Section 3 of the federal Constitution is directly on point. The Property Clause contains no express limit on Congress's power to dispose of property owned by the United States. Such property includes all species, such as leasehold interests and electrical energy as well as ordinary realty and personalty. Disposal may include direct competition with private enterprise (such as TVA and the High Grasslands hypothetical) and has never been invalidated on that ground. (A) is incorrect because the General Welfare Clause allows Congress to spend for the general welfare, and here Congress is not spending, but disposing of property. (C) is not as good an answer as (B) because it is not direct. The Commerce Clause gives Congress the power to regulate interstate commerce, which encompasses any activity that either in itself or in combination with other activities has a substantial economic effect on, or effect on movement in, interstate commerce. When this power is combined with the Necessary and Proper Clause, it might allow Congress to regulate disposition of federal lands in a specified manner, but the property power is much more direct. (D) is incorrect because the Supremacy Clause merely states that federal law takes precedence over conflicting state law, but no state law is involved here. A private company is suing because the federal government is undercutting the company's price.

Answer to Question 39

(A) The annual is admissible as an adoptive admission of the defendants. Admissions of party opponents are nonhearsay under the Federal Rules (801(d)(2)) and an exception to the hearsay rule under the common law. Furthermore, a party may expressly adopt someone else's statement as his own, thus giving rise to an "adoptive" admission. The manufacturers have done this by referring Peck to the figures in *Insulation Manufacturer's Annual Journal* as accurate in their response to the interrogatory. The defendant is estopped, at trial, from denying their admissibility. (B) is incorrect because the *Journal* does not clearly contain entries made in the ordinary course of business. (C) is incorrect because admissions of party opponents are nonhearsay under the Federal Rules. (D) is incorrect because party admissions waive the authentication requirement.

Answer to Question 40

(C) The agreement between the parties is a type of requirements contract that obligates GM to buy from FGF all of the red cheese that it will sell and obligates FGF to supply GM's needs up to FGF's entire output. GM does not have to buy any FGF red cheese if it acts in good faith. Requirements contracts (a promise by the buyer to buy all of his requirements from the seller, who promises to sell that amount to the buyer) and output contracts (a promise by the seller to sell all of his output to the buyer, who agrees to buy that amount from the seller) are enforceable under section 2-306 of the Uniform Commercial Code. Consideration exists on both sides in these contracts. In a requirements contract, the buyer's consideration is the good faith operation of his business and the promise that he will only buy from the seller; the seller's consideration is the promise to sell at an agreed-upon per unit price whatever the buyer requires. In an output contract, the seller's consideration is the good faith operation of business and the promise to sell the goods only to the buyer, and the buyer's consideration is the promise to buy at an agreed-upon unit price whatever the seller produces. The agreement here is essentially a requirements contract that puts an upper limit on what GM can require—the total output of FGF—and also requires FGF to sell its red cheese only to GM. It is not an output contract because GM is not required to buy all of FGF's output even though it has retained the right to do so. Under the U.C.C., the buyer in a requirements contract is required to conduct his business in good faith and according to commercial standards of fair dealing in the trade so that his requirements will approximate a reasonably foreseeable figure. However, good faith variations from prior requirements are permitted even when the variation may be such as to result in discontinuance. Thus, a shutdown by a requirements buyer for lack of orders may be permissible if the buyer is acting in good faith. [U.C.C. §2-306, comment 2] In this case, then, choice (C) best states the obligations of the parties: GM is not obligated to buy any red cheese from FGF as long as it acts in good faith, but any red cheese it sells must come from FGF.

Answer to Question 41

(D) The court should determine that title to Greenacre is one-half in the heirs of Susan, one-quarter in the heirs of Henry, and one-quarter in the heirs of Audrey. Henry and Audrey held the one-half interest in Greenacre as joint tenants with right of survivorship. Thus, had one of them survived, he or she would own the entire one-half interest. The operation of the simultaneous death statute in the jurisdiction, which disposes of property as if each survived, results in their property being distributed as though they were tenants in common; *i.e.,* one-half of their interest passes through Henry's estate as though he survived and one-half of their interest passes through Audrey's estate as though she survived. Susan always held her one-half interest as a tenant in common, so her one-half interest clearly passes to her heirs without any need to resort to the simultaneous death statute. (A) is wrong because Constance effectively conveyed her entire interest in Greenacre to Audrey, Henry, and Susan, and Constance is not the sole heir of the decedents. No consideration is required for a valid conveyance, and both deeds were properly delivered. Acceptance is presumed. (B) is wrong because it ignores Susan's interest. Henry and Audrey never owned the whole of Greenacre; therefore, they cannot pass the whole of Greenacre to their respective heirs. (C) is wrong because it implies that the one-half interest was not effectively conveyed to Susan. The delivery of the deed to Susan's parent during the time that she was a minor is effective delivery. The fact that the deed was not recorded has no effect on its effectiveness.

Answer to Question 42

(B) The court should find the tax constitutional because it is nondiscriminatory. Nondiscriminatory, indirect taxes on the federal government or its property are permissible if they do not unreasonably burden the federal government. The tax here is a nondiscriminatory "doing business" tax directed at the gross receipts of *all* business conducted within the state, and there is no indication that the tax unreasonably burdens the transaction of business by the federal government. Hence, the fact that the corporation was acting as a federal contractor will not immunize it from liability for the tax. (A) is incorrect because it is too broad. A state's power over purely intrastate commercial transactions is subject to the Due Process Clause and, where the federal government is involved such as here, the Supremacy Clause. However, the tax here does not violate the Supremacy Clause, as (C) states, because it is not targeted at, nor does it unreasonably burden, the federal government. (D) is incorrect because, even if interstate commerce is involved here, the three factors evaluated by a court in determining whether an undue burden exists (substantial nexus, fair apportionment, and fair relationship) do not appear to be lacking in this case.

Answer to Question 43

(A) The subpoena should be upheld because the information about hours billed is not within the privilege. There is no privilege regarding a communication that is relevant to an issue of breach of duty by the lawyer to his client or by the client to her lawyer. Thus, the billing data does not fall within the ambit of the privilege. (B) is incorrect because the information here is not covered by the privilege. Furthermore, if the privilege were applicable, Able would be able to invoke the privilege on behalf of his clients. The lawyer's authority to do this is presumed in the absence of any evidence to the contrary. (C) is a correct statement of law, but the work product rule does not apply to these facts. Documents prepared by the lawyer for his own use *in prosecuting his client's case* are protected by this rule. Time records are not prepared for litigation purposes; they are not related to the substance of the client's case. (D) is incorrect because the other clients are protected by the blacking out of confidential information. Moreover, since the time records are not communications to or from the client and the identity of clients is often not considered to be within the privilege, the billing records of other clients may not be privileged and their consent may not have been necessary even without the deletions.

Answer to Question 44

(D) The grandchildren take nothing because the purported conveyance to them violates the Rule Against Perpetuities. Under the Rule Against Perpetuities, an interest in property is not valid unless it will vest, if at all, not later than 21 years after a life in being at the creation of the interest. The validity of interests under the Rule is determined at the time the interests are created, taking into account the facts then existing. The "lives in being plus 21 years" period begins to run, and the measuring lives used to show the validity of an interest must be in existence, at that time. The problem in this case is that there is an age contingency beyond age 21 in an open class. The perpetuities period begins to run on the date Torgeson conveyed Fruitacre to Fran. After that date, Diana could have additional children, shortly after which the lives in being (she, Fran, Hubert, Dubert, and Luberta) might all die. The additional children's interest would vest when they reach age 25, which is more than 21 years after lives in being. (A) is wrong because the interest violates the Rule Against Perpetuities. Except for the Rule, the grandchildren's interest would be classified as contingent remainder. It is contingent because of the condition precedent of their reaching a certain age before taking an interest. (B) is wrong because, even if the Rule Against Perpetuities had not been violated, the grandchildren's interest would not have been vested because their taking was subject to a condition precedent. (C) is wrong because, even if the Rule Against Perpetuities had not been violated, the grandchildren's interest would be a remainder rather than an executory interest. Their interest follows a life estate and as a rule of thumb, remainders always follow life estates. An executory interest is an interest that divests the interest of another, and under these facts, Fran would not have been divested of her interest; she was entitled to retain the property for the remainder of her life.

Answer to Question 45

(D) The purported contingent remainder to the Sisters of Charity violates the Rule Against Perpetuities and consequently they take nothing. As noted in the above answer, the grandchildren are not certain to reach age 25 (or to die before reaching 25) within 21 years after any life in being. Thus, the interest to the grandchildren violates the Rule Against Perpetuities and, hence, any interest being conveyed subsequent in time, such as that to the Sisters of Charity, will automatically violate the Rule Against Perpetuities. Like any other gift, a gift for charitable purposes is void for remoteness if it is contingent upon the happening of an event that may not occur within the perpetuities period. The only exception to this rule is that if there is a gift to a charity, followed by a gift over to another charity upon a possibly remote event, the gift over is valid. Remember, this is a charity-to-charity exception; the Rule Against Perpetuities still applies to dispositions over from an individual to a charity on a remote condition. In this case, there is a disposition over from an individual to a charity on a remote condition in violation of the Rule. (A) is wrong because the interest is void under the Rule Against Perpetuities. If the Rule did not apply, the Sisters of Charity would have a contingent remainder, and (A) would be correct. The grandchildren would have a contingent remainder and the Sisters' interest is contingent on none of the grandchildren attaining age 25. (B) is incorrect because a vested remainder subject to total divestment arises when: (i) the remainderman is in existence and ascertained, (ii) his interest is not subject to any condition precedent, but (iii) his right to possession and enjoyment is subject to being defeated by the happening of some condition subsequent. The remainder here at all times remains subject to the condition precedent that none of the grandchildren attain age 25 and therefore the remainder can never be vested. Furthermore, there is no condition subsequent that would ever divest the Sisters of Charity of their interest once they acquired such interest. (C) is incorrect because without regard to the Rule, any interest that the Sisters of Charity would ever take would not divest Fran of her life estate. Thus, their interest could not be described as an executory interest.

Answer to Question 46

(D) The strongest argument against the validity of the state action is that state provision of textbooks to this segregated private school violates the Equal Protection Clause by giving state support to a racially segregated educational process. The practice amounts to significant state involvement in these activities. Note that a party challenging the state involvement here would also have to show a discriminatory motive, because the distribution of textbooks to all public and private schools is neutral on its face. (A) is incorrect because it is nonsensical. Providing textbooks necessarily serves a legitimate educational function; and even if it did not, there is no requirement that a state serve such a function in the exercise of its power to tax and spend. For example, denial by the Internal Revenue Service of tax-exempt status to racially discriminatory religious schools does not violate the Constitution since the governmental interest in ending racial discrimination outweighs the burden on these religious schools. (B) is wrong because a state may aid anyone as long as its acts are not constitutionally prohibited. (C) is incorrect because the Constitution does not forbid any private bias; it only forbids discriminatory state action. To the extent that private discrimination is forbidden under various federal civil rights acts, the source of the prohibition is legislative, not constitutional.

Answer to Question 47

(C) If it can be shown that there is neither a religious purpose nor an effect on religion, and that there is not excessive entanglement between government and religion, then the government is not involved in an establishment of religion. The fact that private sectarian schools fulfill an important function (A) would not justify a violation of the Establishment of Religion Clause. That religious instruction in private schools is not objectionable (B) is true—but the issue here is whether the government is involved in the establishment of religion, not whether what is being taught is objectionable or unobjectionable. The Free Exercise Clause (D) does not require identical treatment of public and private schools and, furthermore, the relevant issue here involves the Establishment Clause, not the Free Exercise Clause.

Answer to Question 48

(A) Edgewater probably will be vicariously liable to Parka because Edgar's deviation did not take him outside the scope of the employment relationship. Under the doctrine of respondeat superior, an employer will be vicariously liable for tortious acts committed by its employee if the tortious acts occur within the scope of the employment relationship. What the scope of employment is in a particular case is a question of fact determined by factors such as the specific authorization by the employer, the employee's motivation, and the normal routines of the employee. Ordinarily, an employee heading home after work is no longer within the scope of employment. Here, however, Edgar was required to be "on call" 24 hours a day and was required to drive the company van to his home so that he would be ready to provide emergency service whenever a call would come in. Most likely, then, Edgar was still within the scope of his employment when he was driving the van home. The next issue is whether his deviation from his route home took him outside the scope of his employment. Most courts today consider the foreseeability of the deviation to be the most important factor in determining whether the employee was still within the scope of employment or was on a "frolic" of his own. Thus, minor deviations in time and geographic area from the employer's business are still within the scope of employment because they are foreseeable. Here, Edgar's deviation of a few blocks from his normal route home to pick up some groceries was not a substantial enough departure from his employment purposes so as to be unforeseeable, and therefore Edgewater can be held vicariously liable for Edgar's negligence. (B) is incorrect because Parka can recover even without showing that Edgewater knew of Edgar's potential for negligence. While that might make Edgewater independently liable for its own negligence in allowing Edgar to drive a company van, Edgewater is vicariously liable even without the assumption stated in choice (B). (C) is wrong because, as discussed above, a minor deviation of a few blocks is not considered a "frolic" by most courts unless it is unforeseeable. (D) is incorrect even though it is a true statement as a general rule. While an employee traveling to and from work ordinarily is not acting within the scope of his employment, Edgar was "on call" for his employer under the facts in this question even while he was driving home from work.

Answer to Question 49

(C) The best defense that Smythe's testimony offers is insanity. Under the *M'Naghten* test for insanity, defendant must show that (i) a disease of the mind (ii) caused a defect of reason (iii) such that defendant lacked the ability at the time of his actions to either know the wrongfulness of his actions or understand the nature and quality of his actions. Under the A.L.I./Model Penal Code test for insanity, the defendant is entitled to acquittal if the proof shows that he suffered from a mental disease or defect and as a result lacked substantial capacity to either: (i) appreciate the criminality (wrongfulness) of his conduct; or (ii) conform his conduct to the requirements of law. Smythe's testimony indicates insanity under either test. Smythe's hospitalizations indicate a mental disease and his delusion regarding his wife's basement activities indicates a defect of reason and an inability to appreciate the wrongfulness of his conduct. (A) is incorrect because Smythe intended to kill his wife; hence, the mens rea required for homicide, malice aforethought, is satisfied. (B) is incorrect because Smythe performed the act that killed his wife. (D) is incorrect because Smythe's belief was not a reasonable one and does not, by itself, establish a defense.

Answer to Question 50

(B) Scholastica will lose because Rector can raise consent as a complete defense to her libel action. A defamation action at common law required plaintiff to prove (i) defamatory language on defendant's part that is (ii) "of or concerning" the plaintiff, (iii) publication of the defamatory language to a third person, and (iv) damage to the reputation of the plaintiff. (Because the defamation here does not refer to a public figure or involve a matter of public concern, the elements of falsity and fault do not need to be proved.) In this case, Rector uttered a statement to a third person, Loretta, that linked Scholastica to the sale of drugs; this satisfies the first three elements of the prima facie case. Because the statement was libel (uttered in a writing), general damages will be presumed by law; Scholastica does not need to show actual damages from the statement. Hence, Scholastica can establish a prima facie case for libel against Rector. As with all torts, however, consent, whether express or implied, is a complete defense to a defamation action. Implied consent includes apparent consent, which is consent that a reasonable person would infer from plaintiff's conduct. Here, it was reasonable for Rector to infer that Scholastica's dispatch of her lawyer to request the reasons for her dismissal included a consent for Rector to make defamatory statements to the lawyer as long as they related to the reasons for Scholastica's dismissal. Thus, Scholastica impliedly consented to the statement in the letter and will not prevail in her suit against Rector. (A) is incorrect even though Rector should have verified the statement before repeating it. His defense is that Scholastica impliedly consented to the statement rather than that he did not originate the statement. (C) is incorrect because the fact that Rector did not originate the statement does not provide a defense. One who repeats a defamatory statement will be held liable on the same general basis as the primary publisher even though the repeater states the source or makes it clear that he does not believe the defamation. (D) is incorrect because whether Scholastica was dealing in drugs only affects whether Rector can also raise the defense of truth in this defamation action. Rector will win by raising the defense of consent; the fact that Scholastica was not dealing in drugs does not change this result.

Answer to Question 51

(B) Rose's motion should be denied because a prosecution for conspiracy is distinct from a prosecution for any substantive offense involving the same conduct as the conspiracy. The Fifth Amendment provides that no person shall be twice put in jeopardy for the same offense. The general rule is that two crimes do not constitute the same offense if each crime requires proof of an additional element that the other crime does not require, even though some of the same facts may be necessary to prove both crimes. [Blockburger v. United States (1932)] Furthermore, a prosecution for conspiracy is not barred merely because some of the alleged overt acts of that conspiracy have already been prosecuted. [United States v. Felix (1992)] Here, both the conspiracy charge and the possession charge require proof of an element that the other charge does not; hence, there is no double jeopardy problem with the indictment. (A) is incorrect because it is too broad a statement. The fact that separate statutes are involved does not establish that these are not the "same offense" for purposes of double jeopardy. (C) is incorrect because the "same conduct" test is not currently used by the Supreme Court to evaluate a double jeopardy claim. (D) is incorrect because the question involves defendant's motion to quash an indictment and not her ultimate punishment.

Answer to Question 52

(B) Where a statutory classification is challenged as violating the Equal Protection Clause, one of three tests is used. If the classification relates to exercise of a fundamental right or is based on a suspect trait, a compelling state interest must justify the classification. If a quasi-suspect classification is involved (*i.e.,* one based on gender or legitimacy), the law will be upheld if it is substantially related to an important government interest. In other cases, the classification is valid if there is a rational basis for the classification. This rational basis test is used for classifications that relate to matters of economics or social welfare. The Midland statute does not infringe on a fundamental right, nor is it based on a suspect or quasi-suspect trait. Thus, it is judged under the rational basis test. (C) is incorrect because the compelling state interest test is inapplicable here. (A) is incorrect because the existence of a protected property interest is a consideration more appropriate to a due process argument than to one based on equal protection. (D) is incorrect because, although interstate travel is a fundamental right subject to the compelling state interest test, not every restriction on the right to cross state lines is an impairment of the right to travel. Prohibiting possession of snipe traps would not penalize or unduly burden the right of interstate travel.

Answer to Question 53

(D) A valid federal statute or regulation may expressly or impliedly occupy the entire field regulated, so as to preclude even nonconflicting state or local regulation of the same general subject. Here, the federal rule relates to the subject of consumer product safety, while the Midland statute relates to animal conservation. Thus, even if the federal rule is deemed to occupy the entire field that it regulates, that field differs from the field to which the state statute relates. Consequently, there is no preemption. It follows that (A) is incorrect. (B) is incorrect because the mere absence of affirmative authorization for continued state regulation does not establish preemption. (C) is simply an incorrect statement of the law; it is much too broad.

Answer to Question 54

(B) This videotape, after being properly authenticated, would be considered to be real evidence going to show the intoxicated state of Dryden shortly after he was driving. It would be admitted as relevant because its value would not be substantially outweighed by undue prejudice. (A) is incorrect because the videotape is not being offered to prove the truth of any statements that Dryden made; it is offered to prove only that he was intoxicated. Thus, there is no statement being made that would constitute an admission. (C) is wrong because Dryden is not being asked to give any testimony. Rather, the matter in question is the introduction of real proof. (D) is wrong because a videotape of the defendant at the time in question has nothing to do with specific instances of conduct, which have to do with past actions of the defendant.

Answer to Question 55

(C) The seller of land is obligated to deliver a title that is free from reasonable doubt either in fact or law. This does not require a perfect title, but rather one that is free from questions which might present an unreasonable risk of litigation. Title is marketable if a reasonably prudent buyer will accept it in the exercise of ordinary prudence. An inability to establish a record chain of title will generally render the title unmarketable. If the seller attempts to rely on adverse possession to show that defects have been cleared, courts traditionally do not favor such an argument, because proof of adverse possession normally rests on *oral* evidence, which might not be available to the buyer at a later time. Here, although Simmons may have acquired title by adverse possession, Boyd should not be faced with the prospect of having to prove this in court in the future. Thus, (A) is incorrect. (If Simmons had written proof or a quiet title judgment, title would be marketable.) (D) is incorrect because it does not appear that Simmons's conduct amounted to fraud. (B) is nonsensical.

Answer to Question 56

(D) Susan takes subject to State National Bank's mortgage. A foreclosure sale wipes out all junior mortgages (those that came later in time than the mortgage that was foreclosed) but does not wipe out senior mortgages (those that came earlier). Since State National Bank's mortgage preceded Home Finance's, it is senior and is not wiped out. Susan takes subject to this mortgage. Thus, (B) is wrong. Although Susan is not personally liable on this debt (she did not sign the note, Jane did), she must pay the mortgage or face foreclosure by State National. Since Property Equity Lenders's mortgage came later than Home Finance's, it is junior and is wiped out. Thus, (A) and (C) are wrong. If, after paying the cost of the foreclosure and paying off Home Finance's mortgage, there is money left over from the sale, it will first go to paying off Property Equity Lenders's mortgage. But regardless of whether Property Equity Lenders is paid off or not, Susan takes completely free of this obligation.

Answer to Question 57

(C) (C) is the least correct statement because a condition subsequent is one the occurrence of which cuts off an already existing absolute duty of performance. Beta's tendering of good title would not cut off Alpha's duty to perform. (A) and (B) are wrong because they are not inaccurate statements. A condition precedent is one that must occur before an absolute duty of immediate performance arises in the other party. When conditions are concurrent as they are here (as discussed below), it can be said that each condition is a condition precedent to the other. (D) is wrong because conditions concurrent are those that are capable of occurring together (which describes Alpha and Beta's relationship regarding the exchange of the farm and the apartment house) and the parties are bound to perform at the same time. In effect, each is a condition precedent to the other.

Answer to Question 58

(A) (A) is correct for the following reasons: A condition subsequent is one the occurrence of which cuts off an already existing duty of performance. The *form* of the condition requiring removal of the shed is that of a condition subsequent because, under the language of the contract, failure to do so will cut off Beta's duty to pay the $1,000. A condition precedent is one that must occur before an absolute duty of immediate performance arises in the other party. The *substance* of the shed removal provision is that of a condition precedent because no duty to pay $1,000 arises until *after* Alpha has removed the shed. (B) and (C) are wrong because Beta is not under a duty to pay the $1,000 before Alpha is required to remove the shed. (D) is wrong because removal of the shed is a condition precedent to Beta's duty to pay the $1,000.

Answer to Question 59

(C) A land occupier has an affirmative duty to warn or protect children against dangerous artificial conditions on the land. Thus, the best answer to the question is what Cantebury Trails should have done to best protect the children in this factual situation. (B) is thus easily eliminated, since it has nothing to do with this particular issue; regardless of the neighborhood, Cantebury Trails was aware that children played among the buses. (A) is not the best answer because Cantebury Trails must do what is necessary to protect the children, consistent with the business it is operating on the premises. This answer only goes to one narrow possibility of injury. There are many other ways the children could have been injured playing with these abandoned and wrecked buses. Due care could also have required installation of a higher fence or more diligent patrol of the yard. (D) is also not the best answer because the maintenance of the fence is not in issue; the facts indicate that the children were able to climb the fence without problem. Hence, (C) is the best answer because it states a breach of duty in the broadest terms. Donny would be best able to show a breach of duty by proving that Cantebury Trails could have taken precautionary steps to prevent any injury to children who were tempted to come on the premises.

Answer to Question 60

(B) The record should be admitted because its direct relevance to the ultimate issue of the case outweighs the danger of prejudice against the defendant. (A) is wrong because evidence of this prior conviction would not be admissible as character evidence against Davidson. (C) is wrong because the process leading to conviction is irrelevant. (D) is wrong because an exception to the hearsay rule applies. Federal Rule 803(22) provides that judgments of felony convictions are admissible in both criminal and civil actions to prove any fact essential to the judgment. Felony convictions are those for which the *potential* punishment is imprisonment in excess of one year; hence, the hearsay exception applies here.

Answer to Question 61

(C) Defendant will not be guilty of burglary in situation (C) because he did not have an intent to commit a felony at the time he entered Victor's house. The elements of burglary as defined by the jurisdiction here are (i) a breaking (ii) and entry (iii) of a dwelling or other building (iv) of another (v) at nighttime (vi) with the intent of committing a felony therein. In situation (C),

Defendant entered Victor's house with the intent only to obtain repayment of a debt, which does not satisfy the intent required for larceny. Since Defendant believed he was entitled to take the money as repayment of the debt, he did not intend to permanently deprive Victor of his property. The fact that he later decided to steal the painting will not establish the requisite intent; it must exist at the time of entry for burglary to be established. (A) is wrong because Defendant committed a constructive breaking by gaining entry to the store by means of fraud, and the other elements of burglary are present from the facts. (Note that the fact that he broke *out* of the store after he committed the felony is irrelevant.) (B) is incorrect because Defendant committed an entry of the premises by reaching his hand through the mail slot. Since he had the intent to commit a felony at that point, he has committed a burglary; his withdrawal is irrelevant. (D) is wrong because Defendant made an entry by inserting an inanimate object (the bullet) into the dwelling by breaking (the window) with the intent to commit a felony (since he knew he did not have authority to use deadly force). Hence, he has committed a burglary.

Answer to Question 62

(D) Violet's objection should be overruled because the opportunity for immediate cross-examination protects Violet's rights. Federal Rule 705 provides that a hypothetical question need not be asked. Examining counsel may ask the expert for an opinion and then immediately allow the opposing side to cross-examine, without any disclosure of the data underlying the opinion (unless the trial court requires advance disclosure). It follows that (B) is incorrect. (A) is incorrect because the Federal Rules repudiate the ultimate issue limitation. (C) is simply an incorrect statement of the law—no presumption is created by the qualification of an expert.

Answer to Question 63

(C) Lane, as the beneficiary of the nonassignment clause, could have taken positive action to avoid the transfer, but by accepting rent from Andrews, he waived his right to avoid the transfer. Talbot has no such right to contest the transfer because he was not the beneficiary of the nonassignment clause. (A) is wrong because one co-tenant generally does not need the consent of other co-tenants to assign his interest. Only Lane's consent was necessary under the lease clause. Since Lane waived his right to avoid the transfer, the transfer became valid. (B) is wrong because the right to enforce this lease provision was waived by Lane. (D) is wrong because nonassignment clauses in leases are valid. They are not considered to be void restraints on alienation.

Answer to Question 64

(D) The judge should overrule the objection because lay opinion is permissible (and often essential) to identify handwriting. A foundation must first be laid to establish familiarity with the handwriting. (A) is wrong because expert testimony is not necessary to identify handwriting. (B) is incorrect because only a proper foundation is required for the admission of testimony identifying handwriting. The fact that there are other individuals who may be more familiar with or in more recent contact with the handwriting does not, of itself, preclude admissibility of the teacher's testimony. The fact that the teacher has not seen John's handwriting for 10 years goes to the credibility of her testimony but not to its admissibility. (C) is wrong because expert testimony is not required for handwriting identification and, therefore, the witness need not be qualified as an expert.

Answer to Question 65

(A) Wanda will prevail on a theory of intentional infliction of emotional distress. To establish liability for intentional infliction of emotional distress, the defendants must have intended to cause severe emotional distress (*i.e.,* either acted with the goal of bringing about such distress or knew with substantial certainty that such distress would result from their conduct). It is also sufficient if the defendants acted recklessly, *i.e.,* in deliberate disregard of a high probability that their conduct would cause emotional distress. Here, Grandmaw and Grandpaw caused Wanda to spend four years not knowing where her young son was. Grandmaw and Grandpaw acted in deliberate disregard of the high probability that a mother would be severely distressed by being kept from her child, not knowing whether he was safe or even alive. (A) correctly states the requisite intent for this tort. (B) is incorrect because, as explained above, it is not required that defendant actually know that the conduct would cause severe emotional distress. (C) is incorrect because it is not necessary to prove physical injuries to recover for intentional infliction of emotional distress. (D) is incorrect because the "zone of danger" is more appropriately used in determining liability for *negligent* infliction of emotional distress. Here, Wanda has a cause of action for intentional infliction of emotional distress.

Answer to Question 66

(D) The government will most likely prevail because Fritz had no judicial discretion or powers in his position. Under Article III of the Constitution, a federal judge is protected from termination of tenure during good behavior. This necessarily requires that a person who seeks protection under this provision be able to show that he is a federal "judge." From the facts, Fritz was clearly no more than an administrative hearing officer, without discretion or power. Thus, he would not be a judge within the meaning of this article, and its provisions would not apply to him. Therefore (B) is wrong. (A) is wrong because anybody can recommend that Congress enact or repeal a statute. Just because an executive branch's commission does so, it does not mean that there is a violation of the separation of powers doctrine. (C) is factually incorrect and does not explain the proper reason for the result.

Answer to Question 67

(B) The loyalty oath is valid if it merely requires the candidate to affirm that she will oppose the violent overthrow of the government. The government may require employees and other public officers to take a loyalty oath. Such an oath must not be overbroad, so as to prohibit constitutionally protected activities, nor can it be vague. An oath has been upheld that requires state employees to oppose the overthrow of the government by force, violence, or by an illegal or unconstitutional method. [Cole v. Richardson (1972)] This type of oath (which is virtually the same as that set forth in (B)) was deemed to be similar to an oath requiring the taker simply to commit herself to live by the constitutional processes of our system. (D) is incorrect because, as noted above, a requirement for a loyalty oath as a condition of holding public office or employment is valid, as long as the oath is within constitutionally acceptable limits. (A) is incorrect because it has been held that a loyalty oath that disavows *advocating* the violent overthrow of the government as an abstract doctrine is invalid. The First Amendment prohibits statutes regulating advocacy that are not limited to advocacy of action. [Communist Party v. Whitcomb (1974)] The oath in (A) appears to be overbroad in that it regulates mere advocacy of violent overthrow of the government, rather than regulating only advocacy of action. Therefore, the oath is invalid. (C) is incorrect because only knowing membership in an organization with specific intent to further unlawful aims is unprotected by the First Amendment. [Keyishian v. Board of Regents (1967)] The oath in (C) would in effect punish mere membership in an organization, without showing knowledge of or a specific intent to further any unlawful aims of the organization.

Answer to Question 68

(C) Burro and the paper should prevail. The Constitution prohibits Congress or the states from abridging freedom of the press. While this freedom is no greater than the freedom of speech granted to all citizens, the information printed by the paper here is protected. The media may not be punished for publishing a true fact once it is lawfully obtained from the public records or is otherwise released to the public. It does not matter that the release was inadvertent. Therefore, (C) is correct and (B) is incorrect. [*See* The Florida Star v. B.J.F. (1989)] (A) is partially true—a state might have a compelling interest in protecting the privacy of its citizens—but the state generally cannot protect the interest by prohibiting publication of public information; the most that the state may do is keep such records sealed. (D) is incorrect because it is too broad; freedom of the press is not absolute. For example, the press would not be allowed to reprint copyrighted material regardless of whether it was legally obtained.

Answer to Question 69

(D) An offer must be accepted within a reasonable time. Eureka's reply letter constituted an offer to sell 24 LBVCs for $39.99. Gourmet accepted this offer by a memo plus full performance. If this occurred within a reasonable time, a contract was formed. (A) is incorrect because contracts may be formed by nonmerchants. (B) is incorrect because the contract would have already been formed by Gourmet's acceptance; it is irrelevant whether Eureka has enough stock on hand. (C) is incorrect because Eureka's offer called for prompt acceptance and so did not constitute a firm offer, which must be kept open for a reasonable time, not to exceed three months.

Answer to Question 70

(C) If Eureka's original reply was not an offer, then Gourmet's sending the check and memo would have been an offer and Eureka's shipment of the LBVCs would have been an acceptance. The acceptance would have included terms altering the offer (the no resale provision), but under the U.C.C., between merchants such terms generally become part of the contract. Thus, Gourmet could be held liable for breaching the no resale provision. (A) is wrong because under Article 2, the status of Eureka does not change the result. (B) is wrong because if the invoice by Eureka was a material alteration, Eureka would not prevail. (D) is incorrect because the phrase "not available in stores" is not sufficient to restrict subsequent resale. It merely indicates that the LBVCs were not currently available in stores.

Answer to Question 71

(B) Donna's best defense is that the statute was not reasonably available because she did not receive the explanatory booklet. Generally, it is not a defense to a crime that the defendant was unaware that her acts were prohibited by the criminal law or that she mistakenly believed that her acts were not prohibited. However, the defendant has a defense if the statute proscribing her conduct was not published or made reasonably available prior to the conduct. The statute under which Donna is charged was presumably published prior to her filing her income tax return. However, the statute was exceedingly complicated, as were the computation schedules and other information accompanying the tax forms. Consequently, the failure of the state to include the explanatory booklet with the tax forms may amount to a situation in which the pertinent statute was not made reasonably available to Donna prior to filing her return. If this is the case, then Donna will have a defense. (C) is incorrect. At common law, it was no defense that the defendant relied upon an official interpretation of the law by the public officer or body responsible for its interpretation or administration. Under modern law, it is a defense if the defendant relies upon an erroneous official statement of the law by one charged by law with responsibility for the interpretation, administration, or enforcement of the law. However, even under this rule Donna would not have a strong defense because Michael, as a law student working at the revenue department part-time, is not the type of public officer charged by law with responsibility for interpreting or enforcing the statute, upon whose advice Donna would be entitled to rely. (D) is incorrect because generally it is no defense that a defendant simply relied on the erroneous advice of counsel. An emerging trend provides that if reasonable reliance on the advice of counsel negates the necessary state of mind for the crime, such reliance may be a defense. However, choice (D) focuses on Donna's reliance on Lem's advice rather than her lack of intent, so (B) is the better answer. (A) is incorrect because Donna's mistake as to the scope of the law does not negate the required state of mind. If the mental state for a crime requires a certain belief concerning a collateral aspect of law, ignorance or mistake as to that aspect of law will negate the requisite state of mind. Such a situation involves ignorance of some aspect of the *elements* of the crime rather than the *existence* of the statute making the act criminal. The statute here simply penalizes one who knowingly fails to declare monies received that fall within the statute. Donna knew that she was not declaring certain money that she received; her ignorance that the law applied to those funds does not negate her state of mind and is not a defense.

Answer to Question 72

(C) Sassoon will win if O'Shaunessy acted willfully and wantonly. Because Sassoon was contributorily negligent in making himself appear to be a deer on opening day of deer hunting season, his recovery depends on the effect of his contributory negligence. Without comparative negligence principles, Sassoon's contributory negligence might bar his recovery unless he can show that O'Shaunessy's conduct was willful and wanton, as to which conduct contributory negligence is no defense. Thus, (C) is the correct pick. (A) is wrong because O'Shaunessy's liability is not dependent on intentional tort theories. He can be liable if he acted willfully or wantonly. (B) is not the best answer because even if O'Shaunessy did not have the last clear chance (the doctrine of last clear chance overcomes contributory negligence), he may still be liable if his actions are characterized as willful and wanton. (D) is wrong because, absent the factors discussed above, O'Shaunessy's negligence would be counterbalanced by Sassoon's contributory negligence.

Answer to Question 73

(B) A state may require that those enrolled to vote be bona fide residents of the community. However, any law regulating the right of persons over age 18 to vote must be narrowly tailored to promote a compelling interest. (A) is incorrect because a state *does* have a compelling interest in the integrity of the voting process that will support narrowly tailored restrictions. (C) is incorrect because whether persons have attained the age of majority has nothing to do with their status as bona fide residents. (D) is incorrect because there does not appear to be any discriminatory effect on interstate commerce. (B) is correct because it is the only answer that recognizes that the state may limit ballot access to actual residents, albeit with safeguards against over-inclusiveness; *e.g.,* the state should provide means by which the students can show that they are bona fide residents.

Answer to Question 74

(C) Perry is entitled to the proceeds of the sale because under the doctrine of equitable conversion a deceased seller's interest generally passes as personal property. If the seller dies, "bare" legal title passes to the takers of his real property, but they must give up the title to the buyer when the contract closes. When the purchase price is paid, the money passes as personal property to those who take the seller's personal property (unless the seller **specifically** devises the land in question to a devisee). Thus, Perry, as the personal property devisee, is entitled to the proceeds of the sale. (A) is incorrect as a matter of law. A real estate contract survives the death of either party unless the agreement itself provides otherwise. (B) is wrong because the doctrine of equitable conversion came into play as soon as the contract of sale was signed. (D) is wrong because marketable title is title reasonably free from doubt. Generally, this involves either defects in the chain of title or encumbrances that might present an unreasonable risk of litigation. Such problems are not present in these facts.

Answer to Question 75

(A) Buyer's heir may specifically enforce the agreement. Under the doctrine of equitable conversion and principles applicable in most states, if the buyer dies, the takers of his real property can demand a conveyance of the land at the closing of the contract. (B) is incorrect because the death of either Seller or Buyer does not render the agreement cancellable at the will of either party. (C) is wrong because a real estate contract survives the death of either party unless the agreement itself provides otherwise. (D) is wrong because marketable title is title reasonably free from doubt. Generally, this involves either defects in the chain of title or encumbrances that might present an unreasonable risk of litigation. Such problems are not present in these facts.

Answer to Question 76

(D) By process of elimination: (A) is not the best answer because it cannot be determined whether the eyewitness was under the influence of the exciting event when he spoke to the police, and there are multiple levels of hearsay involved. (B) suffers from the same defects. (C) is wrong because inability to cure an error by jury instruction is not a valid reason for denying a motion to strike. Therefore, (D) must be the best answer—since Dellacourt's counsel was being argumentative, and asked how the witness knew a certain fact, the specific response to counsel's question might be admitted as precisely what counsel asked for.

Answer to Question 77

(A) In a strict liability action, the plaintiff must prove that a product was so defective that it is unreasonably dangerous. The defect causing the harm must have existed when the product left the defendant's control. The defendant must be a commercial supplier of the product in question. Brake failure on a bicycle is an unreasonably dangerous defect. If this defect existed when the bicycle left the factory of Cycle Company, then Roth has a viable cause of action sounding in strict liability against Bike Shop, a supplier in the distributive chain. Thus, (A) is correct. (B) is wrong because it implies **absolute** liability, not **strict** liability; *i.e.,* Bike Shop is not liable simply because the brakes failed. It must be established that the brakes were defective when placed in commerce. (C) is wrong because, in jurisdictions retaining traditional contributory negligence rules, ordinary contributory negligence does not bar recovery in strict liability cases where the plaintiff fails to discover the defect or to take steps to guard against its existence. (D) is wrong because a careful inspection would be relevant to a negligence action, but not to one based on strict liability.

Answer to Question 78

(B) To prevail on a negligence claim, Perez must show negligent conduct by Cycle Company, leading to the supplying of a defective product by the company. (B) is the correct answer because the failure to exercise reasonable care is a major element in a negligence action. (A) is wrong because simply placing a defective bicycle into the stream of commerce would present grounds for a strict liability action, but not one for negligence. Some negligence must be shown. (C) is wrong because privity is not required. The duty of due care is owed to any foreseeable plaintiff. (D) is wrong because any negligence on the part of Roth is reasonably foreseeable and will not relieve Cycle Company of the consequences of its negligence.

Answer to Question 79

(D) Hiker will most likely be found not guilty if the jury believes Hiker's claim. Although the statute does not clearly indicate what state of mind is required, the statute appears to be a larceny-type offense. Larceny requires a specific intent to steal. Therefore, if Hiker honestly believed that the sign was abandoned property, he did not have the intent to steal and so will be found not guilty. (A) and (B) are wrong because a statute that closely resembles a traditional common law offense requiring mens rea is seldom held to be a strict liability offense; rather, it is interpreted to require the mens rea of the common law crime. (C) is incorrect because, even if the state had taken those steps, Hiker would not be guilty if he honestly believed that the sign had been abandoned. A mistake of fact need not be reasonable when offered as a defense to a specific intent crime.

Answer to Question 80

(C) Williams's testimony is hearsay, because it relates to a statement made by the driver, while not testifying at the trial, and it is offered in evidence to prove the truth of the matter asserted; *i.e.,* that the blue convertible was involved in the hit-and-run accident. (B) is incorrect because the fact that the driver's statement came 10 minutes after the accident probably indicates that the statement was not made close enough to the time of receipt of the sense impression to qualify for the present sense impression exception. (A) is incorrect because there is no "recent perception" exception to the hearsay rule. (D) is incorrect because the evidence is very probative and would not be excluded as prejudicial simply because its receipt in evidence would disadvantage the defendant Dorry.

Answer to Question 81

(D) Claret is not an intended beneficiary of the contract between Bouquet and Vintage. Although Claret was mentioned in the contract, it seems clear that Bouquet and Vintage did not intend to confer any benefits or rights on Claret. Rather, the parties seem to have been simply expressing a preference as to the distributor of the wine, with no indication that the validity of the contract depended on use of Claret as the distributor. (A) is incorrect because Vintage was contractually bound to perform only with regard to Bouquet, rather than to Claret. (B) is incorrect because Bouquet and Vintage could not foresee that Claret would act in reliance on a contract that conferred no rights on him. (C) is incorrect because an express agreement between Bouquet and Vintage would not have been necessary to a determination that Claret had some rights under the contract. For example, if Claret stood in such a relationship to Bouquet that one could infer that Bouquet wished to make an agreement for his benefit, then it would be more likely that the contract was primarily for the benefit of Claret. (D) is the best answer because the key factor is that Bouquet and Vintage were simply protecting their own interests, with no thought of conferring a benefit upon Claret.

Answer to Question 82

(C) The only theory under which Amicusbank can recover Bouquet's share of the profits is that Amicusbank is an assignee of Bouquet's rights. (D) would not provide a strong defense for

Vintage, because it is clear that Amicusbank was not an intended beneficiary of the Bouquet-Vintage contract. (A) is incorrect because there is no presumption that an assignment is invalid absent express authorization in the contract. (B) is incorrect because, even if Bouquet and Vintage are partners, Bouquet would still be able to assign his rights to profits. (C) is the best answer, because Amicusbank's only hope of prevailing is for it to be considered an assignee of Bouquet's rights. It appears that the written instrument executed by Bouquet lacks the present words of assignment necessary to manifest the intent of the assignor to transfer his rights under the contract completely and immediately to the assignee. The instrument merely allows Amicusbank to collect the debt from Bouquet's share of the profits. Thus, Vintage has a fairly strong argument that Amicusbank is not an assignee of Bouquet's rights under the Bouquet-Vintage contract.

Answer to Question 83

(A) A contractual duty may not be delegated if performance by the delegate will materially change the obligee's expectancy under the contract. Here, substitution of Agribiz, a company with no experience in the wine-grape business, for Vintage, an established entity in the business, greatly decreases the probable profits which will accrue to Bouquet, the obligee. Thus, a court should rule that the attempted delegation by Vintage of its duty to grow grapes for the venture is invalid. It follows that (C) is incorrect. (B) is incorrect because a delegation can be effective absent a contractual provision authorizing the same. (D) is incorrect because, although Vintage certainly must delegate duties to its individual employees, here it is attempting to delegate duties to an entirely different company, one with no experience or reputation in the industry.

Answer to Question 84

(A) In defamation actions involving a private person plaintiff and a defamatory statement relating to a matter of public concern, the plaintiff must show that the defendant acted, if not with malice, then at least negligently. This principle applies where the defamatory potential of the statement was apparent. Here, Miller is a private person plaintiff. His application for transfer of a liquor license, as the subject of public hearing held by a governmental entity, is a matter of public concern. The defamatory potential of Hammond's accusations of Miller's underworld connections is apparent. Therefore, Hammond must have, at the very least, been negligent for Miller to recover; *i.e.,* no strict liability. (A) reflects this fact. (B) is incorrect because Miller's reputation could have been damaged even if his application were granted. (C) is incorrect because it implies liability without fault, simply because a false statement was made. (D) is incorrect because, even if Hammond's appearance was voluntary, there still must be a showing of fault.

Answer to Question 85

(C) Actual possession of property held in concurrent ownership by one concurrent owner for the statutory adverse possession period will not be sufficient to give that possessor title to the whole estate to the exclusion of his co-tenant, unless there has been an ouster. Here, Arthur occupied Goodacre under unity of possession with Celia. Thus, his possession is not adverse to that of Celia and (A) is incorrect. (D) is incorrect because, had Arthur ousted Celia prior to possessing the land for the required period, he could claim title to all of Goodacre because his possession would have been adverse. (B) is incorrect because the facts do not indicate that Celia intended to renounce her rights in the property.

Answer to Question 86

(A) The choice to testify will be Wanda's. In federal court, one spouse may testify against the other in a criminal case, with or without the consent of the party-spouse. Thus, the witness-spouse may not be compelled to testify, but neither may she be foreclosed from testifying (except as to a confidential communication made between the spouses while they were husband and wife). Here, Wanda is being asked to testify about a meeting in which her husband participated that took place before her marriage to David. Thus, the privilege for confidential marital communications is inapplicable, making (C) incorrect. Of (A), (B), and (D), only (A) reflects the fact that Wanda may not be compelled to testify, nor may she be foreclosed from testifying.

Answer to Question 87

(C)   The motion to dismiss should be denied. For purposes of the Double Jeopardy Clause, two crimes do not constitute the "same offense" if each crime requires proof of an additional element that the other crime does not require, even though some of the same facts may be necessary to prove both crimes. Here, even though the same facts are involved for both crimes, the robbery charge requires proof of a taking by force but not a death, while the murder charge requires proof of a death but not of a taking of property. Thus, (C) is correct and (A) is incorrect. (B) is incorrect because armed robbery is not a lesser included offense of premeditated murder. (D) is incorrect because the prosecution would be estopped if violation of one statute constituted a lesser in-cluded offense of the other statute.

Answer to Question 88

(B)   Under Article I, Section 8, Congress may spend to "provide for the common defense and general welfare," which means, in effect, that spending may be for any public purpose. Furthermore, the Necessary and Proper Clause grants Congress the power to make all laws appropriate for carry-ing into execution any power granted to any branch of the federal government. The power to require that the weapons system be purchased falls within this rubric. Furthermore, the President has no constitutional authority to "impound" (*i.e.,* refuse to spend) funds whose expenditures Congress has expressly mandated. (A) is incorrect as a matter of law. Whether a bill is passed with the President's signature or over his veto is not relevant to the question of whether spending is permissive or mandatory. (C) is incorrect because even though the President's powers do not expressly refer to spending, the President has extensive military powers as commander in chief that could include spending for military necessities in the event of actual hostilities against the United States. (D) is wrong because, in the event of actual hostilities, the President, as com-mander in chief of the armed forces and militia, could exercise his inherent power to allocate funds. There is also some case law implying that the President has some inherent powers, even in internal affairs, to meet national emergency needs.

Answer to Question 89

(B)   Potts can testify as to any first-hand knowledge he has and need not rely on any written records if he presently remembers the facts. First-hand knowledge is considered to be reliable testimony. (A) is wrong because the records themselves are not being introduced. (C) is wrong because the best evidence rule applies only in situations where the content of the writing is in issue. Here, Potts is testifying about facts he perceived; facts that exist apart from the writing. The notebooks merely describe what Potts saw and knows personally. (D) is wrong because no such summary is sought to be introduced, and even if it were, (D) is an incorrect statement of the law.

Answer to Question 90

(B)   Testimony obtained by a promise of immunity is by definition coerced and therefore involuntary. Thus, immunized testimony may not be used for impeachment of the defendant's testimony at trial. Simmons's testimony will not be permitted to be used against Taylor because it resulted from Taylor's immunized testimony. (A) is wrong because it is an inaccurate statement of the law. Prosecutors can bargain away the rights of co-defendants. (C) is wrong because police suspicion is not the equivalent of actual testimony. (D) is wrong. Even though a witness wants to testify, various privileges such as lawyer/client, doctor/patient, etc., may bar the testimony. Here, the grant of immunity to Taylor is a bar to Simmons's derived testimony because use immunity bars use of one's testimony or anything derived from it.

Answer to Question 91

(C) Dino owed to a foreseeable plaintiff a general duty to behave as a reasonable person would under the same or similar circumstances. If, upon noticing that the car was once again pulling to the left when braking, Dino should have been on notice that further operation of the car was dangerous, then he should have had the car towed to the repair shop. Continuing to drive the car with knowledge of an attendant danger would create an unreasonable risk of injury to people such as Pedestrian, and would constitute a breach of Dino's duty of care. However, Dino had no reason to know of the dangerous underlying problem (the defective master cylinder), and he had been assured by Dealer's mechanic that the car was safe to drive. (A) is incorrect because Dino had been assured by Dealer's mechanic that a recurrence of the problem would not result in total brake failure. Thus, Dino had a reasonable belief that he could safely drive the car to Dealer. (B) is incorrect because Dino's duty to maintain his car's brakes does not make him strictly liable for a brake failure. Dino reasonably relied on the advice of Dealer's mechanic in believing that the car was safe to drive. It is true that, as (D) states, Dino had diligently had his brakes repaired, but if he had reason to know, subsequent to the repairs, that the brakes were dangerous, he should not have driven the car. Because Dino reasonably relied on the advice of Dealer's mechanic, Dino had no reason to know of the danger involved in continuing to drive the car. Thus, (C) is a better answer than (D).

Answer to Question 92

(B) To hold Belchfire, a manufacturer, strictly liable for a defect in the car, the car must have reached the consumer without substantial change in the condition in which it was supplied. If the master cylinder was defective when the car left Belchfire's control, then Belchfire has produced a product that is so defective as to be unreasonably dangerous. This defective product actually and proximately caused Pedestrian's personal injuries, and so Belchfire will be liable. (A) is wrong because, unlike (B), it ignores the requirement that the defect be attributable to the manufacturer. (C) is wrong because Pedestrian's strict liability action is based on failure of the master cylinder. The facts do not establish that the mechanic's readjustment of the brakes effected any alteration in the master cylinder. Thus, the work performed on the brakes does not preclude the success of Pedestrian's action against Belchfire. (D) is wrong because a history of brake defects would show that Belchfire should have had notice of the problem. Such notice would be relevant to a negligence action, but not to an action for strict liability.

Answer to Question 93

(C) While inspecting and repairing Dino's car, Dealer's mechanic owed a general duty of due care to Dino and to any other foreseeable plaintiff. If a reasonably competent mechanic would have discovered the defective cylinder while inspecting and repairing the brakes, then Dealer's mechanic breached the duty of due care by failing to discover the defective cylinder. This breach of duty caused injury to Pedestrian, a foreseeable plaintiff. Dealer would be vicariously liable, under the doctrine of respondeat superior, for the negligence of his employee, the mechanic. (C) is correct because it recognizes that Dealer's liability in negligence hinges on whether the mechanic should have discovered the defective master cylinder. (B) is incorrect because it ignores the possibility that the mechanic should not have been expected to discover the defective cylinder while seeking to remedy the problem originally complained of by Dino. (A) is incorrect because merely selling the car with an unreasonably dangerous defect, without knowing or being expected to know of the defect, will not subject Dealer to liability for negligence. The statement in (A) is more appropriate in an action based on strict liability. (D) is incorrect because, absent any reason to believe that Belchfire is not a reputable manufacturer, Dealer is not liable for Belchfire's negligence.

Answer to Question 94

(A) Gaint is seeking to enforce the covenant by means of an equitable remedy. Thus, this question concerns an equitable servitude. An equitable servitude relates to a promise that touches and concerns the land. A covenant touches and concerns the land when it makes the land itself more useful or valuable to the benefited party. Here, an agreement to purchase electrical power only from a specified source probably does not touch and concern the land. (B) is incorrect because a common development scheme is not necessary for an equitable servitude. (C) is incorrect because the covenant here does not restrain alienation. (D) is incorrect because privity of estate is not required for enforcement of an equitable servitude, and in any event, privity is present here.

Answer to Question 95

(B) The Supreme Court has specifically upheld requirements that public employees take an oath to "support the Constitution of the United States" and the state constitution [Connell v. Higgenbotham (1971)] and that state employees take an oath "to oppose the overthrow of the government . . . by force, violence, or by an illegal or unconstitutional method." [Cole v. Richardson (1972)] The Court held that such oaths merely required the takers "to commit themselves to live by the processes of our system." (B) is, therefore, correct because it reflects these Supreme Court precedents involving loyalty oaths. (A) is incorrect because the Supreme Court has moved away from the old privilege vs. right analysis, and, in any case, there is no justification based upon "privilege" that would permit oaths that are overbroad or vague, resulting in a chilling effect on First Amendment activities. (C) is wrong because it is overbroad. States may not infringe on First Amendment rights in employment. (D) is wrong. It is doubtful that a college instructor position would be considered to be a position of governmental trust.

Answer to Question 96

(B) Charlie's use of the Kumquats is an acceptance only if the use was more than reasonably necessary to determine whether they were suitable, since they did not conform to the contract. The U.C.C. gives a buyer the right to reject goods that do not conform to the contract until he has accepted the goods. Acceptance occurs when the buyer: (i) indicates that he will keep the goods, after reasonable inspection, even though they are nonconforming; (ii) fails to reject within a reasonable time after tender or delivery of the goods or fails to seasonably notify the seller of his rejection; or (iii) does an act inconsistent with the seller's ownership. Thus, the buyer is allowed a reasonable time to inspect the goods before accepting or rejecting them. Here, Charlie used the Kumquats for a week and then found them to be unacceptable substitutes for the MBIs that he ordered. If this trial period was reasonable, he did not accept the goods and therefore may reject them. If the period is more than what reasonably would be required to test them, Charlie will be seen as having accepted them and can no longer reject them. (A) is wrong because it does not provide for Charlie's right to reasonably inspect. It is not enough that Charlie simply knew that the Kumquats were nonconforming; he is entitled to inspect them to determine whether he will keep them even though they are not what he ordered. (C) is wrong because even nonconforming goods can be accepted. After reasonable inspection a buyer may decide to keep the goods despite the nonconformity, and this is an acceptance. (D) is wrong because under the U.C.C., if a buyer accepts nonconforming goods, he may still sue for damages. Here, as explained above, it is unclear whether Charlie accepted the Kumquats (he did so only if the week trial period was unreasonable). But even if there was an acceptance, Charlie could still recover damages due to the nonconforming shipment. Thus, he has not waived a claim for damages due to the nondelivery of the three MBIs.

Answer to Question 97

(B) Because the subject matter of the contract became illegal after Flipper's offer but before Arcade's acceptance, the supervening illegality is deemed to revoke the offer. It will be a defense to enforcement of a contract if either the consideration or the subject matter is illegal. If the illegality is present at the time of the offer, there is no valid offer. If the illegality arises after the offer but before acceptance, the illegality operates to revoke the offer. If the illegality arises after formation of a valid contract, it discharges the contract because performance has become impossible. Here, Arcade received Flipper's offer to sell the games on August 5. Generally, an offer not supported by consideration can be revoked at will, even if the offeror has promised not to revoke for a certain period. However, an offer by a merchant to buy or sell goods in a signed writing that, by its terms, gives assurances that it will be held open is not revocable for lack of consideration during the time stated. Flipper is a merchant who deals in goods of the kind being sold. Its offer contained in the letter of August 3 assured Arcade that its terms would be open until September 2. Thus, the offer was not revocable until September 2, and Flipper's purported revocation of August 17 was ineffective. The legislation rendering illegal the sale of the type of machines to be sold by Flipper to Arcade took effect on August 28, two days prior to Arcade's acceptance. Thus, the illegality arose after Flipper's offer and before Arcade's acceptance. Hence, the state law serves to revoke the offer. (C) is incorrect because, as explained above, Flipper's attempted revocation was ineffective. (D) is incorrect because the state law would only create a condition of impossibility of performance if it became effective after formation of a valid contract. Here, the law was effective prior to Arcade's acceptance. (A) is incorrect because if the state law had not been enacted, Flipper would have been bound by the terms of its offer until September 2. The fact that Flipper was able to obtain a higher price for the machines would not permit it to revoke its offer prior to expiration of the specified period.

Answer to Question 98

(D) The entry into Desmond's apartment and his arrest, without a warrant, probable cause, or circumstances permitting an exception from these requirements, were illegal. The statements he made thereafter were fruits of the original illegality and must be suppressed unless the taint was purged. The giving of *Miranda* warnings was not sufficient. Hence, (D) is the best answer. If probable cause for a warrant is based on information from an informer, usually that informer's identity need not be revealed. Thus, (A) is incorrect. (B) is a misstatement of law. There was no interrogation by the police to trigger the *Miranda* requirements. (C) is attractive but not as accurate an answer as (D). If the police had been acting with probable cause to arrest, their forced entry into the apartment would not have made Desmond's statements involuntary.

Answer to Question 99

(D) Don can introduce all of the items of character evidence as part of his defense. The general rule is that evidence of character to prove the conduct of a person in the litigated event is not admissible in a civil case. However, when a person's character itself is one of the issues in the case, character evidence is not only admissible, but in fact is the best method of proving the issue. Where the plaintiff brings a defamation action for injury to reputation and the defendant pleads as an affirmative defense that his statements were true, plaintiff's character is directly at issue in the case. Under the Federal Rules, any of the types of evidence (reputation, opinion, or specific acts) may be used to prove character when character is directly in issue. [Fed. R. Evid. 405(b)] Here, William's character is at issue and Don is offering character evidence to show that his assertion that the mayor is corrupt is a true statement. Item I. is evidence of a specific act that demonstrates the mayor's character for corruption; Item II. is testimony regarding the mayor's general reputation in the state as a corrupt politician; and Item III. is opinion testimony about the mayor's corrupt character. All of these items of evidence are admissible; hence, (D) is the correct choice.

Answer to Question 100

(B) Purr will be entitled to obtain specific performance. If the vendor of land cannot give marketable title but the purchaser wishes to proceed with the transaction, the purchaser can usually obtain specific performance with an abatement of the purchase price in an amount representing the title defect. Here, Kuzz's legitimate claim to 1/10 of the property constituted a defect that would make title unmarketable. The title defect was cured by Purr at a cost of $10,000. Thus, an abatement will be applied to the purchase price. The certified check for $140,000 in choice (B) represents the purchase price ($160,000) less the earnest money already paid ($10,000) less the abatement to obtain marketable title ($10,000), leaving the amount to be tendered as $140,000. (A) is wrong because either the abatement or the earnest money is not taken into account with that figure. (C) is wrong because Purr acted reasonably in clearing the title defect himself. The rule that a buyer must notify a seller of title defects is intended to prevent the buyer from avoiding the closing by raising a title defect problem at the last minute. Here, Purr was trying to facilitate the closing by resolving the title problem himself, which he did. Prior notice to Venn was not necessary in this case. (D) is wrong because the action is based on a contract that was signed before any potential co-tenancy occurred, and there is no rule that precludes a co-tenant from obtaining specific performance from another co-tenant on an otherwise valid contract.

Answer to Question 101

(D) Egbert prevails if he believed the truth of the assertion. Charles is a candidate for public office and, as such, to recover he must establish (i) falsity, and (ii) "actual malice"—*i.e.*, knowledge of falsity or reckless disregard of truth or falsity. Thus, if Egbert honestly believed the truth of his statement, Charles could not show actual malice, and Egbert would prevail. (A) is wrong because it goes to malice in the sense of "ill will." That type of malice is not the standard for defamation; it is irrelevant that defendant wanted to "get even" with Charles. (B) is wrong because a showing of negligence is not sufficient to recover for defamation of a public official or figure; knowledge of falsity or reckless disregard of truth or falsity is required. (C) is wrong because even if the story is a matter of public concern, Charles might still prevail if he can show fault on the part of Egbert—such as Egbert's reckless disregard for whether the statement was true.

Answer to Question 102

(D) Mathews will not be convicted of an attempt to violate the statute if her employee did not have the requisite intent. Although the statute has been interpreted to create a strict liability crime, which does not require proof of criminal intent, to **attempt** a strict liability crime requires proof that the defendant acted with the intent to bring about the proscribed result. Therefore, for Mathews to be charged vicariously with attempt, her employee must have acted with the requisite intent; he must have intended to sell the ammunition to a minor. If he did not so intend, Mathews will not be convicted of attempt. (A) is incorrect because this is a case of factual impossibility, which is not a defense to attempt. (B) is incorrect because careful instructions will not, in and of themselves, absolve an employer from vicarious liability. (C) is incorrect because the strict liability elements of the underlying offense make it clear that knowledge of the age of the purchaser is not an element of the underlying offense. Thus, the clerk (and Mathews) can be liable for selling ammunition to a minor no matter how old the purchaser looked or how old he claimed to be. Duncan's lie may have bearing on the clerk's lack of intent, but this is not as direct an answer as (D).

Answer to Question 103

(B) Where a dispute exists as to the meaning of a written agreement's terms, parol evidence can be received to aid the fact finder in reaching a correct interpretation of the agreement. The Uniform Commercial Code, which governs the contract here, follows the modern approach that permits evidence of interpretation even when the terms are not patently ambiguous. [*See* U.C.C. §2-202, comment 1] Here, the terms may be explained by the previous course of dealing between the parties, because it suggests that the parties understood that specifying "Yellow Giant" in the contract did not mean that a Yellow Giant was being ordered. In addition, the fact that the purchase price for the "Yellow Giant" is $25,000 more than the going price for a Yellow Giant creates enough uncertainty to warrant admission of testimony explaining what the parties meant by the term "Yellow Giant." While Cruncher will have the burden of proving that the term meant something different from what it appears to mean, any evidence it offers will be considered by the trier of fact. (A) is incorrect because reformation is generally available only when a writing incorrectly reflects a valid antecedent agreement, such as where a mistake was made in transcribing the agreement. Here, the writing correctly reflects the antecedent agreement, since the parties agreed to use the words "Yellow Giant"; the problem now lies in determining what was meant by "Yellow Giant." Also, this answer overconfidently states the outcome of the controversy, since Technix may have evidence of its own contradicting Cruncher's. (C) is incorrect on these facts because the president is seeking to explain, not contradict, the terms of the written contract. Before it can be determined that testimony is being offered to contradict the terms of a written agreement, the meaning of the terms must be resolved. Thus, the parol evidence rule does not bar admission of this testimony. (D) is incorrect because the requirements of the Statute of Frauds [U.C.C. §2-201] are satisfied here. The U.C.C. requires only (i) a writing sufficient to indicate that a contract was formed, (ii) a quantity term, and (iii) the signature of the party to be charged. All other terms of the contract, including the meaning of a contract term, can be established by parol evidence without implicating the Statute of Frauds.

Answer to Question 104

(A) The licensing requirement is constitutional. The state may "within the proper purpose of the exercise of its police powers" require licensing of anyone who deals with the public in general, and the Supreme Court has particularly been very liberal when the state is attempting legislation that is remedial in effect to cure a social evil that exists within the state. (B) is incorrect because the designation of the attorney general does not affect the constitutionality. (C) is wrong because this is a permissible burden (if it is one at all). (D) is wrong because there is no indication that the state is treating nonresident garment makers differently than those residing in the state. (Note also that the Interstate Privileges and Immunities Clause does not protect corporations.)

Answer to Question 105

(A) It is unlikely that this provision could survive even the traditional rationality test. There is no apparent rational relationship between the classifications of citizens and noncitizens, and particularly residents and nonresidents, and the proper state purpose of discouraging the hiring of illegal aliens. Furthermore, state alienage classifications are suspect and will be upheld only if necessary to promote a compelling state interest. The classification in this case is not necessary because there are less burdensome means available to accomplish the state's purpose. (B) is wrong because the Fourteenth Amendment Privileges and Immunities Clause is limited to rights arising out of national citizenship. (Note that the durational residence requirement, but not the United States citizenship requirement, may violate the Article IV Privileges and Immunities Clause.) (C) is wrong because the Due Process Clause of the Fifth Amendment applies only to federal government action. (D) is wrong because the Tenth Amendment reserves power to the states; it does not include restrictions on state power.

Answer to Question 106

(C) Either an authenticated copy of the tape or the testimony of the lawyers is admissible. Hearsay is a statement, other than one made by the declarant while testifying at the trial or hearing, offered to prove the truth of the matter asserted. Wandrus is obviously not testifying at the current trial, and his statements are being offered for their truth. Thus, his deposition testimony is hearsay. The next issue is whether it falls within an exception to the hearsay rule. Ordinarily, a now unavailable declarant's statements made in a deposition are admissible under the former testimony exception to the hearsay rule. That rule, however, requires that the statements be made under oath. Since Wandrus was not under oath when he testified, this exception would not apply. When a declarant is unavailable, a statement not specifically covered under the specific hearsay exceptions but having equivalent guarantees of trustworthiness is admissible if: (i) it is offered as evidence of a material fact; (ii) it is more probative of the issue than any other evidence the proponent can procure with reasonable efforts; (iii) the purposes of the rules of evidence and the interests of justice will best be served by admission of the statement; and (iv) the proponent gives the adverse party sufficient notice of his intention to use the statement and the statement's particulars. [Fed. R. Evid. 807—the "catch-all" exception] Here, Wandrus's statements are being offered as evidence of the material fact—the accident. Clearly, since Wandrus was the only neutral eyewitness, his statements are more probative of the issue than any other evidence that can be produced. Because Wandrus was the only neutral eyewitness and because the statement comes with guarantees of trustworthiness (*e.g.,* Wandrus was subject to cross-examination by the parties involved in this trial), the interests of justice would best be served by admission of the testimony. Since both sides agree that Wandrus had no motive to lie, the oath is a less important guarantee of trustworthiness, and the lack of an oath should not affect the admissibility of the statements. Since both parties were present (in the form of their attorneys) when the statements were made and knew that Wandrus was being questioned for the purpose of this suit, the notice requirement was probably satisfied. Therefore, Wandrus's deposition is admissible. Since Wandrus's statements exist independently of the recording, the best evidence rule, which requires that the original "document" be produced to prove its terms, does not apply, and either the authenticated recording *or* the lawyers' testimony would be admissible. Thus (A) and (B) are both true but not as good as (C) because (C) contains both options. (D) is incorrect because, as stated, the tape or the testimony is admissible. (D) would have been the correct choice were it not for the unusual set of circumstances making this declarant's statements extraordinarily useful and trustworthy.

Answer to Question 107

(D) Mark and Martha each own an undivided one-half interest because the Statute of Frauds applies. The Statute of Frauds requires that any transfer of an interest in land be in writing. The right of survivorship Taylor and Scott tried to create by their oral agreement is an interest in land. As such, it must be in writing to be enforceable. Furthermore, to create a joint tenancy with right of survivorship, the unities of time, title, interest, and possession must be present; *i.e.,* a tenancy in common cannot be converted to joint tenancy by agreement. Therefore, Taylor and Scott remained tenants in common at their deaths, with each undivided one-half interest passing through their respective estates. (A) is incorrect because reliance on a mistake of law cannot convert a tenancy in common to a joint tenancy, and for Martha to take the entire interest, Scott would have to have a right of survivorship. (B) is incorrect because, as discussed above, Scott and Taylor's mistake as to the operation of law is an insufficient basis to reform the deed. A joint tenancy is not created without the four unities and the use of the specific language required by the jurisdiction. (C) is incorrect because the deaths of Scott and Taylor resulting from the same accident is irrelevant. The deaths were not simultaneous and it would not have mattered if they were. The share of each tenant in common goes to each tenant's heirs, and death resulting from the same accident or simultaneous death would not entitle the other co-tenant to take as if he or she had survived because a tenancy in common is involved.

Answer to Question 108

(D) The state must demonstrate that the requirement is necessary to advance a compelling state interest. The Equal Protection Clause requires that similarly situated persons not be discriminated against unreasonably. Where a suspect class is involved, it is unreasonable to discriminate unless the government can show that the discrimination is narrowly tailored to achieve a compelling governmental interest. As to state government regulation, alienage is a suspect class. Thus, (D) is correct. (A) is incorrect because it states the wrong test (rational basis). (B) is incorrect because it places the burden on the wrong party (the alien). (C) is incorrect because it states the wrong test (rational basis). This test applies only to laws restricting alien participation in the functioning of the state government.

Answer to Question 109

(C) Tina will not recover because she was a trespasser on Owner's land. The general rule is that one who possesses an animal not customarily domesticated in that area is strictly liable for all harm done by the animal as a result of the harmful or dangerous characteristics of the animal. For trespassers, however, strict liability is not imposed against landowners. Trespassers cannot recover for injuries inflicted by the landowner's wild animals in the absence of negligence, such as where the landowner knows that trespassers are on the land and fails to warn them of the animal. Under this standard, even though Owner could anticipate that trespassers like Tina would cross his property, he will not be liable because he exercised reasonable care by posting a sign warning about the bobcat and by attempting to make the animal less dangerous. (A) is incorrect because, as discussed above, Owner is not strictly liable to Tina, a trespasser. (B) is incorrect because Tina cannot recover regardless of whether she saw the sign. Had strict liability applied, Tina's awareness of the sign may have allowed Owner to raise an assumption of risk defense. With regard to Owner's exercise of reasonable care, however, it does not matter that Tina did not see the sign as long as the sign was noticeable enough that it could have been seen. (D) is wrong because Vet's negligent conduct is the type of foreseeable intervening cause that would not supersede any fault on Owner's part. If Owner were negligent, he could be jointly liable with Vet for Tina's injuries.

Answer to Question 110

(C) The strongest argument for admission of Pullen's testimony concerning the telephone call is that, after hearing Denison speak in chambers, Pullen recognized Denison's voice as that of the person on the telephone. Aural voice identification is not a subject of expert testimony; *i.e.*, lay opinion is sufficient. Familiarity with the voice may be acquired before *or after* the speaking that is the subject of the identification. Thus, the fact that Pullen became familiar with Denison's voice later, in the judge's chambers, does not disqualify the identification. That identification, coupled with Denison's self-identification during the call, is sufficient to authenticate the telephone conversation. (A) and (B) are wrong because they state requirements for identifying the person called, not the caller. (D) is wrong because self-identification of the caller is insufficient evidence of identity; additional evidence of identity, such as the testimony in (C), is required.

Answer to Question 111

(B) Drake can be guilty of arson because his failure to put out the fire that he started establishes the malice necessary for arson. Arson at common law consists of the malicious burning of the dwelling of another. All that malice requires is that defendant have acted with the intent or knowledge that the structure would burn, or with reckless disregard of an obvious risk that the structure would burn. Here, it is not enough that Drake accidentally or negligently caused the fire to start. However, since he was the cause of the fire, he had a duty to take reasonable steps to try to prevent it from spreading. His failure to do anything when the fire was probably small enough to put out would suffice as reckless disregard of an obvious risk that the building would burn, which it did. With regard to the dwelling requirement, most states extend the crime of arson to structures other than dwellings, and questions on the MBE testing on other arson issues will often assume without saying that the jurisdiction's arson law applies to other buildings. The requirement that the building be "of another" pertains to possession rather than ownership. Thus, a landlord could be guilty of arson for burning down his own building if his tenants were in possession of it rather than him; hence, (D) is incorrect. (A) is wrong because the malice requirement is not established by the fact that Drake harbored ill will against Teague, and there is no "felony arson" doctrine comparable to the felony murder doctrine. (C) is wrong because, as discussed above, Drake need not have intended to start the building on fire; all that need be shown is a reckless disregard of an obvious risk that the structure would burn.

Answer to Question 112

(A) Dietz should be found guilty of robbery because his accomplice obtained the wallet by means of force. Robbery consists of (i) a taking (ii) of personal property of another (iii) from the other's person or presence (iv) by force or intimidation (v) with the intent to permanently deprive him of it. Thus, robbery is basically an aggravated form of larceny in which the taking is accomplished by force or threats of force. The force must be used either to gain possession of the property or to retain possession immediately after such possession has been accomplished, but the defendant need not have intended to use force to complete the crime; the only intent required is the intent to permanently deprive the victim of his property. Here, Dietz and Atkins had such an intent, and they were able to carry out that intent in part because Atkins slashed Verner's hand with the knife, incapacitating him. The fact that he did not intend to injure Verner is irrelevant; hence, (C) is wrong. (B) is wrong because Verner's erroneous belief that he was being threatened does not establish the element of threat or intimidation. Dietz's conduct was merely an attempt to distract Verner and did not constitute a threat or intimidation; the fact that Verner's intoxication caused him to believe otherwise does not change that result. (D) is incorrect because the unreasonableness of Verner's belief does not change the fact that Dietz is liable as an accomplice to the robbery by Atkins, since robbery (the use of force) was a foreseeable consequence of the pickpocketing.

Answer to Question 113

(A) David will probably be required to pay Peterson $105 under an implied-in-fact contract. An implied-in-fact contract is a contract formed by manifestations of assent other than oral or written language, *i.e.,* by conduct. Even if there is no subjective "meeting of the minds," the parties will be bound if their conduct objectively appears to manifest a contractual intent. Where an offeree silently takes the benefit of offered services with reasonable opportunity to reject them and reason to know that they were offered with the expectation of compensation, the offeree's inaction may constitute an acceptance. [Rest. 2d Contracts §69(1)(a)] Here, David's silence in the face of Professor Peterson's offer and his conduct in staying within earshot of the group is a sufficient objective manifestation of contractual intent for the court to find an implied-in-fact contract. Hence, a court will probably allow Peterson to recover the contract price. (B) is wrong because it states the wrong rationale. The Statute of Frauds would not be applicable even if the cost of the tour were over $500; the $500 provision of the Statute of Frauds is applicable only to the sale of goods. (C) is incorrect because it states a restitutionary remedy available in a quasi-contract action. A quasi-contract action for restitution is a legal remedy to prevent unjust enrichment where an enforceable contract is not present, and allows the claimant to recover the reasonable value of the benefits that he rendered to the other party. While Peterson probably could pursue a quasi-contract action for restitution because he rendered services with a reasonable expectation of being compensated, he is not limited to that remedy because he can establish an implied-in-fact contract. Hence, he can recover the contract price for the tour without having to establish that it was a reasonable fee for the lectures. (D) is wrong because, as stated above, David's conduct would be sufficient for a court to find the existence of an implied-in-fact contract here, or, at a minimum to grant restitution in a quasi-contract action.

Answer to Question 114

(B) The court could find the title marketable by finding that an implied easement for the benefit of Blackacre was created from the existing use when Blackacre was severed from Whiteacre by the sale. The requirement that the seller provide the buyer with marketable title means that the title must be free from questions that present an unreasonable risk of litigation. A significant encroachment constitutes a title defect, regardless of whether an adjacent landowner is encroaching on the seller's land or vice versa. However, under the circumstances in choice (B), a court will be able to avoid the encroachment problem by implying an easement from the existing use (a quasi-easement). If a use exists on the "servient" part of the tract that is reasonably necessary for the enjoyment of the "dominant" part, and a court determines that the parties intended the use to continue after division of the property, an easement will be implied. Given that title will not be marketable otherwise, the court will deem that the parties intended for the use to continue. (A) is wrong because the fact that the law requires a ramp would not prevent the adjacent property owner from bringing a lawsuit to have the encroachment removed. (C) is incorrect because an encroachment of 10 inches is significant enough to make title unmarketable. Whether an encroachment is significant enough to make title unmarketable is ultimately a question of fact; however, structures that encroach an inch or more over the property line are generally found by the courts to be significant encroachments. (D) is incorrect because the type of deed required by the contract does not establish marketability. Also, the fact that a contract calls for a quitclaim deed, which does not contain any covenants for title, does not eliminate the implied warranty to provide marketable title.

Answer to Question 115

(C) Ned will not recover because Parker did not breach a duty owed to him when he parked the car. This question can be analyzed in terms of either the extent of the duty of care or proximate cause. Where defendant's conduct creates an unreasonable risk of injury to persons in the position of the plaintiff, the general duty of care extends from the defendant to the plaintiff. However, no duty is imposed on a person to take precautions against events that cannot reasonably be foreseen. And in terms of proximate cause, intervening forces that produce unforeseeable results (results not within the increased risk created by defendant's negligence) will be deemed to be unforeseeable and superseding, and thus break the causal connection between the defendant's negligent act and the ultimate injury. Here, Parker's allegedly negligent parking did not increase the risk that Driver would sideswipe his car; Driver's conduct was an unforeseeable intervening force that cuts off Parker's liability for his conduct. (A) is incorrect for two reasons. For breach of a statute to establish negligence per se, plaintiff must show that the statute was designed to prevent the type of harm that occurred, which does not seem to be the case with the fire hydrant ordinance here. Furthermore, proving breach of an applicable statute establishes only duty and breach of duty. Actual and proximate cause must still be established for recovery, and proximate cause is lacking here. (B) is incorrect because the fact that Parker's conduct was a cause in fact of Ned's injury, even assuming that leaving the car there was negligent, does not establish the necessary element of proximate cause. (D) is incorrect because violation of an ordinance may establish negligence per se if the statutory standard is applicable to the situation.

Answer to Question 116

(B) Byer probably will be required to pay $6,000 for all but lot 101. Since the facts stipulate that there was an enforceable contract at $5,000 as to lot 101, there was no consideration for Byer's agreeing to pay more for that lot; hence, that promise is unenforceable. However, as to the other lots, Ohner's telephone call would act as a revocation of the original offer, and a new offer at $6,000; Byer's telegram occurred after revocation of the original offer and therefore was an acceptance of this new offer and bound Byer to pay the raised price.

Answer to Question 117

(D) Byer probably will not succeed because Byer was notified of the sale of the lots to a third party. Notice to an offeree that the offeror has made an inconsistent contract with a third party operates as a revocation of the offer. (A) is incorrect because there was apparently no consideration given by Byer for Ohner's promise to keep the offer open until June 1, and hence it too was revocable. (C) is not as good an answer as (D) because it is the *notice* to the offeree that constitutes the revocation (rather than the inconsistent contract with the third party).

Answer to Question 118

(C) Arguably, Byer's telegram on May 2 could reasonably be interpreted as a rejection of Ohner's offer as to all other lots except 101; *i.e.,* having accepted only 101, he was impliedly rejecting the rest. Once rejected, the offer is terminated and the offeree's power of acceptance is extinguished; thus, the May 6 attempt to accept would be ineffective. None of the other alternatives makes sense. For impossibility of performance in (A) to apply, the impossibility must be "objective"; *i.e.,* the duties could not be performed by anyone. Also, the impossibility must arise *after* the contract has been entered into. (D) is wrong because a condition precedent must be distinguished from a promise. A condition is the occurrence of an event that will create, limit, or extinguish the absolute duty to perform. In this case, it would probably be determined that the intention of the parties was an exchange of promises. (B) is incorrect because a unilateral mistake in most cases will not prevent formation of a contract. Only mutual mistake going to the heart of the bargain may prevent the formation of the contract.

Answer to Question 119

(D) The court will likely find that the statute is a bill of attainder. A bill of attainder is a legislative act that inflicts punishment without a judicial trial on individuals who are designated either by name or in terms of past conduct. Past conduct acts to define who those particular persons are. The prohibition against bills of attainder mandates the use of judicial machinery for trial and punishment of crime as well as the drafting of the definition of criminal conduct in such general terms that it will not single out a particular individual or small group for punishment because of past behavior. In *United States v. Brown* (1965), the Court found that a provision making it a crime for an officer of a labor union to have been a member of the Communist Party was an unconstitutional bill of attainder. Hence, (A) is wrong. (B) is wrong because regardless of whether a rational basis exists for the adoption of the statute, if it constitutes a bill of attainder it cannot be upheld. (C) is incorrect because it is too broad. While the right to join together with other persons for political activity is protected by the First Amendment, infringements on that right may be justified by compelling government interests.

Answer to Question 120

(A) The phone message is admissible because it is an admission by a party-opponent. An admission is a statement made or an act done that amounts to a prior acknowledgment by one of the parties to an action of one of the relevant facts in dispute. The statement may be in writing and need not be against that party's interest at the time it was made. Here, Peters is offering a statement made by Dietrich that is directly relevant to the issue in the lawsuit. The phone message should therefore be ruled admissible. (B) is incorrect. While statements of a declarant's then-existing intent are admissible as an exception to the hearsay rule to allow an inference that the intent was probably carried out, statements of memory or belief are not admissible to prove the truth of the fact remembered or believed. Thus, even if Dietrich left the message shortly after he made the agreement with Peters, it would not be admissible under the state of mind exception to the hearsay rule. (C) is incorrect because the privilege for confidential communications between a husband and wife does not extend to routine communications of a business nature that were not made in confidence. Here, Dietrich gave the message to the switchboard operator to relay to his wife. Thus, the communication was not made in reliance on the intimacy of the marital relationship. (D) is incorrect because the statement is admissible as an admission of a party-opponent, which is not hearsay under the Federal Rules.

Answer to Question 121

(A) Patrick will prevail if Hotel's management breached its duty of care by not improving the locks. Innkeepers have a duty to use a high degree of care to aid or assist their guests and to prevent injury to them from third persons. Included in this duty is the duty to take reasonable precautions against foreseeable criminal acts of third parties. If, as stated in (A), Hotel's management had reason to believe the locks were inadequate, it breached its duty of care to Patrick, and this breach caused his injury. (C) is incorrect because the burglary would be a superseding intervening force only if it was unforeseeable. Also, if Hotel's management had reason to believe the locks were inadequate, it is likely that the burglary and assault will be deemed to be a foreseeable risk of the inadequate locks. (B) is incorrect because the fact that innkeepers owe a high degree of care to their guests does not make them strictly liable for their injuries; some breach of that duty of care must be shown. (D) is incorrect because compliance with the statute is not determinative. The statute sets forth a minimum standard of conduct regarding installation of locks in hotel rooms. Despite compliance with this statute, a careful hotel proprietor would be required to take additional precautions if he was or should have been aware of special circumstances; *e.g.*, a history of prior criminal acts despite use of the statutorily mandated locks.

Answer to Question 122

(A) Patrick is liable for the type of invasion of privacy of intrusion upon plaintiff's private affairs or seclusion. Husband could reasonably expect that what he did in the woman's hotel room would be free from intrusion. Patrick violated Husband's seclusion by listening to the activities in the room. This intrusion would certainly be objectionable to a reasonable person. (D) is wrong because the viability of this cause of action does not depend upon publication by the defendant; the interest protected by this type of invasion of privacy is the plaintiff's right to be let alone, rather than his interest in not having the information disseminated. (B) is wrong because illegality of the defendant's actions is not an element of the prima facie case for this form of invasion of privacy. Even if the eavesdropping is legal, Patrick's conduct would still be an objectionable intrusion upon Husband's private domain. Finally, the fact that Husband may have been engaging in illegal adulterous conduct does not justify a private individual's intrusion on his solitude. (The situation might be different if Patrick were a law enforcement officer acting pursuant to previously obtained judicial authorization.) Thus, (C) is incorrect.

Answer to Question 123

(D) The gifts are valid under the Rule. Hubert's will created a life estate in Waverly, contingent remainders in the class consisting of Hubert's children (contingent upon their attaining age 30), and contingent remainders in the class consisting of any children of Hubert's children (contingent on their surviving their parent, and the parent dying before attaining age 30). There are two keys to understanding the question. The first is that a will speaks at death, no matter when it was executed. Here, Hubert's will became an effective conveyance only when he died in 1990. The second key is that the grandchildren (*i.e.*, the children of Allan, Beth, or Carter) do not themselves have to survive to any particular age to take their gifts. The wording of the question is somewhat confusing on this point, but it is clear when read carefully. Since there are two future interests in the question, each must be analyzed separately under the Rule Against Perpetuities. The gift to Hubert's children is a class gift, and the Rule makes class gifts entirely void unless it is certain that the gift will vest or fail as to all members of the class within the perpetuities period. However, it is clear that this will be true here. The three children (Allan, Beth, and Carter) are all alive when the will speaks in 1990. Hence, they are all lives in being. (If Hubert's wife had been pregnant when Hubert died, that child, when born, would also have been considered a "life in being" as of Hubert's death.) The gift is certain to vest as to each of Hubert's children when each reaches age 30, which is obviously within each's lifetime. Likewise, if one of the children dies before age 30, his interest will fail; again, that is certain to happen within his or her lifetime. Since this is so, the class gift to the children of Hubert is certain to vest or fail as to each member within "lives in being." The gift is therefore valid under the Rule. It is not even necessary to add the 21-year period as permitted by the Rule. As to the class gift to the grandchildren of Hubert, a similar analysis follows. If any grandchild's interest ever becomes vested, it will do so immediately upon the death of that grandchild's parent (Allan, Beth, or Carter) prior to reaching age 30. Since those three persons are "lives in being" at Hubert's death, the grandchildren's interests are certain to vest or fail in every case at the end of a life in being. Again, it is not necessary to add the 21-year period as permitted by the Rule. (A) is wrong because the time of execution of the will is irrelevant; it is the date of the testator's death that commences the running of the perpetuities period. (B) is wrong for the same reason. (C) is wrong for the reasons discussed above.

Answer to Question 124

(D) To have a Fourth Amendment right, a defendant must have a reasonable expectation of privacy in the object seized. A person does not have such an expectation in objects held out to the public, such as account records held by a bank. Thus, (D) is correct. (A) is incorrect because a search warrant is not required where the defendant does not have a Fourth Amendment right. (B) is incorrect because Downs did not have a Fourth Amendment right in the records. Also, the period covered by the records was not necessarily overextensive. It could be that Downs was suspected of being involved in bribery for the preceding two years. (C) is incorrect because, even if the facts here presented describe an exigent situation, such a situation is actually an exception to the warrant requirement; and, like the warrant requirement, will not arise unless and until the defendant has a Fourth Amendment right.

Answer to Question 125

(B) Jason will be liable for false imprisonment because he deprived Mark of access to the person that the court had determined should be his primary caretaker. This fairly difficult question is testing your knowledge of the issue of awareness in a false imprisonment action. A prima facie case for false imprisonment consists of: (i) an act or omission to act by defendant that confines or restrains plaintiff; (ii) intent on the part of defendant to confine; and (iii) causation. Under the general rule, confinement is not present unless the plaintiff is aware of the confinement at the time. However, most courts recognize an exception to the awareness requirement if the plaintiff is actually injured by the confinement. Here, there is no indication that Mark was aware of any confinement. However, even though Mark enjoyed living on the farm, he has been deprived of his mother's custody and care for two years during a time in which the divorce court had decided that his best interests would be served by having his mother as the primary custodial parent. Even though Mark was not physically harmed, Mary would have little difficulty establishing that Mark's lengthy separation from his mother during his formative years constituted harm to Mark. [*See* Restatement (Second) of Torts, §42, illus. 4] (A) is wrong because it implies that a person with legal custody cannot be liable for false imprisonment. An intentional confinement of a child by his legal custodian could constitute false imprisonment if the other requirements for the tort are met. (C) is wrong because the fact that Mark was not aware of his confinement will not prevent recovery for false imprisonment if he was harmed by the confinement. (D) is wrong because the fact that Mark enjoyed living on the farm does not establish that he was not harmed by the confinement. As discussed above, the deprivation of contact with his mother for two years constituted harm to Mark.

Answer to Question 126

(C) Crane's testimony is not admissible because Drake's statement that he told Crane that he acted in self-defense is extrinsic evidence on a collateral matter. A witness's statement on a collateral matter may be impeached only by cross-examination. A collateral matter is one that is not directly relevant to the issues in the case. Here, Officer Crane's testimony is being offered to disprove Drake's claim that he told the officer that he acted in self-defense, which Drake related just to bolster his self-defense claim. While the *circumstances* of Drake's altercation itself are relevant to a self-defense claim and could be the proper subject of testimony, his *statement* to Officer Crane is just an assertion of his innocence and is not directly relevant to whether his self-defense claim was proper. (The prosecution could have objected to Drake's statement as irrelevant, and could have challenged it on cross-examination, but it cannot impeach the statement with extrinsic evidence.) (A) is incorrect because for silence to be an admission, the party must have remained silent when faced with an accusatory statement. Here, Drake was not confronted with an accusatory statement at his arrest. (B) is incorrect because, as discussed above, the testimony constitutes impeachment by extrinsic evidence on a collateral matter. While it may cast doubt on Drake's overall credibility, it is not directly relevant to the issue of self-defense in the case. (D) is incorrect. The Fifth Amendment privilege against self-incrimination would prevent the prosecution from using Drake's silence for substantive purposes as an admission. Here, however, Drake's silence is not being offered as an admission, but only for the limited purpose of impeaching his claim that he made a statement to Officer Crane.

Answer to Question 127

(D) The Secretary must distribute $100 million, because the President's executive order constitutes an attempted exercise of legislative power. Although the Supreme Court has not fully resolved the scope of the President's power over internal affairs, it has held that the President has no power to refuse to spend appropriated funds when Congress has expressly mandated that they be spent. Congress has the power to spend money for the general welfare under Article I, and the President's action here infringes on that power. It follows that (A) and (B) are incorrect. (C) is incorrect because, although it presupposes a less drastic spending cut than (A) or (B), the President may not unilaterally impose even a cut of 10% when Congress has clearly required the spending of the full amount.

Answer to Question 128

(B) The outcome will turn on the definition of "value," because Crider, having received his deed after Price, is the junior claimant. His recordation prior to Price will protect Crider's right to Blackacre only if Crider took the deed in good faith and for value. Here, Owen apparently gave the deed to Crider in exchange for a release from the antecedent debt. If the jurisdiction in question considers this "value," Crider will benefit from the recording act because he is a subsequent bona fide purchaser for value, the very person the recording acts seek to protect. (A) is wrong because the form of deed has no effect on bona fide purchaser status. A quitclaim deed merely means the seller is not making any warranties of title. (C) is wrong because whether Price paid value is irrelevant. Price is not the subsequent purchaser. The recording act protects subsequent purchasers, so Price's interest depends on whether Crider benefits from the protection of the act. (D) is wrong because Price's title is good as against anyone except a subsequent bona fide purchaser for value. Thus, unless Crider is shown to qualify for the protection of the recording act, Price's title is good. There is no estoppel component to the recording acts.

Answer to Question 129

(B) The scenario in (B) provides the best defense because it would enable Green to rescind based on unilateral mistake. Rescission of a contract is available when one party is mistaken about material facts relating to a contract, the mistake adversely affects that party, and the other party knows of the mistake. (A) is wrong because in this case it is the nonmistaken party who is adversely affected. (Note that under choices (A) and (B) it is unclear whether Brown's claim is based on a contract. If it is, the promissory note will be treated as a modification. The modification could be rescinded as discussed above, but there also is an issue of whether there was valid consideration for the modification under the preexisting duty rule. (B) is still the best answer. Under the preexisting legal duty rule, past consideration is valid consideration if there is an honest dispute as to duty owed. There would be no honest dispute under (B) because the nonmistaken party is taking advantage of the mistaken party, but this is not true in (A).) (C) is wrong. The Statute of Frauds is not a problem here because Brown is seeking to enforce the promissory note—which complies with the Statute of Frauds—and not the original agreement. Neither does the preexisting legal duty rule negate the consideration here since there is an exception to the rule for reaffirmations of voidable promises (*e.g.*, promises unenforceable under the Statute of Frauds, promises by infants, promises based on fraud, etc.). (D) is wrong because the statute of limitations would run anew on the note that Brown is trying to enforce, and there is no preexisting legal duty consideration problem because of the exception to the rule for "technical defense bars"—a new promise to pay a legal obligation barred by a technical defense (such as the statute of limitations) is enforceable according to the terms of the new promise.

Answer to Question 130

(A) Generally, a joint tortfeasor may recover indemnification from another joint tortfeasor where there is a considerable difference in the degree of fault. Here, Ellis, the person whose improper design actually caused Carla's injuries, is a "more wrongful" tortfeasor than Toyco. Thus, Toyco should prevail in its claim against Ellis, which result is reflected in (A). (B) is incorrect because indemnity is not available simply because Toyco and Ellis are joint tortfeasors. (C) is incorrect because Toyco's liability to Carla does not preclude it from obtaining indemnity from Ellis. (D) is incorrect because, even if Toyco was negligent in failing to discover the defect, it may still be entitled to indemnity from the person who negligently designed the game.

Answer to Question 131

(C) The Due Process Clause has been interpreted to require the prosecution to prove each element of the crime charged beyond a reasonable doubt. The "malice aforethought" element of murder has traditionally been defined as encompassing the absence of provocation engendering a passion. Putting the burden of persuasion as to the existence of provocation and passion on the defendant relieves the prosecution of its burden as to their absence. Therefore, (C) is the best answer and (A) is incorrect on the facts. (B) is incorrect because the presumption of "malice aforethought" is not a legitimate presumption. (D) is incorrect as a matter of law. Presumptions are permitted as long as they are not mandatory for the jury.

Answer to Question 132

(B) Tommy had a reasonable expectation of privacy, as evidenced by the obscuring of the window so that passersby could not see into the shop. Hence, the officer's search would have to be based on a valid warrant or qualify under one of the exceptions to the warrant requirement. Climbing on the trash cans and peering through a narrow opening eight feet above the pavement would be considered a violation of Tommy's Fourth Amendment rights and not a "plain view" of criminal activity. Since the seizure of the cocaine, mirror, and razor was based on the illegal search, the evidence could not be used by the state. (A) is wrong; absolute certainty of illegal activity is not required for a valid search. A reasonable belief is required. (C) is wrong. The arrest itself is probably invalid, and in any event a search of the next room would not be an area within the immediate control of the defendant. (D) is wrong. Consent to enter the shop is not a consent to search the back room.

Answer to Question 133

(B) The evidence is admissible as evidence of Wade's possible bias in favor of Dexter. Evidence that a witness is biased tends to show that the witness has a motive to lie. A witness may always be impeached by extrinsic evidence of bias, provided a proper foundation is laid. Bias may be shown by evidence of a business relationship or friendship with a party. Here, the fact that Wade is Dexter's partner in a gambling operation is admissible to impeach Wade for bias. (A) is wrong because the only relevant facet of Wade's character in this case is his veracity, and extrinsic evidence of bad acts is not admissible to impeach a witness. Under the Federal Rules, instances of a witness's conduct may be inquired into on cross-examination if they are probative of truthfulness (*i.e.,* acts of deceit or lying), but extrinsic evidence is not allowed. It is doubtful that running a gambling operation would be found to be probative of Wade's truthfulness. Even if it were, extrinsic evidence would be inadmissible. (C) misstates the law. Criminal conduct can be shown by means other than admission or record of conviction. As discussed above, a party may be impeached by instances of bad or criminal conduct (even if it does not result in a conviction) if it is probative of truthfulness and it is brought out on cross-examination (no extrinsic evidence). (D) is wrong because extrinsic evidence of bias is admissible. (Note, however, that many states require that the bias be inquired into on cross-examination before extrinsic evidence is admissible.)

Answer to Question 134

(B) Cost of completion minus installments is the correct measure of damages because the facts give us the breach of a construction contract by the builder during construction. In such cases where the builder breaches after partially performing, the owner of the land is entitled to the cost of completion plus reasonable compensation for any delay in performance. Courts generally allow the builder to offset or recover for work performed to date to avoid the unjust enrichment of the owner. Hence, the unpaid installments should be deducted. Although this option does not mention reasonable compensation for delay, it is clearly a more accurate statement of the correct measure of damages than the other options. (A) is wrong because Farquart's damage relates to the cost of having the house completed. This cost could either exceed or be less than the restitution of the installments. If the amount is less, Farquart would be unjustly enriched. (C) is incorrect because damage relates to cost of completion and not market value. The house might have minimal market value in its partially completed state, and to measure damages based on the differences between such minimal value at the time of breach and market value when completed according to specifications could dramatically overstate Farquart's real damages. (D) is incorrect because damages for mental distress are too speculative and are not awarded in a contract situation.

Answer to Question 135

(C) Farquart's additional expense in providing temporary housing would be the best basis for a claim of consequential damages. In addition to the standard measure of damages, consequential damages may be awarded for further losses resulting from the breach that any reasonable person would have foreseen would occur from a breach *at the time of entry* into the contract. Temporary housing expenses would have been foreseeable at the time Sawtooth and Farquart entered into the contract. (A) is incorrect because it would be consequential damage to Junior rather than Farquart, because it is Junior who will incur the expense. (B) is incorrect because the fiancee's jilting of Junior is not a foreseeable consequence of the breach. (D) is incorrect because at the time Sawtooth and Farquart entered into the contract, both parties would have reasonably assumed that the house would be built and completed by experienced construction personnel. Farquart's attempt to complete the house himself and the ensuing negligence were not foreseeable.

Answer to Question 136

(B) The legal effect of the two circumstances is best stated by (B). When a condition or duty of performance (*i.e.,* payment) is broken, the beneficiary of the condition or duty has an election: he may (i) terminate his liability; or (ii) continue under the contract. If he chooses the latter course, he will be deemed to have waived the condition or duty. Since Sawtooth did not terminate his liability to complete construction of the house, but rather treated the contract as ongoing, he is deemed to have waived the delay in payment. Farquart's failure to require a certificate from Builders would be deemed a revocable waiver. At any time Farquart could insist on the certificate before making a monthly payment. Because the certificate represents that the work performed during a particular month met the specifications, Farquart would always retain the right to condition his payment for a particular month on receipt of the certificate. (A) is incorrect because there was no estoppel waiver as to either I. or II. Whenever a party indicates that he is "waiving" a condition before it is to happen, or some performance before it is rendered, and the person addressed detrimentally relies upon such an indication, the courts will hold this to be a binding (estoppel) waiver. Sawtooth never indicated in advance that he was waiving the four monthly payments and there was no detrimental reliance by Farquart. Likewise, Farquart never indicated in advance that he was waiving the certificate requirement and there was no detrimental reliance by Sawtooth. (C) is incorrect because mutual rescission requires an ***express agreement*** between the parties to rescind. The agreement to rescind is itself a binding contract supported by consideration (the giving up by each party of his right to counterperformance from the other). The parties did not rescind the contract here. (D) is wrong because, as noted above, there was no estoppel waiver as to II. Also, there was never any discharge of Farquart's duty to make the four payments. (Although Farquart's duty might be excused because no work was done between November and February, this does not necessarily follow from the terms of the contract.)

Answer to Question 137

(D) The outcome of Stone's suit will be governed by whether the power to "sell and convey" is construed to include the power to execute the usual form of deed used to convey realty. If Mitchell lacked the authority to include covenants for title, Rogers will probably not be bound by those covenants. (A) is wrong because the deed included covenants. It may be slightly relevant on the issue of how the power of attorney should be construed, but the outcome of the case will not be governed by this determination. (B) is wrong for a couple of reasons. Covenants for title are not like real covenants; they are not characterized as personal or running with the land. Covenants for title are either present or future. Even if the terminology of personal or running with the land were used, (B) would be incorrect because the suit concerns the original parties; thus, whether the covenant runs with the land would be irrelevant. (C) is wrong because bona fide purchaser status is irrelevant to the enforcement of covenants for title. This status is important mostly for purposes of the recording statute.

Answer to Question 138

(A) The court should dismiss the action because Midwest cannot show that any injury it allegedly suffered will be remedied by a decision enjoining performance of the Great Plains contract. Even if a federal court has jurisdiction over the subject matter of a case, it will not decide a constitutional challenge to a government action unless the party challenging the action has "standing" to raise the constitutional issue, *i.e.,* a concrete stake in the outcome of the controversy. This requires plaintiff to show an injury in fact—caused by the government—that will be remedied by a decision in its favor. Here, Midwest cannot establish that whatever injury it might have suffered by having its bid rejected will be remedied by an injunction preventing Great Plains from performing its contract with the government; hence, it does not have standing to bring this action. (B) is incorrect because it is too broad; even in the absence of express constitutional limitations, the government is restricted by the Bill of Rights in the exercise of its contracting power. (C) is wrong because Midwest does not have standing to raise a claim on behalf of minorities potentially affected by the waiver. Even if the court were to consider the merits of the case, the government, while it might have had to show a compelling government interest to *institute* its affirmative action policies, would not have to show a compelling interest to *suspend* the policies. (D) is wrong because Midwest does not have standing to assert a violation of its rights in an action to enjoin another party's performance of a contract with the government.

Answer to Question 139

(B) Under pure comparative negligence, the plaintiff may recover no matter how great her negligence. In this case, Phyllis has suffered damages of $100,000. Because she was 40% negligent, she may recover only $60,000 ($100,000 less $40,000). Therefore, (B) is correct, and (A) is wrong. Absent a statute, damages are not reduced or mitigated because of benefits received from collateral sources (*e.g.,* health insurance). Thus, Phyllis's receipt of $10,000 under her insurance plan does not diminish her recovery. (C) is therefore wrong. Andrew and Brett are jointly and severally liable for Phyllis's injuries because their negligent acts combined to proximately cause an indivisible injury to Phyllis. Because Andrew and Brett are jointly and severely liable, Phyllis may recover the entire $60,000 from Andrew. Thus, (D) is wrong.

Answer to Question 140

(A) Ben, who is apparently a purchaser at arm's length, had ample opportunity to inspect the property and discover the conduit. The law will not protect a party in Ben's situation who failed to protect himself. Owen, in the absence of a fiduciary relationship with Ben or of any affirmative representations that Owen knows or discovers to have been false, has no duty to disclose the existence of the conduit except (in some jurisdictions) if he knows that Ben is laboring under a misapprehension as to a basic assumption and the act of nondisclosure is made in bad faith. The facts do not support either of these exceptions. It does not appear that Owen acted in bad faith, particularly because Owen permitted an inspection and Ben had ample opportunity to discover the truth. Furthermore, it does not appear that Ben will be unable to build the high-rise simply because of the presence of the conduit. (B) is incorrect because Ben's purpose is not irrelevant: if Owen knew about Ben's purpose, Owen may have a duty to disclose any fact that would preclude that purpose. (C) is incorrect because the existence of the conduit does not make title unmarketable. (D) is incorrect because nothing in the facts indicates that Ben could not build the high-rise on the property despite the existence of the conduit; there are no facts indicating that Ben will experience grossly excessive costs in attempting to do so; and the existence of the conduit, which was discoverable, is not the sort of unforeseeable supervening event that would give rise to a frustration defense.

Answer to Question 141

(B) Burglary requires a breaking and entering with the intent to commit a felony therein. Because what Donaldson intended to do when he broke in was not a crime, it cannot be said that he entered with the intent to commit a felony. For this reason, he should be acquitted of burglary. It follows that (B) is correct and (C) is incorrect. (D) is incorrect. While the fact that Donaldson was unable to retrieve the exams would not have been a defense to the burglary charge, the decisive fact in this case involves *legal* impossibility, not *factual* impossibility. (A) is incorrect because the crime of burglary would have been complete at the moment of breaking and entering with intent to commit a felony therein. However, because looking at exam questions was not a crime, Donaldson could not be convicted of either burglary or attempted burglary.

Answer to Question 142

(C) Martha will lose unless she was in the "zone of danger" with Sue. Under the traditional approach for negligent infliction of emotional distress, one of the elements for recovery by a bystander is that she must have been within the "zone of danger" or "target zone" of defendant's negligent conduct. Unless Martha was crossing the street with Sue and therefore in the "zone of danger," she will not recover. Thus, (A) is incorrect. (The modern "foreseeability" approach would permit Martha to recover even though she was outside the "zone of danger"—her relationship to the person injured and her presence at the scene would establish foreseeability under this approach.) (B) is wrong even though severe shock to the nervous system may be a sufficient physical injury; Martha will lose because of the "zone of danger" requirement. (D) is incorrect because Martha's relationship to Sue is not relevant under the traditional "zone of danger" approach.

Answer to Question 143

(B) The testimony of Watts should be admitted as a statement to a physician made for purposes of diagnosis or treatment. The Federal Rules allow the admission of statements not only of past symptoms and medical history, but also of the cause or source of the condition as reasonably pertinent to diagnosis or treatment. This is an exception to the hearsay rule. (A) is incorrect because this is not a statement of **present** bodily condition which falls under a different exception to the hearsay rule. (C) is incorrect because, as explained above, this testimony is admissible under an exception to the hearsay rule. (D) is incorrect because this hearsay exception does not require unavailability of the declarant.

Answer to Question 144

(A) If a law burdens a fundamental right, the state must demonstrate that the law is necessary to promote a compelling state interest. In all other cases, a law is valid if it rationally relates to a legitimate end of government. Where the "rational basis" test applies, the law is presumed valid and the burden is on the challenging party to prove its invalidity. The statute at issue infringes on Zeller's right of parental custody, which is almost certainly a fundamental right. Thus, the **state** bears the burden of showing that this statute is needed to promote a compelling state interest. (A) is correct. (B) and (D) are wrong because showing a rational relationship is not enough since a fundamental right is involved. (C) and (D) are wrong because the burden is on the state, not Zeller.

Answer to Question 145

(D) A conviction for felony murder requires that the defendant have had the intent to commit the underlying felony. Here, because Dunbar believed that the $200 rightfully belonged to her, she did not have the intent to permanently deprive Stone of his money. Thus, Dunbar lacked the intent required for conviction of the underlying felony, and she cannot be found guilty of felony murder. (A) is wrong because it fails to account for the necessary intent to commit the underlying felony. (B) is wrong because taking Balcom to the store did not in and of itself create a risk of death. Also, (B), like (A), fails to account for the necessary intent to commit the underlying felony. (C) is wrong because the required mental state for felony murder (*i.e.*, intent to commit the underlying felony) has nothing to do with knowledge that Balcom was armed.

Answer to Question 146

(C) Conviction as an accessory requires that the defendant have given aid, counsel, or encouragement with the intent that an offense be committed or, in some cases, knowing that she was contributing to the commission of a crime. If Dunbar neither planned to use force nor knew that Balcom was armed, and she believed that the $200 was rightfully hers, then she cannot be said to have aided, counseled, or encouraged Balcom with the intent that an offense be committed, or knowing that she was contributing to the commission of a crime. (A) and (B) are incorrect because they ignore the encouragement and intent necessary for conviction as an accessory. (D) is incorrect because, even if Dunbar was only exercising self-help, this alternative does not address her state of mind regarding the charge of being an accessory to murder.

Answer to Question 147

(D) The accused in a criminal case may introduce evidence of a *pertinent* character trait because it may tend to show that he did not commit the crime charged. But here, evidence of Duncan's character for truth is not pertinent to a charge of a violent crime (aggravated assault). (A) is wrong because the character evidence is admissible only if it is pertinent to the charged crime. (B) is wrong because Duncan's credibility is not in issue, since he did not testify. (C) is wrong because in a criminal trial such evidence may be admitted, if pertinent, at the initiative of the accused.

Answer to Question 148

(B) If the decision is for Andy, it will be because the right to take minerals is an incident of a fee simple interest. The owner of a defeasible fee has the same right to possession and privileges of use as the owner of a fee simple absolute. Only unconscionable conduct by the owner that substantially reduces the value of the land could possibly be enjoined by the person who would take the land should the current owner's estate terminate. (A) is incorrect because Bob has an executory interest. (C) is an incorrect statement of the law. A person in possession (*e.g.,* a life tenant), absent other circumstances, does not have the right to exploit mineral resources. (D) is incorrect because it is irrelevant. Andy's mental state or "good faith" or lack thereof has no bearing on his right to take minerals from his fee estate.

Answer to Question 149

(D) Norris will not prevail if Josephs had reasonable grounds for his statement. As a former employer responding to queries of a prospective employer about a job applicant, Dr. Josephs has a qualified privilege. Such a privilege is not absolute; it exists only if exercised in a reasonable manner and for a proper purpose. The privilege may be lost if the speaker made a statement not within the scope of the privilege or if the speaker acted with "malice" (*i.e.,* knowledge that the statement was untrue or with reckless disregard as to its truth or falsity). If Josephs had reasonable grounds for his belief, he was not acting with malice. (A) is incorrect because of the reasons stated in the analysis of option (D). A statement of opinion may be actionable if it appears to be based on specific facts which, if expressly stated, would be defamatory. However, because of the qualified privilege, Dr. Josephs will not be liable for his mistake as long as his belief was reasonable. (B) is incorrect because the fact that the statement was in a category that is slander per se (*i.e.,* adversely reflecting on Norris's abilities to practice her profession) goes to whether Norris must plead special damages. It does not, however, undermine the qualified privilege. (C) is incorrect because permission to make inquiry is not tantamount to consent to be defamed.

Answer to Question 150

(D) Marketable title is one that is free from reasonable doubt in fact or in law. Here, there is confusion because the building restrictions apply to all the lots shown on the map, but the parcel at issue is not one of the 10 numbered lots. Thus, it is unclear whether the parcel is subject to restrictions that will reduce the uses of the lot or its market value. Thus, (D) is correct. (A) is wrong because it is not clear that the undesignated parcel is not subject to the subdivision restrictions. It was included on the map and the restrictions apply to "all lots shown." (B) is wrong because even though it is not one of the 10 lots, it may be bound by the restrictions. Since this is unclear, title is not marketable. (C) is wrong because there could be marketable title without government approval.

Answer to Question 151

(C) Venus is entitled to the contract price for the grapes delivered and accepted, but Tipple is entitled to cover—to purchase grapes at the market price prevailing at the time of performance and to deduct any increase over the Venus-Tipple contract price. (A) is wrong because Tipple is entitled to cover, and does not "waive" the breach by accepting a part performance. (B) is wrong because the price for the grapes delivered is the contract price, not the prevailing market price. (D) is wrong because Venus is entitled to payment for the grapes she delivered, and would be able to enforce her claim through litigation, if necessary.

Answer to Question 152

(C) Wall's testimony is admissible as prior identification by the witness. Under the Federal Rules of Evidence, a statement of prior identification by the witness of another person is nonhearsay. Thus, (A) is incorrect. (B) is incorrect because Wall is testifying at the trial and is subject to cross-examination. Thus, Dray's right of confrontation is not violated. (D) is incorrect because past recollection recorded is an *exception* to the hearsay rule, and the statement here at issue is nonhearsay. Also, past recollection recorded involves use of a writing made when the events were fresh in the mind of the witness. There is no such writing involved here.

Answer to Question 153

(A) The modification is fully enforceable. Although there was no consideration for Barnes's promise to take only half of the bargained-for production, none is required because this is a contract for the sale of goods and hence subject to U.C.C. section 2-209(1), which provides that a good faith modification is enforceable regardless of lack of consideration. Hence, (C) is wrong. (B) and (D) are wrong because they imply that the original agreement was not fully enforceable. The agreement between Barnes and Stevens is basically an output contract and is fully enforceable under the U.C.C. Although generally the subject matter of a contract must be definite and certain, an agreement to buy or sell all of one's requirements or output is deemed capable of being made certain by reference to objective, extrinsic facts. It is assumed that the parties will act in good faith.

Answer to Question 154

(D) Discharge of contractual duties by impossibility must be objective; *i.e.,* the duties could not be performed by anyone. Generally, physical incapacity of a person necessary to effectuate the contract only excuses performance where the services are deemed "unique." That would not be the case here. Stevens's allergy to the bees does not constitute objective impossibility of performance because his duties are delegable. Hence, his failure to deliver is not excused. (B) is wrong because his performance would be excused only if the parties had entered into a contract for personal services. (A) is wrong because Stevens promised to supply at least 100 lbs. per month. (C) is wrong because such notice would not excuse a breach.

Answer to Question 155

(C)   The basis for finding that the bank's due process rights have been violated is that it should have received notice through personal service or by mail. When the government seeks to use a judicial or administrative process to take or terminate property interests, it must give notice to those persons whose property interests may be taken by that process. The form of notice must be reasonably designed to insure that those persons will in fact be notified of the proceedings. Here, the bank had recorded its mortgage and presumably could have been notified by mail that the property was being seized by the government. Being deprived of the opportunity to protect its interest in the property violated the bank's due process rights under the three-part test of *Mathews v. Eldridge. Mathews* lists three criteria that the courts should weigh in determining what consti- tutes fair process: (i) the importance of the individual interest involved, (ii) the value of specific procedural safeguards to that interest, and (iii) the governmental interest in fiscal and administra- tive efficiency. Here, the Bank has an important property right that is being terminated, the procedure of publishing a general notice was not sufficient to safeguard its interests, and the government interest in efficiency would not have been overburdened by requiring notice by mail to parties with a recorded interest in the property. (A) is wrong because it is too broad. Under *Mathews*, the government is not required to provide personal notice to all parties if it is not feasible, nor is it required to provide a preseizure hearing if exigent circumstances make it im- practicable. (B) is incorrect because even when a private party is seeking to use a judicial or administrative process, state action is involved and the Due Process Clause must be satisfied; hence, notice to a record mortgage holder would be required even if a private party were seeking to seize the property through judicial means. (D) is incorrect because the state's characterization of the mortgagee's interest is not critical; the mortgagee has legal rights to the property that are protected by the Due Process Clause, regardless of how the rights are characterized.

Answer to Question 156

(C)   The court should deny Darren's motion if it finds that he voluntarily consented to the search that revealed the drugs. The police may conduct a valid warrantless search of an area otherwise protected by the Fourth Amendment if they have a voluntary and intelligent consent to do so. The scope of the search is governed by the scope of the consent, but consent extends to all areas to which a reasonable person under the circumstances would believe it extends. The fact that a defendant has been placed under arrest does not mean that he cannot otherwise give valid consent to a search, and the search that led to the discovery of the cocaine in this case was within the scope of the consent that Darren provided. Thus, he has no Fourth Amendment grounds to ex- clude evidence of the cocaine. (A) is wrong because the fact that Darren was arrested did not mean that his consent was not voluntary. Whether consent is voluntary is judged by the totality of the circumstances. He does not necessarily need to be told that he has a right to withhold consent or be informed of the specific items being sought in the search. As long as his consent was not the product of express or implied coercion, it will be valid. (B) is incorrect even though it is a true statement. After making a lawful arrest of the occupant of an automobile, the police may conduct a warrantless search of the passenger compartment of the automobile but may not search the trunk. Here, however, the search of the trunk was based on Darren's consent rather than as incident to his arrest. (D) is incorrect. The lesser expectation of privacy in vehicles permits the police to search a vehicle without a warrant if they have probable cause to believe that the vehicle contains contraband or evidence of a crime. However, the facts in this question do not indicate that Officer Jones had probable cause to search the trunk of Darren's car. The more certain basis for upholding the validity of the search is the consent given by Darren.

Answer to Question 157

(B) Defendant is guilty of larceny because he had the intent to deprive the victim permanently of his car at the time of the taking. Neither victim's fraudulently procured consent nor defendant's later return of the car negates the larceny. (A) is wrong because, since the defendant intended to return the car within a reasonable time and, at the time of the taking, had a substantial ability to do so, his unauthorized borrowing of the car does not constitute larceny. (C) is wrong because the elements of false pretenses have not been met. False pretenses involves the obtaining of title to the property of another by an intentional false statement with intent to defraud the owner. Here, since defendant did not get title, it cannot be false pretenses. (D) is wrong because no conversion occurred. For embezzlement to have occurred, the defendant who was in legal possession of the car would have actually had to convert it for his own gain. Returning the car within a reasonable time would not constitute embezzlement.

Answer to Question 158

(A) The testimony should be admissible as sufficiently authenticated. Where the identity of the speaker of an oral statement is important, authentication as to the speaker's identity is required. A statement made during a telephone conversation may be authenticated by a party to the call who testifies that: (i) he recognized the other party's voice; (ii) the speaker had knowledge of certain facts that only a particular person would have; or (iii) he called a certain person's telephone number, and a voice answered, "This is (the person whose number was called)." Here, the identity of the person with whom Jones spoke on the telephone is important because the speaker admitted that his horse caused the damage. Thus, authentication is required. Because Jones called the listed phone number for Smith, and the answering voice identified itself as Smith, authentication is proper under (iii) above. (B) is incorrect because the accuracy of phone books is not an accurately verifiable fact or a matter of common knowledge. (C) is incorrect because, as noted above, familiarity with the speaker's voice is only one means of authentication. (D) is incorrect because there is no requirement of corroboration by the speaker.

Answer to Question 159

(A) Photographs are admissible only if identified by a witness as a portrayal of certain facts relevant to the issue and verified by the witness as a correct representation of those facts. The witness who identifies the photograph need only be familiar with the scene or object that is depicted. It is not necessary to call the photographer to authenticate the photograph. Jones, as the owner of the cornfield, is familiar with the field that is depicted. Thus, Jones may testify to the photograph as an accurate portrayal of the condition of the field after the damage was done. (B) is incorrect because, if the photograph accurately depicts the damage, the photograph need not have been taken within a week after the occurrence. The fact that it was taken within a week does not establish that it was an accurate portrayal of the damage to the field. (C) is incorrect because, as noted above, it is not necessary to call the photographer. (D) is incorrect because, as long as the photograph is properly authenticated, it is admissible.

Answer to Question 160

(C) State laws based on alienage are subject to strict scrutiny, meaning that a compelling state interest must be shown to justify the disparate treatment. However, if the law discriminates against alien participation in the self-governance process, the "rationality" test is applied. Here, Clovis's application for tuition assistance does not relate to participation in the governmental process, thus the strict scrutiny test applies. (B) is incorrect, because it is based on the assumption that the "rationality" test is appropriate. (C) is the only answer that addresses the fact that the state must demonstrate a compelling interest to justify the restriction. It follows that (A) is incorrect. (D) is incorrect because aliens are excluded from the protection of the Privileges and Immunities Clause of Article IV.

Answer to Question 161

(D) Fenster may not remove the windows because they are fixtures and the bank's mortgage on the real property takes priority. Under the concept of fixtures, a chattel that has been annexed to real property is converted from personalty to realty. As an accessory to the real property, it is subject to any mortgage on the real property. In all common ownership cases (*i.e.,* those in which the person who brings the chattel onto the land owns both the chattel and the realty), whether an item that is not incorporated into a structure is a "fixture" (*i.e.,* part of the realty) depends upon the objective intention of the party who made the "annexation." This intention is determined by considering: (i) the nature of the article; (ii) the manner in which it is attached to the realty; (iii) the amount of damage that would be caused by its removal; and (iv) the adaptation of the item to the use of the realty. Under this analysis the windows are fixtures. It should first be noted that Dickens is the fee simple owner of the house rather than a tenant and intended to make numerous permanent improvements to the house in future years; the state-of-the-art windows were simply the first step in what he believed would be a long-term process. The fact that the windows were easily removable (and therefore would cause minimal damage in the event of removal) would ordinarily indicate less of an intention to permanently improve the freehold, but here the facts indicate that they were easily removable to make it easier to clean them. Another important factor indicating that the windows are fixtures is that they cannot readily be used at any other house unless the window sizes happen to correspond to those at Dickens's house. They were custom-made specifically for that house and therefore they were specially adapted to the use of the realty. They serve both functional and aesthetic purposes, they are an integral part of the house, and are necessary and appropriate to the use of the premises. Thus, in view of factors (i) and (iv) above, and considering Dickens's fee simple ownership and long-term plans for the house, they should be deemed fixtures.

The fact that the windows are fixtures does not resolve the dispute between Fenster and the bank, however. Under Article 9 of the Uniform Commercial Code, a seller of a chattel that will become a fixture can grant a security interest in the chattel for a portion of the purchase price and protect his interest by making a "fixture filing" even though the real property has a mortgage. Under U.C.C. section 9-313(4), a seller who provides a purchase money security interest in an affixed chattel will prevail (to the extent of his claim) over a prior recorded mortgage on the land as long as the chattel interest is recorded within 20 days after the chattel is affixed to the land; this allows the seller to remove the chattel without having to reimburse the mortgagee for any diminution in the property's value. However, if this exception does not apply, the general rule that the first interest to be recorded prevails will be applied by the court. Here, while Fenster has a purchase money security interest in the windows, there is no indication that he made a fixture filing within 20 days of when the windows were installed. Thus, the bank's recorded mortgage interest is superior to Fenster's security interest, so Fenster will not be permitted to remove the windows. (A) is incorrect. In determining whether a chattel is a fixture in landlord-tenant cases, courts will generally allow the tenant to remove any chattel that he installed (*i.e.,* deem it not to be a fixture) if removal does not cause substantial damage to the premises or the virtual destruction of the chattel. However, that reflects the probable intent of the tenant who purchased the chattel, since he has no interest in permanently improving the freehold. Here, however, Dickens was the fee simple owner of the house. The fact that he saved the old windows does not negate his intent to permanently improve the real estate with the new ones. (B) is incorrect because, as discussed above, the ease of removing the windows was for purposes of cleaning and does not negate an intent to permanently improve the real estate. (C) is incorrect even though it states an important factor for concluding that the windows are fixtures. As discussed above, that fact would not have precluded Fenster from prevailing had he recorded his security interest in the windows.

Answer to Question 162

(B) Phil cannot recover damages in a misrepresentation action against Donna because he has suffered no pecuniary loss as a result of reliance on the false statement. An action for intentional misrepresentation requires plaintiff to show (i) a misrepresentation by defendant, (ii) scienter, (iii) an intent to induce plaintiff's reliance on the misrepresentation, (iv) causation (*i.e.*, actual reliance on the misrepresentation), (v) justifiable reliance by plaintiff on the misrepresentation, and (vi) damages. The damages element permits plaintiff to recover only if he has suffered actual pecuniary loss as a result of reliance on the false statement. Here, Phil received a fair price for the powder horn and would not have obtained a higher amount had he sold it to someone else. His distress over selling it to her because of her false statement does not satisfy the damages requirement for intentional misrepresentation. (A) is incorrect not only because Phil suffered no actionable damages but also because Donna need not *know* that her statements were false. The element of scienter also encompasses statements that were made with reckless disregard as to their truth or falsity. (C) is wrong even though it correctly states the causation element of intentional misrepresentation. Without the element of pecuniary harm, the prima facie case is not complete. (D) is wrong because statements of law are viewed as statements of opinion that cannot be justifiably relied upon only if they are merely predictions as to the legal consequences of facts. In contrast, a statement of law that includes an express or implied misrepresentation of fact is actionable. Here, Donna's assertions that she had a power of attorney and the legal right to seize the horn through a replevin action are fact-based assertions that Phil had the right to rely upon.

Answer to Question 163

(C) The court should hold against Roy because the Supreme Court has permitted Congress to remove the states' Eleventh Amendment immunity from suit only when it acts to enforce the Fourteenth Amendment. The Eleventh Amendment generally prohibits a federal court from hearing private parties' claims against the government, including claims for damages such as Roy's claim here. While Congress's power to prevent discrimination under the Fourteenth Amendment has enabled it to abrogate state immunity, it has no such power under the Commerce Clause. [*See* Seminole Tribe of Florida v. Florida (1996)] Hence, the court should dismiss the action as barred by the Eleventh Amendment, and (A) is therefore incorrect. (B) is incorrect because while Congress does have the power to regulate the jurisdiction of the federal courts, it does not have the power to grant jurisdiction in violation of another constitutional provision, such as the Eleventh Amendment in this case. (D) is wrong because Congress does have power under certain circumstances to remove the states' Eleventh Amendment immunity. Under the power given to Congress in the enabling clause of the Fourteenth Amendment (and perhaps the Thirteenth and Fifteenth Amendments), it could pass anti-discrimination legislation that permits a state to be sued in federal court.

Answer to Question 164

(B) Janet's testimony is admissible to impeach Elliot's credibility and as substantive evidence of

Evans's guilt. As long as the witness is given an opportunity to explain or deny the statement, extrinsic proof of a prior inconsistent statement is admissible to impeach the witness's testimony. If the prior inconsistent statement was made under oath at a prior trial, hearing, or other proceeding, it is admissible nonhearsay; *i.e.,* it is admissible as substantive evidence. In this case, the prior inconsistent statement was made under oath at Elliot's trial and thus is admissible for its substance as well as for impeachment. (A) is incorrect because, as discussed above, Janet's testimony is admissible as substantive evidence of Evans's guilt. (C) is incorrect because jurors are incompetent to testify only (i) before the jury on which they are sitting, and (ii) in postverdict proceedings as to certain matters occurring during jury deliberations. Since Janet is not testifying before the jury on which she was sitting and is not testifying about jury deliberations, she is a competent witness. (D) is incorrect because the best evidence rule does not apply to this situation. Janet is not being called to prove the terms of a writing or to testify about knowledge she gained from reading a writing. The facts as to which she is testifying exist independently of any writing; thus, the best evidence rule does not apply.

Answer to Question 165

(A) Because stopping a car is a seizure for Fourth Amendment purposes, police generally may not stop a car unless they have at least a reasonable suspicion that a law has been violated. However, even absent that suspicion, police may set up roadblocks to stop cars if (i) the cars are stopped on the basis of some neutral, articulable standard, and (ii) the stops are designed to serve a purpose closely related to a particular problem arising from automobiles and their mobility. [*See* Indianapolis v. Edmund (2000)] The use of a checkpoint to detect evidence of ordinary criminal wrongdoing unrelated to use of cars or highway safety, such as the conduct here, was improper and thus the marijuana would be inadmissible under the exclusionary rule. (B) is wrong because if the car had been properly stopped, the use of the flashlight would not have been improper. (C) is wrong because the established police plan cannot overcome the constitutional objection to the random stopping. (D) is wrong because the stopping of the car was improper. If it had been proper, the subsequent search would have been proper since it would have been based on probable cause.

Answer to Question 166

(C) Hunko is likely to prevail because of the preexisting duty rule. At common law, a modification of a contract required consideration because the parties were under a preexisting legal duty to perform. Since there was no consideration for the modification, Adman is not entitled to the $2,000. (B) would be correct if the U.C.C. applied, but it does not apply to this fact situation. (A) is wrong; the parol evidence rule does not apply to subsequent modifications. (D) is wrong. It is a true statement but it is not the reason Hunko will prevail. There is nothing in the facts to indicate that Adman did not use his best efforts.

Answer to Question 167

(D) Judgment could be for either Purvis or Rand, because there is a split of authority as to whether a recorded deed, obtained from a grantor who had no title at that time, but who afterwards obtains title, is constructive notice to a subsequent purchaser from the same grantor. Thus, the answer to this question turns on whether the deed from Vine to Purvis constitutes constructive notice to Rand. (A) is incorrect because it does not address the issue of Rand's notice of the prior deed. (B) is incorrect because of the possibility that the deed to Purvis should have put Rand on notice of Purvis's claim. (C) is incorrect because it does not address the issue of notice.

Answer to Question 168

(B) The rehabilitation will most likely be permitted to rebut testimony of Willie's perjury conviction. Under Federal Rule 608(a), a witness can be rehabilitated with evidence of his good reputation for truthfulness after the character of the witness for truthfulness has been attacked by "opinion or reputation evidence or otherwise." The commentary to 608 specifically states that impeachment through a prior conviction is covered by the "or otherwise" provision and therefore will give rise to rehabilitation through reputation for truthfulness evidence. (A) and (D) are wrong because the commentary to 608 specifically states that impeachment through bias does not allow rehabilitation with reputation for truthfulness evidence. (C) is possible. It could be argued that the impeachment in (C) qualifies under the "or otherwise" provision. (C) is not, however, as good an answer as (B), where the rehabilitation through good reputation evidence would clearly be allowed.

Answer to Question 169

(D) This question involves spoken defamation (slander). Ordinary slander is not actionable in the absence of pleading and proof of special damages. The defamation here does not fall within one of the slander per se categories (adverse reflection on plaintiff's abilities in his profession, loathsome disease, crime involving moral turpitude, unchastity of a woman). Thus, Poe will not prevail without a showing of special damages. (A) is incorrect because it implies that Poe can prevail without proof of special damages. (C) is incorrect because proof that the defendant knew of the falsity of the defamatory statement is not required in cases involving a private person plaintiff and a matter of private concern. (B) is incorrect because "extreme and outrageous conduct" is part of the prima facie case for intentional infliction of emotional distress, not for defamation.

Answer to Question 170

(A) Extreme and outrageous conduct is an element of the prima facie case for intentional infliction of emotional distress. Because Kane's conduct was extreme and outrageous, intentional, and likely caused Poe severe distress, Poe will probably prevail. (B) is incorrect because mere intrusion on the plaintiff's property does not constitute intentional infliction of emotional distress. (C) is incorrect because physical injury is not required to recover for this tort. (D) is incorrect because, even if Poe still owed Store for the merchandise, this would not justify extreme and outrageous methods of bill collection. Thus (A) is the best answer.

Answer to Question 171

(B) The requisite intent for intentional torts (such as battery) is satisfied if the actor knows with substantial certainty that the consequences of his conduct will result. Here, by slamming the door shut, Poe set in motion a force that brought about harmful contact to Kane. (A) is wrong because a request to leave the property would not have justified commission of the battery. Generally, one may use reasonable force to prevent the commission of a tort against his property, if use of force is preceded by a request to desist. Kane was not engaged in the commission of a tort against Poe's property. Thus, Poe's use of force was not justified, with or without a request to leave the property. (C) is wrong because, although Kane's conduct undoubtedly did trigger Poe's response, there are no circumstances indicating justification for such a response. (D) is wrong because, as explained above, Kane was not committing a tort against Poe's property so as to justify the use of force.

Answer to Question 172

(B) The judge should give the manslaughter instruction and allow the jury to consider the earlier altercation. Provocation will reduce a killing to voluntary manslaughter only if four requirements are met: (i) the provocation was a type that would arouse sudden and intense passion that would cause a reasonable person to lose self-control, (ii) the defendant in fact was provoked, (iii) there was not sufficient time between the provocation and the killing for the passion of a reasonable person to cool, and (iv) the defendant in fact did not cool off between the provocation and the killing. While at common law some provocations were defined as inadequate as a matter of law, modern courts are more likely to submit to the jury the question of what constituted adequate provocation. Similarly, whether there has been a sufficient time for a reasonable person to cool off is a factual question that depends on the nature of the provocation and the attendant circumstances. Here, Dan's belief that he was being shoved again by Rick and set up for another punch in the face may have rekindled his rage at the earlier punch and taunting by Rick. The jury should be allowed to consider all of the circumstances, including the earlier altercation, to decide whether there was a sufficient provocation or a sufficient time for a reasonable person to cool off. Hence, the judge should agree to give the manslaughter instruction. (A) is incorrect. Some states recognize an "imperfect self-defense" doctrine under which a murder may be reduced to manslaughter even though the defendant unreasonably but honestly believed in the necessity of responding with deadly force. However, the doctrine is not necessary here; Dan should be entitled to a manslaughter instruction regardless of whether he shows that he believed in the need to use deadly force in self-defense. (C) is wrong because under the principle of transferred intent, which would transfer Dan's intent from the intended person to the person actually harmed, any mitigating circumstances that the defendant could have asserted against the intended victim (such as provocation) will also be transferred. While the jury could decide that Dan, even if adequately provoked, acted with reckless disregard by stabbing at a person before looking to see who it was and thus is guilty of murder, Dan is at least entitled to have the jury consider the manslaughter issue. (D) is incorrect because, as discussed above, the court would probably allow the jury to consider the earlier altercation as well as the later shove in deciding whether Dan was adequately provoked.

Answer to Question 173

(C) The statute will probably be found to violate the First Amendment because it is overbroad. The state can adopt a specific definition of obscenity applying to materials sold to minors, even though the material might not be obscene in terms of an adult audience. However, government may not prohibit the sale or distribution of material to adults merely because it is inappropriate for children. Here, there is no indication that the state has attempted less restrictive means of keeping minors from the objectionable video games, such as requiring arcade operators to put these games in a limited access area and monitor their use. While an outright ban on these games may be the most certain means of denying minors access to them, the denial of adult access to them indicates that the statute will probably be found unconstitutional. (A) is incorrect even though it is a true statement. As indicated above, a statute designed to protect minors must be narrowly drawn to avoid a First Amendment violation. (B) is incorrect because the fact that the statute precisely defines the content that is prohibited indicates only that it probably is not unconstitutionally vague; it does not affect its overbreadth problem. (D) is wrong because, as indicated above, restrictions on materials available to minors do not necessarily have to satisfy the constitutional test for obscenity. In addition, choice (D) misstates the test: the element of serious social value is determined by a national standard, rather than community standards.

Answer to Question 174

(C) Wren's testimony is inadmissible hearsay because it is an out-of-court statement by the declarant (Dent) offered to prove that Dent's wife had driven through a red light, and no hearsay exceptions apply here. (A) is wrong because Dent is not a party to the litigation, and the husband-wife relationship does not suffice to allow the use of the statement against his wife as a vicarious admission. (B) is wrong because there is no indication that Dent is unavailable as a witness, which is required for the statement against interest exception to apply. (D) is incorrect because Dent's statement was a statement of fact, rather than opinion; further, even if it were opinion, that would not make it inadmissible if it otherwise qualified as an admission.

Answer to Question 175

(C) Judgment should be for Jose. Luis, by quitclaim deed, conveyed to Jose his future *interest* in Blackacre; technically, it is an executory interest. When Eugenia died survived by a husband and no children, Luis would have taken title to Blackacre pursuant to Ortega's will. However, because of the quitclaim deed, Jose takes title to the property. (A) is incorrect because no after-acquired title is involved; Luis had his future interest from the moment of Ortega's death, and that is what his deed transferred. (B) is incorrect because, although it is true that Jose took nothing under Ortega's will, Luis chose to convey his interest in Blackacre to Jose, as permitted by the applicable statute. (D) is incorrect because after-acquired title is inapplicable to these facts. Moreover, the after-acquired title doctrine applies to conveyances by warranty deed. The conveyance here was effected by quitclaim deed.

Answer to Question 176

(A) In single delivery contracts, the buyer can reject goods for any defect in the goods, even if the breach is not material. Here, the ties sent by Kravat were nonconforming goods. Thus, Clothier properly rejected the ties delivered on June 3. (B) is incorrect because even if Kravat had notified Clothier that the ties were shipped as an accommodation, this would merely be a counteroffer, and Clothier would not have been obligated to accept the ties. (C) is incorrect because acceptance of an offer by shipment of nonconforming goods results in a breach of the contract, giving the buyer the right to reject. (D) is incorrect because, after rejection of goods in his possession, the buyer's obligation is to hold the goods with reasonable care at the seller's disposition for a time sufficient to permit the seller to remove them. The buyer is not obligated to promptly return the goods to the seller in order to preserve his remedies.

Answer to Question 177

(C) Where a buyer has rejected goods because of defects, the seller may, within the time originally provided for performance, cure by giving reasonable notice of intention to do so and making a new tender of conforming goods, which the buyer must then accept. Kravat took all of the steps necessary to cure. Consequently, Clothier's rejection of the ties tendered on June 30 was improper. It follows that (A) is incorrect. (B) is incorrect because Kravat's prompt dispatch of a telegram on June 4, indicating his intention to cure the defect, does not indicate a clear unwillingness or inability to perform, as is required for anticipatory repudiation. (D) is incorrect because modification of the contract is not at issue here. By curing the defective delivery, Kravat is simply performing according to the terms of the contract.

Answer to Question 178

(A) Deanna is not guilty of larceny of the computer because her mistake prevented her from having the requisite mens rea for larceny. Larceny requires an intent to permanently deprive another of her interest in the property taken. Deanna did not have such an intent because she believed that the computer was her own and that Vanessa had no possessory interest in it. Therefore, she did not have the intent required for larceny. (B) is wrong because Deanna's mistake need not have been reasonable. When mistake is offered to negate the existence of general intent or malice, it must be a reasonable mistake. However, any mistake of fact, reasonable or unreasonable, is a defense to a specific intent crime, and larceny is a specific intent crime. (C) is wrong because, as stated above, she did not have the intent to deprive Vanessa of Vanessa's computer; her mistake negates such an intent. (D) is incorrect because the "continuing trespass" doctrine is inapplicable. While larceny generally requires that the intent to deprive another person of her interest in the property must have existed at the moment of the taking of the property, the continuing trespass doctrine provides that if a defendant takes property with a wrongful state of mind but without the intent to steal, and later forms the intent to steal it, the trespass involved in the initial wrongful taking is regarded as "continuing" and the defendant is guilty of larceny. However, this doctrine has no application if the defendant's initial taking of the property, although trespassory, was not motivated by a wrongful state of mind. Here, Deanna took Vanessa's computer as a result of an innocent mistake. Even if she decides to keep the computer, she will not be guilty of larceny because her initial taking was done with an innocent state of mind.

Answer to Question 179

(B) Walter's testimony is admissible to show the effect of the statement on Dent's state of mind. A statement is hearsay if it is offered to prove the truth of the matter asserted in the statement. If the statement is offered for another purpose, it is not considered a hearsay statement. Statements offered for the purpose of showing the effect on the listener are generally not classified as hearsay. Thus, (B) is correct, and (C) is wrong. (A) is wrong; the statements are not hearsay, and the state of mind exception applies to the state of mind of the speaker. (D) is wrong. Clearly, if Dent heard the statement, that would tend to establish the fear necessary for a self-defense claim.

Answer to Question 180

(C) Because the appropriation by the village council implicates the Establishment Clause and a portion of Curmudgeon's taxes are paying for the appropriation, the Court should entertain his suit. The Supreme Court will not decide a constitutional challenge to a government action unless the person who is challenging it has standing to raise the constitutional issue. To have standing, a person must be able to assert that he is injured by a government program. This injury must be more than the merely theoretical injury that all persons suffer by seeing their government engage in unconstitutional actions. In cases where a taxpayer is claiming injury from the use of his taxes for an unconstitutional appropriation or expenditure of public funds, the Supreme Court has required the taxpayer to show that the challenged measure (i) was enacted under the governmental body's power to tax and spend (rather than as an incidental expenditure in the administration of an essentially regulatory statute), and (ii) exceeds some specific limitation on that power. The only specific limitation that the Court has recognized when an appropriation measure has been challenged is the First Amendment's Establishment Clause. [See Flast v. Cohen (1968)] Here, Curmudgeon is challenging a specific appropriation of money by the village council that has been earmarked to benefit the property of the local church. The Establishment Clause, which is applicable to the states through the Fourteenth Amendment, requires that government programs (i) must have a secular purpose, (ii) must have a primary effect that neither advances nor inhibits religion, and (iii) must not produce excessive government entanglement with religion. Because the council's appropriation may violate these requirements, Curmudgeon has standing as a taxpayer to sue the council. (A) is incorrect even though the portion of Curmudgeon's taxes that would be used for the appropriation is minimal. While this factor has been relied on by the Supreme Court in its general refusal to grant federal and state taxpayers standing, it has not been used to deny municipal taxpayers standing in federal courts. [*See* Asarco, Inc. v. Kadish (1989)] Furthermore, the Court has carved out a narrow exception for federal taxpayers to challenge an appropriation, despite the fact that any one taxpayer's contribution would be minute and indeterminable, where the measure was enacted under Congress's taxing and spending powers and violates the Establishment Clause (as discussed above). This exception would be equally applicable to the village council's appropriation here if the court were to follow the federal taxpayer approach. Thus, the minimal contribution by Curmudgeon's taxes would be irrelevant. (B) is incorrect because it does not recognize the limited exception discussed above. (D) is incorrect because generally taxpayers do not have standing to sue on constitutional grounds. The Supreme Court has not expanded the standing rules beyond what *Flast v. Cohen* had established.

Answer to Question 181

(D) Landesmann can recover all of his damages. Where two or more tortious acts combine to proximately cause an indivisible injury to a plaintiff, each tortfeasor will be jointly and severally liable for that injury. This is so even though each defendant acted entirely independently. Here, the tortious acts of Acorp and Beeco combined to proximately cause the poisoning of Landesmann's cattle. Thus, each company will be jointly and severally liable for the entire amount of Landesmann's damages. Thus, (D) is correct. (A) is wrong. Where two or more acts combine to cause the injury, but none of the acts standing alone would be sufficient, each of the acts is an actual cause of the injury (because but for either of the acts, the injury would not have occurred). Thus, Landesmann can recover because the combined actions of the defendants caused his injury. (B) is wrong because to recover Landesmann need not show the amount of fault of each defendant. (C) is wrong because, as mentioned, in this type of case the defendants are jointly and severally liable for the entire injury.

Answer to Question 182

(B) Barton's right to purchase is a preemptive option, which is subject to the Rule Against Perpetuities. If the option could be exercised more than 21 years after some life in being at its creation, it is void. Obviously, Barton's right to purchase will vest or fail within 21 years after Amato's death. Thus, the Rule's provisions are satisfied. (D) is incorrect because a preemptive right, such as is held by Barton, is not so onerous a restriction on transfer of property as to constitute an unreasonable restraint on alienation. (A) is incorrect because recordation is not essential to the validity of the instrument, as between the grantor and grantee. Recordation merely gives notice to the world that an interest affecting title has been conveyed. (C) is incorrect because there is no prohibition against the owner of property conveying her property so that it will pass outside of her will. Here, Amato has chosen freely to dispose of Riveracre in the manner described, and her choice will be given effect.

Answer to Question 183

(A) Pretrial familiarization of a signature by a nonexpert is not an accepted method of authentication because lay opinion as to the authenticity of handwriting must be based on personal familiarity with the handwriting. Here, the nonexpert's only familiarity with Drake's usual signature has come from pretrial preparation. An expert witness or the trier of fact can determine the genuineness of a writing by comparing the questioned writing with another writing proved to be genuine.

Thus, (B) would be an accepted method of authenticating Drake's signature. (C) is an accepted method of authentication because it describes the requirements under the Federal Rules for authentication of an ancient document. (D) is acceptable as an admission by a party-opponent— *i.e.,* a prior acknowledgment by one of the parties of a relevant fact.

Answer to Question 184

(D) If Dennison believed that the building was abandoned, he probably will not be found to have the requisite mens rea for murder. Murder is the unlawful killing of another human being with malice aforethought. Malice aforethought exists when the defendant has (i) intent to kill, (ii) intent to inflict great bodily injury, (iii) reckless indifference to an unjustifiably high risk to human life ("abandoned and malignant heart"), or (iv) intent to commit a felony (under the felony murder doctrine). Here, the jury could find that spraying a building with submachine gun fire demonstrates a reckless indifference to an unjustifiably high risk to human life even though Dennison was not intending to shoot anyone. However, if the jury accepts his assertion that he believed that the building was abandoned and had no idea that there would be any people inside it, the jury will probably find that he did not have a sufficient awareness of an unjustifiably high risk to human life to be liable for murder. (A) is not as strong a defense as (D) because Dennison may still be found liable for the murder as an accomplice. Dennison will be an accomplice to the drive-by shooting even if he was only the driver because he assisted the principal in the commission of the crime and had the intent to do so. An accomplice is liable not only for the crime he intended to aid but also for any other crimes committed during commission of the intended crime if the other crimes were probable or foreseeable. Here, even though the Assassins knew that the store was closed, a jury could find that it was foreseeable that someone would be killed when they sprayed the building with submachine gun fire. Even if Dennison was only the driver, his best defense would be his belief that the building was abandoned. (B) is incorrect because Dennison's voluntary intoxication would not be a defense to a murder charge that was based on reckless indifference to an unjustifiably high risk to human life. Voluntary intoxication caused by alcohol or drugs is a defense to a crime that requires purpose (intent) or knowledge as long as the intoxication prevents the defendant from formulating the purpose or obtaining the knowledge. It is no defense to crimes involving recklessness or negligence, however. Even though recklessness requires a conscious disregard of the risk, and the defendant's intoxication may make him unaware of the risk, courts hold him liable for recklessness offenses because his initial act of becoming voluntarily intoxicated was reckless. Thus, for murder based on a malice aforethought of reckless indifference to an unjustifiably high risk to human life, voluntary intoxication would not be a defense. (C) is wrong because duress is not a defense to murder. A criminal offense may be excused if the defendant does the act under threat of imminent infliction of death or great bodily harm, as long as the defendant reasonably believes that the threat will be carried out. However, no threat will suffice as a defense to a homicide crime. Dennison may still be liable for murder if he acted with an awareness of an unjustifiably high risk to human life.

Answer to Question 185

(A) Hull acquired title to Brownacre by adverse possession. He possessed the property for longer than the required 10 years. Although Hull entered Brownacre without Orris's knowledge, he dealt with the property in such a manner as to put the true owner and the community on notice of the fact of his possession. Also, Hull's possession was continuous, exclusive, and hostile. Thus, the elements of adverse possession are present. Because Orris lost title to the land due to Hull's adverse possession, it follows that (B) is incorrect. (D) is incorrect because Powell, who supposedly took title to Brownacre by a quitclaim deed from Orris, cannot take title from someone who had none to convey. (C) is incorrect because Burns never possessed the land for the requisite statutory period. Also, he did not hold the land in a hostile manner for a continuous period.

Answer to Question 186

(A) Title to the dam resided in the fee simple owner of Brownacre. Under the concept of fixtures, the dam was converted from personalty into realty. The dam is an accessory to the land and passes with the ownership of the land. (A) expresses this fact. (B) is wrong because the document purporting to transfer Hull's interest in the dam to Burns was insufficient to transfer real property. (C) is an incorrect statement of the law. (D) is wrong because the dam, as an accessory to the land, belongs to the owner of the land.

Answer to Question 187

(B) If the legislation is found to be unconstitutional, it will be because the commission will be exercising administrative powers. Under Article II, Section 2, Congress may not appoint members of a body with administrative or enforcement powers. Such persons are "officers of the United States" and must be appointed by the President with senatorial confirmation unless Congress has vested their appointment in the President alone, in federal courts, or in heads of departments. Here, selection of two members of the commission by a committee of the House of Representatives would violate the Appointments Clause because the commission has investigative and administrative powers. (A) is incorrect because the problem with the legislation is not that the President is infringing on the legislative branch's power by being able to veto congressional appointments, but rather that the congressional appointments are infringing on the executive branch appointment power. (C) is incorrect because Congress may by law vest appointment power of inferior officers in the federal courts. Hence, the judiciary has been properly granted the power by Congress to appoint members of the commission. (D) is incorrect because only Cabinet-level officers require Senate confirmation for their appointment. Inferior officers, which would include members of this commission, may be appointed by the President without Senate approval if provided for by Congress, as is the case here.

Answer to Question 188

(C) Title to Brownacre is vested half in Tenniel, free of the mortgage, and half in Stokes subject to the mortgage. Because the jurisdiction in which Brownacre is located recognizes the title theory of mortgages, Johnson's execution of the mortgage on Brownacre effected a severance of the joint tenancy, by passing a title interest from Johnson to Lowden. Following severance of the joint tenancy, Johnson and Tenniel held as tenants in common, with no right of survivorship. The interest of a tenant in common passes by succession. When Johnson died, Tenniel could not take Brownacre by right of survivorship, because of the severance of the joint tenancy. Thus, (A) and (B) are incorrect. Upon Johnson's death, Stokes succeeded to his interest in Brownacre, subject to the mortgage. However, Tenniel's interest in the property, as a tenant in common, is not subject to the mortgage. Therefore, (D) is incorrect and (C) is correct.

Answer to Question 189

(B) Both damages and an injunction would be ordered. Church has a life estate pur autre vie, and a life tenant as a general rule is not entitled to consume or exploit natural resources on the property; this constitutes affirmative (voluntary) waste that injures the interests of the future interest holders. Any award of damages will be held until the class gift to the grandchildren closes at Carl's death. (A) is wrong since the church's action did not terminate its interest. The "provided that" language creates a condition subsequent. An estate subject to a condition subsequent does not terminate automatically on the happening of the condition. To terminate, the grantor must exercise a right of entry, and here no right of entry was reserved. (C) is wrong because it is entirely unnecessary for Omar and Carl to be parties, since neither of them has any interest in the land. Omar has given up his interest entirely, and Carl is present in the conveyance only to serve as a measuring life for the life estate; he owns no interest in the land itself. (D) is wrong because the injury to the land is permanent and therefore should be prevented by an injunction.

Answer to Question 190

(B) Dolly can be convicted of either kidnapping or false imprisonment, but not both. False imprisonment consists of unlawful confinement of a person without her valid consent. Confinement requires that the victim either be compelled to go where she does not wish to go or to remain where she does not wish to remain. A confinement is unlawful unless specifically authorized by law or by the victim's consent. Any consent must be freely given by one with capacity to give such consent; *i.e.,* consent is invalidated if obtained by coercion, threats, deception, or incapacity arising from mental illness, retardation, or youth. Here, Dolly compelled Jane to go with her for the weekend by lying to her about her mother's having to go out of town and asking Dolly to care for Jane. This constitutes a confinement because, despite the fact that Jane enjoyed her time with Dolly, Jane was only four years old and incapable of validly consenting to go and remain with Dolly for the weekend. This confinement was not authorized by law. Consequently, Dolly can be convicted of false imprisonment. Kidnapping under modern statutes is confinement of a person that involves either some movement of the victim or concealment of the victim in a secret place. As with false imprisonment, consent freely given by a person competent to do so precludes a confinement or movement from being kidnapping. However, a young child is incapable of giving valid consent to her detention or movement. Dolly "moved" Jane by taking her home. This was a confinement because Jane was compelled to go where she did not wish to go. The fact that the experience apparently was totally enjoyable for Jane does not mean that there was a valid consent that would preclude a conviction of kidnapping. As explained above, Jane is incapacitated by her age from giving a valid consent to Dolly's actions. For the foregoing reasons, Dolly can be properly convicted of kidnapping. However, Dolly cannot be convicted of both kidnapping and false imprisonment, because false imprisonment is a lesser included offense of kidnapping (*i.e.,* kidnapping is a form of aggravated false imprisonment). A lesser included offense is one that consists entirely of some, but not all, elements of the greater crime. A person may not be convicted of both the greater offense and a lesser included offense. False imprisonment and kidnapping both consist of unlawfully confining a person against her will, with kidnapping containing the added elements of either moving or concealing the victim. Thus, false imprisonment is a lesser included offense of kidnapping. Consequently, Dolly may be convicted of *either* of these offenses, but *not both* of them. (A) is incorrect because kidnapping is not the only crime of which Dolly can be convicted. (C) is incorrect because, as discussed above, there can be a conviction for either of these crimes, but not for both of them. (D) is incorrect because these facts support a conviction for either of the crimes mentioned.

Answer to Question 191

(A) Since White persists in refusing to testify as to matters covered in his earlier testimony, he should be considered "unavailable" at Dean's trial. Thus, his former testimony should be admissible as an exception to the hearsay rule. It will be considered to be trustworthy since it was given during formal proceedings, under oath, and subject to cross-examination. (B) is wrong because this is not the applicable exception to the hearsay rule. In this case there is no evidence that White does not presently remember the facts in question. (C) is wrong because White could have asserted his privilege against self-incrimination when the former testimony was given. He can assert his privilege at present to keep from testifying. (D) is wrong because there is an applicable exception to the hearsay rule.

Answer to Question 192

(D) Having created a forum generally open for use by all groups, Hometown must justify its exclusions therefrom under applicable constitutional norms. To justify discriminatory exclusion from a public forum based on the religious content of a group's intended speech, Hometown must show that the ordinance is necessary to serve a compelling state interest, and that it is narrowly drawn to achieve that end. Alternative (B) suggests that the ordinance serves the compelling interest of maintaining separation of church and state. However, the former "equal access" policy did not offend the Establishment Clause. The former policy had a secular purpose (providing a forum in which citizens can exchange ideas); it avoided excessive entanglement with religion; and it did not have a primary effect of either advancing or inhibiting religion (permitting religious groups to use the auditorium would result in, at most, an incidental benefit). Thus, (B) is incorrect. (A) is incorrect because an unjustified content-based exclusion of religious speech is not made more acceptable by virtue of the fact that it treats all religions equally. (C) is incorrect because, although there is no authoritative constitutional definition of religion, it is unlikely that the term "religious groups" will be deemed to be impermissibly vague.

Answer to Question 193

(A) Light Company had notice that the insulators were being destroyed, causing the power lines to fall. Certainly, it was foreseeable that children, or anyone else, in the vicinity of a fallen line might be injured by such a dangerous condition. Consequently, Light Company had a duty to take reasonable steps, if possible, to prevent the lines from falling. Breach of this duty will lay the foundation for a recovery by Paul. (B) is simply an incorrect statement of the law. (C) is incorrect because, even if the company took measures to stop the destruction of the insulators, it also had a duty to take precautions against the danger of falling power lines. (D) is incorrect because Light Company had a duty to make its operations safe in light of the destruction of which it had notice. This is true even though the destruction was intentional. Criminal acts and intentional torts of third persons are not superseding forces where they are foreseeable, such as here.

Answer to Question 194

(D) When a purchaser has paid only part of the purchase price under an installment land contract, most courts hold that the purchaser is protected by the recording acts only to the extent of payment made. Depending on the equities involved in the case, the court has three options: (i) create a tenancy in common in the property, with the contract purchaser receiving a share of the property equal to the proportion of payments made; (ii) award the land to the prior claimant, but give the contract purchaser a right to recover the amount she paid (with interest), secured by a lien on the property; or (iii) award the land to the contract purchaser, but require the contract purchaser to make the remaining payments to the prior claimant. This last obligation is also secured by a lien on the property. Thus, I., II., and III. are all appropriate actions for the court. (A) is wrong because it does not include the remedy under which the property is awarded to Date and the remaining payments are made to Bay. (B) is wrong because IV. misstates the law. When only partial payment of the purchase price has been paid, the subsequent purchaser is protected only to the extent of payment. Thus, even if the equities favored Date and he were allowed to retain the property, Bay would be entitled to the remaining payments. (C) is wrong because the subsequent contract purchaser, Date, is protected by the recording act to the extent of his payment even though he acquired his interest from a donee. Since Bay did not record, he will have to pay Date $40,000 if he is awarded Whiteacre.

Answer to Question 195

(B) Restrictions on the ability of persons to be candidates may violate the First Amendment rights of speech and political association or the Fourteenth Amendment Equal Protection Clause. The Supreme Court uses a balancing test in determining whether a regulation of the electoral process is valid: if the restriction on First Amendment activities is severe, it will be upheld only if it is *narrowly tailored* to achieve a compelling interest, but if the restriction is reasonable and nondiscriminatory, it generally will be upheld on the basis of the state's important regulatory interests. Thus, if the ballot restriction here is deemed to be a severe and unreasonable burden on independent candidates, Roderick's best argument is choice (B)—that the objectives of the statute could be satisfactorily achieved by less burdensome means. [*See* Norman v. Reed (1992)] A state may require that independent candidates obtain a reasonable number of signatures. Although such a requirement may be burdensome, that factor alone does not make it invalid. Thus, (A) is not as strong an argument as (B). (D) is incorrect because signature requirements may be justified by a state interest in assuring that candidates have at least minimal support before they are allowed to appear on the ballot. (C) is incorrect because the fact that few independent candidates have obtained ballot status may simply reflect the absence of even the minimal popular support which the state may legitimately require.

Answer to Question 196

(D) The court should deny the motion to suppress because the police had a warrant to search Johnny's home. Johnny's expectation of privacy extended only to his own home, which was searched under a warrant. Johnny does not have standing to assert a Fourth Amendment claim regarding the search of Mildred's apartment because Mildred's apartment was not Johnny's home, and Johnny did not own it or have a right to possession of it. Thus, (A) is incorrect. Since Johnny cannot object to the search that provided the probable cause for the search of his apartment, (B) is also incorrect. (C) is not a valid justification because there is nothing to indicate that the seizure would fall under the "inevitable discovery" exception to the exclusionary rule.

Answer to Question 197

(D) Garrison is liable by virtue of his negligence, and Astin is vicariously liable for Garrison's negligence by virtue of the statute. Where such joint liability exists, the plaintiff may recover the entire judgment amount from either defendant. Further, where one is held liable for damages caused by another simply because of his relationship to that person (*i.e.*, vicarious liability), such person may seek indemnification from the person whose conduct actually caused the damage. Applying the foregoing principles to the facts of this question, Placek may recover the entire $100,000 from Astin and Garrison jointly. This eliminates (A) and (B). Because Astin is only liable vicariously, she is entitled to indemnification from Garrison for any amount collected from Astin by Placek. Therefore, (D) is the correct answer and (C) is incorrect.

Answer to Question 198

(B) If the Smiths had a reasonable (*i.e.*, good faith) belief in the enforceability of their claim, their surrender of the claim is valid consideration. (A) is wrong because the reason they made the gift is immaterial if neither Herb nor Edna deliberately misled them. (C) is irrelevant because the accounts were held in joint tenancy and any interest Edna may have had in the funds ended when she died. (D) is wrong because there was no consideration given for Edna's promise and the fact that it was in writing does not change the lack of consideration.

Answer to Question 199

(D) If the Smiths have given up a good faith claim, their agreement with Herb is a compromise supported by valid consideration. Thus, there is an enforceable contract. (A) is wrong because Herb was requesting a promise from the Smiths, not an act. (B) is wrong because Herb was under no obligation to reject a gift if he did not deliberately induce the Smiths to give it. (C) is wrong because there is no evidence that the Smiths gave the food in reliance on any promise made by Herb.

Answer to Question 200

(A) Walter's testimony, although hearsay, should be admissible under the exception for present sense impressions. Hearsay is defined under the Federal Rules as "a statement, other than one made by the declarant while testifying at the trial or hearing, offered in evidence to prove the truth of the matter asserted." Walter's testimony as to what Vincent said on the phone is hearsay: Vincent's statement that "Dornbach is here" is being offered in evidence by someone other than Vincent to prove that Dornbach was present at Vincent's house shortly before he was killed. Walter's testimony is therefore not admissible under Fed. R. Evid. 802 unless an exception to the hearsay rule applies. Rule 803(1) recognizes an exception for a statement "describing or explaining an event or condition made while the declarant was perceiving the event or condition, or immediately thereafter." Because the statement is made concurrently with the event it is describing, it is safe from defects in memory and there is usually little or no time for calculated misstatements. Here, Vincent's statement that "Dornbach is here" was made to Walter immediately after he went to the door and perceived Dornbach to be there. Thus, the statement is Vincent's present sense impression that Walter may testify to at trial. (B) is incorrect because Vincent's statement is not being offered to show his state of mind or his intent to do something in the future. The prosecution is using Vincent's statement simply to establish Dornbach's presence at Vincent's house the day he was killed. (C) is wrong because the prior identification must be by the witness testifying at trial to be admissible. Had Vincent survived an attempted homicide and testified at Dornbach's trial, Fed. R. Evid. 801(d)(1)(C) would permit his prior statement to Walter identifying Dornbach to be admitted as nonhearsay and substantive evidence. (D) is incorrect. While the testimony is hearsay, it falls within the exception to the hearsay rule for present sense impressions.

BAR REVIEW

Released Multistate Questions and Analytical Answers

CONSTITUTIONAL LAW QUESTIONS

Question 1

A newly enacted criminal statute provides, in its entirety, "No person shall utter to another person in a public place any annoying, disturbing or unwelcome language." Smith followed an elderly woman for three blocks down a public street, yelling in her ear offensive four-letter words. The woman repeatedly asked Smith to leave her alone, but he refused.

In the subsequent prosecution of Smith, the first under this statute, Smith will:

(A) Not prevail.

(B) Prevail, because speech of the sort described here may not be punished by the state because of the First and Fourteenth Amendments.

(C) Prevail, because though his speech may be punished by the state, the state may not do so under this statute.

(D) Prevail, because the average user of a public street would think his speech/action here was amusing and ridiculous rather than "annoying," etc.

Question 2

Congressional legislation regulating the conditions for marriages and divorces would be most likely upheld if it:

(A) Applied only to marriages and divorces by members of the armed services.

(B) Applied only to marriages performed by federal judges and to divorces granted by federal courts.

(C) Implemented an executive agreement seeking to define basic human rights.

(D) Applied only to marriages and divorces in the District of Columbia.

Question 3

Assume for the purposes of this question that you are counsel to the state legislative committee that is responsible for real estate laws in your state. The committee wants you to draft legislation to make all restrictions on land use, imposed by deeds (now or hereafter recorded), unenforceable in the future so that public land-use planning through zoning will have exclusive control in matters of land use.

Which of the following is *least* likely to be a consideration in the drafting of such legislation?

(A) Compensation for property rights taken by public authority.

(B) Impairment of contract.

(C) Sovereign immunity.

(D) Police power.

Questions 4-6 are based on the following fact situation:

Congress provides by statute that any state that fails to prohibit automobile speeds of over 55 miles per hour on highways within the state shall be denied federal highway construction funding. The state of Atlantic, one of the richest and most highway-oriented states in the country, refuses to enact such a statute.

4. Which of the following potential plaintiffs is most likely to be able to obtain a judicial determination of the validity of this federal statute?

(A) A taxpayer of the United States and the state of Atlantic who wants his state to get its fair share of his tax monies for highways, and fears that, if it does not, his state taxes will be increased to pay for the highway construction in the state of Atlantic that federal funds would have financed.

(B) Contractors who have been awarded contracts by the state of Atlantic for specified highway construction projects, which contracts are contingent on payment to the state of the federal funds to which it would otherwise be entitled.

(C) An automobile owner who lives in the state of Atlantic and regularly uses its highway system.

(D) An organization dedicated to keeping the federal government within the powers granted it by the Constitution.

5. The best argument that can be made in support of the constitutionality of this federal statute is that:

(A) The states conceded their authority over highways to the national government when the states accepted federal grants to help finance the highways.

(B) The federal government can regulate the use of state highways without limitation because the federal government paid for most of their construction costs.

(C) Reasonable legislators could believe that the 55 mile-per-hour speed limit will ensure that the federal money spent on highways results in greater benefit than harm to the public.

(D) A recent public opinion survey demonstrates that 90% of the people in this country support a 55 mile-per-hour speed limit.

6. The federal statute relating to disbursement of highway funds, conditioned on the 55 mile-per-hour speed limit, is probably:

(A) Unconstitutional.

(B) Constitutional only on the basis of the spending power.

(C) Constitutional only on the basis of the commerce power.

(D) Constitutional on the basis of both the spending power and the commerce power.

Questions 7-8 are based on the following fact situation:

A recently enacted state law forbids nonresident aliens from owning more than 100 acres of land within the state and directs the state attorney general to bring an action of ejectment whenever a nonresident alien owns such land. Zane, a nonresident alien, has obtained title to 200 acres of land in the state, and he brings an action in federal court to enjoin the state attorney general from enforcing the statute. The defendant moves to dismiss the complaint.

7. The best argument for Zane is that:

(A) States are forbidden by the Commerce Clause from interfering with the rights of nonresidents to own land.

(B) The state's power to restrict alien rights is limited by the federal power to control foreign relations.

(C) The state statute adversely affects Zane's right to travel.

(D) The 100-acre restriction means that aliens cannot engage in farming operations requiring larger amounts of land.

8. The federal court should:

(A) Dismiss the action, because under the Constitution, nonresident aliens may not sue in federal court.

(B) Dismiss the action, because a state has plenary power to determine the qualifications for landholding within its boundaries.

(C) Hear the action, because the United Nations Charter forbids such discrimination.

(D) Hear the action, because a federal question is presented.

Question 9

Zall, a resident of the state of Paxico, brought suit in federal district court against Motors, Inc., a Paxico corporation. Zall seeks recovery of $12,000 actual and $12,000 punitive damages arising from Motors's sale to him of a defective automobile. Zall's suit is based only on a common law contract theory.

From a constitutional standpoint, should the federal district court hear this suit on its merits?

(A) Yes, because Article III vests federal courts with jurisdiction over cases involving the obligation of contracts.

(B) Yes, because it is an action affecting interstate commerce.

(C) No, because this suit is not within the jurisdiction of an Article III court.

(D) No, because there is no case or controversy within the meaning of Article III.

Questions 10-11 are based on the following fact situation:

The state of Missoula has enacted a new election code designed to increase voter responsibility in the exercise of the franchise and to enlarge citizen participation in the electoral process. None of its provisions conflict with federal statutes.

10. Which of the following is the strongest reason for finding unconstitutional a requirement in the Missoula election code that each voter must be literate in English?

   (A) The requirement violates Article I, Section 2 of the Constitution, which provides that representatives to Congress be chosen "by the people of the several States."

   (B) The requirement violates Article I, Section 4 of the Constitution, which gives Congress the power to "make or alter" state regulations providing for

the "times" and "manner" of holding elections for senators and representatives.

   (C) The requirement violates the Due Process Clause of the Fourteenth Amendment.

   (D) The requirement violates the Equal Protection Clause of the Fourteenth Amendment.

11. The Missoula election code provides that in a special-purpose election for directors of a state watershed improvement district, the franchise is limited to landowners within the district, because they are the only ones directly affected by the outcome. Each vote is weighted according to the proportion of the holding of that individual in relation to the total affected property. The best argument in support of the statute and against the application of the "one person, one vote" principle in this situation is that the principle:

   (A) Applies only to election of individuals to statewide public office.

   (B) Does not apply where property rights are involved.

   (C) Does not apply because the actions of such a district principally affect landowners.

   (D) Does not apply because of rights reserved to the states by the Tenth Amendment.

Questions 12-14 are based on the following fact situation:

The state of Yuma provides by statute, "No person may be awarded any state construction contract without agreeing to employ only citizens of the state and of the United States in performance of the contract."

12. In evaluating the constitutionality of this state statute under the Supremacy Clause,

which of the following would be most directly relevant?

(A) The general unemployment rate in the nation.

(B) The treaties and immigration laws of the United States.

(C) The need of the state for this particular statute.

(D) The number of aliens currently residing in Yuma.

13. If the Yuma statute is attacked as violating the Commerce Clause, which of the following defenses is the *weakest*?

(A) The statute will help protect the workers of the state of Yuma from competition by foreign workers.

(B) The statute will help ensure that workers with jobs directly affecting the performance of public contracts are dedicated to their jobs.

(C) The statute will help ensure a continuously available and stable work force for the execution of public contracts.

(D) The statute will help ensure that only the most qualified individuals work on public contracts.

14. Suppose the state supreme court declares the statute to be unconstitutional on the ground that it violates the Privileges and Immunities Clause of the Fourteenth Amendment to the federal Constitution and the Equal Protection Clause of the state constitution. If the state seeks review in the United States Supreme Court, which of the following statements is most accurate?

(A) The United States Supreme Court may properly review that decision by certiorari only.

(B) The United States Supreme Court may properly review that decision by appeal only.

(C) The United States Supreme Court may properly review that decision by appeal or certiorari.

(D) The United States Supreme Court may not properly review that decision.

Questions 15-16 are based on the following fact situation:

The state of Champlain enacts the Young Adult Marriage Counseling Act, which provides that, before any persons less than 30 years of age may be issued a marriage license, they must receive at least five hours of marriage counseling from a state-licensed social worker. This counseling is designed to ensure that applicants for marriage licenses know their legal rights and duties in relation to marriage and parenthood, understand the "true nature" of the marriage relationship, and understand the procedures for obtaining divorces.

15. Pine, aged 25, contemplates marrying Ross, aged 25. Both are residents of the state of Champlain. Pine has not yet proposed to Ross because he is offended by the counseling requirement.

Pine sues in federal court seeking a declaratory judgment that the Young Adult Marriage Counseling Act is unconstitutional. Which of the following is the clearest ground for dismissal of this action by the court?

(A) Pine and Ross are residents of the same state.

(B) No substantial federal question is presented.

(C) The suit presents a nonjusticiable political question.

(D) The suit is unripe.

16. In a case in which the constitutionality of the Young Adult Marriage Counseling Act is in issue, the burden of persuasion will probably be on the:

(A) Person challenging the law, because there is a strong presumption that elected state legislators acted properly.

(B) Person challenging the law, because the Tenth Amendment authorizes states to determine the conditions on which they issue marriage licenses.

(C) State, because there is a substantial impact on the right to marry, and that right is fundamental.

(D) State, because there is a substantial impact on the discrete and insular class of young adults.

Question 17

A statute of the state of Tuscarora made it a misdemeanor to construct any building of more than five stories without an automatic fire sprinkler system.

A local construction company built, in Tuscarora, a 10-story federal office building. It constructed the building according to the precise specifications of a federal contract authorized by federal statutes. Because the building was built without the automatic fire sprinkler system required by state law, Tuscarora prosecutes the private contractor.

Which of the following is the company's strongest defense to that prosecution?

(A) The state sprinkler requirement denies the company property or liberty without due process.

(B) The state sprinkler requirement denies the company equal protection of the laws.

(C) As applied, the state sprinkler requirement violates the Supremacy Clause.

(D) As applied, the state sprinkler requirement violates the Obligation of Contracts Clause.

Question 18

A state accredits both public and private schools, licenses their teachers, and supplies textbooks on secular subjects to all such schools. Country Schoolhouse, a private school that offers elementary and secondary education in the state, denies admission to all non-Caucasians.

In a suit to enjoin as unconstitutional the continued racially exclusionary admissions policy of the Country Schoolhouse, which of the following is the strongest argument *against* the school?

(A) Because education is a public function, the Country Schoolhouse may not discriminate on racial grounds.

(B) The state is so involved in school regulation and support that the Equal Protection Clause of the Fourteenth Amendment is applicable to the school.

(C) The state is constitutionally obligated to eliminate segregation in all public and private educational institutions within the state.

(D) Any school with teachers who are licensed by the state is forbidden to discriminate on racial grounds.

Question 19

A federal statute requires United States civil service employees to retire at age 75. However, that statute also states that civil service employees of the armed forces must retire at age 65.

Prentis, a 65-year-old civil service employee of the Department of the Army, seeks a declaratory judgment that would forbid his mandatory retirement until age 75.

The strongest argument that Prentis can make to invalidate the requirement that he retire at age 65 is that the law:

(A) Denies him a privilege or immunity of national citizenship.

(B) Deprives him of a property right without just compensation.

(C) Is not within the scope of any of the enumerated powers of Congress in Article I, Section 8.

(D) Invidiously discriminates against him on the basis of age in violation of the Fifth Amendment.

Question 20

Congress passes a law regulating the wholesale and retail prices of "every purchase or sale of oil, natural gas, and electric power made in the United States."

The strongest argument in support of the constitutionality of this statute is that:

(A) The Constitution expressly empowers Congress to enact laws for "the general welfare."

(B) Congress has the authority to regulate such products' interstate transportation and importation from abroad.

(C) Congress may regulate the prices of every purchase and sale of goods and services made in this country, because commerce includes buying and selling.

(D) In inseverable aggregates, the domestic purchases or sales of such products affect interstate or foreign commerce.

Question 21

Congress enacted a statute providing that persons may challenge a state energy law on the ground that it is in conflict with the federal Constitution in either federal or state court. According to this federal statute, any decision by a lower state court upholding a state energy law against a challenge based on the federal Constitution may be appealed directly to the United States Supreme Court.

The provisions of this statute that authorize direct United States Supreme Court review of

specified decisions rendered by lower state courts are:

(A) Constitutional, because congressional control over questions of energy use is plenary.

(B) Constitutional, because Congress may establish the manner by which the appellate jurisdiction of the United States Supreme Court is exercised.

(C) Unconstitutional, because they infringe the sovereign right of states to have their supreme courts review decisions of their lower state courts.

(D) Unconstitutional, because under Article III of the Constitution, the United States Supreme Court does not have authority to review directly decisions of lower state courts.

Question 22

Congress enacts a criminal statute prohibiting "any person from interfering in any way with any right conferred on another person by the Equal Protection Clause of the Fourteenth Amendment."

Application of this statute to Jones, a private citizen, would be most clearly constitutional if Jones, with threats of violence, coerces:

(A) A public school teacher to exclude black pupils from her class, solely because of their race.

(B) Black pupils, solely because of their race, to refrain from attending a privately owned and operated school licensed by the state.

(C) The bus driver operating a free school bus service under the sponsorship of a local church to refuse to allow black pupils on the bus, solely because of their race.

(D) The federal official in charge of distributing certain federal benefits directly to students from distributing them to black pupils, solely because of their race.

Questions 23-24 are based on the following fact situation:

All lawyers practicing in the state of Erewhon must be members of the State Bar Association, by order of the state supreme court. Several state officials serve on the Bar Association's Board of Bar Governors. The Board of Bar Governors authorizes the payment of dues for two staff members to the Cosmopolitan Club, a private dining club licensed to sell alcoholic beverages. The Cosmopolitan Club is frequented by affluent businessmen and professionals and by legislators. It is generally known that the purpose of the membership of the Bar Association staff is to enable them to go where members of the "elite" meet and to lobby for legislation in which the Bar Association is interested. The State Association has numerous committees and subcommittees concerned with family law, real estate law, unauthorized practice, etc., and its recommendations often influence state policy. Some committee meetings are held at the Cosmopolitan Club. The club is known to have rules which restrict membership by race, religion, and sex.

Plaintiffs, husband and wife, who are members of the Erewhon Bar Association, petition the Board of Bar Governors to adopt a resolution prohibiting the payment of club dues to and the holding of meetings of the Bar Association or its committees at places that discriminate on the basis of race, religion, or sex. After substantial public discussion, the Board of Bar Governors, by a close vote, fails to pass such a resolution. These events receive extensive coverage in the local newspapers. Plaintiffs bring an action in federal court seeking an injunction against such payments and the holding of meetings in such places as the Cosmopolitan Club.

23. The strongest argument for Plaintiffs is:

(A) Private rights to discriminate and associate freely must defer to a public interest against discrimination on the basis of race, religion, or sex.

(B) The failure of the State Bar Association to pass a resolution forbidding discrimination on the basis of race,

religion, or sex constitutes a denial of equal protection.

(C) The State Bar Association is an agency of the state and its payment of dues to such private clubs promotes discrimination on the basis of race, religion, and sex.

(D) The State Bar Association's payment of dues to such private clubs promotes discrimination on the basis of race, religion, and sex.

24. Which of the following actions should a federal district court take with respect to jurisdiction?

(A) Hear the case on the merits, because a federal claim is presented.

(B) Hear the case on the merits, because the expenditure of state funds in support of segregation is forbidden by the Fifth Amendment.

(C) Abstain from jurisdiction, because the constitutional issue should be litigated first in a state court.

(D) Dismiss the case for lack of jurisdiction, because the issue of Bar Association activities is solely within the domain of state law.

Question 25

Congress enacts a statute punishing "each and every conspiracy entered into by any two or more persons for the purpose of denying black persons housing, employment, or education, solely because of their race."

Under which of the following constitutional provisions is the authority of Congress to pass such a statute most clearly and easily justifiable?

(A) The Obligation of Contracts Clause.

(B) The General Welfare Clause of Article I, Section 8.

(C) The Thirteenth Amendment.

(D) The Fourteenth Amendment.

Question 26

A federal criminal law makes it a crime for any citizen of the United States not specifically authorized by the President to negotiate with a foreign government for the purpose of influencing the foreign government in relation to a dispute with the United States.

The strongest constitutional ground for the validity of this law is that:

(A) Under several of its enumerated powers, Congress may legislate to preserve the monopoly of the national government over the conduct of United States foreign affairs.

(B) The President's inherent power to negotiate for the United States with foreign countries authorizes the President, even in the absence of statutory authorization, to punish citizens who engage in such negotiations without permission.

(C) The law deals with foreign relations and therefore is not governed by the First Amendment.

(D) Federal criminal laws dealing with international affairs need not be as specific as those dealing with domestic affairs.

Question 27

A state statute requires that all buses which operate as common carriers on the highways of the state shall be equipped with seat belts for passengers. Transport Lines, an interstate carrier, challenges the validity of the statute and the right of the state to make the requirement.

What is the best basis for a constitutional challenge by Transport Lines?

(A) Violation of the Due Process Clause of the Fourteenth Amendment.

(B) Violation of the Equal Protection Clause of the Fourteenth Amendment.

(C) Unreasonable burden on interstate commerce.

(D) Difficulty of enforcement.

Question 28

Congress passes an act requiring that all owners of bicycles in the United States register them with a federal bicycle registry. The purpose of the law is to provide reliable evidence of ownership to reduce bicycle theft. No fee is charged for the registration. Although most stolen bicycles are kept or resold by the thieves in the same cities in which the bicycles were stolen, an increasing number of bicycles are being taken to cities in other states for resale.

Is this act of Congress constitutional?

(A) Yes, because Congress has the power to regulate property for the general welfare.

(B) Yes, because Congress could determine that, in inseverable aggregates, bicycle thefts affect interstate commerce.

(C) No, because most stolen bicycles remain within the state in which they were stolen.

(D) No, because the registration of vehicles is a matter reserved to the states by the Tenth Amendment.

Question 29

A statute of the state of Lanape flatly bans the sale or distribution of contraceptive devices to minors. Drugs, Inc., a national retailer of drugs and related items, is charged with violating the Lanape statute.

Which of the following is the strongest constitutional argument Drugs, Inc., could make in defending itself against prosecution for violation of this statute?

(A) The statute constitutes an undue burden on interstate commerce.

(B) The statute denies minors one of their fundamental rights without due process.

(C) The statute denies Drugs, Inc., a privilege or immunity of state citizenship.

(D) The statute violates the First Amendment right to freedom of religion because it regulates morals.

Question 30

Congress enacted a law prohibiting the killing, capture, or removal of any form of wildlife upon or from any federally owned land.

Which of the following is the most easily justifiable source of national authority for this federal law?

(A) The Commerce Clause of Article I, Section 8.

(B) The Privileges and Immunities Clause of Article IV.

(C) The Enforcement Clause of the Fourteenth Amendment.

(D) The Property Clause of Article IV, Section 3.

Question 31

The President of the United States recognizes the country of Ruritania and undertakes diplomatic relations with its government through the Secretary of State. Ruritania is governed by a repressive totalitarian government.

In an appropriate federal court, Dunn brings a suit against the President and Secretary of State to set aside this action on the ground that it is inconsistent with the principles of our constitutional form of government. Dunn has a lucrative contract with the United States Department of Commerce to provide commercial information about Ruritania. The contract expressly terminates, however, "when the President recognizes the country of Ruritania and undertakes diplomatic relations with its government."

Which of the following is the most proper disposition of the Dunn suit by the federal court?

(A) Suit dismissed, because Dunn does not have standing to bring this action.

(B) Suit dismissed, because there is no adversity between Dunn and the defendants.

(C) Suit dismissed, because it presents a nonjusticiable political question.

(D) Suit decided on the merits.

Question 32

Congress passes an Energy Conservation Act. The Act requires all users of energy in this country to reduce their consumption by a specified percentage, to be set by a presidential executive order. The Act sets forth specific standards the President must use in setting the percentage and detailed procedures to be followed.

The provision that allows the President to set the exact percentage is probably:

(A) Constitutional, because it creates a limited administrative power to implement the statute.

(B) Constitutional, because inherent executive powers permit such action even without statutory authorization.

(C) Unconstitutional as an undue delegation of legislative power to the executive.

(D) Unconstitutional, because it violates the Due Process Clause of the Fifth Amendment.

Question 33

The federal government has complete jurisdiction over certain park land located within the state of Plains. To conserve the wildlife that inhabits that land, the federal government enacts a statute forbidding all hunting of animals in the federal park. That statute also forbids the hunting of animals that have left the federal park and have entered the state of Plains.

Hanson has a hunting license from the state of Plains authorizing him to hunt deer anywhere in the state. On land within the state of Plains located adjacent to the federal park, Hanson shoots a deer he knows has recently left the federal land.

Hanson is prosecuted for violating the federal hunting law. The strongest ground supporting the constitutionality of the federal law forbidding the hunting of wild animals that wander off federal property is that:

(A) This law is a necessary and proper means of protecting United States property.

(B) The animals are moving in the stream of interstate commerce.

(C) The police powers of the federal government encompass protection of wild animals.

(D) Shooting wild animals is a privilege, not a right.

Question 34

A state statute makes fraud for personal financial gain a crime. Jones was convicted of violating this statute on three separate occasions. Following his most recent conviction, he professed to have undergone a religious conversion and proclaimed himself to be the divine minister of "St. Rockport," an alleged messiah who would shortly be making his appearance on earth. Jones solicited cash donations from the public to support his efforts to spread the word of St. Rockport and his coming appearance on earth.

Following complaints by several contributors who claimed he defrauded them, Jones was again charged with fraud under this state statute. The charge was that Jones "should have known that his representations about St. Rockport were false and, therefore, that he made them solely to collect cash donations for his personal gain." A witness for the prosecution in Jones's trial stated that Jones had admitted that, at times, he had doubts about the existence of St. Rockport. Jones was the only religious minister prosecuted for fraud under this state statute.

The strongest constitutional defense that Jones could assert would be that this prosecution:

(A) Deprived him of the equal protection of the laws because other religious ministers have not been charged under this statute.

(B) Denied him procedural due process because it placed upon Jones the burden of rebutting evidence, submitted by the state, of his bad faith in raising this money.

(C) Denied him rights conferred by the Obligation of Contracts Clause by preventing him from taking money from persons who wished to contract with him to spread the word of St. Rockport.

(D) Denied him the free exercise of religion in violation of the First and Fourteenth Amendments because it required the state to determine the truth or falsity of the content of his religious beliefs.

Questions 35-37 are based on the following fact situation:

As part of a comprehensive federal aid-to-education program, Congress included the following provisions as conditions for state receipt of federal funds: (1) Whenever textbooks are provided to students without charge, they must include no religious instruction and must be made available on the same terms to students in all public and private schools accredited by the state educational authority. (2) Salary supplements can be paid to teachers in public and private schools, up to 10% of existing salary schedules, where present compensation is less than the average salary for persons of comparable training and experience, provided that no such supplement is paid to any teacher who instructs in religious subjects. (3) Construction grants can be made toward the cost of physical plants at private colleges and universities, provided that no part of the grant is used for buildings in which instruction in religious subject matters is offered.

35. Federal taxpayer Allen challenges the provision that allows the distribution of free textbooks to students in a private school where religious instruction is included in the curriculum. On the question of the adequacy of Allen's standing to raise the constitutional question, the most likely result is that standing will be:

(A) Sustained, because any congressional spending authorization can be challenged by any taxpayer.

(B) Sustained, because the challenge to the exercise of congressional spending power is based on a claimed violation of specific constitutional limitations on the exercise of such power.

(C) Denied, because there is insufficient nexus between the taxpayer and the challenged expenditures.

(D) Denied, because, in the case of private schools, no state action is involved.

36. Federal taxpayer Bates also challenges the salary supplements for teachers in private schools where religious instruction is included in the curriculum. On the substantive constitutional issue, the most likely result is that the salary supplements will be:

(A) Sustained, because the statute provides that no supplements will be made to teachers who are engaged in any religious instruction.

(B) Sustained, because to distinguish between private and public school teachers would violate the Free Exercise Clause of the First Amendment.

(C) Held unconstitutional, because some religions would benefit disproportionately.

(D) Held unconstitutional, because the policing of the restriction would amount to an excessive entanglement with religion.

37. Federal taxpayer Bates also challenges the construction grants to church-operated private colleges and universities. The most likely result is that the construction grants will be:

(A) Sustained, because aid to one aspect of an institution of higher education not shown to be pervasively sectarian does not necessarily free it to spend its other resources for religious purposes.

(B) Sustained, because bricks and mortar do not aid religion in a way forbidden by the Establishment Clause of the First Amendment.

(C) Held unconstitutional, because any financial aid to a church-operated school strengthens the religious purposes of the institution.

(D) Held unconstitutional, because the grants involve or cause an excessive entanglement with religion.

Question 38

Leonard was the high priest of a small cult of Satan worshippers living in New Arcadia. As a part of the practice of their religious beliefs, a cat was required to be sacrificed to the glory of Satan after a live dissection of the animal in which it endured frightful pain. In the course of such a religious sacrifice, Leonard was arrested on the complaint of the local Humane Society and charged under a statute punishing cruelty to animals.

On appeal, a conviction of Leonard probably will be:

(A) Sustained, on the grounds that belief in or worship of Satan does not enjoy constitutional protection.

(B) Sustained, on the grounds that sincere religious belief is not an adequate defense on these facts.

(C) Overturned, on the grounds that the constitutionally guaranteed freedom of religion and its expression was violated.

(D) Overturned, on the grounds that the beliefs of the cult members in the need for the sacrifice might be reasonable, and their act was religious.

Question 39

Congress enacts a law providing that all disagreements between the United States and a state over federal grant-in-aid funds shall be settled by the filing of suit in the federal district court in the affected state. "The judgment of that federal court shall be transmitted to the head of the federal agency dispensing such funds, who, if satisfied that the judgment is fair and lawful, shall execute the judgment according to its terms."

This law is:

(A) Constitutional, because disagreements over federal grant-in-aid funds necessarily involve federal questions within the judicial power of the United States.

(B) Constitutional, because the spending of federal monies necessarily includes the authority to provide for the effective settlement of disputes involving them.

(C) Unconstitutional, because it vests authority in the federal court to determine a matter prohibited to it by the Eleventh Amendment.

(D) Unconstitutional, because it vests authority in a federal court to render an advisory opinion.

Question 40

A statute authorizes a specified federal administrative agency to issue rules governing the distribution of federal grant funds for scientific research. The statute provides that, in issuing those rules, the agency must follow procedures and substantive standards contained in the statute. In a severable provision, the statute also provides that otherwise valid rules issued by the agency under authority delegated to it by this statute may be set aside by a majority vote of a designated standing joint committee of Congress.

The provision of this statute relating to the power of the designated standing joint committee of Congress is:

(A) Constitutional, because it is a necessary and proper means of ensuring that the rules issued by this agency are actually consistent with the will of Congress.

(B) Constitutional, because discretionary money grants authorized by statute are privileges, not rights, and, therefore, Congress has greater freedom to intervene in their administration than it has to intervene in the administration of regulatory laws.

(C) Unconstitutional, because it denies equal protection of the laws to members of Congress who are not appointed to the joint legislative committee authorized to set aside rules of this agency.

(D) Unconstitutional, because it authorizes a congressional change of legal rights and obligations by means other than those specified in the Constitution for the enactment of laws.

CONSTITUTIONAL LAW ANSWERS

Answer to Question 1

(C) The statute at issue is void for vagueness. If a criminal law or regulation fails to give persons reasonable notice of what is prohibited, it may violate the Due Process Clause. This principle is applied somewhat strictly when First Amendment activity is involved in order to avoid the chilling effect a vague law might have on speech (*i.e.,* if it is unclear what speech is regulated, people might refrain from speech that is permissible for fear that they will be violating the law). Here, the statute does not give reasonable notice as to what language is being prohibited, and no court decisions have limited its construction. Thus, it is impermissibly vague, and Smith will prevail. Therefore, (A) incorrectly states that Smith will not prevail. (B) is incorrect because it is too broad a statement. First Amendment freedoms are not absolute; for instance, obscenity may be punished under a properly drawn statute. The problem here is that it cannot be determined what speech is being prohibited. (D) is incorrect because there is no **constitutional** "average person test."

Answer to Question 2

(D) (D) is the "safest" answer because Congress has the same legislative authority over the District of Columbia as a state legislature has over matters internal to its state. This clearly includes the authority to regulate marriage and divorce. It could be argued that Congress's military and war powers could sustain (A); that Congress's power to regulate the jurisdiction of federal courts could sustain (B); that Congress's power over external affairs, which includes the power to implement executive agreements, could sustain (C), but these arguments are more speculative than that for (D).

Answer to Question 3

(C) (A) is incorrect because, depending upon specific applications of the proposed legislation, a "taking of property," requiring just compensation, could result. This would raise the issue as to whether the governmental action amounts to a taking (in which case the state must fairly compensate the owner of property) or a regulation (in which case there is no need for compensation), and would certainly be a consideration in the drafting of the subject legislation. (B) is incorrect because the proposed legislation could be seen as constituting a prohibited retroactive impairment of contract rights. (D) is incorrect because questions of "taking" often arise in connection with the state's exercise of its police power (*i.e.,* the power to legislate for the health, welfare, or safety of the people). (C) appears least relevant because the proposed legislation does not seem to contemplate suits against the state.

Answer to Question 4

(B) In order to have standing, a person must usually show a direct and immediate personal injury due to the challenged government action. The claimant must be in a position to demonstrate a concrete stake in the outcome of the suit and a direct impairment of his own constitutional rights. The contractors in (B) satisfy the criteria. The plaintiffs in (C) and (D) do not. As to (A), federal taxpayers generally have no standing to challenge the validity of federal expenditures; in any event, the federal taxpayer here is not complaining of any added tax burdens. State taxpayers may challenge the validity of state programs that involve measurable state expenditures, but here it is a federal program whose constitutionality is in issue and, in any event, the state expenditure is only hypothetical.

Answer to Question 5

(C) (A) is incorrect because the mere acceptance of federal money to help pay for highways does not amount to a concession of authority over such highways. Federal authority over the highways must be derived from a specific source, rather than from the mere supplying of funds for the highways. Thus, (B) also is incorrect. (D) is incorrect because the constitutionality (or lack thereof) of an exercise of federal legislative power is in no way based on public opinion. (C) is correct because Congress has power to condition federal spending if Congress reasonably finds that the spending program is for the general welfare. Even where Congress otherwise has no power to regulate an area, it can use its spending power to so regulate by requiring entities that accept government money to act in a certain manner.

Answer to Question 6

(D) (D) is correct, because Congress clearly has the right to place conditions on appropriated funds under the spending power and because highways fall within the purview of interstate commerce and are thus subject to Commerce Clause regulation. Few cases have ever declared a generally applicable federal statute based on commerce power to be an unconstitutional interference with state functions, and spending power conditions were upheld in *South Dakota v. Dole* (1987). It follows that (A), (B), and (C) are incorrect.

Answer to Question 7

(B) (B) is an accurate statement of constitutional doctrine. Congress has plenary power over aliens. A state or local law that is based on alienage is subject to strict scrutiny (*i.e.*, a compelling state interest must be shown to justify disparate treatment). When, as with the state law here at issue, state action regulates aliens, Congress's plenary power over aliens arising from its power over naturalization is more directly implicated than Congress's commerce power; thus (B) is a better choice than (A). (C) is incorrect because the state law does not penalize anyone for exercising the right to travel from state to state. (D)'s relevance is remote, at best.

Answer to Question 8

(D) The federal judicial power extends to cases arising under the Constitution of the United States. (D) is correct because the recently enacted state law discriminates against aliens, and many state discriminations against aliens have been held unconstitutional. Thus, there is a federal question. (A) is incorrect because aliens are permitted to bring certain actions in federal court challenging constitutionally suspect governmental action. (B) is incorrect because a state's regulation of land ownership may not be exercised in a manner that runs afoul of constitutional parameters. (C) is incorrect because, even assuming that there is a United Nations charter provision on point, this would not give the court jurisdiction; there must be a federal question.

Answer to Question 9

(C) The court should not hear this suit on the merits because Article III courts are not empowered to hear suits between citizens of the same state where no federal question jurisdiction is involved. Article III lists the cases to which federal jurisdiction extends. It includes suits arising under federal law, and suits between citizens of two or more states. Zall's suit against Motors involves two citizens of the state of Paxico and no federal question is raised. No provision of Article III covers such a suit. Thus, Zall should have brought suit in Paxico state court. (A) is incorrect because the Contracts Clause deals with state *legislation* impairing contracts and no such legislation is implied by the facts. Article III has no general provision for suits involving the obligation of contracts. (B) is incorrect because while it might be said that the action can affect interstate commerce and thus is subject to federal regulation, absent such federal regulation, there is no basis under Article III for jurisdiction. Article III does not provide for federal court jurisdiction in all cases affecting interstate commerce. (D) is incorrect because a "case or controversy" exists. The case or controversy requirement only prohibits federal courts from rendering advisory opinions, such as where the case is moot or unripe, or the parties are not truly adverse. The parties here are clearly adverse and there is a real, live controversy; the only thing missing is a basis for federal court jurisdiction.

Answer to Question 10

(D) The Fourteenth Amendment prevents states from discriminating against the exercise of "fundamental rights," one of which is the right to vote, unless the state shows a compelling interest. The English requirement suggests discrimination against the right to vote of people who cannot speak English. (A) is clearly inapplicable. (B) is clearly incorrect. (C) may be correct, but it is not as good as (D). Note that the Supreme Court has not specifically decided whether a "discriminatory purpose" is required for a violation of the Fifteenth Amendment's bar against governmental racial discrimination in voting.

Answer to Question 11

(C) When a governmental body establishes voting districts for the election of representatives, the number of persons in each district may not vary significantly ("one person, one vote"). This principle applies to almost every election where a person is being elected to perform normal governmental functions. However, the government can limit the class of persons who are allowed to vote in an election of persons to serve on a special purpose government unit if the unit has a special impact on the class of enfranchised voters. The watershed improvement districts referred to in this question are so specialized that election of their directors is not subject to the "one person, one vote" principle. These districts disproportionately affect landowners and do not perform general governmental functions. Thus, (C) is correct. (A) is incorrect because "one person, one vote" has a broader reach than merely election to statewide office. As noted above, the principle applies to almost every election for the performance of normal governmental functions. (B) is incorrect because conditioning the right to vote on property ownership normally would be invalid under the Equal Protection Clause. Only certain special purpose elections can be based on property ownership. (D) incorrectly implies that "one person, one vote" does not apply to states. In fact, the principle is binding on states through the Equal Protection Clause of the Fourteenth Amendment.

Answer to Question 12

(B) An act of Congress or federal regulation supersedes any state or local action that actually conflicts with the federal rule, whether by commanding conduct inconsistent with that required by the federal rule, or by forbidding conduct that the federal rule is designed to foster. The conflict need not relate to conduct; it is sufficient if the state law interferes with achievement of a federal objective. In addition, note that Congress has exclusive power over naturalization and denaturalization. Thus, United States treaties and immigration laws would supersede an inconsistent state law, making them relevant to the constitutionality of the state Yuma statute. (A), (C), and (D) all refer to some perceived justification for the statute. However, they are irrelevant because, even if a state law was enacted for a valid purpose, it will be rendered void if it conflicts with federal law.

Answer to Question 13

(A) The acknowledgment that the statute will protect Yuma workers from outside competition is the weakest defense because it indicates that the law has a discriminatory impact. State legislation that is challenged on Commerce Clause grounds (i) must not discriminate against out-of-state competition to benefit local economic interests, and (ii) must not be unduly burdensome. A discriminatory law will be valid only if it furthers an important *noneconomic* state interest and there are no reasonable alternatives available, whereas a nondiscriminatory law will be valid as long as the legitimate state interests outweigh the burden on interstate commerce. Here, choices (B), (C), and (D) all attempt to provide a nondiscriminatory rationale for the statute, making it easier to pass muster under the Commerce Clause, while choice (A) amounts to a concession by the state that the statute discriminates in favor of state economic interests, making it more likely to be invalidated.

Answer to Question 14

(D) The Supreme Court will hear a case from a state court only if the state court judgment turned on federal grounds. The Court will refuse jurisdiction if it finds adequate and independent non-federal grounds to support the state decision. The nonfederal grounds must be adequate in that they are fully dispositive of the case, so that even if the federal grounds are wrongly decided, it would not affect the outcome of the case. Also, the nonfederal grounds must be independent. If the state court's interpretation of its state provision was based on federal case law interpreting an identical federal provision, the state law grounds for the decision is not independent. Here, the state supreme court rested its decision on the ground of violation of the state constitution, without any interpretation based on an identical federal provision. Thus, the decision is supported by adequate and independent nonfederal grounds, and the Supreme Court should refuse jurisdiction. (A), (B), and (C) are all based on the incorrect premise that the Supreme Court may somehow properly review the decision.

Answer to Question 15

(D) This issue would not be considered ripe because there is no real harm or immediate threat of harm. If Pine and Ross were actually engaged to be married, refused to undergo the counseling, and then requested that a license be issued, the issue would be ripe, because at that point they would have been denied the license on the basis of the statute. As it is, they have not even come to the point of requesting a license. (A) is wrong because diversity is not the only basis for federal jurisdiction. (B) is wrong because there is a substantial federal question—the right to marry is part of the constitutionally protected right of privacy. (C) is wrong because no political question is presented. Political questions include those issues committed by the Constitution to another branch of government and those inherently incapable of resolution and enforcement by the judicial process.

Answer to Question 16

(C) Where a fundamental right, such as the right to marry, is substantially affected, the state bears the burden of persuading the court that the statute in question is necessary to achieve a compelling or overriding government purpose. (A) is wrong because there is no presumption that state legislators acted properly. Also, as can be seen from the analysis at the beginning of this answer, (A) places the burden on the wrong party. (B) also places the burden on the wrong party. In addition, the Tenth Amendment provides that all powers not delegated to the federal government by the Constitution are reserved to the states. The Tenth Amendment does not authorize states to place unconstitutional burdens on fundamental rights. (D) is wrong, because "young adults" are not a discrete and insular class entitled to judicial scrutiny of laws that arguably require equal protection under the law.

Answer to Question 17

(C)   Whenever Congress acts within the scope of a delegated power such as that of the Commerce Clause, the Supremacy Clause renders any conflicting state or local law or action void. Thus, as applied, the state sprinkler requirement violates the Supremacy Clause. (A) is wrong because a substantive due process claim would be almost guaranteed to fail, since business regulation is now invariably sustained as reasonable state action under the Due Process Clause. (B) is wrong because classifications that relate only to matters of economics or social welfare (not fundamental rights) and do not employ suspect or quasi-suspect classifications are almost always upheld. The classification of building story size is not arbitrary. (D) is wrong because the contract has not been breached, so no Obligation of Contracts Clause issue is presented.

Answer to Question 18

(B)   Race is a "suspect category" under the Equal Protection Clause, but the Fourteenth Amendment does not apply to purely private acts of discrimination. However, if state action is found, the clause can be invoked against Country Schoolhouse. State action can be found in the actions of seemingly private individuals who (i) perform exclusive public functions or (ii) have significant state involvement in their activities. (B) states an example of significant state involvement and is, therefore, correct. (A) is wrong because to be state action, the activity must be both a traditional and exclusive government function. Education does not so qualify. The Supreme Court has only found running a town and running an election for public office to be such exclusive government functions. (C) is wrong because the statement is overbroad. Only intentional discrimination will be found to create discriminatory classifications calling for strict scrutiny. (D) is wrong because state involvement must be "significant" to trigger state action. Mere licensure is generally not "significant."

Answer to Question 19

(D)   Prentis's strongest argument would be that his Fifth Amendment due process rights have been abridged. While the Equal Protection Clause of the Fourteenth Amendment only applies to state action, it is clear that arbitrary or invidious discrimination by the federal government violates the Due Process Clause of the Fifth Amendment. Thus, there are really two equal protection guarantees. Since age is not a suspect category, this legislation would only be subject to the rational basis test. Because other civil service employees can work until the age of 75, Prentis would have an argument that the state had invidiously discriminated against him on the basis of age. His argument would probably fail, but is the "strongest" argument of the four alternatives given. (A) is wrong because employment is not a privilege or immunity of national citizenship. (B) is wrong because, where a public employee holds his position at the will of an employer, there is no property interest in continued employment. Since Prentis was dismissed on the basis of his age, rather than for cause, he had no property interest in continued employment. (C) is wrong because under the Necessary and Proper Clause, Congress may do anything that is arguably appropriate to relate to a federal interest.

Answer to Question 20

(D)   This would be the strongest argument in support of the constitutionality of this statute. Article I, Section 8, Paragraph 3 empowers Congress to "regulate commerce with foreign nations and among the several states, and with the Indian tribes." Only rarely has a modern case invalidated a federal law regulating nongovernmental persons because it exceeded the commerce power. (A) is wrong because Congress does not have a general welfare power to regulate all activity in this country. (B) is wrong because it would not justify the statute at issue. (C) is wrong because it overstates congressional power by failing to connect the activity to "commerce."

Answer to Question 21

(B) Congress has the power to regulate and limit the appellate jurisdiction of the Supreme Court. Thus, the statute here, which was enacted by Congress, properly authorizes direct appeal of a specified decision to the Supreme Court. (A) is incorrect because there is nothing to support the proposition that Congress has plenary control over matters involving energy use. Also, (A) does not address the issue of jurisdiction of the Supreme Court. (C) is incorrect because states possess no such sovereign right. Federal review of state acts (whether they be executive, legislative, or judicial) is well established. (D) is incorrect because Article III actually provides that the Supreme Court shall have appellate jurisdiction under such regulations as Congress shall make.

Answer to Question 22

(A) Application (A) is the most clearly constitutional. Section 1 of the Fourteenth Amendment guarantees equal protection; it applies directly only to "state action," which is most clearly indicated in answer (A). Thus, answers (B) and (C) are not as clearly constitutional. Answer (D) is incorrect because the Fourteenth Amendment does not directly apply to federal action. Congress's power to prohibit federal acts would be easier to justify under Article I (*e.g.*, as necessary and proper to carry out the spending power). Thus, (D) is not as clear a Fourteenth Amendment case as (A).

Answer to Question 23

(C) Race is a suspect classification under the Equal Protection Clause. However, the Fourteenth Amendment only applies if there is action by a state or local government office, or a private individual whose behavior meets the requirement of "state action." State action exists where seemingly private individuals (i) perform exclusive public functions, or (ii) have significant state involvement in their activities. "State action" also exists where a state affirmatively facilitates, encourages, or authorizes acts of discrimination by its citizens. However, there must be some sort of affirmative act by the state approving the private action. It is not enough that the state merely permits the conduct to occur. Under these facts, several state officials serve on the Bar Association's Board of Bar Governors. Furthermore, the state supreme court requires all lawyers to be members of the State Bar Association. Thus, the State Bar Association does not operate independently of the state and, therefore, Plaintiffs' strongest argument would be to demonstrate that "state action" is involved in payment of dues by the Association to private clubs that discriminate. Thus, (C) is correct. (A) is wrong because "state action" is required to invoke the antidiscrimination protections of the Fourteenth Amendment. Only the Thirteenth Amendment's ban on badges or incidents of slavery applies to purely private actions. (B) is wrong because the failure of the Association to pass a resolution forbidding discrimination does not, in and of itself, constitute a denial of equal protection, and the argument for state action being present is much weaker than in option (C). (D) is wrong because, unless it is shown that the Association is an instrumentality of the state or closely intertwined with state action, the mere fact of its payment of dues to such private clubs will not invoke the Equal Protection Clause. (C) is the only answer that clearly focuses on the state action issue.

Answer to Question 24

(A) The court should hear the case on the merits. Federal judicial power extends to all cases and controversies arising under the Constitution, laws, or treaties of the United States. Because the activities of the State Bar Association present a federal claim arising under the Equal Protection Clause of the United States Constitution, the federal district court should hear the case on its merits. Therefore, (A) is correct. (B) is wrong because it is the Fourteenth Amendment that applies to the states. The Fifth Amendment Due Process Clause forbids *federal* discrimination. (C) is wrong because the doctrine of abstention is applicable when a federal constitutional claim is premised on an unsettled question of state law. These facts present no such unsettled state law question. (D) is wrong because the Bar Association's activities encroach on federally protected constitutional rights and, therefore, are not solely within the domain of state law, nor are there any "adequate and independent state grounds" here.

Answer to Question 25

(C) (C) is correct because the Thirteenth Amendment addresses private acts of racial discrimination. (D) is incorrect because the Supreme Court has not recognized any power of Congress to regulate private persons under Section 5 of the Fourteenth Amendment. (A) is incorrect because the Obligation of Contracts Clause prohibits states from impairing contractual obligations. Thus, this clause is inapplicable to this case. (B) is incorrect because the General Welfare Clause authorizes Congress to spend to provide for the common defense and general welfare. There is no connection between this clause and the statute at issue.

Answer to Question 26

(A) Congress has the power to declare war, raise and support armies, provide for and maintain a navy, and spend to provide for the common defense and general welfare, as well as the power to make all laws that are necessary and proper for carrying into execution the foregoing powers or any other federal power (including the power of the President and Senate to enter into treaties in conformity with Article II). Pursuant to these enumerated powers, Congress can take preventive measures against activities that may cause international misunderstandings, which in turn may lead to war, as well as against endeavors to undermine the government. The statute here shows a congressional intent to ensure that only properly authorized persons negotiate with foreign governments, and it is a legitimate means of implementing Congress's powers. (B) is incorrect because, although the President has broad discretion in foreign affairs, it is doubtful that such discretion would include the authority to unilaterally punish citizens who encroach on that discretion, absent legislative authorization to impose such punishment. (C) and (D) are incorrect because they are based on the mistaken notion that laws dealing with foreign affairs need not pass constitutional muster.

Answer to Question 27

(C) A challenge based on interstate commerce would be most effective. Sometimes a nondiscriminatory law that regulates commerce may place a burden on interstate commerce. Such a law will be invalidated if the burden on interstate commerce outweighs local interests. This is a case-by-case balancing test, and it is by no means clear that the law in question *would* be ruled invalid. However, the Commerce Clause issue is the only answer where there is any reasonable likelihood that the legislation could be declared invalid. Thus, (C) is the correct answer. (A) is wrong because no fundamental right is involved and, therefore, the mere rationality test is applied, and the law will be upheld if it is rationally related to any conceivable legitimate end of government. The seat belt law clearly meets this minimal standard and any challenge based on due process would surely fail. (B) is wrong because the legislation does not involve a fundamental right, a suspect classification, or a quasi-suspect classification. In equal protection analysis, if any other classification is involved, the action will be upheld unless the challenger proves that the action is not rationally related to a legitimate government interest. Transport Lines cannot carry such a burden of proof. (D) is wrong because a constitutional challenge should be based on the infringement of rights guaranteed by the Constitution. Difficulty of enforcement is not relevant here.

Answer to Question 28

(B) Congress may regulate any activity, local or interstate, which either in itself, or in combination with other activities, has a substantial effect upon interstate commerce. Here, although most stolen bicycles remain within the state in which they were stolen, the cumulative effect of many instances of stolen bicycles being transported across state lines for resale could be felt in interstate commerce. It follows that (C) is incorrect. (A) is incorrect because Congress has the power to *spend* for the general welfare. The *property power* involves the disposal and acquisition of property belonging to the United States, and is not at all relevant to this question. (D) is incorrect because the Tenth Amendment reserves to the states those powers not delegated to the United States nor prohibited to the states by the Constitution. As noted above, the power to regulate commerce is conferred upon Congress by the Constitution. Thus, this matter is not reserved to the states.

Answer to Question 29

(B) The purchase of contraceptives is encompassed by the fundamental right of privacy. Because this statute contains no procedural safeguards, it denies minors a fundamental right without due process. Because Drugs, Inc., may assert the minors' rights, (B) is the correct answer. (A) is incorrect because there does not appear to be an undue burden on interstate commerce. (C) is incorrect because the statute does not treat state residents differently from out-of-state residents. (D) is nonsensical. *Note:* Under the Supreme Court's decisions regarding the sale of contraceptives to minors, the best possible answer would have been that the statute violated equal protection because it denied a fundamental right to a class of persons (minors) without sufficient justification. Since that answer was not given, the due process answer (which mentioned fundamental rights) was the best choice.

Answer to Question 30

(D) It has been held that the Property Clause empowers Congress to protect wildlife wandering onto federally owned lands. (B) is incorrect because the Privileges and Immunities Clause of Article IV pertains to discrimination by states against out-of-state citizens. (A) is incorrect because the commerce power is not as *easy a way to justify* the law as is the property power, which clearly and literally applies here (note the wording of the question). (C) is incorrect because the enabling clause of the Fourteenth Amendment gives Congress the power to enforce the amendment by appropriate legislation. The Fourteenth Amendment, which prevents the states from depriving any person of life, liberty, or property without due process of law and equal protection of the law, is not at issue here.

Answer to Question 31

(C) A federal court will not decide political questions, which are: (i) those issues committed by the Constitution to another branch of government; and (ii) those issues inherently incapable of resolution and enforcement by the judicial process. Political questions include those regarding the conduct of foreign relations. Based on Supreme Court cases, the recognition of and establishment of diplomatic relations with a foreign country appear to be political questions. Thus, (D) is incorrect. (A) and (B) are incorrect because Dunn will be injured economically by the actions of the President and Secretary of State. Therefore, Dunn can demonstrate such a concrete stake in the outcome of this controversy as to ensure the adversariness which sharpens the presentation of issues.

Answer to Question 32

(A) Legislative power can be delegated to executive officers and/or administrative agencies. Any delegated power must not be uniquely confined to Congress. The delegation must include intelligible standards for action by the delegatee. The statutory provision here meets these criteria for a permissible delegation. It follows that (C) is incorrect. (B) is an incorrect statement of law. Even if the executive had the inherent power, that would not make the legislation constitutional. (D) is incorrect because this statute does not represent arbitrary governmental action. It serves a proper governmental purpose and provides for specific standards and procedures relative to its implementation.

Answer to Question 33

(A) In addition to its enumerated powers, Congress possesses auxiliary powers that are necessary and proper to carrying out all powers vested in the federal government. The statute here at issue is necessary and proper to carry out Congress's property power. By proscribing even the hunting of animals that have left the federal park, the statute will help protect the wildlife, which is property belonging to the United States. (B) is not the "strongest ground" because nothing in the facts points to interstate commerce. (C) is incorrect because the police power is a power of state government, not the federal government. (D), as a general statement of law, is incorrect. Also, it apparently is based on the rejected "right" vs. "privilege" distinction relative to deprivation of liberty and property without procedural due process, an issue not raised by these facts.

Answer to Question 34

(D) Jones's strongest defense is that the statute violates his free exercise of religion. The Free Exercise Clause forbids government from making laws that prohibit the free exercise of religion. The Court has held that this means that the government may not punish a person for his or her religious beliefs. In determining what is a religious belief, the court may delve into the sincerity of the belief, but it may not find religious beliefs to be false. Thus, the prosecution here may be unconstitutional because it was based on the alleged falsity of a religious belief. (A) could be correct but it is not as good a basis as (D). Under the Equal Protection Clause, government must not unreasonably discriminate against similarly situated people. If a law discriminates (on its face or in its application) on the basis of a suspect class or where a fundamental right is involved, the law will be held invalid unless it is narrowly tailored to achieve a compelling government interest. Here, the law interferes with freedom of religion (a fundamental right), but it is not clear from this one prosecution that the law is being applied in a discriminatory manner. Therefore, (D) is a better answer. (B) is incorrect because the Due Process Clause requires only that the prosecution prove each element of a crime. Once the prosecution proves an element, there is no due process violation in having the defendant rebut the evidence; otherwise no one could ever be convicted of a crime. (C) is wrong because it is not clear that there was a Contract Clause violation. The Contract Clause forbids the retroactive impairment of contract rights unless the impairment is narrowly tailored to meet an important government interest. Here, the statute was apparently in existence when Jones "contracted" with his donors (although presumably the donations were gratuitous and not contractual). Thus, there is no retroactive impairment of contract. Moreover, even if this were a retroactive impairment, it could be argued that it was justified because preventing fraud is an important government interest. In any case, this clearly is not as good a defense as (D).

Answer to Question 35

(B) The general rule is that people do not have standing as taxpayers to challenge the way tax dollars are spent because their interest is too remote. However, there is an exception to the general rule. A federal taxpayer has standing to challenge federal appropriations and spending measures if she can establish that the challenged measure: (i) was enacted under Congress's taxing and spending power; and (ii) exceeds some specific limitation on the power. To date, the only limit that the Supreme Court has found on the taxing power is the Establishment Clause. Here, Allen's challenge is based upon such an Establishment Clause matter. Hence, the exception applies and (B) is correct. (A) is incorrect because it is overbroad. Only spending falling within the exception described above may be challenged by taxpayers. (C) is incorrect because sufficient "nexus" is a concept applied to state taxation of interstate commerce—a state can tax only those persons with a sufficient relationship to the state. Here, the complaint is not that Allen is being taxed, but that the tax money is being spent in violation of the Constitution. (D) is wrong. First, state action *is* involved—the government is giving money for textbooks. Second, standing depends on whether the party has a concrete stake in the outcome of the litigation and is not dependent on whether the action complained of is state action.

Answer to Question 36

(D) The salary supplements probably will be held unconstitutional. The controlling case in this area is *Lemon v. Kurtzman* (1971), which determined that supplements to salaries of teachers in religious school raised "excessive entanglement" problems. The current Establishment Clause test is that the government program must: (i) have a secular purpose; (ii) have a primary effect that neither advances nor inhibits religion; and (iii) not produce excessive government entanglement with religion. The instant case raises both "primary purpose" and, from the policing of the restriction on use of the funds, "entanglement" problems. Option (D) goes most directly to the issue in question and is, therefore, correct. (A) is incorrect because it does not consider the "entanglement" problems of the "no religious instruction" restriction. The answer given in option (A) goes only to the "secular purpose" issue. (B) is incorrect because: (i) no "free exercise" issues are involved here; and (ii) distinguishing between public and private schools *avoids* Establishment Clause problems. (C) is incorrect because the facts do not indicate disproportionality. Even if disproportionality can be assumed, the courts have elected to invalidate similar laws on the basis of the three-pronged test discussed above rather than couching the issues in terms of "sect preference."

Answer to Question 37

(A) The Supreme Court applies the Establishment Clause prohibitions less strictly when the benefited institution is a religiously affiliated college or hospital rather than a grade or secondary school. The Court will uphold a government grant of aid to such a college or hospital as long as the government program requires that the aid be used only for nonreligious purposes and the recipient so agrees in good faith. Option (A) most nearly approximates this test and is, therefore, correct. (B), on the other hand, is incorrect because it is overbroad. "Bricks and mortar" may not be used, *e.g.,* to build a college chapel. (C) is incorrect because it is overbroad in another direction. Certain grants (*e.g.,* state-approved textbooks, transportation to and from school, expenses of compiling state-required data) have been allowed even for grade and secondary schools. (D) is incorrect because the Supreme Court has found that no excessive entanglement is involved when government funds are used to build "secular" buildings at colleges and universities.

Answer to Question 38

(B) Leonard's conviction will be sustained because states can prohibit or regulate conduct in general, and this is true even if the prohibition or regulation happens to interfere with a person's religious practices. The Free Exercise Clause cannot be used to challenge a neutral law of general applicability (such as the law against cruelty to animals) unless it can be shown that the law was motivated by a desire to interfere with religion. [See Church of the Lukumi Babalu Aye, Inc. v. Hialeah (1993)] A law that regulates the conduct of all persons, as this statute appears to do, can be applied to prohibit the conduct of a single person even if the person's religious beliefs prohibit him from complying with the law. (A) is incorrect because the constitutional protection of religious beliefs does not require that the belief arise from a traditional, or even an organized, religion. Beliefs in Satan could have constitutional protection. (C) is wrong for the reasons given in the analysis of option (B). (D) is incorrect because the reasonableness of religious beliefs is not a suitable subject for constitutional inquiry. The courts may not, for example, declare a religion to be "false." The courts may inquire into the sincerity of religious belief, but the reasonableness of the belief is not relevant.

Answer to Question 39

(D) Federal courts are barred from rendering advisory opinions. The legislation here calls for a federal court to transmit to the head of a federal agency an opinion regarding the proper disbursement of federal funds, and the agency head is not required to follow the opinion. This would be an advisory opinion. (A) is incorrect because it fails to consider the necessity for a case and controversy prior to the exercise of federal judicial power. (B) may be a true statement, but the rendition of advisory opinions by a federal court is not a permissible method to settle disputes involving the spending of federal monies. (C) is incorrect because the Eleventh Amendment pertains to suits brought against a state by citizens of that or any other state. Such a suit is not at issue here.

Answer to Question 40

(D) The provision is unconstitutional. The Supreme Court has found "legislative vetoes" to be unconstitutional because they are not subject to presidential review and they violate the separation of powers guaranteed by the federal Constitution. The mechanism set up here has even less basis for constitutionality because the legislative veto that the Supreme Court held unconstitutional at least envisioned votes by one or both full houses of Congress (rather than a mere committee). (A) is incorrect because the Necessary and Proper Clause does not allow Congress to exceed its powers or violate the separation of powers. It merely allows Congress to adopt laws necessary and proper to the powers granted by the Constitution. (B) is incorrect because there is no such rule. Furthermore, the Supreme Court has generally abandoned the "privileges vs. rights" dichotomy. (C) is incorrect because the Equal Protection Clause applies only to actions by the states. Moreover, since no fundamental right or suspect class is involved, the discrimination here would be upheld as long as it is rational.

CONTRACTS QUESTIONS

Questions 1-2 are based on the following fact situation:

Addie, who has been in the painting and contracting business for 10 years and has a fine reputation, contracts to paint Boone's barn. Boone's barn is a standard red barn with a loft. The contract has no provision regarding assignment.

1. If Addie assigns the contract to Coot, who has comparable experience and reputation, which of the following statements is correct?

   (A) Addie is in breach of contract.

   (B) Boone may refuse to accept performance by Coot.

   (C) Boone is required to accept performance by Coot.

   (D) There is a novation.

2. If Addie assigns the contract to Coot and thereafter Coot does not meet the contract specifications in painting Boone's barn, Boone:

   (A) Has a cause of action against Addie for damages.

   (B) Has a cause of action only against Coot for damages.

   (C) Has a cause of action against Addie for damages, only after he has first exhausted his remedies against Coot.

   (D) Does not have a cause of action against Addie for damages because he waived his rights against Addie by permitting Coot to perform the work.

Questions 3-5 are based on the following fact situation:

Johnston purchased 100 bolts of standard blue wool, No. 1 quality, from McHugh. The sales contract provided that Johnston would make payment prior to inspection. The 100 bolts were shipped and Johnston paid McHugh. Upon inspection, however, Johnston discovered that the wool was No. 2 quality. Johnston thereupon tendered back the wool to McHugh and demanded return of his payment. McHugh refused on the ground that there is no difference between No. 1 quality wool and No. 2 quality wool.

3. Which of the following statements regarding the contract provision for preinspection payment is correct?

   (A) It constitutes an acceptance of the goods.

   (B) It constitutes a waiver of the buyer's remedy of private sale in the case of nonconforming goods.

   (C) It does not impair a buyer's right of inspection or his remedies.

   (D) It is invalid.

4. What is Johnston's remedy because the wool was nonconforming?

   (A) Specific performance.

   (B) Damages measured by the difference between the value of the goods delivered and the value of conforming goods.

   (C) Damages measured by the price paid plus the difference between the contract price and the cost of buying substitute goods.

   (D) None, since he waived his remedies by agreeing to pay before inspection.

5. Can Johnston resell the wool?

   (A) Yes, in a private sale.

   (B) Yes, in a private sale but only after giving McHugh reasonable notice of his intention to resell.

(C) Yes, but only at a public sale.

(D) No.

Questions 6-8 are based on the following fact situation:

Duffer and Slicker, who lived in different suburbs 20 miles apart, were golfing acquaintances at the Interurban Country Club. Both were traveling salesmen—Duffer for a pharmaceutical house and Slicker for a widget manufacturer. Duffer wrote Slicker by United States mail on Friday, October 8:

> I need a motorcycle for transportation to the country club, and will buy your Sujocki for $1,200 upon your bringing it to my home address above [stated in the letterhead] on or before noon, November 12 next. This offer is not subject to countermand.
>
> Sincerely,
>
> [signed]   Duffer

Slicker replied by mail the following day:

> I accept your offer and promise to deliver the bike as you specified.
>
> Sincerely,
>
> [signed]   Slicker

This letter, although properly addressed, was misdirected by the postal service and not received by Duffer until November 10. Duffer had bought another Sujocki bike from Koolcat for $1,050 a few hours before.

Koolcat saw Slicker at the Interurban Country Club on November 11 and said: "I sold my Sujocki to Duffer yesterday for $1,050. Would you consider selling me yours for $950?" Slicker replied, "I'll let you know in a few days."

On November 12, Slicker took his Sujocki to Duffer's residence; he arrived at 11:55 a.m.

Duffer was asleep and did not answer Slicker's doorbell rings until 12:15 p.m. Duffer then rejected Slicker's bike on the ground that he had already bought Koolcat's.

6. In Duffer's letter of October 8, what was the legal effect of the language: "This offer is not subject to countermand"?

(A) Under the Uniform Commercial Code, the offer was irrevocable until noon, November 12.

(B) Such language prevented an effective acceptance by Slicker prior to noon, November 12.

(C) At common law, such language created a binding option in Slicker's favor.

(D) Such language did not affect the offeror's power of revocation of the offer.

7. In a lawsuit by Slicker against Duffer for breach of contract, what would the court probably decide regarding Slicker's letter of October 9?

(A) The letter bound both parties to a unilateral contract as soon as Slicker mailed it.

(B) Mailing of the letter by Slicker did not, of itself, prevent a subsequent effective revocation by Duffer of his offer.

(C) The letter bound both parties to a bilateral contract, but only when received by Duffer on November 10.

(D) Regardless of whether Duffer's offer had proposed a unilateral or a bilateral contract, the letter was an effective acceptance upon receipt, if not upon dispatch.

8. What is the probable legal effect of Koolcat's conversation with Slicker and

report that he (Koolcat) had sold his Sujocki to Duffer on November 10?

(A) This report had no legal effect because Duffer's offer was irrevocable until November 12.

(B) Unless a contract had already been formed between Slicker and Duffer, Koolcat's report to Slicker operated to terminate Slicker's power of accepting Duffer's offer.

(C) This report had no legal effect because the offer had been made by a prospective buyer (Duffer) rather than a prospective seller.

(D) Koolcat's conversation with Slicker on November 11 terminated Duffer's original offer and operated as an offer by Koolcat to buy Slicker's Sujocki for $950.

Questions 9-10 are based on the following fact situation:

Tortfeasor tortiously injured Victim in an auto accident. While Victim was recovering in Hospital, Tortfeasor's liability insurer, Insurer, settled with Victim for $5,000. Victim gave Insurer a signed release and received a signed memorandum wherein Insurer promised to pay Victim $5,000 by check within 30 days. When Victim left Hospital two days later, Hospital demanded payment of its $4,000 stated bill. Victim thereupon gave Hospital his own negotiable promissory note for $4,000, payable to Hospital's order in 30 days, and also, as security, assigned to Hospital the Insurer settlement memorandum. Hospital promptly assigned for value the settlement memorandum and negotiated the note to Holder, who took the note as a holder in due course. Subsequently, Victim misrepresented to Insurer that he had lost the settlement memorandum and needed another. Insurer issued another memorandum identical to the first, and Victim assigned it to ABC Furniture to secure a $5,000 credit sale contract. ABC immediately notified Insurer of this assignment.

Later it was discovered that Hospital had mistakenly overbilled Victim by the amount of $1,000 and that Tortfeasor was an irresponsible minor.

9. If Victim starts an action against Insurer 40 days after the insurance settlement agreement, can Victim recover?

(A) Yes, because his attempted assignments of his claim against Insurer were ineffective, inasmuch as Insurer's promise to pay "by check" created a right in Victim that was too personal to assign.

(B) No, because he no longer has possession of Insurer's written memorandum.

(C) No, because Tortfeasor's minority and irresponsibility vitiated the settlement agreement between Victim and Insurer.

(D) No, because he has made at least one effective assignment of his claim against Insurer, and Insurer has notice thereof.

10. In view of Tortfeasor's age and irresponsibility when Insurer issued his liability policy, can Holder and ABC Furniture recover on their assignments?

(A) Neither can recover because Victim, the assignor, is a third-party beneficiary of the liability policy, whose rights thereon can be no better than Tortfeasor's.

(B) Neither can recover unless Insurer knowingly waived the defense of Tortfeasor's minority and irresponsibility.

(C) Neither can recover because the liability policy, and settlement thereunder, are unenforceable because of Tortfeasor's minority.

(D) Either Holder or ABC Furniture, depending on priority, can recover as assignee (or subassignee) of Victim's claim because the latter arose from Insurer's settlement agreement, the latter agreement not being vitiated by Tortfeasor's minority and irresponsibility when he obtained the policy.

Question 11

On January 15, Carpenter agreed to repair Householder's house according to certain specifications and to have the work completed by April 1. On March 1, Householder's property was inundated by flood waters which did not abate until March 15. Householder could not get the house in a condition which would permit Carpenter to begin the repairs until March 31. On that date Carpenter notified Householder that he would not repair the house.

Which one of the following facts, if it was the only one true and known to both parties on January 15, would best serve Carpenter as the basis for a defense in an action brought against him by Householder for breach of contract?

(A) Carpenter's busy schedule permitted him to work on Householder's house only during the month of March.

(B) Any delay in making the repairs would not seriously affect Householder's use of the property.

(C) The cost of making repairs was increasing at the rate of 3% a month.

(D) The area around Householder's property was frequently flooded during the month of March.

Question 12

In a telephone call on March 1, Adams, an unemployed, retired person, said to Dawes, "I will sell my automobile for $3,000 cash. I will hold this offer open through March 14." On March 12, Adams called Dawes and told her that he had sold the automobile to Clark. Adams in fact had not sold the automobile to anyone. On March 14, Dawes learned that Adams still owned the automobile, and on that date called Adams and said, "I'm coming over to your place with $3,000." Adams replied, "Don't bother. I won't deliver the automobile to you under any circumstances." Dawes protested, but made no further attempt to pay for or take delivery of the automobile.

In an action by Dawes against Adams for breach of contract, Dawes probably will:

(A) Succeed, because Adams had assured her that the offer would remain open through March 14.

(B) Succeed, because Adams had not in fact sold the automobile to Clark.

(C) Not succeed, because Dawes had not tendered the $3,000 to Adams on or before March 14.

(D) Not succeed, because on March 12, Adams had told Dawes that he had sold the automobile to Clark.

Question 13

Carver is a chemical engineer. She has no interest in or connection with Chemco. Carver noticed that Chemco's most recent publicly issued financial statement listed, as part of Chemco's assets, a large inventory of a certain special chemical compound. This asset was listed at a cost of $100,000, but Carver knew that the ingredients of the compound were in short supply and that the current market value of the inventory was in excess of $1 million. There was no current public quotation of the price of Chemco stock. The book value of Chemco stock, according to the statement, was $5 per share; its actual value was $30 per share.

Knowing these facts, Carver offered to purchase from Page at $6 per share the 1,000 shares of Chemco stock owned by Page. Page and Carver had not previously met. Page sold the stock to Carver for $6 per share.

If Page asserts a claim based on misrepresentation against Carver, will Page prevail?

(A) Yes, because Carver knew that the value of the stock was greater than the price she offered.

(B) Yes, if Carver did not inform Page of the true value of the inventory.

(C) No, unless Carver told Page that the stock was not worth more than $6 per share.

(D) No, if Chemco's financial statement was available to Page.

Questions 14-15 are based on the following fact situation:

In a written contract Singer agreed to deliver to Byer 500 described chairs at $20 each F.O.B. Singer's place of business. The contract provided that "neither party will assign this contract without the written consent of the other." Singer placed the chairs on board a carrier on January 30. On February 1, Singer said in a signed writing, "I hereby assign to Wheeler all my rights under the Singer-Byer contract." Singer did not request and did not get Byer's consent to this transaction. On February 2, the chairs, while in transit, were destroyed in a derailment of the carrier's railroad car.

14. In an action by Wheeler against Byer, Wheeler probably will recover:

   (A) $10,000, the contract price.

   (B) The difference between the contract price and the market value of the chairs.

   (C) Nothing, because the chairs had not been delivered.

   (D) Nothing, because the Singer-Byer contract forbade an assignment.

15. In an action by Byer against Singer for breach of contract, Byer probably will:

   (A) Succeed, because the carrier will be deemed to be Singer's agent.

(B) Succeed, because the risk of loss was on Singer.

(C) Not succeed, because of impossibility of performance.

(D) Not succeed, because the risk of loss was on Byer.

Question 16

After several days of negotiations, Ohner wrote to Plummer: "Will pay you $3,000 if you will install new plumbing in my office building according to the specifications I have sent you. I must have your reply by March 30." Plummer replied by a letter that Ohner received on March 15: "Will not do it for less than $3,500." On March 20, Plummer wrote to Ohner: "Have changed my mind. I will do the work for $3,000. Unless I hear from you to the contrary, I will begin work on April 5." Ohner received this letter on March 22 but did not reply to it. Plummer, without Ohner's knowledge, began the work on April 5.

Which of the following best characterizes the legal relationship between Ohner and Plummer as of April 5?

(A) A contract was formed on March 20 when Plummer posted his letter.

(B) A contract was formed on March 22 when Ohner received Plummer's letter.

(C) A contract was formed on April 5 when Plummer began work.

(D) There was no contract between the parties as of April 5.

Questions 17-18 are based on the following fact situation:

On January 15, in a signed writing, Artisan agreed to remodel Ohner's building according to certain specifications, Ohner to pay the agreed price of $5,000 to Artisan's niece, Roberta Neese, as a birthday present. Neese did not learn of the agreement until her birthday on May 5.

Before they signed the writing, Artisan and Ohner had orally agreed that their "written agreement will be null and void unless Ohner is able to obtain a $5,000 loan from the First National Bank before January 31."

17. For this question only, assume that Ohner was unable to obtain the loan and, on January 31, phoned Artisan and told him, "Don't begin the work. The deal is off." In an action for breach of contract brought against Ohner by the proper party, will Ohner be successful in asserting as a defense his inability to obtain a loan?

   (A) Yes, because obtaining a loan was a condition precedent to the existence of an enforceable contract.

   (B) Yes, because the agreement about obtaining a loan is a modification of a construction contract and is not required to be in writing.

   (C) No, because the agreement about obtaining a loan contradicts the express and implied terms of the writing.

   (D) No, because Ohner is estopped to deny the validity of the written agreement.

18. For this question only, assume that Ohner obtained the loan, that Artisan completed the remodeling on May 1, and that on May 3, at Artisan's request, Ohner paid the $5,000 to Artisan. If Neese learns of Ohner's payment to Artisan on May 5, at the same time she learns of the written Artisan-Ohner contract, will she succeed in an action against Ohner for $5,000?

   (A) Yes, because she is an intended beneficiary of the written Artisan-Ohner contract.

   (B) Yes, because the written Artisan-Ohner contract operated as an assignment to Neese, and Artisan thereby lost whatever rights he may have had to the $5,000.

   (C) No, because Neese had not furnished any consideration to support Ohner's promise to pay $5,000 to her.

   (D) No, because on May 3, Artisan and Ohner effectively modified their written contract, thereby depriving Neese of whatever rights she may have had under that contract.

Questions 19-20 are based on the following fact situation:

When Esther, Gray's 21-year-old daughter, finished college, Gray handed her a signed memorandum stating that if she would go to law school for three academic years, he would pay her tuition, room, and board, and would "give her a $1,000 bonus" for each "A" she got in law school. Esther's uncle, Miller, who was present on this occasion, read the memorandum and thereupon said to Esther, "and if he doesn't pay your expenses, I will." Gray paid her tuition, room, and board for her first year but died just before the end of that year. Subsequently, Esther learned that she had received two "As" in the second semester. The executor of Gray's estate has refused to pay her anything for the two "As" and has told her that the estate will no longer pay her tuition, room, and board in law school.

19. In an action by Esther against Miller on account of the executor's repudiation of Gray's promise to pay future tuition, room, and board, which of the following would be Miller's strongest defense?

   (A) The parties did not manifestly intend a contract.

   (B) Gray's death terminated the agreement.

   (C) The agreement was oral.

   (D) The agreement was divisible.

20. In an action against Gray's estate for $2,000 on account of the two "As," if the only defense raised is lack of consideration, Esther probably will:

(A) Succeed under the doctrine of promissory estoppel.

(B) Succeed on a theory of bargained-for exchange for her father's promise.

(C) Not succeed, because the $1,000 for each "A" was promised only as a bonus.

(D) Not succeed, because Esther was already legally obligated to use her best efforts in law school.

Question 21

Zeller contracted in writing to deliver to Baker 100 bushels of wheat on August 1 at $3.50 per bushel. Because his suppliers had not delivered enough wheat to him by that time, Zeller on August 1 had only 95 bushels of wheat with which to fulfill his contract with Baker.

If Zeller tenders 95 bushels of wheat to Baker on August 1, and Baker refuses to accept or pay for any of the wheat, which of the following best states the legal relationship between Zeller and Baker?

(A) Zeller has a cause of action against Baker, because Zeller has substantially performed his contract.

(B) Zeller is excused from performing his contract because of impossibility of performance.

(C) Baker has a cause of action against Zeller for Zeller's failure to deliver 100 bushels of wheat.

(D) Baker is obligated to give Zeller a reasonable time to attempt to obtain the other five bushels of wheat.

Questions 22-23 are based on the following fact situation:

On May 1, Selco and Byco entered into a written agreement in which Selco agreed to fabricate and sell to Byco 10,000 specially designed brake linings for a new type of power brake manufactured by Byco. The contract provided that Byco would pay half of the purchase price on May 15 in order to give Selco funds to "tool up" for the work; that Selco would deliver 5,000 brake linings on May 31; that Byco would pay the balance of the purchase price on June 5; and that Selco would deliver the balance of the brake linings on June 30.

On May 10, Selco notified Byco that it was doubtful whether Selco could perform because of problems encountered in modifying its production machines to produce the brake linings. On May 15, however, Selco assured Byco that the production difficulties had been overcome, and Byco paid Selco the first 50% installment of the purchase price. Selco did not deliver the first 5,000 brake linings on May 31, or at any time thereafter; and on June 10, Selco notified Byco that it would not perform the contract.

22. Which of the following correctly states Byco's rights and obligations immediately after receipt of Selco's notice on May 10?

(A) Byco can treat the notice as an anticipatory repudiation, and has a cause of action on May 10 for breach of the entire contract.

(B) Byco can treat the notice as an anticipatory repudiation, and can sue at once to enjoin an actual breach by Selco on May 31.

(C) Byco has no cause of action for breach of contract, but can suspend its performance and demand assurances that Selco will perform.

(D) Byco has no cause of action for breach of contract, and must pay the installment of the purchase price due on May 15 to preserve its rights under the contract.

23. Which of the following is **not** a correct statement of the parties' legal status

immediately after Selco's notice on June 10?

(A) Byco has a cause of action for total breach of contract because of Selco's repudiation, but that cause of action will be lost if Selco retracts its repudiation before Byco changes its position or manifests to Selco that Byco considers the repudiation final.

(B) Byco can bring suit to rescind the contract even if it elects to await Selco's performance for a commercially reasonable time.

(C) Byco can await performance by Selco for a commercially reasonable time, but if Byco awaits performance beyond that period, it cannot recover any resulting damages that it reasonably could have avoided.

(D) Byco has a cause of action for breach of contract that it can successfully assert only after it has given Selco a commercially reasonable time to perform.

Questions 24-25 are based on the following fact situation:

The Kernel Corporation, through its president, Demeter Gritz, requested from Vault Finance, Inc., a short-term loan of $100,000. On April 1, Gritz and Vault's loan officer agreed orally that Vault would make the loan on the following terms: (1) the loan would be repaid in full on or before the following July 1 and would carry interest at an annual rate of 15% (a lawful rate under the applicable usury law); and (2) Gritz would personally guarantee repayment. The loan was approved and made on April 5. The only document evidencing the loan was a memorandum, written and supplied by Vault and signed by Gritz for Kernel, that read in its entirety:

April 5

In consideration of a loan advanced on this date, Kernel Corporation hereby promises to pay Vault Finance, Inc., $100,000 on September 1.

> Kernel Corporation
> by /s/ Demeter Gritz
> Demeter Gritz, President

Kernel Corporation did not repay the loan on or before July 1, although it had sufficient funds to do so. On July 10, Vault sued Kernel as principal debtor and Gritz individually as guarantor for $100,000, plus 15% interest from April 5.

24. At the trial, can Vault prove Kernel's oral commitment to repay the loan on or before July 1?

(A) Yes, because the oral agreement was supported by an independent consideration.

(B) Yes, because evidence of the parties' negotiations is relevant to their contractual intent concerning maturity of the debt.

(C) No, because such evidence is barred by the preexisting duty rule.

(D) No, because such evidence contradicts the writing and is barred by the parol evidence rule.

25. At the trial, can Vault prove Gritz's oral promise to guarantee the loan?

(A) Yes, because Gritz signed the memorandum.

(B) Yes, because, as president of the debtor-company, Gritz is a third-party beneficiary of the loan.

(C) No, because there was no separate consideration for Gritz's promise.

(D) No, because such proof is barred by the Statute of Frauds.

Question 26

Osif owned Broadacres in fee simple. For a consideration of $5,000, Osif gave Bard a written option to purchase Broadacres for $300,000. The option was assignable. For a consideration of $10,000, Bard subsequently gave an option to Cutter to purchase Broadacres for $325,000. Cutter exercised his option.

Bard thereupon exercised his option. Bard paid the agreed price of $300,000, and took title to Broadacres by deed from Osif. Thereafter, Cutter refused to consummate his purchase.

Bard brought an appropriate action against Cutter for specific performance, or, if that should be denied, then for damages. Cutter counterclaimed for return of the $10,000.

In this action, the court will:

(A) Grant money damages only to Bard.

(B) Grant specific performance to Bard.

(C) Grant Bard only the right to retain the $10,000.

(D) Require Bard to refund the $10,000 to Cutter.

Questions 27-28 are based on the following fact situation:

Mater, a wealthy widow, wishing to make a substantial and potentially enduring gift to her beloved adult stepson, Prodigal, established with the Vault Savings and Loan Association a passbook savings account by an initial deposit of $10,000.

27. For this question only, assume the following facts. The passbook was issued solely in Prodigal's name; but Mater retained possession of it, and Prodigal was not then informed of the savings account. Subsequently, Mater became disgusted with Prodigal's behavior and decided to give the same savings account solely to her beloved adult daughter Distaff. As permitted by the rules of Vault Savings and Loan, Mater effected this change by agreement with Vault. This time she left possession of the passbook with Vault. Shortly thereafter, Prodigal learned of the original savings account in his name and the subsequent switch to Distaff's name.

If Prodigal now sues Vault Savings and Loan for $10,000 plus accrued interest, will the action succeed?

(A) Yes, because Prodigal was a third-party intended beneficiary of the original Mater-Vault deposit agreement.

(B) Yes, because Prodigal was a constructive assignee of Mater's claim, as depositor, to the savings account.

(C) No, because Prodigal never obtained possession of the passbook.

(D) No, because Prodigal's right, if any, to the funds on deposit was effectively abrogated by the second Mater-Vault deposit agreement.

28. For this question only, assume the following facts. The passbook was issued by Vault to Mater solely in her own name. That same day, disinterested witnesses being present, she handed the passbook to Prodigal and said, "As a token of my love and affection for you, I give you this $10,000 savings account." Shortly thereafter, she changed her mind and wrote Prodigal, "I hereby revoke my gift to you of the $10,000 savings account with Vault Savings and Loan Association. Please return my passbook immediately. Signed: Mater." Prodigal received this letter but ignored it, and Mater died unexpectedly a few days later.

In litigation between Prodigal and Mater's estate, which of the following is a correct statement of the parties' rights with respect to the money on deposit with Vault?

(A) The estate prevails, because Mater's gift to Prodigal was revocable and was terminated by her death.

(B) The estate prevails, because Mater's gift to Prodigal was revocable and was terminated by her express revocation.

(C) Prodigal prevails, because he took Mater's claim to the savings account by a gratuitous but effective and irrevocable assignment from Mater.

(D) Prodigal prevails, because his failure to reject the gift, even if the assignment was revocable, created an estoppel against Mater and her estate.

Questions 29-30 are based on the following fact situation:

On October 1, Toy Store, Inc., entered into a written contract with Fido Factory, Inc., for the purchase at $20 per unit of 1,000 mechanical dogs, to be specially manufactured by Fido according to Toy Store's specifications. Fido promised to deliver all of the dogs "not later than November 15, for the Yule shopping season," and Toy Store promised to pay the full $20,000 price upon delivery. In order to obtain operating funds, Fido as borrower entered into a written loan agreement on October 5 with the High Finance Company. In relevant part, this agreement recited, "Fido Factory hereby transfers and assigns to High Finance its (Fido Factory's) October 1 mechanical dog contract with Toy Store, as security for a 50-day loan of $15,000, the advance and receipt of which are hereby acknowledged by Fido Factory. . . ." No copy of this agreement, or statement relating to it, was filed in an office of public record.

On October 15, Fido notified Toy Store, "We regret to advise that our master shaft burned out last night because our night supervisor let the lubricant level get too low. We have just fired the supervisor, but the shaft cannot be repaired or replaced until about January 1. We can guarantee delivery of your order, however, not later than January 20." Toy Store rejected this proposal as

unacceptable and immediately contracted with the only other available manufacturer to obtain the 1,000 dogs at $30 per unit by November 15.

29. For this question only, assume that on November 1, Toy Store sues Fido for damages and alleges the above facts, except those relating to the Fido-High Finance loan agreement. Upon Fido's motion to dismiss the complaint, the court should:

(A) Sustain the motion, because Fido on October 15 stated its willingness, and gave assurance of its ability, to perform the contract in January.

(B) Sustain the motion, because Toy Store's lawsuit is premature in any case until after November 15.

(C) Deny the motion, because Toy Store's complaint alleges an actionable tort by Fido.

(D) Deny the motion, because Toy Store's complaint alleges an actionable breach of contract by Fido.

30. For this question only, assume that by November 16, Fido, without legal excuse, has delivered no dogs, and that Toy Store has brought no action against Fido. In an action brought on November 16 by Toy Store against High Finance Company because of Fido's default, Toy Store can recover:

(A) Nothing, because the October 5 assignment by Fido to High Finance of Fido's contract with Toy Store was only an assignment for security.

(B) Nothing, because no record of the October 5 transaction between Fido and High Finance was publicly filed.

(C) $10,000 in damages, because Toy Store was a third-party intended beneficiary of the October 5 transaction between Fido and High Finance.

(D) $10,000 in damages, because the October 5 transaction between Fido and High Finance effected, with respect to Toy Store as creditor, a novation of debtors.

Question 31

In March, when Ohm was 17, Stereo delivered to Ohm a television set. At that time Ohm agreed in writing to pay $400 for the set on July 1, when he would reach his 18th birthday. Eighteen is the applicable statutory age of majority, and on that date Ohm was to receive the proceeds of a trust. On July 1, when the reasonable value of the television set was $250, Ohm sent Stereo a signed letter stating, "I'll only pay you $300. That is all the set is worth."

In an action against Ohm for money damages on July 2, what is the maximum amount that Stereo will be entitled to recover?

(A) Nothing.

(B) $250, the reasonable value of the set.

(C) $300, the amount Ohm promised to pay in his letter of July 1.

(D) $400, the original sale price.

Question 32

Ann leased commercial property to Brenda for a period of 10 years. The lease contained the following provision: "No subleasing or assignment will be permitted unless with the written consent of the lessor." One year later, Brenda assigned all interest in the lease to Carolyn, who assumed and agreed to perform the lessee's obligations under the terms of the lease. Ann learned of the assignment and wrote to Brenda that she had no objection to the assignment to Carolyn and agreed to accept rent from Carolyn instead of Brenda. Thereafter, Carolyn paid rent to Ann for a period of five years. Carolyn then defaulted and went into bankruptcy. In an appropriate action, Ann sued Brenda for rent due.

If Ann loses, it will be because there was:

(A) Laches.

(B) An accord and satisfaction.

(C) A novation.

(D) An attornment.

Questions 33-34 are based on the following fact situation:

Furrow leased in writing a 100-acre farm from Quark for five years at $2,000 per year, with an option to purchase "five acres of the land for $10,000 cash" at the end of the lease term. Before the lease was executed, Quark orally promised to have a five-acre parcel surveyed before the end of the lease term. Furrow took possession of the farm and paid the rent for five years. During the fifth year, having decided that he would exercise the purchase option, Furrow planted several fruit trees and built a large grain silo on the property. At the end of the term, Furrow tendered Quark $10,000 and demanded a conveyance, but Quark repudiated the option agreement and retook possession of the farm. He had never had the five-acre parcel surveyed.

33. In an action by Furrow against Quark for specific performance of the option agreement, which of the following is Quark's best defense?

(A) The option part of the agreement is unenforceable because it lacked a separate consideration.

(B) The description of the property to be sold in the parties' written agreement is too indefinite to permit the remedy sought.

(C) Quark's failure to have the five-acre parcel surveyed was failure of a condition precedent to his own duty of performance.

(D) The option part of the agreement is unenforceable under the parol evidence rule.

34. Assume for this question only that Quark is not liable to Furrow for breach of a land-sale contract. In an action by Furrow against Quark for the reasonable value of the improvements that Furrow added to the farm, which of the following theories would best support Furrow's claim?

(A) Quasi-contract, for benefits unofficiously and non-gratuitously conferred upon Quark by Furrow.

(B) Tort, for conversion by Quark in retaking possession of the improvements.

(C) Breach of trust by Quark as trustee of a resulting trust of the improvements.

(D) Breach by Quark of an implied-in-fact promise (manifested by his retaking possession of the farm and improvements) to compensate Furrow for the improvements.

Questions 35-36 are based on the following fact situation:

On January 2, Hugh Homey and Sue Structo entered into a written contract in which Structo agreed to build on Homey's lot a new house for Homey, according to plans and specifications furnished by Homey's architect, Barbara Bilevel, at a contract price of $200,000. The contract provided for specified progress payments and a final payment of $40,000 upon Homey's acceptance of the house and issuance of a certificate of final approval by the architect. Further, under a "liquidated damages" clause in the agreement, Structo promised to pay Homey $500 for each day's delay in completing the house after the following October 1. Homey, however, told Structo on January 2, before the contract was signed, that he would be on an around-the-world vacation trip most of the summer and fall and would not return to occupy the house until November 1.

35. For this question only, assume the following facts: Because she was overextended on other construction jobs, Structo did not complete the house until October 15. Homey returned on November 1 as planned and occupied the house. Ten days later, after making the $40,000 final payment to Structo, Homey learned for the first time that the house had not been completed until October 15.

If Homey sues Structo for breach of contract on account of the 15-day delay in completion, which of the following will the court probably decide?

(A) Homey will recover damages as specified in the contract, *i.e.,* $500 multiplied by 15.

(B) Homey will recover his actual damages, if any, caused by the delay in completion.

(C) Having waived the delay by occupying the house and making the final payment, Homey will recover nothing.

(D) Homey will recover nothing because the contractual completion date was impliedly modified to November 1 when Homey on January 2 advised Structo about Homey's prospective trip and return date.

36. For this question only, assume the following facts: Structo completed the house on October 14 and, when Homey returned on November 1, requested the final payment of $40,000 and issuance of a certificate of final approval by the architect, Bilevel. Homey, however, refused to pay any part of the final installment after Bilevel told him, "Structo did a great job and I find no defects worth mentioning, but Structo's contract price was at least $40,000 too high, especially in view of the big drop in housing values within the past 10 months. I will withhold the final certificate, and you just hold on to your money."

If Structo sues Homey for the $40,000 final payment after Bilevel's refusal to issue a final certificate, which of the following will the court probably decide?

(A) Structo wins, because nonoccurrence of the condition requiring Bilevel's certificate of final approval was excused by Bilevel's bad-faith refusal to issue the certificate.

(B) Structo wins, but, because all contractual conditions have not occurred, her recovery is limited to restitution of the benefit conferred on Homey, minus progress payments already received.

(C) Homey wins, provided he can prove by clear and convincing evidence that the fair-market value of the completed house is $160,000 or less.

(D) Homey wins, provided he can prove by clear and convincing evidence that total payments to Structo of $160,000 will yield a fair net profit.

CONTRACTS ANSWERS

Answer to Question 1

(C) Although this assignment of rights would result in the performance of personal services, the nature of the personal service described here appears to be routine rather than unique and thus the duty is delegable. Note also that the contract contains no language restricting assignment or delegation. (Note also that language "assigning the contract" may be construed to include a delegation of duties.) Thus, Boone (the obligee) would be required to accept performance by the delegate (Coot). Therefore, (B), which states that Boone may refuse to accept such performance, is incorrect. Because the contract does not prohibit Addie's assignment thereof, (A) incorrectly states that such assignment renders Addie in breach. (D) is incorrect because a novation substitutes a new party for an original party to the contract, and requires the assent of all parties, and completely releases the original party. The facts here do not indicate that Boone agreed to any such new arrangement.

Answer to Question 2

(A) The delegator remains personally liable on his contract, even if the delegate has expressly assumed the duties. Thus, Addie remains liable for any defective performance of the painting. (B) and (C) each are based on the incorrect assumption that the obligee is required to look to the delegate for a remedy in the event of defective performance. As explained above, the obligee (Boone) may hold the delegator (Addie) liable on the contract. (D) is incorrect because the facts do not indicate that Boone accepted performance by a new party with knowledge that there was an intent to substitute that party for an original party to the contract. Therefore, Boone did not waive his rights against Addie.

Answer to Question 3

(C) Because Johnston promised to pay without inspecting the goods, he had no right to inspect *prior to payment*. If payment is due before inspection, the fact that the goods are defective does not excuse nonpayment, unless the defect appears without inspection or there is fraud in the transaction. However, the buyer is not prevented from inspecting the goods after making payment, and thereafter pursuing all available remedies for defective performance. (D) is incorrect because, as explained above, nothing prevents a buyer from promising to pay prior to inspection. (A) is incorrect because the contractual provision at issue does not constitute an acceptance. There is no acceptance until Johnston has had an opportunity to inspect. (B) also incorrectly implies that the provision effectuates a waiver of the buyer's rights.

Answer to Question 4

(C) Where the seller does not deliver or the buyer properly rejects or revokes acceptance of tendered goods, the buyer's basic remedy is the difference between the contract price and either the market price or the cost of buying replacement goods (cover). (C) reflects the latter measure of damages. (A) is incorrect because specific performance is only available where the goods are unique or in other proper circumstances. Here, the wool does not appear to be unique. (B) is incorrect because it sets forth a measure of damages that is properly applicable where the buyer accepts goods that breach one of the seller's warranties; here, the goods have not been accepted. (D) is incorrect because, as explained in the answer to the preceding question, agreeing to pay before inspection does not waive any of the buyer's rights.

Answer to Question 5

(B) Where the buyer has paid for goods which are nonconforming, and the seller has refused the buyer's offer to restore the goods and the buyer's demand for repayment, the buyer may resell the goods and credit the proceeds to the amount owed by the seller (under the same rules that apply to a seller's resale of wrongfully rejected goods). The buyer may sell at either a public or private sale; but if it is a private sale, reasonable advance notice must be given to the seller. [U.C.C. §§2-711(3), 2-706(2), (3)] (A) and (C) each incorrectly limit the sale to being either private or public. (D) incorrectly states that the sale is not permitted at all.

Answer to Question 6

(D) Generally, offers are revocable unless the offeror receives consideration to keep the offer open. If a *merchant* signs a written offer giving assurances that it will be held open, the offer is irrevocable for the stated period or for a reasonable time if no period is stated. Here, the language at issue would probably be interpreted as a promise not to revoke; however, the offeror (Duffer) is not a merchant (*i.e.*, he does not deal in goods of the kind being sold). Thus, in the absence of consideration being given for this promise, it remains revocable. (A) is incorrect because, although there is a sale of goods, neither of the parties is a merchant, and hence, the "firm offer" provision of the U.C.C. does not apply. (B) makes no sense because the very terms of the offer state that Slicker can accept prior to noon on November 12. (C) is incorrect because no consideration was given for the promise not to countermand.

Answer to Question 7

(B) Duffer's letter would be construed as an offer that unambiguously calls for completion of performance, rather than a promise, as the only manner of acceptance. This would be an offer for a unilateral contract. An offer for a unilateral contract cannot be accepted by promising to perform. Hence, Slicker's letter of October 9 by itself wouldn't prevent Duffer from revoking his offer. (A) is wrong because a unilateral contract is created only on completion of performance of the bargained-for act, not by simply mailing a purported acceptance. (C) is wrong because the offer was for a unilateral contract. (D) is wrong because, as a response to an offer to enter into a unilateral contract, the promise to perform had no legal effect regardless of when it was received.

Answer to Question 8

(B) An offer is effectively revoked when the offeree acquires knowledge that the offeror has made an inconsistent contract with another, whether such knowledge is obtained from the offeror or some independent source. (A) is wrong because there was no consideration for the promise to keep the offer open. (C) makes no sense. Whether Slicker's power of accepting the offer is terminated does not depend on the fact that the offer was made by a prospective buyer rather than a prospective seller. (D) is incorrect insofar as it states that the November 11 conversation was also an offer to purchase; the wording used by Koolcat ("would you consider . . .") seems too preliminary in nature and thus more an invitation than an offer.

Answer to Question 9

(D) An assignor may not enforce rights against an obligor that have been previously assigned, as is the case here. An assignment establishes privity of contract between the obligor and the assignee while extinguishing privity between the obligor and assignor. Thus, the assignee replaces the assignor as the real party in interest, and the assignee alone is entitled to performance under the contract. (A) is incorrect because a promise to pay by check does not create a right too personal to assign. An attempted assignment is invalid where the rights "assigned" would result in the obligor having to perform unique personal services to someone other than the original obligee. Paying by check does not constitute such a personal service. (B) is incorrect because possession of the memorandum of settlement has no bearing on the effectiveness of an assignment. (C) is wrong because minority does not vitiate a contract, but makes it *voidable* by the minor. Furthermore, insurance contracts usually cannot be voided by minors.

Answer to Question 10

(D) Insurance contracts usually cannot be voided by infants. Thus, the liability insurance, and settlement agreement arising out of it, are valid. (A) seems to be based on the incorrect assumption that, because of Tortfeasor's minority at the time the liability policy was issued, Insurer might not be bound on the contract of insurance. Actually, the effect of a contract entered into between an infant and an adult is that the contract is voidable by the infant but binding on the adult. Thus, there is no question that Tortfeasor has rights under the liability policy. (B) assumes that Tortfeasor's minority constitutes a defense. As explained above, this is incorrect. (C) is incorrect for the same reason.

Answer to Question 11

(A) If both parties knew of Carpenter's schedule limitation at the time the contract was entered into, the supervening flood would discharge the duty to perform by impossibility, because no one could have performed during the month of March. The requirement that the impossibility must arise after the contract was entered into has been met. Since the impossibility is temporary, it could be argued that the impossibility only suspends contractual duties rather than discharging them. However, if it was specifically understood that the only time for performance was the month of March, then the contract should be discharged by impossibility. (B) is wrong because this would actually argue for a continuing duty on the part of Carpenter to make the repairs. (C) is wrong because it would not be relevant. With no additional facts, Carpenter could have begun performance in January and incurred no extra costs. (D) is wrong because it does not speak to whether Carpenter could have performed either before or after March.

Answer to Question 12

(D) On March 12, Adams terminated his offer by communicating his revocation to the offeree before Dawes had accepted. Since the revocation was directly communicated to the offeree, it was immediately effective. Because the offer was revoked, Dawes no longer had any power of acceptance. (A) is wrong because Adams's assurance did not create an option contract. Dawes gave no value for an option contract, and Adams did not assure Dawes that the offer would remain open to her personally until March 14, but only that the offer would remain open generally until that date. (B) is wrong because Adams's failure to sell the car is of no import. Adams's statement clearly communicated the intent to revoke the offer and thus terminated the offer to Dawes. (C) is wrong because even if Dawes had tendered the $3,000 on March 13, Adams need not have conveyed the automobile because he had already terminated the offer.

Answer to Question 13

(C) Carver had no duty to disclose to Page the true value of the stock. If, however, Carver had represented that the stock was not worth more than $6 a share, this would have constituted material misrepresentation and no contract would result. (A) is wrong because Carver's knowledge of the true value did not create a duty to disclose that knowledge. (B) is wrong because there was no duty to inform Page of the true value of the inventory. (D) is wrong because if Carver had misrepresented the value of the stock, availability of Chemco's financial statement to Page would not relieve Carver of liability.

Answer to Question 14

(A) Since the contract stipulated F.O.B. Singer's place of business, the risk of loss passed to Byer on January 30 when Singer placed the chairs on board a carrier. Thus, the loss of the chairs must be borne by Byer, and Singer is entitled to the contract price. Wheeler, as Singer's assignee, is entitled to the contract price. (B) is wrong as this is the measure where the buyer refuses the goods and the seller then resells them to someone else. Here, since the chairs do not exist any more, the measure of damages would be the entire contract price. (C) is wrong because the contract stipulated F.O.B. Singer's place of business. If it had not so stated, the statement in (C) would be correct. (D) is wrong because, absent circumstances suggesting otherwise, a clause prohibiting the assignment of "the contract" will be construed as barring only the delegation of the assignor's duties, not the assignment of the right to receive payment.

Answer to Question 15

(D) In a contract that specifies that delivery is F.O.B. (free on board) a particular point, the F.O.B. point is the delivery point. If the contract is F.O.B. the seller's place of shipment, the seller need only, at his expense and risk, put the goods in the hands of the carrier. If the contract is F.O.B. destination, the seller must, at his expense and risk, tender delivery of the goods at the designated destination. Here, the risk of loss had passed to Byer because the contract specifically stated that delivery was to be F.O.B. Singer's place of business. (A) and (B) are incorrect because, as explained above, the terms of the contract establish that the risk of loss was not on Singer. (C) is wrong because Singer had already performed by delivering the chairs to the carrier.

Answer to Question 16

(D) No contract was formed between the parties because Plummer gave Ohner a counteroffer rather than an acceptance. If the language had been different, this might have been an acceptance conditioned on higher payment, but given the wording, there were no clear words of acceptance. The making of the counteroffer made acceptance of the original offer impossible, and since Ohner never accepted the counteroffer, no contract was formed between the parties. (A) is wrong because at that point Plummer no longer had power of acceptance on the original offer. (B) is wrong because if Plummer's writing had been a valid acceptance, it would have been valid upon posting under the mailbox rule. (C) is wrong because Ohner's original offer was to be accepted by reply rather than by conduct, and it terminated when Plummer made his counteroffer.

Answer to Question 17

(A) A condition precedent is one which must occur before an absolute duty of immediate performance arises in the other party. Here, because performance was expressly conditioned upon Ohner's obtaining a loan and since that loan was refused, no duty to perform exists. (B) is wrong because the agreement was made before the signing of the contract. (C) is wrong because the agreement does not contradict and is in addition to the meaning of the written contract. (D) is wrong because Ohner is not attempting to deny the validity of the written agreement.

Answer to Question 18

(D) Parties to a contract may modify it by mutual assent. While consideration is necessary to modify a contract, courts usually find consideration to be present in that each party has limited his right to enforce the original contract on its own terms. On May 3, the parties modified the original contract by making other arrangements for payment which were then met. This modification served to discharge the terms in the original contract regarding payment, so Neese has no claim to the $5,000. (A) is wrong because even though Neese was an intended beneficiary of the contract, her rights in it had not vested when the modification was made on May 3, because she had not yet learned of the contract. (B) is wrong because the contract was not assigned to Neese. Rather, she was an intended beneficiary of the contract. (C) is wrong because an intended beneficiary need not furnish any consideration, so long as the original contract is supported by consideration.

Answer to Question 19

(C) Miller's strongest argument is that since the contract, by its own terms, could not be performed within a year, it was subject to the Statute of Frauds and should have been in writing. Since it was not, it is void under the Statute of Frauds. (A) would be a possible argument, but it is not as strong as the Statute of Frauds argument. Further, it would probably fail as there does appear to be manifest intent to contract. (B) is wrong because if there was a valid contract, it would not have been terminated by Gray's death. Rather, Gray's estate would have been liable for the monies owed. (D) is wrong because this was not a divisible contract.

Answer to Question 20

(B) Esther's argument would be that her hard work academically constituted her consideration for the agreement. It is not required that consideration be economic in nature. (A) is wrong because if the only defense is lack of consideration, Esther should keep arguing on contractual terms. Even in arguing under the doctrine of promissory estoppel, Esther would have to establish that she relied on the promise to her detriment. (C) is wrong because the "bonus" provision was an integral part of the contract. (D) is wrong because there is no legal duty to try one's hardest in academic pursuits, so Esther had no preexisting duty to excel.

Answer to Question 21

(C) Since Baker contracted for 100 bushels on August 1, Zeller had a contractual duty which was breached by the tendering of only 95 bushels. Baker has a cause of action for that breach. (A) is wrong because substantial performance does not excuse total performance of contractual duties. (B) is wrong because discharge by impossibility only occurs where impossibility is objective. The fact that Zeller only had 95 bushels created a subjective rather than an objective impossibility of performance, and thus did not excuse his breach. (D) is wrong because Baker was entitled to performance on August 1.

Answer to Question 22

(C) Under Article Two of the U.C.C., Selco's notice of May 10 would be considered an action which increases the risk of nonperformance, but does not clearly indicate that performance will not be forthcoming. Thus, it will not immediately be treated as a repudiation. The notice constitutes reasonable grounds for insecurity, entitling Byco to demand adequate assurance of due performance. Until Byco receives such assurance, it may suspend its own performance. (C) is the only answer embodying these principles. (A) and (B) are incorrect because they treat Selco's notice as an anticipatory repudiation. (D) is incorrect because it implies that Byco may not suspend its own performance until receipt of adequate assurances.

Answer to Question 23

(D) Selco's notice of June 10 made it clear that it was unable or unwilling to perform. In such circumstance, the aggrieved party may: (i) await performance for a commercially reasonable time; (ii) resort to any remedy for breach even though he has also urged the other party to perform; or (iii) suspend his own performance. The repudiating party may, at any time before his next performance is due, withdraw his repudiation unless the other party has canceled, materially changed her position in reliance on the repudiation, or otherwise indicated that she considers the repudiation final. From the foregoing, (A), (B), and (C) are clearly correct statements of the parties' legal status after June 10. (D) is an incorrect statement (and, thus, the correct answer) because, in actuality, Byco may assert its cause of action immediately, without giving Selco a commercially reasonable time to perform.

Answer to Question 24

(D) Where the parties to a contract express their agreement in a writing with the intent that it embody the full and final expression of their bargain, any other expressions made prior to or contemporaneous with the writing are inadmissible to vary the terms of the writing. This is the parol evidence rule. In this case, the memorandum clearly states the time of repayment as September 1. If Vault were permitted to prove Kernel's oral commitment to repay the loan by July 1, this would be permitting the introduction of an expression prior to the writing, to vary the terms of the writing. (A) is incorrect because the parol evidence rule bars evidence of the oral agreement regardless of whether such agreement was supported by consideration. (B) is incorrect because the memorandum contains no ambiguity requiring further exposition of the parties' intent. (C) is incorrect because the preexisting duty rule relates to the issue of consideration, which is not at issue here.

Answer to Question 25

(D) The Statute of Frauds provides, inter alia, that a promise to answer for the debt or default of another must be in writing, except where the main purpose of the promisor is to serve a pecuniary interest of his own. Gritz's oral promise to guarantee the loan falls within the ambit of the Statute. Proof of such promise is barred, regardless of whether it was supported by separate consideration. Thus, (C) is incorrect. (A) is incorrect because Gritz signed the memorandum in his capacity as president of Kernel, not in an individual capacity. (B) is incorrect because Gritz, as president of Kernel, appears to be a mere employee, not someone with an ownership interest. There is no indication that Gritz will benefit from the loan.

Answer to Question 26

(B) Specific performance is appropriate where the legal remedy is inadequate. The legal remedy is inadequate where land is the subject of the contract. Although theoretically the seller of land will be fully compensated by money damages, the courts will usually grant specific performance to the seller, because land is considered unique. Thus, (A) is incorrect. Although Bard did not have title to Broadacres at the time he entered into the option contract with Cutter, he did own the option to buy the property. By exercising his option under his agreement with Osif, Bard could have obtained title to Broadacres. This, in turn, would have enabled Bard to convey to Cutter, if the latter exercised his option. Thus, Bard could have been compelled to perform. Because Bard is able to perform, and Cutter has exercised his option for purchase of the land, the case is an appropriate one for specific performance. Only (B) reaches this conclusion.

Answer to Question 27

(D) Prodigal was a third-party beneficiary of the original Mater-Vault deposit agreement. A third-party beneficiary's rights do not vest (*i.e.*, are modifiable) until he: manifests assent to the promise, brings suit to enforce the promise, or materially changes position in justifiable reliance on the promise. None of these vesting acts occurred before the modification here; in fact, Prodigal did not even know of the first contract until after the modification. Thus, his rights had not vested, and the terms of the second Mater-Vault deposit agreement control the disposition of the funds. Thus, (A) is incorrect. (B) is incorrect, because even if Prodigal were an assignee, this gratuitous assignment would be revocable. (C) is incorrect because Prodigal's rights could have vested without obtaining possession of the passbook.

Answer to Question 28

(C) This question involves an assignment. Generally, a gratuitous assignment is revocable. However, an assignment is irrevocable if a token chose involving the rights to be assigned (*e.g.*, a savings account passbook) is delivered. In such a case, the assignor loses both the right and the power to revoke. (C) is the only alternative that embodies these principles. (A) and (B) are wrong because they are based on the revocability of the gift. (D) is wrong because there is no showing of detrimental reliance on the part of Prodigal. Thus, there is no estoppel.

Answer to Question 29

(D) Where the other party's words, actions, or circumstances make it clear that she is unwilling or unable to perform, the aggrieved party may, inter alia, resort to any remedy for breach. By informing Toy Store that the shaft cannot be repaired or replaced until January, Fido has made it clear that it is unable to perform by the agreed-upon date of November 15. This is a material breach, because the contract indicates that delivery must be made in time for the Christmas shopping season. Thus, Toy Store is entitled to bring an action for damages. Thus, (B) is incorrect. (A) is incorrect because performance by January does not satisfy Fido's contractual undertaking. (C) is incorrect because, although Fido's night supervisor may have been negligent, it is clear that the appropriate cause of action against Fido is based on breach of its contractual agreement to deliver the dogs by November 15.

Answer to Question 30

(A) An assignment of "the contract" or an assignment in similar general terms is an assignment of rights and, unless the language or the circumstances (as in an assignment for security) indicate the contrary, it is also a delegation of performance of the assignor's duties. Here, the October 5 assignment constituted an assignment for security, pursuant to which only Fido's rights, not its duties, under its contract with Toy Store were transferred. (B) is incorrect because even if the October 5 transaction had been filed, this would not change the fact that High Finance had not assumed Fido's duties under the contract. (C) is incorrect because Toy Store was never intended to benefit from this assignment for security. (D) is incorrect because High Finance was not substituted as a new party in place of Fido, nor did Toy Store consent thereto, both of which are requirements for a novation.

Answer to Question 31

(C) A contract entered into by a minor is voidable at his election. Upon reaching majority, the minor may affirm, *i.e.*, choose to be bound by the contract. If he retains the benefits of the contract after reaching majority, he is liable for the fair market value of the goods. Here, Ohm, who contracted to pay for the television while still an infant, could have chosen to avoid the entire contract. However, upon reaching majority, Ohm not only retained the set, but expressly affirmed the contract to the extent of $300. Therefore, Stereo may recover against Ohm on the contract, but only to the extent that he has chosen to be bound ($300). Thus, (C) is correct. (A) is wrong because Ohm affirmed the contract after reaching 18 and so must pay for the set. (B) is wrong because Ohm expressly agreed to pay more than fair market value. (D) is wrong because Ohm was not liable on the contract made while he was a minor.

Answer to Question 32

(C) If Ann loses it will be because there was a novation. A novation occurs when a new contract substitutes a new party to receive benefits and assume duties that had belonged to one of the original parties under the terms of an old contract. All the parties must agree to the substitution. A novation discharges the old contract. The elements of a valid novation are: (i) a previous valid contract; (ii) an agreement among all parties, including the new party to the new contract; (iii) the immediate extinguishment of contractual duties as between the original parties; and (iv) a valid and enforceable new contract. When lessor Ann wrote to Carolyn agreeing to accept rent and Carolyn began to do so, a new contract was formed, and Ann's rights against Brenda were extinguished. (A) is incorrect because laches is not available here. Laches is an equitable defense available when a party delays in bringing an equitable suit and the delay prejudices the defendant. The action here (for back rent) is at law, not equity. Moreover, nothing in the facts indicates that Ann delayed in bringing her action. Thus, laches is not available. (B) is incorrect because there was no accord and satisfaction. An accord occurs when the parties to a contract agree to substitute a different duty for an existing duty under the contract. Satisfaction occurs when the new duty is performed. There was no new duty here; rather, the parties agreed to substitute a new party under an existing contract (a novation). (D) is incorrect because attornment arises when the tenant agrees to accept a new landlord, and here Ann remained the landlord at all times.

Answer to Question 33

(B) Quark's best defense is that the description is too indefinite. Specific performance will not be granted unless there is an enforceable contract. For a contract for the sale of land to be enforceable, there must be an adequate description of the subject property. A description of "five acres" from a 100-acre tract is not sufficient because it does not describe which five acres were intended. Thus, specific performance will not be available. (A) is incorrect because the option agreement was a term of the contract between Quark and Furrow. As such, it was fully supported by the consideration (payment of the rent) on the contract. It was not an additional agreement requiring further consideration. (C) is incorrect because a condition precedent is one that must occur before an absolute duty of immediate performance arises in the other party. The survey was not such a condition. When Furrow tendered the $10,000 for the five acres, Furrow had a duty to perform. Nowhere in the contract itself, or extrinsically, is there an indication that Furrow's option may not be exercised until a survey is made. (D) is incorrect because the option term of the contract is a part of the written contract and does not require proof via parol evidence.

Answer to Question 34

(A) Quasi-contract is the best theory because a quasi-contract action to recover restitution is the standard remedy to avoid unjust enrichment in the case of a failed contract. Here, Furrow did not intend to gratuitously confer a benefit on Quark, but rather he conferred the benefit in reliance on Quark's promise that Quark would convey five acres to Furrow. If Quark were allowed to keep the benefits under such conditions, he would be unjustly enriched. (B) is incorrect because conversion deals with the wrongful taking or retention of chattels. Here, the fruit trees became part of the land and so were not chattels. Moreover, it was not wrongful for Quark to keep the trees since they were affixed to his property. (C) is incorrect because resulting trusts arise only where an attempted trust has failed. There was no attempt to create a trust here. (D) is incorrect because the general rule is that at the end of a lease, the owner is entitled to keep any improvements that the tenant has made that have become securely affixed to the premises. Retaining such property does not imply a promise to pay for the improvements.

Answer to Question 35

(B) Homey will only be able to recover his actual damages; the liquidated damages clause is unenforceable because it constitutes a penalty. A liquidated damages clause will be enforced only if: (i) damages in case of breach were difficult to ascertain at the time the contract was made, and (ii) the amount agreed upon was a reasonable approximation of what the damages would be. The liquidated damages clause here fails the second test. The facts indicate that Homey knew that he would not be moving into the new house until November. Thus, there is no reason for assuming that Structo's late performance would cause any damages until November. The $500 a day late fee during October can thus only be viewed as a penalty. Therefore, the liquidated damages clause will be unenforceable and Homey will be able to collect only actual damages. (C) is incorrect because there was no valid waiver here. For a waiver of rights to be valid, one must at least know of the rights being waived. Here, Homey did not know of Structo's late performance when Homey paid. Thus, the payment cannot constitute a waiver of Homey's rights arising from the late performance. (D) is incorrect—there was no enforceable modification here—because of the parol evidence rule. The parol evidence rule prohibits a party to a written contract from bringing into court evidence of prior or contemporaneous oral communications that seek to vary the terms of the written contract. Here, the oral statement was made before the written contract was signed, and the evidence seeks to vary the completion date provided in the written contract. This will not be allowed under the parol evidence rule. Thus, Structo will not be able to bring in evidence seeking to vary the written date.

Answer to Question 36

(A) Structo will win because the condition of the architect's certificate will be excused by Bilevel's bad faith. While the issuance of the certificate was an express condition precedent to Homey's duty to pay, the condition will be excused by Homey's hindrance. If a party having a duty of performance that is subject to a condition wrongfully prevents the condition from occurring, the condition will be excused. Here, Homey's duty of payment was subject to the condition precedent that Bilevel issue a certificate of approval, and Homey wrongfully hindered the occurrence of the condition by agreeing to allow Bilevel to not issue the certificate for an improper reason—Structo had done all that it was obliged to do under the contract properly and the only reason for refusing the certificate is that Bilevel and Homey believe the price Homey agreed to is now too high. This is not a valid reason for withholding the certificate. Thus, the condition of the certificate will be excused and Structo can collect the full $40,000. (B) is incorrect because, as explained above, the condition of the architect's certificate will be excused. Thus, the contract is fully enforceable. (C) and (D) are incorrect because, as explained above, the contract is fully enforceable. Thus, Homey will have to pay the contract price. It is not a defense that the price is higher than it should have been at current prices.

CRIMINAL LAW QUESTIONS

Question 1

In which of the following situations is Defendant's claim of intoxication most likely to result in his being found not guilty?

(A) Defendant is charged with manslaughter for a death resulting from an automobile accident. Defendant, the driver, claims he was so drunk he was unable to see the other car involved in the accident.

(B) Defendant is charged with assault with intent to kill Watts, as a result of his wounding Watts by shooting him. Defendant claims he was so drunk he did not realize anyone else was around when he fired the gun.

(C) Defendant is charged with armed robbery. He claims he was so drunk he did not know whether the gun was loaded.

(D) Defendant is charged with statutory rape, after he had sexual intercourse with a girl aged 15, in a jurisdiction where the age of consent is 16. Defendant claims he was so drunk he did not realize the girl was a minor.

Question 2

Jackson and Brannick planned to break into a federal government office to steal food stamps. Jackson telephoned Crowley one night and asked whether Crowley wanted to buy some "hot" food stamps. Crowley, who understood that "hot" meant stolen, said, "Sure, bring them right over." Jackson and Brannick then successfully executed their scheme. That same night they delivered the food stamps to Crowley, who bought them for $500. Crowley did not ask when or by whom the stamps were stolen. All three were arrested. Jackson and Brannick entered guilty pleas in federal court to a charge of larceny in connection with the theft. Crowley was brought to trial in the state court on a charge of conspiracy to steal food stamps.

On the evidence stated, Crowley should be found:

(A) Guilty, because, when a new confederate enters a conspiracy already in progress, he becomes a party to it.

(B) Guilty, because he knowingly and willingly aided and abetted the conspiracy and is chargeable as a principal.

(C) Not guilty, because, although Crowley knew the stamps were stolen, he neither helped to plan nor participated or assisted in the theft.

(D) Not guilty, because Jackson and Brannick had not been convicted of or charged with conspiracy, and Crowley cannot be guilty of conspiracy by himself.

Question 3

Jack and Paul planned to hold up a bank. They drove to the bank in Jack's car. Jack entered while Paul remained as lookout in the car. After a few moments, Paul panicked and drove off.

Jack looked over the various tellers, approached one and whispered nervously, "Just hand over the cash. Don't look around, don't make a false move—or it's your life." The teller looked at the fidgeting Jack, laughed, flipped him a dollar bill, and said, "Go on, beat it." Flustered, Jack grabbed the dollar and left.

Paul's best defense to a charge of robbery would be that:

(A) Jack alone entered the bank.

(B) Paul withdrew, before commission of the crime, when he fled the scene.

(C) Paul had no knowledge of what Jack whispered to the teller.

(D) The teller was not placed in fear by Jack.

Question 4

Adam and Bailey, brothers, operated an illicit still. They customarily sold to anyone unless they suspected the person of being a revenue agent or an informant. One day when Adam was at the still alone, he was approached by Mitchell, who asked to buy a gallon of liquor. Mitchell was in fact a revenue officer. After Adam had sold him the liquor, Mitchell revealed his identity. Adam grabbed one of the rifles that the brothers kept handy in case of trouble with the law, and shot and wounded Mitchell. Other officers, hiding nearby, overpowered and arrested Adam.

Shortly thereafter, Bailey came on the scene. The officers in hiding had been waiting for him. One of them approached him and asked to buy liquor. Bailey was suspicious and refused to sell. The officers nevertheless arrested him.

Adam and Bailey were charged with conspiracy to violate revenue laws, illegal selling of liquor, and battery of the officer.

On the charge of battery, which statement concerning Adam and Bailey is true?

(A) Neither is guilty.

(B) Both are guilty.

(C) Adam is guilty but Bailey is not, because the conspiracy had terminated with the arrest of Adam.

(D) Adam is guilty but Bailey is not, because Adam's act was outside the scope of the conspiracy.

Question 5

Dent, while eating in a restaurant, noticed that a departing customer at the next table had left a five-dollar bill as a tip for the waitress. Dent reached over, picked up the five-dollar bill, and put it in his pocket. As he stood up to leave, another customer who had seen him take the money ran over to him and hit him in the face with her umbrella. Enraged, Dent choked the customer to death.

Dent is charged with murder. He requests the court to charge the jury that they can find him guilty of voluntary manslaughter rather than murder. Dent's request should be:

(A) Granted, because the jury could find that Dent acted recklessly and not with the intent to cause death or serious bodily harm.

(B) Granted, because the jury could find that being hit in the face with an umbrella constitutes adequate provocation.

(C) Denied, because the evidence shows that Dent intended to kill or to cause serious bodily harm.

(D) Denied, because the evidence shows that Dent provoked the assault on himself by his criminal misconduct.

Question 6

Brown suffered from the delusion that he was a special agent of God. He frequently experienced hallucinations in the form of hearing divine commands. Brown believed God told him several times that the local Roman Catholic bishop was corrupting the diocese into heresy, and that the bishop should be "done away with." Brown, a devout Catholic, conceived of himself as a religious martyr. He knew that shooting bishops for heresy is against the criminal law. He nevertheless carefully planned how he might kill the bishop. One evening Brown shot the bishop, who was taken to the hospital, where he died two weeks later.

Brown told the police he assumed the institutions of society would support the ecclesiastical hierarchy, and he expected to be persecuted for his God-inspired actions. Psychiatrist Stevens examined Brown and found that Brown suffered from schizophrenic psychosis, that in the absence of this psychosis he would not have shot the bishop, and that because of the psychosis Brown found it extremely difficult to determine whether he should obey the specific command that he do away with the bishop or the general commandment "Thou shalt not kill"; Brown was charged with murder.

If Brown interposes an insanity defense and the jurisdiction in which he is tried has adopted only the *M'Naghten* test of insanity, then the strongest argument for the defense under that test is that:

(A) Brown did not know the nature of the act he was performing.

(B) Brown did not know that his act was morally wrong.

(C) Brown did not know the quality of the act he was performing.

(D) Brown's acts were the product of a mental disease.

Question 7

In which of the following situations is Defendant most likely to be guilty of common law murder?

(A) During an argument in a bar, Norris punches Defendant. Defendant, mistakenly believing that Norris is about to stab him, shoots and kills Norris.

(B) While committing a robbery of a liquor store, Defendant accidentally drops his revolver, which goes off. The bullet strikes and kills Johnson, a customer in the store.

(C) While hunting deer, Defendant notices something moving in the bushes. Believing it to be a deer, Defendant fires into the bushes. The bullet strikes and kills Griggs, another hunter.

(D) In celebration of the Fourth of July, Defendant discharges a pistol within the city limits in violation of a city ordinance. The bullet ricochets off the street and strikes and kills Abbott.

Question 8

Dutton, disappointed by his eight-year-old son's failure to do well in school, began systematically depriving the child of food during summer vacation. Although his son became seriously ill from malnutrition, Dutton failed to call a doctor. He believed that as a parent he had the sole right to determine whether the child was fed or received medical treatment. Eventually, the child died. An autopsy disclosed that the child had suffered agonizingly as a result of the starvation, that a physician's aid would have alleviated the suffering, and that although the child would have died in a few months from malnutrition, the actual cause of death was an untreatable form of cancer.

The father was prosecuted for murder, defined in the jurisdiction as "unlawful killing of a human being with malice aforethought." The father should be:

(A) Acquitted, because of the defendant's good faith belief concerning parental rights in supervising children.

(B) Acquitted, because summoning the physician or feeding the child would not have prevented the child's death from cancer.

(C) Convicted, because the father's treatment of his son showed a reckless indifference to the value of life.

(D) Convicted, because the child would have died from malnutrition had he not been afflicted with cancer.

Question 9

Vance had cheated Dodd in a card game. Angered, Dodd set out for Vance's house with the intention of shooting him. Just as he was about to set foot on Vance's property, Dodd was arrested by a police officer who noticed that Dodd was carrying a revolver. A statute in the jurisdiction makes it a crime to "enter the property of another with the intent to commit any crime of violence thereon."

If charged with attempting to violate the statute, Dodd should be found:

(A) Not guilty, because the statute defines an attempt crime and there cannot be an attempt to attempt.

(B) Not guilty, because to convict him would be to punish him simply for having a guilty mind.

(C) Guilty, because he was close enough to entering the property and he had the necessary state of mind.

(D) Guilty, because this is a statute designed to protect the public from violence, and Dodd was dangerous.

Questions 10-15 are based on the following fact situation and require you to assume that you are in either a TYPE A or a TYPE B jurisdiction:

TYPE A. The homicide statute in this jurisdiction reads in part as follows:

Murder is the unlawful killing of a human being with malice aforethought. Such malice may be express or implied. It is express when there is manifested a deliberate intention unlawfully to take away the life of a fellow creature. It is implied when no considerable provocation appears or when the circumstances attending the killing show an abandoned and malignant heart. Every person guilty of murder shall suffer death or confinement in the state prison for life, at the discretion of the jury trying the same.

TYPE B. The homicide statute in this jurisdiction reads in part as follows:

Murder is the unlawful killing of a human being with malice aforethought. Such malice may be express or implied. It is express when there is manifested a deliberate intention unlawfully to take away the life of a fellow creature. It is implied when no considerable provocation appears or when the circumstances attending the killing show an abandoned and malignant heart. All murder that is perpetrated by willful, deliberate, or premeditated killing or that is committed in the perpetration of or attempt to perpetrate arson, rape, robbery, or burglary is murder of the first degree. All other kinds of murders are of the second degree. Every person guilty of murder in the first degree shall suffer death or confinement in the state prison for life, at the

discretion of the jury trying the same. Every person convicted of murder in the second degree shall be confined in the state prison for life.

Both TYPE A and TYPE B jurisdictions have a statute reading as follows:

Manslaughter is the unlawful killing of a human being without malice. It is of two kinds:

1. Voluntary—upon a sudden quarrel or heat of passion.

2. Involuntary—in the commission of an unlawful act, not amounting to a felony; or in the commission of a lawful act that might produce death in an unlawful manner or without due caution and circumspection.

Manslaughter is punishable by imprisonment in the state prison not exceeding 15 years.

Victor and Defendant were 16 and 17, respectively. Both were old enough to be legally responsible for a crime in the particular jurisdiction. By prearrangement they met at the Dairy Shoppe, a teenage hangout. They were depressed. It had been raining for some days, and school had been out for several weeks. Defendant asked Victor if he would like to play Russian roulette. They played with a revolver, as they had done before. The cylinder of the revolver had six chambers, from which they would remove all but one cartridge. One of them would then spin the cylinder, point the revolver at the other's head, and fire it. With six chambers and one cartridge, the odds were 5 to 1 that the revolver would not fire.

Defendant obtained the revolver from his parents' bedroom. Adam, his father, kept the revolver in the bedroom at all times. Adam repeatedly bragged that he kept a loaded revolver in his room. Defendant took the revolver from the bedroom. He had done this before. He took out all but one cartridge, placed the others in his pocket, and then proceeded to the Dairy Shoppe.

Victor agreed to play Russian roulette. Defendant, pointing the revolver at Victor's head, pulled the trigger. Nothing happened. Victor then spun the cylinder and pointed the revolver at Defendant's head. He pulled the trigger. Nothing happened. Defendant spun the cylinder and pointed the revolver at Victor's head. He pulled the trigger. The gun fired. He was heard to exclaim: "Victor, Victor, I didn't think it would shoot! I'm sorry!" Victor died en route to the hospital.

10. Defendant is charged with murder in a TYPE A jurisdiction. Which of the following is the soundest result?

   (A) Not guilty, because consent is a complete defense.

   (B) Not guilty, because the negligence of Adam is a complete defense.

   (C) Guilty of murder.

   (D) Guilty of involuntary manslaughter.

11. Defendant is charged with first degree murder in a TYPE B jurisdiction. Which of the following is Defendant's soundest theory of defense?

   (A) Laws making a 17-year-old liable for any homicide are unconstitutional as imposing a cruel and unusual punishment.

   (B) A revolver with only one of its six chambers loaded is not a deadly weapon, and its use therefore cannot prove deliberate killing.

   (C) Defendant, because of his youth, could not have the malice aforethought required for murder.

   (D) Defendant is guilty of murder, but his deed does not fall within the definition of first degree murder.

12. Defendant is charged with murder in a TYPE A jurisdiction. The trial judge can properly charge the jury on which of the following theories?

   (A) Involuntary manslaughter only.

   (B) Murder and involuntary manslaughter.

   (C) Murder and voluntary manslaughter.

   (D) First degree murder, second degree murder, and involuntary manslaughter.

13. Defendant is charged with murder in a TYPE A jurisdiction. Which of the following is the soundest argument of the prosecutor?

   (A) Defendant's actions demonstrated an abandoned and malignant heart because he knew his act might cause death or great bodily harm.

   (B) The homicide is a felony murder since Victor's death was the result of an assault with a deadly weapon.

   (C) Defendant by definition is not a juvenile and can be found guilty of a capital crime.

   (D) The negligence of Adam is not a supervening cause which will relieve Defendant of liability.

14. Defendant is charged with first degree murder in a TYPE B jurisdiction. Defendant's best argument for acquittal of first degree murder would be that:

   (A) He committed no arson, rape, robbery, or burglary.

   (B) He did not deliberate or premeditate.

   (C) Victor consented to the homicide.

   (D) He did not deliberate, premeditate, or commit a first degree felony murder.

15. Assuming statutes covering the following offenses, in a TYPE A jurisdiction Adam, the father, can be most appropriately charged with:

    (A) Assault with a deadly weapon.

    (B) Contributing to the delinquency of a minor.

    (C) Murder.

    (D) Voluntary manslaughter.

Questions 16-17 are based on the following fact situation:

Linda was 15 years old, but she appeared and acted older. When asked, she always said she was 22, and she carried false identification saying she was that old. She frequented taverns and drank heavily. One evening in a bar she became acquainted with Duke. He believed her when she told him her claimed age. They had several drinks and became inebriated. Later, they drove in Duke's car to a secluded spot. After they had necked for a while, Duke propositioned Linda and she consented. Before Duke achieved penetration, Linda changed her mind, saying, "Stop! Don't touch me! I don't want to do it." When Duke did not desist, Linda started to cry and said, "I am only 15." Duke immediately jumped from the car and ran away. Duke was indicted for attempted rape, assault with intent to rape, contributing to the delinquency of a minor, and attempted statutory rape. The age of consent in the jurisdiction is 16.

16. If the contributing charge were based on a statute reading, "Whoever shall commit an act affecting the morals of a minor under 16 years of age shall be deemed guilty of contributing to the delinquency of a minor and shall be punished by imprisonment in the state penitentiary for a period not to exceed 5 years," Duke's best legal defense would be that:

    (A) The statute is unconstitutionally vague.

    (B) Linda consented to his actions.

    (C) He was entrapped by Linda's appearance.

    (D) He did not intend to contribute to her delinquency.

17. With respect to the contributing charge under the statute set out in the question above, proof by Duke that he was so inebriated that he could not have formed a criminal intent would be a:

    (A) Good defense, because the charge requires a specific intent.

    (B) Good defense, because at least a general criminal intent is required for every offense.

    (C) Poor defense, because contributing to the delinquency of a minor is an offense against a child.

    (D) Poor defense, because the state of mind of the defendant is irrelevant to this offense, so long as he was legally sane.

Questions 18-20 are based on the following fact situation:

Adams, Bennett, and Curtis are charged in a common law jurisdiction with conspiracy to commit larceny. The state introduced evidence that they agreed to go to Nelson's house to take stock certificates from a safe in Nelson's bedroom, that they went to the house, and that they were arrested as they entered Nelson's bedroom.

Adams testified that he thought the stock certificates belonged to Curtis, that Nelson was improperly keeping them from Curtis, and that he went along to aid in retrieving Curtis's property.

Bennett testified that he suspected Adams and Curtis of being thieves and joined up with them in order to catch them. He also testified that he made an anonymous telephone call to the police alerting them to the crime and that the call caused the police to be waiting for them when they walked into Nelson's bedroom.

Curtis did not testify.

18. If the jury believes Adams, it should find him:

   (A) Guilty, because there was an agreement and the entry into the bedroom is sufficient for the overt act.

   (B) Guilty, because good motives are not a defense to criminal liability.

   (C) Not guilty, because he did not have a corrupt motive.

   (D) Not guilty, because he did not intend to steal.

19. If the jury believes Bennett, it should find him:

   (A) Guilty, because there was an agreement and the entry into the bedroom is sufficient for the overt act.

   (B) Guilty, because he is not a police officer and thus cannot claim any privilege of apprehending criminals.

   (C) Not guilty, because he did not intend to steal.

   (D) Not guilty, because he prevented the theft from occurring.

20. If the jury believes both Adams and Bennett, it should find Curtis:

   (A) Guilty, because there was an agreement and the entry into the bedroom is sufficient for the overt act.

   (B) Guilty, because he intended to steal.

   (C) Not guilty, because a conviction would penalize him for exercising his right not to be a witness.

   (D) Not guilty, because Adams and Bennett did not intend to steal.

Questions 21-25 are based on the four case summaries below. For each question, select the case that would be most applicable as a precedent:

(A) *Commonwealth v. Mason.* Two brothers see a wealthy neighbor's pedigreed dog on the street. They take the dog home, intending to conceal it until the owner offers a reward. Held, guilty of larceny.

(B) *Saferite v. State.* Two young men saw a motor car on the street with the keys in the ignition lock. They drove the car to a neighboring town with the intention, they said, of visiting the wife of one of them. The car was wrecked on their way back. Conviction for larceny reversed.

(C) *People v. Noblett.* Defendant, a tenant of a city apartment, advertised it for sublease. Will agreed to sublease for three months, and on March 12 paid Defendant $550, the total agreed rental. Will was to receive possession on March 20, but possession was never given him. Held, not guilty of common law larceny.

(D) *King v. Pear.* From a stablekeeper, Defendant hired a horse to go to Sutton and back, saying he would be back at 8 p.m. He did not return. Investigation showed that Defendant had given a false address, and that he had sold the horse the same day. Conviction of larceny affirmed.

21. Davis paid Realtor $500 as down payment on a house. That night, Davis broke into a hardware store and took a brace and bit. Davis broke into Realtor's office and used the tools to open the safe, where he had seen Realtor place the $500. The safe was empty. Davis's fingerprints on the tools, left lying in front of the safe, led to his arrest. He is charged with larceny of the tools.

22. Smith placed a newspaper advertisement reading, "Wanted: responsible man to collect for large firm. $500 security required. Address Box 66, Times." Vincent answered the ad and was called on by Smith, who said he represented Ames Advertising Agency. He took Vincent to the office of the company (a large actual firm), but as they were about to enter the building Smith said, "There is Mr. Ames now," and introduced him to a companion of Smith who impersonated Ames. The result of the conversation was that the false Ames agreed to hire Vincent. It was agreed that Vincent would draw $500 from the bank to put up as security, and that this money would be placed in a bank and Vincent given a certificate of deposit in his own name. They went to the bank where Vincent gave Smith the money, after which Smith and "Ames" disappeared. Smith was later charged with larceny.

23. Jones, angry at a neighbor with whom he had quarreled, for revenge surreptitiously removed a piece of stone statuary from the neighbor's garden and concealed it in his garage. He intended to replace it a day or two later, after giving the neighbor a chance to feel bad over its being stolen. Suspecting who was guilty, the neighbor had Jones arrested and charged with larceny.

24. Harris, a heroin addict, broke into a home and took several cameras and watches, which he promptly pawned to obtain cash with which to purchase a "fix." Harris was later charged with larceny of the cameras and watches.

25. Allison told Mark that he, Allison, was the legal representative for a syndicate that had a photoelectric machine for making counterfeit money, and to prove that the money was good enough to "pass anywhere," Allison showed what he said was one of the counterfeit $10 bills. He said that if Mark would invest $1,000, the syndicate would pay him counterfeit money in the amount of $10,000. Mark paid the $1,000

to Allison, who then disappeared. Allison is caught and charged with larceny.

Question 26

Ted frequently visited Janet, his next-door neighbor. Janet was separated from her husband, Howard. Howard resided with his mother but jointly owned the house in which Janet resided. Late one night, Ted and Janet were sitting on the bed in Janet's bedroom drinking when Howard burst through the door and told Ted, "Get out!" When Ted refused, Howard challenged him to go outside and "fight it out." Ted again refused. Howard then pulled a knife from his pocket and lunged at Ted. Ted grabbed a lamp, struck Howard on the head, and killed him. Ted is charged with murder.

On a charge of murder, Ted should be found:

(A) Not guilty, because Ted had as much right as Howard to be in the house.

(B) Not guilty, because Howard attacked Ted with a deadly weapon.

(C) Guilty, because Ted's presence in Janet's bedroom prompted Howard's attack.

(D) Guilty, because Ted's failure to obey Howard's order to leave the house made him a trespasser.

Question 27

Defendant is charged with assault and battery. The state's evidence shows that Victim was struck in the face by Defendant's fist.

In which of the following situations is Defendant most likely to be **not guilty** of assault and battery?

(A) Defendant had been hypnotized at a party and ordered by the hypnotist to strike the person he disliked the most.

(B) Defendant was suffering from an epileptic seizure and had no control over his motions.

(C) Defendant was heavily intoxicated and was shadow boxing without realizing that Victim was near him.

(D) Defendant, who had just awakened from a deep sleep, was not fully aware of what was happening and mistakenly thought Victim was attacking him.

Question 28

Donna was arrested and taken to police headquarters, where she was given her *Miranda* warnings. Donna indicated that she wished to telephone her lawyer and was told that she could do so after her fingerprints had been taken. While being fingerprinted, however, Donna blurted out, "Paying a lawyer is a waste of money because I know you have me."

At trial, Donna's motion to prevent the introduction of the statement she made while being fingerprinted will most probably be:

(A) Granted, because Donna's request to contact her attorney by telephone was reasonable and should have been granted immediately.

(B) Granted, because of the "fruit of the poisonous tree" doctrine.

(C) Denied, because the statements were volunteered and not the result of interrogation.

(D) Denied, because fingerprinting is not a critical stage of the proceeding requiring the assistance of counsel.

Question 29

Driving down a dark road, Defendant accidentally ran over a man. Defendant stopped and found that the victim was dead. Defendant, fearing that he might be held responsible, took the victim's wallet, which contained a substantial amount of money. He removed the identification papers and put the wallet and money back into the victim's pocket.

Defendant is *not guilty* of:

(A) Larceny, because he took the papers only to prevent identification and not for his own use.

(B) Larceny, because he did not take anything from a living victim.

(C) Robbery, because he did not take the papers by means of force or putting in fear.

(D) Robbery, because he did not take anything of monetary value.

Question 30

Tom had a heart ailment so serious that his doctors had concluded that only a heart transplant could save his life. They therefore arranged to have him flown to Big City to have the operation performed.

Dan, Tom's nephew, who stood to inherit from him, poisoned him. The poison produced a reaction which required postponing the journey. The plane on which Tom was to have flown crashed, and all aboard were killed. By the following day, Tom's heart was so weakened by the effects of the poison that he suffered a heart attack and died.

If charged with criminal homicide, Dan should be found:

(A) Guilty.

(B) Not guilty, because his act did not hasten the deceased's death, but instead prolonged his life by one day.

(C) Not guilty, because the deceased was already suffering from a fatal illness.

(D) Not guilty, because the poison was not the sole cause of death.

Questions 31-32 are based on the following fact situation:

Statutes in the jurisdiction define criminal assault as "an attempt to commit a criminal battery" and criminal battery as "causing an offensive touching."

As Edward was walking down the street, a gust of wind blew his hat off. Edward reached out, trying to grab his hat, and narrowly missed striking Margaret in the face with his hand. Margaret, fearful of being struck by Edward, pushed Edward away.

31. If charged with criminal assault, Edward should be found:

    (A) Guilty, because he caused Margaret to be in apprehension of an offensive touching.

    (B) Guilty, because he should have realized he might strike someone by reaching out.

    (C) Not guilty, because he did not intend to hit Margaret.

    (D) Not guilty, because he did not hit Margaret.

32. If charged with criminal battery, Margaret should be found:

    (A) Guilty, because she intentionally pushed Edward.

    (B) Guilty, because she caused the touching of Edward whether she meant to do so or not.

    (C) Not guilty, because a push is not an offensive touching.

    (D) Not guilty, because she was justified in pushing Edward.

Question 33

A state statute makes it a felony for any teacher at a state institution of higher education to accept anything of value from a student at the same institution. Monroe, a student at the state university, offered Professor Smith, his English teacher, $50 in exchange for a good grade in his English course. Smith agreed and took the money. Professor Smith and Monroe are tried jointly for violation of the state statute. Professor Smith is charged with violating the statute and Monroe with aiding and abetting him.

Monroe's best argument for a dismissal of the charge against him is that:

    (A) A principal and an accessory cannot be tried together, since the principal must be convicted first.

    (B) He cannot be an accessory, since he is the victim of the crime.

    (C) The legislature did not intend to punish the person giving the thing of value.

    (D) He did not assist Professor Smith in violating the statute.

Question 34

In which of the following situations is Defendant most likely to be guilty of larceny?

    (A) Defendant took Sue's television set, with the intention of returning it the next day. However, he dropped it and damaged it beyond repair.

    (B) Defendant went into Tom's house and took $100 in the belief that Tom had damaged Defendant's car to that amount.

    (C) Mistakenly believing that larceny does not include the taking of a dog, Defendant took his neighbor's dog and sold it.

    (D) Unreasonably mistaking George's car for his own, Defendant got into George's car in a parking lot and drove it home.

Question 35

Which of the following is most likely to be found to be a strict liability offense?

(A) A city ordinance providing for a fine of not more than $200 for shoplifting.

(B) A federal statute making it a felony to possess heroin.

(C) A state statute making it a felony to fail to register a firearm.

(D) A state statute making the sale of adulterated milk a misdemeanor.

Question 36

Which of the following is *least* likely to be the underlying felony in a prosecution for felony murder?

(A) Arson.

(B) Manslaughter.

(C) Attempted rape.

(D) Burglary.

Question 37

Rimm and Hill were fooling around with a pistol in Hill's den. Rimm aimed the pistol in Hill's direction and fired three shots slightly to Hill's right. One shot ricocheted off the wall and struck Hill in the back, killing him instantly.

The most serious crime of which Rimm can be convicted is:

(A) Murder.

(B) Voluntary manslaughter.

(C) Involuntary manslaughter.

(D) Assault with a dangerous weapon.

Question 38

Defendant, a worker in a metal working shop, had long been teasing Vincent, a young colleague, by calling him insulting names and ridiculing him. One day Vincent responded to the teasing by picking up a metal bar and attacking Defendant. Defendant could have escaped from the shop. He parried the blow with his left arm, and with his right hand struck Vincent a blow on his jaw from which the young man died.

What is the most serious offense of which Defendant could be properly convicted?

(A) Involuntary manslaughter.

(B) Voluntary manslaughter.

(C) Murder.

(D) None of the above.

Question 39

Alford was a suspect in a homicide committed during a robbery of a liquor store. Barber was a friend of Alford. Police telephoned Barber and asked if he would help locate Alford. Barber agreed and met the police officers at headquarters later that night.

After a discussion during which police asked questions about Alford and the homicide, Barber said that he wanted to get something "off his chest" and advised the officers that he was in on the robbery but that Alford had shot the owner of the store without his permission or prior knowledge. The officers then for the first time gave Barber his *Miranda* warnings.

Barber was indicted for felony murder. He moved to prevent the introduction of his statement into evidence. His motion should be:

(A) Granted, because Barber was effectively in custody and entitled to receive *Miranda* warnings at the beginning of the discussion.

(B) Granted, because Barber's right to counsel and due process were violated by the interrogation at police headquarters.

(C) Denied, because his statement was freely and voluntarily given and he was not entitled to *Miranda* warnings.

(D) Denied, because by visiting headquarters voluntarily, Barber waived his right to have *Miranda* warnings at the beginning of the discussion.

CRIMINAL LAW ANSWERS

Answer to Question 1

(B)   Voluntary intoxication is a defense to a crime that requires **intent** (assault with intent to kill), and in (B) the intoxication prevented Defendant from formulating the intent to commit the crime. (A) and (D) are incorrect because voluntary intoxication is no defense to crimes involving recklessness or strict liability. (C) is incorrect because Defendant's intoxication did not prevent him from formulating the purpose or intent to commit the crime.

Answer to Question 2

(C)   Crowley should be found not guilty because what he did was commit the crime of **receiving** stolen property knowing it to be stolen. This crime would not be necessary if the mere agreement to purchase the loot after another had already stolen it were enough to make the purchaser a conspirator. (A) is wrong. The point of law stated is accurate enough, but it assumes that simply by agreeing to buy the stamps, Crowley joined in the conspiracy to steal them. (B) is wrong because Crowley did not aid and abet the conspiracy to commit larceny because that conspiracy had already accomplished its target object, the stealing of the stamps. (D) is wrong. It is true that one may not conspire with himself. But it is not true that one who does enter into a conspiracy with one or more people cannot be convicted unless the others are at least charged with the conspiracy. If only one conspirator is prosecuted, however, the prosecution must show that, in fact, others were involved with the defendant on trial.

Answer to Question 3

(D)   Paul's best defense is that Jack did not commit a robbery. Robbery is in effect a larceny from the person, committed by force or fear. Here, force was threatened, not actually used. Had the teller felt any apprehension that Jack would use a gun if he did not do what he was told, this would be "fear" even though the victim remained cool and poised while complying with the demands, and knew that as long as he did so, no force would be used. In this case, however, it is obvious that the teller felt no fear at all. (Paul's crime was **attempted** robbery.) (A) is wrong. Paul was an accomplice to Jack. He would incur vicarious liability for crimes committed by Jack. (B) is wrong. Paul would be an accomplice to attempted robbery (and perhaps larceny) because he did not repudiate his assistance before fleeing; thus, he did not effectively withdraw. (C) is wrong. We are told that Paul and Jack planned to hold up a bank. It is not necessary that the accomplice know all the precise details of how this is to be carried out. It suffices that Paul knew that Jack would use the threat of force to obtain property permanently.

Answer to Question 4

(B)   Battery is an unlawful application of force to the person of another resulting in bodily injury or an offensive touching. Adam's shooting and wounding of Mitchell meets all the elements of the crime. Thus, Adam is guilty of battery. Bailey is also guilty of battery because Adam conspired with Bailey to operate an illegal still, and each co-conspirator is liable for the crimes of all other co-conspirators if: (i) the crimes were committed in furtherance of the objective of the conspiracy; and (ii) the crimes were a natural and probable consequence of the conspiracy (*i.e.,* foreseeable). The battery was committed in furtherance of the conspiracy (to keep the still in operation) and was foreseeable because the conspirators kept guns on the site in case of trouble with the law, and the wounding of a peace officer would be a "natural and probable" consequence. Thus, (B) is correct, and it follows that (A) must be incorrect. (C) is wrong because even if the conspiracy was terminated by Adam's arrest, the battery occurred before the arrest, when the conspiracy was clearly ongoing. Bailey made no legally effective withdrawal prior to the battery, and he remains liable for Adam's act. (D) is wrong because, as discussed above, the battery was in furtherance of the objective of the conspiracy and a foreseeable consequence of the conspiracy.

Answer to Question 5

(B) The existence of adequate provocation may reduce a killing to voluntary manslaughter. Being subjected to a serious battery is frequently recognized as constituting adequate provocation. Here, the jury should decide whether being hit in the face with an umbrella qualifies. (A) is incorrect because a finding that Dent acted recklessly would not necessarily suffice to reduce the crime to voluntary manslaughter. Provocation is the key. (C) is incorrect because to the extent that Dent intended to kill or to cause serious bodily harm, he was acting in the wake of a sudden and intense passion that caused him to lose his self-control, which would make voluntary manslaughter applicable. (D) is incorrect because it is questionable whether Dent's taking of the money that had been left for the waitress constituted sufficient reason for the customer to hit him in the face with an umbrella. Thus, the jury should be allowed to consider voluntary manslaughter as an option.

Answer to Question 6

(B) The traditional *M'Naghten* rule provides that a defendant is entitled to acquittal if the proof establishes that: (a) a disease of the mind; (b) caused a defect of reason; (c) such that the defendant lacked the ability at the time of his actions to either: (i) know the wrongfulness of his actions; or (ii) understand the nature and quality of his actions. (B) is the best answer here, because this option goes directly to the wrongfulness issue and is supported by the facts, which indicate Brown's moral dilemma. His conclusion that direct orders from God overrode the general prohibition against killing indicates that Brown did not know the wrongfulness of his act. (A) and (C) are incorrect because the *M'Naghten* test speaks of nature **and** quality, and each of these options contains only one of these two elements. In addition, the facts are less likely to support an assertion that Brown was ignorant of either the nature or quality of his act than that he did not understand it was wrong. (D) is wrong because mental disease is but one element of the *M'Naghten* test. Acts that occur as a "product of mental disease or defect" fall under the insanity defense in jurisdictions that apply the *Durham* rule, which is substantially broader than *M'Naghten*.

Answer to Question 7

(B) The defendant is guilty of felony murder in this fact situation, since even an accidental killing committed during the course of a felony constitutes common law murder. Malice is implied from the intent to commit the underlying felony. Since defendant did have the requisite intent to commit the robbery with no defense to cut off liability, he would be liable at common law for the accidental death as well. (A) is wrong, since this fact situation would give the defendant a possible self-defense claim, and if that failed, it would be manslaughter, not common law murder. (C) is wrong because here there was no malice aforethought. At most, the defendant would be guilty of involuntary manslaughter. (D) is not as good a choice as (B) because a jury could find that there was no malice aforethought. Defendant then would be guilty only of misdemeanor manslaughter while committing an "unlawful act," not common law murder.

Answer to Question 8

(B) Dutton would have to be acquitted because his actions did not cause the death of the child. (A) is wrong because the defendant's beliefs about his rights are irrelevant. If the child had died of malnutrition, the defendant's good faith belief concerning parental rights in supervising children would have been of no help to him. (C) is wrong because that reckless indifference did not cause the child's death. (D) is wrong because the child did not actually die from malnutrition.

Answer to Question 9

(C) Vance could not be convicted of actually violating the statute because he did not enter the property of another. However, since he was approaching the property with the requisite state of mind, he could be charged with attempting to violate that statute. (A) is wrong because the statute does not define an attempt crime. Entering onto the property of another is an affirmative action. (B) is wrong because entering the property of another with the intent to commit a crime of violence constitutes more than merely "having a guilty mind." (D) is wrong because it is overbroad and overly subjective.

Answer to Question 10

(C) Defendant's conduct qualifies as a killing with "an abandoned and malignant heart" because it exhibited a reckless indifference to the "very high" risk of death or serious injury. (A) is wrong because consent is not a defense to acts involving serious bodily injury. (B) is wrong because the misconduct of Adam is not a defense to homicide. (D) is wrong because the manslaughter statute requires that the killing be without malice. Here, malice is implied from Defendant's "abandoned and malignant heart."

Answer to Question 11

(D) Since the felony murder rule is not involved here, the only theory of first degree murder available would be that killing was "willful, deliberate, or premeditated." First degree murder requires an actual intent to kill, which Defendant lacked. (A) is wrong under common law. At common law, it was possible to convict a seven-year-old of a crime. Also, there is nothing under this statute to indicate that a 17-year-old could not be convicted of a crime. Nor is youthfulness (of a defendant over the age of 14) a legally recognized source of "mitigating" a criminal homicide to manslaughter. Hence, (C) is wrong. (B) is wrong because a revolver is a deadly weapon and intentional use of it would support an inference that Defendant intended to kill.

Answer to Question 12

(B) This is the best alternative. The choice as to whether this behavior is wanton or reckless (murder) or criminal or gross negligence (involuntary manslaughter) is best left to the jury. Hence, it would be wrong to instruct the jury "only" on involuntary manslaughter, and thus (A) is incorrect. (D) is wrong because the question relates to a Type A jurisdiction where murder is not divided into degrees. (C) is wrong as there is no way that Defendant would be guilty of voluntary manslaughter, which would involve an unjustified, unexcused but mitigated, intentional homicide. Defendant did not intend to kill or seriously injure.

Answer to Question 13

(A) This question tests your understanding of the "abandoned and malignant heart" terminology still found in many murder statutes. (B) is wrong because "assault with a deadly weapon" is not the "independent" or "collateral felony" required for the felony murder rule. (C) and (D) are wrong because they do not concern issues that would be the most relevant to the murder charges. Both of these cover responses to defenses raised by the defendant rather than a necessary element to be proved by the prosecutor.

Answer to Question 14

(D) This answer covers all the possible ways to commit a first degree murder under a Type B statute (felony murder **and** premeditative or deliberate). Hence, both (A) and (B) are incomplete and wrong. (C) is wrong because consent of the victim will not excuse, mitigate, or reduce the level of a criminal homicide.

Answer to Question 15

(B) This is the only possible charge. Although the 17-year-old son is old enough to be "legally" responsible for a crime, he is still a minor, and the father's bragging about a loaded revolver in his room could be deemed contributory to his delinquency. At best, the father's act was "criminally" negligent, and therefore any liability on the father's part would not rise above the level of involuntary manslaughter. Therefore, (C) is wrong; merely leaving a loaded gun about is not an "abandoned and malignant heart" situation. (D) is also wrong; the father did not kill Victor as a result of a sudden quarrel or in the heat of passion. (A) is wrong because the father did not assault anyone and also because the assault charge would merge into the murder charge.

Answer to Question 16

(A) The best defense is challenging the statute, because all of the other choices do not offer defenses. Linda's consent is irrelevant under the statute, as is her appearance of being older. Duke's intent is likewise irrelevant under this type of statute, which is a strict liability statute. Therefore, his only possible challenge is that the statute is void for vagueness because it does not apprise a defendant of which acts are proscribed.

Answer to Question 17

(D) This is a strict liability crime. Voluntary intoxication is no defense to crimes of strict liability because a defense that negates intent is not a defense to a strict liability crime. Thus, (D) is the correct answer and (A) is incorrect. (B) is misleading because voluntary intoxication is an insufficient defense to general intent offenses. (C) is irrelevant.

Answer to Question 18

(D) Adams is not guilty if he did not intend to achieve the objective of the conspiracy—*i.e.,* to permanently deprive the owner of his property, since Adams thought that Curtis was the owner and that Nelson was improperly keeping the certificates from Curtis. (A) is incorrect because an agreement and overt act are insufficient for conspiracy if Adams did not have the intent to commit larceny. (B), while a correct statement of law, is irrelevant to the required specific intent element. The corrupt motive doctrine is a minority view requiring conspirators to know that their objective is illegal. However, (C) is inapplicable to these facts since Adams had no intent to commit larceny.

Answer to Question 19

(C) The crime of conspiracy requires that each conspirator intend to achieve an unlawful goal. If the jury believes Bennett, he must be found not guilty because he did not intend to achieve an unlawful goal. (A) is therefore incorrect. (D) is incorrect because Bennett's act of prevention would not have excused the conspiracy if he had the proper mental state. (*Note:* The Model Penal Code recognizes such a defense.) (B) is incorrect because the privilege to apprehend criminals is not in issue here.

Answer to Question 20

(D) If the jury believes both Adams and Bennett, neither could be guilty of conspiracy because of absence of intent. Therefore, Curtis could not be guilty of conspiracy at common law because there was never an agreement to achieve an unlawful purpose. (A) is wrong because there was never an agreement between two or more persons. (B) is incorrect because intent is but one element of conspiracy—there must also be an agreement. (C) is a nonsensical statement.

Answer to Question 21

(A) Case squib (A) is the most applicable. Case squib (A) illustrates that the state of mind required for larceny is satisfied when the defendant intends to deal with the property in a manner that involves a substantial risk of loss to the owner, such as intending to sell the property back to the owner or hold it until a reward is offered. In this question, Davis used the tools to break open a safe. While he probably never intended to keep the tools, he also never intended to return them either—he did not care whether the hardware store ever got the tools back. Thus, the charge of larceny here is based on an intent to deal with the property in a manner that involves a high risk of loss to the owner, just as in squib (A). Squib (B) is not as applicable because the decisive element there was the defendants' intent only to borrow the car and to return it within a reasonable time. Squibs (C) and (D) are inapplicable because they involved a taking by means of false representations, which is not the case here.

Answer to Question 22

(D) Squib (D) is the most applicable precedent. That squib establishes that the "trespassory" aspect of the taking is satisfied when the victim consents to defendant's taking possession of the property only as a result of defendant's misrepresentations. In this question, Vincent transferred possession of the $500 as a result of the false representations of Smith. Squib (C) is not applicable because it establishes that one obtaining *title* to property as a result of false representations is not guilty of larceny. Here, Vincent only transferred *possession* of the $500—he was expecting to receive a certificate of deposit for it.

Answer to Question 23

(B) Squib (B) is most applicable because it establishes that an intent to borrow another's property without permission for a short period of time is not sufficient for common law larceny. Here, Jones took the statuary with the intent to return it within a day or two. Despite his vindictive motive, Jones would not be liable for larceny if the jury decides that he did not intend to keep it for an unreasonable length of time. Regardless of the verdict, squib (B) is the most applicable precedent. Squib (A) is not applicable because the defendants in that case were not planning to return the dog until the owner offered a reward, which is not the case here.

Answer to Question 24

(A) Squib (A) is most applicable. That case squib establishes that an intent to deal with another's property in any manner that creates a substantial risk of loss of the property is a sufficient intent for larceny. Here, Harris's conduct in pawning the property after taking it from the owner created a substantial risk of loss to the owner—enough to make Harris liable for larceny. Squib (B) is inappropriate because pawning the property negates any intent to return it. Squibs (C) and (D) are inapplicable because there were no misrepresentations in this case.

Answer to Question 25

(C) Case squib (C) is most applicable because it establishes that common law larceny does not apply in the fact situation here. In squib (C), the decisive element is that the victim, Will, gave the cash to the defendant with the intent that he keep it (*i.e.,* with the intent to convey title to the cash to defendant in exchange for possession of the apartment). As a result, defendant was not guilty of common law larceny of the cash because more than possession was transferred. Similarly, here Mark passed *title* to the money to Allison based on Allison's false representations. Squib (C) is therefore more applicable than squib (D) because (C) establishes that common law larceny does not apply in this case.

Answer to Question 26

(B) It seems clear from the facts that Ted has killed in self-defense. Even if striking Howard with the lamp were seen as the use of deadly force, it was necessary in response to the latter's use of deadly force. (A) is simply irrelevant. (C) might have been relevant to a defense for Howard if he had killed Ted, but it is irrelevant to the facts of this case. (D) is a misstatement of law.

Answer to Question 27

(B) Battery is a general intent crime that may be satisfied by a showing of recklessness or criminal negligence. (B) involves facts that are most clearly inconsistent with the defendant having any mental state whatever. Alternatively, (B) is to be preferred because it most clearly indicates that there was not a willed act, since convulsive acts are not considered to be voluntary. Even while in a hypnotic state, Defendant's striking Victim was a voluntary physical movement. (A) is therefore incorrect. (C) is wrong because voluntary intoxication is not a defense to crimes requiring recklessness. (D) is inapplicable because, although he was mistaken as to Victim's actions, Defendant willed himself to hit Victim.

Answer to Question 28

(C) Answer (A) is to be rejected because the request for the attorney means interrogation must cease and not that the attorney be produced immediately. In this case, interrogation had not yet begun. (B) is inapplicable since there is no suggestion that the arrest was unlawful. (D) is accurate but nonsensical. It is the introduction of the statement, not the fingerprints, that is in issue. The best answer is (C), because truly volunteered statements are not the product of custodial interrogation.

Answer to Question 29

(C) It is clear that the taking was not achieved by the use of force, an element of robbery. (It would be different if Defendant had run down the victim with the intent to appropriate his property.) (A) and (B) are based on mistaken legal premises and are thus incorrect. The Defendant's motive is irrelevant, and larceny does not require a taking from a living person. (D) might be accurate at common law but modern statutes normally include documents as being property subject to larceny and thus, robbery.

Answer to Question 30

(A) Dan should be found guilty. The problem here is whether Dan caused Tom's death. Dan's act was not only the "but for" cause but also, since the death as it happened was the natural and foreseeable result, the "proximate" cause. The fact that other preexisting conditions contributed to the death does not absolve Dan. Therefore, (D) is incorrect. (B) is irrelevant to whether Dan committed murder. (C) is a misstatement of the facts relating to Tom's "serious" illness. Moreover, an act that hastens an inevitable result is still a legal cause of that result.

Answer to Question 31

(C) The statute defines assault as "an attempt to commit a battery." Attempts require the specific intent to commit the crime. We are told Edward had no such intent. Hence, (C) is the best answer. Thus, (A) and (B) are incorrect. (D) is incorrect because an assault is an attempt to cause an offensive touching, and thus it would not be necessary for him to actually hit Margaret.

Answer to Question 32

(D) There is no doubt that Margaret committed a battery. Hence, (C) is to be rejected. The question is whether it was justified. Since she is permitted to use nondeadly force when she reasonably believes such is necessary to avoid the danger of harm from an aggressor and the facts indicate this was her position, the best answer is (D). (A) is incorrect because, even though her conduct was intentional, she has a defense of self-defense. (B) is incorrect because of her justification for the pushing.

Answer to Question 33

(C) A court, in enforcing a criminal statute, will construe legislative intent in assessing criminal liability. If a statute defines a crime in a way that necessarily involves more than one participant and provides for the liability of only one participant, it is presumed that the legislative intent was to immunize the other participant from liability as an accomplice (*e.g.,* the buyer in an illegal sale of drugs is neither guilty of being an accessory to the sale nor in a conspiracy with the seller). Further, the rule of lenity requires that an ambiguous criminal statute must be strictly construed in favor of the defendant. (A) is wrong because those who provide inducement for a crime that requires two parties are not accessories. Further, Monroe was not an accessory at common law because accessories were not present when the crime was committed. (B) is wrong because Monroe is not the victim; the state is. (D) is wrong because Monroe did assist Professor Smith in violating the statute by offering him the $50.

Answer to Question 34

(C) Answer (A) is wrong because we are told Defendant did not have the requisite intent to steal. (B) is incorrect because Defendant's mistake may have gone to civil law—his right to use self-help in recovering a debt—rather than to the former type of mistake. (D) is to be rejected because of the facts; Defendant did not intend to steal the property of another. (C) is the best answer because Defendant's mistake is as to the coverage of the criminal law and that is not an excuse.

Answer to Question 35

(D) A strict liability offense does not require awareness of all of the factors constituting the crime. Strict liability offenses are generally part of a regulatory scheme. They generally involve a relatively low penalty. Here, (A) and (B) are incorrect because the offenses described do not appear to be part of a regulatory scheme. Also, they appear to require awareness of all of the factors constituting the crime; *i.e.,* a defendant probably could not be convicted under (A) without an awareness that he was shoplifting, and a defendant probably could not be convicted under (B) without an awareness that he possessed heroin. (C) presents a closer question. The offense described in (C) appears to be part of a scheme to regulate firearms. The offense described in (D) is part of a scheme to regulate the sale of milk for the purpose of protecting the public from the threat of consumption of tainted milk. Such statutes, in protecting the public health and safety, almost always provide for culpability, regardless of the seller's knowledge of the tainted nature of the product. Also, the statute in (D) describes a misdemeanor, meaning that a violation thereof carries a lesser penalty than does violation of the felony statute in (C). Consequently, because (D) fits more closely the classic concept of a strict liability offense, it is a better answer than (C).

Answer to Question 36

(B)   Manslaughter will not serve as the underlying felony in a felony murder prosecution. The felony murder rule can be applied only where the underlying felony is independent of the killing. With a felony such as manslaughter, there is ordinarily no intent to commit a felony independent of the killing itself; hence, felony murder does not apply. In contrast, the other crimes listed would satisfy the requirement that the defendant intend to commit an underlying felony. One who is guilty of arson (choice A) would have intended that a burning take place. Attempted rape (choice C) requires the intent to perform an act which, if achieved, would constitute rape. Burglary (choice D) requires intent to commit a felony at time of entry.

Answer to Question 37

(A)   Rimm can be convicted of murder because the way Rimm employed the firearm was sufficient to fulfill the "malice" requirement for murder. Murder is the unlawful killing of a human being with malice aforethought. Malice aforethought may be express or implied. In addition to obvious malice situations where there is intention to kill, malice is implied where there is: (i) intent to inflict great bodily injury; (ii) reckless indifference to an unjustifiably high risk to human life (also called acting with "an abandoned and malignant heart"); or (iii) felony murder situations. Here, Rimm's firing of the gun when aimed slightly to the side of Hill in an enclosed room (where ricochet was likely) constituted acting with reckless disregard of an unjustifiably high risk to human life. Rimm's malice is thus implied. (B) is incorrect because the provocation that would reduce murder to voluntary manslaughter is not present in the facts. (C) is incorrect because Rimm's activities could be found to be more dangerous than "criminal negligence." (D) is incorrect. Although Hill's conduct of aiming a pistol at Rimm and firing could constitute assault with a deadly weapon, the more serious crime of which Rimm can be convicted is murder, because Hill was killed by Rimm's reckless conduct.

Answer to Question 38

(D)   Defendant acted in self-defense and, therefore, should not be convicted of a homicide. A person may use deadly force in self-defense if: (i) he is without fault; (ii) he is confronted with unlawful force; and (iii) he is threatened with imminent death or great bodily harm. All three elements are present under these facts. Because Vincent initiated the attack, he will be considered the aggressor, and Defendant will be deemed "without fault." Mere teasing words should not be sufficient to deem Defendant the aggressor, but even if the words were such a provocation, Vincent's sudden escalation of the fight into one involving deadly force would allow Defendant to use force in his own defense. Unlawful force is defined as force that constitutes a crime or a tort. Vincent's attack with the metal bar so qualifies. The defendant must reasonably believe that he is threatened with imminent death or great bodily harm if he does not respond with deadly force. Defendant had such a reasonable belief. Furthermore, Defendant had no duty to retreat under the prevailing rule. It follows that (A), (B), and (C) are incorrect, because Defendant's use of deadly force was justified by self-defense.

Answer to Question 39

(C) *Miranda* warnings are required only where the accused has made a statement during custodial interrogation. Barber voluntarily complied with a request to come to police headquarters, where he was not arrested and was free to leave. During his discussion with the police officers, he voluntarily made a spontaneous inculpatory statement. Thus, he was not entitled to *Miranda* warnings, and (A) is incorrect. (B) is incorrect because, in circumstances such as these, the right to counsel would attach only if there was a custodial police interrogation. "Interrogation" refers not only to express questioning, but also to other words or actions reasonably likely to elicit an incriminating response from the suspect. However, routine questions that the police had no reason to believe would elicit an incriminating response do not constitute an interrogation. Also, there is no due process violation arising from the making of a free and voluntary statement. (D) is incorrect primarily because Barber was not entitled to *Miranda* warnings simply by visiting the police station. Thus, he had nothing to waive. However, even if Barber was entitled to the warnings, the facts do not indicate a waiver. A waiver must be knowing, voluntary and intelligent. Merely agreeing to visit police headquarters does not constitute a knowing, voluntary, and intelligent waiver of *Miranda* warnings.

EVIDENCE QUESTIONS

Questions 1-2 are based on the following fact situation:

Paula sued for injuries she sustained in a fall in a hotel hallway connecting the lobby of the hotel with a restaurant located in the hotel building. The hallway floor was covered with vinyl tile. The defendants were Horne, owner of the hotel building, and Lee, lessee of the restaurant. The evidence was that the hallway floor had been waxed approximately an hour before Paula slipped on it, and although the wax had dried, there appeared to be excessive dried wax caked on several of the tiles. Horne's defense was that the hallway was a part of the premises leased to Lee over which he retained no control, and Lee denied negligence and alleged contributory negligence.

1. Lee offered to prove by Marks, the restaurant manager, that in the week immediately preceding Paula's fall at least 1,000 people had used the hallway in going to and from the restaurant, and Marks had neither seen anyone fall nor received reports that anyone had fallen. The trial judge should rule this evidence:

    (A) Admissible, because it tends to prove that Paula did not use the care exercised by reasonably prudent people.

    (B) Admissible, because it tends to prove that Lee was generally careful in maintaining the floor.

    (C) Inadmissible, because Marks's testimony is self-serving.

    (D) Inadmissible, because it does not bear on the issue of Lee's exercise of due care on this specific occasion.

2. If Paula offered to prove that the day after she fell, Horne had the vinyl tile taken up and replaced with a new floor covering, the trial judge should rule the evidence:

    (A) Admissible, because it is relevant to the issue of whether Horne retained control of the hallway.

    (B) Admissible, because it is relevant as to the issue of awareness of the unsafe condition of the hallway at the time of Paula's fall.

    (C) Inadmissible, because there was no showing that the new floor covering would be any safer than the old.

    (D) Inadmissible, because to admit such would discourage a policy of making repairs to prevent further injury, regardless of fault.

Question 3

Powers sued Debbs for battery. At trial, Powers's witness, Wilson, testified that Debbs had made an unprovoked attack on Powers.

On cross-examination, Debbs asks Wilson about a false claim that Wilson had once filed on an insurance policy. The question is:

(A) Proper, because the conduct involved untruthfulness.

(B) Proper, provided that the conduct resulted in conviction of Wilson.

(C) Improper, because the impeachment involved a specific instance of misconduct.

(D) Improper, because the claim form would be the best evidence.

Question 4

In a tort action, Fisher testified against Dawes. Dawes then called Jones, who testified that Fisher had a bad reputation for veracity. Dawes then also called Weld to testify that Fisher once perpetrated a hoax on the police.

Weld's testimony is:

(A) Admissible, because a hoax involves untruthfulness.

(B) Admissible, provided that the hoax resulted in conviction of Fisher.

(C) Inadmissible, because it is merely cumulative impeachment.

(D) Inadmissible, because it is extrinsic evidence of a specific instance of misconduct.

Questions 5-6 are based on the following fact situation:

Peters sued Davis for $100,000 for injuries received in a traffic accident. Davis charges Peters with contributory negligence and alleges that Peters failed to have his lights on at a time when it was dark enough to require them.

5. Davis calls Bystander to testify that Passenger, who was riding in Peters's automobile and who was injured, confided to him at the scene of the accident that "we should have had our lights on." Bystander's testimony is:

(A) Admissible as an admission of a party-opponent.

(B) Admissible as a statement against interest.

(C) Inadmissible, because it is hearsay not within any exception.

(D) Inadmissible, because it is opinion.

6. Davis offers to have Bystander testify that he was talking to Witness when he heard the crash and heard Witness, now deceased, exclaim, "That car doesn't have any lights on." Bystander's testimony is:

(A) Admissible as a statement of present sense impression.

(B) Admissible, because Witness is not available to testify.

(C) Inadmissible as hearsay not within any exception.

(D) Inadmissible, because of the Dead Man's Statute.

Questions 7-8 are based on the following fact situation:

Owner and his employee, Driver, consult Attorney about a motor vehicle collision resulting in a suit by Litigant against Owner and Driver as joint defendants. Attorney calls Irving, his investigator, into the conference to make notes of what is said, and those present discuss the facts of the collision and Owner's insurance. Owner thereafter files a cross-claim against Driver for indemnity for any damages obtained by Litigant.

7. Litigant calls Driver to testify in Litigant's case-in-chief to admissions made by Owner in the conference. On objection by Owner, the court should rule that Driver's testimony is:

(A) Admissible, because of the presence of persons in the conference other than Attorney and Owner.

(B) Admissible, because Driver is an adverse party in the lawsuit.

(C) Inadmissible, because of the attorney-client privilege.

(D) Inadmissible, because the best evidence is Irving's notes of the conference.

8. Driver calls Irving in his defense against the cross-claim. He seeks to have Irving testify to admissions made by Owner in the conference. On objection by Owner, the court should rule Irving's testimony:

(A) Admissible, because the attorney-client privilege does not apply, in suits between those conferring with him, to joint consultations with an attorney.

(B) Admissible, because the attorney-client privilege does not apply to testimony by one who does not stand in a confidential relationship with the person against whom the evidence is offered.

(C) Admissible, because the conference was not intended to be confidential, since it concerned anticipated testimony in open court.

(D) Inadmissible, because Owner has not waived the attorney-client privilege.

Questions 9-11 are based on the following fact situation:

Pemberton and three passengers, Able, Baker, and Charley, were injured when their car was struck by a truck owned by Mammoth Corporation and driven by Edwards. Helper, also a Mammoth employee, was riding in the truck. The issues in *Pemberton v. Mammoth* include the negligence of Edwards in driving too fast and in failing to wear glasses, and of Pemberton in failing to yield the right of way.

9. Pemberton's counsel proffers evidence showing that shortly after the accident, Mammoth put a speed governor on the truck involved in the accident. The judge should rule the proffered evidence:

(A) Admissible as an admission of a party.

(B) Admissible as res gestae.

(C) Inadmissible for public policy reasons.

(D) Inadmissible, because it would lead to the drawing of an inference on an inference.

10. Pemberton's counsel seeks to introduce Helper's written statement that Edwards, Mammoth's driver, had left his glasses (required by his operator's license) at the truck stop which they had left five minutes before the accident. The judge should rule the statement admissible only if:

(A) Pemberton first proves that Helper is an agent of Mammoth and that the statement concerned a matter within the scope of his agency.

(B) Pemberton produces independent evidence that Edwards was not wearing corrective lenses at the time of the accident.

(C) Helper is shown to be beyond the process of the court and unavailable to testify.

(D) The statement was under oath in affidavit form.

11. Mammoth's counsel seeks to have Sheriff testify that while he was investigating the accident he was told by Pemberton, "This was probably our fault." The judge should rule the proffered evidence:

(A) Admissible as an admission of a party.

(B) Admissible, because it is a statement made to a police officer in the course of an official investigation.

(C) Inadmissible, because it is a mixed conclusion of law and fact.

(D) Inadmissible, because it is hearsay not within any exception.

Question 12

In a contract suit between Terrell and Ward, Ward testified that he recalls having his first conversation with Terrell on January 3. When asked how he remembers the date, he answers, "In the conversation, Terrell referred to a story in that day's newspaper announcing my daughter's engagement." Terrell's counsel moves to strike the reference to the newspaper story.

The judge should:

(A) Grant the motion on the ground that the best evidence rule requires production of the newspaper itself.

(B) Grant the motion, because the reference to the newspaper story does not fit within any established exception to the hearsay rule.

(C) Deny the motion on the ground that the court may take judicial notice of local newspapers and their contents.

(D) Deny the motion on the ground that a witness may refer to collateral documents without providing the documents themselves.

Question 13

In Peel's personal injury action, Wilson, a physician who had no previous knowledge of the matter, sat in court and heard all of the evidence about Peel's symptoms and conditions.

Wilson is called to give her opinion whether Peel's injuries are permanent. May Wilson so testify?

(A) Yes, provided she first identifies the data on which her opinion is based.

(B) Yes, because an expert may base her opinion on facts made known to her at the trial.

(C) No, because she has no personal knowledge of Peel's condition.

(D) No, because permanence of injury is an issue to be decided by the jury.

Questions 14-15 are based on the following fact situation:

Rider, a bus passenger, sued Transit Company for injuries to his back from an accident caused by Transit's negligence. Transit denies that Rider received any injury in the accident.

14. Rider's counsel seeks to introduce an affidavit he obtained in preparation for trial from Dr. Bond, who has since died. The affidavit avers that Dr. Bond examined Rider two days after the Transit Company accident and found him suffering from a recently incurred back injury. The judge should rule the affidavit:

(A) Admissible as a statement of present bodily condition made to a physician.

(B) Admissible as prior recorded testimony.

(C) Inadmissible, because it is irrelevant.

(D) Inadmissible, because it is hearsay not within any exception.

15. Transit Company calls Observer to testify that right after the accident, Rider told him that he had recently suffered a recurrence of an old back injury. The judge should rule Observer's testimony:

(A) Admissible as an admission of a party-opponent.

(B) Admissible as a spontaneous declaration.

(C) Inadmissible, because it is irrelevant.

(D) Inadmissible, because it is hearsay not within any exception.

Question 16

Patty sues Mart Department Store for personal injuries, alleging that while shopping she was knocked to the floor by a merchandise cart being pushed by Handy, a stock clerk, and that as a consequence her back was injured.

Handy testified that Patty fell near the cart but was not struck by it. Thirty minutes after Patty's fall, Handy, in accordance with regular practice at Mart, had filled out a printed form, "Employee's Report of Accident—Mart Department Store," in which he stated that Patty had been leaning over to spank her young child and in so doing had fallen near his cart. Counsel for Mart offers in evidence the report, which had been given him by Handy's supervisor.

The judge should rule the report offered by Mart:

(A) Admissible as res gestae.

(B) Admissible as a business record.

(C) Inadmissible, because it is hearsay not within any exception.

(D) Inadmissible, because Handy is available as a witness.

Question 17

Pace sues Def Company for injuries suffered when Pace's car collided with Def Company's truck. Def's general manager prepared a report of the accident at the request of the company's attorney, in preparation for the trial, and delivered the report to the attorney. Pace demands that the report be produced.

Will production of the report be required?

(A) Yes, because business reports are not generally privileged.

(B) No, because it is a privileged communication from client to the attorney.

(C) No, because such reports contain hearsay.

(D) No, because such reports are self-serving.

Question 18

At the trial of Davis for a murder that occurred in Newtown, the prosecution called Waite, who testified that she saw Davis kill the victim. Davis believed that Waite was 600 miles away in Old Town, engaged in the illegal sale of narcotics, on the day in question. On cross-examination by Davis, Waite was asked whether she had in fact sold narcotics in Old Town on that date. Waite refused to answer on the ground of self-incrimination.

The judge, over the prosecutor's objection, ordered that if Waite did not testify, her direct testimony should be stricken.

The order to testify or have the testimony stricken can best be supported on the basis that:

(A) Waite had not been charged with any crime and, thus, could claim no privilege against self-incrimination.

(B) Waite's proper invocation of the privilege prevented adequate cross-examination.

(C) The public interest in allowing an accused to defend himself or herself outweighs the interest of a nonparty witness in the privilege.

(D) The trial record, independent of testimony, does not establish that Waite's answer could incriminate her.

Question 19

Alex and Sam were arrested for holding up a gas station. They were taken to police headquarters and placed in a room for interrogation. As a police officer addressing both started to give them *Miranda* warnings prior to the questioning, Alex said, "Look, Sam planned the damned thing and I was dumb enough to go along with it. We robbed the place—what else is there to say?" Sam said nothing. Sam was escorted into another room and a full written confession was then obtained from Alex.

If Sam is brought to trial on an indictment charging him with robbery, the fact that Sam failed to object to Alex's statement and remained silent after Alex had implicated him in the crime should be ruled:

(A) Admissible, because his silence was an implied admission by Sam that he had participated in the crime.

(B) Admissible, because a statement of a participant in a crime is admissible against another participant.

(C) Inadmissible, because under the circumstances there was no duty or responsibility on Sam's part to respond.

(D) Inadmissible, because whatever Alex may have said has no probative value in a trial against Sam.

Question 20

Pack sued Donlon for slander, alleging that Donlon had publicly accused Pack of being a thief. In his answer, Donlon admitted making the accusation, but alleged that it was a true statement.

At trial, Donlon offers evidence that Pack stole a ring worth $10,000 from a jewelry store.

Evidence concerning this theft should be:

(A) Admitted, because specific instances of conduct may be proved when character is directly in issue.

(B) Admitted, because Pack's actions constituted a felony.

(C) Excluded, because character must be shown by reputation or opinion.

(D) Excluded, because its relevance is substantially outweighed by the danger of unfair prejudice.

Question 21

In a suit attacking the validity of a deed executed 15 years ago, Plaintiff alleges mental incompetency of Joe, the grantor, and offers in evidence a properly authenticated affidavit of Harry, Joe's brother. The affidavit, which was executed shortly after the deed, stated that Harry had observed Joe closely over a period of weeks, that Joe had engaged in instances of unusual behavior (which were described), and that Joe's appearance had changed from one of neatness and alertness to one of disorder and absentmindedness.

The judge should rule Harry's affidavit:

(A) Inadmissible as opinion.

(B) Inadmissible as hearsay not within any exception.

(C) Admissible as an official document.

(D) Admissible as an ancient document.

Question 22

Park brought an action against Dan for injuries received in an automobile accident, alleging negligence in that Dan was speeding and inattentive. Park calls White to testify that Dan had a reputation in the community for being a reckless driver and was known as "Daredevil Dan."

White's testimony is:

(A) Admissible as habit evidence.

(B) Admissible, because it tends to prove that Dan was negligent at the time of this collision.

(C) Inadmissible, because Dan has not offered testimony of his own good character.

(D) Inadmissible to show negligence.

Question 23

In Polk's negligence action against Dell arising out of a multiple-car collision, Witt testified for Polk that Dell went through a red light. On cross-examination, Dell seeks to question Witt about her statement that the light was yellow, made in a deposition that Witt gave in a separate action between Adams and Baker. The transcript of the deposition is self-authenticating.

On proper objection, the court should rule the inquiry:

(A) Admissible for impeachment only.

(B) Admissible as substantive evidence only.

(C) Admissible for impeachment and as substantive evidence.

(D) Inadmissible, because it is hearsay not within any exception.

Questions 24-25 are based on the following fact situation:

Price sued Derrick for injuries Price received in an automobile accident. Price claimed Derrick was negligent in (a) exceeding the posted speed limit of 35 m.p.h., (b) failing to keep a lookout, and (c) crossing the center line.

24. Bystander, Price's eyewitness, testified on cross-examination that Derrick was wearing a green sweater at the time of the accident. Derrick's counsel calls Wilson to testify that Derrick's sweater was blue. Wilson's testimony is:

    (A) Admissible as substantive evidence of a material fact.

    (B) Admissible as bearing on Bystander's truthfulness and veracity.

    (C) Inadmissible, because it has no bearing on the capacity of Bystander to observe.

    (D) Inadmissible, because it is extrinsic evidence of a collateral matter.

25. Derrick testified in his own behalf that he was going 30 m.p.h. On cross-examination, Price's counsel did not question Derrick with regard to his speed. Subsequently, Price's counsel calls Officer to testify that, in his investigation following the accident, Derrick told him he was driving 40 m.p.h. Officer's testimony is:

    (A) Admissible as a prior inconsistent statement.

    (B) Admissible as an admission.

    (C) Inadmissible, because it lacks a foundation.

    (D) Inadmissible, because it is hearsay not within any exception.

Question 26

Drew is charged with the murder of Pitt. The prosecutor introduced testimony of a police officer that Pitt told a priest administering the last rites, "I was stabbed by Drew. Since I am dying, tell him I forgive him." Thereafter, Drew's attorney offers the testimony of Wall that the day before, when Pitt believed he would live, he stated that he had been stabbed by Jack, an old enemy.

The testimony of Wall is:

(A) Admissible under an exception to the hearsay rule.

(B) Admissible to impeach the dead declarant.

(C) Inadmissible, because it goes to the ultimate issue in the case.

(D) Inadmissible, because irrelevant to any substantive issue in the case.

Question 27

Post sued Dean for personal injury alleged to have been caused by Dean's negligence. A major issue at trial was whether Post's disability was caused solely by trauma or by a preexisting condition of osteoarthritis.

Post called Dr. Cox, who testified that the disability was caused by trauma. On cross-examination, Dr. Cox testified that a medical textbook entitled *Diseases of the Joints* was authoritative and that she agreed with the substance of passages from the textbook that she was directed to look at, but that the passages were inapplicable to Post's condition because they dealt with rheumatoid arthritis rather than with the osteoarthritis that Post was alleged to have.

Dean then called his expert, Dr. Freed, who testified that, with reference to the issue being litigated, there is no difference between the two kinds of arthritis. Dean's counsel then asks permission to read to the jury the textbook passages earlier shown to Dr. Cox.

The judge should rule the textbook passages:

(A) Admissible only for the purpose of impeaching Cox.

(B) Admissible as substantive evidence if the judge determines that the passages are relevant.

(C) Inadmissible, because they are hearsay not within any exception.

(D) Inadmissible, because Cox contended that they are not relevant to Post's condition.

Question 28

Pratt sued Danvers for injuries suffered by Pratt when their automobiles collided. At trial, Pratt offers into evidence a properly authenticated letter from Danvers that says, "Your claim seems too high, but, because I might have been a little negligent, I'm prepared to offer you half of what you ask."

The letter is:

(A) Admissible as an admission by a party-opponent.

(B) Admissible as a statement against pecuniary interest.

(C) Inadmissible, because Danvers's statement is lay opinion on a legal issue.

(D) Inadmissible, because Danvers's statement was made in an effort to settle the claim.

Question 29

Parker sued Dodd over title to an island in a river. Daily variations in the water level were important.

For many years Wells, a commercial fisherman, kept a daily log of the water level at his dock opposite the island in order to forecast fishing conditions. Parker employed Zee, an engineer, to prepare graphs from Wells's log.

Wells was called to testify to the manner in which he kept the log, which had been available for inspection. His testimony should be:

(A) Excluded on a general objection because not admissible for any purpose.

(B) Excluded on a specific objection that it calls for hearsay.

(C) Admitted to support the credibility of Wells and Zee as witnesses.

(D) Admitted as part of the foundation for admission of Zee's graphs.

Question 30

Polk sued DeVore on a written contract. In her case-in-chief, DeVore testified that she withdrew from the contractual arrangement, as the contract permitted, by notifying Polk by means of a letter. She testified that she put the letter in an envelope, with proper postage, addressed to Polk at his place of business, and that she placed it in a United States Post Office mailbox.

In rebuttal, Polk testified that he got his mail each day from a locked post office box and that he had never received any such letter. There was no other evidence relating to receipt of the notice letter.

When the case is ready to go to the jury, the trial judge should:

(A) Withdraw from the jury's consideration the issue of whether Polk received the notice.

(B) Instruct the jury that it may presume that Polk received the notice.

(C) Instruct the jury that it should find that Polk received the notice.

(D) Submit the case to the jury without instruction concerning a presumption of receipt.

Question 31

Park sued Dent for breach of an oral contract which Dent denied making. Weston testified that he heard Dent make the contract on July 7. Dent discredited Weston, and Park offers evidence of Weston's good reputation for truthfulness.

The rehabilitation is most likely to be permitted if the discrediting evidence by Dent was testimony that:

(A) Weston had been promoting highly speculative stocks.

(B) Weston had been Park's college roommate.

(C) Weston had attended a school for mentally retarded children.

(D) Weston had been out of town the whole week of July 4-10.

Question 32

In a will case, Paula seeks to prove her relationship to the testator Terrence by a statement in a deed of a gift from Terrence, "I transfer to my niece Paula . . ." The deed was recorded pursuant to statute in the office of the county recorder and is kept there. Paula calls Recorder, who authenticates an enlarged print photocopy of the deed. The photocopy was made from the microfilm records kept in Recorder's office pursuant to statute.

The photocopy is:

(A) Admissible as a record of a document affecting an interest in property.

(B) Admissible as recorded recollection.

(C) Inadmissible as hearsay not within any recognized exception.

(D) Inadmissible as not the best evidence.

Question 33

Alice was held up at the point of a gun, an unusual revolver with a red-painted barrel, while she was clerking in a neighborhood grocery store. Dennis is charged with armed robbery of Alice.

The prosecutor calls Winthrop to testify that, a week after the robbery of Alice, he was robbed by Dennis with a pistol that had red paint on the barrel. Winthrop's testimony is:

(A) Admissible as establishing an identifying circumstance.

(B) Admissible as showing that Dennis was willing to commit robbery.

(C) Inadmissible, because it is improper character evidence.

(D) Inadmissible, because its probative value is substantially outweighed by the danger of unfair prejudice.

Question 34

Darden was prosecuted for armed robbery. At trial, Darden testified in his own behalf, denying that he had committed the robbery. On cross-examination, the prosecutor intends to ask Darden whether he had been convicted of burglary six years earlier.

The question concerning the burglary conviction is:

(A) Proper if the court finds that the probative value for impeachment outweighs the prejudice to Darden.

(B) Proper, because the prosecutor is entitled to make this inquiry as a matter of right.

(C) Improper, because burglary does not involve dishonesty or false statement.

(D) Improper, because the conviction must be proved by court record, not by question on cross-examination.

Question 35

Pitt sued Dow for damages for injuries that Pitt incurred when a badly rotted limb fell from a curbside tree in front of Dow's home and hit Pitt. Dow claimed that the tree was on city property and thus was the responsibility of the city. At trial, Pitt offered testimony that, a week after the accident, Dow had cut the tree down with a chainsaw.

The offered evidence is:

(A) Inadmissible, because there is a policy to encourage safety precautions.

(B) Inadmissible, because it is irrelevant to the condition of the tree at the time of the accident.

(C) Admissible to show the tree was on Dow's property.

(D) Admissible to show the tree was in a rotted condition.

Question 36

In litigation over the estate of Baggs, who died intestate, Payton, who is 18 years old, claimed to be Baggs's niece and entitled, therefore, to a share of his large estate. In support of her claim, Payton offered in evidence a Bible, properly identified as having belonged to Baggs's family, in the front of which was a list of family births, marriages, and deaths. The list recorded Payton's birth to Baggs's oldest sister.

To prove that Payton is Baggs's niece, the Bible listing is:

(A) Admissible as an ancient document.

(B) Admissible as a family record.

(C) Inadmissible, because it is hearsay not within any exception.

(D) Inadmissible, because there was no showing of firsthand knowledge by the one who wrote it.

Question 37

Paulsen sued Daly for nonpayment of a personal loan to Daly, as evidenced by Daly's promissory note to Paulsen. Paulsen called Walters to testify that he knows Daly's handwriting and that the signature on the note is Daly's. On direct examination, to identify himself, Walters gave his name and address and testified that he had been employed by a roofing company for seven years.

During presentation of Daly's case, Daly called Wilson to testify that she is the roofing company's personnel manager and that she had determined, by examining the company's employment records, that Walters had worked there only three years.

The trial judge should rule that Wilson's testimony is:

(A) Inadmissible, because it is not the best evidence.

(B) Inadmissible, because it is impeachment on a collateral question.

(C) Admissible as evidence of a regularly conducted activity.

(D) Admissible as tending to impeach Walters's credibility.

Question 38

In a civil suit by Pine against Decker, Decker called Wall, a chemist, as an expert witness and asked him a number of questions about his education and experience in chemistry. Over Pine's objection that Wall was not shown to be qualified in chemistry, the trial court permitted Wall to testify as to his opinion in response to a hypothetical question.

On cross-examination, Pine asked Wall if he had failed two chemistry courses while doing his graduate work. The answer should be:

(A) Admitted, because it is relevant to the weight to be given Wall's testimony.

(B) Admitted, because specific acts bearing on truthfulness may be inquired about on cross-examination.

(C) Excluded, because the court has determined that Wall is qualified to testify as an expert.

(D) Excluded, because Wall's character has not been put in issue.

EVIDENCE ANSWERS

Answer to Question 1

(D) The testimony of Marks presents a problem of relevance. When evidence that relates to a time, event, or person other than the time, event, or persons directly involved in the controversy being litigated is offered, the relevance of that evidence is suspect. However, such evidence may be relevant if it is probative of the material issue involved, and if such probative value outweighs the risk of confusion or unfair prejudice. Specifically, the evidence being offered here is evidence of the absence of similar accidents. Many courts are reluctant to admit evidence of the absence of similar accidents or complaints to show absence of negligence, or lack of a defect. Thus, (D) correctly concludes that the testimony cannot be admitted to show that, at the time of Paula's injury, Lee was exercising due care. For the same reason, (B) is incorrect in stating that the evidence may be used to show that Lee was generally careful in maintaining the floor. (A) is incorrect because, if this type of evidence cannot be used to show that the defendant was not negligent, then it certainly cannot be used to show that the plaintiff was negligent. (C) is incorrect because the fact that evidence may be self-serving does not render it inadmissible; virtually all evidence is self-serving to its proponent, or else it would not be offered by that party.

Answer to Question 2

(A) The law encourages the repair of defective conditions that cause injury. Thus, evidence of repairs or other precautionary measures made following an injury is inadmissible to prove negligence or culpable conduct. However, such evidence may be admissible for other purposes. One such purpose is to show ownership or control, since it is unlikely that a stranger would make repairs. Here, Horne has denied that he had control of the hallway in which the injury occurred. Thus, evidence that he had a new floor covering placed in the hallway is relevant to show that he did in fact have control of the subject premises. This conclusion is accurately reflected in (A). (B) is incorrect because it points precisely to a reason why the evidence might *not* be admissible (*i.e.,* it tries to use the evidence to show that Horne was negligent). (D) is incorrect because proof of ownership or control is, as detailed above, an exception to the general rule that evidence of subsequent repairs is inadmissible. Regarding (C), we have already established that the evidence is admissible to show control. Whether the new floor covering is actually safer than the old will not change this result.

Answer to Question 3

(A) A witness may be interrogated upon cross-examination, in the discretion of the court, with respect to any act of misconduct that is probative of truthfulness, regardless of whether the witness was convicted as a result of the "bad act." Thus, (A) is correct. (B) is incorrect because, although it arrives at the correct conclusion that the question is proper, it incorrectly requires that the misconduct have resulted in a conviction. (C) is incorrect because impeachment may be based on specific acts of misconduct. (D) is incorrect because such specific acts of misconduct can only be elicited on cross-examination of the witness; extrinsic evidence is not permitted.

Answer to Question 4

(D) A witness may be interrogated upon cross-examination, in the discretion of the court, with respect to any act of misconduct that is probative of truthfulness, regardless of whether the witness was convicted as a result of the "bad act." Such specific act of misconduct *can only be elicited on cross-examination* of the witness. Extrinsic evidence is not permitted. Weld's testimony would constitute extrinsic evidence of a specific instance of misconduct. Thus, (D) is correct. It follows that (A) and (B) are incorrect. (C) is incorrect because there is no rule limiting cumulative impeachment.

Answer to Question 5

(C) Hearsay is a statement, other than one made by the declarant while testifying at the trial or hearing, offered in evidence to prove the truth of the matter asserted. Bystander's testimony as to Passenger's statement is offered to prove the truth of the matter asserted therein; *i.e.*, that Peters did not have his lights on and was thus contributorily negligent. Therefore, the statement is not admissible unless it comes within one of the hearsay exceptions. (A) is incorrect because Passenger is not a party, and there is no indication either that Peters adopted Passenger's statement or that Peters and Passenger had such a relationship that would render the statement a vicarious admission by Peters. (B) is incorrect because the statement against interest exception requires that the declarant be unavailable as a witness. Passenger does not appear to be unavailable. Also, the statement does not seem to be against the interest of Passenger (although it certainly is against the interest of Peters). (D) is incorrect because the matter is one about which laypersons regularly form opinions.

Answer to Question 6

(A) Witness's statement is hearsay but within the present sense impression exception to the hearsay rule. This exception comes into play when a person perceives some event that is not particularly shocking, yet that person nevertheless is moved to comment on what he perceived at the time of receipt of the sense impression or immediately thereafter. Here, the statement conveys what Witness perceived at the time of the accident; thus, it is allowed into evidence as a present sense impression. Because the statement falls within one of the hearsay exceptions, (C) is incorrect. (B) is incorrect because, for the present sense impression exception, the declarant's availability is immaterial. (D) is incorrect because a Dead Man's Statute prohibits testimony as to a personal transaction or communication with a decedent when such testimony is offered against the representative or successors in interest of the deceased. This question does not involve a suit against a decedent's estate.

Answer to Question 7

(C) A communication is confidential, for purposes of the attorney-client privilege, if it was not intended to be disclosed to third persons, other than those to whom disclosure would be in furtherance of the rendition of legal services to the client. Also, where a lawyer acts for two parties, the privilege can be claimed in a suit between either or both of the parties and third persons. Here, Attorney's investigator is someone to whom disclosure was in furtherance of the rendition of legal services. Thus, any statements made in Irving's presence will still be confidential. In addition, the fact that Owner made statements in the presence of a joint client does not deprive those statements of the protection of the attorney-client privilege. For these reasons, (A) is incorrect in holding the privilege inapplicable because of the presence of third persons in the conference. (B) is incorrect because Driver and Owner are both defendants in Litigant's suit, and communications made by joint clients are privileged as against third parties. (D) is incorrect because the best evidence rule does not apply to these facts. According to the rule, in proving the terms of a writing, where the terms are material, the original writing must be produced. Testimony is not offered here to prove the contents of Irving's notes.

Answer to Question 8

(A) Where a lawyer acts for joint clients, no privilege can be invoked in a suit between the two parties, as they could not have desired nor could they have expected confidentiality as between themselves in a joint consultation. There is a suit (a cross-claim) between Owner and Driver.

Thus, in this suit, Owner cannot claim the privilege as to statements made during the joint conference. Therefore, (A) is correct. (B) is wrong because where a privilege attaches, the holder can prevent disclosure by anyone. (C) is incorrect because the lack of confidentiality arises from the fact that the two litigants participated in a joint conference, rather than from the fact that the conference related to testimony to be given in open court. (D) reaches the incorrect conclusion that the testimony is inadmissible, because the privilege has not been waived. As explained above, the requisite confidentiality is missing.

Answer to Question 9

(C) Evidence of repairs or other precautionary measures made following an injury is inadmissible to prove negligence or culpable conduct. This is because public policy encourages people to make such repairs. Such evidence *is* admissible for other purposes, *e.g.*, to prove ownership or control. Here, we are told that the issues involve negligence. Thus, the evidence as to the speed governor is being offered to prove culpable conduct or negligence, and therefore is inadmissible. (A) and (B) each incorrectly conclude that the evidence is admissible. (D) makes absolutely no sense.

Answer to Question 10

(A) The statement by Helper is one made by the declarant (Helper) other than while testifying at the trial, offered to prove the truth of the matter asserted (*i.e.*, that Edwards was not wearing his glasses at the time of the accident). This presents a hearsay issue. However, an admission by a party-opponent is not considered hearsay under the Federal Rules. Here, the party-opponent is Mammoth Corporation, while the statement is by an employee of Mammoth. Statements by an agent concerning any matter within the scope of his agency, made during the course of the employment relationship, are not hearsay and are admissible against the principal. Thus, (A) correctly states that the statement is admissible only if Helper is an agent of Mammoth and the statement concerned a matter within the scope of the agency. (B) is incorrect because admissibility of the statement is not dependent on independent corroboration of the truth thereof. (C) is incorrect because unavailability of the declarant is not a prerequisite for an admission of a party-opponent. (D) is incorrect because an admission need not be under oath in order to be admissible.

Answer to Question 11

(A) As detailed in the answer to the preceding question, an admission by a party-opponent is non-hearsay under the Federal Rules. An admission is a statement made or act done that amounts to a prior acknowledgment by one of the parties of a relevant fact. Here, a fact in issue is whether Pemberton failed to yield the right of way. Pemberton's statement to Sheriff acknowledges fault. Thus, the testimony as to the statement is admissible as an admission by a party-opponent of Mammoth's. Because the evidence is not considered hearsay, (D) incorrectly concludes that it *is* hearsay. (B) is incorrect because statements made in such a manner may be inadmissible multiple hearsay. (C) is incorrect because the admissibility of the testimony centers on a party's admission of a relevant fact. The declarant's use of the word "fault," which may be a legal conclusion, does not affect the admissibility of the statement.

Answer to Question 12

(D) Pursuant to the best evidence rule, when proving the terms of a writing (where the terms are material), the original writing must be produced. The rule does not apply to writings of minor importance to the matter in controversy. Thus, a witness may refer to collateral documents without providing the documents themselves. Here, the newspaper issue is tangential. As a result, there is no need to produce the newspaper. Therefore, (A) incorrectly concludes that the best evidence rule requires production of the newspaper. (B) is wrong because the newspaper story is not offered to prove the truth of its contents. (C) is incorrect because courts may take judicial notice of the *existence* of a local newspaper (a matter of common knowledge within the community) but not the *contents* of articles appearing therein.

Answer to Question 13

(B) An expert's opinion may be based upon one or more of three possible sources of information: (i) facts that he knows from his own observation; (ii) facts presented in evidence at the trial and submitted to the expert; or (iii) facts not in evidence that were supplied to the expert out of court, which facts are of a type reasonably relied upon by experts in the particular field in forming opinions on the subject. (B) correctly refers to (ii), above, as a proper source of information for the expert. (A) is incorrect because, where an expert bases her opinion on facts made known to her at the trial, the expert need not disclose the reasons for the opinion on direct examination unless the court orders it. (C) is incorrect because, although personal observation is one of the sources upon which an expert opinion may be based, it is not the only such source. (D) is incorrect because permanence of injury is an issue that requires specialized knowledge to assist the jury.

Answer to Question 14

(D) The statement is inadmissible hearsay. Hearsay is an out-of-court statement offered in evidence to prove the truth of the matter asserted. Here, the affidavit is being offered to prove that Rider incurred a recent back injury. Because Dr. Bond is dead, the adverse party is denied the opportunity to cross-examine him and test the veracity of his statement. Furthermore, the statement falls within no recognized exception to the hearsay rule. Thus, (D) is correct. (A) is incorrect because declarations of present bodily condition are statements made contemporaneously with the symptoms. Here, the affidavit was prepared later in contemplation of trial. It does not contain Rider's contemporaneous statements regarding his symptoms, but rather the physician's observation that Rider suffered from a recent back injury. Hence, the statement does not fall within the exception. (B) is incorrect because the former testimony exception requires that the statement be given during formal proceedings and under oath by a witness subject to cross-examination. (C) is incorrect because the statement relates to a time, event, or person in controversy. Whether Rider's back injury was an old or a recent injury is such a matter in controversy. Hence, the statement is relevant.

Answer to Question 15

(A) An admission by a party-opponent is considered nonhearsay under the Federal Rules. An admission is a statement that amounts to a prior acknowledgment by one of the parties to an action of one of the relevant facts. If the party said or did something inconsistent with his contentions at trial, the law regards him as estopped from preventing its admission into evidence. (A) is correct because Rider's statement that his back injury was a recurrence of an old injury is inconsistent with his assertion that the injury resulted from the recent accident. (B) is wrong because a spontaneous declaration (or "excited utterance") must concern the immediate facts of a startling occurrence. Rider's statement does not refer to the accident itself. Nor is it clear from the facts that the statement was made under the stress of the excitement. (C) is wrong because the statement relates to a time, event, or person in controversy (*i.e.*, whether Rider's back injury resulted from Transit Company's negligence). Hence, it is relevant. (D) is wrong because (as noted in the discussion of option (A), above) an admission by a party-opponent is nonhearsay under the Federal Rules of Evidence.

Answer to Question 16

(C) The report is hearsay, as it is a statement, not made by the declarant while testifying at the trial, offered to prove the truth of the matter asserted. Thus, the report is inadmissible unless it comes within a hearsay exception. The only applicable exception is the business records exception, under which a writing or record made as a memorandum of any act, transaction, occurrence, or event is admissible as proof of such act, etc., if made in the regular course of a business, and if it was the regular course of such business to make it at the time of the act, or within a reasonable time thereafter. Many courts exclude self-serving employee accident reports that are prepared primarily for litigation by someone with a strong motive to misrepresent. Under the Federal Rules, courts have discretion to exclude a business record if the source of information indicates a lack of trustworthiness. The report at issue was prepared primarily for litigation purposes by Handy, who had a strong motive to misrepresent the facts. Therefore, the report is sufficiently lacking in trustworthiness so as to not qualify for admission as a business record. Because the report is inadmissible, (A) and (B) are incorrect for concluding that it is admissible. (D) is incorrect because unavailability is not germane to the business records exception.

Answer to Question 17

(B) Communications between attorney and client, made during professional consultation, are privileged from disclosure. A business report prepared as a communication from client to attorney is privileged. Here, Def's general manager prepared the report at the request of the company's attorney. This report constitutes a privileged, confidential communication between a client (Def Company) and its attorney. Therefore, production of the report will not be required. (A) is incorrect because the facts indicate that this particular business report is of a privileged nature. (C) and (D) are wrong because the fact that a report contains hearsay or is self-serving does not prevent its discovery by the opponent.

Answer to Question 18

(B) Waite's invocation of the privilege meant that Davis could not cross-examine her on a critical issue in the case. If Waite actually was in Old Town, she could not have witnessed the murder, and her testimony would be impeached. Because she cannot be adequately cross-examined on this matter, her testimony should be stricken in its entirety. (A) is wrong because it is not necessary for a person to have been charged with a crime in order to claim a privilege against self-incrimination. (C) is wrong because a non-party's privileges are not outweighed by the rights of the accused. (D) is wrong because it is not necessary for one claiming a privilege against self-incrimination to establish that she would actually be self-incriminated by her testimony.

Answer to Question 19

(C) Under the Fifth Amendment to the United States Constitution, a witness cannot be compelled to testify against himself. A prosecutor may not comment on a defendant's silence after being arrested and receiving *Miranda* warnings. The warnings carry an implicit assurance that silence will carry no penalty. Thus, Sam's silence after Alex's incriminating statement is inadmissible against Sam and (C) is correct. It follows that (A) is incorrect. The self-incrimination privilege negates the "adoptive admission" doctrine, and failure to reply to an accusation or statement made by police in a criminal case can almost never be used as an implied admission of a criminal act. (B) is wrong because the statement is overbroad, and because the issue of admissibility involves Sam's silence (which is protected by the Fifth Amendment) rather than Alex's confession. (D) is an incorrect statement of fact. Alex's statement relates to a time, person, or event in controversy, and thus is relevant and obviously has probative value. However, the issue of admissibility in this question involves Sam's silence and not Alex's statement. Thus, option (D) is unresponsive to the call of the question.

Answer to Question 20

(A) Evidence concerning the theft should be admitted because specific instances of conduct may be proved when character is directly in issue. Although character evidence, including evidence of specific acts, is generally inadmissible in a civil case, there is an exception where character is directly in issue. In defamation cases, character is always in issue, and evidence is admissible as to the trait in question. Here, the issue is whether Pack is a thief. Evidence of acts of theft by Pack are admissible. (B) is wrong because whether the act is a felony is only important if it is offered as a prior conviction to attack the character for truthfulness of a testifying witness. Any act of theft, felony or misdemeanor, would be admissible here to show that Pack is a thief; it is not being offered for impeachment purposes. (C) is incorrect because, under the Federal Rules, any of the types of character evidence (reputation, opinion, or specific acts) may be used to prove character when character is directly in issue. (D) is wrong because the evidence is central to the ultimate issue in the case—the truth of Donlon's statement. Its relevance could not be greater and could not be substantially outweighed by the danger of unfair prejudice.

Answer to Question 21

(B) Harry's affidavit is inadmissible. Hearsay is an out-of-court statement offered in evidence to prove the truth of the matter asserted. Here, the affidavit is an out-of-court statement Plaintiff seeks to introduce to prove that Joe was incompetent when he conveyed the property. Hence, it is hearsay. The affidavit does not fall within any recognized exception to the hearsay rule. Hence, (B) is correct. (A) is wrong because opinion testimony by lay witnesses is admissible when: (i) it is rationally based on the perception of the witness; and (ii) it is helpful to a clear understanding of testimony or to the determination of a fact in issue. Opinions of laypersons as to the general appearance or condition of a person are generally admissible. The problem here does not involve "opinion," but rather the fact that the affidavit is hearsay. (C) is wrong because the affidavit does not qualify as an official document. The official records exception to the hearsay rule covers records, reports, statements, or data compilations of public offices and agencies made by, and within the scope of duty of, the public employee. Harry and his affidavit have no such official standing. (D) is wrong because the affidavit is 15 years old, and the Federal Rules of Evidence require that a document be at least 20 years old to qualify as an "ancient document." (It should also be noted that statements affecting an interest in property are not subject to the 20-year rule. However, the affidavit is not a deed, a will, or a document that otherwise disposes of property. Therefore, it does not qualify under the exception.)

Answer to Question 22

(D) White's testimony is inadmissible to show negligence. Evidence of character to prove the conduct of a person in the litigated event is generally not admissible in civil cases, because the slight probative value of character is outweighed by the danger of prejudice, the possible distraction of the jury from the main question in issue, and the possible waste of time required by examination of collateral issues. There is an exception to this general rule when a person's character itself is one of the issues in the case. Here, Dan's character is not in issue. Thus, the general rule applies, and (D) is correct. (A) is incorrect because habit describes one's regular response to a specific set of circumstances. Here, however, what is involved is character evidence rather than habit evidence. Character describes one's disposition with respect to general traits (*i.e.*, Dan's reputation in the community as a reckless driver). (B) is wrong because reputation evidence in civil cases is admitted only for the purpose of proving character. Negligence of Dan on a particular occasion does not raise character issues. (C) is wrong because it applies the general rule for criminal cases, and the case in question is a civil one.

Answer to Question 23

(C)   Under Federal Rule 801(d)(1), Witt's statement made in the earlier deposition is considered nonhearsay as a prior inconsistent statement made by a witness while testifying under oath at some prior proceeding, and thus is admissible as substantive proof. It can be admitted for impeachment purposes so long as a proper foundation is laid. Federal Rule 613 requires that the witness must be first examined "so as to give him an opportunity to explain or deny" the allegedly inconsistent statement unless "the interests of justice otherwise require." (A) is wrong because this was a former statement made under oath, is considered not to be hearsay, and is admissible as substantive proof. (B) is wrong because so long as a proper foundation is laid, it can be introduced for impeachment purposes as well. (D) is wrong because it is not hearsay.

Answer to Question 24

(D)   Where a witness makes a statement not directly relevant to the issues in the case, the opponent is barred from proving the statement untrue either by extrinsic contradictory facts or by a prior inconsistent statement. The color of the sweater worn by Derrick is collateral to the issues in this case. Thus, allowing testimony contradicting Bystander's testimony on this matter would raise the possibility of unfair surprise, confusion of issues, and inefficient use of the court's time. For these reasons, Wilson's testimony is inadmissible. (A) is wrong because nothing in the facts indicates that the color of Derrick's sweater is of consequence to the action. (B) and (C) are wrong because even if the evidence has some bearing on the witness's credibility, it is excluded because of possible confusion of issues or waste of time.

Answer to Question 25

(B)   The statement made by Derrick to Officer is an admission by a party-opponent (*i.e.*, a statement that amounts to a prior acknowledgment by a party of one of the relevant facts). We are told that the rate of speed at which Derrick was traveling is in issue. Thus, Derrick's statement that he was driving 40 m.p.h. comes in as an admission. (D) is wrong because, under the Federal Rules, an admission is not hearsay. (A) is wrong because an admission is admissible whether or not it discredits later testimony. (C) is wrong because no foundation is necessary for the admission into evidence of an admission by a party-opponent.

Answer to Question 26

(B)   Where an out-of-court statement is admitted into evidence under one of the exceptions to the hearsay rule, the party against whom the statement has been admitted may impeach the credibility of the declarant. The declarant's credibility may be attacked by evidence that would be admissible if the declarant had testified. The testimony of Wall is admissible to show that Pitt made a statement that was inconsistent with the statement related by the police officer. (A) is incorrect because impeachment evidence is *excluded* from the hearsay rule. (C) refers to the traditional rule prohibiting expert witnesses from expressing opinions on the ultimate issue in the case. This rule has been repudiated by the Federal Rules. Also, this case does not involve expert testimony. In addition, the testimony does not relate an opinion. For these reasons, (C) is incorrect. (D) is wrong because Pitt's credibility is crucial to Drew's culpability.

Answer to Question 27

(B) The Federal Rules allow for substantive admissibility of learned treatises, if such treatises are called to the attention of the expert witness upon cross-examination or relied upon by her during direct examination and they are established as reliable authority by the testimony or admission of the witness, or by other expert testimony, or by judicial notice. This is an exception to the hearsay rule. Here, the medical textbook was called to the attention of Dr. Cox on cross-examination, and she testified that it was authoritative. Thus, the passages from the textbook are admissible as substantive evidence. It logically follows that (A) and (C) are incorrect. (D) is incorrect because it is not Dr. Cox's job to determine the relevancy of proffered evidence.

Answer to Question 28

(D) Evidence of compromises or offers to compromise a claim disputed as to either liability or damages is inadmissible to prove liability for or invalidity of a claim. Also, any conduct or statement made in the course of negotiating a compromise is inadmissible. It follows that (A) and (B) are incorrect. (C) is incorrect because, were it not for the rule excluding offers of compromise, the statement would be an admission of a party-opponent. Such an admission can be in the form of an opinion.

Answer to Question 29

(D) Zee's graphs are demonstrative evidence, offered to illustrate the daily variations in water level at issue here. Because the graphs are reproductions of the data contained in Wells's log, Wells's testimony regarding the compilation of the log is necessary to determine whether the graphs are based on a foundation strong enough to justify their admission into evidence. It follows that (A) is incorrect. (B) is incorrect because this is not hearsay. Wells is going to testify to the manner in which he kept the log, not to an out-of-court statement offered to prove the truth of the matter asserted. (C) is incorrect because, generally, credibility may not be bolstered until it has been impeached.

Answer to Question 30

(D) A letter shown to have been properly addressed, stamped, and mailed is presumed to have been delivered in the due course of mail. Under the Federal Rules, such a presumption is overcome when the party against whom it is directed produces sufficient evidence contradicting the presumed fact. Here, DeVore's testimony raises a presumption of due delivery of the notice letter. However, Polk, by his testimony, has produced enough evidence to rebut this presumption. Thus, when the case goes to the jury, the judge should not instruct the jury regarding a presumption of receipt, because that presumption is gone. (A) is incorrect because the jury must determine questions of fact, such as whether Polk received the notice. (B) is incorrect because, as explained above, there is no longer a presumption that Polk received the notice. (C) is incorrect because it goes even further than to call for a presumption. Rather, it calls for a "conclusive" presumption, which cannot be rebutted by contrary evidence. Such a presumption runs afoul of the Federal Rules, which permit a presumption to be rebutted.

Answer to Question 31

(D)   A witness's good reputation for truth and veracity may be shown after attack. However, only under certain circumstances will it be proper. (A) is not correct because selling speculative stocks does not need the response of good reputation for truth. (B) is not correct because good reputation for truth and veracity does not refute bias. (C) is not correct since attending a school for the mentally retarded does not go to credibility. (D) is a fundamental attack going to the credibility of Weston's entire testimony. It is thus the best answer.

Answer to Question 32

(A),(C)   (A) and (C) were both given credit by the examiners. (B) is wrong because for past recollection recorded there must be a record made at or near the event by someone with firsthand knowledge who has no present recollection but who can say it was accurate when written. That is not present here. (D) is wrong because the best evidence rule requires the production of the original unless it is accounted for. Photocopies would be admissible, absent a genuine dispute about the authenticity of the original or other unfairness. Either (A) or (C) could be correct depending upon interpretation. This is a document affecting an interest in property. Statements in documents affecting an interest in property are admissible if they are "relevant to the purpose of the document." If one interprets the statement that the recipient of the deed of gift is related to the donor to be "relevant to the purpose of the document," then (A) would be correct. If not, then (C) would be correct.

Answer to Question 33

(A)   Other crimes or wrongs are not generally admissible. They may be shown, however, to prove identity (among a few other relevant things). Other crimes are admissible on identity only when they are highly individual and amount to a "signature." Red paint on a gun is individual enough to qualify. Thus, (A) is right and (D) is wrong. (B) is an incorrect theory. Having a red gun does not show anything about the defendant's willingness to commit a crime. (C) is wrong, too. This is not character evidence.

Answer to Question 34

(A)   The Federal Rules allow impeachment by: (i) any felony conviction, if the trial judge decides that the probative value of the conviction outweighs its prejudicial effect; and (ii) conviction of any other crime requiring proof or admission of an act of dishonesty or false statement. The prior conviction may be shown either by cross-examination of the witness or by introducing a record of the judgment. It follows that (D) is incorrect. (C) is incorrect because impeachment may be accomplished by showing any felony conviction (if the probative value outweighs the prejudicial effect), not just by showing conviction of crimes involving dishonesty or false statement. (B) is incorrect because it fails to account for the need to find that the probative value outweighs the prejudicial effect.

Answer to Question 35

(C)   The evidence is admissible to show that the tree was on Dow's property. While evidence of repairs made following an accident is generally inadmissible to prove negligence or culpable conduct under Federal Rule 407, such evidence may be introduced to show ownership or control, since a stranger would hardly make repairs. (A) is wrong because while there is such a public policy, in this case a valid exception applies. (B) is wrong because the evidence is not being introduced to show the condition of the tree at the time of the accident. (D) is wrong because Dow's cutting down of the tree cannot be admitted to show the tree was in a rotted condition. This would contravene the policy of the rule, which has the purpose of encouraging people to make such repairs.

Answer to Question 36

(B) The Bible listing is admissible as a family record. Federal Rule of Evidence 803(13) provides a specific exception to the hearsay rule allowing admission of family records, such as family Bibles, genealogies, engravings, etc. A family Bible with a record of births and deaths is exactly the type of document intended by this exception. (A) is incorrect because the inscription concerning Baggs's niece is less than 20 years old. (C) is incorrect because the hearsay exception described above applies to the family Bible. (D) is incorrect because there is no such foundational requirement in the exception to the hearsay rule. The family Bible is considered to have inherent indicia of trustworthiness. The Bible has been properly identified as having belonged to Baggs's family, and there is no reason to consider the inscription untrustworthy.

Answer to Question 37

(B) Where a witness makes a statement not directly relevant to the issues in the case, the rule against impeachment on a collateral matter applies to bar the other side from proving the statement untrue by extrinsic evidence or by a prior inconsistent statement. Here, the actual number of years during which Walters was employed by the roofing company is irrelevant to the genuineness of Daly's signature on the note. Thus, this is a collateral matter, and Daly will not be permitted to impeach Walters on it. (D) then is incorrect. (C) is incorrect, not only because Wilson's testimony is irrelevant to any issue in the case, but also because such testimony is not evidence of a regularly conducted activity. (A) is incorrect. Although the witness is testifying orally about matters contained in a writing (the employment records), the records here are collateral to the issue being litigated. Accordingly, the collateral document exception applies and the best evidence rule is inapplicable.

Answer to Question 38

(A) The credibility of an expert witness may be attacked by cross-examining him as to: (i) his general knowledge of the field in which he is claiming to be an expert; and (ii) his particular knowledge of the facts upon which his opinion is based. Pine's question on cross-examination relates to Wall's general knowledge of the field of chemistry. This bears directly on the weight to be given Wall's testimony. Thus, (A) is correct. (C) is incorrect because any determination of Wall's qualifications as an expert does not preclude an attack on his credibility or on the weight to be given the opinion. (B) and (D) are incorrect because the question relates to neither Wall's truthfulness nor his character.

REAL PROPERTY QUESTIONS

Questions 1-3 are based on the following fact situation:

Sue owned a five-acre tract of land, one acre of which had previously been owned by Opal, but to which Sue had acquired title by adverse possession. Sue contracted to convey the full five-acre tract to Peg, but the contract did not specify the quality of title Sue would convey.

1. Suppose Peg pays the purchase price and accepts a deed. Subsequently, Sue's title to the one acre proves inadequate and Opal ejects Peg from that acre. Peg sues Sue for damages. Which of the following statements applies most accurately to the determination of Peg's rights?

    (A) Sue's deed was fraudulent.

    (B) The terms of the deed control Sue's liability.

    (C) The only remedy available for breach of warranty of title is rescission.

    (D) Peg's rights are based on the implied covenants that the title conveyed shall be marketable.

2. Suppose Sue's contract had called for the conveyance of "a good and marketable title." Pursuant to that contract, Peg paid the purchase price and accepted a deed from Sue containing no covenants of title. Sue's title to the one acre subsequently proved defective and Peg was ejected by Opal. Peg sued Sue. Which of the following results is most likely?

    (A) Peg will win, because Sue's deed was fraudulent.

    (B) Peg will win, because the terms of the deed control Sue's liability.

    (C) Sue will win, because the terms of the deed control her liability.

    (D) Sue will win, because the deed incorporates the terms of the contract.

3. Suppose that before closing, the house on the property had been totally destroyed by fire. In determining the rights of Sue and Peg, the court would most likely consider the doctrine of equitable:

    (A) Marshaling.

    (B) Sequestration.

    (C) Subrogation.

    (D) Conversion.

Question 4

Owens contracted to sell a tract of land, Overlea, to Painter by general warranty deed. However, at the closing Painter did not carefully examine the deed and accepted a quitclaim deed without covenants of title. Painter later attempted to sell Overlea to Thompson, who refused to perform because Owens had conveyed an easement for a highway across Overlea before Painter bought the property.

Painter sued Owens for damages. Which of the following arguments will most likely succeed in Owens's defense?

(A) The existence of the easement does not violate the contract.

(B) The mere existence of an easement that is not being used does not give rise to a cause of action.

(C) Painter's cause of action must be based on the deed and not on the contract.

(D) The proper remedy is rescission of the deed.

Question 5

Lord leased a warehouse building and the lot on which it stood to Taylor for a term of 10 years. The lease contained a clause prohibiting Taylor from subletting his interest.

Can Taylor assign his interest under the lease?

(A) Yes, because restraints on alienation of land are strictly construed.

(B) Yes, because disabling restraints on alienation are invalid.

(C) No, because the term "subletting" includes "assignment" when the term is employed in a lease.

(D) No, because even in the absence of an express prohibition on assignment, a tenant may not assign without the landlord's permission.

Question 6

The following facts concern a tract of land in a state which follows general law. Each instrument is in proper form, recorded, marital property rights were waived when necessary, and each person named was adult and competent at the time of the named transaction.

1. In 1940, Oleg, the owner, conveyed his interest in fee simple "to my brothers Bob and Bill, their heirs and assigns as joint tenants with right of survivorship."

2. In 1950 Bob died, devising his interest to his only child, "Charles, for life, and then to Charles's son, Sam, for life, and then to Sam's children, their heirs and assigns."

3. In 1970 Bill died, devising his interest "to my friend, Frank, his heirs and assigns."

4. In 1972 Frank conveyed by quitclaim deed "to Paul, his heirs and assigns, whatever right, title, and interest I own."

Paul has never married. Paul has contracted to convey marketable record title in the land to Patrick. Can Paul do so?

(A) Yes, without joinder of any other person in the conveyance.

(B) Yes, if Charles, Sam, and Sam's only child (Gene, aged 25) will join in the conveyance.

(C) No, regardless of who joins in the conveyance, because Sam may have additional children whose interests cannot be defeated.

(D) No, regardless of who joins in the conveyance, because a title acquired by quitclaim deed is impliedly unmarketable.

Questions 7-8 are based on the following fact situation:

Oscar, the owner in fee simple, laid out a subdivision of 325 lots on 150 acres of land. He obtained governmental approval (as required by applicable ordinances) and, between 1968 and 1970, he sold 140 of the lots, inserting in each of the 140 deeds the following provision:

> The Grantee, for himself and his heirs, assigns and successors, covenants and agrees that the premises conveyed herein shall have erected thereon one single-family dwelling and that no other structure (other than a detached garage, normally incident to a single-family dwelling) shall be erected or maintained; and, further, that no use shall ever be made or permitted to be made other than occupancy by a single family for residential purposes only.

Because of difficulty encountered in selling the remaining lots for single-family use, in January 1971, Oscar advertised the remaining lots with prominent emphasis: "These lots are not subject to any restrictions and purchasers will find them adaptable to a wide range of uses."

7. Payne had purchased one of the 140 lots and brought suit against Oscar to establish that the remaining 185 lots, as well as the 140 sold previously, can be used only for residential purposes by single families. Assuming that procedural requirements have been met, to permit adjudication of the issue Payne has tendered, which of the following is the most appropriate comment?

(A) Oscar should win because the provision binds only the grantee.

(B) The outcome turns on whether a common development scheme had been established for the entire subdivision.

(C) The outcome turns on whether there are sufficient land areas devoted to multiple family uses within the municipality to afford reasonable opportunity for all economic classes to move into the area so as to satisfy the standards of equal protection of the law.

(D) Payne should win under an application of the doctrine, which requires construction of deeds, to resolve any doubt against the grantor.

8. Suppose that Oscar sold 50 lots during 1971 without inserting in the deeds any provisions relating to structures or uses. Doyle purchased one of the 50 lots and proposes to erect a service station and to conduct a retail business for the sale of gasoline, etc.

Pringle purchased a lot from Boyer. Boyer had purchased from Oscar in 1968 and the deed had the provision that is quoted in the fact situation.

Pringle brings suit to prevent Doyle from erecting the service station and from conducting a retail business.

In the litigation between Pringle and Doyle, which of the following constitutes the best defense for Doyle?

(A) Oscar's difficulty in selling with provisions relating to use establishes a change in circumstances which renders any restrictions which may once have existed unenforceable.

(B) Enforcement of the restriction, in view of the change of circumstances, would be an unreasonable restraint on alienation.

(C) Since the proof (as stated) does not establish a danger of monetary loss to Pringle, Pringle has failed to establish one of the necessary elements in a cause of action to prevent Doyle from using his lot for business purposes.

(D) The facts do not establish a common building or development scheme for the entire subdivision.

Question 9

Odum owned Brightacre (a tract of land) in fee simple. He conveyed it "to Pike, his heirs and assigns; but if Farley shall be living 30 years from the date of this deed, then to Farley, his heirs and assigns."

The limitation "to Farley, his heirs and assigns" is:

(A) Valid, because Farley's interest is a reversion.

(B) Valid, because the interest will vest, if at all, within a life in being.

(C) Valid, because Farley's interest is vested subject to divestment.

(D) Invalid.

Questions 10-11 are based on the following fact situation:

Trease owned Hilltop in fee simple. By his will, he devised as follows: "Hilltop to such of my grandchildren who shall reach the age of 21; and by this provision I intend to include all grandchildren whenever born." At the time of his death, Trease had three children and two grandchildren.

10. Courts hold such a devise valid under the common law Rule Against Perpetuities. What is the best explanation of that determination?

(A) All of Trease's children would be measuring lives.

(B) The rule of convenience closes the class of beneficiaries when any grandchild reaches the age of 21.

    (C) There is a presumption that Trease intended to include only those grandchildren born prior to his death.

    (D) There is a subsidiary rule of construction that dispositive instruments are to be interpreted so as to uphold interests rather than to invalidate them under the Rule Against Perpetuities.

11. Which of the following additions to or changes in the facts of the preceding question would produce a violation of the common law Rule Against Perpetuities?

    (A) A posthumous child was born to Trease.

    (B) Trease's will expressed the intention to include all afterborn grandchildren in the gift.

    (C) The instrument was an inter vivos conveyance rather than a will.

    (D) Trease had no grandchildren living at the time of his death.

Question 12

Assume for the purposes of this question that you are counsel to the state legislative committee that is responsible for real estate laws in your state. The committee wants you to draft a statute, governing the recording of deeds, that fixes priorities of title, as reflected on the public record, as definitely as possible.

Which of the following, divorced from other policy considerations, would best accomplish this particular result?

(A) Eliminate the requirement of witnesses to deeds.

(B) Make time of recording the controlling factor.

(C) Make irrebuttable the declarations in the deeds that valuable consideration was paid.

(D) Make the protection of bona fide purchasers the controlling factor.

Questions 13-15 are based on the following fact situation:

Owen held in fee simple Farmdale, a large tract of vacant land. The state wherein Farmdale is situated has a statute which provides, in substance, that unless the conveyance is recorded, every deed or other conveyance of an interest in land is void as to a subsequent purchaser who pays value without notice of such conveyance. The following transactions occurred in the order given.

First: Owen conveyed Farmdale, for a fair price, to Allred by general warranty deed. Allred did not immediately record.

Second: Owen executed a mortgage to secure repayment of a loan concurrently made to Owen by Leon. Leon had no notice of the prior conveyance to Allred and promptly recorded the mortgage.

Third: Owen, by general warranty deed, gratuitously conveyed to Niece, who promptly recorded the deed.

Fourth: Allred recorded his deed from Owen.

Fifth: Niece, by general warranty deed, conveyed Farmdale to Barrett. Barrett had no actual notice of any of the prior transactions, paid full value, and promptly recorded the deed.

13. Asserting that his title was held free of any claim by Barrett, Allred instituted suit against Barrett to quiet title to Farmdale. If Barrett prevails, it will be because:

    (A) Allred's prior recorded deed is deemed to be outside Barrett's chain of title.

    (B) Barrett's grantor, Niece, recorded before Allred.

    (C) As between two warranty deeds, the later one controls.

    (D) Barrett's grantor, Niece, had no notice of Allred's rights.

14. Asserting that his title was held free of any claim by Leon, Allred instituted suit against Leon to quiet title to Farmdale. Judgment should be for:

    (A) Allred, because Leon is deemed not to have paid value.

    (B) Allred, because a mortgagee is not a subsequent purchaser within the meaning of the statute mentioned.

    (C) Leon, because he recorded before Allred.

    (D) Leon, because he advanced money without notice of Allred's rights.

15. Assume for this question only that Niece had not conveyed to Barrett. After Allred recorded his deed from Owen, Allred, asserting that Allred's title was held free of any claim by Niece, instituted suit against Niece to recover title to Farmdale. Judgment should be for:

    (A) Niece, because she had no notice of Allred's rights when she accepted the deed from Owen.

    (B) Niece, because she recorded her deed before Allred recorded his.

    (C) Allred, because Niece was not a bona fide purchaser who paid value.

    (D) Allred, because he had paid value for Farmdale and had no actual or constructive notice of the deed to Niece.

Questions 16-17 are based on the following fact situation:

Ogden was the fee simple owner of three adjoining vacant lots fronting on a common street in a primarily residential section of a city which had no zoning laws. The lots were identified as Lots 1, 2, and 3. Ogden conveyed Lot 1 to Akers and Lot 2 to Bell. Ogden retained Lot 3, which consisted of three acres of woodland. Bell, whose lot was between the other two, built a house on his lot. Bell's house included a large window on the side facing Lot 3. The window provided a beautiful view from Bell's living room, thereby adding value to Bell's house.

Akers erected a house on his lot. Ogden made no complaint to either Akers or Bell concerning the houses they built. After both Akers and Bell had completed their houses, the two of them agreed to and did build a common driveway running from the street to the rear of their respective lots. The driveway was built on the line between the two houses so that one-half of the way was located on each lot. Akers and Bell exchanged right-of-way deeds by which each of them conveyed to the other, his heirs and assigns, an easement to continue the right of way. Both deeds were properly recorded.

After Akers and Bell had lived in their respective houses for 30 years, a new public street was built bordering on the rear of Lots 1, 2, and 3. Akers informed Bell that, since the new street removed the need for their common driveway, he considered the right-of-way terminated; therefore, he intended to discontinue its use and expected Bell to do the same. At about the same time, Ogden began the erection of a six-story apartment house on Lot 3. If the apartment house is completed, it will block the view from Bell's window and will substantially reduce the value of Bell's lot.

16. In an action brought by Bell to enjoin Akers from interfering with Bell's continued use of the common driveway between the two lots, the decision should be for:

    (A) Akers, because the termination of the necessity for the easement terminated the easement.

    (B) Akers, because the continuation of the easement after the change of circumstances would adversely affect the marketability of both lots without adding any commensurate value to either.

(C) Bell, because an incorporeal heredita-ment lies in grant and cannot be terminated without a writing.

(D) Bell, because the removal of the need for the easement created by express grant does not affect the right to the easement.

17. In an action brought by Bell to enjoin Ogden from erecting the apartment build-ing in such a way as to obstruct the view from Bell's living room window, the decision should be for:

(A) Bell, because Ogden's proposed building would be an obstruction of Bell's natural right to an easement for light and air.

(B) Bell, because Bell was misled by Ogden's failure to complain when Bell was building his house.

(C) Ogden if, but only if, it can be shown that Ogden's intention to erect such a building was made known to Bell at or prior to the time of Ogden's convey-ance to Bell.

(D) Ogden, because Bell has no easement for light, air, or view.

Question 18

Morgan conveyed Greenacre, her one-family residence, to "Perez for life, remainder to Rowan, her heirs and assigns, subject, however, to First Bank's mortgage thereon." There was an unpaid balance on the mortgage of $10,000, which is payable in $1,000 annual installments plus interest at 6% on the unpaid balance, with the next payment due on July 1. Perez is now occupying Greenacre. The reasonable rental value of the property exceeds the sum necessary to meet all current charges. There is no appli-cable statute.

Under the rules governing contributions between life tenants and remaindermen, how should the burden for payment be allocated?

(A) Rowan must pay the principal payment, but Perez must pay the interest to First Bank.

(B) Rowan must pay both the principal and interest payments to First Bank.

(C) Perez must pay both the principal and interest payments to First Bank.

(D) Perez must pay the principal payment, but Rowan must pay the interest to First Bank.

Question 19

Anders conveyed her only parcel of land to Burton by a duly executed and delivered war-ranty deed, which provided:

To have and to hold the described tract of land in fee simple, subject to the under-standing that within one year from the date of the instrument said grantee shall con-struct and thereafter maintain and operate on said premises a public health center.

The grantee, Burton, constructed a public health center on the tract within the time speci-fied and operated it for five years. At the end of this period, Burton converted the structure into a senior citizens' recreational facility. It is consid-ered by all parties in interest that a senior citi-zens' recreational facility is not a public health center.

In an appropriate action, Anders seeks a declaration that the change in the use of the facility has caused the land and structure to revert to her. In this action, Anders should:

(A) Win, because the language of the deed created a determinable fee, which leaves a possibility of reverter in the grantor.

(B) Win, because the language of the deed created a fee subject to condition subse-quent, which leaves a right of entry or power of termination in the grantor.

(C) Lose, because the language of the deed created only a contractual obligation and did not provide for retention of property interest by the grantor.

(D) Lose, because an equitable charge is enforceable only in equity.

Question 20

Homer conveyed his home to his wife, Wanda, for life, remainder to his daughter, Dixie. There was a $20,000 mortgage on the home, requiring monthly payment covering interest to date plus a portion of the principal.

Which of the following statements about the monthly payment is correct?

(A) Wanda must pay the full monthly payment.

(B) Wanda must pay a portion of the monthly payment based on an apportionment of the value between Wanda's life estate and Dixie's remainder.

(C) Wanda must pay the portion of the monthly payment that represents interest.

(D) Dixie must pay the full monthly payment.

Questions 21-22 are based on the following fact situation:

The owner of Newacre executed and delivered to a power company a right-of-way deed for the building and maintenance of an overhead power line across Newacre. The deed was properly recorded. Newacre then passed through several intermediate conveyances until it was conveyed to Sloan about 10 years after the date of the right-of-way deed. All the intermediate deeds were properly recorded, but none of them mentioned the right-of-way.

Sloan entered into a written contract to sell Newacre to Jones. By the terms of the contract, Sloan promised to furnish an abstract of title to Jones. Sloan contracted directly with Abstract Company to prepare and deliver an abstract to Jones, and Abstract Company did so. The abstract omitted the right-of-way deed. Jones delivered the abstract to his attorney and asked the attorney for an opinion as to title. The attorney signed and delivered to Jones a letter stating that, from the attorney's examination of the abstract, it was his "opinion that Sloan had a free and unencumbered marketable title to Newacre."

Sloan conveyed Newacre to Jones by a deed which included covenants of general warranty and against encumbrances. Jones paid the full purchase price. After Jones had been in possession of Newacre for more than a year, he learned about the right-of-way deed. Sloan, Jones, Abstract Company, and Jones's attorney were all without actual knowledge of the existence of the right-of-way prior to the conveyance from Sloan to Jones.

21. If Jones sues Abstract Company for damages caused to Jones by the presence of the right-of-way, the most likely result will be a decision for:

(A) Jones, because Jones was a third-party creditor beneficiary of the contract between Sloan and Abstract Company.

(B) Jones, because the abstract prepared by Abstract Company constitutes a guarantee of Jones's title to Newacre.

(C) Abstract Company, because Abstract Company had no knowledge of the existence of the right-of-way.

(D) Abstract Company, because there was no showing that any fraud was practiced upon Jones.

22. If Jones sues Sloan because of the presence of the right-of-way, the most likely result will be a decision for:

(A) Jones, because Sloan is liable for his negligent misrepresentation.

(B) Jones, because the covenants in Sloan's deed to Jones have been breached.

(C) Sloan, because Jones relied upon Abstract Company, not Sloan, for information concerning title.

(D) Sloan, because Sloan was without knowledge of any defects in the title to Newacre.

Question 23

Testator devised his farm "to my son, Selden, for life, then to Selden's children and their heirs and assigns." Selden, a widower, had two unmarried adult children.

In an appropriate action to construe the will, the court will determine that the remainder to the children is:

(A) Indefeasibly vested.

(B) Contingent.

(C) Vested subject to partial defeasance.

(D) Vested subject to complete defeasance.

Questions 24-25 are based on the following fact situation:

Ohner holds title in fee simple to a tract of 1,500 acres. He desires to develop the entire tract as a golf course, country club, and residential subdivision. He contemplates forming a corporation to own and to operate the golf course and country club; the stock in the corporation will be distributed to the owners of lots in the residential portions of the subdivision, but no obligation to issue the stock is to ripen until all the residential lots are sold. The price of the lots is intended to return enough money to compensate Ohner for the raw land, development costs (including the building of the golf course and the country club facilities), and developer's profit, if all of the lots are sold.

Ohner's market analyses indicate that he must create a scheme of development that will offer prospective purchasers (and their lawyers) a very high order of assurance that several aspects will be clearly established:

1. Aside from the country club and golf course, there will be no land use other than for residential use and occupancy in the 1,500 acres.

2. The residents of the subdivision will have unambiguous right of access to the club and golf course facilities.

3. Each lot owner must have an unambiguous right to transfer his lot to a purchaser with all original benefits.

4. Each lot owner must be obligated to pay annual dues to a pro rata share (based on the number of lots) of the club's annual operating deficit (whether or not such owner desires to make use of club and course facilities).

24. In the context of all aspects of the scheme, which of the following will offer the best chance of implementing the requirement that each lot owner pay annual dues to support the club and golf course?

(A) Covenant.

(B) Easement.

(C) Mortgage.

(D) Personal contractual obligation by each purchaser.

25. Of the following, the greatest difficulty that will be encountered in establishing the scheme is that:

(A) Any judicial recognition will be construed as state action which, under current doctrines, raises a substantial question whether such action would be in conflict with the Fourteenth Amendment.

(B) The scheme, if effective, renders title unmarketable.

(C) One or more of the essential aspects outlined by Ohner will result in a restraint on alienation.

(D) There is a judicial reluctance to recognize an affirmative burden to pay money in installments and over an indefinite period as a burden that can be affixed to bind future owners of land.

Question 26

Oaks, the owner of Blackacre, conveyed a right-of-way to United Utility "for the underground transportation of gas by pipeline, the location of right-of-way to be mutually agreed upon by Oaks and United Utility." United Utility then installed a six-inch pipeline at a location selected by it and not objected to by Oaks. Two years later, United Utility advised Oaks of its intention to install an additional six-inch pipeline parallel to and three feet laterally from the original pipeline. In an appropriate action, Oaks sought a declaration that United Utility has no right to install the second pipeline.

If Oaks prevails, it will be because:

(A) Any right implied to expand the original use of the right-of-way creates an interest that violates the Rule Against Perpetuities.

(B) The original installation by United Utility defined the scope of the easement.

(C) Oaks did not expressly agree to the location of the right-of-way.

(D) The assertion of the right to install an additional pipeline constitutes inverse condemnation.

Question 27

Martinez, a widower, owns in fee simple a ranch, Ranchacre. Martinez has one child, Enrique, who is married. Enrique has one child, Ana Maria, who is also married but has no children. In an effort to dispose of Ranchacre to his descendants and to honor a request by Ana Maria that she be skipped in any such disposition, Martinez conveys Ranchacre to his son, Enrique, for life with the remainder to Ana Maria's children in fee simple.

What interest, if any, is created in favor of Ana Maria's unborn children at the time of the conveyance?

(A) A contingent remainder.

(B) A vested remainder subject to divestment.

(C) A springing use.

(D) None.

Question 28

While hospitalized, Marsh requested her attorney to draw a deed conveying her home to her son, Simon. While Marsh remained in the hospital, the deed was drawn, properly executed, and promptly and properly recorded. On being informed of the existence of the deed, Simon told his mother, "I want no part of the property; take the deed right back." Marsh recovered and left the hospital, but shortly thereafter, before any other relevant event, Simon died intestate.

Marsh brought an appropriate action against Simon's heirs to determine title.

If Marsh wins, it will be because:

(A) The court will impose a constructive trust to carry out the intent of the deceased son.

(B) The presumption of delivery arising from the recording is not valid unless the grantee has knowledge at the time of the recording.

(C) Simon's declaration was a constructive reconveyance of the land.

(D) There was no effective acceptance of delivery of the deed.

Question 29

Andres conveyed Applewood Farm "to Bogatz, her heirs and assigns, so long as the premises are used for residential and farm purposes, then to Cohen and his heirs." The common law Rule Against Perpetuities, unmodified by statute, is part of the law of the jurisdiction in which Applewood Farm is located.

As a consequence of the conveyance, Cohen's interest in Applewood Farm is:

(A) Nothing.

(B) A valid executory interest.

(C) A possibility of reverter.

(D) A right of entry for condition broken.

Question 30

Metterly, the owner in fee simple of Brownacre, by quitclaim deed conveyed Brownacre to her daughter, Doris, who paid no consideration for the conveyance. The deed was never recorded. About a year after the delivery of the deed, Metterly decided that this gift had been ill-advised. She requested that Doris destroy the deed, which Doris dutifully and voluntarily did. Within the month following the destruction of the deed, Metterly and Doris were killed in a common disaster. Each of the successors in interest claimed title to Brownacre.

In an appropriate action to determine the title to Brownacre, the probable outcome will be that:

(A) Metterly was the owner of Brownacre, because Doris was a donee and therefore could not acquire title by quitclaim deed.

(B) Metterly was the owner of Brownacre, because title to Brownacre reverted to her upon the voluntary destruction of the deed by Doris.

(C) Doris was the owner of Brownacre, because her destruction of the deed to Brownacre was under the undue influence of Metterly.

(D) Doris was the owner of Brownacre, because the deed was merely evidence of her title, and its destruction was insufficient to cause title to pass back to Metterly.

Question 31

By her validly executed will, Sallie devised a certain tract of land to her son, Ben, for his life with remainder to such of Ben's children as should be living at his death, "Provided, however, that no such child of Ben shall mortgage or sell, or attempt to mortgage or sell, his or her interest in the property prior to attaining 25 years of age; and, if any such child of Ben shall violate this provision, then upon such violation his or her interest shall pass to and become the property of the remaining children of Ben then living, share and share alike."

Sallie's will included an identical provision for each of her four other children concerning four other tracts of land. The residuary clause of the will gave the residuary estate to Sallie's five children equally. Sallie died and was survived by the five children named in her will and by 11 grandchildren. Several additional grandchildren have since been born.

In an action for a declaration of rights, it was claimed that the attempted gifts to Sallie's grandchildren were entirely void and that the interests following the life estates to Sallie's children passed to the children absolutely by the residuary clause.

Assuming that the action was properly brought with all necessary parties and with a guardian ad litem appointed to represent the interests of unborn and infant grandchildren, the decision should be that:

(A) The attempted gifts to grandchildren are void under the Rule Against Perpetuities.

(B) The attempted gifts to grandchildren are void as unlawful restraints on alienation.

(C) The provisions concerning grandchildren are valid and will be upheld according to their terms.

(D) Even if the provisions against sale or mortgage by the grandchildren are void, the remainders to grandchildren are otherwise valid and will be given effect.

Questions 32-33 are based on the following fact situation:

Meadowview is a large tract of undeveloped land. Black, the owner of Meadowview, prepared a development plan creating 200 house lots in Meadowview with the necessary streets and public areas. The plan was fully approved by all necessary governmental agencies and duly recorded. However, construction of the streets, utilities, and other aspects of the development of Meadowview has not yet begun, and none of the streets can be opened as public ways until they are completed in accordance with the applicable ordinances of the municipality in which Meadowview is located.

College Avenue, one of the streets laid out as part of the Meadowview development, abuts Whiteacre, an adjacent one-acre parcel owned by White. Whiteacre has no access to any public way except an old, poorly developed road which is inconvenient and cannot be used without great expense. White sold Whiteacre to Breyer. The description used in the deed from White to Breyer was the same as that used in prior deeds except that the portion of the description which formerly said, "thence by land of Black, northeasterly a distance of 200 feet, more or less," was changed to "thence by College Avenue as laid out on the Plan of Meadowview North 16° East 201.6 feet," with full reference to the plan and as recording data.

Breyer now seeks a building permit which will show that Breyer intends to use College Avenue for access to Whiteacre. Black objects to the granting of a building permit on the grounds that he has never granted any rights to White or Breyer to use College Avenue. There

are no governing statutes or ordinances relating to the problem. Black brings an appropriate action in which the right of Breyer to use College Avenue without an express grant from Black is at issue.

32. The best argument for Black in this action is that:

(A) Breyer's right must await the action of appropriate public authorities to open College Avenue as a public street, since no private easements arose by implication.

(B) The Statute of Frauds prevents the introduction of evidence which might prove the necessity for Breyer to use College Avenue.

(C) Breyer's right to use College Avenue is restricted to the assertion of a way by necessity and the facts preclude the success of such a claim.

(D) Breyer would be unjustly enriched if he were permitted to use College Avenue.

33. The best argument for Breyer in this action is that:

(A) There is a way by necessity over Meadowview's lands to gain access to a public road.

(B) The deed from White to Breyer referred to the recorded plan and therefore created rights to use the streets delineated on the plan.

(C) Sale of lots in Meadowview by reference to its plan creates private easements in the streets shown on the plan.

(D) The recording of the plan is a dedication of the streets shown on the plan to public use.

Question 34

Lester, the owner in fee simple of a small farm consisting of 30 acres of land improved with a house and several outbuildings, leased the same to Tanner for a 10-year period. After two years had expired, the government condemned 20 acres of the property and allocated the compensation award to Lester and Tanner according to their respective interest so taken. It so happened, however, that the 20 acres taken embraced all of the farm's tillable land, leaving only the house, outbuildings, and a small woodlot. There is no applicable statute in the jurisdiction where the property is located nor any provision in the lease relating to condemnation. Tanner quit possession and Lester brought suit against him to recover rent.

Lester will:

(A) Lose, because there has been a frustration of purpose which excuses Tanner from further performance of his contract to pay rent.

(B) Lose, because there has been a breach of the implied covenant of quiet enjoyment by Lester's inability to provide Tanner with possession of the whole of the property for the entire term.

(C) Win, because of the implied warranty on the part of the tenant to return the demised premises in the same condition at the end of the term as they were at the beginning.

(D) Win, because the relationship of landlord and tenant was unaffected by the condemnation, thus leaving Tanner still obligated to pay rent.

Question 35

Allen and Barker are equal tenants in common of a strip of land 10 feet wide and 100 feet deep which lies between the lots on which their respective homes are situated. Both Allen and Barker need the use of the 10-foot strip as a driveway, and each fears that a new neighbor might seek partition and leave him with an unusable five-foot strip.

The best measure to solve their problem is:

(A) A covenant against partition.

(B) An indenture granting cross-easements in the undivided half interest of each.

(C) A partition into two separate five-foot-wide strips and an indenture granting cross-easements.

(D) A trust to hold the strip in perpetuity.

Question 36

Santos agreed to sell and Perrine agreed to buy a described lot on which a single-family residence had been built. Under the contract, Santos agreed to convey marketable title subject only to conditions, covenants, and restrictions of record and all applicable zoning laws and ordinances. The lot was subject to a 10-foot side line setback originally set forth in the developer's duly recorded subdivision plot. The applicable zoning ordinance zones the property for single-family units and requires an 8.5-foot side line setback.

Prior to closing, a survey of the property was made. It revealed that a portion of Santos's house was 8.4 feet from the side line.

Perrine refused to consummate the transaction on the ground that Santos's title is not marketable. In an appropriate action, Santos seeks specific performance.

Who will prevail in such an action?

(A) Santos, because any suit against Perrine concerning the setback would be frivolous.

(B) Santos, because the setback violation falls within the doctrine of *de minimis non curat lex*.

(C) Perrine, because any variation, however small, amounts to a breach of contract.

(D) Perrine, because the fact that Perrine may be exposed to litigation is sufficient to make the title unmarketable.

REAL PROPERTY ANSWERS

Answer to Question 1

(B) Every land sale contract (not deed) contains an implied warranty of marketable title. For bar examination purposes, title acquired by adverse possession is unmarketable. However, the buyer's acceptance of a deed discharges the seller's contractual obligation to furnish marketable title, and leaves the buyer with remedies only on the covenants in the deed. (D) is wrong because a deed contains no implied covenant of marketability. (A) is wrong because it is not supported by the facts, and (C) is an incorrect statement of law; a buyer can choose to rescind, sue for damages for breach, get specific performance with abatement of the purchase price, or, in some jurisdictions, require the seller to quiet title.

Answer to Question 2

(C) Acceptance of a deed discharges the seller's liability on the contract. Since the deed here contained no covenants of title, it was a quitclaim deed. Conveyances under a quitclaim deed give the buyer only that which the seller owns. If Sue did not own the one acre she believed that she had acquired by adverse possession, then her quitclaim deed conveyed only the four remaining acres to Peg. Thus, Peg cannot prevail and (B) and (D) are wrong. (A) is not supported by the facts.

Answer to Question 3

(D) Once a land sale contract is signed, the doctrine of equitable conversion applies, making the buyer the equitable owner of the property. Under the majority view, the risk of loss then rests on the buyer; Peg must pay the purchase price. Thus, (D) is correct and the other choices are incorrect. Note that if Sue had insured the house for loss by fire, most courts would require her to give Peg credit, in the amount of the insurance proceeds, against the purchase price.

Answer to Question 4

(C) Painter's acceptance of the deed constituted a discharge of Owens's liability on the contract. A quitclaim deed contains no warranties and conveys only what the seller owns—here, property encumbered by an easement. Therefore, (C) is correct and (D) is inapplicable since there was no breach. (A) and (B) are not valid defenses, since existence of the easement was violative of the contract. The contract contained an implied warranty of marketable title, which generally means an unencumbered fee simple with good record title. An easement is an encumbrance. Note that if Owens had conveyed a general warranty deed to Painter, it would have contained a covenant against encumbrances.

Answer to Question 5

(A) Anti-transfer covenants are strictly construed; therefore, a prohibition against subleasing does not prevent assignment, and (C) is thus incorrect. (D) is wrong because an anti-assignment covenant must be express. Regarding (B), disabling restraints on a legal interest are always void. However, lease provisions restricting assignments and subleases are valid restraints. These are considered promissory restraints, breach of which will void an attempted assignment or transfer. Thus, (B) is wrong.

Answer to Question 6

(A) Oleg expressly conveyed a fee simple to Bob and Bill as joint tenants with the right of survivorship. Since the joint tenancy was not severed, Bill became the owner in fee simple at the instant of Bob's death. Bob's will was not effective until his death, at which time he no longer had an interest in the property; the act of making a will containing a testamentary devise of the land is not sufficient to sever the joint tenancy. Hence, Bob's attempt to devise his interest was inoperative, and (B) and (C) are thus incorrect. (D) is wrong because conveyance by quitclaim deed does not render title unmarketable.

Answer to Question 7

(B) If Oscar had a scheme for an exclusively residential subdivision, the court could *imply* a reciprocal negative servitude limiting the remaining lots to the same use. Reciprocal negative servitudes are implied only when the sales begin. Since all 140 lots already sold contain the covenant restricting the land use to single-family residential dwellings, a common scheme will be implied. Any subsequent purchaser will be bound by the covenant if there was notice. The appearance of an area containing only single-family residences is sufficient to constitute inquiry notice. Hence, (A) is wrong. (C) is incorrect because covenants are a private land use control. (D) is wrong because the issue does not concern construction of the deeds.

Answer to Question 8

(D) If Oscar had no uniform development scheme, there is no basis for implying a residential restriction in Doyle's deed. (A) is not the best defense because selling difficulties probably do not establish changes such as would render enforcement of the covenants inequitable. (B) is wrong because restraints upon use (as opposed to restraints upon alienation) of land are valid and enforceable. (C) is wrong because monetary loss is irrelevant in an action to establish an implied equitable servitude.

Answer to Question 9

(B) Pike had a fee simple subject to a shifting executory interest in Farley. If Farley lives 30 more years, the fee simple will shift to him. Therefore, (B) is correct and (D) is wrong. The Rule Against Perpetuities requires that the interest vest, if at all, within 21 years after a life in being and, using Farley's life as the measuring life, it is clear that his interest will vest, if at all, within his lifetime. (A) is wrong because a reversion occurs by operation of law when a grantor conveys less than the entire estate. Here, Odum transferred a fee simple in Brightacre to either Pike or Farley; there was no interest left to revert to Odum. (C) is wrong because an executory interest is not vested.

Answer to Question 10

(A) The class of Trease's grandchildren would close at the death of his last surviving child, who was necessarily a life in being at Trease's death (when the gift took effect); the gift would then vest (or fail) within 21 years thereafter. (C) is wrong because the express language of the will controls. The rule of convenience is used to determine when a class closes only absent an express intent to include all persons described no matter when born. Since Trease expressed such an intention, the rule is inapplicable and (B) is incorrect. (D) is wrong because the gift is valid without resort to preferential rules of construction.

Answer to Question 11

(C) If Trease had made the gift by inter vivos conveyance, he might have had another child thereafter who would not have been a life in being at the creation of the interest (and whose children might have reached 21 after the permissible perpetuities period). (A) is wrong because the Rule Against Perpetuities allows for periods of gestation. (B) is wrong because it changes nothing; the will already expresses an intention to include afterborn grandchildren. Further, (B) and (D) are wrong because all of Trease's grandchildren would be born to his children, who were lives in being at his death.

Answer to Question 12

(B) Priorities based on time of recording would protect most persons obtaining an interest in land that is timely recorded. Since the purpose of recordation is to give notice to others of a convey-ance of title, prospective purchasers could easily determine the status of the title. Furthermore, priorities based on recording generally protect bona fide purchasers. (D) is wrong because simply protecting bona fide purchasers would not assure an accurate reflection of priority of title on the public record (*e.g.*, "notice" statutes). (A) and (C) alone have no bearing on priority of title. Moreover, they are misstatements of law; witnesses to a deed are generally unnecessary and no recital of consideration is required for a valid deed.

Answer to Question 13

(A) A subsequent grantee has constructive knowledge of all prior recorded deeds except those outside of his chain of title. (B) and (D) are wrong because Niece's recordation would be relevant only if she had been a bona fide purchaser who could "shelter" Barrett. Under the shelter rule, a person who takes from a bona fide purchaser will prevail against any interest that the bona fide pur-chaser would have prevailed against—even if the grantee knew of the prior unrecorded interest. However, donees are not bona fide purchasers and, thus, are not protected. (C) is wrong because the state statute governs priority of title.

Answer to Question 14

(D) Leon will prevail because he had no actual or constructive notice of the conveyance to Allred, since it was not recorded at the time of the mortgage. A mortgagee who gives a concurrent loan is considered a purchaser for value within state recording acts. Hence, (A) and (B) are incorrect. (C) is wrong because the statute is a pure notice statute, which does not require that the subsequent purchaser be the first to record to protect his rights against a ***prior*** purchaser.

Answer to Question 15

(C) Judgment should be for Allred. Under the statute, unrecorded conveyances are void only as against bona fide purchasers. Since Niece took by a gratuitous conveyance, her prior recordation without notice is irrelevant. Thus, (A) and (B) are incorrect because Niece is not protected by the recording statute. (D) is incorrect because, absent a bona fide purchaser, priority is determined by the first-in-time rule.

Answer to Question 16

(D) Because the easement was validly created and recorded, the removal of the need for the easement does not affect the continuing right to the easement. (A) is wrong because there is no such auto-matic termination. If the parties had failed validly to create the easement in this case, a court might still have found an easement by necessity. If that had been the case, the end of the neces-sity would result in the expiration of the easement. But that was not the case here. Because an easement was created and recorded, the fact that the easement is no longer necessary has no bearing on its continued existence. The easement could be terminated by release or abandonment, but Bell does not wish to terminate the easement. (B) is wrong because an easement is a right that exists even if it adversely affects the marketability of land. (C) is wrong because easements can be terminated in ways other than by a writing. For example, Bell could abandon his easement by long nonuse accompanied by intent to abandon.

Answer to Question 17

(D) Bell has no claim because he had no easement for light, air, or view. (A) is wrong because there is no "natural right" to an easement for light and air. (B) is wrong because Bell's building of his house has no relationship to whether an easement for light and air was created. (C) is wrong because even if Ogden had no plans, at the time of his conveyance to Bell, to erect such a building, no easement for light and air would automatically be created. Bell could have requested and could have been granted an easement for light, air, or view, but there is no evidence that he did so.

Answer to Question 18

(A) A life tenant is obligated to pay interest on any encumbrances to the extent of the income or profits from the land. He does not, however, have to pay anything on the principal. The remainderman, here Rowan, must pay off the principal in order to protect her own interests. (B) is wrong because Rowan is only liable for the principal. (C) is wrong because Perez is only liable for the interest payments. (D) is wrong because it reverses the duties of the life tenant and the remainderman.

Answer to Question 19

(C) Anders could have constructed a deed such that she would have retained a property interest in the parcel of land, but she did not do so. Rather, she only created a contractual obligation which was met in the first five years after the conveyance. Because she retained no property interest, she has no claim to the land. (A) is wrong because this could have been a determinable fee only if durational language, such as "for as long as," "while," "during," or "until," had been used in the deed. Because it was not, no possibility of reverter was created in Anders. (B) is wrong because the grantor did not reserve the right to terminate the grantee's estate on the happening of a specified condition subsequent, and thus reserved no right of entry for condition broken. (D) is wrong because it has been stated that Anders has instituted an appropriate action, so it is assumed that she is in the proper court. In any event, the contract or covenant obligation of Burton would probably be enforceable both at law (for damages) and in equity (for an injunction). In most jurisdictions today the same court could order either remedy.

Answer to Question 20

(C) The application of a basic allocation rule is involved here. A life tenant is obligated to pay interest on any encumbrances on the land to the extent of the income or profits from the land (or in their absence to the extent of the reasonable rental value of the land). However, she does not have to pay anything on the principal of the debt: reversioners or remaindermen must pay the principal in order to protect their interests. Thus, (C) is correct because it applies the rule correctly. (A) is incorrect because Dixie must make the portion of the monthly payment allocated to principal. (B) is wrong because the allocation between life tenant and remainderman is a simple allocation between interest and principal and hence the actual value of the life estate and the remainder are not considered. (D) is wrong because Wanda must make the portion of the monthly payment allocated to interest.

Answer to Question 21

(A) Jones was the intended third-party creditor beneficiary of the contract between Sloan and the Abstract Company to prepare and deliver the abstract. Abstract Company is liable because it failed to uncover the existence of the right-of-way deed which was in the chain of title. Jones should recover because he was the intended beneficiary. (B) is wrong because Abstract Company is liable on breach of its contract to describe accurately the state of the record title. It gave no title guarantee. (C) is wrong because, while Abstract Company may have had no actual knowledge of the deed, it had a contractual duty to find any encumbrances in the record chain of title. (D) is wrong because fraud is not necessary for a showing of breach of contract.

Answer to Question 22

(B) Sloan conveyed a deed including covenants of general warranty and against encumbrances. Because an encumbrance exists in the form of the right-of-way, Sloan is in breach of the covenant against encumbrances. (A) is wrong because Sloan was diligent in his attempt to establish clear title through the Abstract Company. (C) is wrong because it was Sloan and not the Abstract Company which actually made the covenant against encumbrances. (D) is wrong because Sloan covenanted that there were no encumbrances at all. It makes no difference whether he had any actual knowledge of such encumbrances.

Answer to Question 23

(C) Because the remainder is created in a class of persons (*i.e.*, Selden's children) that is certain to take on the termination of the preceding estate, but is subject to diminution by reason of other persons becoming entitled to share in the remainder (*i.e.*, additional children that Selden could sire), the remainder is vested subject to partial defeasance (or divestment). This is also sometimes called a vested remainder subject to open. (A) is wrong because an indefeasibly vested remainder must not be subject to being diminished in size, which could be the case if Selden has more children. (B) is incorrect because the remainder here is not subject to a condition precedent or in favor of unborn or unascertained persons. Hence, it is not contingent. (D) is wrong because a vested remainder subject to complete defeasance arises when the remainderman is in existence and ascertained and his right to possession and enjoyment is subject to being defeated by the happening of some condition subsequent. Under the facts, Selden's children or their heirs under all circumstances will be entitled to a portion of the fee.

Answer to Question 24

(A) A covenant is the best choice because a real covenant, normally found in deeds, is a written promise to do something on the land or a promise not to do something on the land. Real covenants run with the land at law, which means that subsequent owners of the land may enforce or be burdened by the covenant. In cases where the covenant involves a promise to pay money, the majority rule is that if the money is to be used in a way connected with the land, the burden will run with the land. The most common example is a covenant to pay a homeowners' association an annual fee for maintenance of common ways, parks, etc., in a subdivision. Such a situation is analogous to the golf course and country club dues presented in the facts. (B) is incorrect because the holder of an easement has the right to use a tract of land (called the servient tenement) for a special purpose but has no right to possess and use the land. The annual dues requirement does not constitute the right to use another's land for a special purpose. (C) is incorrect because a mortgage is a security interest in real estate (usually to secure a promise to repay a loan represented by a promissory note). The payment of dues does not result in a security interest in the golf course, and is thus inapplicable to the facts. (D) is wrong because a personal contractual obligation by each purchaser does not bind subsequent purchasers, who would, therefore, be under no obligation to pay the annual dues.

Answer to Question 25

(D) (D) is the correct answer by a process of elimination. (A) is incorrect because there is no racial discrimination or other constitutionally questionable activity presented in the facts. (B) is wrong because marketable title is title reasonably free from doubt. Generally, this involves either defects in the chain of title or encumbrances that might present an unreasonable risk of litigation. The dues scheme is not such an encumbrance. (C) is incorrect because the scheme does not impose a direct restraint on alienation of the fee. There are no disabling restraints, forfeiture restraints, or promissory restraints on transferability of property. Thus, by a process of elimination, (D) presents the greatest obstacle to establishing the scheme, even though a majority of courts today allow real covenants that require payment of an annual fee for maintenance of common ways, parks, etc.

Answer to Question 26

(B) If Oaks prevails, it will be because the original installation defined the scope of the easement. The scope of the easement depends on the intent of the parties. In determining the intent of the parties, the courts look at the subsequent conduct of the parties respecting the arrangement as well as the language of the instrument. Here, the instrument states the location is to be mutually agreed upon. Oaks and United agreed to the original pipeline and its location, but have not agreed upon the location of the second set of pipes. The parties' subsequent conduct could also lead to the conclusion that the first installation was the full extent of what the parties intended. (A) is incorrect because the Rule Against Perpetuities has absolutely no application to these facts. The easement was vested when it was created, and easements are presumed to be perpetual. (C) is incorrect because Oaks will be deemed to have acquiesced in the location of the original easement. (D) is wrong because inverse condemnation is the term for a landowner's lawsuit for damages to recover for a governmental taking without exercising its formal power of eminent domain (e.g., regulatory takings that deprive the owner of all economically viable uses of the property). Even if United were a government agency and this were a regulatory taking, inverse condemnation would not be correct since Oaks is seeking an injunction, not compensation.

Answer to Question 27

(A) A remainder is a future interest created in a transferee that is capable of becoming a present interest upon the natural termination of the preceding estates created in the same disposition. A contingent remainder is a remainder that is subject to a condition precedent, or a remainder that is created in favor of unborn or unascertained persons. Here, Ana Maria's unborn children will take a remainder, because their interest will become a present interest upon the natural termination of the preceding estate (upon Enrique's death). Because this remainder is created in favor of unborn and unascertained persons, it is contingent. A vested remainder subject to divestment arises when the remainderman is in existence and ascertained and his interest is not subject to any condition precedent, but his right to possession is subject to being defeated by some condition subsequent. (B) is incorrect because the remaindermen are neither in existence nor ascertained. A springing use is a form of executory interest (a future interest in a transferee that is not capable of taking on the natural termination of the preceding estate). (C) is incorrect because Ana Maria's children's interest will become a present interest upon the natural termination of the preceding estate. Finally, because (A) is correct, (D) is obviously incorrect.

Answer to Question 28

(D) If Marsh wins, it will be because there was no effective acceptance of delivery of the deed. There must be acceptance by the grantee to complete a conveyance. Although acceptance is presumed, this presumption is rebutted by evidence of rejection. Here, Simon expressly rejected the conveyance, and therefore, title never passed to Simon. (A) is incorrect because a constructive trust presumes that Simon had legal title. As discussed above, title did not pass to Simon. Furthermore, even had title passed, a constructive trust would probably be inappropriate here. Constructive trust is the appropriate remedy for unjust enrichment, and there is no indication of any wrongdoing under these facts. (B) is an incorrect statement of law. If the grantor intends the recording of the deed to be the final act in vesting title in the grantee, such recording creates a presumption of delivery even though the grantee did not know of the recordation. (C) is wrong because there is no such thing as a constructive reconveyance. Had Simon accepted the deed and then changed his mind, he would have had to execute a new deed to reconvey the property back to Marsh.

Answer to Question 29

(A) Cohen's interest purports to be an executory limitation. However, Cohen cannot take the land until such time as the premises are no longer used for residential and farm purposes. This could happen more than 21 years after the death of Bogatz or Cohen, the relevant lives in being. Thus, this interest violates the Rule Against Perpetuities. It follows that (B), (C), and (D) are incorrect. Note also that, regarding (C) and (D), possibilities of reverter and rights of entry for condition broken are future interests left in a *grantor*. Cohen is not a grantor.

Answer to Question 30

(D) The deed, once it has been delivered, is merely evidence of its own existence, and its destruction does not cause any change in the title. Doris therefore continued to own the property. (A) is wrong because a title can be acquired by a quitclaim deed and that is true, even though the grantee has paid no consideration. (B) is wrong because destruction of the deed does not cause title to revert. (C) is wrong because there is no evidence of undue influence, and, in any event, destruction of the deed would cause no change in the status of the title.

Answer to Question 31

(D) The question is somewhat confusing, since there are really two gifts to grandchildren. The first is the vested remainder in the grandchildren that follows Ben's life estate. The second is the executory interest that is given to the other grandchildren if one of the grandchildren purports to mortgage or sell in violation of the condition. This latter gift is void both as a violation of the Rule Against Perpetuities and as an unlawful restraint on alienation. It violates the Rule because by its terms it could purport to vest possession in the "other" grandchildren more than 21 years after the termination of a life in being. However, these objections apply only to the second of the two gifts to the grandchildren. The first gift, that is, the remainder to them, is entirely valid. The language dealing with the restraint on alienation would probably be stricken by the court, leaving the initial gift intact. (D) is the answer that best expresses this result.

Answer to Question 32

(A) The best argument is that Breyer's rights depend on the existence of a public street. (B) is wrong because no issue of the Statute of Frauds is present. There has been no purported conveyance to Breyer of rights in the street by anyone who owns such rights. (C) is wrong because, if a public street exists, Breyer need not assert a way of necessity. (D) is wrong because there is no legal objection to the enrichment that results if persons other than the dedicator are permitted to use a public street.

Answer to Question 33

(D) The dedication argument is Breyer's strongest, although even it is not likely to be successful unless and until the city bodies accept the dedication. (A) is wrong because Breyer does not need a way of necessity, since he has other access to his land. (B) is wrong because the deed from White to Breyer, while referring to the plan, used it only as a boundary reference and did not create any rights to the use of the streets. (C) is wrong because, while the sale of lots by reference to a plan does create private easements in the streets, the easements serve only the lots in the subdivision plan itself and not such land as Whiteacre that is outside the plan.

Answer to Question 34

(D) In a partial condemnation case, the landlord-tenant relationship continues, as does the tenant's obligation to pay the entire rent for the remaining lease term. (A) is wrong because the law of landlord and tenant traditionally refuses to recognize frustration of purpose as a ground for termination of a lease. (B) is wrong because the covenant of quiet enjoyment can be breached only by actions of the landlord and not those of a third party, such as the government. (C) is wrong because, while the tenant generally is obligated to return the premises in the same condition as when received (except for ordinary wear and tear), that obligation would not be considered breached by the actions of a third party such as the government.

Answer to Question 35

(C) Partition and cross-easements is the best approach because the holder of an easement has the right to use a tract of land (called the servient tenement) for a special purpose, but has no right to possess and enjoy the tract of land. Typically, easements are created to give their holder the right of access over a tract of land. An easement is deemed appurtenant when the right of special use benefits the holder in his physical use or enjoyment of another tract of land. For an easement appurtenant to exist, there must be *two tracts* of land. The dominant tenement has the benefit of the easement, and the servient tenement is subject to the easement right. One consequence of appurtenance is that the benefit passes with transfers of the benefited land, regardless of whether the easement is mentioned in the conveyance. Partition is necessary to create the required two tracts of land. (A) is incorrect because a covenant not to partition is personal to the parties and thus subsequent owners will not be bound by the covenant. It is also wrong because under the principles of the Rule Against Restraints on Alienation, the courts will enforce prohibitions against partition by any one co-tenant only if the restriction is to last for a reasonable time. (B) is wrong because, as noted above, easements appurtenant require two tracts of land. As long as the strip remains undivided, a new neighbor, as a tenant-in-common, would have the right to partition the strip and thus terminate the cross-easement. (D) is incorrect because a trust in perpetuity would violate the Rule Against Restraints on Alienation. The effect of the trust would be to create a disabling restraint.

Answer to Question 36

(D) Generally, an existing violation of a zoning ordinance renders title unmarketable. Here, the location of the house in relation to the side line setback exposes Perrine to the threat of litigation, both for violation of the zoning ordinance and for violation of a restriction in the recorded subdivision plot. Regardless of the likelihood that such litigation may be initiated, and of the likelihood that Perrine would ultimately prevail, he cannot be required to "buy a lawsuit." Thus, (D) is the correct answer. It follows that (A) and (B) are incorrect. (C) is incorrect because it fails to address the issue of unmarketability of title through exposure to potential litigation, which forms the basis for Perrine's refusal to consummate the transaction.

TORTS QUESTIONS

Questions 1-2 are based on the following fact situation:

Innes worked as a secretary in an office in a building occupied partly by her employer and partly by Glass, a retail store. The two areas were separated by walls and were in no way connected, except that the air conditioning unit served both areas and there was a common return-air duct.

Glass began remodeling, and its employees did the work, which included affixing a plastic surfacing material to counters. To fasten the plastic to the counters, the employees purchased glue, with the brand name Stick, that was manufactured by Steel, packaged in a sealed container by Steel, and retailed by Paint Company.

In the course of the remodeling job, one of Glass's employees turned on the air conditioning and caused fumes from the glue to travel from Glass through the air conditioning unit and into Innes's office. The employees did not know that there was common ductwork for the air conditioners. Innes was permanently blinded by the fumes from the glue.

The label on the container of glue read, "DANGER. Do not smoke near this product. Extremely flammable. Contains Butanone, Toluol, and Hexane. Use with adequate ventilation. Keep out of the reach of children."

The three chemicals listed on the label are very toxic and harmful to human eyes. Steel had received no reports of eye injuries during the 10 years that the product had been manufactured and sold.

1. If Innes asserts a claim against Paint Company, the most likely result is that she will:

    (A) Recover if she can recover against Steel.

    (B) Recover, because Innes was an invitee of a tenant in the building.

    (C) Not recover, unless Paint Company was negligent.

    (D) Not recover, because the glue came in a sealed package.

2. If Innes asserts a claim against Glass, the most likely result is that she will:

    (A) Recover, because a user of a product is held to the same standard as the manufacturer.

    (B) Recover, because the employees of Glass caused the fumes to enter her area of the building.

    (C) Not recover, because Glass used the glue for its intended purpose.

    (D) Not recover, because the employees of Glass had no reason to know that the fumes could injure Innes.

Questions 3-4 are based on the following fact situation:

When Denton heard that his neighbor, Prout, intended to sell his home to a minority purchaser, Denton told Prout that Prout and his wife and children would meet with "accidents" if he did so. Prout then called the prospective purchaser and told him that he was taking the house off the market.

3. If Prout asserts a claim against Denton for assault, Prout will:

    (A) Recover if Denton intended to place Prout in fear of physical harm.

    (B) Recover, because Denton's conduct was extreme and outrageous.

    (C) Not recover if Denton took no action that threatened immediate physical harm to Prout.

    (D) Not recover, because Prout's action removed any threat of harmful force.

4.   If Prout asserts a claim against Denton for intentional infliction of emotional distress, Prout will:

(A)   Recover if Prout suffered severe emotional distress as a consequence of Denton's conduct.

(B)   Recover, because Denton intended to frighten Prout.

(C)   Not recover, because Denton made no threat of immediate physical harm to Prout or his family.

(D)   Not recover if Prout suffered no physical harm as a consequence of Denton's conduct.

Question 5

Doctor, a licensed physician, resided in her own home. The street in front of the home had a gradual slope. Doctor's garage was on the street level, with a driveway entrance from the street.

At two in the morning, Doctor received an emergency call. She dressed and went to the garage to get her car and found a car parked in front of her driveway. That car was occupied by Parker, who, while intoxicated, had driven to that place and now was in a drunken stupor in the front seat. Unable to rouse Parker, Doctor pushed him into the passenger's side of the front seat and got in on the driver's side. Doctor released the brake and coasted the car down the street, planning to pull into a parking space that was open. When Doctor attempted to stop the car, the brakes failed to work, and the car crashed into the wall of Owner's home, damaging Owner's home and Parker's car and injuring Doctor and Parker. Subsequent examination of the car disclosed that the brake linings were badly worn. A state statute prohibits the operation of a motor vehicle unless the brakes are capable of stopping the vehicle within specified distances at specified speeds. The brakes on Parker's car were incapable of stopping the vehicle within the limits required by the statute. Another state statute makes it a criminal offense to be intoxicated while driving a motor vehicle. The state follows traditional contributory negligence rules.

If Parker asserts a claim against Doctor for his injuries, Parker will probably:

(A)   Recover, because Doctor was negligent as a matter of law.

(B)   Recover, because Doctor had no right to move the car.

(C)   Not recover, because his brakes were defective.

(D)   Not recover, because he was in a drunken stupor when injured.

Question 6

Construction Company contracted to build a laundry for Wash Company on the latter's vacant lot in a residential area. As a part of its work, Construction Company dug a trench from the partially completed laundry to the edge of a public sidewalk; waterlines were to be installed in the trench. Because of the contour of the land, the trench was dug to a depth ranging from seven to nine feet. Construction Company did not place any barriers around the trench and permitted it to lie open for almost a week while waiting for the delivery of water pipes. This was known to Wash Company, but it raised no objection.

During the time the trench was open, a series of heavy rains fell, causing five feet of surface water to gather in the bottom of the trench. While this condition existed, five-year-old Tommy, who was playing on the vacant lot with friends, stumbled and fell into the trench. Robert, an adult passerby, saw this and immediately lowered himself into the trench to rescue Tommy. However, his doing so caused the rain-soaked walls of the trench to collapse, killing both him and Tommy.

In a claim for wrongful death by Tommy's administrator against Construction Company, the most likely result is that plaintiff will:

(A) Recover, because the defendant left the open trench unprotected.

(B) Recover, because construction companies are strictly liable for inherently dangerous conditions.

(C) Not recover, because Tommy was a trespasser.

(D) Not recover, because Tommy's death was a result of the collapse of the trench, an independent intervening cause.

Question 7

Philip was a 10-year-old boy. Macco was a company that sold new and used machinery. Macco stored discarded machinery, pending sale for scrap, on a large vacant area it owned. This area was unfenced and was one-quarter mile from the housing development where Philip lived. Macco knew that children frequently played in this area and on the machinery. Philip's parents had directed him not to play on the machinery because it was dangerous.

One day Philip was playing on a press in Macco's storage area. The press had several wheels, each geared to the other. Philip climbed on the largest wheel, which was about five feet in diameter. Philip's weight caused the wheel to rotate, his foot was caught between two wheels that were set into motion, and he was severely injured.

A claim for relief was asserted by Philip through a duly appointed guardian. Macco denied liability and pleaded Philip's contributory fault as a defense.

In determining whether Macco breached a duty to Philip, which of the following is the most significant?

(A) Whether the press on which Philip was injured was visible from a public way.

(B) Whether the maintenance of the area for the storage of discarded machinery was a private nuisance.

(C) Whether the maintenance of the area of the storage of discarded machinery was a public nuisance.

(D) Whether Macco could have eliminated the risk of harm without unduly interfering with Macco's normal operations.

Question 8

Householder hired Contractor to remodel Householder's kitchen. She had learned of him through a classified advertisement he placed in the local newspaper. During the telephone conversation in which she hired him, he stated he was experienced and qualified to do all necessary work. Because of his low charge for his work, they agreed in writing that on acceptance of his job by Householder, he would have no further liability to her or to anyone else for any defects in materials or workmanship, and that she would bear all such costs.

Householder purchased a dishwasher manufactured by Elex Company from Dealer, who was in the retail electrical appliance business. The washer was sold by Dealer with only the manufacturer's warranty and with no warranty by Dealer; Elex Company restricted its warranty to 90 days on parts and labor. Contractor installed the dishwasher.

Two months after Householder accepted the entire job, she was conversing in her home with Accountant, an acquaintance who had agreed to prepare her income tax return gratuitously. As they talked, they noticed that the dishwasher was operating strangely, repeatedly stopping and starting. At Householder's request, Accountant gave it a cursory examination and, while inspecting it, received a violent electrical shock which did him extensive harm. The dishwasher had an internal wiring defect that allowed electrical current to be carried into the framework and caused the machine to malfunction. The machine had not been adequately grounded by Contractor during installation; if it had been, the current would have been led harmlessly away. The machine carried instructions for correct grounding, which Contractor had not followed.

If Accountant asserts a claim based on strict liability against Elex Company for damages, the probable result is that Accountant will:

(A) Recover, because the dishwasher was defectively made.

(B) Recover, because Elex Company is vicariously liable for the improper installation.

(C) Not recover, because he assumed the risk by inspecting the machine.

(D) Not recover, because he was not the purchaser.

Question 9

Diner, a drive-in hamburger and ice cream stand, recently opened for business in the suburban town of Little City. Diner's business hours are from 9 a.m. to midnight. It is in an area that for 15 years has been zoned for small retail businesses, apartment buildings, and one- and two-family residences. The zoning code specifies that "small retail businesses" include "businesses where food and drink are dispensed for consumption on the premises." Diner was the first drive-in in Little City. For seven years Mr. and Mrs. Householder have owned and lived in their single-family residence, which is across the street from Diner.

On opening day a brass band played in the parking lot of Diner until midnight, and the noise of cars and the usual activity as a result of the new business prevented the Householders from getting to sleep until well after midnight, long after their usual time. Diner is heavily patronized during the day and night by high school students. The noise of cars, the lights of the cars, the lights illuminating the parking lot at Diner, and the noise from the loudspeaker of the ordering system prevented the Householders from sleeping before midnight. Paper cups, napkins, and other items from the drive-in are regularly blown into the Householders's front yard by the prevailing wind. The traffic to and from Diner is so heavy on the street in front of

their house that the Householders are afraid to allow their small children to play in the front yard.

The Householders have asserted a claim against Diner based on private nuisance.

The most likely effect of the fact that the Householders were in the area before Diner is that it:

(A) Requires that the Householders' interest be given priority.

(B) Is irrelevant because of the zoning ordinance.

(C) Is irrelevant because conforming economic uses are given priority.

(D) Is some, but not controlling, evidence.

Questions 10-11 are based on the following fact situation:

In City of State Y, Maple Street is a local public thoroughfare, designated as a one-way street for northbound traffic. Pine Street is a public thoroughfare, designated as a one-way street for eastbound traffic. Maple and Pine Streets intersect at right angles. The intersection is controlled by traffic lights. There are two sets of lights, one at the northeast corner and one at the northwest corner, for traffic on Maple Street. There are two sets of lights, one at the northeast corner and one at the southeast corner, for traffic on Pine Street.

Trucker was making a delivery to a market on the east side of Maple Street, just north of its intersection with Pine Street. There being insufficient space for his truck and enclosed trailer, he parked it with the rear of the trailer extending entirely across the crosswalk on the north side of the intersection. The height of the trailer was such that it entirely obscured the traffic light on the northeast corner from the view of traffic moving east on Pine Street. Unknown to Trucker, the traffic light at the southeast corner was not functioning, because a collision 72 hours earlier had knocked down the pole from which the light was suspended.

Visitor, on his first trip to City, was driving east on Pine Street. Not seeing any traffic light or pole, he entered the intersection at a time when the light was red for eastbound traffic and green for northbound traffic. Driver, proceeding north on Maple Street and seeing the green light, entered the intersection without looking for any cross traffic and struck Visitor's car. Driver received personal injuries, and Visitor's car was damaged severely as a result of the impact.

Statutes of State Y make it a misdemeanor (1) to park a motor vehicle so that any part projects into a crosswalk and (2) to enter an intersection contrary to a traffic signal.

10. If Driver asserts a claim against Trucker and establishes that Trucker was negligent, the likely result is that Trucker's negligence is:

   (A) A legal but not an actual cause of Driver's injuries.

   (B) An actual but not a legal cause of Driver's injuries.

   (C) Both an actual and a legal cause of Driver's injuries.

   (D) Neither an actual nor a legal cause of Driver's injuries.

11. If Driver asserts a claim against City, the theory on which he has the best chance of prevailing is that City:

   (A) Is strictly liable for harm caused by a defective traffic signal.

   (B) Was negligent in not replacing the broken pole within 72 hours.

   (C) Had an absolute duty to maintain installed signals in good operating order.

   (D) Created a dangerous trap by not promptly replacing the broken pole.

Question 12

Henry hated Wanda, his former wife, for divorcing him and marrying John a short time thereafter. About a month after Wanda married John, Henry secretly entered Wanda and John's rented apartment during their absence by using a master key. Henry placed a microphone behind the bookstand in the bedroom of the apartment and drilled a hole in the nearby wall, with the result that the microphone appeared to be connected with wires going into the adjoining apartment. Actually, the microphone was not connected to anything. Henry anticipated that Wanda would discover the microphone in a few days and would be upset by the thought that someone had been listening to her conversations with John in their bedroom.

Shortly thereafter, as he was putting a book on the stand, John noticed the wires behind the bookstand and discovered the hidden microphone. He then called Wanda and showed her the microphone and wires. Wanda fainted and, in falling, struck her head on the bookstand and suffered a mild concussion. The next day John telephoned Henry and accused him of planting the microphone. Henry laughingly admitted it. Because of his concern about Wanda and his anger at Henry, John is emotionally upset and unable to go to work.

If Wanda asserts a claim against Henry based on infliction of mental distress, the fact that John was the person who showed her the microphone will:

(A) Relieve Henry of liability, because John was careless in so doing.

(B) Relieve Henry of liability, because John's conduct was the immediate cause of Wanda's harm.

(C) Not relieve Henry of liability, because Henry's goal was achieved.

(D) Not relieve Henry of liability, because the conduct of a third person is irrelevant in emotional distress cases.

Questions 13-14 are based on the following fact situation:

Peter was rowing a boat on a mountain lake when a storm suddenly arose. Fearful that the boat might sink, Peter rowed to a boat dock on shore and tied the boat to the dock. The shore property and dock were the private property of Owner.

While the boat was tied at the dock, Owner came down and ordered Peter to remove the boat because the action of the waves was causing the boat to rub against a bumper on the dock. When Peter refused, Owner untied the boat and cast it adrift. The boat sank.

Peter was wearing a pair of swimming trunks and nothing else. He had a pair of shoes and a parka in the boat, but they were lost when Owner set it adrift. Peter was staying at a cabin one mile from Owner's property. The only land routes back were a short rocky trail that was dangerous during the storm, and a 15-mile road around the lake. The storm continued with heavy rain and hail, and Peter, having informed Owner of the location of his cabin, asked Owner to take him back there in Owner's car. Owner said, "You got here by yourself and you'll have to get back home yourself." After one hour the storm stopped, and Peter walked home over the trail.

13. A necessary element in determining if Peter is liable for a trespass is whether:

(A) Owner had clearly posted his property with a sign indicating that it was private property.

(B) Peter knew that the property belonged to a private person.

(C) Peter had reasonable grounds to believe the property belonged to a private person.

(D) Peter had reasonable grounds to believe his boat might be swamped and might sink.

14. If Peter asserts a claim against Owner for loss of the boat, the most likely result is that Owner will:

(A) Have no defense under the circumstances.

(B) Prevail, because Peter was a trespasser ab initio.

(C) Prevail, because the boat might have damaged the dock.

(D) Prevail, because Peter became a trespasser when he refused to remove the boat.

Questions 15-16 are based on the following fact situation:

Dave is a six-year-old boy who has a well-deserved reputation for bullying younger and smaller children. His parents have encouraged him to be aggressive and tough. Dave, for no reason, knocked down, kicked, and severely injured Pete, a four-year-old. A claim has been asserted by Pete's parents for their medical and hospital costs and for Pete's injuries.

15. If the claim is asserted against Dave's parents, the most likely result is they will be:

(A) Liable, because parents are strictly liable for the torts of their children.

(B) Liable, because Dave's parents encouraged him to be aggressive and tough.

(C) Not liable, because a child under seven is not liable in tort.

(D) Not liable, because parents cannot be held liable for the tort of a child.

16. If the claim is asserted against Dave, the most likely result is Dave will be:

(A) Liable, because he intentionally harmed Pete.

(B) Liable, because, as a six-year-old, he should have known his conduct was wrongful.

(C) Not liable, because a child under seven is not liable in tort.

(D) Not liable, because he is presumed to be under his parents' control and they have the sole responsibility.

Questions 17-18 are based on the following fact situation:

Mrs. Ritter, a widow, recently purchased a new uncrated electric range for her kitchen from Local Retailer. The range has a wide oven with a large oven door. The crate in which Stove Company, the manufacturer, shipped the range carried a warning label that the stove would tip over with a weight of 25 pounds or more on the oven door. Mrs. Ritter has one child—Brenda, age three. Recently, at about 5:30 p.m., Brenda was playing on the floor of the kitchen while Mrs. Ritter was heating water in a pan on the stove. The telephone rang and Mrs. Ritter went into the living room to answer it. While she was gone Brenda decided to find out what was cooking. She opened the oven door and climbed on it to see what was in the pan. Brenda's weight (25 pounds) on the door caused the stove to tip over forward. Brenda fell to the floor and the hot water spilled over her, burning her

severely. Brenda screamed. Mrs. Ritter ran to the kitchen and immediately gave her first aid treatment for burns. Brenda thereafter received medical treatment.

Brenda's burns were painful. They have now healed and do not bother her, but she has ugly scars on her legs and back. Brenda's claim is asserted on her behalf by the proper party.

17. If Brenda asserts a claim based on strict liability against Local Retailer, she must establish that:

(A) Local Retailer did not inform Mrs. Ritter of the warning on the crate.

(B) The stove was substantially in the same condition at the time it tipped over as when it was purchased from Local Retailer.

(C) Local Retailer made some change in the stove design or had improperly assembled it so that it tipped over more easily.

(D) Local Retailer knew or should have known that the stove was dangerous because of the ease with which it tipped over.

18. If Brenda asserts a claim based on strict liability against Stove Company, she must establish that:

(A) The defendant negligently designed the stove.

(B) Stoves made by other manufacturers do not turn over with a 25-pound weight on the oven door.

(C) The defendant failed to warn the Ritters that the stove would turn over easily.

(D) The stove was defective and unreasonably dangerous to her.

Question 19

Paulsen was eating in a restaurant when he began to choke on a piece of food that had lodged in his throat. Dow, a physician who was sitting at a nearby table, did not wish to become involved and did not render any assistance, although prompt medical attention would have been effective in removing the obstruction from Paulsen's throat. Because of the failure to obtain prompt medical attention, Paulsen suffered severe brain injury from lack of oxygen.

If Paulsen asserts a claim against Dow for his injuries, will Paulsen prevail?

(A) Yes, if the jurisdiction relieves physicians of malpractice liability for emergency first aid.

(B) Yes, if a reasonably prudent person with Dow's experience, training, and knowledge would have assisted Paulsen.

(C) No, because Dow was not responsible for Paulsen's condition.

(D) No, unless Dow knew that Paulsen was substantially certain to sustain serious injury.

Questions 20-21 are based on the following fact situation:

Parents purchased a new mobile home from Seller. The mobile home was manufactured by Mobilco and had a ventilating system designed by Mobilco with both a heating unit and an air conditioner. Mobilco installed a furnace manufactured by Heatco and an air conditioning unit manufactured by Coolco. Each was controlled by an independent thermostat installed by Mobilco. Because of the manner in which Mobilco designed the ventilating system, the first time the ventilating system was operated by Parents, cold air was vented into Parents' bedroom to keep the temperature at 68° F (20° C). The cold air then activated the heater thermostat, and hot air was pumped into the bedroom of Child, the six-month-old child of Parents. The temperature in Child's room

reached more than 170° F (77° C) before Child's mother became aware of the condition and shut the system off manually. As a result, Child suffered permanent physical injury.

Claims have been asserted by Child, through a duly appointed guardian, against Mobilco, Seller, Heatco, and Coolco.

20. If Child's claim against Seller is based on negligence, the minimum proof necessary to establish Seller's liability is that the ventilating system:

(A) Was defective.

(B) Was defective and had not been inspected by Seller.

(C) Was defective and had been inspected by Seller, and the defect was not discovered.

(D) Was defective, and the defect would have been discovered if Seller had exercised reasonable care in inspecting the system.

21. If Child's claims against Mobilco, Heatco, and Coolco are based on strict liability in tort, Child will probably recover against:

(A) Mobilco only, because the ventilating system was defectively designed by Mobilco.

(B) Heatco only, because it was the excessive heat from the furnace that caused Child's injuries.

(C) Mobilco and Heatco only, because the combination of Mobilco's design and Heatco's furnace caused Child's injuries.

(D) Mobilco, Heatco, and Coolco, because the combination of Mobilco's design, Heatco's furnace, and Coolco's air conditioning unit caused Child's injuries.

Question 22

Hank owned a secondhand goods store. He often placed merchandise on the sidewalk, sometimes for short intervals, sometimes from 7 a.m. until 6 p.m. Pedestrians from time to time stopped and gathered to look at the merchandise. Fred had moved into an apartment that was situated immediately above Hank's store; a street-level stairway entrance was located about 20 feet to the east. On several occasions, Fred had complained to Hank about the situation because not only were his view and peace of mind affected, but also his travel on the sidewalk was made more difficult. Fred owned and managed a restaurant two blocks to the west of his apartment and made frequent trips back and forth. There was a back entrance to his apartment through a parking lot; this entrance was about 200 feet farther in walking distance from his restaurant. Once Fred complained to the police, whereupon Hank was arrested under a local ordinance which prohibited the placing of goods or merchandise on public sidewalks and imposed, as its sole sanction, a fine for its violation.

One day, the sidewalk in front of Hank's store was unusually cluttered because he was cleaning and mopping the floor of his shop. Fred and his 15-year-old son, Steve, saw a bus they wished to take, and they raced down the stairs and onto the cluttered sidewalk in front of Hank's store, Fred in the lead. While dodging merchandise and people, Fred fell. Steve tripped over him and suffered a broken arm. Fred also suffered broken bones and was unable to attend to his duties for six weeks.

If, prior to the day of his personal injuries, Fred had asserted a claim based on public nuisance for injunctive relief against Hank for his obstruction of the sidewalk in violation of the ordinance, the defense on which Hank would have most likely prevailed is that:

(A) Fred consented to the obstruction by continuing to rent his apartment.

(B) The violation of the ordinance was not unreasonable.

(C) Remedy of abatement by self-help was adequate.

(D) There was no claim for special damage.

Question 23

The city of Metropolis has an ordinance that makes it an offense, punishable by fine, for the owner of a dog to permit the dog to run unleashed on a public way.

Smythe, a police officer, observed a small dog running loose in the street. As Smythe picked the dog up, Nelson, who was seated in her car lawfully parked at the curb, called out, "Oh, thank you, Officer, for returning Fido." Smythe asked Nelson whether the dog was hers, and when she acknowledged ownership, he asked to see her driver's license. Nelson gave her name and address, but she refused to produce a driver's license. Smythe then told her to produce her driver's license if she did not want to go to jail. Nelson responded by saying, "Isn't this ridiculous?" Smythe took her by the arm and said, "Let's go. You are under arrest."

Nelson cried out that Smythe was hurting her but he refused to release her arm, and she struck him with her free hand. Smythe then dragged Nelson from her car, forced her into his squad car, and took her to the police station.

The incident took place on the street in front of the apartment where Nelson and her aged father, Joplin, lived. Smythe did not know that Joplin had observed what took place from a window in the apartment.

If Nelson's father, Joplin, asserts a claim against Smythe for the intentional infliction of emotional distress, will Joplin prevail?

(A) Yes, if Smythe's acts caused Joplin severe emotional distress.

(B) Yes, if it is found that Smythe's behavior was extreme and outrageous with respect to Nelson.

(C) No, because Smythe did not know that Joplin was watching.

(D) No, because Joplin was not within the zone of physical danger.

Questions 24-25 are based on the following fact situation:

Gasco owns a storage facility where flammable gases are stored in liquefied form under high pressure in large spherical tanks. The facility was constructed for Gasco by Acme Company, a firm that specializes in the construction of such facilities. After the facility had been in use for five years, an explosion in the facility started a large fire that blanketed the surrounding countryside with a high concentration of oily smoke and soot.

Farber owns a large truck farm near the facility. His entire lettuce crop was destroyed by oily deposits left by the smoke.

24. If Farber asserts a claim against Gasco for the loss of his lettuce crop and is unable to show any negligence on the part of Gasco, will Farber prevail?

(A) Yes, because the operation of the storage facility was an abnormally dangerous activity.

(B) Yes, because the intrusion of the smoke onto Farber's farm amounted to a trespass.

(C) No, if the explosion was caused by internal corrosion that reasonable inspection procedures would not have disclosed.

(D) No, if the explosion was caused by negligent construction on Acme's part.

25. If Farber asserts a claim against Acme Company for the loss of his lettuce crop, will Farber prevail?

(A) No, if Acme did not design the storage facility.

(B) No, because Acme was an independent contractor.

(C) Yes, because the operation of the storage facility was an abnormally dangerous activity.

(D) Yes, if the explosion resulted from a defect of which Acme was aware.

Question 26

Siddon worked as a private duty nurse and on occasion worked in Doctors' Hospital. The hospital called Registry, the private duty referral agency through which Siddon usually obtained employment, and asked that in the future she not be assigned to patients in Doctors' Hospital. Registry asked the hospital why it had made the request. Doctors' Hospital sent a letter to Registry giving as the reason for its request that significant amounts of narcotics had disappeared during Siddon's shifts from the nursing stations at which she had worked.

If Siddon asserts a claim based on defamation against Doctors' Hospital, Siddon will:

(A) Recover, because the hospital accused Siddon of improper professional conduct.

(B) Recover if Siddon did not take the narcotics.

(C) Not recover if narcotics disappeared during Siddon's shifts.

(D) Not recover if the hospital reasonably believed that Siddon took the narcotics.

Question 27

When Mary Weld visited Dugan's Alleys to participate in the weekly bowling league competition held there she brought her two-year-old son, Bobby, along and left him in a nursery provided by Dugan for the convenience of his customers. The children in the nursery were normally supervised by three attendants, but at this particular time, as Mary Weld knew, there was only one attendant present to care for about 20 children of assorted ages.

About 30 minutes later, while the attendant was looking the other way, Bobby suddenly started to cry. The attendant found him lying on his back, picked him up, and called his mother. It was later discovered that Bobby had suffered a skull fracture.

If a claim is asserted against Dugan on Bobby's behalf, will Bobby prevail?

(A) Yes, because Dugan owed the child the highest degree of care.

(B) Yes, because a two-year-old is incapable of contributory negligence.

(C) No, unless Dugan or his employees failed to exercise reasonable care to assure Bobby's safety.

(D) No, if Mary Weld assumed the risk by leaving Bobby in the nursery.

Question 28

Dever drove his car into an intersection and collided with a fire engine that had entered the intersection from Dever's right. The accident was caused by negligence on Dever's part. As a result of the accident, the fire engine was delayed in reaching Peters's house, which was entirely consumed by fire. Peters's house was located about 10 blocks from the scene of the accident.

If Peters asserts a claim against Dever, Peters will recover:

(A) That part of his loss that would have been prevented if the collision had not occurred.

(B) The value of his house before the fire.

(C) Nothing if Dever had nothing to do with causing the fire.

(D) Nothing, because Dever's conduct did not create an apparent danger to Peters.

Question 29

Purvis purchased a used car from Daley, a used-car dealer. Knowing them to be false, Daley made the following statements to Purvis prior to the sale:

Statement 1.   This car has never been involved in an accident.

Statement 2.   This car gets 25 miles to the gallon on the open highway.

Statement 3.   This is as smooth-riding a car as you can get.

If Purvis asserts a claim against Daley based on deceit, which of the false statements made by Daley would support Purvis's claim?

(A) Statement 1. only.

(B) Statement 2. only.

(C) Statements 1. and 2. only.

(D) Statements 2. and 3. only.

Question 30

Customer, age 20, went into Store at approximately 6:45 p.m. to look at some suits that were on sale. The clerks were busy, and one of them told him that he should wait on himself. Customer selected three suits from a rack and went into the dressing room to try them on. Signs posted on the walls of the Store state that closing time is 9 p.m.; however, because of a special awards banquet for employees, Store was closed at 7 p.m. on this day. The employees, in a hurry to get to the banquet, did not check the dressing rooms or turn off the lights before leaving. When Customer emerged from the dressing room a few minutes after 7 p.m., he was alone and locked in. Customer tried the front door but it was secured on the outside by a bar and padlock, so he went to the rear door. Customer grabbed the doorknob and vigorously shook the door. It did not open, but the activity set off a mechanism that had been installed because of several recent thefts committed by persons who had hidden in the store until after closing time. The mechanism sprayed a chemical mist in Customer's face, causing him to become temporarily blind. The mechanism also activated an alarm carried by Store's employee, Watchman, who was just coming to work. Watchman unlocked the front door, ran into the store, and grabbed Customer. Customer, who was still unable to see, struck out at this person and hit a metal rack, injuring his hand. Watchman then identified himself, and Customer did the same. After assuring himself that Customer was telling the truth, Watchman allowed him to leave.

If Customer is to prevail on a claim against Store based on battery from the use of the chemical spray, Customer must establish that:

(A) He suffered severe bodily harm.

(B) The spray mist was an offensive or harmful contact.

(C) He suffered severe emotional distress.

(D) His conduct was not a factual cause of the chemical's spraying him.

Question 31

Dock had been the unsuccessful suitor of Mary, who had recently announced her engagement to Paul. Angered by her engagement, Dock sent Mary the following letter: "I hope you know what you are doing. The man you think you love wears women's clothes when at home. A Friend."

The receipt of this letter caused Mary great emotional distress. She hysterically telephoned Paul, read him the letter, and told him that she was breaking their engagement. The contents of the letter were not revealed to others. Paul, who was a young attorney in the state attorney's office, suffered serious humiliation and emotional distress as a result of the broken engagement.

If Paul asserts a claim against Dock based on defamation and it is proved that Dock's statement was true, such proof will be:

(A) A defense by itself.

(B) A defense only if Dock was not actuated by malice.

(C) A defense only if Dock reasonably believed it to be true.

(D) No defense by itself.

Question 32

Auto Company, a corporation, was a small dealer in big new cars and operated a service department. Peter wanted to ask Mike, the service manager, whether Auto Company would check the muffler on his small foreign car. Peter parked on the street near the service department with the intention of entering that part of the building by walking through one of the three large entrances designed for use by automobiles. There was no street entrance to the service department for individuals, and customers as well as company employees often used one of the automobile entrances.

As Peter reached the building, he glanced behind him to be sure no vehicle was approaching that entrance. Seeing none, he walked through the entrance, but immediately he was struck on the back of the head and neck by the large overhead door which was descending. The blow knocked Peter unconscious and caused permanent damage.

Peter did not know how the door was raised and lowered; however, the overhead door was operated by the use of either of two switches in the building. One switch was located in the office of the service manager and the other was located near the door in the service work area for the convenience of the mechanics. On this occasion, no one was in the service work area except three Auto Company mechanics. Mike, who had been in his office, and the three mechanics denied having touched a switch that would have lowered the door. Subsequent investigation showed, however, that the switches were working properly and that all of the mechanisms for moving the door were in good working order.

If Peter asserts a claim based on negligence against Auto Company, Peter probably will:

(A) Recover, because Auto Company is strictly liable under the circumstances.

(B) Recover, because an employee of Auto Company was negligent.

(C) Not recover, because Peter was a licensee.

(D) Not recover, because Peter assumed the risk.

Questions 33-34 are based on the following fact situation:

Si was in the act of siphoning gasoline from Neighbor's car, in Neighbor's garage and without his consent, when the gasoline exploded and a fire followed. Rescuer, seeing the fire, grabbed a fire extinguisher from his car and put out the fire, saving Si's life and Neighbor's car and garage. In doing so, Rescuer was badly burned.

33. If Rescuer asserts a claim against Si for personal injuries, Rescuer will:

(A) Prevail, because he saved Si's life.

(B) Prevail, because Si was at fault in causing the fire.

(C) Not prevail, because Rescuer knowingly assumed the risk.

(D) Not prevail, because Rescuer's action was not a foreseeable consequence of Si's conduct.

34. If Rescuer asserts a claim against Neighbor for personal injuries, Rescuer will:

(A) Prevail, because he saved Neighbor's property.

(B) Prevail, because he acted reasonably in an emergency.

(C) Not prevail, because Neighbor was not at fault.

(D) Not prevail, because Rescuer knowingly assumed the risk.

Question 35

Telco, a local telephone company, negligently allowed one of its telephone poles, located between a street and a sidewalk, to become termite-ridden. Rhodes, who was intoxicated and driving at an excessive rate of speed, lost control of her car and hit the weakened telephone pole. One week later, the pole fell and struck Walker, a pedestrian who was walking on the sidewalk. The pole fell because of the combination of the force of the impact and the pole's termite-ridden condition.

If Walker asserts a claim against Telco and Rhodes, will Walker prevail?

(A) Yes, against Telco but not Rhodes.

(B) Yes, against Rhodes but not Telco.

(C) Yes, against Telco and Rhodes, each for one-half of his damages.

(D) Yes, against both Telco and Rhodes for the full amount of his damages.

Question 36

While on a hiking trip during the late fall, Page arrived toward the end of the day at a clearing where several similar cabins were located, none of which was occupied. One of the cabins belonged to Levin, Page's friend, who had given Page permission to use it. Page entered one of the cabins, which she thought was Levin's, and prepared to spend the night. In fact the cabin was owned, not by Levin, but by Dwyer.

When the night turned cold, Page started a fire in the stove. Unknown to Page, there was a defect in the stove that allowed carbon monoxide fumes to escape into the cabin. During the night the fumes caused serious injury to Page.

If Page asserts a claim against Dwyer for her injury, will Page recover?

(A) Yes, if Dwyer knew that the stove was defective.

(B) Yes, if Dwyer could have discovered the defect in the stove by a reasonable inspection.

(C) No, because Dwyer had no reason to anticipate Page's presence in the cabin.

(D) No, unless Page needed to use the cabin for her own protection.

Question 37

A group of children, ranging in age from 8 to 15, regularly played football on the common area of an apartment complex owned by O'Neill. Most of the children lived in the apartment complex, but some lived elsewhere. O'Neill knew that the children played on the common area and had not objected.

Peter, a 13-year-old who did not live in the apartment complex, fell over a sprinkler head while running for a pass and broke his leg. Although Peter had played football on the common area before, he had never noticed the sprinkler heads, which protruded one inch above the ground and were part of a permanently installed underground sprinkler system.

If a claim is asserted on Peter's behalf, Peter will:

(A) Prevail, if the sprinkler head was a hazard that Peter probably would not discover.

(B) Prevail, because O'Neill had not objected to children playing on the common area.

(C) Not prevail, because Peter did not live in the apartment complex.

(D) Not prevail, unless the sprinkler heads were abnormally dangerous to users of the common area.

Question 38

Chemco designed and built a large tank on its premises for the purpose of storing highly toxic gas. The tank developed a sudden leak and escaping toxic gas drifted into the adjacent premises, where Nyman lived. Nyman inhaled the gas and died as a result.

In a suit brought by Nyman's personal representative against Chemco, which of the following must be established if the claim is to prevail?

I. The toxic gas that escaped from Chemco's premises was the cause of Nyman's death.

II. The tank was built in a defective manner.

III. Chemco was negligent in designing the tank.

(A) I. only.

(B) I. and II. only.

(C) I. and III. only.

(D) I., II., and III.

Question 39

Plummer, a well-known politician, was scheduled to address a large crowd at a political dinner. Just as Plummer was about to sit down at the head table, Devon pushed Plummer's chair to one side. As a result, Plummer fell to the floor. Plummer was embarrassed at being made to look foolish before a large audience but suffered no physical harm.

If Plummer asserts a claim against Devon for damages because of his embarrassment, will Plummer prevail?

(A) Yes, if Devon knew that Plummer was about to sit on the chair.

(B) Yes, if Devon negligently failed to notice that Plummer was about to sit on the chair.

(C) No, because Plummer suffered no physical harm along with his embarrassment.

(D) No, if in moving the chair Devon intended only a good-natured practical joke on Plummer.

Question 40

In 1956, Silo Cement Company constructed a plant for manufacturing ready-mix concrete in Lakeville. At that time Silo was using bagged cement, which caused little or no dust. In 1970, Petrone bought a home approximately 1,800 feet from the Silo plant. One year ago, Silo stopped using bagged cement and began to receive cement in bulk shipments. Since then at least five truckloads of cement have passed Petrone's house daily. Cement blows off the trucks and into Petrone's house. When the cement arrives at the Silo plant, it is blown by forced air from the trucks into the storage bin. As a consequence, cement dust fills the air surrounding the plant to a distance of 2,000 feet. Petrone's house is the only residence within 2,000 feet of the plant.

If Petrone asserts a claim against Silo based on nuisance, will Petrone prevail?

(A) Yes, unless using bagged cement would substantially increase Silo's costs.

(B) Yes, if the cement dust interfered unreasonably with the use and enjoyment of Petrone's property.

(C) No, because Silo is not required to change its industrial methods to accommodate the needs of one individual.

(D) No, if Silo's methods are in conformity with those in general use in the industry.

TORTS ANSWERS

Answer to Question 1

(A)   Because Steel had no notice that the product would cause eye injuries, an action against Steel must be predicated on strict liability, not negligence. The strict duty in such cases extends to any supplier in the distributive chain. Thus, if Steel, the manufacturer of the glue, is liable, then Paint Company, the retailer, may also be subject to liability. Conversely, if there is a determination that Steel did not manufacture an unreasonably dangerous product, then there will be no basis for holding the retailer liable. (B) is incorrect. It addresses Innes's status as a foreseeable victim of the fumes. However, it fails to address the basic issue of liability. Innes could be a foreseeable victim, yet she still must establish the unreasonably dangerous character of the product. (C) is incorrect because negligence is irrelevant to a strict liability action, which Innes can pursue against Paint Company as a commercial supplier. (D) is incorrect because the dangerous character of the glue emanates from its properties during use, not its packaging. The fact that Paint Company had no opportunity to inspect the product is irrelevant to its liability.

Answer to Question 2

(D)   Innes probably cannot recover against Glass. An action against Glass would have to be based on the actions of its employees. Because it was not functioning as a commercial supplier in this case, it cannot be held liable on a strict liability theory. A successful action against it must be based on negligence. The employees had no notice of the dangerous character of the glue, nor were they even aware of the common ductwork. Therefore, a cause of action for negligence will not lie against the employees, and obviously will not lie against Glass. (A) is an incorrect statement of the law. (B) is incorrect. The employees did cause the fumes to enter Innes's area of the building. However, as has been shown, they were unaware of the damage the fumes could cause, or that they were sending fumes into the other area. (C) is incorrect because use of a product for its intended purpose does not negate the possibility of liability. If Glass's employees acted negligently while using the product for its intended purpose, Glass could be held vicariously liable for their actions.

Answer to Question 3

(C)   Prout will not recover if Denton's conduct did not threaten immediate physical harm. A prima facie case for tortious assault requires that the defendant create a reasonable apprehension in the plaintiff of *immediate* harmful or offensive contact to the plaintiff's person. Threats of *future* harm do not give rise to an action for assault. (A) is incorrect because mere intent to place in fear of physical harm is not enough. There must be a creation of reasonable apprehension of immediate harm. (B) is incorrect; extreme and outrageous conduct is an element of intentional infliction of emotional distress, but not of assault. (D) is incorrect because it is irrelevant, and later actions would not vitiate any threat of immediate harm.

Answer to Question 4

(A)   Prout will recover if he suffered severe emotional distress. The tort of intentional infliction of emotional distress requires: (i) an act by defendant amounting to extreme and outrageous conduct; (ii) intent to cause severe emotional distress or recklessness as to the effect of the conduct; (iii) causation; and (iv) damages. If Prout suffered severe emotional distress resulting from Denton's conduct (which was extreme and outrageous and, at the very least, reckless), he can recover from Denton. (B) is incorrect because intent, without more, does not establish intentional infliction of emotional distress. (C) is incorrect because immediate threat of physical harm is an element of assault rather than intentional infliction of emotional distress. (D) is incorrect because, even though actual damages are required to win a case grounded on intentional infliction of emotional distress, physical injuries are not required.

Answer to Question 5

(C) Parker will not prevail because at common law Parker's contributory negligence will completely bar his right to recover. Parker was contributorily negligent because he was operating a car with defective brakes in violation of the statute. (A) is wrong because Parker was not in the class intended to be protected by the statute. It was Parker's obligation to ensure that the brakes complied with the statute. (B) is incorrect because the existence of an emergency, presenting little time for reflection, may be considered as among the circumstances under which the defendant acted (*i.e.*, he must act as the reasonable person would act in the same emergency). Applying this criterion, Doctor was justified in moving the car. (D) is incorrect because a person who is injured while intoxicated does not automatically lose a cause of action against the person causing the injury. In addition, the harm in this case was not the type of harm which the drunk driving statute was designed to prevent.

Answer to Question 6

(A) (A) is correct because leaving the trench uncovered was the proximate cause of Tommy's death. Generally, rescuers are viewed as foreseeable intervening forces, and the original tortfeasor will be liable for their negligence. (B) is wrong as a matter of law. Construction companies are subject to strict liability based on the same criteria applied to other companies and individuals. The activity must be deemed "ultrahazardous" or "abnormally dangerous" to subject the party performing the activity to strict liability. Leaving the trench uncovered was negligent, but it is not ultrahazardous or abnormally dangerous. (C) is wrong because under the attractive nuisance doctrine, the defendant had a duty to exercise ordinary care to avoid reasonably foreseeable harm to children caused by artificial conditions on the property. The fact that children played on the vacant lot made it possible for the defendant to anticipate infant trespassers. The defendant also knew of the dangerous condition, and the expense of covering the trench would be slight in comparison with the magnitude of the risk. (D) is incorrect, because even if the collapse of the trench was unforeseeable, Construction Company's conduct still threatened to cause injury, and most courts find liability where there is a foreseeable result of an unforeseeable cause.

Answer to Question 7

(D) The most significant factor pertains to the burden on Macco to eliminate the danger. Under the attractive nuisance doctrine, most courts impose on a landowner the duty to exercise ordinary care to avoid reasonably foreseeable risks of harm to children caused by artificial conditions on the property. To assess this special duty on the landowner, the plaintiff must show, among other things, that the expense of remedying the situation is slight compared with the magnitude of the risk. Choice (D) most closely reflects that requirement. (A) is incorrect because most jurisdictions no longer require that the child plaintiff be lured onto the property by the dangerous condition. Thus, whether the press was visible from a public way would only be relevant to show that the trespass was foreseeable, and here the facts indicate that the landowner was already aware that children played on the machinery. (B) and (C) are incorrect because the doctrine of attractive nuisance is distinct from nuisance law. The landowner may be liable even if the danger is neither a public nor a private nuisance as to adjoining landowners.

Answer to Question 8

(A) Accountant will recover because the dishwasher was defective. A prima facie products liability action based on strict liability in tort requires: (i) strict duty owed by a commercial supplier; (ii) breach of that duty; (iii) actual and proximate cause; and (iv) damages. Accountant can make such a case because he need not prove that the defendant was at fault in selling or producing a defective product—only that the product in fact is so defective as to be "unreasonably dangerous." The product also must have reached the user without substantial change in the condition in which it is supplied. The fact that the dishwasher had an internal wiring defect causing the machine to malfunction is a sufficient basis to impose strict liability. Any negligence by Contractor as an intermediary does not void the manufacturer's liability. Suppliers must anticipate reasonably foreseeable uses even if they are misuses. (B) is wrong because Contractor was an independent contractor with no relationship to Elex Company that vicarious liability would support. (C) is wrong even though assumption of risk may sometimes be successfully raised in strict liability cases. Here, Accountant did not know of the risk and did not voluntarily assume it. (D) is incorrect because privity is not required to bring a strict liability action. A majority of courts extend protection not only to buyers, but also to members of the buyer's family, guests, friends, and employees of the buyer, as well as foreseeable bystanders.

Answer to Question 9

(D) Absent a valid defense, a defendant may not cause a substantial, unreasonable interference with a neighbor's use or enjoyment of his property. Whether the Householders were there before or after Diner opened does not control the result; plaintiffs' right to the reasonable use or enjoyment of their land is the test. (A) is wrong because the fact that one type of land use was entered into before another is relevant but not conclusive evidence as to reasonableness of use. (B) is wrong because a use permitted under a zoning ordinance may be shown to be unreasonable. (C) is a misstatement of law.

Answer to Question 10

(C) Driver's injuries were actually caused by Trucker since they would not have occurred "but for" Trucker's negligent parking. Trucker was also the legal (proximate) cause of Driver's injuries. It was foreseeable that an eastbound car might proceed into the intersection when the traffic signal was obstructed and possibly collide with another car possessing the right of way—a foreseeable result caused by a foreseeable intervening force. Therefore, (A), (B), and (D) are incorrect.

Answer to Question 11

(B) Nothing in the facts indicates that City was under an absolute duty to maintain its traffic poles. Hence, (A) and (C) are incorrect. (D) states no legal theory for Driver's claim and so is not as good an answer as (B). The best theory for Driver is that City was negligent in not replacing the broken pole within 72 hours.

Answer to Question 12

(C) Henry intended to cause Wanda the severe emotional distress that did, in fact, result from his outrageous conduct. Hence, his conduct satisfies the prima facie case and (C) is the correct response. John's conduct was a foreseeable response to Henry's act and hence did not break the chain of causation leading to the result intended by Henry. Thus, (B) is wrong. (A) is unsupported by the facts, and (D) is a misstatement of law; if the third person's conduct was unforeseeable, it may affect the defendant's liability.

Answer to Question 13

(D) Although Peter intended to go onto Owner's property, his entry was privileged if Peter believed it was necessary to protect himself and/or his boat. Note that this privilege is qualified in that Peter must pay for any damage he caused to Owner's property. (A), (B), and (C) are incorrect because knowledge that the land is privately owned is irrelevant to the privilege of necessity.

Answer to Question 14

(A) The privilege to invade land as a private necessity supersedes the occupant's right to protect the property from invasion; hence, the landowner is liable to the invader for any harm suffered if entry is denied. (C) is wrong because Owner could have recovered for injury to his dock, but had no right to resist Peter's entry. (B) and (D) are incorrect because Peter's entry was privileged.

Answer to Question 15

(B) Parents may be liable for *negligence* for failing to prevent the tortious conduct of their children. Further, if parents know of their child's propensity to harm, they have a duty to exercise due care to control the child's behavior. Here, they did just the opposite. Hence, (D) is wrong. (C) is wrong because children are considered capable of committing torts. (A) is wrong because parents' liability is based on *negligence*.

Answer to Question 16

(A) A child is liable for his intentional torts whether or not he knows of their "wrongfulness." Hence, (B) is incorrect. (C) is wrong because there is no minimum age for capacity to commit torts. Children generally are deemed to have the capacity to form the intent to commit intentional torts. (D) is wrong because parents are not vicariously liable for their children's torts.

Answer to Question 17

(B) Brenda must establish the facts in (B) because to hold the commercial supplier strictly liable for a product defect, the product must be expected to, and must in fact, reach the user or consumer without substantial change in the condition in which it is supplied. (A) is wrong because warnings are only one consideration in determining whether a product is in a "defective condition unreasonably dangerous" as required for strict liability purposes. Strict liability can apply even if the customer is informed of the warnings. (C) is wrong because it goes to an issue of negligence on the retailer's part. It is unnecessary for a retailer to affirmatively contribute to the defectiveness of the product for strict liability to apply. (*See* the analysis of option (B), above.) (D) is incorrect because in a strict liability case it is unnecessary to prove that the defendant was at fault in selling or producing a dangerous product—only that the product is in fact so defective as to be unreasonably dangerous. Thus, plaintiff need not show that Local Retailer was aware or should have been aware of the danger. Options (A), (C), and (D) all deal with fault on Local Retailer's part, and are, therefore, wrong in a strict liability analysis.

Answer to Question 18

(D) Brenda must show that the stove had an unreasonably dangerous defect to establish a breach of duty by the manufacturer. To establish a prima facie case based on strict liability in tort, the plaintiff must prove: (i) strict duty owed by a commercial supplier; (ii) breach of that duty; (iii) actual and proximate cause; and (iv) damages. To establish breach of duty for a strict liability action, the plaintiff need not prove that the defendant was at fault in selling or producing a dangerous product—only that the product in fact is so defective as to be "unreasonably dangerous." (A) is wrong because negligence need not be proven in a strict liability case. (B) is wrong because the availability of safer product alternatives is only one factor to be considered by the courts in determining whether a product is defective. (C) is incorrect because even though the warnings may well have been inadequate because they were placed on the crate rather than on the stove itself, the role of instructions and warnings is but one of many factors the courts will consider in determining the defective nature of a given product.

Answer to Question 19

(C) At issue is Dow's duty to Paulsen. Generally, the law imposes no duty to affirmatively act for the benefit of others. There are exceptions to this rule—*e.g.*, one who places another in a position of peril must use reasonable care to aid that person; one who gratuitously acts for the benefit of another thereby assumes a duty to act like an ordinary reasonable person. None of the exceptions is applicable to the case at bar. Therefore, (B) and (D) are clearly incorrect. The "Good Samaritan" statute, described in (A), generally exempts from liability medical personnel who voluntarily and gratuitously render emergency treatment. However, it does not *require* them to provide such treatment. Thus, (A) is incorrect.

Answer to Question 20

(D) Under a negligence analysis, the defendant's conduct must fall below the standard of care expected of a reasonable person under like circumstances. In the instant case, Seller had a duty, at the time of transfer of possession of the home to Parents, to disclose concealed, unreasonably dangerous conditions, of which he knew or had reason to know, and of which he knew Parents were ignorant and not likely to discover on reasonable inspection. Thus, if Seller did not know of a defect in the ventilating system, and could not have discovered the defect through reasonable care, a cause of action for negligence would not lie. (B) and (C) imply that Seller would be liable in negligence merely for failure to inspect or for failure to discover the defect upon inspection. However, there must also be a showing that a reasonable inspection would have disclosed the defect. Consequently, (B) and (C) are incorrect. (A) is more appropriate to a strict liability case, since it does not even mention the necessity for knowledge or discovery of the defect. Therefore, it is an incorrect alternative.

Answer to Question 21

(A) The issue is causation. But for Mobilco's defective design of the ventilating system, the injury to Child would not have occurred. Since Child can trace the injury to a defect in the ventilating system that existed when it left Mobilco's control, cause in fact is established. The same concepts of proximate cause which govern negligence actions are applicable to strict liability actions for defective products. Child's injury is the direct result of Mobilco's defective design, which is the cause in fact of the injury. Thus, proximate cause is established. Heatco's furnace and Coolco's air conditioning unit contained no defects and did not cause injury to Child. As the facts make clear, both units were controlled by a thermostat independent of the units themselves. Thus, (B), (C), and (D) are incorrect.

Answer to Question 22

(D) Hank would prevail in the absence of a claim for special damage. Public nuisance is an act that unreasonably interferes with the health, safety, or property rights of the *community*. Recovery is available for public nuisance only if a private party has suffered some unique damage not suffered by the public at large. Thus, without a claim of special damage by Fred, Hank would be able to defend against Fred's public nuisance suit. (A) is wrong because it is a form of the largely discredited "coming to the nuisance" defense. Fred is entitled to the reasonable use and enjoyment of his leasehold. Remaining in the apartment does not constitute "consent." (B) is incorrect because the ordinance is enforceable against Hank even if his violation is "reasonable." This option is a "distractor," designed to lure you into wrongfully applying the "unreasonable interference" test from *private* nuisance cases. (C) is incorrect because only one who has suffered some unique damage has a privilege to abate a public nuisance by self-help. In the absence of such unique damage, a public nuisance may be abated or enjoined only by public authority.

Answer to Question 23

(C)   Where the defendant intentionally causes severe physical harm to one person, and another person suffers severe emotional distress because of that person's relationship to the injured party, problems of intent and causation arise. To sustain a claim for intentional infliction of emotional distress under such circumstances, the plaintiff generally must show: (i) he was present when the injury occurred to the other person; (ii) he is a close relation of the injured person; and (iii) the defendant knew that the plaintiff was present and a close relation to the injured person. In the case at bar, we do not know that Nelson suffered severe physical harm. However, we do know that Smythe was unaware that Joplin observed the incident. (A) and (B) are incorrect, because they ignore the issue of whether Smythe knew that Joplin was watching. (D) is incorrect, because the term "zone of physical danger" is more appropriate to an action for *negligent* infliction of emotional distress.

Answer to Question 24

(A)   An activity may be characterized as ultrahazardous if it (i) involves a substantial risk of serious harm to person or property; (ii) cannot be performed without risk of serious harm no matter how much care is taken; and (iii) is not a commonly engaged-in activity in the particular community. In such cases, the duty owed is an absolute duty to make safe the ultrahazardous condition. Liability will be imposed for any injuries to persons or property resulting from the condition. Pursuant to the foregoing criteria, Gasco's operation of the storage facility constitutes an abnormally dangerous activity, subjecting Gasco to liability for damage caused by the explosion, regardless of any negligence on the part of Gasco. Thus, (C) is incorrect. (D) is incorrect because any negligence on the part of Acme will not absolve Gasco of liability for maintenance of an ultrahazardous condition. (B) is incorrect because where, as here, no physical object enters the plaintiff's land, a court will generally treat the matter as a nuisance case or one involving strict liability if ultrahazardous activity is involved, rather than as a trespass case.

Answer to Question 25

(D)   Acme, as the manufacturer of the facility, owed a duty of due care to any foreseeable plaintiff. Farber, whose farm is located near the facility, is a foreseeable plaintiff. Therefore, if the explosion resulted from a defect of which Acme was aware, Acme would be liable to Farber for the resultant loss of his lettuce crop. (B) is incorrect because Acme's status as an independent contractor relative to Gasco has no bearing on the duty owed by Acme to Farber. (A) is incorrect because Acme will be liable for manufacturing the facility with knowledge of a defect, regardless of the identity of the facility's designer. (C) is incorrect because Acme was the *manufacturer*, rather than the *operator*, of the facility.

Answer to Question 26

(D)   In a defamation action, a defendant may assert a claim of qualified privilege for statements made in the interest of the publisher of the statement, the recipient of the statement, or both. The privilege will be lost only if the statement is not within the scope of the privilege or if it was made with malice (*i.e.*, knowledge of falsity or reckless disregard of truth or falsity). In this case, Hospital's response to Registry on a matter of common interest was within the scope of the privilege. Thus, (D) is correct because Hospital's reasonable belief would negate any malice on its part. (A) is incorrect, because the accusation alone does not establish defamation when a claim of qualified privilege is raised. (B) is incorrect, because the falsity of the statement does not dispose of the question of qualified privilege. (C) is incorrect, because the disappearance of the narcotics does not, by itself, establish a reasonable belief on the part of the hospital that Siddon was responsible for the disappearance.

Answer to Question 27

(C) (A) is incorrect because Dugan owed the child the duty to act as an ordinary, prudent, reasonable person—not the "highest degree of care." (B) is incorrect because, even if a two-year-old were incapable of contributory negligence, the plaintiff could prevail only if the defendant or his employees were negligent—*i.e.*, failed to exercise reasonable care to ensure the plaintiff's safety. Because (C) reflects this principle, it is the correct answer. (D) is incorrect because, even if Mary assumed the risk, the mother's assumption of risk will not be imputed to the plaintiff-child.

Answer to Question 28

(A) In negligently causing the collision with the fire engine, it was foreseeable that Dever's actions could cause injury to someone else (*e.g.*, a local resident who the fire engine would be unable to reach because of the accident). Peters, whose house was located only 10 blocks from the scene of the accident, falls within the foreseeable zone of danger. It follows that (D) is incorrect. (C) is incorrect because, even if Dever was not involved in causing the fire, his negligence caused the delay in the arrival of the fire engine. In turn, this delay may well have caused all or part of the damage suffered by Peters. (B) is incorrect because it assumes, without a factual basis, that Dever's negligence caused the entire loss. (A) is correct because it recognizes that Dever breached a duty of due care owed to Peters, and that Dever will be liable for that part of Peters's damages that was actually and proximately caused by Dever's breach of duty.

Answer to Question 29

(C) A cause of action for deceit requires: (i) a false representation of a material past or present fact; (ii) scienter; (iii) intent to induce reliance; (iv) causation; (v) justifiable reliance; and (vi) damages. Generally, reliance upon false statements of opinion, value, or quality is unjustified. Here, Daley's statements regarding the car's not having been involved in an accident and the gasoline mileage constitute knowingly false representations of material fact that will form the basis of a cause of action for deceit. Thus, statements 1. and 2. are correct. Statement 3., regarding the smooth ride of the car, is an opinion, upon which Purvis would not be justified in relying. Consequently, statement 3. would not support Purvis's claim for deceit. Therefore, (C) is correct, and (A), (B), and (D) are wrong.

Answer to Question 30

(B) In order to establish a prima facie case for battery, Customer must show (i) an act by the defendant Store that brings about harmful or offensive contact to Customer's person, (ii) intent by Store to bring about such contact, and (iii) causation. (B) is correct since this is one of the elements necessary to establish a battery. (A) is wrong because there need not be severe bodily harm for a battery to occur. The contact may be merely offensive without causing any bodily injury.

(C) is wrong because there need not be any emotional distress for a battery to occur. (D) is wrong because Customer's conduct of vigorously shaking the door was indeed the factual cause of the spray. However, there was causation on the Store's part in the sense of the Store having set in motion a force that would bring about a harmful or offensive contact to Customer's person where there was any attempt to open the door.

Answer to Question 31

(A) Truth is an absolute defense to a claim of defamation. (B) is wrong because it is irrelevant whether Dock made the statement out of malice as long as the statement was in fact true. (C) is wrong because it is equally irrelevant whether Dock reasonably believed the statement to be true. The fact that the statement is true is the only requirement for the defense to prevail. (D) is wrong for the reason that (A) is correct. Note that Paul's claim is based on defamation. Even though Dock can defend the defamation action by showing that the statement is true, Paul might nonetheless be able to successfully assert a cause of action based on intentional infliction of emotional distress.

Answer to Question 32

(B) (B) is correct because res ipsa loquitur applies. When the facts are such as to strongly indicate that the plaintiff's injuries resulted from the defendant's negligence, the trier of fact may be permitted to infer the defendant's liability. The circumstantial evidence doctrine of res ipsa loquitur requires the plaintiff to show: (i) the accident causing his injury is of the type that would not normally occur unless someone was negligent; (ii) the negligence was attributable to the defendant; and (iii) the plaintiff was free from negligence. All of these elements are satisfied from the facts of this case. Because the switches and the doors were found to be in good working order, the injury can reasonably be inferred to be attributable to one of Auto Company's employees, because they had access to the switches. (A) is wrong because strict liability applies to ultrahazardous or abnormally dangerous activities that cannot be performed without risk of serious harm no matter how much care is taken. The operation of the door cannot be characterized as ultrahazardous or abnormally dangerous. (C) is incorrect because the owner has a duty to exercise reasonable care in the conduct of "active operations" (such as opening and closing the door) for the protection of licensees known to be on the property. (D) is incorrect because to have assumed the risk, the plaintiff must have known of the risk and voluntarily assumed it. Peter had no reason to know of any risk involving the overhead door and consequently could not assume it.

Answer to Question 33

(B) It is foreseeable that where a defendant's wrongful conduct places him in a position of peril, a rescuer may suffer injuries while reasonably attempting to aid him, *i.e.,* "danger invites rescue." Hence, (B) is correct and (D) is incorrect. (C) is wrong because a rescue is not a "voluntary" assumption of the risk. (A) is not a reason for imposing liability.

Answer to Question 34

(C) Since Neighbor's conduct did not endanger Si, Neighbor owed no duty to Si or his rescuer. Generally, there is no duty owed to an undiscovered trespasser such as Si, whose conduct was unforeseeable. (A) and (B) are wrong because the facts that Rescuer acted reasonably or saved Neighbor's property are irrelevant to the issue of Neighbor's duty. (D) is wrong because an act of rescue is not an assumption of the risk.

Answer to Question 35

(D) Telco and Rhodes are liable for the full amount as joint tortfeasors. In cases where there are joint tortfeasors and the injury suffered is not divisible, each tortfeasor will be jointly and severally liable for that injury. The rule of joint and several liability applies even where (as in the case described by the facts) each defendant acted entirely independently. Both defendants were negligent and contributed to the injuries suffered by the plaintiff when the pole fell. (A) is incorrect because Telco's prior negligence has no effect on Rhodes's liability. Her conduct was the direct cause of the foreseeable harmful result of the pole falling; the fact that it did not happen immediately is irrelevant. (B) is incorrect because Rhodes's reckless driving was not a superseding intervening force that would cut off Telco's liability for its original negligence. Because of Telco's negligence, it was foreseeable that the pole would fall. The fact that it was caused by another's reckless conduct, whether foreseeable or unforeseeable, does not cut off Telco's liability. (C) is incorrect because there is no basis to divide the plaintiff's injuries as 50% caused by Telco and 50% caused by Rhodes.

Answer to Question 36

(C) Page will not recover because she was an unforeseeable plaintiff to whom Dwyer owed no duty. A duty of care is owed only to foreseeable plaintiffs. A trespasser is not a foreseeable plaintiff unless the landowner has discovered her presence or should reasonably know of trespassers who constantly cross over a section of his land. Neither of these situations is indicated by the facts. Thus, Page was an undiscovered trespasser to whom no duty is owed. Dwyer was under no obligation to inspect his premises to determine if trespassers were entering his cabin. (A) is incorrect. Because Dwyer owed no duty to Page, it is irrelevant whether Dwyer knew that the stove was defective. (B) is incorrect for the same reason. Dwyer had no duty to inspect the appliances in his cabin to make it safe for undiscovered trespassers. (D) is incorrect because it mitigates Page's liability for trespass but has no effect on Dwyer's duty to Page.

Answer to Question 37

(A) Most courts impose upon a landowner the duty to exercise ordinary care to avoid reasonably foreseeable risk of harm to children caused by artificial conditions on his property. Under the general rule, the plaintiff must show: (i) that there is a dangerous condition present on the land that the owner is (or should be) aware of; (ii) that the owner knows or should know that young persons frequent the vicinity of this dangerous condition; (iii) that the condition is likely to cause injury because of the child's inability to appreciate the risk; and (iv) that the expense of remedying the situation is slight compared to the magnitude of the risk. If the sprinkler head was a hazard that Peter would probably not discover, it would meet the requirements for a showing of attractive nuisance, and O'Neill would be liable. (B) is incorrect because O'Neill would continue to be responsible even if he had objected to the children playing on the common area. (C) is incorrect because it is of no consequence where Peter lived. (D) is incorrect because there is a higher standard of care where attractive nuisances to children are concerned.

Answer to Question 38

(A) The only proposition that must be established is that the gas caused Nyman's death. The storage of highly toxic gas is an activity for which strict liability is imposed. Proposition I. relates to an element required in a strict liability case, while propositions II. and III. relate to additional matters that might be necessary to prove if negligence were the issue. In strict liability the plaintiff need only prove: (i) the existence of an absolute duty on the part of the defendant to make safe; (ii) breach of that duty; (iii) that such breach was the actual and proximate cause of the plaintiff's injury; and (iv) damages. Ultrahazardous or abnormally dangerous activities fall into the strict liability category because they: (i) involve risk of serious harm to persons or property; (ii) cannot be performed without risk of serious harm no matter how much care is taken; and (iii) are not commonly engaged-in activities in the community. The storage of toxic gas is such an ultrahazardous activity. Nyman's personal representative need only prove that the escaping toxic gas was the cause of Nyman's death. It follows that (B), (C), and (D) are incorrect because they state propositions that need not be proved for the plaintiff to recover in a strict liability case.

Answer to Question 39

(A) Devon's knowledge that Plummer was about to sit on the chair makes his action a battery. A prima facie case for battery requires an act by defendant that brings about harmful or offensive contact to plaintiff, intent on the part of defendant to do the act, and causation. Here, Devon's act in pulling out Plummer's chair brought about offensive contact to Plummer. The causation element is satisfied not only by direct contact but also by indirect contact. Here, since Devon set in motion the events that brought about the offensive contact, causation exists. The intent element is satisfied if defendant knew with substantial certainty the consequences of his act. Here, if Devon knew that Plummer was about to sit on the chair, he also knew with substantial certainty that Plummer would fall if the chair were moved. Thus, Plummer will prevail on a battery cause of action. (B) is incorrect because Devon's negligence would not suffice for battery, and the only alternative cause of action based on negligence is negligent infliction of emotional distress, which requires that defendant's negligent conduct cause some physical injury to plaintiff. Here, Plummer suffered no physical harm. (C) is incorrect because the prima facie case for battery does not require physical harm to be shown. Even if Plummer cannot prove any actual damages, he will be entitled to a judgment for nominal damages. (D) is incorrect because it merely states Devon's motive for moving the chair. Regardless of the fact that Devon did not have an evil motive or intend to cause injury, he knew with substantial certainty that his conduct would cause an offensive contact to Plummer; this satisfies the intent requirement for battery.

Answer to Question 40

(B) Petrone will prevail if the cement dust constituted an unreasonable interference. For a private nuisance to be actionable, defendant's conduct must amount to a substantial, unreasonable interference with plaintiff's use and enjoyment of property. The operative language in the choice is "interfered unreasonably," and in most MBE nuisance questions such language usually can be found in the correct choice. (A) is incorrect because, even though a balancing test is sometimes used in nuisance cases, mere increased costs is not a sufficient justification to allow continued unreasonable interference with plaintiff's rights. (C) is incorrect because the number of individuals affected is not determinative of whether a nuisance exists. (D) is similarly incorrect; conformity to general methods in the industry will not preclude Silo from being liable for nuisance.

barbri®

BAR REVIEW

Practice Questions by Subject and Analytical Answers

CONSTITUTIONAL LAW
ANSWER SHEET

1. Ⓐ Ⓑ Ⓒ Ⓓ
2. Ⓐ Ⓑ Ⓒ Ⓓ
3. Ⓐ Ⓑ Ⓒ Ⓓ
4. Ⓐ Ⓑ Ⓒ Ⓓ
5. Ⓐ Ⓑ Ⓒ Ⓓ

19. Ⓐ Ⓑ Ⓒ Ⓓ
20. Ⓐ Ⓑ Ⓒ Ⓓ
21. Ⓐ Ⓑ Ⓒ Ⓓ
22. Ⓐ Ⓑ Ⓒ Ⓓ
23. Ⓐ Ⓑ Ⓒ Ⓓ

6. Ⓐ Ⓑ Ⓒ Ⓓ
7. Ⓐ Ⓑ Ⓒ Ⓓ
8. Ⓐ Ⓑ Ⓒ Ⓓ
9. Ⓐ Ⓑ Ⓒ Ⓓ
10. Ⓐ Ⓑ Ⓒ Ⓓ

24. Ⓐ Ⓑ Ⓒ Ⓓ
25. Ⓐ Ⓑ Ⓒ Ⓓ
26. Ⓐ Ⓑ Ⓒ Ⓓ
27. Ⓐ Ⓑ Ⓒ Ⓓ
28. Ⓐ Ⓑ Ⓒ Ⓓ

11. Ⓐ Ⓑ Ⓒ Ⓓ
12. Ⓐ Ⓑ Ⓒ Ⓓ
13. Ⓐ Ⓑ Ⓒ Ⓓ
14. Ⓐ Ⓑ Ⓒ Ⓓ
15. Ⓐ Ⓑ Ⓒ Ⓓ

29. Ⓐ Ⓑ Ⓒ Ⓓ
30. Ⓐ Ⓑ Ⓒ Ⓓ
31. Ⓐ Ⓑ Ⓒ Ⓓ
32. Ⓐ Ⓑ Ⓒ Ⓓ
33. Ⓐ Ⓑ Ⓒ Ⓓ

16. Ⓐ Ⓑ Ⓒ Ⓓ
17. Ⓐ Ⓑ Ⓒ Ⓓ
18. Ⓐ Ⓑ Ⓒ Ⓓ

34. Ⓐ Ⓑ Ⓒ Ⓓ
35. Ⓐ Ⓑ Ⓒ Ⓓ

CONSTITUTIONAL LAW QUESTIONS

Question 1

The state of Ohio enacted legislation providing for a program of testing the skills of all high school students to perform tasks considered necessary to effective functioning in the adult world, such as following instructions on a form, balancing a checkbook, preparing a shopping list, and similar items. The test was given annually to all public school students by government employees on campus, and both religious and secular private schools were reimbursed for the costs of administering the tests and reporting the results to the state using their own personnel. The state office of education regularly audited the reimbursement program to make sure that the private schools were paid for no more than the reasonable costs, in terms of what government employees would be paid for similar services, of giving the test and recording and reporting the results.

Citizens for Religious Freedom filed suit seeking to enjoin the reimbursement to the religious schools, claiming that the legislation violates the Establishment Clause of the First Amendment to the United States Constitution.

The trial court should:

(A) Grant the injunction, because direct state payment to religious schools violates the Establishment Clause.

(B) Grant the injunction, because the state may not require the religious schools to conduct tests that violate their religious principles.

(C) Deny the injunction, because the legislation has a secular purpose which neither advances nor inhibits religion and which will not entangle the state in religion.

(D) Deny the injunction, because the tests do not involve matters of religion.

Question 2

Davis City decided that it wanted to limit to the extent possible the proliferation of unsightly commercial advertising, and so it amended its zoning ordinance so that billboards were permitted only within 100 yards of the interstate highway that passed through town, and on no other streets within the city limits. A year after the amended zoning ordinance took effect, the state converted the old two-lane road connecting the nearby town of Woodland to the interstate into a divided, four-lane freeway. The new freeway intersected the interstate within the city limits of Davis City and remained therein for about five miles of its northward course to Woodland. Design Concepts, a firm whose business includes renting billboard space to advertising agencies, has contracted with the landowners adjacent to the new freeway and obtained permission to erect 10 billboards, all of which would be within the city limits. You are an attorney consulted by Design Concepts about the likelihood of success of an action to challenge the constitutionality of the Davis City zoning ordinance.

You should advise your client that a court would most likely rule that the zoning ordinance is:

(A) Unconstitutional, because it is "spot zoning."

(B) Unconstitutional, because it restricts freedom of expression.

(C) Valid, because commercial speech is not entitled to protection by the First Amendment.

(D) Valid, because freedom of expression is subject to reasonable time, place, and manner restrictions.

Questions 3-4 are based on the following fact situation:

When the President was unable to convince the Federal Reserve to lower the interest rate it charged financial institutions for money, so that the prime rate would drop and stimulate the national economy, he succeeded in having Congress pass a federal usury law, which proscribed loans at interest higher than 10% per annum or 2% above the rate set by the Federal Reserve, whichever was higher at the time the loan was made. The Conference Committee report on the usury statute stated that it was an emergency measure designed to alleviate the destructive effect of high interest rates on businesses of all sizes throughout the United States.

The Commercial Bank of West Rabbit's Foot, Texas, a statewide bank with several billion dollars in assets, operates primarily as a factor for wholesalers and retailers in Texas, lending money to cover inventory which is repaid when the inventory is sold. It is currently charging its customers between 14% and 15% interest per annum, and the rate charged by the Federal Reserve is 8%. Commercial Bank determines that if it is forced to loan money at 10%, its profits will be reduced by 80%. The Texas usury statute prohibits loans made for more than 7% over the rate charged by the Federal Reserve.

3. If Commercial Bank attempts to challenge the federal usury statute on the grounds that it is not within the enumerated powers of the federal government, it will most likely:

    (A) Win, because the federal government may not regulate the interest charged by private lenders who do not lend in interstate markets.

    (B) Lose, because the commerce power permits Congress to regulate commerce in money, and Commercial Bank's activities have a substantial effect on that commerce.

    (C) Lose, because the general welfare power permits Congress to aid the national economy, and any measure which in the opinion of Congress will aid that economy is necessary and proper.

    (D) Win, because interest rates are a particularly local problem not amenable to treatment on a national level.

4. If the state of Texas seeks to enjoin enforcement of the federal usury statute within its boundaries on the grounds that no financial institution in the state can make an adequate profit at a 10% or lower interest rate, and that all lending will cease, the federal court should rule that:

    (A) The issue should be certified to the court of appeals immediately because of the importance of the issue.

    (B) The issue is a peculiarly local one that is better addressed on a state level, and should enjoin enforcement of the federal law.

    (C) The federal statute preempts the state usury law, and the latter is invalid pursuant to the Supremacy Clause.

    (D) It has no jurisdiction to hear the case, since a state is a party and original jurisdiction lies with the United States Supreme Court.

Questions 5-6 are based on the following fact situation:

Roger was hired as a registered nurse by Watsonville Community Hospital and given an information booklet explaining that during the first nine months of employment he would be on probationary status and could be dismissed for any reason and without an explanation. After six months, Roger was notified by hospital administrators that he was dismissed. If he had been employed for over nine months, hospital regulations required that he could be dismissed only for cause and after notice and a hearing.

5. Which of the following, if true, most strongly supports Roger's dismissal without notice or hearing?

    (A) He could be replaced with a more competent nurse.

    (B) His performance as a nurse had been unsatisfactory.

(C) He had not been employed for at least nine months.

(D) He had violated hospital regulations by talking with a newspaper reporter about the hospital's policy of allowing registered nurses to dispense medication without doctor authorization.

6. Which of the following, if true, most strongly supports Roger's argument that he should have been afforded notice and a hearing before dismissal?

(A) He was the only newly hired nurse not to have survived the probationary period for the past three years.

(B) There is no evidence that nurses with permanent status are any more competent than Roger.

(C) He moved his household from out of state to Watsonville in reliance upon an oral promise by the hospital chief administrator that the job would be permanent and that he could be dismissed only for cause.

(D) He purchased a home with a large mortgage in Watsonville in the expectation that he would become a permanent employee of the hospital.

Question 7

Pursuant to statute, the department of education of the state of North Washabama provides model lesson plans complete with sample examinations, suggested class activities, and additional reading lists for any subject taught in the elementary schools of North Washabama to any school or school district in the state requesting such plans.

The Tenfold Path is a Zen-Baptist school whose curriculum is more than 50% religious matters. The Path applied for and received model lesson plans for the nonreligious subjects taught in its classrooms.

Which of the following is the best argument supporting the constitutionality of the state of North Washabama's statutory policy of providing model lesson plans to The Tenfold Path?

(A) The teaching of religious matters in private schools is not constitutionally prohibited.

(B) The purpose and effect of the lesson plan program is secular and does not entangle government and religion.

(C) Private religious schools fulfill an important educational function.

(D) The state's refusal to provide lesson plans to private religious schools would violate the Free Exercise Clause of the First Amendment by discriminating against their students in favor of students in secular private and public schools.

Question 8

To combat the problem of obesity among the nation's youth, Red, a state located in the northeastern part of the United States, adopted a statute providing funds to train a corps of nutritionists who could go to schools and run six-week seminars designed to encourage healthy eating and exercise habits. The Jefferson Davis Academy is a private school that has a stated policy of admitting only white students. Its administration has requested that a state nutrition corps member be sent to the school to run a six-week seminar.

Which of the following is the best constitutional argument supporting the state's rejection of the Jefferson Davis Academy request?

(A) The Constitution prohibits private discrimination.

(B) The state may not aid private schools.

(C) Segregation would be furthered by the provision of the seminar.

(D) No legitimate educational function is served by giving nutrition seminars at private schools.

Question 9

After the collapse of a large energy corporation, a congressional committee was formed to look into possible violations of federal law and investigate ways in which future similar collapses could be avoided. During the investigation, the committee subpoenaed Mr. Powers to appear before the committee and answer certain questions. Mr. Powers appeared before the committee but refused to answer any questions. The committee notified the Speaker of the House of Mr. Powers's refusal to cooperate. The Speaker called a special session of the House. At the special session, a majority of the members of the House voted to order the Attorney General of the United States to prosecute Mr. Powers pursuant to a federal statute that establishes the penalties for contempt of Congress.

Is the Attorney General constitutionally obligated to prosecute Mr. Powers pursuant to the congressional order?

(A) No, if Mr. Powers is an appointive official of the executive branch, because he would then be immune from prosecution for acts performed in the course of his duties.

(B) No, because the decision to prosecute is exclusively within the discretion of the executive branch.

(C) Yes, because the Attorney General may not lawfully disobey a directive from Congress to punish a contempt.

(D) Yes, because the Attorney General may not refuse to prosecute one who has violated federal law.

Questions 10-12 are based on the following fact situation:

The legislature of Mississippi recently enacted statutes regulating the auto repair business. Numerous problems had arisen with unprincipled auto repair operations that were opened in the state by nonresidents who would leave the state to avoid civil liability for their fraud. The new legislation provided, among other things, that all auto mechanics or auto repair business owners must be licensed by the state department of consumer affairs, and it also established licensing standards. Licensees must be residents of Mississippi, defined as any United States citizen whose domicile has been that state for one year prior to the application for a license. Any applicant for an auto repair business license must demonstrate financial responsibility by purchasing business failure insurance from an insurance company whose principal place of business is in Mississippi. To become a licensed auto mechanic, the applicant must demonstrate one year of related experience within the state of Mississippi or five years of auto mechanic experience elsewhere.

Wilcox, who just moved to Mississippi from the state of New York, where he has been an auto mechanic for two years, wants to open an auto repair business in which he will be the sole mechanic. He applies to the state department of consumer affairs for a license and is denied one. He decides to open his garage anyway and does excellent business, with no dissatisfied customers. The state department of justice brings an action in state court to enjoin Wilcox's business and for civil penalties.

10. If Wilcox attacks the state legislation's provision that licensees be residents of the state for a year prior to the application, his challenge should be based upon:

(A) The Privileges and Immunities Clause of Article IV.

(B) The Commerce Clause.

(C) The Equal Protection Clause of the Fourteenth Amendment.

(D) All of the above.

11. Assume for the purposes of this question only that Wilcox had lived in Mississippi for the last five years. If Wilcox challenges the power of the state to require him to obtain a license to practice his livelihood, he will probably:

(A) Lose, because the state has plenary power regarding commerce.

(B) Lose, because licensing is within the police power of the state and infringes no specific constitutional prohibition.

(C) Win, because the license requirement substantially burdens interstate commerce.

(D) Win, because the license requirement violates the Equal Protection Clause of the Fifth Amendment.

12. Assume for the purposes of this question only that Wilcox meets all the requirements for a mechanic's license, but when he seeks to purchase the necessary insurance, he discovers that Mississippi insurance firms charge about three times as much for business insurance as firms that operate out of New York. He purchases insurance by mail from a reputable New York firm and is denied a business license. His challenge to this aspect of the state legislation will:

(A) Succeed, because the requirement that the insurer be a Mississippi firm violates the Due Process Clause of the Fourteenth Amendment.

(B) Succeed, because the requirement constitutes discrimination against interstate commerce.

(C) Fail, because the state can enforce its laws governing the sale of insurance only if the firm is located in Mississippi.

(D) Fail, because the requirement is reasonably related to the legislation's purpose to protect auto repair consumers.

Questions 13-14 are based on the following fact situation:

Following a number of poisoning incidents of consumers of over-the-counter headache remedies, Congress enacted legislation prescribing in great detail the specifications for various types of containers that all manufacturers, wholesalers, and retailers of nonprescription drugs were required to use in marketing their products. The containers mandated by the new legislation were considerably more expensive than those formerly in wide use in the industry and would result in considerably smaller sales volumes. The same legislation established a Commission on Nonprescription Drug Use whose purpose was to gather information about the number, type, and costs to the consumer of nonprescription drugs used in the United States and report its findings on an annual basis to Congress. The members of the commission were all Representatives or Senators who served on the committees in their respective chambers concerned with legislation relating to food and drugs.

13. General Ingestion, a manufacturer of pharmaceuticals, objects to the notion of having to supply the government with any information about the manufacture and sale of nonprescription drugs and so resists a subpoena for its chief executive officer to testify before the commission. Insofar as Congress's power to investigate is concerned, the general rule is:

(A) The power of Congress is limited only by the concept of separation of powers.

(B) Congress's power to investigate is coextensive with its power to legislate.

(C) Congress's power to investigate is limited to the appointment of its own members to make such investigations.

(D) There are no limitations upon Congressional powers of investigation as to the domestic economy.

14. Congress's power to prescribe standards for the manufacture of nonprescription drug packaging is derived from:

(A) The Necessary and Proper Clause.

(B) The Commerce Clause.

(C) The General Welfare Clause.

(D) The Tenth Amendment.

Question 15

The legislature of the state of Blue enacts a statute that provides for loaning certain textbooks on secular subjects to students in all public and private schools. In accordance with the statute, the state board of education distributes textbooks to Redbrick School, a private school that offers religious instruction and admits only Caucasian students.

Which of the following is the strongest argument against the constitutionality of free distribution of textbooks to the students at Redbrick School?

(A) A state may not constitutionally aid private schools through distribution of textbooks.

(B) Segregation is furthered by the distribution of textbooks to these students.

(C) The distribution of textbooks advances religion because it is impossible to separate their secular and religious uses.

(D) The distribution of textbooks fosters excessive government entanglement with religion.

Questions 16-17 are based on the following fact situation:

In response to a growing number of injuries and fires occurring as the result of the improper manufacture and use of fireworks, Congress adopted the Federal Firework Control Act, which established certain safety and performance standards for all fireworks manufactured in the United States. The Act also created a seven-member safety commission to investigate firework safety, to make recommendations to

Congress for new laws, to make further rules for establishing safety and performance standards, and to prosecute violations of the Act. The chairman of the committee was appointed by the President. Three members were selected by the Speaker of the House of Representatives and three members were selected by the President pro tempore of the Senate. Big Blast, Inc., a manufacturer of fireworks offered for sale in the northeastern portion of the country, seeks to enjoin enforcement of the Commission's rules.

16. The best argument that Big Blast can make is that:

(A) The commerce power does not extend to the manufacture of fireworks sold solely within a state.

(B) Legislative power may not be delegated by Congress to an agency in the absence of clear guidelines.

(C) Big Blast is denied due process of law because it is not represented on the commission.

(D) The commission lacks authority to enforce its standards, because some of its members were appointed by Congress.

17. The appropriate decision for the court is to:

(A) Forbid the commission to take any action under the Act.

(B) Order that all members of the commission be appointed by the President by and with the advice and consent of the Senate.

(C) Allow the commission to prosecute violations of the act but not allow it to issue rules.

(D) Allow the commission to continue investigating firework safety and making recommendations to Congress.

Questions 18-19 are based on the following fact situation:

Oral is a member of the legislature of State. He is prosecuted in federal court for violating the civil rights of a member of the janitorial staff of the state legislature's building in connection with a sexual assault that occurred in Oral's office late at night during the Christmas recess. Oral raises as a defense the claim that the allegedly wrongful acts were committed in the course of legislative business and are immune from scrutiny by the federal government.

18. Which of the following is the strongest constitutional argument in favor of Oral's defense?

   (A) The application of federal civil rights statutes to state legislators would violate the Due Process Clause.

   (B) A federal court must follow state law respecting the scope of legislative immunity.

   (C) State legislators enjoy the protection of the Speech and Debate Clause of the United States Constitution.

   (D) Because of doctrines of federalism, federal law generally cannot be applied to state legislators acting in the course of their official duties.

19. Which of the following is the strongest argument against Oral's constitutional defense?

   (A) Congress may impose liability on state legislators by virtue of the Necessary and Proper Clause.

   (B) Congress does not significantly interfere with state government by applying the civil rights statutes to state legislators.

   (C) Congress may impose liability on the state legislators as a means of guaranteeing a Republican form of government.

   (D) Congress has plenary power under the General Welfare Clause.

Questions 20-21 are based on the following fact situation:

Hoping to help control a growing gang problem and to give teenagers a place to go, the city of Centreville established a youth center. Originally, the center was open to all young people between the ages of 13 and 19, but trouble often occurred when male gang members showed up at the youth center. There were frequent fights and incidents of alcohol and drug abuse. The City Council threatened to close the center, but social workers who work at the center suggested a compromise, pointing out that the trouble invariably involved single men who came to the center without dates. Therefore, the Council passed an ordinance forbidding any male between the ages of 13 and 19 to enter the center unless accompanied by a female.

Rick, an 18-year-old who was new to Centreville, went to the youth center to try to meet new friends. He was refused admission because he was not escorted by a female.

20. Angered, Rick filed suit in federal district court seeking admission to the center and asking the court to strike down the ordinance as unconstitutional. The court should find the ordinance:

   (A) Constitutional, because in these situations, the government is performing a parens patriae function.

   (B) Constitutional, if the city can show a rational relationship between the ordinance and maintaining order at the center.

   (C) Unconstitutional, if Rick can show that the ordinance was not necessary to promote a compelling government interest.

   (D) Unconstitutional, unless the city can show that the ordinance is substantially related to important government objectives.

21. Assume for purposes of this question only that by the time the trial date arrived, Rick was 20 years old and married. Furthermore, after receiving numerous complaints about the ineffectiveness of the ordinance (the gangs simply moved their activity outside the doors of the center), the City Council has slated a vote to repeal the ordinance within a month of Rick's trial date.

When Rick's suit comes before the federal district court, the court should:

(A) Dismiss, because Rick is 20 years old.

(B) Dismiss, if Rick has been permitted to enter the center with his wife.

(C) Hear the case on the merits, because regardless of any change in Rick's circumstances, he has already suffered a deprivation of his constitutional rights.

(D) Dismiss, if it appears that the City Council will repeal the ordinance.

Questions 22-24 are based on the following fact situation:

The state of Pacific enacted legislation that permits parents to pay for the education of their children at the school of their choice by means of a voucher system. The system provides that when a residential real property owner pays his state real property tax, the taxpayer is given a voucher that can be used to pay the tuition at the school in which his children are enrolled. The school, if accredited by the state, can turn in the vouchers to the state and receive funds represented by these vouchers. If the taxpayer has no children in school, the taxpayer can assign the voucher to a relative by blood or marriage who has children in school, but the voucher cannot otherwise be sold or assigned except to the state. Residential taxpayers who have neither children nor close relatives with children can return the vouchers to the state and receive a 50% credit on their real property taxes.

In addition, Pacific raised its state sales tax from 3% to 5%, the additional 2% to be used exclusively to pay the costs of the public school system in addition to any voucher payments made for those children attending private school.

Roberts, a state legislator who fought against the enactment of the bill, brought suit in federal court to have the voucher system declared unconstitutional. In his suit, Roberts contends that parents are using the vouchers to send their children to parochial school and to send their children to segregated private schools. Roberts also alleged that 60% of the residential real property taxpayers are white, and 53% of the blacks in Pacific are inner-city dwellers who live in rental property.

22. For Roberts to bring suit against Pacific, at the very least Roberts must show that:

(A) He rents his home.

(B) He rents his home and has children who are of school age.

(C) He owns residential real property on which he pays taxes.

(D) He owns residential real property, on which he pays taxes, and has children who are of school age.

23. To prevail in his contention that the voucher system is unconstitutional with regard to the segregated private schools, Roberts is *least likely* to rely on which of the following arguments:

(A) The purpose of the legislation was to promote segregation.

(B) Voucher funds are being used by the majority of parents to send their children to segregated schools.

(C) The voucher system has no valid purpose other than to promote segregation.

(D) Segregation is furthered by the use of the voucher system.

24. Of the following, which is Pacific's best argument in support of its use of tax money to pay tuition at religious schools?

    (A) The Equal Protection Clause requires that both private and public schools be treated in the same manner.

    (B) Private religious schools, like public schools, fulfill a function important to the general welfare of the citizens of the state.

    (C) The purpose and effect of the taxes is secular in nature and is not intended to involve the state in religious institutions.

    (D) Only the taxes of the parents of the children who attend private religious schools are used to pay tuition at those schools; general tax revenues are not.

Questions 25-27 are based on the following fact situation:

A statute in the state of Utopia makes it unlawful to sell soft drink beverages in any type of container except refundable glass containers. A violation of the statute is a misdemeanor, subjecting the violator to a fine of up to $1,000.

25. Assume that CanCo, an out-of-state corporation that manufactures aluminum soft drink cans, brings suit in a state court contesting the constitutionality of the statute. The highest court in Utopia ruled against CanCo's claim that the statute was unconstitutional. If CanCo sought to appeal the matter to the Supreme Court, the Court may:

    (A) Deny a hearing, because the Eleventh Amendment forbids the exercise of judicial power by the federal government in a suit prosecuted against any state by a citizen of another state.

    (B) Deny the hearing, because the highest court of any state is the final arbiter of the constitutionality of its own laws.

    (C) Grant a hearing, because a federal question is involved.

    (D) Grant a hearing, because jurisdiction exists on the basis of diversity.

26. Assume that CanCo is a manufacturer doing business in Utopia, and it brings suit for declaratory judgment in the federal court, contending that the bottle statute violates a constitutional prohibition. The federal court should:

    (A) Entertain the suit, because a federal question is involved.

    (B) Entertain the suit, because an action for declaratory relief is a proper method of deciding constitutional questions.

    (C) Abstain from the assertion of jurisdiction until a state court has the opportunity to construe the statute.

    (D) Dismiss the suit, because CanCo is not being prosecuted for the violation of the statute.

27. Assume that in addition to fines, the statute provides for the suspension or revocation of a retail business license where there have been "repeated violations" of the statute by any one individual or business. Allman, a store owner, had already been fined three times under the statute when an inspector purchased from him a soft drink in a can. Several days later, Allman received a notice from the regulatory agency that was created by the statute stating that his business license was suspended for 21 days for violation of the statute. In a suit filed by Allman in the court to set aside the suspension, the most likely finding a court would make is that Allman:

    (A) Prevails, because the statute fails to set forth the exact number of violations that a business would have to commit before its business license was revoked.

(B) Prevails, because he was not given a hearing before the agency.

(C) Does not prevail, because the agency could by its rules construe the term "repeated violations" in such a manner as to comport with due process requirements.

(D) Does not prevail, because the agency is merely a regulatory agency, and therefore Allman has no right to a hearing.

Questions 28-29 are based on the following fact situation:

Lawrence, a chief commissioner on a federal trade board, is cited for contempt of the Senate for refusing to answer certain questions concerning discussions during a closed meeting of the board. The contempt citation is prepared and given to a federal grand jury for indictment. The grand jury returns the indictment, but the United States Attorney General refuses to prosecute Lawrence.

28. Can the Senate force the Attorney General to prosecute Lawrence in accordance with the grand jury indictment?

(A) Yes, provided that two-thirds of the Senate concur in the resolution.

(B) Yes, because the indictment charges Lawrence with a crime against the Senate.

(C) No, because the Attorney General is a member of the executive branch, and he has the exclusive right to determine whether to prosecute.

(D) No, because Lawrence, as a federal trade commissioner, is a member of the executive branch, and it violates the separation of powers doctrine for the Senate to seek testimony from him.

29. If Lawrence were prosecuted for this contempt charge, he would be **least likely** to be convicted if he is able to show that:

(A) The questions he refused to answer related to his duties as a member of the executive branch.

(B) If he answered the questions, he could be subject to dismissal from his position as chief of the board.

(C) The questions do not relate to any matter concerning which the Senate intended to legislate.

(D) Disclosure of the substance of the discussions that occurred during the closed meeting of the board would have a chilling effect on the free exchange of views.

Questions 30-32 are based on the following fact situation:

To practice acupuncture in the state of Missouri, one must have a license issued by the Missouri Board of Health. Missouri statutes specify that an applicant for an acupuncture license must establish that (i) he was trained, in Missouri, by a person licensed to practice acupuncture; (ii) he has been a resident of Missouri for the three years preceding the date of application for the license; and (iii) he is a citizen of the United States.

Victor Chan, a citizen of the United Kingdom permanently admitted as a resident alien to the United States, has recently moved from San Francisco, California, to South Rabbit's Foot, Missouri, at the request of that town's only physician. When Victor Chan applied to the Missouri Board of Health for a license to practice acupuncture, his application was denied because he was not trained in Missouri (having been trained in Hong Kong), has not resided in Missouri for the preceding three years, and is not a United States citizen. The citizens of South Rabbit's Foot and Victor Chan bring an action in federal district court against the Missouri Board of Health and the state of Missouri seeking to compel them to issue a license to practice acupuncture to Mr. Chan.

30. If the plaintiffs challenge the constitutionality of the Missouri statute that predicates issuance of a license on United States citizenship, their best argument would be:

    (A) That it is a bill of attainder.

    (B) That it violates the Equal Protection Clause of the Fifth Amendment.

    (C) That it violates the Equal Protection Clause of the Fourteenth Amendment.

    (D) That it invades the foreign policy power reserved to the federal government.

31. Chan's strongest argument against the requirement that an applicant be trained in Missouri is:

    (A) The requirement violates the Privileges and Immunities Clause of the Fourteenth Amendment.

    (B) The requirement violates the Privileges and Immunities Clause of Article IV.

    (C) The requirement burdens his fundamental right to practice a particular profession.

    (D) The requirement bears no relationship to the interests the state seeks to protect.

32. The plaintiffs' challenge to the residency requirement of the Missouri statutes will probably:

    (A) Succeed, because the requirement violates the Privileges and Immunities Clause of the Fourteenth Amendment.

    (B) Succeed, because the requirement violates the Equal Protection Clause of the Fourteenth Amendment.

    (C) Succeed, because the requirement violates the Due Process Clause of the Fourteenth Amendment.

    (D) Fail, because the state has a compelling interest in furthering the welfare of its residents.

Questions 33-35 are based on the following fact situation:

The state of Red has long been known for the quality of its silver-tip fox furs. Recently, however, the size of the silver-tip fox population has dwindled to dangerously low proportions. This is due in part to increased hunting caused by the increased demand for the furs and also to a reduction in the size of the foxes' habitat caused by increased population in Red.

Both the government of Red and the federal government have decided to take action to protect the foxes. The state government has enacted a statute that reads as follows:

1. No fox shall be hunted or captured within the state unless it is at least 24 inches in length (the purpose being to allow young foxes to breed before being taken).

2. A tax of $5 per fox shall be levied on all foxes taken within the state. All fees so collected shall be used for conservation and protection of the foxes' habitat.

3. All hunters must report in person any foxes taken within the state to the nearest State Department of Fish and Game office, which shall then levy the $5 fee.

The federal government enacts legislation that provides $2.5 million for research into ways to increase the state's fox population. The legislation also imposes a special excise tax of $100 per fox taken in violation of state law if later shipped via interstate commerce.

33. Act Now, a consumer action group, brings suit in federal court to stop the expenditure of the $2.5 million on a "frivolous and

unnecessary project." The suit challenges the expenditure as an improper exercise of congressional power. Which of the following defenses raised by the federal government are valid?

I. The legislation is a valid exercise of the federal taxing and spending powers.

II. The federal court lacks jurisdiction to enjoin such expenditures voted by Congress, under the doctrine of separation of powers.

III. Act Now lacks standing to sue (even though all of its members are federal taxpayers).

(A) I. and II. only.

(B) I. and III. only.

(C) I. only.

(D) III. only.

34. Hunter, who is engaged in the business of hunting and trapping foxes and selling the furs, is a resident of the state of Blue, which borders Red. Blue has no laws restricting the taking of silver-tip foxes. While hunting foxes in Blue, Hunter accidentally crossed into Red. She was arrested by Red game wardens for taking foxes less than 24 inches in length. If Hunter challenges the constitutionality of the Red statute, which of the following is the most likely result?

(A) The statute will be held invalid because it violates the interstate Privileges and Immunities Clause of Article IV, Section 2.

(B) The statute will be held invalid because it is preempted by the federal legislation regarding the taking of foxes.

(C) The statute will be upheld because Congress may allow the states to adopt legislation that would otherwise violate the Commerce Clause.

(D) The statute will be upheld because it is not unduly burdensome on interstate commerce.

35. Gamer, a resident of the state of Green who hunts foxes in Red and sells the furs in other states, filed suit challenging the constitutionality of the $5 per fox tax imposed by the Red statute. Which of the following is the most likely result?

(A) Gamer will win, because the tax is invalid under the Commerce Clause.

(B) Gamer will win, because the tax is invalid under the Import-Export Clause.

(C) Gamer will lose, because the tax is valid under the Commerce Clause.

(D) Gamer will lose, because the tax is valid under the Import-Export Clause.

CONSTITUTIONAL LAW ANSWERS

Answer to Question 1

(C) In *Committee for Public Education and Religious Liberty v. Regan* (1980), the United States Supreme Court held that a similar statute passed by the state of New York did not violate the Establishment Clause because it had a secular legislative purpose. Its principal effect did not advance or inhibit religion, and it did not foster an excessive government entanglement with religion. (A) is therefore incorrect; aid can be given to religious schools that pass this test. (B) is wrong. It misstates the facts given, which make no mention of a specific religious group. Rather, the suit is filed by an association challenging the reimbursement. (D) is irrelevant. The question is not whether the tests involve "matters of religion," but whether the reimbursement program impermissibly advances religion.

Answer to Question 2

(D) The city may ban billboards in a particular area for purposes of traffic safety or aesthetics if the ordinance constitutes a valid time, place, and manner regulation; *i.e.*, it must be content neutral, it must be narrowly tailored to further a significant government interest, and there must be alternative media available for the protected expression. (A) is wrong because this is not "spot zoning," which describes zoning actions that burden a single or limited number of properties in ways inconsistent with the general scheme. This ordinance simply enacts a general rule. (B) is wrong because it is overbroad. As indicated, expression may be subjected to reasonable time, place, and manner regulations. (C) is a misstatement of law; commercial speech is protected by the First Amendment, but it is subject to greater regulation than other forms of speech.

Answer to Question 3

(B) Congress may regulate, under the commerce power, anything that has a substantial economic effect upon interstate commerce. Since the lending of money within Texas has a substantial economic effect on the interstate traffic in money, Commercial Bank would not prevail. (A) is wrong because the commerce power is broad enough to regulate intrastate activities that have a substantial economic effect on interstate commerce. (C) is wrong because the General Welfare Clause is a limitation on Congress's power, not a source of its power. (D) is wrong because interest rates can be and are regulated on a national basis.

Answer to Question 4

(C) The court should rule that the federal statute preempts the state law. Even if Congress had not preempted the subject of interest rates, the state would not be permitted to establish a standard less strict than the federal rule. (A) is wrong because there is no basis for certification under the facts presented. While (B) might state an alluring policy choice, it is both outside the purview of the court and inappropriate in the face of the express determination by Congress to preempt local control. (D) is incorrect because while the Constitution gives the Supreme Court original jurisdiction over cases in which a state is a party, that jurisdiction is not exclusive. Congress has given the lower federal courts concurrent jurisdiction over all cases in which the Supreme Court has original jurisdiction except those between states. This is a case between the United States and a state. Therefore, the Supreme Court's jurisdiction is not exclusive and the case can be heard in a lower federal court.

Answer to Question 5

(C) Since Roger is an at-will employee, the hospital is not required to provide any justification. Absent this fact, Roger would have been entitled to notice and a hearing, regardless of the substantive merit in his dismissal. (C) is, accordingly, the hospital's strongest defense. (A) and (B) state grounds the hospital could conceivably raise, but since it is not required to, it should not. (D), in turn, raises the possibility of a First Amendment defense to the firing (assuming "community" equals "public," giving rise to state action), since the allegation regarding dispensing medicine would fall within the public policy comment privilege recognized by the Court.

Answer to Question 6

(C) Breaching the oral contract between Roger and the chief administrator deprived Roger of a property right created as a result of the voluntary promise made by the chief administrator, and such deprivation may not be accomplished without due process, meaning notice and an opportunity to respond. None of the other answers raises any constitutional issues or alters his status as a terminable-at-will employee. Thus, (A), (B), and (D) are wrong.

Answer to Question 7

(B) Government is not involved in the establishment of religion if its acts have neither a religious purpose nor an effect on religion, and if the measure does not foster an excessive government entanglement with religion. While religious schools may fulfill an important educational function and the teaching of religious matters is not prohibited, neither statement is material as to the constitutionality of state action. Thus, (A) and (C) are incorrect. (D) is incorrect because the state is compelled by the Establishment Clause not to provide certain types of aid to religious schools; in such cases, the Free Exercise Clause is not violated.

Answer to Question 8

(C) The state's policy is a significant involvement in the segregated educational activities of the Academy, and thus violates the Equal Protection Clause. The Constitution forbids discriminatory state action, not private bias (federal legislation that prohibits private discrimination is not constitutionally mandated), and a state may aid anyone as long as it does not violate a specific constitutional restriction. Thus, (A) and (B) are incorrect. (D) is also incorrect. Running nutrition and exercise seminars at private schools does serve a "legitimate" state interest. A state may not, however, escape the express constitutional prohibition against invidious discrimination by asserting that its support of the education programs in a school like Jefferson Davis is somehow "legitimate" in spite of the discriminatory character of the overall program.

Answer to Question 9

(B) The Attorney General is not obligated to prosecute Mr. Powers, regardless of whether he is an appointive official of the executive branch. The doctrine of separation of powers prohibits legislative interference with the executive discretion as to whether to prosecute. Thus, (C) and (D) are incorrect. (A) is incorrect because officials of the executive branch are not immune from prosecution relating to their duties.

Answer to Question 10

(C) Classifications distinguishing between residents and nonresidents of a state are not suspect, provided the focus is, as here, on individuals who are "citizens" and the challenge is not posed by an alien. Since the state could probably show a rational relationship between most provisions in the law and the state's interest in protecting its citizens from unscrupulous mechanics, the measure would pass constitutional muster. However, the durational residency requirement arguably burdens the fundamental right to interstate travel, thus triggering strict scrutiny analysis. (A) is wrong because Wilcox is now a resident of Mississippi, which takes him outside the operation of the Article IV Privileges and Immunities Clause and, in any case, most of the regulations are closely related to the substantial state purpose of protecting its citizens from fraudulent businesspersons. Thus, (D) is also wrong, since it postulates that "all" of the challenges are appropriate. (B) is wrong because there is no indication that Congress has preempted the field, and the residency provision probably does not constitute an invasion of the federal commerce power, since it is largely a valid exercise of the police power whose benefits outweigh any incidental burdens that might be imposed on commerce.

Answer to Question 11

(B) Licensing of persons who deal with the general public is a valid exercise of the state's police power. Since there could be circumstances within which the various requirements, including five years' experience, could be rationally related to the state's objectives, the licensing scheme as a general matter is valid. (A) is a misstatement of law; Congress, not the states, has plenary power over interstate commerce. (C) is not supported by the facts. While an argument could be made that Wilcox's activities have some impact on commerce, there is nothing here to indicate that these regulatory requirements fail applicable tests. (D) is wrong because the equal protection guarantee of the Fifth Amendment applies only to federal government action.

Answer to Question 12

(B) Since the state seeks simply to protect its citizens, which will presumably occur if insurance is provided by a reputable company, there are reasonable alternatives to the discriminatory regulation challenged here. Thus, the insurance regulation violates the Commerce Clause. (A) is incorrect. Since this case involves a classification, it does not implicate due process, which is concerned with how individuals are treated as an absolute matter. (C) is wrong because Mississippi can enforce its regulations within the state even if the insurer is from out of state, provided it does not discriminate when it does so. (D) is incorrect, because even if there is a rational relationship between the state interest and the particular requirement that Wilcox is challenging, there are reasonable nondiscriminatory alternatives available to regulate the out-of-state insurers.

Answer to Question 13

(B) (B) states the general rule: the power of Congress to investigate is coextensive with the power to legislate created by Article I, Section 8 of the Constitution. (A) and (D) are accordingly incorrect statements of the limitations on this power. (A) is wrong since it postulates that "only" separation of powers doctrines limit the power. (D) is wrong because it is too sweeping. Congressional investigation is limited to matters over which the Congress has jurisdiction. (C) is simply wrong. Congress may use appropriate means to investigate, provided the means selected do not themselves violate separation of powers principles.

Answer to Question 14

(B) The Supreme Court has construed the scope of the commerce power very broadly, so that it covers the regulation of drug packaging, which has a substantial economic effect on interstate commerce. (A) is wrong because this type of regulation definitely falls under the Commerce Clause, and there is no need to imply a power (under the Necessary and Proper Clause) when an enumerated power controls. (C) is wrong because the General Welfare Clause presents a limitation on Congress's spending and taxing powers which is not relevant here. (D) is wrong because the Tenth Amendment generally does not bar Congress from exercising its powers under the Commerce Clause, even when the legislation might arguably invade areas that might have traditionally been left to the state via its police powers.

Answer to Question 15

(B) State provision of textbooks to the segregated private school violates the Equal Protection Clause by giving state support to a racially segregated educational process. (A) is wrong because a state may, under certain situations, aid a private school. (C) and (D) are parts of the test for violation of the Establishment Clause. The Supreme Court has held that a state lending textbooks on secular subjects to all students, including those at religious schools, does not violate the Establishment Clause. Thus, (C) and (D) are incorrect.

Answer to Question 16

(D) The Appointments Clause of the Constitution permits Congress to vest appointments of inferior officers only in the President, the courts, or the heads of departments. Enforcement is an executive act; therefore, Congress cannot appoint members of a commission that exercises enforcement powers. Legislative power can be delegated under very vague guidelines without creating an unconstitutional delegation. Thus, (B) is incorrect. (A) is incorrect because the commerce power would probably extend to the manufacture of fireworks, whether or not the fireworks were actually sold in interstate commerce, because, taken as a whole, the activity has a substantial economic effect on interstate commerce. There is no constitutional provision requiring that a party or group to be regulated be represented on the commission that regulates it. (C) is therefore incorrect.

Answer to Question 17

(D) Congress may appoint its own members to a legislative or investigative commission; therefore, for the limited purposes indicated, the Appointments Clause is not violated. Thus, (B) is incorrect. (C) is incorrect because prosecution of violations is an executive act and the Appointments Clause governs. (A) is incorrect because forbidding the commission to take any action is too strong a remedy and is not constitutionally required.

Answer to Question 18

(D) The general principles of intergovernmental immunity prevent federal interference with state governmental functions. There is no indication of any violation of due process, and federal courts need follow state law only in cases where jurisdiction is based upon diversity of citizenship or when a federal statute specifically incorporates state law. Thus, (A) and (B) are incorrect. (C) is incorrect because the protection of the Speech and Debate Clause extends only to federal legislators.

Answer to Question 19

(B) Even though the claim of "legislative business" is raised, the facts indicate that Oral's activities cannot have had much to do with the operation of state government. Oral may, accordingly, be subject to sanction under a variety of federal statutes that either proscribe such conduct or characterize it as a violation of the victim's civil rights. The courts have consistently refused to decide what a "republican form of government" specifically entails. (C) is therefore incorrect. (A) is incorrect because the Necessary and Proper Clause alone does not furnish authorization for federal action. Congress must be acting in the exercise of one of its express powers, and the answer as phrased does not indicate that this is the case. (D) is incorrect because the general welfare power is a taxing and spending authorization, and would not justify criminal sanctions.

Answer to Question 20

(D)   Classifications based on gender are quasi-suspect and violate equal protection unless the government shows by exceedingly persuasive justification that they are substantially related to an important government objective. (A) is incorrect; even if the government were performing a parens partriae function, it would not be permitted to violate equal protection. (B) states the wrong equal protection test. (C) states the wrong test and places the burden of proof on the wrong party.

Answer to Question 21

(A)   A real, live controversy must exist at all stages of review, not merely when the complaint is filed. If a true controversy no longer exists, the court will dismiss the complaint as moot. A case becomes moot, for example, when, as here, a party can no longer be affected by the challenged statute. The fact that parties unconnected to the litigation may still be affected by the ordinance does not affect this lawsuit's mootness. (C) is therefore incorrect. (B) is incorrect because the fact that Rick was permitted to enter the center with his wife is not the reason that there is no longer a controversy. Had he attempted to enter alone, he would have been allowed in because he is now 20 years old. (D) is incorrect because what the City Council might do in the future should not affect the court's decision.

Answer to Question 22

(C)   One of Roberts's challenges in the suit against Pacific is that the funds collected from the property taxes are used to send children to parochial schools. In general, a taxpayer has no standing to challenge the expenditure of the taxes. The major exception to this rule is where the taxpayer alleges that the taxes were enacted under Congress's taxing and spending power, and exceed some specific limitation on that power, in particular the Establishment Clause. Roberts would not have to have children to make this challenge; hence (D) is wrong. (A) and (B) are wrong, because Roberts is only challenging the voucher system and not the sales tax increase. Therefore, he must show that he is paying the taxes he contends are being spent for unconstitutional purposes.

Answer to Question 23

(B)   State taxes used to pay tuition to segregated private schools would sanction discrimination and arguably violate the Equal Protection Clause. It makes no difference how many parents send their children to such schools: the question is whether the program was intended to have, and did in fact have, the discriminatory effect. (B) is therefore the weakest argument, since (A) and (C) illustrate the intent requirement and (D) indicates that the effect is present.

Answer to Question 24

(C)   The only argument that the state can use to support this scheme is that there is neither a religious purpose nor an effect on religion; thus, the government does not violate the Establishment Clause. (A) is wrong because the Fourteenth Amendment does not change the prohibition of the First Amendment. (B) is wrong because the fact that private religious schools fulfill an important function does not justify a violation of the Establishment Clause. (D) is wrong because when the parents pay the tax to the state, it becomes state funds. The prohibition goes to the state's involvement in its most basic sense. The fact that the state is arguably acting in accordance with the wishes of the taxpayers involved makes no difference.

Answer to Question 25

(C) (A) is wrong because the purpose of the Eleventh Amendment is to protect the sovereignty of a state by preventing lawsuits against that state being brought in a federal court; the appeal in this case deals only with the constitutionality of a state statute. (B) is wrong because the highest court in a state is only the final arbiter on a state law decided in accordance with the state's constitution, not the federal Constitution. (D) makes no sense, since diversity refers only to the jurisdictional basis of the federal district court.

Answer to Question 26

(D) This question tests your ability to spot procedural problems. Under the rationale of *Poe v. Ullman* (1961), the suit should be dismissed because of the ripeness problem. The statute in question forbids only the sale of soft drink beverages in aluminum cans within the state, not the manufacture. There is no showing in the facts that CanCo even sells its cans to bottling companies that sell soft drinks within Utopia, so there is no reason to assume that CanCo is being affected by the statute. (A) and (B) are wrong because they discuss only the most general reason why the court can assert jurisdiction, not why it should. (C) is wrong because there is no reason, under these circumstances, for the federal court to defer to a state court. The statute in question is not ambiguous or complex, and thus the constitutional question is fairly obvious.

Answer to Question 27

(B) The most obvious problem in this situation is that Allman was not afforded the right to a hearing either before or after his license was suspended. A business license is a valid property right, and procedural due process requires a hearing if it is suspended. Thus, (C) is wrong. The agency obviously had enforcement powers; thus (D) is wrong. (A) is an arguable complaint by Allman, but since there appears to be a regulatory agency that can make rules regarding the enforcement of the statute, the agency can construe "repeated violations" so as to comport with due process requirements.

Answer to Question 28

(C) The exercise of prosecutorial discretion is an exercise of executive power, and the doctrine of separation of powers forbids legislative interference with its exercise. (A) is wrong because the number of senators voting for the resolution is irrelevant; the question is one of constitutional power, not degree of support. (B) is wrong for much the same reason; it does not matter that the alleged criminal act was committed against the Senate. (D) is a misstatement of law; Congress can seek testimony from members of the executive branch without violating the separation of powers doctrine.

Answer to Question 29

(C) Congress's power to investigate is limited to matters on which it can legislate. These facts do not state that the Senate could not legislate concerning the subject matter of these questions, but only that it did not *intend* to legislate. However, the question asks under which facts would Lawrence be *least* likely to be convicted of a contempt charge, and out of these answers this will be his best choice. (A) is wrong because Congress can question a member of the executive branch concerning his duties. (B) is wrong because he would only have a privilege not to answer if he is subject to criminal liability. Merely because he may get fired is not sufficient grounds for him to refuse to answer a lawful question posed by a member of the Senate in an appropriate hearing. (D) seems to have some validity, because it speaks to a question of freedom of speech. However, there is nothing in the facts that shows that the board has a right to have closed meetings and confidential discussions. Generally, the workings of a federal board are a matter of public record, so unless there is some fact that shows that the board had the right to have an unrecorded meeting, this is not the best answer.

Answer to Question 30

(C) Alienage is a suspect classification when used by the states in matters not involving the self-government process, and must be justified by a compelling state interest or be considered a violation of the Equal Protection Clause of the Fourteenth Amendment. (B) is wrong because the Fifth Amendment applies only to the federal government. While the federal government is responsible for foreign policy, and, as a consequence, is given great latitude in that area by the courts, this alone would not be a reason to invalidate the citizenship requirement. Thus, (D) is wrong. (A) is wrong because a bill of attainder is a legislative determination of guilt.

Answer to Question 31

(D) Chan's best argument is that the requirement bears no rational relationship to the state's interest in making certain that individuals in the health professions are qualified to practice. The classification here, between those trained in the state and those trained elsewhere, does not on its face implicate either a suspect class or a fundamental right. Chan will, accordingly, need to argue that it is either irrational in and of itself, or is unconstitutional as applied to him, a resident alien. (C) is wrong because there is no fundamental right to practice a profession. (A) and (B) are wrong because both Privileges and Immunities Clauses protect citizens, and Chan is not a citizen.

Answer to Question 32

(B) Residency requirements have been successfully challenged as violative of the Equal Protection Clause. These durational residency requirements can be construed as burdening the fundamental right of interstate travel, thus triggering a strict scrutiny analysis. The desire to benefit state residents is not alone a compelling state interest. Thus, (D) is wrong. This requirement might even be struck down under the traditional mere rationality test. (A) is wrong because the Privileges and Immunities Clause does not apply to aliens. (C) is wrong because the classification makes an equal protection analysis more appropriate.

Answer to Question 33

(B) The legislation is a valid exercise of federal power and Act Now lacks standing to sue. Congress has the power to lay and collect taxes (as long as they are uniform) and the power to spend to "provide for the common defense and the general welfare." A tax measure will be upheld if it bears some reasonable relationship to revenue production or if Congress has the power to regulate the taxed activity. Spending may be for any public purpose—not merely the accomplishment of other enumerated powers. These independent powers enable Congress to address matters it otherwise could not regulate directly under the commerce power. Both the excise tax and the appropriation are valid exercises of congressional power, so I. is a valid defense. III. is a valid defense because the organization has standing to sue on behalf of its members only if the individual members would have a right to sue on their own behalf. As a general rule, federal taxpayers have no standing to challenge the way tax dollars are spent by the federal government, because their interest is too remote. The only exception recognized by the Court has been expenditures under Congress's taxing and spending power that violate the Establishment Clause. Here, the appropriation does not violate the Establishment Clause or any other specific constitutional limitation. II. is not a valid defense because it is a well-established principle of judicial review that federal courts have the power to review and, if necessary, enjoin expenditures voted by Congress.

Answer to Question 34

(D) The statute will be upheld because it is a valid state regulation of commerce. In the absence of congressional action preempting the area of regulation, a state may regulate local aspects of interstate commerce if the regulation (i) does not discriminate against out-of-state competition to benefit local economic interests, and (ii) is not unduly burdensome (*i.e.*, the incidental burden on interstate commerce does not outweigh the legitimate local benefits produced by the regulation). Here, the federal legislation does not conflict with the state law, nor does it preempt state regulation of foxes; in fact, the excise tax supports state laws regulating fox hunting. The state law here does not discriminate against interstate commerce or out-of-state competition because it applies to all hunting of foxes within the state. Nor is the state law unduly burdensome because the state's legitimate interest in trying to preserve one of its natural resources outweighs the incidental burden on interstate commerce that is created by the law. (A) is incorrect because the Privileges and Immunities Clause of Article IV prohibits discrimination by a state against nonresidents engaging in commercial activities. Here, the law does not discriminate against nonresidents—it applies equally to hunters residing in the state of Red. (B) is incorrect because, as discussed above, the federal legislation regarding the taking of foxes supports the state statute; it has not preempted state laws in that area. (C) is incorrect because, while Congress may allow the states to adopt discriminatory regulations that would otherwise violate the Commerce Clause, that is not the case here. The state of Red statute is nondiscriminatory and would not violate the Commerce Clause even in the absence of any congressional regulation on the topic, and the fact that the congressional excise tax reinforces state laws regulating foxes does not establish a congressional grant to the states of power over interstate commerce.

Answer to Question 35

(C) Gamer will lose because the tax is valid under the Commerce Clause. The same general considerations applicable to state regulation of commerce apply to taxation. A nondiscriminatory state tax affecting interstate commerce will be deemed to be an undue burden on the free flow of commerce unless three criteria are met: (i) there must be a substantial nexus between the activity taxed and the taxing state, (ii) the tax must be fairly apportioned according to a rational formula, and (iii) the tax must be fairly related to the benefits or services provided by the state. Here, the tax satisfies all three tests because the capture of foxes within the state has a nexus to the state, it is imposed on a per-fox basis, and it is used for the conservation of the foxes' habitat, a legitimate purpose for which a state may exercise its power to tax. Thus, (A) is incorrect. (B) and (D) are incorrect because the Import-Export Clause prohibits states from imposing taxes on goods imported from or exported to foreign nations. The Clause is inapplicable here because nothing in the facts suggests that Gamer exports fox furs to other countries.

CONTRACTS
ANSWER SHEET

1. Ⓐ Ⓑ Ⓒ Ⓓ
2. Ⓐ Ⓑ Ⓒ Ⓓ
3. Ⓐ Ⓑ Ⓒ Ⓓ
4. Ⓐ Ⓑ Ⓒ Ⓓ
5. Ⓐ Ⓑ Ⓒ Ⓓ

19. Ⓐ Ⓑ Ⓒ Ⓓ
20. Ⓐ Ⓑ Ⓒ Ⓓ
21. Ⓐ Ⓑ Ⓒ Ⓓ
22. Ⓐ Ⓑ Ⓒ Ⓓ
23. Ⓐ Ⓑ Ⓒ Ⓓ

6. Ⓐ Ⓑ Ⓒ Ⓓ
7. Ⓐ Ⓑ Ⓒ Ⓓ
8. Ⓐ Ⓑ Ⓒ Ⓓ
9. Ⓐ Ⓑ Ⓒ Ⓓ
10. Ⓐ Ⓑ Ⓒ Ⓓ

24. Ⓐ Ⓑ Ⓒ Ⓓ
25. Ⓐ Ⓑ Ⓒ Ⓓ
26. Ⓐ Ⓑ Ⓒ Ⓓ
27. Ⓐ Ⓑ Ⓒ Ⓓ
28. Ⓐ Ⓑ Ⓒ Ⓓ

11. Ⓐ Ⓑ Ⓒ Ⓓ
12. Ⓐ Ⓑ Ⓒ Ⓓ
13. Ⓐ Ⓑ Ⓒ Ⓓ
14. Ⓐ Ⓑ Ⓒ Ⓓ
15. Ⓐ Ⓑ Ⓒ Ⓓ

29. Ⓐ Ⓑ Ⓒ Ⓓ
30. Ⓐ Ⓑ Ⓒ Ⓓ
31. Ⓐ Ⓑ Ⓒ Ⓓ
32. Ⓐ Ⓑ Ⓒ Ⓓ
33. Ⓐ Ⓑ Ⓒ Ⓓ

16. Ⓐ Ⓑ Ⓒ Ⓓ
17. Ⓐ Ⓑ Ⓒ Ⓓ
18. Ⓐ Ⓑ Ⓒ Ⓓ

34. Ⓐ Ⓑ Ⓒ Ⓓ
35. Ⓐ Ⓑ Ⓒ Ⓓ

CONTRACTS QUESTIONS

Questions 1-2 are based on the following fact situation:

Sherwood and Thurman owned summer homes adjacent to each other on the lake. One summer, after Sherwood's 20-year-old son, Wesley, had spent a few weeks at the summer home, Sherwood received a telephone call from Thurman. Thurman told Sherwood that he had just gone up to his own home and found that his boat dock had been badly damaged. Another neighbor told him that Wesley and some friends had gotten drunk and accidentally crashed their boat into Thurman's dock. Sherwood was very surprised at the accusation because he was sure that if Wesley had caused the damages, Wesley would have told him. However, Thurman wanted Sherwood to give him Wesley's address at college, and since Sherwood was in the middle of some important business negotiations and did not want to become distracted by a dispute with his neighbor, he told Thurman that if he agreed not to bring a claim against Wesley for the damage to the dock, he would arrange to have it repaired and pay for the repairs.

Thurman agreed, and Sherwood had one of the local carpenters, Kerry, repair the dock. However, Kerry was not really a good carpenter and the job he did on the dock was very poor.

1. Thurman was forced to hire another to do the repairs on the dock and he had to sue Sherwood for reimbursement of the money he had to pay on the repairs. Sherwood was able to show at trial that, in fact, the damages were done to Thurman's dock after Wesley had returned to college and that the neighbor was mistaken when he identified Wesley as one of the persons involved in the accident. Is Sherwood obligated to pay Thurman for the repairs?

    (A) No, because Sherwood never really believed that Wesley caused the damage.

    (B) No, because Wesley in fact did not cause the damage.

    (C) No, because Thurman was wrong when he accused Wesley of causing the damage, and it would be unfair to enforce an agreement when there was a mutual mistake of fact.

    (D) Yes.

2. Assuming that there is an enforceable agreement between Thurman and Sherwood, would Thurman have an action against Kerry?

    (A) No, because there was no agreement between Kerry and Thurman with regard to the repairs on the dock.

    (B) No, because Thurman was only an incidental beneficiary of the contract between Kerry and Sherwood.

    (C) Yes, because Thurman was a creditor beneficiary of the contract between Kerry and Sherwood.

    (D) Yes, because Thurman was a donee beneficiary of the contract between Kerry and Sherwood.

Questions 3-4 are based on the following fact situation:

AeroFlyte was given the opportunity to enter into contract negotiations with a foreign country to sell military aircraft and parts. Accordingly, it entered into a written agreement with Rudy for her to act as its agent in what were expected to be lengthy negotiations. Rudy was a highly respected salesperson in the industry and one of the most qualified to act as an agent in these types of negotiations.

Rudy was required by the contract to begin meetings with the representatives of the foreign country on August 1. However, on July 19, Rudy accepted a job with Bowing, a large aircraft manufacturer, and could not thereafter represent AeroFlyte. To fulfill her contractual obligations with AeroFlyte, Rudy called her friend Cliff, who was reputed to be "the best in the business," and orally assigned the AeroFlyte contract to him, paying him $600.

3. Assume for this question only that Aero-Flyte does not want Cliff to represent it and sues Rudy for damages for breach. What result?

    (A) AeroFlyte will prevail, because the assignment was oral.

    (B) AeroFlyte will prevail, because Rudy's performance was personal.

    (C) Rudy will prevail, because Cliff is a better negotiator than Rudy and so AeroFlyte was not damaged.

    (D) Rudy will prevail, because damages are speculative.

4. Assume for this question only that Aero-Flyte agrees to allow Cliff to represent it, but before the negotiations have begun, Cliff informs AeroFlyte that he will not represent it. AeroFlyte sues Cliff for breach. What result?

    (A) Cliff will prevail, because AeroFlyte's only remedy is against Rudy.

    (B) Cliff will prevail, because $600 is grossly inadequate consideration.

    (C) AeroFlyte will prevail, because there has been a novation.

    (D) AeroFlyte will prevail, because it is an intended third-party beneficiary of the Rudy-Cliff contract.

Questions 5-6 are based on the following fact situation:

Alex wanted to have his driveway resurfaced. He called a number of commercial establishments that do such work and received bids ranging from $4,500 to $5,000. Bart submitted a bid to do the work for $4,000, and Alex entered into a contract with him to have the driveway resurfaced.

Shortly before Bart was scheduled to begin work, he called Alex and said, "I just found out my secretary made a mistake in adding the figures. I couldn't possibly do the work for less than $4,600 or I'd lose money."

5. If Alex sues Bart for breach of contract, who will prevail?

    (A) Alex, but only if it is too late for Alex to accept the bid of the next lowest bidder.

    (B) Alex, but only if Alex did not have reason to know of Bart's erroneous bid.

    (C) Bart, because he had not yet commenced performance under the contract.

    (D) Bart, because he can successfully assert the defense of mistake.

6. Assume that Alex responded to Bart's statement by saying, "O.K., I'll pay you the extra $600, but I think you're being unfair." After Bart finished the driveway, he asked Alex for his money. Alex handed Bart $4,000 in cash and said, "This is all I'm going to pay you because you had no right to up the price on me." If Bart sues Alex for the additional $600, who will prevail?

    (A) Alex, because Bart was already under a preexisting duty to resurface the driveway for $4,000.

    (B) Alex, because the promise to pay the additional money was not in writing.

    (C) Bart, because he relied on Alex's promise to pay the additional money to his detriment.

    (D) Bart, because the promise to pay the additional money was the settlement of a good faith dispute.

Questions 7-9 are based on the following fact situation:

At the start of the academic year, September 1, Professor announced to his class that he would pay the tuition of the bar review course of the student's choice for the student who receives the highest grade in Professor's Constitutional Law class. Professor reduced his offer to writing and posted it on the student bulletin board the next day, stating the same essential terms with the added statement, "Maximum award, $1,000."

Stillwell, a student in Professor's class, told Professor prior to the September 8 class that: "I'm really going to give my best effort to get the highest grade in your class and win that prize. I started studying three days ago and yesterday I purchased every substantive constitutional law outline on the market just so I can win the prize."

Shortly thereafter, the Dean of the law school told Professor that she had been receiving complaints from many of the other law professors about the lack of study on the part of the students because the students were concentrating their efforts on constitutional law only. The Dean also stated that she felt that Professor's offer could be interpreted as an improper school policy. Professor stated that, although he still wished to perform on his agreement, he would post a notice announcing the withdrawal of his offer. Professor posted the withdrawal notice on October 1 and stated the reasons why he was forced to withdraw his offer to his class. He apologized, but said that in the interest of the school, he had no choice.

Later that day, Stillwell told Professor that the offer could not be withdrawn after he, Stillwell, had started to perform by purchasing the outlines and devoting his studying exclusively to Constitutional Law for the past month. Professor again stated that he had no choice. Stillwell received the highest grade in Professor's class and now requests performance by Professor.

7. Professor's offer to his class on September 1 and the announcement posted on the bulletin board the next day would be interpreted as:

(A) Preliminary negotiations.

(B) A promise to make a conditional gift.

(C) A contractual offer, creating a power of acceptance.

(D) A mere statement designed to induce the students to study harder and achieve higher grades.

8. If Professor's announcement to his class was held to be an offer, it would be an offer for:

(A) A bilateral contract.

(B) A unilateral contract.

(C) A bilateral contract or a unilateral contract, according to the offeree's intentions.

(D) A unilateral contract that became a bilateral contract when Stillwell began to perform.

9. Professor's announcement of withdrawal of the offer to his class and the posting of the withdrawal notice on the bulletin board would most likely be interpreted as:

(A) Having no legal effect, because no offer had been made.

(B) An effective revocation of the offer.

(C) An ineffective revocation as to any student who failed to hear Professor's announcement or read the notice on the bulletin board.

(D) An ineffective revocation as to Stillwell because Stillwell relied on the promise.

Questions 10-12 are based on the following fact situation:

Futsworth, a lawyer, and Green, a carpenter, entered into an oral contract in which Green agreed to build a redwood deck in Futsworth's backyard for $1,500 plus the cost of materials. Futsworth intended to have a hot tub installed and wanted everything ready for the upcoming summer, and so he told Green that "time is of the essence" and that the deck must be completed by May 15. Futsworth also made Green promise that he would complete the deck "in a good and workmanlike manner."

Green completed work on the deck on May 14, and asked Futsworth for immediate payment of the $1,500 because Green needed the money to finish another project for which he was also on a deadline. Futsworth refused to pay, asserting that Green had not built the deck as agreed and that inferior materials and workmanship prevented installation of the hot tub Futsworth had purchased. The next day, Green mailed to Futsworth via registered mail an invoice demanding payment for all the materials used to construct the redwood deck, listing them, and for the agreed contract price for services of $1,500. The total amount demanded by Green is $2,300.

Futsworth consulted with another carpenter who stated that he could modify the deck at a cost of $300 in additional materials and $150 in labor costs so that the hot tub Futsworth had purchased could be installed. Futsworth purchased the necessary additional materials, then mailed Green a letter offering to pay him $2,150 if he would make the modifications, using Futsworth's materials, to enable installation of the hot tub. When Futsworth received no reply within a week, Futsworth mailed Green a check for $2,150 on which he had written, "Payment in full for construction of redwood deck." Upon receipt of the check from Futsworth, Green cashed it and used the proceeds to complete another project he was working on.

10. Green brings an action against Futsworth for $150, the difference between the agreed contract price and the amount paid. Futsworth defends on the basis of an accord and satisfaction. The trial court should rule for:

(A) Green, because he cashed the check from Futsworth under economic duress.

(B) Futsworth, because Green cashed the check without objection.

(C) Green, if he can establish that the deck was completed in a good and workmanlike manner.

(D) Futsworth, because Green is entitled to only the reasonable value of his services, or $1,500.

11. If the trial court is called upon to determine whether Futsworth has breached his contract with Green, it should conclude that:

(A) Futsworth totally breached the agreement only if Green completed the deck in a good and workmanlike manner.

(B) Futsworth totally breached the agreement regardless of the nature of Green's performance.

(C) Futsworth partially breached the agreement only if Green completed the deck in a good and workmanlike manner.

(D) Futsworth partially breached the agreement regardless of the nature of Green's performance.

12. Futsworth files a cross-complaint seeking to recover the $150 he was forced to pay another carpenter to complete the modifications necessary to permit installation of the hot tub. As to the cross-complaint, the trial court should probably rule for:

(A) Futsworth, because Green accepted Futsworth's offer by not replying to the latter's letter.

(B) Futsworth, because Green accepted Futsworth's offer by cashing the latter's check.

(C) Green, because there was no consideration to support a promise by Green to make the modifications.

(D) Green, because he never accepted the offer contained in Futsworth's letter.

Questions 13-15 are based on the following fact situation:

Steven was the owner in fee simple of Gold Acre, an undivided tract of land. On January 1, Steven decided to sell Gold Acre. On January 10, Steven orally agreed to sell Gold Acre to Barny for $79,000 to be paid on February 28. As a condition of the sale, Barny orally agreed to pay $30,000 of the purchase price to Terry in satisfaction of a debt that Steven had promised to pay to Terry. On February 1, Barny told his secretary of his agreement to buy Gold Acre from Steven and asked her to prepare a formal, typewritten copy of the contract. In so doing, Barny's secretary accidentally typed $74,000 rather than $79,000 as the purchase price. Both Barny and Steven read the document before signing, but neither noticed the mistake in the purchase price. The signed document made no reference of the payment of $30,000 to Terry.

13. Terry files suit against Barny for $30,000. Which of the following is a correct statement?

I. Barny could successfully raise the Statute of Frauds as a defense because the Barny/Steven agreement was to answer to the debt of another.

II. Barny could successfully raise the Statute of Frauds as a defense because the Barny/Steven agreement was for the sale of an interest in land.

(A) I. only.

(B) II. only.

(C) Both I. and II.

(D) Neither I. nor II.

14. Which of the following would be most important in deciding an action by Terry against Barny for $30,000?

(A) Whether Barny was negligent in not having carefully read the written agreement.

(B) Whether the Barny/Steven agreement was completely integrated.

(C) Whether Steven was negligent in not having carefully read the agreement.

(D) Whether the omission of Terry from the written document was intentional or accidental.

15. Assume for this question only that Barny refuses to pay more than $74,000 for Gold Acre. If Steven brings suit against Barny to recover the additional $5,000, which of the following, if proved, would be of the most help to Steven?

(A) There was a mistake in integration.

(B) There was a misunderstanding between Steven and Barny concerning the purchase price.

(C) The writing was only a memorialization.

(D) The writing was only a partial integration.

Questions 16-18 are based on the following fact situation:

Duncan, the owner of a large chain of small doughnut shops, decided to add fresh-baked cookies to his menus. To that end, Duncan developed a line of cookies. Since each of his doughnut shops is small, Duncan decided that it would be most cost-efficient and would ensure the highest quality if he created cookie mixes at a central location and shipped the mixes to each shop. One of Duncan's better-tasting cookies was his chocolate chip. Duncan decided to make that his flagship cookie, and sought out the very best ingredients for this mix. After a little research, Duncan found out what the rest of the country already knew: the best semisweet chocolate chips in the country were made by Chipco. Although Chipco's chocolate chips were more expensive than any other on the market, Duncan thought they were well worth the cost because he would be able to benefit from the chips' reputation as "the best." Duncan met with Chipco and impressed them with the quality of his products. They offered to supply him with whatever amount of chocolate chips he needed. Duncan entered into a written contract with Chipco whereby Chipco agreed to send Duncan 5,000 pounds of chips on the first day of each month. Duncan was to pay $12,500 for each shipment by the 10th day of each month. The contract was to expire at the end of one year.

16. Assume for this question only that when Duncan opened the first shipment of chips, he found that 60% of them were tainted with rat hairs. He immediately called Chipco and informed them of the breach. Chipco offered to send replacements, but Duncan, having become uncertain of the probable success of the cookie venture, refused the offer and told Chipco that he was canceling the contract. Will Chipco prevail in an action to enforce the contract?

(A) No, because Chipco breached the contract and Duncan was entitled to a perfect tender.

(B) No, because damages are speculative.

(C) Yes, because Duncan's notice of breach had to be in writing.

(D) Yes, because Chipco had a right to cure.

17. Assume for this question only that Chipco and Duncan properly fulfilled their contractual obligations for two months. The day

after Chipco made the third delivery, Chipco's president ventured into one of Duncan's shops and tasted a chocolate chip cookie made with Chipco chips. Finding the cookie to be the worst he had ever tasted, the president called Duncan and told him that to protect Chipco's reputation, Chipco will absolutely not send Duncan any more chips. Duncan immediately files an action for breach. What result?

(A) Chipco will prevail because it was not in breach when the action was filed.

(B) Chipco will prevail if it can show that Duncan's cookies tasted bad.

(C) Duncan will prevail because the president's action amounts to an anticipatory repudiation.

(D) Duncan will prevail because the president's action amounts to a prospective inability to perform.

18. Assume for this question only that after three months of proper performance, Chipco refuses to send Duncan any more chips because of Chipco's president's perception that Duncan's cookies taste bad and thus will harm Chipco's reputation. If Duncan sues to force Chipco to ship the chips, will he prevail?

(A) Yes, if Chipco's chips really are the best, and no other chip would be sufficient.

(B) Yes, because Duncan relied to his detriment.

(C) No, because specific performance is not available for a contract for the sale of goods.

(D) No, if Duncan's cookies will harm Chipco's reputation since that would be inequitable and specific performance is an equitable remedy.

Questions 19-21 are based on the following fact situation:

Lucy needed a new television set. She went from store to store looking for the perfect set but always was disappointed. Finally, when she was just about to give up, she walked by the local Azimuth Television Co. store and saw the television of her dreams: the Azimuth 360. Lucy walked right into the store and up to the nearest salesperson and asked, "How much for that black 360 in the window?" The salesperson replied, "$500," and Lucy said, "Fine, I'll take one." The salesperson happily complied, and within minutes Lucy was on her way home with the new television set.

When Lucy got home, she opened the box containing the television. Inside, she found an owner's manual that contained instructions on how to operate the set, warnings regarding the danger of electricity, and a warranty that stated:

> Azimuth expressly warrants that this set shall be free of manufacturing defects for five days. If a set is defective, Azimuth's liability shall be limited to the cost of repair or replacement of defective parts. **AZIMUTH HEREBY DISCLAIMS ANY AND ALL OTHER WARRANTIES, EXPRESS OR IMPLIED, INCLUDING THE WARRANTY OF FITNESS FOR PARTICULAR PURPOSE AND THE WARRANTY OF MERCHANTABILITY.**

19. Assume for this question only that when Lucy takes the set out of the box, she discovers that it is not black, but green. She takes it back to Azimuth and demands an exchange or refund. Azimuth refuses, on the ground that the set is not defective. If Lucy sues for a refund, who will prevail?

   (A) Lucy, because in consumer transactions a consumer has an absolute right to return goods within 24 hours under the "buyer's remorse" laws.

   (B) Lucy, because an express warranty that the television would be black arose and was breached.

   (C) Azimuth, because the television is not defective in that color does not affect the television's operation.

   (D) Azimuth, because the express warranty has not been breached.

20. Assume now that 10 days later, after the set was properly installed and Lucy had read the owner's manual, she turned on the set, heard a crackling noise, and watched as her television exploded. The television was destroyed. Under which of the following theories will Lucy most likely recover?

   (A) Breach of express warranty.

   (B) Breach of the implied warranty of merchantability.

   (C) Breach of the implied warranty of fitness for a particular purpose.

   (D) None of the above.

21. If in addition to destroying the television, the explosion injured Lucy and caused damage to her house, in a breach of warranty action, what damages may Lucy recover?

   I.   The cost of the television.

   II.   Her personal injuries.

   III. The damage to her house.

   (A) I. and II., but not III.

   (B) I. and III., but not II.

   (C) I., II., and III.

   (D) None of the above.

Questions 22-24 are based on the following fact situation:

Mary, 17 years old, was an unemployed disappointment to her parents. To teach Mary to be more self-sufficient, Mary's parents took a one-month trip to Europe, leaving Mary at home to take care of the house. They left Mary $400, which she promptly spent on her first weekend party. By the end of the next week, Mary ran out of food and became hungry. She walked to the local grocery store (the family car was out of gas) and explained her predicament to the manager. He told Mary that if she agreed to work at the store for 20 hours a week for three weeks, she could have $75 worth of groceries. Although it seemed like a lot of work for $75 worth of groceries, Mary needed to eat, and so she accepted, picked up her groceries, promised to report for work the next day, and left.

While on the way home, Mary decided that the idea of credit was not so bad—for a mere promise she obtained $75 worth of groceries. Just then, she passed Buddy's Budget Autos and decided that she would really impress her parents if she had her own car when they returned. She negotiated with Buddy, the owner of Buddy's, to obtain an $800 car in exchange for her promise to work for Buddy 20 hours a week for eight weeks. When Buddy agreed, they drew up a written contract.

While driving home from Buddy's, Mary lost control of the car and crashed into a tree. Both the car and the groceries were completely destroyed. Mary suffered minor injuries. Mary's parents immediately flew home to care for their injured daughter.

22. If the grocery store sues Mary for the cost of the groceries and *wins*, it will be because:

(A) Mary promised to pay for them.

(B) Mary cannot return the groceries so she cannot return the store to the status quo ante.

(C) Mary needed the food.

(D) The contract was not within the Statute of Frauds.

23. If the grocery store sues Mary for the cost of the groceries and *loses*, it will be because:

(A) Mary was a minor.

(B) The groceries were destroyed and thus there was a failure of consideration.

(C) The contract was unconscionable.

(D) It was impossible for Mary to perform.

24. If Buddy sues Mary for the price of the car and *loses*, it will be because:

(A) The contract was unconscionable.

(B) Mary did not need the car.

(C) Since the car was destroyed, there is no consideration to support the bargain.

(D) The purpose of the contract has been frustrated.

Questions 25-26 are based on the following fact situation:

Integrated Circuit Technology, Inc. ("ICT") was having difficulty finding qualified engineers to work in its expanding production facilities because the hardware needed to train top-flight engineering students was so expensive that most colleges could not afford to purchase more than a minimal amount of such equipment, which limited program sizes and held down the number of available engineering degree candidates. ICT's chief executive officer, Cruz, wrote the following letter to the heads of several universities: "If you will commit your institution to accepting in your engineering degree program every junior-year undergraduate who wishes to pursue that major, ICT will provide your institution with all the necessary electronic hardware to instruct such students. Our engineers have informed me that one set of equipment (*i.e.*, one each of every machine used by ICT in its production process) is sufficient for use by five students; therefore, for every five engineering degree majors you accept in excess of your current engineering degree population, ICT will provide one such set of equipment."

25. Marchand, chancellor of Middle States University ("MSU"), received a letter from Cruz and immediately mailed a reply letter accepting ICT's generous offer. A few weeks later, Marchand received another letter from Cruz explaining that the response to his original letter had been so overwhelming that schools such as MSU who had no history of supplying graduates to ICT as employees would have to be omitted from ICT's equipment program. If MSU brings an action for breach of contract against ICT, what result?

   (A) Judgment for ICT, because it could not be determined with sufficient specificity what MSU's needs for equipment would be, there having been no time to ascertain how many new engineering degree students would apply to the expanding degree program.

   (B) Judgment for ICT, because MSU's obligation under any contract is illusory—no additional students will necessarily apply to an expanded engineering degree program.

   (C) Judgment for MSU, because ICT is classified as a merchant under the U.C.C. and its offer was therefore irrevocable.

   (D) Judgment for MSU, because Marchand's letter was an effective acceptance of ICT's offer and an enforceable contract was thereby formed.

26. Jackson, chancellor of Seaport College of Engineering ("SCE"), also received a letter from Cruz. The ICT letter arrived during SCE's annual budget review process, and Jackson was called upon to decide how much of the college's limited funds to apply to engineering equipment purchases. The day that she received Cruz's letter, Jackson informed the budget committee that no funds would be needed from that year's budget for engineering equipment purchases. A few days later, as Jackson was dictating the acceptance letter to ICT, she received a second letter from Cruz indicating that the ICT equipment program was being canceled due to an influx of qualified foreign engineers to the United States. Because the budget had been approved and all available funds had been committed to nonengineering equipment purchases, Jackson mailed the acceptance letter anyway and it was delivered to Cruz at ICT. If SCE brings a breach of contract action against ICT, what result?

   (A) Judgment for SCE, if Jackson's removal of funds from the engineering department's budget was a reasonable and foreseeable response to ICT's offer.

   (B) Judgment for SCE, because Jackson's removal of funds from the engineering department's budget converted ICT's offer into an express option.

   (C) Judgment for ICT, because its promise to supply equipment to SCE was not supported by consideration.

   (D) Judgment for ICT, because its revocation was received by Jackson before she dispatched the acceptance letter.

Questions 27-28 are based on the following fact situation:

Upon graduation from high school, Nephew could not decide whether he wanted to go on to college or start working for a living. Uncle told Nephew that if Nephew would attend college, Uncle would pay his tuition and expenses for the full year, and that Uncle would pay him a $1,000 bonus for each "A" Nephew earned as a final grade in a class. Nephew told Uncle that he would attend college. The next day, Grandfather called Nephew and told him that he had learned of the offer that Uncle had made him and that if Uncle failed to pay Nephew as promised he (Grandfather) would. Nephew attended college and earned "A"s as final grades in three classes. Shortly thereafter, Uncle died, and the executor of Uncle's estate refused to pay Nephew the bonus for each of the three "A"s.

27. Nephew will be unsuccessful in trying to enforce Grandfather's promise because:

   (A) The contract was illusory.

   (B) The contract was oral.

   (C) There was no consideration flowing to Grandfather.

   (D) The fact that Nephew received a year's worth of free education and tuition was sufficient compensation for Nephew's efforts in earning the three "A"s.

28. If Nephew brings suit against Uncle's estate for failure to pay $1,000 for each "A" as a bonus, will Nephew succeed?

   (A) Yes, because there was a bargained-for exchange between Nephew and Uncle.

   (B) Yes, because Uncle, had he been alive, clearly would have paid the bonus to Nephew.

   (C) No, because Uncle's promise was personal, and the obligation was extinguished at Uncle's death.

   (D) No, because the agreement between Uncle and Nephew was oral, and it would be impossible for Nephew to prove its terms after Uncle's death.

Questions 29-31 are based on the following fact situation:

On July 1, Sam offered to sell Durham, his prize bull, to Bill for $15,000. In return for $100 which Bill paid Sam, Sam handed to Bill a signed written statement that recited the offer and stated that Sam promised not to revoke for a period of 30 days. Both Bill and Sam are cattle ranchers.

On July 10, Bill wrote Sam as follows: "I cannot pay more than $12,500 for Durham. If you cannot accept this amount, I will not be able to go through with the deal."

Bill did not know that Sam had already sold Durham to another party on July 9.

On July 27, Bill wrote Sam: "I accept your offer to sell Durham. Enclosed is my check for $15,000."

Sam received Bill's letter of July 27 on July 29.

29. In a suit by Bill against Sam for damages, a court would most likely find that:

   (A) No contract was formed because Bill's letter of July 10 terminated Sam's offer.

   (B) No contract was formed because Sam had already sold Durham, and this operated as a revocation of his offer since Sam was no longer able to perform.

   (C) A contract was formed because the acceptance was effective prior to the expiration of 30 days.

   (D) A contract was formed because Sam had no power to sell Durham to another party.

30. Assume Sam had not sold Durham on July 9 but instead sold Durham on July 20 after receiving Bill's letter of July 10. Also assume that Bill learned of the sale on July 21. Bill's power to accept the offer:

   (A) Terminated when Sam received Bill's letter of July 10.

   (B) Terminated when Sam sold the bull.

   (C) Terminated on July 21 when Bill learned of the sale.

   (D) Continued until July 30 because Bill paid $100 for a 30-day option.

31. Assume Bill's letter of July 10 had read:

> I have decided to take Durham. A
> check for $15,000 is enclosed. I am
> leaving for Canada for six months
> and will pick up Durham on January 1. I will pay you for his board
> and care.

Bill's letter is:

(A) A counteroffer, because it changes the terms of the offer.

(B) A counteroffer, because it was not a definite expression of acceptance.

(C) An acceptance, and Sam must board the bull but is entitled to the reasonable value of that service.

(D) An acceptance, and Sam may refuse to board the bull.

Questions 32-35 are based on the following fact situation:

Wholesale Electronics Supply ("WES"), located in Los Angeles, California, sells integrated circuits to manufacturers of electronic components throughout the United States. Last year, these sales brought in gross revenues of $100 million. WES also operates a chain of retail outlets in the Southern California area which sell stereo equipment and electric guitars manufactured by others with components purchased in part from WES. WES purchases integrated circuits from five or six different Japanese and American firms, one of which is Silicon Industries ("Silicon"), a corporation with its main offices in San Jose, California. On January 19, WES mailed an order for $200,000 worth of 64-byte microprocessors to Silicon, specifying that the account was payable in full on or before March 1 and that delivery was to be not later than February 25, F.O.B. Southern Pacific Railroad Depot, San Jose, California. Silicon delivered the microprocessors to the railroad depot on February 15 and notified WES by fax that their order was scheduled to arrive at the Southern Pacific Railroad Depot in Los

Angeles on February 20. On February 17 Silicon learned that WES had defaulted on a $700 million loan from the United States Government and that the Attorney General is considering filing an involuntary petition for bankruptcy against WES.

32. Assume that Silicon wires WES that it demands immediate payment in cash for the microprocessors. Is this permissible?

(A) No, but Silicon may refuse to tender delivery of the goods by stopping them in transit.

(B) No, because the contract terms specifying delivery F.O.B. at the Southern Pacific Railroad Depot passed title of the goods to WES.

(C) No, because the payment terms were expressly stated in the purchase order of January 19.

(D) Yes, if WES is in fact insolvent.

33. Assume that the microprocessors were picked up by WES at the Los Angeles Southern Pacific Depot. Two days later, Silicon learned of the default by WES on the government loan and learned that, according to Dunn & Bradstreet, WES is unable to pay its debts as they become due. Silicon now seeks to reclaim the goods. Is this permissible?

(A) No, because the date specified for payment of the account, March 1, has not yet passed.

(B) Yes, unless WES assures Silicon that it will make payment on or before March 1.

(C) Yes, because Silicon relied on WES's representations of solvency.

(D) Yes, if WES is in fact insolvent.

34. Assume for the purposes of this question that Silicon successfully reclaimed the goods from WES after learning that WES was unable to pay its debts as they became due. Silicon then attempted to resell the microprocessors to computer manufacturers in New York. Shortly after Silicon reclaimed the microprocessors, electronics manufacturers announced the availability of a 128-byte microprocessor that renders 64-byte chips obsolete for those purposes. Silicon quickly sold the reclaimed goods for $25,000 and now seeks to recover $175,000 from WES in an action at law. Will Silicon prevail?

    (A) No, because a seller who reclaims waives all other remedies.

    (B) No, because the measure of damages is the market value of the goods at the time and place of delivery.

    (C) No, because the measure of damages is the market value of the goods on the date that payment was originally to be made.

    (D) Yes, because WES's insolvency was a breach of the purchase contract.

35. Assume that on February 21, WES wired Silicon that it was rejecting the microprocessors because they did not meet quality control standards specified in the purchase order. Also assume that this rejection is proper. Silicon discovered that the defects in the goods shipped to WES were caused by an impure batch of silicon and that by using untainted microprocessors made from other batches it can make a perfect tender of conforming goods by February 25. Silicon timely notified WES of its intention to cure. Silicon delivers conforming microprocessors to the Southern Pacific Railroad Depot on February 25, as required by the purchase order. WES refuses to accept these microprocessors. Is this permissible?

    (A) No, because if Silicon notified WES of its intent to tender conforming goods, such tender on or before the date specified in the contract for tender cures the previous imperfect tender.

    (B) Yes, because the right to cure an imperfect tender is waived if delivery is to be to a common carrier instead of directly to the buyer.

    (C) No, unless WES had purchased conforming goods from another manufacturer before the date Silicon tendered the conforming goods.

    (D) Yes, because tender of the original nonconforming goods permitted WES to rescind the purchase contract.

CONTRACTS LAW ANSWERS

Answer to Question 1

(D) Modern courts would hold that a promise to forbear suit on a claim that the promisor *honestly and reasonably* believes to be valid is good consideration to support an agreement, even if the claim ultimately turns out not to be valid. Hence, (A) and (B) are wrong. (C) is wrong because the mutual mistake was only as to the reason for entering the contract, not the terms of the contract. There is no reason why a contract should not be enforced when the parties were mistaken as to the need for the contract if the contract is otherwise valid. Additionally, it is not "unfair" to enforce it because Sherwood always had the right to investigate the truth of the facts before he agreed to pay for the dock.

Answer to Question 2

(C) Sherwood bargained with Kerry to discharge an obligation Sherwood had to Thurman, therefore Thurman was the third-party creditor beneficiary of the agreement to repair the dock and could sue on this agreement. Hence, (A) and (D) are wrong. (B) is wrong because performance of Sherwood's duty is clearly *intended* to benefit Thurman alone.

Answer to Question 3

(B) The general rule is that all contracts can be assigned. However, where a contract is assigned in total, such as the contract here, the assignment includes a delegation of duties. A duty that calls for personal service is nondelegable, and a contract calling for service of a skilled negotiator is personal. (A) is wrong because assignments can be oral. (C) is wrong because the damage lies in taking away the negotiator that AeroFlyte has chosen. (D) is wrong because the damage could be measured by the cost of hiring another negotiator of AeroFlyte's choosing.

Answer to Question 4

(D) Ordinarily, when a duty is delegated, the obligee (here AeroFlyte) cannot force the delegate (Cliff) to perform because the delegate has made no promise to the obligee. However, where the delegate's promise is supported by consideration, a contract arises and the obligee is a third-party beneficiary of that contract. As such, the obligee can enforce the contract. Thus, (A) is wrong. (B) is wrong because a court would probably not even inquire into adequacy. (C) is wrong because nothing in the facts indicates that there has been a novation (*i.e.*, release).

Answer to Question 5

(B) Bart's only defense is unilateral mistake. A contract generally cannot be rescinded for a unilateral mistake. One exception to this rule is where the other party knew of the mistake. However, if the facts are as stated in (B), Bart has no defense, and Alex will win. Therefore, (B) is correct, and (D) is wrong. (A) is wrong because it is irrelevant whether the nonmistaken party can make an alternative contract. (C) is incorrect because it is irrelevant that the contract is still executory.

Answer to Question 6

(A) Bart was already under contract to resurface a driveway for $4,000. Therefore, Alex's promise to pay Bart an additional $600 to do the same work was not supported by consideration. (B) is wrong because contracts for services do not come within the Statute of Frauds unless they cannot be performed within one year of their making. (C) is wrong, because reliance would not cure the lack of consideration. (D) is wrong, because there was no dispute between the parties.

Answer to Question 7

(C) Since Professor had stated the nature of the performance he was requesting, and had specified the terms, Professor would be held to have made an offer, creating a power of acceptance in the student who received the highest grade. Thus, (A) and (D) are incorrect. (B) is incorrect because Professor's motive was to induce a detriment (intensive study), and gratification from influencing the mind of another may be sufficient to establish bargained-for consideration. Thus, this was not to be a gift.

Answer to Question 8

(B) Since Professor's offer could be accepted only by completion of performance (that is, obtaining the highest grade in his class), when Stillwell received the highest grade a unilateral contract was formed. (A), (C), and (D) are therefore incorrect.

Answer to Question 9

(D) A unilateral contract is revocable until performance is begun. Here, Stillwell's purchase of every substantive Constitutional Law outline, while it may be preparation to perform rather than the beginning of performance, was in reliance on Professor's promise. Furthermore, his devoting his studying exclusively to Constitutional Law at the expense of other subjects probably did constitute beginning performance, making the offer irrevocable. Even if his studying were deemed only preparation to perform, it was sufficiently substantial and foreseeable to make the promise binding on Professor. Thus, the offer is irrevocable as to Stillwell. (A) is wrong, because the offer was valid. (B) is wrong as to Stillwell, although it would be correct as to anyone who had not detrimentally relied on the offer. (C) is wrong because a revocation need only be published in the same manner as the offer; it need not actually reach everyone who knew of the offer.

Answer to Question 10

(B) Cashing a check offered as payment in full, where there is a bona fide dispute as to the amount owed, will establish an accord and satisfaction. (A) is incorrect because mere economic duress is insufficient to avoid a contract. (C) is incorrect because the accord and satisfaction would release the parties from their obligations on the original contract. (D) is incorrect because Green, if entitled to recover under the contract, would be entitled to recover the contract price not limited by the reasonable value of his services.

Answer to Question 11

(C) Since Futsworth's performance is to pay money, a total refusal to pay would be a total breach; since he has paid some (in fact most) of the amount he was obligated to pay, he can be only in partial breach. Thus, (A) and (B) are incorrect. The condition that Green perform in a workman-like manner is not too vague to be enforceable (in fact, such a condition would be implied if not expressly included); thus, Futsworth would be bound only if Green fulfilled this condition. Thus, (D) is incorrect.

Answer to Question 12

(B) Communications concerning a contract must be interpreted in context and in proper sequence. When Green cashed Futsworth's check shortly after receiving a letter offering the check as part of an agreement to do additional work, he is considered to have accepted the offer. Thus, (B) is correct, and (D) is incorrect. (A) is incorrect since an offer cannot be accepted by silence except in the most unusual circumstances. (C) is incorrect since consideration would be found in Green's promise to perform additional work and Futsworth's forbearance to sue for any breach of contract claim that he believed he had.

Answer to Question 13

(D) I. is wrong because Barny is not promising to act as a guarantor when he promises to pay some of the money to Terry. II. is wrong because Barny's oral promise to pay part of the purchase price to Terry would most likely be interpreted as collateral to the land transaction itself, all the terms of which must be in writing to be enforceable. Therefore, (D) is the correct answer.

Answer to Question 14

(D) (B) is wrong because even if the Barny/Steven agreement was completely integrated, the contract could still be reformed for mutual mistake if the omission of Terry was accidental. However, if it was intentional, the valid modification would invalidate Terry's rights because they had not vested. (A) and (C) are wrong because the negligence of either Barny or Steven should not adversely affect Terry's claim.

Answer to Question 15

(A) Where the parties have actually made a mistake in integrating their agreement into a writing, then the court will grant relief from the drafting error. (B) is wrong because the presence of a misunderstanding between the parties would not necessarily entitle one of them to relief. (C) is immaterial. (D) is wrong because one does not need to show that the writing was only partially integrated to prove a mistake in drafting. In the case of an actual mistake by both parties, parol evidence would be admissible to show the mistake.

Answer to Question 16

(D) The contract here is an installment contract and the U.C.C. provides that a buyer cannot cancel the entire contract because of a defect in one installment if the defect can be cured. (A) is wrong because "perfect tender" is not the rule for installment contracts. (B) is wrong because damages could be measured by lost profits or by standard contract measure. (C) is wrong because a notification of rejection need not be in writing.

Answer to Question 17

(C) An anticipatory repudiation arises where a promisor expressly and unequivocally indicates, prior to the time of performance, that he will not perform. In such a case, the other party has several options, including treating the repudiation as an immediate breach and suing for damages. Thus, (A) is wrong. (B) is wrong because the poor quality of the cookies would not be a defense under the contract since the contract made no provision regarding the quality of Duncan's product. (D) is wrong because prospective inability to perform involves *conduct* rather than expression, indicating an intent not to perform.

Answer to Question 18

(A) The buyer of goods may obtain specific performance where the seller refuses to deliver goods if the goods are unique or circumstances are otherwise proper. Thus, (C) is wrong. (B) is wrong because if the chips are not unique, damages could be measured by the cost of buying substitute goods or by other U.C.C. measures. (D) is a misstatement of the law.

Answer to Question 19

(B) An express warranty will arise from any affirmation of fact or promise or from any model or description if the statement, promise, model, or description is part of the basis of the bargain. Here, Lucy based her decision to buy on the model in the window; thus, an express warranty arose that the television she purchased would conform to the model. This warranty was not negated by the attempted disclaimer since that came too late to be part of the parties' contract. (A) is a misstatement of the law. (C) and (D) both go to the warranty included in the box, which came too late to be part of the bargain.

Answer to Question 20

(B) In every sale of goods, unless expressly disclaimed, there arises a warranty that the goods shall be merchantable, which means that the goods shall be fit for ordinary purposes. A television that explodes after 10 days of use breaches this warranty. Furthermore, the warranty here was not effectively disclaimed since the disclaimer came too late to be included in the parties' contract. Thus, (D) is wrong. (A) is wrong because no express warranty was made as to quality at a time sufficient to become part of the bargain. (C) is wrong because such a warranty arises only where the buyer relies on the seller's expertise to pick suitable goods, and here Lucy picked the television herself.

Answer to Question 21

(C) A buyer of defective goods may recover as damages "loss resulting in the normal course of events from the breach," which includes damages to the goods themselves plus all foreseeable incidental and consequential damages, including injuries to persons and property. Thus, Lucy may recover damages for all of these injuries, and so (C) is correct, and (A), (B), and (D) are wrong.

Answer to Question 22

(C) Generally, a contract by a minor is not enforceable against the minor, and persons under age 18 are considered minors. However, minors are bound for the reasonable value of necessities for which they contract. (A) is wrong because a mere promise to pay by a minor is not sufficient to bind the minor. (B) is irrelevant. (D) is wrong because it does not address the issue of Mary's minority.

Answer to Question 23

(C) U.C.C. section 2-302 allows a court to refuse to enforce a contract that it finds unconscionable. Unconscionability usually arises where bargaining power is unequal and one party dictates unfair terms to the other party. Here, Mary told the manager that she needed food and he forced her to agree to work for, in essence, $1.25 per hour. (A) is not a defense because the contract was for necessaries. (B) is wrong since Mary did in fact receive the groceries. (D) is wrong because nothing in the facts indicates that performance is impossible.

Answer to Question 24

(B) Since Mary is a minor, she will not be bound to her contract unless some exception to the general rule applies. No exception applies here. The car is not a necessity. (A) is wrong since the terms seem fair. (C) is wrong since a minor does not need to return the goods in the same condition as received. (D) is wrong because no basic assumption on the part of both parties has been frustrated.

Answer to Question 25

(D) Marchand's letter of acceptance created an enforceable contract. (A) is wrong because requirements contracts are now recognized as sufficiently definite to be enforced. (B) is incorrect because MSU's promise was not illusory; it agreed to expand its degree program and to accept anyone who applied. (C) is not the best answer because ICT's offer was accepted before the purported revocation, and so the revocability of the offer is immaterial.

Answer to Question 26

(A) Under the modern, majority view, where the offeror could reasonably expect that the offer would induce the offeree to detrimentally change position in reliance on the offer, the courts will hold the offer to be an irrevocable option due to the detrimental reliance. (D) would be the correct answer under the older, minority view, which did not recognize the application of promissory estoppel in this situation, and would thus apply the rule that the revocation, effective on receipt, predated dispatch of the acceptance. (B) is wrong because the offer is converted into an equitable option, not an express option. (C) is incorrect because SCE's agreement to expand its degree program and accept applying students is adequate consideration to support ICT's promise.

Answer to Question 27

(B) Grandfather's promise was a promise to answer for the debt of another, which is required to be in writing under the Statute of Frauds. (A) is wrong because the contract clearly is not illusory; Uncle promised to pay if Nephew received "A"s. Uncle would be paying money and Nephew would be giving Uncle the satisfaction of Nephew's receiving "A"s. (C) is wrong because the consideration for Grandfather's promise is Nephew's act of getting "A"s. (D) is incorrect because this was not the bargained-for exchange Nephew expected.

Answer to Question 28

(A) Nephew and Uncle had entered into a valid contract, and Uncle's estate would be liable to pay the consideration promised by Uncle. (B) is irrelevant and is not supported by the facts. (C) is an incorrect statement of the law. (D) is wrong because Nephew could still prove the existence of the oral agreement, even after Uncle's death.

Answer to Question 29

(C) Bill has an option for 30 days. His July 10 counteroffer does not terminate that option. (A) is therefore wrong. His July 27 acceptance forms a contract between Sam and himself. Sam cannot perform the deal because he has already sold the bull to an innocent third party. He had the power but not the right to sell. Thus, (D) is wrong. Therefore, Sam has breached his contract with Bill.

Thus, (B) is wrong because sale of the bull constitutes breach of the option contract; the offer was irrevocable for 30 days.

Answer to Question 30

(B) The rejection of the offer in an option contract does not terminate the power to accept the offer. Nevertheless, if the optionor (Sam) detrimentally relies upon the rejection, the power to accept the offer terminates at the time of reliance; *i.e.*, when Sam sells the bull. Thus, (B) is correct and (C) is wrong. (A) is wrong because, as stated, the rejection of the offer does not terminate the power of acceptance. (D) is wrong because Sam detrimentally relied on the rejection and thus the power of acceptance terminated earlier than 30 days.

Answer to Question 31

(D) Under U.C.C. section 2-207, proposed new terms in a deal between merchants do not terminate the offer (*i.e.*, do not constitute a counteroffer) and they become part of the deal unless (i) the offer is limited to its own terms, (ii) the new terms materially alter the deal, or (iii) the offeror objects within a reasonable time. (D) is correct and (C) is incorrect because Bill's proposal would materially alter the terms of the contract. (A) and (B) are wrong because the letter is not a counteroffer.

Answer to Question 32

(D) If a buyer is actually insolvent, U.C.C. section 2-702 permits the seller to refuse to deliver except for cash, including payment for all goods previously delivered under the contract. Thus, it does not matter that title passed on delivery to the Southern Pacific Depot. (A) is wrong because while Silicon could stop the goods in transit under U.C.C. section 2-705, even after title passes (thus rendering (B) wrong), it could also demand cash payment. (C) is wrong because the U.C.C. provisions allow the above modifications to payment terms upon finding the buyer insolvent.

Answer to Question 33

(D) U.C.C. section 2-702(2) permits the seller to reclaim goods upon demand within 10 days after the buyer receives them if the seller discovers that the buyer received the goods on credit while insolvent. (A) is incorrect because it does not matter whether the time for payment has passed. (B) is incorrect because, when the buyer is actually insolvent, the U.C.C. allows the seller to do more than merely demand assurances. (C) is incorrect because reliance upon a representation of solvency is not important unless more than 10 days have elapsed since delivery.

Answer to Question 34

(A) U.C.C. section 2-702(3) provides that the successful reclamation of goods from an insolvent buyer excludes all other remedies with respect to them. Thus, (A) is correct and (D) is incorrect. (B) and (C) are incorrect because they do not accurately state remedies for the seller. If the seller did have a right to recover damages, it would be measured by the *difference* between the contract price and the market value of the goods.

Answer to Question 35

(A) U.C.C. section 2-508 provides that where a tender of goods by the seller is rejected because of nonconformance of the goods and the time for performance has not passed, the seller may seasonably notify the buyer of his intention to cure and may then make a conforming delivery within the time specified in the contract. Thus, (A) is correct and (D) is incorrect. (B) is an untrue statement. (C) is incorrect because Silicon timely notified WES of its intention to cure.

CRIMINAL LAW
ANSWER SHEET

1. Ⓐ Ⓑ Ⓒ Ⓓ
2. Ⓐ Ⓑ Ⓒ Ⓓ
3. Ⓐ Ⓑ Ⓒ Ⓓ
4. Ⓐ Ⓑ Ⓒ Ⓓ
5. Ⓐ Ⓑ Ⓒ Ⓓ

6. Ⓐ Ⓑ Ⓒ Ⓓ
7. Ⓐ Ⓑ Ⓒ Ⓓ
8. Ⓐ Ⓑ Ⓒ Ⓓ
9. Ⓐ Ⓑ Ⓒ Ⓓ
10. Ⓐ Ⓑ Ⓒ Ⓓ

11. Ⓐ Ⓑ Ⓒ Ⓓ
12. Ⓐ Ⓑ Ⓒ Ⓓ
13. Ⓐ Ⓑ Ⓒ Ⓓ
14. Ⓐ Ⓑ Ⓒ Ⓓ
15. Ⓐ Ⓑ Ⓒ Ⓓ

16. Ⓐ Ⓑ Ⓒ Ⓓ
17. Ⓐ Ⓑ Ⓒ Ⓓ
18. Ⓐ Ⓑ Ⓒ Ⓓ

19. Ⓐ Ⓑ Ⓒ Ⓓ
20. Ⓐ Ⓑ Ⓒ Ⓓ
21. Ⓐ Ⓑ Ⓒ Ⓓ
22. Ⓐ Ⓑ Ⓒ Ⓓ
23. Ⓐ Ⓑ Ⓒ Ⓓ

24. Ⓐ Ⓑ Ⓒ Ⓓ
25. Ⓐ Ⓑ Ⓒ Ⓓ
26. Ⓐ Ⓑ Ⓒ Ⓓ
27. Ⓐ Ⓑ Ⓒ Ⓓ
28. Ⓐ Ⓑ Ⓒ Ⓓ

29. Ⓐ Ⓑ Ⓒ Ⓓ
30. Ⓐ Ⓑ Ⓒ Ⓓ
31. Ⓐ Ⓑ Ⓒ Ⓓ
32. Ⓐ Ⓑ Ⓒ Ⓓ
33. Ⓐ Ⓑ Ⓒ Ⓓ

34. Ⓐ Ⓑ Ⓒ Ⓓ
35. Ⓐ Ⓑ Ⓒ Ⓓ

CRIMINAL LAW QUESTIONS

Question 1

Edgar owned and operated a used car dealership in the City of Oakridge. For several months, Philmont, an agent for the Internal Revenue Service, has been investigating Edgar and his car dealership because of suspected fraudulent tax returns Edgar had been filing. In addition, Oscar, a detective for State, which had been investigating a stolen car ring, uncovered evidence indicating that Edgar might be a part of the ring. Oscar went to Edgar's car lot and found evidence indicating that the ring was operating through Edgar's used car sales lot. Oscar asked Edgar to go with him to the police station to make a statement regarding the evidence Oscar had just uncovered, and Edgar agreed. While in the police car on the way to the station, Edgar voluntarily informed Oscar about the fraudulently filed tax returns, because he believed that by revealing these facts he might receive a lighter sentence for his involvement in the stolen car ring.

Edgar was tried for filing false tax returns. At the trial, Edgar's attorney moved to exclude the statements made to Oscar in the police car. The prosecuting attorney argued strongly against granting the motion. The best argument for admitting the statement is that:

(A) Oscar was not an agent of the Internal Revenue Service.

(B) Edgar had not been formally charged at the time that the statement was made.

(C) The statement was volunteered by Edgar.

(D) The statement was made prior to the arrest of Edgar.

Question 2

Xavier and Zack agreed to break into Alice's house and steal two paintings hanging in Alice's den. They were arrested shortly after they pried open Alice's back door. Both were charged with conspiracy to commit larceny, among other crimes. Xavier testified that he suspected Zack of being a thief, that he agreed to the plan in order to catch Zack, and that he had made an anonymous telephone call to the police alerting them to the crime, enabling the police to arrest them "in the act." Zack did not testify. The jurisdiction follows common law conspiracy rules.

As to a charge of conspiracy to commit larceny, if the jury believes Xavier, it should find him:

(A) Not guilty, because he did not intend to steal.

(B) Not guilty, because he prevented the theft from occurring.

(C) Guilty, because there was an agreement, and the prying open of the back door was sufficient for the overt act.

(D) Guilty, because he is not a police officer, and thus cannot claim any privilege of apprehending criminals.

Question 3

Gordon was weaving all over the road and driving very erratically when stopped by state troopers and arrested for drunk driving. He was advised of his constitutional rights and elected to remain silent. At trial for his drunk driving charge, Gordon testified in his own defense, stating that he had just left his doctor's office and had been administered medication without being told that it would seriously and immediately hamper his coordination. On cross-examination, the prosecutor asks, "Didn't you just make up this medication story after the fact to evade legitimate liability for driving while intoxicated?" When Gordon replied that he had not, the prosecutor asked, "Then why didn't you tell the arresting officer about the medication?" Defense counsel objects.

The trial court should rule that the question is:

(A) Improper, because to require the defense to inform the prosecution of defendant's testimony prior to trial would be unconstitutional pretrial discovery.

(B) Improper, because use of defendant's post-arrest silence violates his right to due process of law.

(C) Proper, since defendant's silence was not used as direct evidence but only for impeachment on cross-examination.

(D) Proper, because defendant's post-arrest silence is a prior inconsistent statement which is admissible to show recent fabrication.

Question 4

Bob and his employer, Don, had a dispute over how much money Bob was due for work done at the garage. Don alleged that he had paid Bob $300 that month for work on cars that Bob did not do, and Bob contended that he had done the work. At the conclusion, Bob said he was going to quit, and Don said it was fine with him but he was going to keep Bob's tools until Bob repaid him the money he had been overpaid.

Bob, still very angry, went down the street to a bar where he saw a friend of his, Greg, a small-time thief. They had a few drinks together, and Bob told Greg what happened. Greg suggested to Bob that he could go to the garage and get an estimate of how much it would cost to replace the transmission in his car. Then, while Don was writing the estimate, Greg would take Bob's tool box and put it in the trunk of his car. Bob thought this was a great idea and described the location of his tool box and gave its description to Greg.

Greg went to the garage as planned, and when Don went into the office to write up an estimate, Greg grabbed what he believed to be Bob's tool kit and put it in his car. But Don had locked Bob's tool kit in the storage room, and another mechanic who worked in the garage had taken over Bob's station, so the kit taken by Greg was the other mechanic's.

After Greg left, Don realized that Greg must have stolen the tool kit. He took the license number he had on the work sheet and gave it to the police. Several minutes later, the police spotted Greg's car outside the bar, and, as Bob and Greg came out to go to the car, arrested them both.

Of the following, which is the best argument for Greg as a defense to a charge of larceny?

(A) He had the consent of the owner to take the tool box.

(B) He thought the tool box belonged to Bob.

(C) He was not intending to keep the tool box, but to give it to Bob.

(D) He was apprehended by the police before Bob could inspect the tool box.

Question 5

Asher planned to rob a bank. He asked Frederick to join him in the robbery and proposed that Frederick supply his car and driving skills to assist in getting to the bank and making a successful escape. Although Frederick had no desire to participate in the robbery, he pretended to agree to aid Asher and planned to report Asher's plan to the police before Asher could commit the crime.

On the day that Asher had appointed for the crime, Frederick drove to Asher's house and picked up Asher. Asher told Frederick to drive him to the Third National Bank. Frederick took a direct route, but approximately two miles from the bank he told Asher that he needed a pack of cigarettes and drove into the parking lot of a convenience store. Inside the store, Frederick used a pay telephone to call the local police. He told them that a robbery was about to take place at the Third National Bank and that units should be assigned there to prevent the crime. The desk sergeant, Stella, thought that Frederick was making a "crank call." She laughed at him and hung up the phone. Frederick made another attempt to call the police, but Stella answered again, laughed at him, and hung up. Frederick was now out of quarters and he went back to the parking lot, intending to talk Asher out of going to the bank. When he reached the lot, he found the car missing. Frederick had left his keys in the ignition and also had left the engine running. When Frederick had not emerged from the store in five minutes, Asher had grown nervous and had driven off in the car. Asher drove to the bank and robbed it at gunpoint. Asher fled the scene in Frederick's car, but was apprehended a short time later.

If Frederick is charged with conspiracy, the trial court is most likely to find him:

(A) Guilty, because his withdrawal was ineffective since it was not communicated to Asher in time for him to change his plans.

(B) Guilty, because he provided Asher with an instrumentality of the crime.

(C) Not guilty, because Frederick withdrew from any conspiracy.

(D) Not guilty, because Frederick lacked criminal intent.

Question 6

Frank planned to rob the local currency exchange but needed a getaway car and somebody to be a lookout. Frank asked Jeff, who had a car, if he wanted to take part in the scheme. Jeff immediately refused and warned him against carrying it out. Frank did not want Jeff to tell anyone so he showed Jeff his gun and said that he would use it on him if he did not go along with the plan. In the face of this threat, Jeff consented to help Frank and the pair left for the currency exchange, with Jeff driving. When they arrived, Jeff left the car running so that he could get away and contact the police while Frank was inside. However, Frank ordered Jeff to go inside with him. During the robbery attempt, the clerk pulled out a gun, and Frank and the clerk shot and killed each other.

If Jeff is charged with the killing of the store clerk, should the jury find him criminally liable if it accepts Jeff's version of the facts?

(A) Yes, because duress is not a defense to murder.

(B) Yes, because the clerk's death occurred in furtherance of and during the perpetration of a robbery in which Jeff was participating.

(C) No, because Jeff lacked the requisite intent.

(D) No, because Jeff withdrew from the conspiracy to commit robbery and thus is not liable for any acts committed in furtherance of the conspiracy.

Question 7

Harfo, Groufo, and Chifo met in a room in the Hotsheetz Hotel on a Saturday night and agreed that they would rob a nearby branch of the Last Bank and Trust Company on the following Tuesday. Harfo was assigned the task of stealing a car to be used for the getaway, Chifo agreed to procure weapons, and Groufo would "case" the bank to determine the location of cameras, guards, and other security devices. On Sunday night, Harfo stole a car and parked it in a lot behind his girlfriend's apartment building. While visiting his girlfriend on Monday night, Harfo complained of severe chest pain and shortly thereafter suffered a series of convulsive seizures. Harfo's girlfriend called an ambulance and Harfo was rushed to the hospital. Harfo was placed in the intensive care unit and heavily sedated. Groufo and Chifo, unaware of Harfo's illness, met at the appointed place of rendezvous and decided to rob the bank on their own, despite the absence of Harfo and a getaway car. They robbed the bank, but were quickly apprehended as they tried to escape on foot. Groufo and Chifo implicated Harfo under police questioning.

Harfo can be charged with:

(A) Theft of the car only.

(B) Conspiracy to commit robbery and theft of the car only.

(C) Robbery and theft of the car only.

(D) Theft of the car, conspiracy to commit robbery, and robbery.

Question 8

Archie Delphinium and his wife, Edith, were taking an extended motor tour of the United States. When the Delphiniums were driving through the sparsely populated high plains of the Western state of Arapahoe, Edith complained to Archie of severe pains in her abdominal area. She asked if he would please stop in Crow City, the next town of any consequence, to have a doctor examine her. Signs on the interstate highway indicated that Crow City had an emergency hospital facility. Signs on the highway also stated: "Next food, gas, and lodging at Dry Gulch, 118 miles." It was getting to be late in the afternoon, and Archie had a reservation at the Highway Inn in Dry Gulch that would be automatically canceled if the Delphiniums did not arrive before 6 p.m. He, therefore, refused to stop at Crow City and drove on toward Dry Gulch. In fact, Edith was suffering from an attack of acute appendicitis. Her appendix burst about 30 miles from Dry Gulch, and she was on the point of expiring when Archie arrived at the Dry Gulch Clinic. A nurse attended to Edith and called Dr. Holiday, the only physician in the county, and he arrived 30 minutes later. Holiday concluded that it was too late to save Edith's life and she died two hours later. After a coroner's inquest into the death of Edith, Archie was charged with murder.

Which of the following, if true, would be the fact most beneficial to Archie's defense?

(A) Although Edith held herself out as "Mrs. Delphinium," and the couple had lived together for many years, Archie and Edith were never legally married.

(B) The Dry Gulch Clinic had adequate operating facilities and an adequate supply of pharmaceuticals to save Edith's life, but Dr.

Holiday acted incompetently when he failed to make a more serious attempt to save Edith's life.

(C) An autopsy following Edith's death disclosed that she had cancer, from which she would have died within a few months.

(D) Archie did not believe that Edith's complaints of abdominal pain signaled a serious medical problem.

Question 9

Under which of the following circumstances would the named defendant most likely be found *not guilty* of larceny?

(A) Upon leaving his police science class, Jack sees the bicycle of another student leaning against the building, and, without the owner's knowledge or permission, rides away on the bike, intending to sell it at a local swap meet.

(B) Jill, who is moving permanently to Afghanistan, asks an acquaintance if she can borrow the latter's backpack and frame. Jill immediately leaves for Afghanistan after obtaining the backpack and frame.

(C) Reginald, who learned that an accountant had embezzled $100,000 from his employer, went to the accountant's apartment and took the cash, intending to spend it on a wild weekend in Mallorca.

(D) Sherri, needing a ride to work, hot wires her neighbor's Cadillac and drives it into town. Sherri intends to drive the car back at the end of the workday and return it to the neighbor, who is away on vacation.

Question 10

In which of the following situations is Defendant *least* likely to be found guilty of murder?

(A) Not intending to kill, Defendant hits Victim over the head with a lead pipe, and Victim dies from the wound.

(B) Not intending to kill, Defendant while at a party pushes Victim, a 10-year-old child, into the swimming pool, and Victim drowns.

(C) Not intending to kill, Defendant drops bricks from the top of a tall building into the crowd below; one of the bricks strikes and kills Victim.

(D) Not intending to kill, Defendant committing a robbery, pushes Victim, a store clerk; Victim falls, strikes her head on the counter, and dies.

Question 11

After much discussion, Axle, Bowers, and Crandall decided to burglarize the home of King, a prominent businessman. The three agreed that the crime would be committed the following Saturday night. On Thursday, Crandall stole a gun for "insurance" in case they encountered trouble during the burglary. On Friday, Crandall was arrested and jailed for a previous, unrelated crime. He was kept in confinement over the weekend. Axle and Bowers decided to go ahead with the burglary. On Saturday night, as they were about to break open the front door to King's home, they were arrested by a passing police officer.

Crandall is guilty of:

(A) Larceny of the gun only.

(B) Larceny of the gun and conspiracy only.

(C) Larceny of the gun and attempted burglary only.

(D) Larceny of the gun, conspiracy, and attempted burglary.

Question 12

Deal has had a history of epileptic seizures over the last five years. Each seizure comes upon him without warning. One day, Deal decided to attend an afternoon movie in town. As he was driving to the theater he had a seizure. He lost control of the car and struck a pedestrian who was lawfully crossing the street. The pedestrian died on the way to the hospital as a result of his injuries. Deal is charged with involuntary manslaughter.

He will most likely be found:

(A) Guilty, because the law presumes that a person intends the natural and probable consequences of his acts.

(B) Guilty, because he knowingly and recklessly chose to drive his car.

(C) Not guilty, because his failure to control the car was not a voluntary act.

(D) Not guilty, because he had no intent to harm anyone.

Question 13

Print kept a small printing press in one room of his home. He used the printing press to help him in his business. Trout was a classmate of Print's son, Donny. She had been in Print's home on many occasions to visit with Donny and had seen the printing press. Trout decided to print a one-page newsletter critical of the local school board's policies and distribute it around town. On an evening when she knew Print and his family were not at home, Trout broke into Print's home intending to use the printing press to print her newsletter. She believed that the unauthorized use of the printing press constituted a crime, but she was mistaken in this belief. Print and his family returned home while Trout was still in the house. She was arrested and charged with burglary. The jurisdiction defines burglary as the breaking and entering of the dwelling house of another at nighttime with the intent to commit a crime.

Trout should be found:

(A) Guilty, because her mistake was one of law, not of fact.

(B) Guilty, because she broke and entered Print's home believing she was going to commit a crime.

(C) Not guilty, because even if she had been successful, no crime would have occurred.

(D) Not guilty, because there was no dangerous proximity to success.

Question 14

Murphy was convicted after a jury trial of violation of federal statutes prohibiting the sale of automatic weapons to foreign nationals, in connection with his activities as a procurement officer for the Provisional Wing of the Irish Republican Army. It was established at trial that Murphy had purchased a number of stolen U.S. Army heavy machine guns and attempted to ship them to Ireland in crates marked "machine parts." The trial court expressly based its imposition of the maximum possible sentence for the conviction on Murphy's refusal to reveal the names of the persons from whom he purchased the stolen weapons.

You are a court of appeals justice authoring the opinion in Murphy's appeal of the sentence imposed. His counsel argues that the trial court's consideration of Murphy's failure to name the sellers of the stolen weapons is reversible error. You should:

(A) Reverse the trial court, because the consideration of Murphy's silence violates his Fifth Amendment privilege against self-incrimination.

(B) Reverse the trial court, because the consideration of collateral circumstances in sentencing violates his due process rights.

(C) Affirm the trial court, because the right to silence of the Fifth Amendment does not include the right to protect others from incrimination.

(D) Affirm the trial court, because citizens must report violations of the criminal statutes.

Question 15

At Dale's trial for battery, it is established that Viola was struck in the face by Dale's fist. Which of the following, if true, would *least* support a finding that Dale had committed battery?

(A) Dale had just been awakened by Viola, and, still groggy, he thought she was a burglar and struck her before he realized the truth.

(B) Dale was at a party where an amateur hypnotist placed him in a highly suggestible state and instructed him that Viola was Adolf Hitler, whereupon Dale struck her.

(C) Dale was showing a friend how Muhammad Ali knocked Sonny Liston down, and being somewhat tipsy, became too exuberant and struck Viola, who was standing nearby.

(D) In setting up equipment for a polygraph examination of Dale, Viola accidentally touched a live electrical wire to Dale's armpit, causing him to involuntarily twitch his arm forward, striking her in the face.

Question 16

Mark was deer hunting with some friends when he thought he saw a deer in a copse of trees a few hundred yards away. To approach the trees, Mark had to climb over a fence posted with "no hunting" and "no trespassing" signs. Mark carefully stalked the fleet-footed forest creature, fired, and discovered to his chagrin that he had just shot a large bull. Homer, owner of the property, heard the shot and grabbed his shotgun, fearing that hunters had shot another one of his cattle. When he arrived at the copse of trees and discovered that Mark had killed his prize bull, he became enraged and ordered Mark to get off his property in extremely abusive language. Instead of leaving immediately, Mark said, "It's just a damn cow!" Homer raised his shotgun and fired at Mark, narrowly missing him. When Homer operated the pump-action of the shotgun and raised it again, Mark shot and killed him.

In Mark's prosecution for murder, he should be found:

(A) Guilty, because he was a trespasser on Homer's land.

(B) Not guilty, because Homer attacked him with deadly force.

(C) Guilty, because Homer's attack was provoked by Mark.

(D) Not guilty, because Homer had no right to defend his property with deadly force.

Question 17

Jim and Sandy had recently separated, although they had not yet filed for a divorce. Jim lived in a hotel in the downtown area while Sandy resided in the house that was jointly owned by Jim and Sandy. Shortly after the period of separation began, Sandy started to date Nick, whom she had recently met. Upon bringing Sandy home from a date, Nick would quite often stay for a drink before leaving for home. One night while Sandy and Nick were in the house having a drink, Jim burst in and told Nick, "Get out." When Nick refused, Jim said, "Then let's go outside and settle this right now." Nick again refused. Jim then pulled a knife from his pocket and moved toward Nick. Nick immediately grabbed a chair and hit Jim on the head, killing him instantly. Nick was arrested and charged with murder.

Nick will most likely be found:

(A) Guilty, if Nick could have retreated safely once Jim pulled out a knife.

(B) Guilty, because Nick's failure to obey Jim's order to leave the house made Nick a trespasser.

(C) Not guilty, because Jim attacked Nick with a deadly weapon.

(D) Not guilty, because Sandy had invited Nick into the house.

Question 18

In which of the following cases is a conviction of the named defendant for robbery **least likely** to be upheld?

(A) Having induced a woman to return home with him, Philips tells her that she will not be allowed to leave unless she gives him all of her money. Fearing for her safety, the woman gives Philips all of the cash she has in her possession.

(B) While in a bar, Ericson noticed the wallet of the man sitting next to him laying on the counter. Ericson waited until the man was looking away and then picked up the wallet and put it into his pocket. Shortly thereafter, the man realized his wallet was gone and accused Ericson of taking it. Ericson pretended to be insulted, slapped the victim, and went off with the wallet.

(C) Sanders broke into a home he believed was unoccupied. Upon finding a man inside, he tied him up and forced him to tell Sanders where he kept his money. Sanders went to the spot, took the money, and fled.

(D) Billings hired a friend to bump into people at an airport hard enough to cause them to drop their luggage. Billings would then pick up the luggage and run off with it.

Question 19

Prex, the president of a private college, received a report that there was a great deal of cocaine use occurring on the second floor of the old dormitory. Prex persuaded the school security officers to place several concealed microphones in the second-floor student lounge. Conversations occurring in the lounge were monitored by the security officers. Security officers recorded a conversation in which Jackson, a student at the college, offered to sell cocaine to another student. A security officer took a tape of the conversation to the local police, who played it for a local judge. The judge issued a warrant to search Jackson's room.

While searching the room the police discovered a large amount of cocaine. Jackson was arrested and charged with unlawful possession of narcotics. Jackson's attorney moved to prevent the introduction of the cocaine into evidence.

The motion will most likely be:

(A) Granted, because Jackson's privacy was unreasonably invaded.

(B) Granted, because the electronic surveillance was "fundamentally unfair."

(C) Denied, because the police properly obtained a search warrant.

(D) Denied, because Prex was acting on behalf of the college population in general.

Question 20

Mary was walking her dog one evening when the leash slipped out of her hand and the dog began to run away. Mary reached out, trying to grab the leash, and in so doing narrowly missed striking Anne, who was walking along the street in the opposite direction. Anne flinched and raised her arms, believing that she was about to be attacked by Mary.

If charged with criminal assault, Mary should be found:

(A) Guilty, because she should have realized she might strike someone by reaching out to recapture the leash.

(B) Guilty, because she caused Anne to be apprehensive of an offensive touching.

(C) Not guilty, because she did not hit Anne.

(D) Not guilty, because she was reaching out to recapture the leash.

Question 21

Laurel and Hardy were arguing on the front lawn of Laurel's house. Hardy, who was a bigger and slower man, decided to end the argument by pushing Laurel as hard as he could. Laurel, fearful that Hardy would continue or escalate the fight as he has done in the past, tackled Hardy and pinned him to the ground, although Laurel could have easily escaped into his house.

If Laurel is tried for battery, he should be found:

(A) Guilty, because Laurel "offensively touched" Hardy by tackling and pinning him.

(B) Guilty, because Laurel could have retreated.

(C) Not guilty, because Laurel was justified in tackling and pinning Hardy.

(D) Not guilty, because Laurel did not intend to hurt Hardy.

Question 22

In which of the following situations is Defendant most likely to be guilty of larceny?

(A) Unreasonably mistaking another man's hat for his own, Defendant takes the hat off the hat rack and walks off with it.

(B) Wishing to collect on a long-time debt, Defendant went into Fred's house and took $50 in cash, the amount Fred owed him.

(C) Defendant took Phil's car with the intention of returning it the next day. However, he was involved in an automobile accident and totaled the car before he could return it.

(D) Mistakenly believing that larceny only involves the taking of items over $100 in value, Defendant takes his neighbor's lawn mower worth $75 and sells it to a third person.

Question 23

Nan ran a boarding house for local factory workers. One evening she smelled what she believed to be a suspicious odor coming from the room of a young boarder, Hal. She telephoned her daughter Yolanda, who was a police officer, and told her of the smell. Her daughter, suspecting that it was marijuana, told her mother that she wanted her to inspect the room the next day when Hal was at work, and if she found anything, to bring it to her.

The next morning, after Hal had gone, Nan took the master key and went into his room. In a drawer next to his bed, she found a box of tablets and some white powder. She took these to her daughter, who checked with the narcotics division and confirmed that they were drugs. Yolanda had her mother return the items, swear out an affidavit, and she had a search warrant issued.

When Hal returned that night, the police arrested him and searched his room. A quantity of drugs was found, and Hal was charged with possession of narcotics for sale.

At trial Hal moved to prevent the evidence of the drugs from being introduced. The trial judge should:

(A) Grant Hal's motion, because once the drugs had been taken to the police department, they had to be kept there and could not be returned to Hal's room for the purpose of finding them there.

(B) Grant Hal's motion, because his reasonable expectation of privacy had been unreasonably invaded.

(C) Deny Hal's motion, because Nan, as owner of the boarding house, had a legal right to inspect the rooms.

(D) Deny Hal's motion, because even without the drugs found by Nan, the police had reasonable cause to seek a search warrant.

Question 24

Gene, learning that his old friend Bart was out of prison, left the following note in his mailbox: "I'm glad to see that you are finally out. Have just found out that Larry is getting a shipment of stolen fur coats at Walker & Son's Warehouse

next Saturday. I have a way of stealing them late Saturday night when no one is around. Interested? Contact me at 555-1234. Gene."

Bart, however, had gone to see some friends in another city and had left the apartment to Ray, who also just got out of prison. Ray, after reading the note, called Ginger and told her to meet him in her car and bring a gun, because he had just overheard at a bar about this shipment of fur coats that was being delivered on Saturday.

Saturday morning, as Larry was opening the warehouse, Ginger and Ray jumped him. However, the police, who had heard of the shipment, were staking out the warehouse, and when they saw Larry get jumped, they moved in and arrested all of them before the shipment arrived.

On Friday, Gene investigated why Bart had not called. When he learned that Bart had gone out of town, he decided it would be impossible to steal the furs himself. But when the police found his note on Ray, they picked up Gene and arrested him.

Gene is charged with conspiracy in a jurisdiction that follows the common law rules. At Gene's preliminary hearing, the best argument his attorney can make to quash the charge is that:

(A) The note did not contain sufficient details of a "plan" to commit an unlawful act.

(B) Gene did not know Ray.

(C) Gene had made no agreement with Ray or Bart.

(D) Ray and Ginger had been arrested before the shipment arrived, so no crime had been committed.

Question 25

Barney had been seeing Hank's wife for several weeks. One night they were drinking together in a bar, when suddenly Hank walked in. Seeing them together, he yelled, "I'm going to kill you!" and put his hand into his coat. Seeing his actions, Barney grabbed a heavy ashtray from the table and hit him in the head. As a result of the blow, Hank, who had a plate in his head, died. No weapon was found on his person.

Barney is charged with manslaughter. Of the following, which is the best defense Barney can assert?

(A) He did not intend to seriously injure Hank.

(B) He thought Hank had a weapon.

(C) He did not know that Hank had a plate in his head.

(D) He had no time for deliberation or premeditation.

Question 26

In response to a telephone call, a report went out over the police radio requesting an ambulance because of a shooting. Several officers who heard the broadcast arrived at the subject residence and knocked on the front door, identifying themselves as police officers. Believing that someone inside the house had been shot, one of the officers entered the building through an unlocked window and opened the front door for the other officers to enter. While searching for victims, the officers saw, in plain view, several containers of cocaine. Defendant, the occupant of the house, was arrested and charged with possession of narcotics. At his trial, Defendant moved to suppress the evidence of the narcotics on the ground that the police officers' warrantless entry into his residence was improper.

Did the police officers have a right to enter the building without a warrant?

(A) Yes, because exigent circumstances existed as a result of the shooting.

(B) Yes, because the police officers were acting in their official function.

(C) No, because there were no factors to indicate that there was not enough time to obtain a warrant.

(D) No, because there was no probable cause to enter without a warrant.

Question 27

After receiving a telephone call that a gunshot was heard there, the police went to a warehouse. There they found Davis standing over Vic's body. They immediately arrested Davis, gave him his *Miranda* warnings, and when he requested his attorney, took him to jail. At trial, Davis testified in his own defense. He claimed that he was in the warehouse alone when he was attacked by Vic, and that he shot Vic in self-defense. The prosecution, on cross-examination, asked Davis why he did not tell the police when they arrived there that he had shot Vic in self-defense. Davis's attorney objected to this question, but he was overruled. Davis was unable to give a very satisfactory answer, and the prosecution suggested that he was lying.

Davis was convicted. He appealed, contending that the prosecutor's cross-examination was improper. His conviction would most likely be:

(A) Reversed, because once Davis had asked for an attorney, he had no obligation to talk with the police while he was in custody.

(B) Reversed, because post-arrest silence constitutes Davis's exercise of his *Miranda* rights and use of that silence against him at trial would violate due process.

(C) Affirmed, because Davis's silence when the police arrived is tantamount to a prior inconsistent statement, giving rise to an inference that the story was fabricated.

(D) Affirmed, because by taking the stand, Davis waived any right he may have had not to testify against himself.

Question 28

A statute in this jurisdiction makes it a felony for any "married person to enter into a new marriage with another when such married person knows, or should know, that his former marriage has not been terminated by a divorce decree or by the death of a former spouse."

Annie is charged with bigamy when it is discovered that she married Gerald while still being married to Rodney. Annie's best defense to this charge is that:

(A) She filed for a divorce but just never got around to requesting the court to enter a divorce decree.

(B) Rodney left home one night after a bad argument, and she has not seen or heard from him in three years.

(C) She retained an attorney to get her a divorce from Rodney, and she believed she had received a divorce.

(D) When she and Rodney were first married, she was underage and so she believed her first marriage to have been invalid.

Question 29

Mervin, a professional jewel thief, sold some stolen goods, including a sterling silver cigar box, to Giles, an antique dealer who frequently purchased stolen goods from Mervin. Several weeks later, acting on an anonymous tip, the police raided Giles's store and arrested him. In this raid, the police seized the goods Mervin sold to Giles and some records in which Giles had recorded this transaction. However, at Giles's subsequent trial for receiving stolen goods, the charges against him were dismissed when the court ruled that the search warrant had been improperly issued.

The police were able to trace the stolen goods to Mervin because of fingerprint identification and the information contained in Giles's record book. At his trial, Mervin made a motion to suppress the stolen goods and record book.

The judge should:

(A) Grant the motion, because the evidence is the fruit of the poisonous tree in that the search of Giles's store was improper.

(B) Grant the motion, because the trial court in Giles's case has already ruled that the evidence was improper.

(C) Deny the motion, because Mervin's fingerprints on the stolen goods were what led to his identification.

(D) Deny the motion, because Mervin has no standing to object to the search.

Question 30

Gregg was invited over to his friend Jud's house for drinks. After a couple of beers, Jud told Gregg that he wanted to show him something that he just got. Jud went into his bedroom and brought out a pre-WWII German Luger. Jud told Gregg that he had stolen the gun from a local museum several days before. Gregg asked him if he was interested in selling it, but Jud said no.

They then decided that they would go out to a bar. As they got to Gregg's car, Gregg realized that he had left his coat in the house and told Jud that he was going back to get it. Gregg went back into the room, and as he picked up his coat, he saw the stolen pistol on the table. He quickly picked it up and put it in his pocket.

Gregg is charged with larceny and burglary. In this jurisdiction, burglary is defined as the breaking and entering of the dwelling place of another with the intent to commit any theft or felony.

Assuming that the evidence at trial shows that in fact the pistol was stolen, Gregg should be convicted of:

(A) Both larceny and burglary.

(B) Burglary only.

(C) Larceny only.

(D) Neither larceny nor burglary.

Question 31

Dorian is on trial for a federal offense. The government has subpoenaed crucial documents from Dorian's bookkeeper. The documents will clearly incriminate Dorian, and so Dorian wishes to invoke her Fifth Amendment privilege against self-incrimination to prevent the documents from being admitted.

Will Dorian succeed in preventing admission of the documents?

(A) Yes, because the documents will incriminate Dorian.

(B) Yes, because the documents belong to Dorian; the bookkeeper merely has custody of them.

(C) No, unless the documents include records required to be kept by legislation.

(D) No, because the Fifth Amendment privilege applies only to compelled testimony.

Questions 32-34 are based on the following fact situation:

The statutes of State Z define the following crimes (with the most serious listed first):

First degree murder—Premeditated or intentional killing.

Felony murder—Killing while in the act of committing a common law felony.

Second degree murder—Killing with reckless disregard for the safety of others.

Manslaughter—Killing with adequate provocation or through criminal negligence.

State Z has another statute that states: "It shall be a felony to dispense prescription drugs without a prescription."

Alyce, a student activist vehemently opposed to nuclear power, suggested to her boyfriend, Bob, that they put nitroglycerine in the sugar bowls at their college cafeteria so that some of their fellow students would become sick to their stomachs and the anti-nuclear group could claim that toxic emissions from a nearby nuclear power plant were the cause. Bob told Alyce that people could become very ill, or even die, if they consumed too large a quantity of nitroglycerine. Alyce said that they would only put a little nitroglycerine in each bowl and asked Bob to get the drug from his friend Phil, a pharmacist. Bob at first refused, but when Alyce threatened to break up with Bob if he did not get the drug, Bob agreed to obtain nitroglycerine. Bob told Phil that his doctor had prescribed nitroglycerine pills for him, that Bob had lost the prescription, and that the doctor was on an extended visit to Tierra del Fuego and could not be reached. Phil did not know about the statute making it a felony to dispense drugs without prescription and gave Bob a bottle of nitroglycerine pills. Bob gave the bottle to Alyce. Before Bob awoke the next day, Alyce broke open the pills, went to the cafeteria, and put small quantities of nitroglycerine in several sugar bowls. She unintentionally put a much larger amount in the sugar bowl at one table. A number of people became slightly ill from ingesting the drug. However, four persons who sat at the table where Alyce had put a large amount in the bowl became extremely ill, and one of the four eventually died.

32. The most serious crime for which Alyce may be convicted is:

(A) First degree murder.

(B) Felony murder.

(C) Second degree murder.

(D) Manslaughter.

33. In the death of the student, Bob may be liable as:

(A) An accessory before the fact.

(B) A principal in the first degree.

(C) A principal in the second degree.

(D) An accessory after the fact.

34. The most serious crime for which Phil may be convicted is:

(A) Felony murder.

(B) Second degree murder.

(C) Dispensing drugs without a prescription.

(D) No crime, because Phil did not know what Bob was going to do with the drugs and was unaware of the drug dispensing statute.

Question 35

Deft left his horse with Fillmont's Stable while he went on vacation. When he returned, he went to the stable to pick up his horse and was informed by Fillmont that the bill was $500. Deft told Fillmont that he would have to go home and get more money. Deft believed that he was being overcharged by Fillmont; instead of paying Fillmont, he arranged to have Neighbor pick up the horse from the stable. Neighbor thought that the stable bill had been paid and Deft had a right to the horse; thus, Neighbor took the horse without Fillmont's knowledge. Halfway to Deft's house, Neighbor decided to keep the horse and rode away on it to his own home.

Is Neighbor guilty of larceny in taking the horse from Fillmont?

(A) Yes, because Deft had not paid the stable bill.

(B) Yes, because Fillmont had possession of the horse.

(C) No, because Deft was the rightful owner of the horse.

(D) No, because he did not know that Fillmont had not been paid for the stable bill.

CRIMINAL LAW ANSWERS

Answer to Question 1

(C) Even though Edgar may have been in custody and may not yet have received his *Miranda* warnings, no violation of Edgar's constitutional rights occurs if he volunteers revelations of his criminal conduct, especially when they are unrelated to the crime for which he is under arrest. (A) is wrong. The fact that a confession offered in a federal prosecution was made to a state police officer will not automatically allow it into evidence. It will be suppressed if it is the product of some violation of the accused's constitutional rights by the state officer. (B) is wrong; if Edgar had not been formally charged, his Sixth Amendment right to counsel would not be implicated by his confession to Oscar. However, this would not prevent suppression of the confession if his Fifth Amendment *Miranda* rights were violated. (D) is not the best answer because *Miranda* violations can occur before a formal arrest.

Answer to Question 2

(A) The crime of conspiracy requires that each conspirator intends to achieve an unlawful goal. Thus, if the jury believes Xavier that he agreed to the plan in order to have Zack arrested, he must be found innocent, because he would not have the intent to achieve an unlawful goal. (C) is therefore incorrect. (B) is incorrect because, at common law, his act of prevention would not have excused the conspiracy if he had the proper mental state. (D) is incorrect because the privilege to apprehend criminals is not in issue here.

Answer to Question 3

(B) After arrest a defendant has a right to remain silent, and his silence cannot be used against him. (A) is wrong; the question is improper but not for the reason set forth in (A). (C) and (D) are incorrect. Statements made without proper *Miranda* warnings can sometimes be used to impeach, but the defendant's silence would not be classified as a prior statement.

Answer to Question 4

(B) Larceny is a specific intent crime, and the defendant must have had the intent to take the property of another. If Greg, as Bob's agent, was intending to take only Bob's tool box, he had no intent to take the property of another. (A) is wrong, of course, because he did not have the consent of the owner of the tool box he took. (C) is incorrect because it is not a defense to a charge of larceny that the defendant was not intending to keep the item taken for his own use. (D) is incorrect because, although once he found out his mistake, he may have intended to return the tool box, he could have just as easily decided to keep it.

Answer to Question 5

(D) Frederick never had the required mental state for conspiracy. Conspiracy requires three elements: (i) an agreement between two or more persons; (ii) an intent to enter into an agreement (which is often inferred from the act of agreement); and (iii) an intent to achieve the objective of the agreement. The two intent elements indicate that conspiracy is a specific intent crime. A defendant must have had both intents to be found guilty. Here, since Frederick planned to contact the police before Asher could commit the crime, he never intended to achieve the criminal objective of robbing the bank. Thus, he cannot be found guilty of conspiracy. (A) is incorrect because Frederick never entered into the conspiracy to begin with (because he lacked the requisite intent); thus, he did not need to withdraw. (B) is incorrect because merely providing the instrumentality to commit the crime is insufficient by itself to establish liability for conspiracy; there must also be some intent to facilitate the crime. The facts show that Frederick *never intended* to commit the crime, and thus he cannot be guilty of conspiracy. (C) is incorrect because, as stated above, Frederick never entered into the conspiracy. If he had, (C) would still be incorrect because at common law and in most states withdrawal is not a defense to the conspiracy charge itself, merely a limitation on liability for the subsequent acts of the co-conspirators.

Answer to Question 6

(C) Jeff lacked the requisite intent to be liable as either principal to the robbery or as a conspirator with Frank. Thus, he cannot be convicted for the killing of the clerk. A defendant may, by virtue of his participation in a conspiracy, be liable for the crime of all other conspirators if the crimes were committed in furtherance of the objectives of the conspiracy and were a natural and probable consequence of the conspiracy (*i.e.,* were foreseeable). Furthermore, liability for felony murder would attach if the killing were committed during the course of a felony. Thus, Jeff would be criminally liable for the killing of the clerk if he were a co-conspirator or if he were a principal to the underlying felony (the robbery). However, under the facts, Jeff is neither a co-conspirator nor a principal to the robbery because he lacked the requisite intent. Given the threat to his life, Jeff did not freely enter into a conspiracy to commit robbery. Furthermore, a defendant cannot be convicted of felony murder if he has a valid defense to the underlying offense. Here, Jeff was acting under duress during the robbery, and thus he has a defense to the robbery. (A) is incorrect because, while duress is not a defense to murder, it *is* a defense to the underlying felony, and thus is a defense to the felony murder charge. (B) is incorrect because, as stated above, under these facts duress is a good defense to the robbery charge and thus would be a good defense to the felony murder charge. (D) is also incorrect. Although a valid withdrawal would be a good defense to subsequent crimes of any co-conspirator, it is doubtful whether Jeff really entered into a conspiracy in the first place. Because Jeff never had the intent required for participation in the conspiracy, the jury would not be required to consider Jeff's defense of withdrawal.

Answer to Question 7

(D) Harfo can be charged with theft, conspiracy, and robbery. The facts clearly show that Harfo is guilty of the theft of the car that was to be used for the getaway. Conspiracy requires: (i) an agreement between two or more persons; (ii) an intent to enter into the agreement; and (iii) an intent to achieve the objective of the agreement. Most states also require an overt act in furtherance of the conspiracy. Harfo conspired to commit robbery, because he entered into an agreement with Groufo and Chifo to rob the bank, intending both to enter into such an agreement and to achieve the objective thereof. Harfo's theft of the car constituted an overt act in furtherance of the conspiracy. Thus, Harfo can be charged with conspiracy. Each member of a conspiracy is liable for the crimes of all other conspirators if: (i) such crimes were committed in furtherance of the objectives of the conspiracy; and (ii) such crimes were a natural and probable consequence of the conspiracy. A conspirator may *limit his liability for subsequent acts* of the other members of the conspiracy if he withdraws from the conspiracy by performing an affirmative act that notifies all members of the conspiracy in time for them to have the opportunity to abandon their plans. However, withdrawal is not a defense to a charge of conspiracy. Harfo's absence from the robbery scene with the getaway car was due to his sudden illness, rather than any voluntary decision on his part to withdraw from the conspiracy. Having failed to make a legally effective withdrawal from the conspiracy, Harfo continued to be liable for any crimes committed by Groufo and/or Chifo that were in furtherance of the conspiracy and were foreseeable consequences of the conspiracy. The facts state that Groufo and Chifo robbed the bank. Certainly, the robbery of the bank, which was the sole object of the conspiracy, was a crime committed in furtherance of the conspiracy's objectives and was a natural and probable consequence of the conspiracy. Therefore, Harfo is liable for this robbery committed by his co-conspirators. Because Harfo can properly be charged with all three crimes, (A), (B), and (C) are incorrect.

Answer to Question 8

(D) If Archie did not believe that Edith's complaints indicated a serious medical problem, he did not have the mental state required for murder. Murder is the unlawful killing of a human being with malice aforethought. Malice aforethought is present if the defendant acts with: (i) intent to kill; (ii) intent to inflict great bodily injury; (iii) reckless indifference to an unjustifiably high risk to human life; or (iv) intent to commit a felony. Assuming that, as stated in (D), Archie did not believe that Edith's complaints of abdominal pain were indicative of a serious medical problem, it cannot be said that in bypassing the Crow City emergency facility Archie acted with the intent to kill or seriously injure Edith, or that he even acted with reckless indifference to a high risk to Edith's life. If Archie did not believe there was a serious medical problem, he could not have thought he was placing Edith in great danger of death by driving on to Dry Gulch. Under such circumstances, Archie lacked the mens rea required to sustain a murder conviction. (A) refers to the matter of whether Archie had a duty to assist Edith in her distress. A defendant's failure to act will not result in criminal liability unless the defendant has a legal duty to act under the circumstances. Such a duty may exist where there is a sufficiently close relationship between the defendant and the victim; *e.g.,* a spouse has a duty to prevent harm to his or her spouse. Even if Archie and Edith were not legally married, the fact that they had lived together for many years as if they were married indicates that they were in a relationship of such a close nature as to give rise to a duty to act to prevent harm to each other. Thus, the facts set forth in (A) will not be helpful to Archie. Regarding (B), a defendant is responsible for all results that occur as a natural and probable consequence of his conduct, even if he did not anticipate the precise manner in which they would occur. All such results are proximately caused by the defendant's act, and the chain of causation is broken only by a superseding factor. An intervening act will shield the defendant from liability if the act is a mere coincidence or is outside the foreseeable sphere of risk created by the defendant's conduct. Negligent medical care is a foreseeable risk. Being injured or even dying due to incompetent medical care was a risk to which Archie exposed Edith when he refused to stop at Crow City, thereby exacerbating an already serious situation. Although Archie may not have anticipated that Edith would die because of Dr. Holiday's incompetence, Edith's death was a natural and probable consequence of Archie's refusal to stop at Crow City. Thus, the additional fact of Dr. Holiday's incompetent treatment of Edith does not establish any defense for Archie. (C) is incorrect because an act that hastens an inevitable result is still considered a legal cause of that result. Although it may be true that Edith would have died of cancer within a relatively short time, Archie's failure to get her proper care as quickly as possible actually caused her death.

Answer to Question 9

(D) Sherri is most likely to be found not guilty of larceny because she did not have the intent to permanently (or for an unreasonable time) deprive her neighbor of his interest in the Cadillac. Larceny consists of a taking and carrying away of tangible personal property of another by trespass, with intent to permanently (or for an unreasonable time) deprive the person of his interest in the property. The intent to permanently deprive must exist at the moment of the taking. If the defendant intended to return the property within a reasonable time, and at the time of the taking had a substantial ability to do so, the unauthorized borrowing is not larceny. If, however, the defendant intended to deal with the property in a manner that involved a substantial risk of loss, this is sufficient for larceny. In (D), Sherri did not intend to permanently deprive her neighbor of his interest in the Cadillac. Rather, she intended to return it at the end of the workday, and had no intention of dealing with it in a manner that involved a substantial risk of loss. This intent to borrow and to return the car within a reasonable time is insufficient to support a charge of larceny. Thus, Sherri will be found not guilty. (A) is incorrect because Jack, at the time of taking and riding away on a bicycle belonging to another, intended to sell it. Thus, Jack committed the requisite acts, with the intent to permanently deprive, so as to be guilty of larceny. (B) is incorrect, because it is an example of larceny by trick. Larceny requires that the taking be trespassory. In (B), the owner of the backpack and frame consented to Jill's taking them. However, if the victim consents to the defendant's taking possession of the property, but this consent has been induced by a misrepresentation, the consent is not valid. The resulting larceny is called larceny by trick. Jill misrepresented to her acquaintance that she merely wanted to borrow the items, but actually intended to keep them when she left for Afghanistan. Because the victim's consent was induced by this misrepresentation, such consent is not valid. Therefore, Jill's taking was wrongful, and she is guilty of larceny. (C) is incorrect because larceny can be committed even against someone who has previously stolen the property from the true owner. Larceny is a crime against possession, so it is only necessary that the person from whom the property is taken have a possessory interest in the property superior to that of the defendant. Although the accountant from whose apartment Reginald took the money had embezzled the cash, the accountant had possession of the money and thus had a possessory interest in it that was superior to that of Reginald. Consequently, Reginald's taking of the cash, accompanied by the requisite intent to deprive, constitutes larceny.

Answer to Question 10

(B) Defendant is least likely to be found guilty of murder for pushing Victim into the swimming pool. If a person recklessly causes the death of another, the crime is manslaughter. If a person causes the death of another under circumstances that show a "wicked or depraved heart," reckless indifference to a very high risk of death or serious injury, the crime is murder. While it would be a judgment for the jury as to how to characterize the behavior in (B), manslaughter is the probable crime. (B) is therefore correct because (A), (C), and (D) would clearly be murder. (A) is incorrect because hitting someone over the head with a lead pipe demonstrates an intent to inflict great bodily injury, and that is enough to satisfy the malice aforethought requirement for murder. Dropping a brick from a tall building into a crowd demonstrates that Defendant acted in the face of an unusually high risk that his conduct would cause death or serious bodily injury. Thus, malice aforethought is implied, and (C) is incorrect. (D) is incorrect because malice aforethought can also be implied from an intent to commit a felony.

Answer to Question 11

(D) Crandall stole the gun; thus, he is guilty of larceny of the gun. Since he agreed with Axle and Bowers to burglarize King's home, he is guilty of conspiracy. And since Crandall never communicated a withdrawal from the conspiracy to either Axle or Bowers, he would be vicariously liable for the attempted burglary of King's home. (A), (B), and (C) are therefore incorrect.

Answer to Question 12

(B) Since Deal was aware of the fact that he might experience a seizure while driving, his actions constituted criminal negligence (also called recklessness), which is a sufficient state of mind for the crime of involuntary manslaughter. (A) is an incorrect statement of the law. (C) is incorrect because he voluntarily drove knowing that he might experience a seizure, which is sufficient for involuntary manslaughter. (D) is incorrect because the state of mind for involuntary manslaughter can be established by criminal negligence.

Answer to Question 13

(C) Under the statute, Trout could not be convicted of burglary unless she actually intended to commit a crime when she entered Print's home. Since what she intended to do was not a crime, there can be no burglary, even though she thought she was committing a criminal act. (A) and (B) are therefore incorrect. (D) is incorrect because she had "broken" and "entered," which, except for the mental element, is all that is required to complete the crime.

Answer to Question 14

(C) The United States Supreme Court held, in *Roberts v. United States* (1980), that a defendant's refusal to cooperate with an investigation of the criminal conspiracy of which he was a member may properly be considered in imposing sentence because the Fifth Amendment right to silence does not afford a privilege to refuse to incriminate others.

Answer to Question 15

(D) Battery is a general intent crime which may be committed recklessly or with criminal negligence. In (D), Dale's act was involuntary, thus negating criminal liability. (A) might result in a battery conviction. If Dale was reasonable in his belief that he was under attack, he would have the defense of self-defense. If he was unreasonable in that belief, he would be guilty of battery. It would be a jury question as to whether his belief was reasonable or unreasonable. (B) might result in a battery conviction. It is not clear whether Dale was actually placed under hypnosis, and even if he was, some courts do not accept that as a defense. (C) might result in a battery conviction. A jury could find that Dale recklessly struck Viola.

Answer to Question 16

(B) Mark acted in self-defense in response to Homer's deadly attack. This is not affected by the fact that Mark was a trespasser or that Homer was enraged by Mark's negligence. (D) is a correct statement of the law but is irrelevant to Mark's guilt.

Answer to Question 17

(C) Nick will most likely be found not guilty. A person is justified in using deadly force in self-defense when he reasonably believes that it is necessary to prevent the use of unlawful deadly force against him. It seems clear from the facts that Nick has killed in self-defense. Even if striking Jim with the chair were seen as the use of deadly force, it could be justified as a necessary response to Jim's use of deadly force. (A) is wrong because the majority rule is that there is no duty to retreat before using deadly force in self-defense against an initial aggressor threatening deadly force. (B) and (D) are incorrect. Regardless of whether Nick had a right to be on the premises, he was entitled to defend himself against the use of unlawful deadly force. One cannot use deadly force against a trespasser in one's dwelling unless the trespasser poses a threat to a person.

Answer to Question 18

(B) Robbery is the taking and carrying away of the personal property of another from the other's person or presence by force or intimidation. In (A), (C), and (D), a jury could find the defendant guilty of robbery because there are facts to prove each element of the crime. In (B), however, a conviction for robbery is unlikely. The taking of the property was not by force or intimidation; the crime was already completed when Ericson slapped the victim.

Answer to Question 19

(C) A search warrant must be based on probable cause. Here, there was sufficient information for a judge to conclude that there was probable cause to believe that evidence of a crime would be found in Jackson's room. Thus, the warrant was properly obtained. (A) is wrong because Jackson had no reasonable expectation of privacy in a dormitory's lounge. Also, even if his privacy had been invaded, any invasion here was done by private persons, not the state, and thus would not prevent introduction of the evidence. (B) is wrong because it is untrue as a matter of law. (D) is wrong because it is not a sufficient basis to deny Jackson's motion. It is irrelevant that Prex acted on behalf of the college population.

Answer to Question 20

(D) Mary should be found not guilty of criminal assault because she did not have the requisite intent. In a majority of jurisdictions, an assault is either: (i) an attempt to commit a battery; or (ii) the intentional creation, other than by mere words, of a reasonable apprehension in the mind of the victim of imminent bodily harm. Here, Mary is not guilty of either type of assault because she did not attempt to commit a battery, nor did she intend to create apprehension in Anne of imminent bodily harm. (A) is wrong because assault requires intent; negligence ("should have realized") does not suffice. (B) is wrong because, again, assault requires intent. (C) is wrong because it states the definition of battery rather than assault.

Answer to Question 21

(C) Laurel should be found not guilty. Battery is an unlawful application of force to the person of another resulting in either bodily injury or an offensive touching. Battery is not a specific intent crime; criminal negligence meets the state of mind requirement for battery. Given that Laurel tackled and pinned Hardy, an offensive touching occurred. Furthermore, the state of mind requirement has been satisfied because the "criminal negligence" state of mind is satisfied by an intentional act—*i.e.,* acting with a higher state of mind satisfies a lower state of mind requirement. However, Laurel can raise the defense of self-defense: a person is entitled to use such force as is reasonably necessary to protect himself against the use of unlawful force on himself. Here, Laurel was fearful that Hardy would escalate the fight because Hardy had done so in the past. Thus, it appears that Laurel was justified in using nondeadly force to prevent a further battery upon his person. As a result, (C) is the correct answer. (A) is incorrect because it does not account for self-defense. (B) is incorrect because one has no duty to retreat before using nondeadly force. (D) is incorrect because it implies that the intent to cause harm is an element of the crime of battery. As stated above, battery is a general intent crime requiring, at a minimum, criminal negligence. Furthermore, actual physical harm is not required—an "offensive touching" suffices.

Answer to Question 22

(D) Larceny is the taking and carrying away of the personal property of another with the intent to permanently deprive the other of his interest in the property. Defendant's mistake is as to the coverage of the criminal law, and this would not be an excuse to the crime of larceny. (A) is wrong because Defendant clearly did not intend to steal another's property. (B) is wrong because Defendant's intent to obtain repayment of a debt does not satisfy the intent required for larceny. (C) is wrong because the intent to "permanently deprive" did not exist.

Answer to Question 23

(B) Hal had an expectation of privacy with respect to the room he rented from Nan, and the police had no reason to believe that Nan was authorized to invade his privacy. (C) is wrong because although Nan, as the owner of the building, may have had limited rights to inspect a boarder's room, it cannot be said that she is authorized, at the instructions of the police, to go through the private property of her boarders. (D) is wrong because Nan's testimony concerning a "suspicious odor" would not be sufficient to uphold a search warrant. (A) is wrong; there is no such rule of law.

Answer to Question 24

(C) Gene's best argument is that there was no agreement. At common law, a conspiracy was defined as a combination or agreement between two or more persons to accomplish some criminal or unlawful purpose, or to accomplish a lawful act by unlawful means. The mens rea required for conspiracy is specific intent, in that both parties must intend to agree to accomplish some criminal or unlawful purpose. In the instant case, Gene had only made a proposal to Bart, but Bart never accepted the proposal. Thus, as to Bart and Gene, there was no agreement and thus no conspiracy. (In other words, Gene may be guilty of criminal solicitation, but not conspiracy.) There was also no agreement between Gene and Ray; in fact, Ray's apparent intent was to steal the furs for himself, cutting Gene out of the loop. Thus, again, an agreement between Gene and anyone else is lacking. (A) is incorrect. It is no defense to a conspiracy charge that the agreement did not specify the details of the proposed criminal activity. (B) is also incorrect. There is no requirement that the conspirators know one another exactly; the requirement is that they know of the overall objective and agree to it. (D) is incorrect. The fact that the crime may not have been completed is irrelevant. Had Ray and Gene actually entered into an agreement to steal the furs, the fact that Ray was not successful in carrying out the plan would have been irrelevant.

Answer to Question 25

(B) Of the defenses, the best defense Barney would have is self-defense. If he were reasonable in his belief that Hank had a weapon and intended to "kill" him, he could use deadly force to protect himself. (A) is not a good defense because it is unreasonable to assume that hitting a person in the head with a heavy ashtray could not seriously injure him. In addition, manslaughter can be established with a reckless mental state, so Barney could be guilty even if he did not intend to seriously injure. (C) is incorrect because even if he did not know that Hank had a plate in his head, he could be guilty of manslaughter if the jury found that he recklessly caused Hank's death. (D) is wrong because Barney is not charged with murder in the first degree.

Answer to Question 26

(A) A shooting is deemed to create a necessity situation to the extent that a motive to enter and search premises to preserve the life of a person thought to be on the premises and in immediate danger is a recognized exception to the warrant requirement. Therefore, the officers had a right to enter the building without a warrant. Since the officers were legitimately on the premises, they had a right to seize all illegal items in plain view. Thus, (C) and (D) are wrong. (B) is wrong because the fact that the officers were acting in their official function is not enough to allow them to enter a building without a warrant.

Answer to Question 27

(B) After arrest a defendant has a right to remain silent, and his silence cannot be used against him. The Supreme Court has held that the prosecution cannot comment to the jury on the fact that an arrested defendant exercised the privilege against self-incrimination. (A) is not entirely accurate. Even if Davis had not asked for an attorney, he could have invoked the privilege against self-incrimination and refused to talk while in custody. Thus, (A) is not as good an answer as (B), which speaks directly to the reason the conviction will be reversed. (C) is wrong. Even though the silence might give rise to the inference that the story was fabricated, the arrested defendant has a "right" to remain silent and the silence cannot be used against him. (D) is wrong. By testifying he waived his right to be silent at the trial; he did not waive his right to silence before the trial.

Answer to Question 28

(C) Of all the possible defenses, (C) is the one most clearly showing that Annie was justified in her belief that her former marriage was already terminated when she married Gerald. (A) is not the best answer, because Annie should know that if she does not get the divorce decree entered, she is not legally divorced. (B) is not the best answer, because although many jurisdictions will accept a reasonable mistake of fact based on the prolonged absence of a spouse, three years would probably not be considered a "prolonged" absence. (D) is not the best answer, because although it is arguable that her marriage to Rodney may have been void, most jurisdictions would find the marriage only voidable while Annie was still a minor. Thus, in these jurisdictions, if neither party sought to annul the marriage until the minor spouse reached majority, they would no longer be able to annul their marriage. Although it can be argued that Annie is operating under a mistake of fact that her first marriage was invalid, most jurisdictions would not find the first marriage void as a matter of law.

Answer to Question 29

(D) Mervin had no ownership interest in Giles's store; he had no legitimate expectation of privacy with respect to it, *i.e.*, he was not present when the search was made; and he had no ownership interest in the stolen goods. Thus, he lacks the standing to object to their illegal seizure. Giles does have such standing and was successful in having the evidence suppressed at his trial, but what occurred at Giles's trial is not relevant to Mervin's motion. Therefore, (A) and (B) are incorrect. (C) is incorrect because the only evidence containing Mervin's fingerprints were the stolen goods. If it is found that these items were illegally seized, it would follow that the evidence arising out of this illegal seizure, including Mervin's fingerprints, was also illegally seized.

Answer to Question 30

(C) Larceny is the taking and carrying away of the personal property of another with the intent to permanently deprive the other of the property. However, larceny is a trespass against *possession*, not ownership, and therefore, in most jurisdictions, a defendant can be convicted of larceny even when he takes property from someone who only has possession of that property because of some wrongful act. However, Gregg would not be guilty of burglary because there is no evidence that he entered the house with the intent to steal the gun. Therefore, (A), (B), and (D) are incorrect.

Answer to Question 31

(D) The privilege against self-incrimination bars the government from procuring *compelled testimony*. Since the documents here were voluntarily prepared, they cannot be considered to be compelled. Furthermore, documents are considered to be real or physical evidence, not testimonial evidence, and thus are outside the scope of the privilege. Thus, (A) is incorrect. (B) is irrelevant since the documents are beyond the scope of the privilege. (C) is wrong because records required by statute that have a lawful administrative purpose are not protected by the Fifth Amendment.

Answer to Question 32

(C) Alyce consciously disregarded a substantial and unjustifiable risk that the drug she was placing in food could be seriously harmful or even fatal. (A) is wrong because Alyce lacked the necessary intent to kill. (B) is wrong because Alyce did not commit a common law felony; battery was not a felony at common law. (D) is not as good an answer as (C). While a jury could find that her actions were criminally negligent, resulting in manslaughter, a jury could also find that she acted with reckless disregard, resulting in second degree murder. Thus, under the call of the question, (C) is correct.

Answer to Question 33

(A) Bob is an accessory before the fact, and thus subject to the same penalty as Alyce. An accessory before the fact provides assistance before the crime but is not actually or constructively present during the crime. (B) is incorrect because a principal in the first degree actually perpetrates the crime. (C) is incorrect because a principal in the second degree must be actually or constructively present during the commission of the crime, and here, Bob was sleeping. (D) is wrong because Bob's aid was before, not after, the fact.

Answer to Question 34

(C) Phil did not commit felony murder because (i) he did not commit a common law felony and (ii) he did not have the necessary mens rea to be liable as an accomplice. Thus, (A) is incorrect. Not knowing the use to which the nitroglycerine was to be put, he did not act with the reckless disregard for the safety of others required for second degree murder, and, again, he lacked the mens rea required for accomplice liability. Thus, (B) is incorrect. (D) is incorrect because it is generally not a defense to crime that the defendant was unaware that his acts were prohibited by the criminal law (assuming that the statute proscribing his conduct was made reasonably available prior to the conduct). Thus, (C) is correct. Phil dispensed the drugs to Bob without a prescription and so he violated that law.

Answer to Question 35

(D) Neighbor would not be guilty of larceny when he took the horse from Fillmont because Neighbor did not have the mens rea necessary for the crime. Common law larceny required the trespassory taking and carrying away of personal property in the possession of another, with the intent to permanently deprive the other of lawful possession. The intent to permanently deprive was often referred to by the courts as the "intent to steal." If the actor believed that he had a right to the property or was taking the property on behalf of someone who had that right, the actor could not be found guilty of larceny, since there would be no intent to permanently deprive another of lawful possession. As Neighbor thought the bill had been paid and the horse rightfully belonged to Deft, Neighbor did not have the "intent to steal" necessary for larceny at the time he took the horse from Fillmont. (A) is wrong. Even though the bill had not been paid, Neighbor is not guilty if he believed Deft had a lawful right to the horse. (B) is wrong. Even though the horse was in the possession of Fillmont, Neighbor is not guilty if he believed Deft had a lawful right to the horse. (C) is wrong because a person can be guilty of larceny of his own property if another person (usually a bailee) has a superior right to possession of the property at the time of the taking.

EVIDENCE
ANSWER SHEET

1. Ⓐ Ⓑ Ⓒ Ⓓ
2. Ⓐ Ⓑ Ⓒ Ⓓ
3. Ⓐ Ⓑ Ⓒ Ⓓ
4. Ⓐ Ⓑ Ⓒ Ⓓ
5. Ⓐ Ⓑ Ⓒ Ⓓ

6. Ⓐ Ⓑ Ⓒ Ⓓ
7. Ⓐ Ⓑ Ⓒ Ⓓ
8. Ⓐ Ⓑ Ⓒ Ⓓ
9. Ⓐ Ⓑ Ⓒ Ⓓ
10. Ⓐ Ⓑ Ⓒ Ⓓ

11. Ⓐ Ⓑ Ⓒ Ⓓ
12. Ⓐ Ⓑ Ⓒ Ⓓ
13. Ⓐ Ⓑ Ⓒ Ⓓ
14. Ⓐ Ⓑ Ⓒ Ⓓ
15. Ⓐ Ⓑ Ⓒ Ⓓ

16. Ⓐ Ⓑ Ⓒ Ⓓ
17. Ⓐ Ⓑ Ⓒ Ⓓ
18. Ⓐ Ⓑ Ⓒ Ⓓ

19. Ⓐ Ⓑ Ⓒ Ⓓ
20. Ⓐ Ⓑ Ⓒ Ⓓ
21. Ⓐ Ⓑ Ⓒ Ⓓ
22. Ⓐ Ⓑ Ⓒ Ⓓ
23. Ⓐ Ⓑ Ⓒ Ⓓ

24. Ⓐ Ⓑ Ⓒ Ⓓ
25. Ⓐ Ⓑ Ⓒ Ⓓ
26. Ⓐ Ⓑ Ⓒ Ⓓ
27. Ⓐ Ⓑ Ⓒ Ⓓ
28. Ⓐ Ⓑ Ⓒ Ⓓ

29. Ⓐ Ⓑ Ⓒ Ⓓ
30. Ⓐ Ⓑ Ⓒ Ⓓ
31. Ⓐ Ⓑ Ⓒ Ⓓ
32. Ⓐ Ⓑ Ⓒ Ⓓ
33. Ⓐ Ⓑ Ⓒ Ⓓ

34. Ⓐ Ⓑ Ⓒ Ⓓ
35. Ⓐ Ⓑ Ⓒ Ⓓ

EVIDENCE QUESTIONS

Question 1

Dave, while driving north on Grand Avenue, collided with Peter, who was driving east on Sixth Street. A police officer present at the scene cited Dave for running a red light.

At the preliminary hearing, Dave initially pleaded guilty, but he withdrew his plea when the judge told him what she had in mind for a sentence. The judge let Dave change his plea to not guilty. Dave, however, had no success at his trial and was convicted. Peter is now suing Dave in a civil action for the injuries he sustained in the accident.

If Peter tries to introduce evidence of Dave's original guilty plea, on proper motion, this evidence will be:

(A) Excluded, because it is hearsay not within any exception.

(B) Excluded, because the plea was withdrawn.

(C) Admitted, because an admission is not hearsay.

(D) Admitted, because it described Dave's state of mind.

Question 2

Popeye bought some packaged chicken breasts from Grocer. The chicken label indicated that it was processed and packaged by Cluck Co. Popeye cooked several pieces of chicken and froze the remainder. The next day, Popeye was hospitalized with a serious case of salmonella poisoning. After his recovery, Popeye sued Grocer and Cluck Co. for his personal injuries. At trial, Popeye called Taylor, a biochemist, and asked her whether, in her opinion, based on laboratory reports made concerning his illness and the chicken in his freezer, it was possible that the chicken was the source of the salmonella that sickened Popeye. Counsel for Cluck Co. objected to Taylor's testimony on this point.

The court should rule that the testimony is:

(A) Admissible, if such reports are reasonably relied upon by biochemists in the course of their profession.

(B) Admissible, if Taylor has the reports with her and offers them into evidence.

(C) Inadmissible, because Taylor's testimony embraces the ultimate issue in the case.

(D) Inadmissible, because the contents of the laboratory reports are hearsay and not admissible under any exception.

Question 3

An indictment was filed in federal district court charging Warren with violations of federal statutes prohibiting bank robbery. At trial, the government attempted to introduce into evidence the testimony of Warren's wife, Faye, who would testify that she had seen Warren arm himself on several occasions with weapons identical to those used in the bank robberies, had seen him return to their home carrying sacks filled with money with the markings of the robbed banks, and had overheard, while serving meals, Warren and his co-defendants discussing plans for robbing the various banks and concealing the loot. Warren's attorney objected, and the district court judge ruled that Faye's testimony was within the spousal privilege and could not be admitted over Warren's objection.

Was this ruling correct?

(A) No, because the spousal privilege may only be asserted by the testifying spouse—she may not be compelled to testify nor foreclosed from testifying.

(B) Yes, because the privilege not to testify may be asserted by either the testifying or nontestifying spouse.

(C) The question cannot be answered, because state law of spousal privilege controls, and the state law is not presented in the question.

(D) No, because there is no federal common law, and the spousal privilege is a creation of the common law.

Question 4

Engineer Thornton is called as a witness in a professional malpractice action. During direct examination by the attorney for the party who called her, she is asked leading questions. The opposing party objects.

Which of the following is *least* likely to persuade the trial court to permit the leading questions?

(A) The question is necessary to refresh recollection.

(B) The questions relate to preliminary information, such as name, address, etc.

(C) Thornton was called as an adverse witness.

(D) The questions relate directly to an issue of ultimate fact in the lawsuit.

Question 5

Peter was lawfully crossing the street when he was struck and seriously injured by a car driven by Tony. Tony had run a red light. At the time, Tony was on his way home from Donna's Tavern. Peter brings suit against Donna's Tavern for his injuries, claiming that Tony was permitted to drink too much liquor at Donna's Tavern before leaving.

Peter calls Wanda to the stand. Wanda testifies that she and a friend had visited Donna's Tavern on the night in question. Wanda seeks to testify that she remarked to her friend, "Look at that guy. He's so drunk he can't even stand up."

Wanda's testimony concerning her remark to her friend is:

(A) Admissible as a prior consistent statement.

(B) Admissible as a statement by Wanda regarding the condition she observed, made while she was observing it.

(C) Admissible as relevant nonhearsay testimony.

(D) Inadmissible as hearsay not within any exception.

Question 6

Don's vacant lot on Front Street was condemned by River City, which planned to establish a riverfront park on the site. During a proceeding to establish condemnation damages, counsel for River City called Don to the stand, expecting him to say that he had been offered $250,000 for the property one month before it was condemned. However, on direct examination, Don testified that he had received a $400,000 offer for his land a month before condemnation. River City then seeks to confront Don with his statement made at his deposition that the offer was for $250,000.

The statement contained in the deposition is:

(A) Inadmissible, because River City cannot impeach its own witness.

(B) Inadmissible, because it is hearsay not within any exception.

(C) Admissible for impeachment and as substantive evidence that Don received an offer for $250,000.

(D) Admissible, but only for the purpose of impeachment.

Question 7

Ralph instituted suit against a development firm and its employee, Bates, for injuries Ralph suffered when a basement stair collapsed as Ralph was being shown one of the firm's buildings that it was leasing. At trial, Bates claims that he told Ralph about the defective stair. Ralph then offers evidence that after his fall, the owner of the development firm called him at home and offered to pay all of Ralph's medical expenses, saying, "I guess I owe you that much after Bates didn't warn you about the broken stair."

The statement regarding the lack of warning is:

(A) Admissible as a statement against interest.

(B) Admissible as an admission by the owner of the development firm that Bates had not warned Ralph about the stair.

(C) Inadmissible as hearsay not within any exception.

(D) Inadmissible on public policy grounds.

Question 8

Beekeeper purchased from Fabrico a specially designed helmet and faceguard that was designed to protect the wearer from bee stings. Shortly thereafter, as Beekeeper was wearing the helmet and faceguard, he was stung on the left cheek by a bee that had entered through a small tear in the faceguard. One hour later, Beekeeper suffered a heart attack. Beekeeper brought suit against Fabrico to recover for the bee sting and the heart attack.

Doctor Able, a physician, having listened to Beekeeper testify to the foregoing facts, is called by Beekeeper and asked whether, assuming the truth of such testimony, Beekeeper's subsequent heart attack could have resulted from the bee sting. His opinion is:

(A) Admissible, only if Doctor Able was Beekeeper's treating physician.

(B) Admissible, as a response to a hypothetical question.

(C) Inadmissible, because a proper foundation has not been laid.

(D) Inadmissible, because an expert's opinion may not be based solely on information provided by lay persons.

Question 9

Allen brings suit against Berry for a libelous letter received by Employer. Berry allegedly sent the letter. The authenticity and contents of the letter are disputed at the jury trial. In response to a question from Allen's attorney, Employer states that: "I received a letter from Berry, which I seem to have lost, but I remember exactly what it said."

Employer will be allowed to testify as to the contents of the letter if:

(A) Allen's attorney lays a proper foundation by proving Employer's good character for truth.

(B) The judge finds that the original letter is lost.

(C) The jury is satisfied that the original letter is unavailable.

(D) Employer can recall the contents of the letter from his own memory without looking to any other document.

Question 10

In an action for breach of contract, which of the following questions, if asked of a witness for plaintiff on cross-examination by counsel for defendant, would most probably be ruled improper by the trial court?

(A) "Weren't you fired last year after your employer learned you had been using its computerized accounting system to divert company funds to your personal bank account?"

(B) "As a creditor of the plaintiff, isn't it true that you stand to gain several thousand dollars if plaintiff prevails in this lawsuit?"

(C) "Isn't it true that you are currently a resident of the City Detoxification Hospital recovering from addiction to Valium?"

(D) "Weren't you convicted six years ago in the court of Neighboring County of forgery?"

Question 11

Marla filed a personal injury suit against Denny for injuries she sustained when their cars collided in an intersection controlled by stop-lights. Marla's attorney seeks to have Paula, the police officer who investigated the accident and prepared the police report, testify that she took the statement of Rick, the driver of the car immediately behind Marla's car, and that Rick told her that Denny "drove right through the red light."

The judge should rule the testimony:

(A) Inadmissible, because the police report is the best evidence.

(B) Inadmissible, because it is hearsay.

(C) Inadmissible as oral testimony, but the report may be introduced into evidence.

(D) Admissible, because Paula was testifying as to past recollection recorded.

Question 12

Jim and Mary Brink were installing an in-ground swimming pool in their backyard with help from their friends Eric and Matt when one of the pool's walls collapsed, injuring Matt. Matt sued the Brinks on a negligence theory. Matt's attorney seeks to have a paramedic who had responded to the accident testify that Eric, who was a construction worker, made a statement to her that "I told Jim that he needed more reinforcement in the concrete."

The trial judge should rule this evidence:

(A) Inadmissible, as it is not relevant to the issues presented in the trial.

(B) Inadmissible, because it is a hearsay declaration.

(C) Admissible, because it is an admission.

(D) Admissible, because it is a statement against interest.

Question 13

As Emily was driving east on Elm Street, her car collided with a west-bound pickup truck driven by Jodie. The accident was observed by Sherry, a cab driver. Since Sherry had a passenger, she did not stay at the scene of the accident but made some notes shortly thereafter. She made her statement to the police the next day, in which she stated that just before the accident, Emily's car swerved into the west-bound lane, hitting the truck. At the trial of Emily's personal injury action against Jodie, Sherry was having difficulty remembering some of the facts. Jodie's attorney sought to let her review the notes she had made.

The court should rule this:

(A) Permissible, because it is a present recollection refreshed.

(B) Permissible, because it is a past recollection recorded.

(C) Impermissible, because Sherry is required to report all accidents to her employer, and the record is thus privileged.

(D) Impermissible, because there is no showing that Sherry had used her notes when she gave her statement to the police officer.

Question 14

Elbert sued Max for battery. Max claimed that he was attacked for no reason by Elbert and that he hit Elbert with a pipe in self-defense. Frances was called to testify that on the night in question she was watching Max and Ralph across her back fence. She heard Ralph tell Max that Elbert had been flirting with Max's girlfriend, Maxine, and Max seemed very angry. Max's attorney objected to this testimony.

The court should find the evidence:

(A) Admissible, to show provocation for the battery.

(B) Admissible, as a legally operative fact.

(C) Inadmissible, because it is hearsay.

(D) Inadmissible, because it is an opinion.

Question 15

Rocky was seriously injured when an ice shard that fell off a high-rise building hit him as he was walking in front of the building. In the hospital emergency room, Rocky said to Louise, the nurse's aide who was cutting away his clothing, "I can't keep this to myself any longer. My cousin, Gabe, killed my neighbor, Mrs. Brown, when she caught him stealing her television." Rocky died on the operating table. Gabe was arrested and charged with the murder of Mrs. Brown. At Gabe's trial, the prosecutor calls Louise to testify to Rocky's statements. Gabe's attorney objects.

Louise's testimony is:

(A) Admissible, because Rocky's statement constitutes a dying declaration.

(B) Admissible, because Rocky's statement is an excited utterance.

(C) Inadmissible, because of the physician-patient privilege.

(D) Inadmissible, because it is hearsay not within any exception.

Question 16

Phillipe was shopping at the Big Department Store. While riding down an escalator, the escalator malfunctioned, causing Phillipe to fall forward to the floor. After hitting the floor, Phillipe was in too much pain to move. Bert, another customer in the store, called an ambulance. Bert had no medical training, and so he simply tried to make Phillipe comfortable until the ambulance arrived. While waiting for the ambulance, Phillipe told Bert, "My left arm is numb and I have chest pains. I'm afraid I'm having a heart attack." Upon being taken to the hospital, it was determined that Phillipe had not suffered a heart attack, but had sustained severe damage to his chest and to the nerves affecting feeling in his left arm. Phillipe sued Big Department Store for his injuries. Big Department Store denies that Phillipe was injured as seriously as alleged in the complaint. At trial, Phillipe called Bert to testify to the statement made by Phillipe.

Bert's testimony as to Phillipe's statement is:

(A) Admissible to prove the extent of Phillipe's injuries at the time.

(B) Inadmissible, because Phillipe did not suffer a heart attack.

(C) Inadmissible, because Bert is not a doctor.

(D) Inadmissible, because it is hearsay not within any exception.

Questions 17-18 are based on the following fact situation:

Vance is charged with the murder of his employer, Mary. At the trial, the prosecution offered the testimony of another employee, Art, that he had accidentally picked up the phone when Vance was talking to an unidentified man who said, "I hear Mary's going to confess about the money you and she embezzled from the company. What are you going to do about it?"

17. Vance's attorney objects to Art's testimony on the ground that it is irrelevant. The judge should:

(A) Sustain the objection.

(B) Sustain the objection, on the grounds that whatever probative value the testimony has is substantially outweighed by the danger of unfair prejudice, confusion of the issues, or misleading the jury.

(C) Overrule the objection.

(D) Overrule the objection; but if Vance's attorney so requests, instruct the jury not to consider Art's testimony as evidence of Vance's involvement with any embezzlement of funds.

18. Vance's attorney also objects to Art's testimony on the ground that it is hearsay. The judge should:

(A) Sustain the objection.

(B) Overrule the objection, because the testimony, although hearsay, is being introduced to show Vance's state of mind, a hearsay exception.

(C) Overrule the objection because the testimony, although hearsay, qualifies as a business record since the call was made during business hours on a business phone.

(D) Overrule the objection if the evidence is offered to help prove Vance's motive.

Question 19

Raoul, an artist, agreed to sell one of his paintings to a friend, David, for $3,000. David said that he would pay Raoul within a week. The agreement was witnessed by Warren, who was browsing in Raoul's studio. David failed to pay the $3,000. After Raoul repeatedly asked David for payment, to no avail, Raoul asked for the return of the painting. David laughed and said, "Sorry, possession is nine-tenths of the law." Raoul knew that David was wrong in his understanding of the law so that night, while David was at his weekly poker game, Raoul entered David's house through an unlocked window and took the painting. David's neighbor, Sam, observed Raoul leave the house carrying a large frame and called police.

Raoul was charged with burglary, defined in the jurisdiction as breaking and entering the dwelling of another with the intent to commit a felony. At trial, Sam testified for the prosecution as to what he had seen and identified Raoul as the person carrying the painting from David's house. Raoul, asserting that he merely was retrieving his own property, attempts to call Warren to testify to the agreement between Raoul and David. The prosecution objects to the testimony, claiming it is irrelevant.

The judge should rule that Warren's testimony is:

(A) Admissible, because it is relevant in determining whether Raoul had the intent required for burglary.

(B) Admissible, because it is relevant in establishing Sam's credibility.

(C) Inadmissible as irrelevant, because it would tend to impeach Sam's testimony on a collateral matter.

(D) Inadmissible as irrelevant, because the probative value of Warren's testimony is substantially outweighed by the danger of unfair prejudice, confusion of the issues, waste of time, or needless presentation of cumulative evidence.

Question 20

Megan filed a personal injury action against Cup & Mug, a small restaurant serving many varieties of coffee and tea and a small selection of breakfast and lunch items. Megan alleges that she had breakfast at the restaurant to celebrate her birthday and that she suffered food poisoning after consuming the daily special that day: Guatemalan Dark coffee with Café Frittata. Cup & Mug defends by claiming that the special that day was Jamaican Blue and Confetti Frittata and that the Guatemalan Dark coffee drink was not even on the menu that day. Counsel for Cup & Mug called Lee, a former waitress at the restaurant, to testify as to whether the Guatemalan Dark coffee drink was on the menu that day. Lee testified that it was always on the menu. Cup & Mug's attorney then asked, "Didn't you in fact, at your deposition, state that the Guatemalan Dark coffee drink was not on the menu that day?" Megan's attorney objects.

The question is:

(A) Proper, if the judge finds that Lee is hostile.

(B) Proper, because it constitutes refreshing the witness's recollection.

(C) Improper, because this is a leading question on direct examination.

(D) Improper, because Cup & Mug cannot impeach its own witness.

Question 21

Bob was charged with reckless driving when his car hit a car driven by Russ in front of him on an expressway. At his trial, Lou, who was a passenger in Bob's car at the time of the accident, testified that Russ's car slammed on the brakes with no warning before the accident. Bob was acquitted of the reckless driving charge. Subsequently, Russ sued Bob for personal injuries and property damages. At the civil trial, counsel for Bob asked Lou, "Did Russ stop suddenly before Bob hit him?" Lou, who was angry with Bob after an argument, responded, "I don't remember it that way. Russ may have slowed down a bit." Bob's attorney seeks to introduce the transcript of Lou's statement from the criminal trial. Russ's attorney objects.

The transcript is:

(A) Admissible, for impeachment purposes only.

(B) Admissible, for impeachment purposes and as substantive evidence.

(C) Inadmissible, because it is hearsay.

(D) Inadmissible, because Lou is not unavailable.

Question 22

Rob is on trial in federal court for bank robbery. Rob contended that he was out of town on the relevant date. The prosecution calls Barbara, Rob's wife, to testify that three days before the robbery, Rob brought a gun home. She will also testify that she found a bank floor plan in Rob's sock drawer. Rob's attorney objects.

The objection should be:

(A) Sustained, because spousal privilege belongs to the party-spouse.

(B) Sustained, because Rob acted in reliance on the intimacy of the marital relationship.

(C) Overruled, because the Federal Rules do not recognize testimonial privileges.

(D) Overruled, because Barbara may choose to testify.

Question 23

Jason owned a retail store specializing in imported, hand-woven Persian carpets. Caitlyn paid $12,000 for a Persian carpet, which she discovered was a fake when she had it appraised for insurance purposes. Caitlyn sued Jason for damages based on a fraud theory. At trial, Caitlyn's attorney calls Jason's ex-wife to testify that during their marriage Jason told her about the fraud he had pulled on Caitlyn. Jason's attorney objects on the ground of privilege.

The court should rule that Jason's ex-wife:

(A) Can be called as a witness and can testify against Jason because she and Jason are no longer married.

(B) Can be called as a witness but cannot be directed to testify against Jason if the facts were told to her in confidence.

(C) Cannot be called as a witness at all.

(D) Must testify, because the privilege applies to criminal cases only.

Question 24

Martin owned a book shop, Olde Pages, which, in addition to shelving normal book store inventory, also specialized in hard-to-find and antique books. Martin decided to sell Olde Pages so he could fulfill his dream of becoming a dog breeder. William operated a dog breeding business and wanted a more sedentary occupation, so Martin and William agreed to exchange businesses. They agreed that each of their businesses were valued at $250,000 and stated this in the writing, signed by both parties, that effected a transfer of the businesses. After becoming owner of Olde Pages, William, wanting to reduce the inventory, hired a book appraiser to determine which books to discard. The appraiser told William that the entire inventory was worth $150,000. William filed suit against Martin for damages.

At trial, Martin's attorney offers a report, purportedly signed by Stillwell, a well-known local CPA, that was prepared shortly after Martin and William signed the agreement. While reports of this kind were not normally prepared by Stillwell, he prepared this one as a favor to Martin. The report contained an extensive analysis of the financial condition of Olde Pages and concludes that "it is entirely possible, in my opinion, that, due to the highly volatile market for old books, the value of the store and books could be placed at $250,000 instead of $150,000." William's attorney objects to the introduction of the report as evidence of the value of the book store.

The court should rule that the report is:

(A) Admissible nonhearsay, since the report constituted the opinion of Stillwell.

(B) Hearsay, but admissible as a past recollection recorded.

(C) Hearsay, but admissible as a business record.

(D) Inadmissible hearsay.

Question 25

Harry is charged with the federal crime of conspiracy to embezzle $50,000 from his employer, a bank. At trial, the prosecutor calls Harry's wife, Wilma, and asks her to testify about a meeting between Harry and Sybil that Wilma observed three weeks prior to her marriage to Harry.

Which of the following is the most accurate statement of the applicable rule concerning whether Wilma may testify?

(A) The choice is Wilma's.

(B) The choice is Harry's.

(C) Wilma is permitted to testify only if both Wilma and Harry agree.

(D) Wilma may be compelled to testify, even if both Wilma and Harry object.

Question 26

Donald was arrested and charged with the September 15 murder of Wilma. At trial, Donald called as his first witness Able, to testify to Donald's reputation in the community as "a peace-loving man."

Able's testimony will most likely be held to be:

(A) Admissible as tending to prove Donald is innocent.

(B) Admissible as tending to prove Donald is believable.

(C) Inadmissible, because reputation is not a proper way to prove character.

(D) Inadmissible, because Donald has not testified.

Question 27

Taylor was on trial for burglary. At the conclusion of the prosecution's case, Taylor called Daniel as his first witness. Daniel testified that Taylor was with him at an out-of-town sporting event at the time of the burglary. On cross-examination, the prosecutor asked Daniel, "Weren't you on a jury that acquitted Taylor of another criminal charge?"

If the judge sustained an objection to this question, the most likely reason will be that:

(A) The question is leading.

(B) The question goes beyond the scope of direct examination.

(C) The probative value of the answer would be substantially outweighed by its tendency to mislead.

(D) A proper foundation was not laid.

Question 28

Gustave brought a lawsuit against BD&F Laboratories. He alleges that he was prescribed some medicine manufactured by them, and that after he took the medicine, a blood clot formed in his left leg, resulting in its having to be amputated. BD&F Laboratories denies liability, claiming that there is nothing in the medicine that could cause clotting of the blood. Gustave offered to have Dr. Hamilton, the chief surgeon of White Chapel Hospital, testify that in the past 15 months, she has treated four persons (who are otherwise proved to have taken the same medicine as Gustave) who suffered from complications caused by blood clotting in their lower extremities. BD&F Laboratories strongly objected to this testimony.

The trial judge should find the testimony:

(A) Inadmissible, because the testimony of the other patients' condition is hearsay not within any exception.

(B) Inadmissible, because it violates the best evidence rule for the doctor to testify concerning her patients' physical condition when there is no showing that the patients are unavailable to testify.

(C) Admissible, if there is shown to be a connection between these patients' ailments and the medicine manufactured by BD&F Laboratories.

(D) Admissible, but only if the doctor is qualified to testify as an expert.

Question 29

Lucy was seriously injured when the bus in which she was riding ran a red light and was hit broadside by a cement mixer. She has brought an action against the bus company for damages from personal injuries.

Winston, a passenger on the same bus that Lucy was riding on when injured, is called as a witness by Lucy to testify that, just after the bus came to a stop after Lucy was injured, he said to another passenger, "We must have been going at least 50 miles per hour!"

Is this testimony admissible?

(A) Yes, if it is offered as a prior consistent statement as to Winston's trial testimony.

(B) Yes, because the statement was an excited utterance.

(C) No, because the statement is hearsay not within an exception.

(D) No, because the testimony is improper opinion evidence.

Question 30

Which of the following questions is most likely to be subject to the objection that it is leading?

(A) On direct examination, counsel asks his own client: "You live at 555 Northward Avenue, don't you?"

(B) On cross-examination of an expert witness, counsel asks: "Isn't it true that most family practice attorneys routinely asserted a community interest in military pensions at that time?"

(C) On direct examination of the victim, a four-year-old child, the prosecutor asks: "Did the defendant touch you there?"

(D) On direct examination of an eyewitness to an accident, plaintiff's counsel asks: "Was the light red when the defendant drove through the intersection?"

Question 31

Philip, a collector of antique cars, contracted with Owen, the owner of a classic Tucker automobile, to buy the car. However, Owen later decided that he did not want to part with his Tucker, so Philip sued Owen for specific performance of the contract. Philip's attorney asked Owen, "Is it true that you paid $160,000 for one of the other cars in your collection and sold it for only $40,000?" Owen's attorney objected.

The court should rule this question:

(A) Objectionable, because it is leading.

(B) Objectionable, because it is irrelevant.

(C) Unobjectionable, because it shows that Owen is irresponsible.

(D) Unobjectionable, because Owen can testify as to the dollar amount of his transactions even though a receipt may exist.

Question 32

Judith is suing Caryn for personal injuries suffered when she was struck by Caryn's car. Judith testified regarding the extent of her injuries. Caryn seeks to testify that when she visited Judith in the hospital, Judith said that if Caryn paid all of her medical bills and gave her $25,000, she would not institute legal proceedings. Judith's attorney objects to the offered testimony.

The judge should rule that the testimony is:

(A) Inadmissible, because it is hearsay.

(B) Inadmissible, because it was an offer of compromise.

(C) Admissible, because it is a statement against interest, and thus, an exception to the hearsay rule.

(D) Admissible, because it is relevant to show that Judith tried to "blackmail" Caryn, and does not really have a claim.

Question 33

Jerome took the stand to testify on his own behalf during his trial for arson. On cross-examination, the prosecutor asked him, "Isn't it true that you were convicted of forgery six years ago?"

The judge should rule the question:

(A) Proper, because Jerome has waived the privilege against self-incrimination by testifying.

(B) Proper, because the prosecutor may inquire into matters bearing on a witness's credibility.

(C) Improper, because the purpose of the question was to elicit prejudicial evidence.

(D) Improper, because on cross-examination, the prosecutor is limited to matters testified to on direct examination.

Questions 34-35 are based on the following fact situation:

Sam brought suit against Bill for breach of a contract involving the sale of 100 imported, handcarved coffee tables. The basis of Sam's suit was that Bill failed to pay as was required in the contract. Bill defends against Sam's action by introducing evidence that the shipment delivered to his place of business was only 68 handcarved coffee tables, which he rejected. Sam introduced a bill of lading showing that import taxes were paid on 100 handcarved coffee tables.

34. Bill then offers evidence that a clause in the Sam-Bill contract stated, "Bill has no obligation to receive any coffee tables from Sam unless they are delivered in one lot of 100 tables." Sam objected. The most likely result is:

(A) Bill is entitled to introduce evidence of any part of the transaction necessary to make it understood.

(B) By not objecting to the contract, Bill has waived any right to introduce any part of it.

(C) Bill's evidence is inadmissible as irrelevant.

(D) Bill's evidence is inadmissible as hearsay.

35. Assume that Sam introduced a Fast Freight record showing that Fast Freight attempted delivery to Bill on the date specified. May Bill now compel Sam to introduce the remainder of the record, showing that Fast Freight had only 68 coffee tables on its truck?

(A) Yes, but only if a proper foundation is laid.

(B) Yes, because in all fairness it should be considered contemporaneously with what Sam is offering.

(C) No, unless Bill can prove that the information would be relevant to the case.

(D) No, because the record would constitute inadmissible hearsay.

EVIDENCE ANSWERS

Answer to Question 1

(B) A plea of guilty which is later withdrawn may not be used against the defendant who made the plea, except in special cases not applicable to this fact pattern. [Fed. R. Evid. 410] (A) is wrong; since Dave's statement would be considered an admission, it cannot be excluded by the hearsay rule. It will be excluded under Rule 410, which prohibits the use of the withdrawn guilty plea, even if it does qualify as an admission. (C) is wrong because, although an admission is not hearsay, this evidence is excluded by Rule 410. (D) is wrong. While Dave's state of mind might be relevant in the civil suit, the evidence will still be excluded under Rule 410.

Answer to Question 2

(A) The basis of an expert's opinion need not be admissible into evidence for the expert's testimony to be admissible, provided that the information is of a type reasonably relied upon by experts in the particular field. [Fed. R. Evid. 703(B)] (B) is incorrect because Taylor need not offer the reports into evidence in order to base her opinion on them. In fact, the proponent of the expert opinion is not permitted to disclose the reports if they are inadmissible, unless the court determines that their probative value in assisting the jury to evaluate the expert's opinion substantially outweighs their prejudicial effect. (C) is wrong because the Federal Rules reject the traditional prohibition on opinions embracing the ultimate issue in the case, as long as the opinion is helpful to the trier of fact. (D) is wrong because Taylor is only relying on the reports as the basis of making her opinion; she is not offering the reports themselves into evidence. Hence, they would not be governed by the hearsay rule.

Answer to Question 3

(A) Federal Rule 501 provides that federal courts shall apply rules of privilege developed at common law except in diversity cases, wherein state law controls, but this is not a diversity case. The United States Supreme Court has held that the privilege not to testify may be asserted only by the testifying spouse, and if she is willing to so testify against her husband, the marital relationship is so disharmonious that there is nothing left for the privilege to preserve.

Answer to Question 4

(D) The substantive relation of the questions to the issues of the lawsuit has no bearing on whether leading questions are permitted. Use of leading questions on direct examination to refresh the recollection of a witness or to establish preliminary matters is permitted in the discretion of the trial court. Thus, (A) and (B) are incorrect. Where a witness is hostile to the party calling him, the examination is treated as cross-examination, and leading questions may be used. Thus, (C) is incorrect.

Answer to Question 5

(B) Wanda's remark is admissible under the present sense impression exception to the hearsay rule. [Fed. R. Evid. 803(1)] (A) is wrong. A prior consistent statement can be used to rebut evidence that the trial testimony is a lie or an exaggeration because of some motive to falsify that has arisen since the event. The facts do not indicate such a claim was made. The statement is hearsay because the witness is relating an out-of-court statement that she made; therefore, (C) is wrong.

(D) is wrong because the statement comes within the present sense impression exception to the hearsay rule.

Answer to Question 6

(C)   Under the Federal Rules, depositions can be used more broadly than under the rules in many states. Here the prior inconsistent statement can be used for impeachment purposes and as substantive evidence. (A) is wrong because the Federal Rules permit impeachment of your own witness. (B) is wrong because under the Federal Rules, prior inconsistent statements, made under oath and subject to the penalty of perjury in a deposition or prior hearing, are admissible as nonhearsay. (D) is wrong because the statement can be used for more than impeachment.

Answer to Question 7

(B)   The offer to pay medical expenses in itself is not admissible as an admission. Here, however, there is a statement that follows such an offer. This statement is admissible as an admission by the owner of the development firm that Bates had not warned Ralph about the dangerous condition of the stairs. Since this is an admission, under the Federal Rules it is not hearsay. (A) is an exception to the hearsay rule and is thus unnecessary. Furthermore, it is an exception requiring the unavailability of the declarant, and there is no indication in the facts that the owner is now unavailable. (C) is wrong because, as mentioned, the statement is not hearsay under the Federal Rules. (D) is a misstatement of the law; only the offer to pay medical expenses is inadmissible on public policy grounds.

Answer to Question 8

(B)   Under the Federal Rules, an expert witness may learn the basis for the opinion at or before the hearing. (A) is wrong because the basis for an expert's opinion need not be personal observation. (C) is wrong because under the Federal Rules, an expert witness may testify in the form of an opinion without prior disclosure of the underlying facts or data. In addition, here the basis of the expert's testimony was based on evidence already introduced at trial. (D) is wrong because expert opinion may indeed be based on information provided by lay people.

Answer to Question 9

(B)   This is a best evidence rule question; it is an attempt to prove the contents of a document that is the basis of the suit. The best evidence rule applies and therefore the party must produce the original document or offer a satisfactory excuse for not producing it. Under Rule 1004, if the original is lost, that is considered a reasonable excuse for not producing the original. Whether the letter is in fact "lost" would be a preliminary question of fact to be determined by the court under Rule 104(a), rather than the jury. Thus, (B) is correct and (C) is wrong. (A) is wrong; there is no such requirement under the rules. (D) is wrong; there is no such rule of law.

Answer to Question 10

(C)   Federal Rule of Evidence 608(b) permits cross-examination relating to prior bad acts if, in the discretion of the trial court, they are probative of truthfulness. Thus, (A) is wrong. (D) is wrong because Federal Rule 609 permits inquiry into a prior crime less than 10 years old if conviction of the crime required proof or admission of an act of dishonesty or false statement. Since the bias involved in a pecuniary interest is always relevant and admissible, (B) is wrong. Only the question relating to drug abuse—a marginally relevant topic, relating possibly to the witness's ability to perceive or remember—appears improper.

Answer to Question 11

(B) Rick's statement is hearsay, and just because it has become part of a police report, it does not stop being hearsay. (A) and (C) are wrong because although the police report itself may qualify under some exception, Rick's statement contained in the report is still hearsay. (D) is wrong because the facts do not indicate that Paula is testifying from her report, and it does not change the hearsay character of the testimony.

Answer to Question 12

(B) The statement is inadmissible hearsay. (A) is wrong because the statement may tend to show a reason for the accident. (C) is wrong because Eric is not a party, and the statement is not attributable to either of the Brinks. (D) is wrong because the statement against interest exception requires that the declarant be unavailable to testify; nothing in the facts suggests that Eric is unavailable.

Answer to Question 13

(A) Under the rule of present recollection refreshed, a witness may be shown any writing that may refresh her memory of an event. (B) is wrong because the doctrine of past recollection recorded refers to the admissibility of the contents of a writing, and a proper foundation must be laid. (C) is a misstatement of the law and makes no sense in this situation. (D) is wrong because Sherry is not testifying to the contents of her statement, but to her recollection of the accident.

Answer to Question 14

(A) Frances's testimony about Ralph's and Max's conversation is not being offered for its truth (*i.e.*, to prove that Elbert had been flirting with Maxine), but rather to show its effect on Max. Thus, it is not hearsay, and (C) is incorrect. When the words themselves are in issue (*e.g.*, words of contract, gift, defamation, etc.), they are legally operative facts. This concept does not apply to these facts, and so (B) is wrong. (D) is incorrect because opinion testimony by lay witnesses is admissible if it is based on the perception of the witness, helpful in determining a fact in issue, and not based on scientific, technical, or other specialized knowledge. Here, Frances saw Max, and he appeared angry. Whether Max was angry could help determine whether he acted in self-defense or struck the first blow.

Answer to Question 15

(D) Rocky's statement is an out-of-court declaration offered for its truth, and it does not fall within any hearsay exception. It is not a dying declaration because the declaration does not concern the immediate circumstances causing Rocky's grievous injuries. Likewise, an excited utterance must concern the immediate facts of the startling event. (A) and (B) are therefore incorrect. (C) is incorrect because, even if the privilege attached to a nurse's aide, the information that is privileged is limited to that necessary for treatment. Rocky's statements are clearly beyond the scope of the privilege.

Answer to Question 16

(A) Declarations of present bodily condition are admissible as an exception to the hearsay rule, even if not made to a physician. Such statements relate to symptoms, such as pain. Here, Phillipe's statement was one of present bodily condition and is admissible to prove the extent of his injuries, which is an issue in the case. It follows that (D) is incorrect. (C) is incorrect because, as noted above, a declaration of present bodily condition is admissible even if not made to a physician. (B) is incorrect, because Phillipe's statement is admissible as a declaration of present pain, not as proof he had a heart attack.

Answer to Question 17

(C) Evidence is relevant if it tends to establish a material proposition in the case. This evidence, which would help establish a motive, which in turn would help establish the guilt of the defendant, would clearly be relevant. Therefore, an objection based solely on the relevance of the evidence should be overruled. Therefore (A) and (B) are wrong. (D) is wrong. On the facts of this case, the involvement of Vance in embezzlement would be relevant, and since the objection was based on grounds of relevance, the limiting instruction would not be required. The statement might be hearsay when used for that purpose, but it would probably qualify as an admission by silence on the part of the defendant. In any event, the objection was not on hearsay grounds.

Answer to Question 18

(D) Out-of-court statements offered for the purpose of proving knowledge on the part of the listener are not objectionable as hearsay. In addition, the evidence may be admissible as an admission by silence. Therefore, (A) is incorrect. (B) is wrong; the state of mind exception to the hearsay rule applies when the out-of-court statement helps establish the declarant's state of mind. (C) is wrong; phone calls during business hours on business phones do not qualify as a business record.

Answer to Question 19

(A) Evidence that Raoul was retrieving his own painting from David's wrongful possession would help negate the intent required for burglary. Therefore, it would be relevant. The testimony would have no effect on Sam's credibility, so (B) and (C) are incorrect. (D) is not a very good answer. First, the objection is on relevancy, not on Rule 403. In addition, rejecting the evidence on Rule 403 grounds would be extremely unlikely on the facts presented.

Answer to Question 20

(A) Under the Federal Rules, either party may impeach a witness, and leading questions are permitted when a witness is hostile. Thus, (C) and (D) are incorrect. (B) is incorrect because the examiner is not trying to refresh Lee's recollection of whether the drink was on the menu; rather, he is talking about a deposition and is trying to impeach her with an inconsistent statement.

Answer to Question 21

(B) Under Federal Rule 801(d)(1), if the prior inconsistent statement was made at a trial or hearing while the declarant was under oath and subject to the penalty of perjury, it is not hearsay. The statement is admissible to impeach Lou *and* as substantive proof that Russ stopped suddenly on the expressway. Thus, (A) and (C) are incorrect. (D) is incorrect because it imposes the unavailability requirement of the former testimony exception to the hearsay rule. Since this evidence is not hearsay under the Federal Rules, the exception and its requirements do not apply.

Answer to Question 22

(D) In federal court, one spouse may testify against the other in a criminal case, without the consent of the party-spouse. Thus, (A) is incorrect. (B) states an element of the privilege for confidential marital communications, which belongs to both spouses. Unfortunately for Rob, Barbara is not testifying about communications between them; she is testifying about facts that she observed. (C) is incorrect because, although the Federal Rules do not set out specific privileges, they specifically state that the witness's privilege is governed by the common law as interpreted by the courts of the United States.

Answer to Question 23

(B) Under the privilege for confidential marital communications, a person can refuse to disclose, or object to another person disclosing, confidential communications made during the marriage. Under the husband-wife privilege, a spouse cannot be forced to testify against a spouse in a criminal case. (A) is incorrect; the privilege for confidential communications applies even though the parties are divorced, as long as the communication took place during the marriage. (C) is wrong; the spouse can be called as a witness, but cannot be compelled to testify to confidential communications. (D) is wrong; the privilege for confidential communications applies to both civil and criminal cases.

Answer to Question 24

(D) The testimony is hearsay on the issue of the value of Olde Pages. (A) is wrong because the value in the report is being offered as a fact due to Stillwell's expertise. In addition, even if the report only contained an opinion, it would still be hearsay. (B) is wrong, because a past recollection recorded is a record about a matter about which the witness once had knowledge but now has insufficient recollection. Here, Stillwell has not been called as a witness. (C) is wrong because such a report is not made in the normal course of business, since Stillwell does not normally make such reports.

Answer to Question 25

(A) Since this was not a confidential communication between husband and wife, the testimonial privilege would be applicable. In federal court, the testimonial privilege is viewed as belonging to the witness-spouse. (B), (C), and (D) are therefore incorrect.

Answer to Question 26

(A) The accused may introduce evidence of his good character for the trait involved in the case to show his innocence of the alleged crime. Since this evidence is not restricted to impeachment purposes, (B) and (D) are incorrect. Under Federal Rule 405, the witness for the defendant may testify to the defendant's reputation for the trait in question, and he may also give his personal opinion. (C) is therefore incorrect.

Answer to Question 27

(C) Jurors are incompetent as witnesses, but only as to the case in which they are currently sitting or at a later time to impeach their verdict. This is not the case here. The evidence could be excluded, however, if the judge determines that the probative value of the evidence would be substantially outweighed by its tendency to mislead. (A) is wrong because a leading question is permitted on cross-examination. (B) is wrong because the question goes to bias, so it cannot be excluded on the issue of scope of direct examination. (D) is wrong because it makes no sense.

Answer to Question 28

(C) For Dr. Hamilton's testimony to be relevant, Gustave is going to have to offer more evidence to connect the medicine he took to the injuries that he and Dr. Hamilton's other patients suffered. This question is best handled by determining the incorrect answers. (A) is obviously wrong because the hearsay objection is not applicable to percipient observations of a witness. (B) is wrong because the best evidence rule applies when a party is attempting to prove the contents of a writing, recording, or photograph. (D) is wrong because Dr. Hamilton is testifying about matters of which she has personal knowledge, and she is not giving opinion testimony; thus, she does not have to be qualified as an expert.

Answer to Question 29

(B) Winston's statement was made while he was still under the stress of excitement of the startling event, and it concerns the immediate facts of the occurrence. (The tipoff that Winston's statement was made under the stress of excitement of the event is the exclamation mark at the end.) Therefore, it is an excited utterance and an exception to the hearsay rule. Thus, (C) is incorrect. (A) is incorrect because a prior consistent statement is admissible only to rebut a charge that the witness is lying or exaggerating because of some motive. The facts do not indicate such a charge against Winston. (D) is incorrect because the opinion of a lay witness is admissible if it is based on the perception of the witness, helpful in determining a fact in issue, and not based on scientific, technical, or other specialized knowledge.

Answer to Question 30

(D) Each of the other picks presents a situation wherein leading questions are generally allowable, at the discretion of the court: (A) is a preliminary matter as to which there is no dispute; (B) is cross-examination; (C) is examination of a very young child. Leading questions are generally not permitted on direct examination of a disinterested witness, and thus (D) is correct.

Answer to Question 31

(B) Evidence is relevant if it helps decide an issue in dispute. Since the issue is whether Owen is required to sell the Tucker to Philip in accordance with the contract, the fact that Owen paid $160,000 for another car and sold it for $40,000 would probably be considered irrelevant. While that point might be debated, (B) is still the correct answer because (A), (C), and (D) are clearly wrong. (A) is wrong. If the question was asked on cross-examination, it is not objectionable as leading; if the question was asked on direct exam, it would be unobjectionable as leading because the opposing party would be considered a hostile witness. (C) is wrong because evidence of a character trait of irresponsibility would be inadmissible. (D) is wrong. The issue is whether the evidence is relevant, not whether the best evidence rule applies.

Answer to Question 32

(B) The evidence is not hearsay since it is an admission made by and offered against a party; therefore (A) is incorrect. (C) is wrong because Judith is available to testify. (D) may be relevant, but the facts show that it was merely an offer to compromise a disputed claim, and therefore public policy encouraging settlements precludes the introduction of such evidence.

Answer to Question 33

(B) A criminal defendant who takes the stand puts his credibility in issue the same as any other witness; thus, he may be impeached by inquiry into a prior conviction of a crime (such as forgery) that requires proof or admission of dishonesty or false statement. (A) is wrong both because the question asked how the judge should rule on the "question," not whether Jerome would have to answer, and also, because the question is not even directed to any matter on which he can be incriminated. (C) is wrong because many proper questions seek "prejudicial" information, and there is no balancing test for crimes involving dishonesty. (D) is wrong because a party is not prohibited on cross-examination from inquiring into a witness's credibility.

Answer to Question 34

(A) Where Sam has introduced part of a writing, Bill would be entitled to cross-examine or introduce rebuttal evidence as to any other part of the same writing necessary to make it understood. (B) is an incorrect statement of the law. (C) is incorrect because the evidence tends to make it more probable that Bill complied with the contract than it would have been without the evidence. (D) is incorrect because the contract is not hearsay; it is a legally operative fact.

Answer to Question 35

(B) Under the Federal Rules, Bill may compel the proponent of the evidence to introduce any part thereof that ought, in fairness, to be considered contemporaneous with it. (A) is incorrect because no foundation need be laid. (C) is incorrect because Federal Rule 106 does not require proof of relevance. The standard is fairness. (D) is incorrect because, although it is hearsay, it is within the business records exception to the hearsay rule.

REAL PROPERTY
ANSWER SHEET

1.	Ⓐ Ⓑ Ⓒ Ⓓ		19.	Ⓐ Ⓑ Ⓒ Ⓓ
2.	Ⓐ Ⓑ Ⓒ Ⓓ		20.	Ⓐ Ⓑ Ⓒ Ⓓ
3.	Ⓐ Ⓑ Ⓒ Ⓓ		21.	Ⓐ Ⓑ Ⓒ Ⓓ
4.	Ⓐ Ⓑ Ⓒ Ⓓ		22.	Ⓐ Ⓑ Ⓒ Ⓓ
5.	Ⓐ Ⓑ Ⓒ Ⓓ		23.	Ⓐ Ⓑ Ⓒ Ⓓ
6.	Ⓐ Ⓑ Ⓒ Ⓓ		24.	Ⓐ Ⓑ Ⓒ Ⓓ
7.	Ⓐ Ⓑ Ⓒ Ⓓ		25.	Ⓐ Ⓑ Ⓒ Ⓓ
8.	Ⓐ Ⓑ Ⓒ Ⓓ		26.	Ⓐ Ⓑ Ⓒ Ⓓ
9.	Ⓐ Ⓑ Ⓒ Ⓓ		27.	Ⓐ Ⓑ Ⓒ Ⓓ
10.	Ⓐ Ⓑ Ⓒ Ⓓ		28.	Ⓐ Ⓑ Ⓒ Ⓓ
11.	Ⓐ Ⓑ Ⓒ Ⓓ		29.	Ⓐ Ⓑ Ⓒ Ⓓ
12.	Ⓐ Ⓑ Ⓒ Ⓓ		30.	Ⓐ Ⓑ Ⓒ Ⓓ
13.	Ⓐ Ⓑ Ⓒ Ⓓ		31.	Ⓐ Ⓑ Ⓒ Ⓓ
14.	Ⓐ Ⓑ Ⓒ Ⓓ		32.	Ⓐ Ⓑ Ⓒ Ⓓ
15.	Ⓐ Ⓑ Ⓒ Ⓓ		33.	Ⓐ Ⓑ Ⓒ Ⓓ
16.	Ⓐ Ⓑ Ⓒ Ⓓ		34.	Ⓐ Ⓑ Ⓒ Ⓓ
17.	Ⓐ Ⓑ Ⓒ Ⓓ		35.	Ⓐ Ⓑ Ⓒ Ⓓ
18.	Ⓐ Ⓑ Ⓒ Ⓓ			

REAL PROPERTY QUESTIONS

Questions 1-2 are based on the following fact situation:

Art was the owner in fee simple of Redacre, a vacant tract of land. He told his favorite nephew, Phil, "I've always liked you, so I'm going to leave you Redacre when I die."

Phil was being pressured by Sandy to pay off an old debt. To satisfy Sandy, he executed and delivered to her a general warranty deed to Redacre. Sandy immediately recorded the deed. Sandy built a house on Redacre and has resided there ever since.

Art died shortly thereafter. His will left Redacre to Phil. Phil, needing money badly, sold Redacre to Mary by general warranty deed, which Mary promptly recorded. Mary paid Phil a reasonable value for Redacre. Mary purchased Redacre solely as an investment and never visited Redacre. She therefore never knew that Sandy was living there.

1. Which of the following best describes the effect of Phil's deed to Sandy at the time it was recorded?

   (A) It was ineffective as a conveyance of either legal or equitable interest in Redacre.

   (B) It effectively conveyed legal title to Redacre since it was recorded.

   (C) It effectively conveyed equitable title to Redacre.

   (D) It was effective as a quitclaim, conveying to Sandy Phil's expectancy of title.

2. Which of the following best describes the status of titles at the time of Art's death?

   (A) Sandy has title to Redacre.

   (B) Sandy has title if Art was aware of Phil's transfer to her.

   (C) Phil has title, but Sandy can sue to recover title on an estoppel theory.

   (D) Phil has title, and Sandy has no enforceable claim to Redacre.

Questions 3-4 are based on the following fact situation:

Proctor and Gamble owned large adjoining tracts of land. The boundary line between the two properties was never properly determined or clearly known.

In 1977, Proctor installed a gas-powered generator on land he thought he owned, but which was in fact owned by Gamble. Proctor ran electrical wires from the generator across land he knew belonged to Gamble. Gamble orally consented to the wiring crossing his land.

In 1990, Gamble was found to be mentally incompetent. He died in 2001, and his executor filed suit to eject Proctor and quiet title. The statute of limitations for ejectment is 20 years.

3. With respect to the land on which the generator was installed:

   (A) Proctor cannot claim title by adverse possession because the statute of limitations was tolled by Gamble's incompetency.

   (B) Proctor cannot claim title by adverse possession because his occupation was not open and notorious.

   (C) Proctor has acquired title by adverse possession.

   (D) None of the above.

4. With respect to the land over which the electrical wires were laid:

   (A) Proctor has acquired title by adverse possession.

(B) Proctor has acquired a prescriptive easement.

(C) Proctor has acquired both title by adverse possession and a prescriptive easement.

(D) Proctor has acquired neither title by adverse possession nor a prescriptive easement.

Questions 5-6 are based on the following fact situation:

In 1962, Alvin inherited a 200-acre undivided tract of land from his grandfather. The land remained vacant until 1998 when Alvin decided to subdivide the property into 80 two-acre lots. He prepared and duly recorded a subdivision plan that showed the 80 two-acre lots, and the remaining 40 acres in the center of the tract was designated "future public golf course." Alvin named the subdivision Fareway Greens and began to market the 80 two-acre lots. He prepared and distributed a brochure promoting Fareway Greens. The brochure provided that one of the benefits of living in Fareway Greens would be the proximity of the public golf course. Property bordering the 40-acre tract sold for a higher price because it was overlooking the golf course. Alvin sold 60 of the lots to individual purchasers. Each deed referred to the recorded plan and also contained the following clause: "No swimming pools shall be installed on any lots within Fareway Greens." In 2002, wishing to rid himself of the remaining Fareway Greens acreage, Alvin sold the remaining 20 acres and the 40-acre tract to Kerry by a deed that referred to the plan and contained the restriction relating to swimming pools. Kerry sold the 20 two-acre lots to individual purchasers and the 40-acre tract to Donna. None of the deeds from Kerry referred to the plan or contained any reference to the swimming pool restriction.

5. Assume for this question only that Donna has announced her intention of erecting a shopping mall on the 40-acre tract. Benny, an owner of a two-acre lot purchased from

Alvin, brings suit to enjoin Donna. If Benny wins, it will be because:

(A) Donna will be deemed to have taken with actual notice because of the location of the tract.

(B) Benny can sue in equity to enforce the plan against Donna.

(C) Benny is a creditor beneficiary of Alvin's promise with respect to the tract.

(D) Benny was economically benefited by the existence of a golf course within the Fareway Greens development.

6. Assume for this question only that Sally, who purchased her lot from Kerry, decided to install a swimming pool on the rear quarter of her lot. Benny, who owns the adjoining lot, discovers that the pool has been installed and files suit against Sally to force her to remove it. Who will prevail?

(A) Benny, because the restrictive covenant in his deed runs with the land.

(B) Benny, because his land is not benefited by the existence of a swimming pool on the adjoining tract.

(C) Sally, because her deed did not contain the restrictive covenant.

(D) Sally, because she had no notice of the restriction on the installation of swimming pools.

Question 7

Peter and James inherited Orangeacre as joint tenants from their parents. Only half of the acreage was planted with oranges, and Peter decided that to increase productivity, the balance of the land should be planted with a different variety of oranges.

James refused to participate in the project, and Peter brought an action for declaratory relief alleging that he was entitled to be reimbursed for half of the cost of the improvement.

Which of the following correctly describes the result in the action?

(A) Peter will be denied the requested judgment.

(B) Peter will be granted the requested judgment.

(C) The result depends upon whether James will receive an economic benefit.

(D) The result depends upon whether the improvements will produce sufficient income to amortize their cost.

Question 8

Even though Ed Jones and Edith Smith had never been formally married, they lived together for 10 years as husband and wife. During this time Edith identified herself as "Mrs. Jones," with the knowledge and consent of Ed. For the entire period, Ed and Edith maintained joint checking accounts and filed joint income tax returns as Mr. and Mrs. Ed Jones. During this period of cohabitation, Ed Jones decided to buy a home. The deed identified the grantees as "Ed Jones and Edith Jones, his wife, and their heirs and assigns forever as tenants by the entirety." Ed made a down payment of $20,000 and executed a mortgage for the unpaid balance. Both he and Edith signed the note for the unpaid balance as husband and wife. Ed continued to make the monthly payments as they became due until he and Edith had an argument and decided to separate. Ed abandoned Edith and the house. Edith then made the payments for six months. At the end of this period, Edith brought an action against Ed for partition of the land in question. Assume that the jurisdiction does not recognize the common law marriage. Assume further that the jurisdiction has no applicable statute on the subject.

Edith's request for partition should be:

(A) Granted, because the estate created by the deed was not a tenancy by the entirety.

(B) Granted, because the tenancy by the entirety that was created by the deed was severed when Ed abandoned Edith.

(C) Denied, because a tenant by the entirety has no right to partition.

(D) Denied, because Ed has absolute title to the property.

Question 9

Tom leased an apartment from Lon for a period of one year. At the end of the year, Tom continued occupying the apartment, paying Lon the $250 rent in advance each month. Tom had continually complained to Lon about the facilities provided for trash disposal behind the apartment house. Finally, after receiving no response from Lon, Tom complained to the Health Department, who in turn mandated that Lon substantially improve the trash facilities for the apartment building. Shortly thereafter, Lon notified Tom that his rent was being increased to $400 per month. Tom protested and pointed out that all of the other tenants in the apartment building paid rent of $250 per month. Lon then gave Tom the required statutory notice that the tenancy was being terminated at the earliest possible time. By an appropriate action, Tom contested Lon's right to terminate.

If Tom succeeds, it will be because:

(A) The doctrine prohibiting retaliatory eviction is part of the law of the jurisdiction.

(B) A periodic tenancy was created by implication.

(C) A landlord must generally charge the same rent for all units located in one complex.

(D) Lon failed to establish a valid reason why Tom's rent needed to be raised.

Question 10

Employer owned Blackwood in fee simple. Employer was very happy with the service Employee had given him over the years. As a bonus, Employer decided to give Blackwood to Employee. Employer presented a deed conveying Blackwood to Employee. The deed was never recorded. Six months later, Employer found that he was in dire financial straits and needed Blackwood back to complete a sale of the tract of land. He asked Employee to please destroy the deed, which Employee dutifully and voluntarily did. Shortly thereafter, Employer and Employee were killed in an explosion of the factory where they both worked. Each of the successors in interest claimed title to Blackwood.

The probable outcome will be that:

(A) Employer was the owner of Blackwood, because Employee had voluntarily destroyed the deed.

(B) Employer was the owner of Blackwood, because the destruction of the deed by Employee relates back and redates the present transfer of the deed to Employee.

(C) Employee was the owner of Blackwood, because the deed was merely evidence of his title and its destruction was insufficient to cause title to pass back to Employer.

(D) Employee was the owner of Blackwood, because his destruction of the deed to Blackwood was under the undue influence of Employer.

Question 11

Luke and Linda were not married, but lived together for two years. Because they felt that their relationship was very stable, they decided to leave their leased apartment and purchase a home. Luke and Linda each put up 50% of the down payment on Whiteacre. They took title as tenants in common, and each orally promised the other that the survivor should take title to Whiteacre. Luke and Linda lived at Whiteacre for three years, equitably dividing mortgage payments and maintenance expenses. They were then involved in a serious car accident. Linda was killed almost instantly and Luke died in the hospital one week later. Neither Luke nor Linda left a will. Linda was survived only by her mother, Meghan. Luke was survived only by his brother, Bobby.

Who owns Whiteacre?

(A) Meghan owns the whole.

(B) Bobby owns the whole.

(C) Meghan and Bobby each have a one-half interest as tenants in common.

(D) Meghan and Bobby each have a one-half interest as joint tenants.

Questions 12-13 are based on the following fact situation:

Ophelia wished to install an in-ground swimming pool in her backyard. She hired the Acme Pool Company to do the installation. Ophelia chose to locate the pool on the west end of her rather large backyard, close to the property line dividing her yard from her neighbor Norbert's property. She told Norbert that she intended to install the pool, and she told him that, when it was completed, she would invite him and his family to use it.

On the day that Acme began excavation for the pool, Norbert was at home. He stood outside in his backyard to watch the workers to be sure that they did not drive their equipment over his property. The workers wisely kept to Ophelia's property. Unfortunately, when the excavation was nearly completed, subsidence on Norbert's property, caused by the excavation, caused part of Norbert's backyard lawn to collapse. Norbert was understandably upset.

12. If Norbert sues Ophelia for the damage to his lawn, how will a court most likely rule?

(A) For Norbert, because Ophelia is absolutely liable for the damage to Norbert's land.

(B) For Norbert, but only if Ophelia's excavation was negligent.

(C) For Ophelia, because only the lawn was damaged, not any of the buildings located on the property.

(D) For Ophelia, because she had no duty to provide support for Norbert's land.

13. Assume for purposes of this question only that Ophelia's excavation caused Norbert's garage to collapse. What is Ophelia's best defense to an action by Norbert for damage to the garage?

(A) Ophelia gave notice to Norbert of her intention to excavate and he made no objection.

(B) Ophelia had hired Acme based on good recommendations.

(C) Ophelia's excavation was done in a proper manner, and there would have been no subsidence except for the fact that the garage was there.

(D) Norbert's garage was made of solid concrete and thus was unusually heavy.

Questions 14-16 are based on the following fact situation:

In the mid-1990s, Sidney entered into a partnership with Jay to develop some land that had been in Sidney's family for many years.

In 1999, in compliance with all applicable laws, and after receiving all necessary permits, the partnership, BayShore Development, began construction on two projects. The first, BayShore Heights, consisted of 500 single-family residences built on 250 acres. The second, BayShore Mall, was a shopping center built on 100 acres next to the north end of BayShore Heights.

14. With consideration of likely court enforcement of the following, which method should BayShore Development use to ensure that BayShore Heights retains its residential character?

(A) All deeds should contain negative easements.

(B) All deeds should be subject to conditions subsequent.

(C) All deeds should include covenants.

(D) Ensure the residential character by developing the area in accordance with zoning laws.

15. Immediately to the west of BayShore Heights, Sidney owned additional acreage on which, in 2003, he desired to build another group of 250 single-family homes. To ensure their marketability, Sidney desired to sell them like BayShore Heights homes, and to that extent, intended that the deeds to the new homes contain the same restrictions as those in BayShore Heights and be enforceable in the same manner by owners in both developments. Will Sidney be successful in this plan?

(A) No, zoning restrictions will control.

(B) No, because in order to have such restrictions, the entire project must have been built at the same time.

(C) Yes, the restrictions will be equally enforceable for this new project as they were for BayShore Heights.

(D) Yes, provided that a court considers this new project to be part of a common development scheme with BayShore Heights.

16. Clay, a developer who wanted to build high-rise condominiums on the remaining acreage owned by Sidney, seeks to purchase the property. Assuming that the condominiums will block the view of the bay of many of the homes in BayShore Heights, what is the effect the original

BayShore Heights project may have on Clay's title to this property?

(A) Clay, who received title from Sidney, is restricted from using the property for anything but single-family dwellings.

(B) Clay will be subject to an implied easement for light and air, and the BayShore Heights owners can enjoin the building of high-rise condominiums.

(C) The creation of the original BayShore Heights project gives the owners of those homes a right, enforceable at law, of first refusal to buy the acreage offered to Clay.

(D) Clay takes title free of any claim by the owners of BayShore Heights because the owners have no enforceable claim against Sidney.

Question 17

Lou owned Blackacre, a large parcel of land. In 1975, Lou decided to subdivide Blackacre into 20 separate lots. Lou sold Lots 1-19, retaining Lot 20 for himself to live on. The deeds for each of the 19 lots sold by Lou contained the following restriction: "All lots within the Blackacre subdivision shall be used for residential purposes only." The purchasers of Lots 1-19 each built residences on their property. Lou lived on Lot 20 in the Blackacre subdivision until his death, when it was sold without any restrictions to Al. In 1995, Al sold Lot 20 to Neil, furnishing him with an abstract of title and assuring him that the land was unrestricted. The abstract of title showed that Lot 20 was not restricted. In 2005, Neil decided to build a grocery store on Lot 20. Sherry, an adjoining owner in the Blackacre subdivision, informed Neil of the restriction and told him that he would be unable to build the grocery store.

If Sherry brings suit seeking an injunction against Neil's building of the grocery store, will she prevail?

(A) No, because Neil had neither actual nor constructive notice of the restriction.

(B) No, because Neil relied on the abstract of title and Al's representation in good faith.

(C) Yes, because the property owners in the Blackacre subdivision have a right to keep the subdivision in the condition that they want it.

(D) Yes, because Neil would be charged with notice as a result of the residential character of the Blackacre subdivision.

Questions 18-19 are based on the following fact situation:

Emma was the owner in fee simple of Greenacre, a tract of land. In 1975, Emma conveyed Greenacre to Martha, "for life and then to the first child of Martha's sister, Vera, who shall reach the age of 21." Vera was unmarried and childless in 1975. In 1981, Vera married, and in 1983, Vera gave birth to a son, Oscar. In 2004, Oscar reached the age of 21, and Martha was still alive and living on Greenacre.

18. Oscar now seeks to obtain possession of Greenacre and brings an action in ejectment against Martha. Martha's best defense against Oscar's attempt to eject her is that:

(A) Martha's life estate was not subject to termination during her lifetime.

(B) Oscar has no claim to Greenacre, because he was not living at the time of Emma's original conveyance.

(C) A conveyance of Greenacre to Oscar violates the Rule Against Perpetuities.

(D) Oscar's interest, if any, would be that of a contingent remainder, and the contingency is Martha's death.

19. Assume that Martha died before Oscar became 21. Assume also that the jurisdiction has abolished the common law rule of

destructibility of contingent remainders. Who would be the owner of Greenacre?

(A) Oscar.

(B) Oscar's court-appointed guardian ad litem.

(C) Emma and her heirs in fee simple.

(D) Emma and her heirs would take the estate until Oscar became 21 years of age.

Questions 20-22 are based on the following fact situation:

Stevens owned Goldacre, a large tract of land, in fee simple. In 1995, Stevens deeded Goldacre as follows: "To Kent for life; if Roberts and Morris are discharged from the Army before Kent's death, to Roberts and Morris and their heirs. If they are not discharged from the Army before Kent's death, then the remainder is to go to my heirs." In 2004, Stevens and Kent died. Stevens's will left his entire estate to the American Cancer Society. Stevens's nearest relative is his brother, Philips.

20. In a jurisdiction that has codified common law principles, the interests of Morris and Roberts at the time the deed was executed are best described as:

(A) Mere expectancies.

(B) Contingent remainders.

(C) Absolutely vested remainders.

(D) Vested remainders subject to a condition subsequent.

21. Assume that Roberts and Morris were discharged from the Army prior to Kent's death. At the time of their discharge, their interest in Goldacre would be classified as:

(A) Tenants in common to a vested remainder.

(B) Joint tenants to a vested remainder.

(C) Tenants in common to a fee simple absolute.

(D) Tenants by the entirety to a fee simple absolute.

22. Assume the same facts as in the previous question. Assume also that Kent is now deceased. Assume further that Roberts predeceased Morris. Morris had a daughter named Cathy, who was the only heir. After Morris's death, Cathy's interest in Goldacre would be:

(A) Ownership of all of Goldacre in fee simple.

(B) Ownership of one-half of Goldacre in fee simple.

(C) Ownership of an undivided one-half interest in Goldacre along with the heirs of Roberts who own the same interest.

(D) Ownership of one-half of Goldacre as a tenant in common with the heirs of Roberts.

Questions 23-25 are based on the following fact situation:

Anson and Barker were adjoining landowners. Anson's property was situated to the west of Barker's property. On the east of Barker's property was Clear Lake. In 1982, Anson purchased a boat to use for fishing on Clear Lake. Anson asked Barker if it would be all right if Anson moved his boat across an eight-foot patch of land leading from Anson's property to Clear Lake. Anson told Barker that the only other way to get to the lake was to take the highway, which involved a six-mile trip. Barker agreed, and Anson used the strip of land regularly to move the boat from his property to the lake and back again. Over the next few years, Anson's continued use of the eight-foot strip created a dirt roadway leading from his property to Clear

Lake. In 2001, Barker sold his property to Samuels. Samuels noticed the dirt road on the eight-foot strip of his property and noticed Anson moving the boat across the dirt road. Even though Samuels knew that this was his property, he said nothing to Anson and let Anson continue for eight months. During the ninth month, Anson and Samuels had a violent argument, and Samuels told Anson that he was never to use the roadway on the eight-foot strip again. Anson continued to use the road until 2004, when Samuels sought an injunction to prevent Anson from using the roadway. The statutory period for adverse possession in this jurisdiction is 20 years.

23. When Barker gave Anson permission to use the eight-foot strip of land leading from Anson's property to Clear Lake, Anson's interest in Barker's property was:

    (A) An easement in gross.

    (B) An easement appurtenant to Barker's property.

    (C) An easement by necessity.

    (D) Not an easement.

24. Which of the following arguments would best support Samuels's action against Anson to enjoin the use of the road?

    (A) The selling of the property to Samuels terminated any claim Anson might have under adverse possession.

    (B) Anson was told to stop using the road prior to the time that the 20-year statute of limitations period had run.

    (C) Anson could not acquire any interest in Samuels's land because his original agreement was oral.

    (D) Anson's use of Samuels's land was permissive during the ownership of Barker.

25. Assume that Anson was held to have a valid easement over the eight-foot strip leading from his property to Clear Lake. The easement would be:

    (A) An easement in gross.

    (B) An easement appurtenant.

    (C) An easement by necessity.

    (D) An easement by implied reservation.

Questions 26-27 are based on the following fact situation:

Jake, who owned two houses on five acres of land, entered into a written agreement with Bob which stated:

> I agree to sell my house and sufficient land for a pool and garage to Bob for $75,000. Received from Bob $200.
>
> Signed June 10.
> Jake
> Bob

On June 15, Bob entered into a written agreement with Marsha to sell her the house for $125,000.

26. Assume for purposes of this question only that Jake learns of Bob's contract with Marsha and decides to sell her the house for $125,000. Bob sues for specific performance. What will the result most likely be?

    (A) Jake will prevail because $200 is only nominal consideration and cannot support the contract.

    (B) Jake will prevail because the contract is ambiguous.

    (C) Bob will prevail because Jake agreed to the purchase price in writing.

    (D) Bob will prevail because Jake's contract with Marsha is sufficient evidence to show which house he agreed to sell to Bob.

27. Assume that Bob actually purchased the house from Jake and then decided that he could sell the house for more than $125,000; he therefore refused to sell it to Marsha according to their agreement. If Marsha sues for specific performance, how will a court hold?

    (A) Judgment for Marsha, because she did not know Bob was purchasing the house from Jake for less than its market value.

    (B) Judgment for Marsha, because Bob had marketable title at the time she sought to enforce the contract.

    (C) Judgment for Bob, because he had no title to the house as of the date he entered into the agreement with Marsha.

    (D) Judgment for Bob, because his agreement with Marsha was fraudulent to Jake at the time it was entered into, and therefore unenforceable.

Question 28

Mary owned 400 acres of land which she inherited from her late husband. About half of the property was densely wooded, and the rest was almost entirely occupied by a large gravel pit. Until his death, Mary's husband Clyde had operated Clyde's Sand and Gravel. Clyde had often thought of cutting the trees and selling the timber but by the time of his death had not done so.

Two years after Clyde's death, Mary transferred the 400 acres to her son Clyde Jr. for life, with the remainder to go to the State Land Trust for Historic Preservation.

Now Clyde Jr. wants to resume gravel production and to cut and sell the trees. Land Trust, the holder of the remainder, sues to block Clyde Jr. on a theory of waste.

How will the court most likely rule?

(A) Land Trust can stop both the gravel mining and the tree cutting.

(B) Land Trust can stop neither the gravel mining nor the tree cutting.

(C) Land Trust can stop the tree cutting but not the gravel mining.

(D) Land Trust can stop the gravel mining but not the tree cutting.

Questions 29-30 are based on the following fact situation:

Katherine and Amanda were sisters who held record title to Lakeacre as joint tenants with right of survivorship. Katherine moved out of Lakeacre shortly after conveying her interest in Lakeacre to her brother Jeff by quitclaim deed. Jeff did not record his deed.

Several years later, Amanda died, leaving her adopted son Chris as her sole heir.

Shortly after Amanda died, Katherine asked Jeff to return his deed and give up his interest in Lakeacre. Jeff agreed and returned the deed, which Katherine destroyed.

29. Who has title to Lakeacre?

    (A) Jeff and Chris as co-tenants.

    (B) Katherine and Chris as co-tenants.

    (C) Katherine as sole owner.

    (D) Jeff as sole owner.

30. Assume for this question only that after Jeff returned his deed to Katherine, Katherine executed and delivered a deed conveying Lakeacre to Paul. The jurisdiction has the following recording act:

    A conveyance of an interest in land shall not be valid against any subsequent purchaser for value, without notice thereof, unless the conveyance is recorded.

Paul promptly and properly recorded his deed. In a suit between Paul and Jeff, Paul will prevail, if at all, because:

(A) Paul recorded his deed.

(B) Jeff's interest terminated when he returned his deed to Katherine.

(C) There has been no severance because Amanda adopted Chris.

(D) Paul is a bona fide purchaser.

Question 31

Olsen and Larsen were negotiating over the proposed purchase by Olsen of a new home constructed by Larsen in a subdivision owned by Larsen. The subdivision contained four types of floor plans. Houses constructed according to the same floor plan were identical, but the different plans varied in square footage and cost.

Olsen could not decide whether he wanted a house with a swimming pool or one located on an extra-large cul-de-sac lot. Both houses were of the same floor plan and both were offered for sale at $100,000. Larsen, who had many other sales transactions to negotiate, prepared a validly executed deed that was ready for recording but did not identify the property conveyed. He told Olsen to decide which house he wanted, identify it in the deed, and then record the deed. Olsen agonized for a few days, then decided that he liked a house with a more expensive floor plan better than either of his original choices. He entered its description in the deed and recorded the deed. The house described had a fair market value of and had been offered for sale by Larsen at $125,000.

Two weeks later, Olsen offered the house for sale to Snyder for $110,000. A real estate agent working for Snyder reported that Olsen had title of record and that it was marketable and free of encumbrances. Olsen told Snyder that the same type of house was selling for $125,000 in the subdivision, but did not describe how he had come to own it or how much he had paid for it.

Snyder agreed to purchase the home, and Olsen conveyed by a validly recorded warranty deed.

If Larsen brings an action against Snyder to quiet title to the house originally sold to Olsen, which of the following is the most probable reason for a judgment for Snyder?

(A) Larsen is guilty of unclean hands.

(B) Recording of the deed by which Olsen conveyed to Snyder precludes any attack on its validity.

(C) Evidence of Larsen's oral instructions to Olsen is barred by the Statute of Frauds.

(D) Larsen is estopped from relying upon his agreement with Olsen because Snyder is a bona fide purchaser for value.

Questions 32-34 are based on the following fact situation:

Lamont owned a 40-acre farm bordering the city limits of Gridley when the local authorities annexed his land to the city and rezoned it from agricultural to residential use. Nathan, the moving force behind the annexation and rezoning, purchased the 40 acres from Lamont and obtained approval of, filed, and recorded a subdivision map dividing the former farm into 120 quarter-acre lots with two five-acre "city parks." He then announced the opening of "Parkland" and proceeded to sell the quarter-acre lots with houses built by his construction subsidiary.

Parkland included a set of covenants, conditions, and restrictions that had been approved by the local land use planning agencies and filed as part of the subdivision map. Among these was a covenant that all purchasers of the lots promised not to engage in any commercial activity (the zoning applicable to Parkland permitted certain types of businesses).

Nathan's real estate operation sold 100 of the quarter-acre lots over the next two years to individual purchasers; each deed referred to the covenants, conditions, and restrictions filed with the subdivision map. When the last 20 lots—located adjacent to one of the areas originally designated as a city park—did not move, Nathan sold the lots and the park in a single 10-acre package to a large national real estate corporation. The deed from Nathan to the corporation omitted any reference to the covenants, conditions, and restrictions. The corporation sold the quarter-acre lots to individual purchasers via deeds also not mentioning the covenants, etc., and then sold the five-acre "park" to a fundamentalist church.

32. After the sale of the five-acre park, but before the church began construction of its Born Again Worship Center and Christian Education Complex, the city of Gridley passes a resolution designating the two "park" areas in Parkland as the Richard Gridley and Gertrude Gridley Memorial Parks, respectively, and soliciting bids from local landscaping firms to prepare the parks for use by the public. When the church learns of the city's plans, it brings an action to quiet title to the five-acre parcel it purchased from the national corporation. How should the trial court rule?

(A) For the city, since the church had constructive notice that the parcel was to be used for park purposes.

(B) For the church, since the deed by which it purchased the parcel did not contain any reference to the subdivision map that designated the area a "park."

(C) For the city, since Nathan dedicated it and the city accepted the two parcels designated as a "park."

(D) For the church, since the city has committed laches in waiting so long to develop the park.

33. Assume for the purposes of this question only that the city has taken no action with respect to the parks, but Winslow, who purchased an individual lot from Nathan, brings an action seeking to enjoin construction of the Born Again Christian Education Complex, alleging that it violates the covenant against conducting commercial activities. The trial court makes a preliminary determination that the Education Complex is a commercial activity. Should the injunction issue?

(A) Yes, because the church cannot be considered a bona fide purchaser.

(B) Yes, because Winslow is a creditor third-party beneficiary of the promise made by Nathan with respect to all the lots in Parkland.

(C) Yes, because Winslow has an equitable servitude concerning use of the land within Parkland.

(D) No, because the covenant not to conduct commercial activity applies only to purchasers of individual quarter-acre lots.

34. One of the purchasers of a quarter-acre lot from the large real estate corporation was Madame Zorka, a self-proclaimed psychic. She places a tasteful neon sign in the front window of her residence and begins giving psychic readings for a fee, an activity in conformity with the applicable zoning regulations. If Winslow seeks to enjoin this activity, will he succeed?

(A) No, because the deed from the corporation to Zorka did not refer to the covenants, conditions, and restrictions.

(B) No, if Zorka relied on the zoning regulations before purchasing her property.

(C) Yes, because the restrictive covenant relating to commercial activity runs with the land.

(D) Yes, if Winslow can show reciprocal negative servitudes implied from a common scheme.

Question 35

Carol leased 130 square feet of space in a commercial building owned by Barbara pursuant to a written contract specifying a term of three years, renewable at Carol's option for an additional three years. Carol installed sinks, tile, mirrors, special chairs, and other equipment related to her hairstyling business. During the second year of the lease term, Barbara borrowed $60,000 from Commercial Credit Company, and executed a mortgage in that company's favor on the building. Carol was not informed of the existence of the mortgage.

In the last month of her three-year term, Carol decided not to renew and began removing the equipment and other items that she had installed at the beginning of the lease. Barbara had defaulted on the payments due Commercial Credit, and that company had commenced foreclosure proceedings two months earlier. Commercial Credit now brings an action to enjoin removal of the equipment, naming as defendants both Carol and Barbara.

If the trial court refuses to issue the injunction, it will probably be because:

(A) The Statute of Frauds precludes Commercial Credit from asserting any interest in the equipment.

(B) In the absence of an agreement to the contrary, a commercial tenant is entitled to remove any property she voluntarily brings upon the premises.

(C) Chattels installed for the purposes of trade generally may be removed by the tenant if she pays for any damages occasioned thereby.

(D) Carol was given no notice of the mortgage.

REAL PROPERTY ANSWERS

Answer to Question 1

(A) Since Phil did not acquire either legal or equitable title until after Art died, he had nothing to pass on to Sandy. Therefore, (B) and (C) are wrong. (D) is not the strongest answer based on the facts.

Answer to Question 2

(A) The majority of states would hold that, under the estoppel by deed theory, title would pass automatically to Sandy by operation of law. (B) is wrong because estoppel by deed applies regardless of the testator's knowledge of a prior deed. (C) is wrong because it states the minority position under estoppel by deed. Under the majority view, title passes to Sandy automatically; she need not bring suit to recover title. (D) is wrong because title passes to Sandy under the doctrine of estoppel by deed.

Answer to Question 3

(C) Since Proctor treated the land as his own for the statutory period, he acquired title to the land by adverse possession. (D) is therefore wrong. (A) is wrong because an intervening disability does not toll the statute of limitations. (B) is wrong because Proctor's occupation was indeed open and notorious under the facts.

Answer to Question 4

(D) Proctor used the land with Gamble's consent, and there were no facts to indicate that Proctor in any way manifested an intention to claim the land as his own. Therefore the "hostile" requirement is not met. (A), (B), and (C) are therefore wrong.

Answer to Question 5

(B) Benny can enjoin Donna's actions only if he has an equitable servitude. (A) is wrong because the location of the tract will not be sufficient to establish notice. However, Benny will be able to enforce the restriction as an equitable servitude because Donna had *record* notice of it: a deed in her chain of title referred to the recorded plan that designated the tract as a golf course. (C) is wrong because Benny is not a third-party beneficiary of Alvin's promise. Instead, he is a direct promisee, since he dealt directly with Alvin. (D) is not sufficient to grant Benny an injunction against Donna.

Answer to Question 6

(A) The restrictive covenant runs with Benny's land, which is benefited, and with Sally's land, which is burdened. The essential ingredients are that the covenant touch and concern the land and that it be intended to run. Both are present here. (B) is therefore wrong. (C) is wrong because the restriction was contained in a previous deed relating to the property. (D) is wrong because Sally at least had constructive notice of the restriction.

Answer to Question 7

(A) A co-tenant has no duty to improve the property and cannot force the other co-tenants to contribute to the cost of improvements made by him. Thus, (B) is wrong. (C) and (D) are wrong because the results of an improvement are irrelevant; the co-tenant cannot force his other co-tenants to contribute to the improvement.

Answer to Question 8

(A) The estate could not have been a tenancy by the entirety since that estate can exist only between a legally married husband and wife. The estate created would probably be considered either a joint tenancy with right of survivorship or a tenancy in common, either of which may be partitioned. (B) is wrong because, even if the estate had been by the entirety, abandonment by one spouse does not cause a severance. (C) is wrong because although a tenant by the entirety cannot obtain a partition, that is not the type of tenancy involved here. (D) is wrong because Ed could not have absolute title under these facts.

Answer to Question 9

(A) In the present case, Lon is attempting to evict Tom for retaliatory purposes, and many jurisdictions prohibit such evictions. (B) is wrong because the fact that this is very likely a periodic tenancy will not save Tom from eviction, since the proper statutory notice has been given to terminate it. (C) is wrong because the amount of rent charged each tenant is a function of "freedom of contract," and a landlord is free to charge differing amounts of rents for the units. (D) is wrong because a landlord generally does not need to establish a valid reason to raise rent.

Answer to Question 10

(C) The deed, once it has been delivered, is merely evidence of title, and its destruction does not cause any change in the title. To transfer title, Employee would have had to deliver a new deed transferring title back to Employer. (A) and (B) are therefore wrong. (D) is not supported by the facts.

Answer to Question 11

(C) When Linda died, her one-half interest descended to her intestate heir, Meghan; and likewise, when Luke died, his one-half interest passed to his intestate heir, Bobby. There is no right of survivorship in a tenancy in common, and the oral agreement between Luke and Linda does not satisfy the Statute of Frauds or the Statute of Wills. The facts involving the closeness of Luke's death to Linda's are a mere distraction, because no real simultaneous death issues arise here. It follows that (A) and (B) are incorrect. (D) is incorrect because a tenancy in common does not become a joint tenancy upon the death of the co-tenants.

Answer to Question 12

(A) A property owner has a right to the support of his land without any buildings on it. An adjoining neighbor is absolutely liable for any withdrawal of support. Thus, if Ophelia's excavation withdrew support for Norbert's land, she is absolutely liable for the damage. (B) is wrong because Ophelia's negligence is irrelevant; she is absolutely liable. (C) is wrong because damage to the land itself is recoverable if support has been withdrawn. (D) is wrong, because as indicated, adjoining landowners have a right of subjacent and lateral support.

Answer to Question 13

(C) If the land would not have subsided but for the structure, Ophelia is not absolutely liable. She would be liable only if she were negligent in excavating. (C) covers the lack of negligence and the fact that the structure contributed to the collapse; it is therefore her best defense. (A) is wrong because notice of the excavation, and lack of objection, does not preclude recovery by Norbert on the negligence. (B) is wrong because it concerns only the negligence issue. (D) is not as good an answer as (C) because even if the garage was unusually heavy, Ophelia could still be liable if she were negligent in excavating.

Answer to Question 14

(C) Negative easements are of too limited a use to ensure that the project retains its residential character, so (A) is wrong. (D) is wrong because a governmental authority may change zoning laws. (B) is possible, but it is unlikely a court will enforce a forfeiture of an owner's estate, particularly since the same result could be accomplished by the use of covenants in the deeds. In addition, buyers may be reluctant to purchase lots subject to a condition subsequent that could cause the loss of their interest. Thus, (C) is the best method.

Answer to Question 15

(D) Prior purchasers may enforce restrictions in subsequent deeds from a common grantor if there is a general scheme evidencing the developer's intent to benefit the entire subdivision. Hence, (B) is wrong. (C) is wrong because it is too absolute; if a court finds there is no common development, the restrictions are not enforceable by the owners of BayShore Heights. (A) is wrong because zoning regulations do not limit the enforceability of private covenants.

Answer to Question 16

(D) The development of the original projects indicates no scheme or plan for development of the remaining acreage. Hence, (A) and (C) are not supported by the facts. (B) is a misstatement of law.

Answer to Question 17

(D) Since the facts state that the other purchasers of Lots 1-19 each built residences on their property, Neil would at least be charged with inquiry notice. Thus, (A) is incorrect. (B) is incorrect because Neil's reliance on the abstract of title and Al's representation would not negate the inquiry notice. (C)'s reasoning would not be sufficient to bind Neil to the covenant.

Answer to Question 18

(A) The conveyance clearly created an estate in Martha, lasting for Martha's life. (B) is incorrect because Oscar did not have to be alive at the time of the original conveyance in order to now claim an interest in Greenacre. (C) is incorrect because Oscar's interest would vest within 21 years of a life in being (Vera). (D) is incorrect because Oscar's interest would be a vested remainder.

Answer to Question 19

(D) Since Emma retained a reversionary interest in Greenacre, she would take possession of the land until Oscar became 21 years of age. Thus, (C) is wrong. (A) is wrong because Oscar is not entitled to possession until he reaches age 21. (B) is wrong. Oscar has no right to possession; thus, a guardian cannot possess for him.

Answer to Question 20

(B) "If Roberts and Morris are discharged from the Army before Kent's death" is a condition precedent to Roberts's and Morris's taking in possession. Thus, their interests are contingent rather than vested remainders, and (C) and (D) are incorrect. Stevens's deed constitutes a valid conveyance of a future interest to Roberts and Morris; therefore, they have more than mere expectancies, and (A) is incorrect.

Answer to Question 21

(A) Because the condition precedent to their remainder has been satisfied, *i.e.,* Roberts and Morris were discharged from the Army before Kent's death, their contingent remainder has "vested." Also, at common law, it was held that any conveyance to two or more persons was presumed to create a joint tenancy unless a contrary intention was clearly expressed. But today all courts hold that such a conveyance creates a tenancy in common. To create a joint tenancy, words such as "as joint tenants" or "in joint tenancy" must normally be used to show the necessary intent. Thus, Roberts and Morris are tenants in common to a vested remainder. (B) is therefore wrong. (C) is wrong because their estate is in a remainder interest, not a fee simple absolute, because the life tenant is still alive. (D) is wrong for the same reason and, additionally, because a tenancy by the entirety can be held only by a husband and wife—which may not be the case here.

Answer to Question 22

(C) When Roberts died, his one-half interest passed to his heirs. When Morris died, Cathy inherited Morris's interest in Goldacre. Therefore Cathy owns an undivided one-half interest in fee simple and the heirs of Roberts own an undivided one-half interest in fee simple. (A) is wrong because she does not own all of Goldacre in fee simple. (B) is wrong because she owns an *undivided* one-half interest, which is a one-half interest as to all of the tract, as opposed to one-half of Goldacre, which would be *all* interest in a one-half part of the tract. (D) is wrong for the same reason that (B) is wrong; she owns an *undivided* one-half interest therein.

Answer to Question 23

(D) In effect, Anson only had a "license" to use the land. Because the agreement between Anson and Barker was not in writing, the Statute of Frauds requirements for the creation of an express easement were not met. Also, since Anson's use of the land was permissive during Barker's ownership, he would not meet the adverse and hostile requirements of adverse use during that period; and therefore, Anson would not have satisfied the requirements of an easement by prescription. Thus, (A), (B), and (C) are wrong.

Answer to Question 24

(D) Since Anson's use of the land was permissive during Barker's ownership, he would not meet the adverse and hostile requirements of adverse possession during that period; and therefore, Anson would not have satisfied the requirements of an easement by prescription. (A) is wrong because changes in ownership of the land do not terminate adverse possession. (B) is wrong because, even though he was told to stop using the road, he continued to do so. (C) is wrong because it is too broad. While it is true that no express easement was created, the fact that the original agreement was oral would have no bearing on determining the creation of an easement by prescription.

Answer to Question 25

(B) Anson's easement is appurtenant because the right of special use benefits him in the use and enjoyment of another tract of land (his own property). An easement in gross is acquired independent of the ownership and enjoyment of another tract of land; there is no dominant tenement. Thus, (A) is incorrect. Even if the lake were considered a public way, Anson would not have an easement by necessity because he has other means of access. Therefore, (C) is incorrect. (D) is incorrect because the facts do not indicate that Anson once owned the entire parcel and conveyed part of it to Barker, impliedly reserving an easement in the conveyance.

Answer to Question 26

(B) Besides the fact that the contract does not specifically state which house is being sold, the phrase "sufficient land for a pool and garage" is too ambiguous to enforce by specific performance. (A) is wrong because $200 is not necessarily nominal consideration and, even if it were, the mutual promises to buy and sell would be sufficient consideration. (C) is wrong because the contract needs to include more than the purchase price to be enforceable; it must also describe the property. (D) is wrong because it is irrelevant which house Jake wants to sell to Marsha; that does not clear up the problem with enforcing the Jake-Bob contract.

Answer to Question 27

(B) There was no implied condition in the contract that Bob have marketable title at the time he entered into the agreement, just that he be able to deliver marketable title at the time of settlement. (C) is wrong for this reason. (A) is irrelevant. (D) is wrong because it is not fraudulent to buy property for resale.

Answer to Question 28

(C) A life tenant generally may not exploit natural resources on the property. The "open mine" exception exists for those uses existing prior to the granting of the life estate. Since the gravel quarry existed at the time of the grant, it is most likely that the grantor intended that the life tenant have the right to mine the gravel. The trees, on the other hand, cannot be cut by the life tenant because on these facts, there is no apparent intent on the part of the grantor that Clyde Jr. could do this. Thus, (C) is the correct choice, and (A), (B), and (D) are necessarily incorrect.

Answer to Question 29

(A) Jeff takes because Katherine conveyed her interest to him, and Chris takes by inheritance. Thus, (A) is correct, and (C) is wrong. (B) is wrong because Katherine has transferred her interest to Jeff. The destruction of his deed has no effect on his interest. For Katherine to have her interest back, Jeff would have to reconvey by deed to her. (D) is wrong because when Katherine conveyed her interest to Jeff, the joint tenancy was severed and the interest became a tenancy in common. Since a tenancy in common has no right of survivorship, when Amanda died, her interest passed to Chris, her heir.

Answer to Question 30

(D) Paul will prevail because he is a bona fide purchaser. (A) is speaking to the right theory, *i.e.*, the recording act, but *if* Paul is to prevail under the recording act, he must take without notice of Jeff's interest *and* pay value; in other words, he must be a bona fide purchaser. That is why (D) is the best answer. (A) is wrong because the recording act is a "notice" statute. Paul would prevail against Jeff even if Paul had not recorded (in contrast to the result under a "race-notice" statute). (B) is wrong because Jeff's return of his deed does not affect his interest. (C) is nonsense.

Answer to Question 31

(D) Snyder has relied to his detriment upon the agency given by Larsen to Olsen, so Larsen is estopped to deny that it was exercised validly. (B) is incorrect because recording of a deed does not insulate it from attack on its validity. (C) is incorrect because the Statute of Frauds, relating to the *enforceability* of conveyances, would not prevent evidence of Larsen's instructions to Olsen from being proved. (A) is incorrect because Larsen had done nothing inequitable that would raise an unclean hands issue.

Answer to Question 32

(C) Recording of the subdivision map containing the designated city parks was an offer of dedication, and the city's action in naming and preparing them was an acceptance of dedication sufficient to give the city good title. Laches would not be a factor over a two-year period, so (D) is incorrect. The church is bound because it had constructive notice of the dedication (not of the proposed use) through its chain of title. Thus, (A) and (B) are incorrect.

Answer to Question 33

(C) Winslow has an equitable servitude—the right to enforce the covenant in equity. He is not a third-party beneficiary of Nathan's promise, but rather he is a direct promisee. (B) is therefore incorrect. Whether the church is a bona fide purchaser is immaterial, since it would be bound by the covenant because of its presence in public records. Thus, (A) is incorrect. The covenant was never restricted to any particular lot or type of lot in the subdivision. (D) is therefore incorrect.

Answer to Question 34

(C) A covenant runs with the land if it touches and concerns the land and is intended to run. Use of land for commercial purposes touches and concerns, and it is evident that Nathan and Winslow intended it to run with the land. Zorka is bound even though her deed did not refer to the covenant and she did not purchase directly from Nathan. The covenant is in the public records and it runs with the land. Thus, (A) is incorrect. (B) is incorrect because compliance with zoning regulations does not excuse noncompliance with an enforceable covenant; both must be complied with. (D) is incorrect. Winslow need not show a servitude implied from a common scheme to prevail; the covenant was recorded and runs with the land, so Winslow can enforce the covenant as an equitable servitude.

Answer to Question 35

(C) Equipment installed for the purposes of trade by a tenant is usually removable if it is not an integral part of the premises and if the tenant pays any damages caused by the removal. Tenants who attach tools of the trade do not generally intend to improve the real property. The Statute of Frauds does not preclude the mortgagee from claiming an interest in property that has become an integral part of the premises, and so (A) is wrong. (D) is wrong because the mortgagee has the same rights as the former owner, regardless of the tenant's knowledge of the mortgage. (B) is wrong because the usual rule is that personal property that becomes affixed to the real property is a fixture, subject to the "trade fixtures" exception described in (C).

TORTS
ANSWER SHEET

1. Ⓐ Ⓑ Ⓒ Ⓓ   19. Ⓐ Ⓑ Ⓒ Ⓓ

2. Ⓐ Ⓑ Ⓒ Ⓓ   20. Ⓐ Ⓑ Ⓒ Ⓓ

3. Ⓐ Ⓑ Ⓒ Ⓓ   21. Ⓐ Ⓑ Ⓒ Ⓓ

4. Ⓐ Ⓑ Ⓒ Ⓓ   22. Ⓐ Ⓑ Ⓒ Ⓓ

5. Ⓐ Ⓑ Ⓒ Ⓓ   23. Ⓐ Ⓑ Ⓒ Ⓓ

6. Ⓐ Ⓑ Ⓒ Ⓓ   24. Ⓐ Ⓑ Ⓒ Ⓓ

7. Ⓐ Ⓑ Ⓒ Ⓓ   25. Ⓐ Ⓑ Ⓒ Ⓓ

8. Ⓐ Ⓑ Ⓒ Ⓓ   26. Ⓐ Ⓑ Ⓒ Ⓓ

9. Ⓐ Ⓑ Ⓒ Ⓓ   27. Ⓐ Ⓑ Ⓒ Ⓓ

10. Ⓐ Ⓑ Ⓒ Ⓓ   28. Ⓐ Ⓑ Ⓒ Ⓓ

11. Ⓐ Ⓑ Ⓒ Ⓓ   29. Ⓐ Ⓑ Ⓒ Ⓓ

12. Ⓐ Ⓑ Ⓒ Ⓓ   30. Ⓐ Ⓑ Ⓒ Ⓓ

13. Ⓐ Ⓑ Ⓒ Ⓓ   31. Ⓐ Ⓑ Ⓒ Ⓓ

14. Ⓐ Ⓑ Ⓒ Ⓓ   32. Ⓐ Ⓑ Ⓒ Ⓓ

15. Ⓐ Ⓑ Ⓒ Ⓓ   33. Ⓐ Ⓑ Ⓒ Ⓓ

16. Ⓐ Ⓑ Ⓒ Ⓓ   34. Ⓐ Ⓑ Ⓒ Ⓓ

17. Ⓐ Ⓑ Ⓒ Ⓓ   35. Ⓐ Ⓑ Ⓒ Ⓓ

18. Ⓐ Ⓑ Ⓒ Ⓓ

TORTS QUESTIONS

Question 1

Marisa works for an agency that contracts with wealthy homeowners to clean their homes. The agency is given a key to the house by the owner and sends its employees out on a schedule to clean and straighten up while the owners are away.

One day after Marisa had completed her work at the home of Nancy, she remembered that she had left some cleaning materials inside that she would need for her next assignment. Because she was already late for the next job, Marisa neglected to lock the door when she left Nancy's home. When Nancy returned home that evening, she discovered that her house had been ransacked and several items of jewelry stolen. The front door was open, and there were no signs of forced entry.

If Nancy brings an action against the agency that employed Marisa on a respondeat superior theory, will she likely prevail?

(A) No, because she is limited to claims for breach of contract based upon her agreement with the agency.

(B) No, because the act of the burglar was an independent supervening cause of Nancy's loss.

(C) Yes, because Marisa's failure to lock the door created the risk that someone might enter and take Nancy's valuables.

(D) Yes, because when Marisa returned after having completed her work, she was technically a trespasser and liable for any damage she caused to the premises.

Questions 2-3 are based on the following fact situation:

While driving his car down the road, Ashton experienced a heart attack. Because of this, Ashton's car crossed the center line of the highway and headed directly at a car driven by Simpson. Simpson, seeing Ashton's car heading toward him, swerved to avoid the collision. In so doing, Simpson's son, Russell, was thrown through the sun roof of the car when a latch on the sun roof sprung open. Russell landed in a ditch beside the road, filled with water. He suffered severe injuries and almost drowned in the ditch. The automobile driven by Simpson was manufactured by the Modo Automobile Company.

2. If Russell brings suit against Ashton for the injuries sustained in the accident, Russell will:

(A) Prevail if Ashton's act was a substantial factor in causing the car driven by Simpson to swerve.

(B) Prevail if Ashton violated a statute by crossing the center line.

(C) Not prevail if Ashton had no prior history of heart trouble.

(D) Not prevail, because Ashton's actions did not create a foreseeable risk of harm from driving.

3. If Russell brings suit against the Modo Automobile Company for the injuries sustained in the accident, Russell will:

(A) Prevail if it was economically feasible to install a more secure latch.

(B) Prevail, because the latch sprang open when the car swerved.

(C) Not prevail, because the car was not being used in the normal manner when the roof came open.

(D) Not prevail if Simpson was negligent in swerving the car.

Questions 4-6 are based on the following fact situation:

One of the employees of Department Store informed the head of security that he suspected a customer of shoplifting. The employee pointed out Wilma as the suspected shoplifter. The head of security, unfortunately, thought the employee was pointing at Martha. He waited until Martha had left the store and then followed her outside. He went up to Martha, pulled a gun, and requested that Martha return with him to the Department Store offices. Martha did so, even though she insisted that she had not done anything wrong. Martha was kept waiting in the Department Store offices for an hour, until the employee informed the head of security that he had arrested the wrong woman. Martha was terribly embarrassed by the entire incident because a number of her friends had seen the guard take her into the offices.

4. If Martha sues Department Store on the theory of assault, she will:

   (A) Prevail if she saw the gun pointed at her.

   (B) Prevail if Department Store's belief that she was the right woman was unreasonable.

   (C) Not prevail, because Martha suffered no injury.

   (D) Not prevail if there was no intent to injure.

5. If Martha sues Department Store on the theory of false imprisonment, she will:

   (A) Prevail, unless Department Store was reasonable in believing that she was the right woman.

   (B) Prevail, because she was intentionally detained.

   (C) Not prevail, because the period for which Martha was detained was the minimal period necessary to establish her identity.

   (D) Not prevail, because Martha suffered no harm.

6. If Martha sues Department Store for damages for her humiliation, Martha will:

   (A) Prevail if she was falsely imprisoned.

   (B) Prevail if Department Store was negligent in identifying her.

   (C) Not prevail, because humiliation is not actionable.

   (D) Not prevail, unless Department Store's conduct was extremely outrageous.

Questions 7-8 are based on the following fact situation:

One Saturday, Joseph, age 10, was walking past an office building being constructed when he saw several of his playmates from school climbing on the large concrete pipes used by the construction company to install the sewer system for the building. Joseph decided to join his friends, and was soon enjoying the game of "superheroes" they all were playing. During one particularly fierce confrontation between Tammy, also age 10, and Joseph, Tammy struck Joseph in the face with her "sword" (a piece of sheet metal left as scrap by the builders) and seriously injured his eye.

7. Joseph's parents bring an action against Tammy and her parents for negligence and intentional tort. The insurance company representing Tammy's family raises the defense of contributory negligence as to the negligence cause of action, alleging that Joseph was engaged in a mock battle with Tammy with his own pretend "sword," another piece of metal. When the court instructs the jury as to the standard to be applied to Joseph's conduct, it should state that:

   (A) Joseph's conduct is judged by what a person of ordinary prudence and caution would have done in the same circumstances.

(B) Joseph's conduct is judged by what a child of similar age, experience, and intelligence would have done in similar circumstances.

(C) Joseph's conduct is immaterial, because Tammy committed an intentional tort when she purposely struck Joseph in the eye.

(D) Joseph's conduct is immaterial, because it is presumed that a child under the age of 14 cannot be negligent.

8. Assume for the purposes of this question only that Joseph was negligent in engaging in the combat with Tammy. The action against Tammy's family is brought by Joseph's mother on his behalf as his guardian ad litem. Joseph's father also brings an action against Tammy's family for the cost of the medical treatment he paid for his son. If the jurisdiction follows traditional rules of contributory negligence, Joseph's father will:

(A) Not recover, because Joseph was contributorily negligent.

(B) Not recover, because Joseph suffered the injuries, not his father.

(C) Recover, because his action is independent of Joseph's, not derivative of it.

(D) Recover, because contributory negligence does not apply to a child under the age of 14.

Questions 9-10 are based on the following fact situation:

Rancher owned a large parcel of vacant land just outside City which motorcyclists frequently used for impromptu motorcross competitions. Rancher knew about this use of his land and while he was not particularly happy about it, he had no immediate plans for the parcel and took no action. The motorcyclists had been riding there every weekend for about two years. One weekend, Rancher drove out to the parcel to do some target shooting with a new .22 caliber rifle he had just bought. He set up some beer cans left by the motorcyclists and was plinking away when Rider arrived at the area with his dirt bike. Rider had been drinking and continued to drink beer as he drove his bike around Rancher's parcel. Just as Rider was trying a particularly dangerous stunt on his dirt bike, one of Rancher's shots struck a rock and ricocheted, passing through Rider's upper arm. Rider was able to ride his bike one-handed to nearby Hospital, where he was treated for a gunshot wound. The jurisdiction has adopted a "pure" comparative negligence statute and retained joint and several liability.

9. Rider brings an action for negligence against Rancher. Rider will probably:

(A) Recover all of his damages.

(B) Recover a portion of his damages, because he was negligent in driving his motorcycle while drunk and attempting the dangerous stunt.

(C) Not recover, because driving while drunk is gross negligence or worse.

(D) Not recover, because he was a trespasser on Rancher's land.

10. Assume for the purposes of this question only that when Rider was treated at Hospital, the emergency room physician was negligent, and as a result, Rider never recovered full use of his arm and could not ride his motorcycle in motorcross ever again. Rider's earnings as a carpenter were also permanently reduced. It is stipulated at trial that Rancher was negligent in target shooting in the same area as the motorcycle riders. The result will be:

(A) Rider will recover all of his damages, including the permanent disability, from Rancher.

(B) Rider will recover the portion of his damages attributable to a properly treated .22 caliber gunshot wound from Rancher.

(C) Rider will recover nothing from Rancher.

(D) Rider will recover all of his damages from Rancher only if he (Rider) joins the negligent doctor as a defendant and the doctor fails to satisfy that portion of the judgment attributable to his negligence.

Questions 11-13 are based on the following fact situation:

Fixit owns and operates a small repair store. In addition to repairing virtually any broken item, Fixit occasionally purchases items in need of repair, rebuilds them, and resells them. Cutter, who runs a gardening service, stopped by Fixit's shop to purchase a lawn mower. He saw a lawn mower that had been originally manufactured by Lawnco for sale in Fixit's shop. The lawn mower had a sign on it which read, "Totally reconditioned." While inspecting the lawn mower, Cutter noticed that the lawn mower had a heavy duty blade on it designed for cutting thick weeds. Knowing that he needed the lawn mower for lawn cutting only, Cutter told Fixit that he would buy the lawn mower if Fixit could put a lighter weight blade on the lawn mower. Fixit agreed and installed a lightweight blade designed for lawn cutting onto the lawn mower. The blade was manufactured by Grass Master Company and was not designed to be used on a Lawnco mower. Two weeks later, Worker, an employee of Cutter's gardening service, was injured while using the lawn mower. Worker's leg was severely cut. As a result, Cutter had to give up half of his customers for a two-week period until a replacement for Worker could be found. Assume that the jurisdiction follows traditional contributory negligence rules.

11. If Worker was injured because the blade flew off the lawn mower when a restraining bolt holding the blade in place broke, and if

Worker asserts a claim based on strict liability in tort against Lawnco, Worker will probably:

(A) Recover, because Lawnco put the lawn mower in the stream of commerce.

(B) Recover if the restraining bolt that broke was a part of the lawn mower when it was new.

(C) Not recover, because the lawn mower had been rebuilt by Fixit.

(D) Not recover, because Worker was not in privity of contract with Lawnco.

12. If Worker was injured because the blade flew off the lawn mower when the restraining bolt holding the blade in place broke, and if Cutter asserts a claim based on strict liability in tort against Fixit for loss of business because of the injury to Worker, Cutter will probably:

(A) Recover, because the reconditioned lawn mower was the actual and proximate cause of Cutter's loss of business.

(B) Recover, because Fixit knew the lawn mower was to be used in Cutter's gardening business.

(C) Not recover, because economic loss from injury to an employee is not within the scope of Fixit's duty.

(D) Not recover, because Fixit was not the manufacturer of the lawn mower.

13. Assume for purposes of this question only that while Worker was using the lawn mower to cut through a patch of heavy weeds, the blade broke and a piece of it flew off the lawn mower and severely cut Worker's leg. If Worker asserts a claim based on strict liability in tort against Grass Master Company, the defense most likely to prevail is:

(A) Worker was not in privity of contract with Grass Master Company.

(B) Worker was contributorily negligent in using the lightweight blade to cut heavy weeds.

(C) Grass Master used every available means to inspect and discover defects in the blade.

(D) Grass Master could not foresee that the grass blade might be used on heavy weeds.

Questions 14-17 are based on the following fact situation:

Linda sprained her ankle while skiing and went to the emergency clinic at Hospital. A nurse had Linda soak her ankle in ice water to bring down the swelling, and told her to wait in the room as the doctor would be in to check her ankle in a half hour after the swelling had gone down. Only several minutes later, however, Myron came into her room and told her he was her doctor. In fact, Myron was in an outpatient program at Hospital's mental health section.

Myron proceeded to examine Linda's hurt ankle, causing her some discomfort but no injury. However, when he decided to bandage the ankle, Myron made the bandage too tight and Linda was in pain. When Linda complained, Myron told her he would give her a shot that would stop the pain. But Linda was afraid of shots and told Myron she would prefer pain pills instead. Myron said that pain pills would take too long to be of any use, and started to give Linda the shot, but the nurse came back and caught him.

14. In a suit by Linda against Myron for battery, Myron asserted as a defense that he was a mental patient. This defense is:

(A) Not valid, because Myron was only an outpatient.

(B) Not valid, if Myron had the state of mind to commit battery.

(C) Valid, because mental patients cannot be held responsible for their actions.

(D) Valid, if Myron really believed he was a doctor.

15. Myron contends as a defense that Linda consented to his touching her. This defense is:

(A) Invalid, because Linda thought he was a doctor.

(B) Invalid, because Linda did not want a shot.

(C) Valid, because Linda was not injured by Myron's conduct.

(D) Valid, because in an emergency situation, consent is presumed.

16. If Linda sued Myron for false imprisonment, she is most likely to:

(A) Prevail, because her injuries prevented her from leaving the room without being harmed.

(B) Prevail, because she would not have stayed in the room if Myron had not pretended to be a doctor.

(C) Not prevail, because Myron would have let her leave if she wanted.

(D) Not prevail, because she had no reason to believe that she could not leave.

17. If Linda sued Hospital for negligence, which of the following defenses would most likely show that Hospital is not liable?

(A) Linda had been told the doctor would not see her until the swelling had gone down; therefore, she was not justified in believing Myron was a doctor.

(B) Myron's conduct was an independent intervening cause that cuts off Hospital's liability.

(C) Hospital had no reason to believe Myron would impersonate a doctor, and had otherwise taken every precaution.

(D) Linda was not really injured by anything Myron did.

Questions 18-21 are based on the following fact situation:

Ken and Steve worked together for many years as night countermen in Liquor Store. In the last few months, however, Steve became very upset over personal problems and began to drink on the job. Ken knew of Steve's personal problems, so he covered for Steve at the store and would send Steve home when he became too drunk to work. Then one day Ken realized that Steve had been taking money from the cash register. Ken did not want to get Steve fired, so he decided to quit and find another job. He did not tell his employer about Steve because there had not been very much money taken, and Ken believed that if Steve had the sole responsibility of running the store at night, he would quit his drinking.

Not long after Ken left, Jose, a friend of his, who knew the reasons why Ken had quit, came into the store one night to buy some beer and cigarettes. Steve, who obviously had had something to drink, started to talk with him about the store. When Jose asked Steve if he found it difficult to be the only counterman at night now that Ken was gone, Steve said, "Yes, but when we found that Ken was stealing from the cash register we had no choice but to let him go."

18. If Ken sues Steve for defamation, Ken must show:

(A) He suffered special damages by reason of Steve's oral statement.

(B) He was fired from his new position as a liquor clerk.

(C) His former employer at Liquor Store did not think he was a thief.

(D) Only that Steve accused him of being a dishonest employee.

19. The fact that Jose knew the truth of why Ken really left:

(A) Acts as a complete defense to the claim of relief for defamation.

(B) Establishes that Ken has not suffered any injury.

(C) May diminish the damages Ken would be entitled to recover.

(D) Proves that Steve had no reasonable ground for believing that Ken was fired for dishonesty.

20. If Steve had accused Ken of the thievery without any other person being present, Ken may:

(A) Sue Steve for defamation, because Steve had no reason to believe that the accusation was true.

(B) Sue Steve for defamation, because the money was really missing, and Ken might have been arrested for embezzlement.

(C) Sue Steve for intentional infliction of emotional distress.

(D) Sue Steve for negligent infliction of emotional distress.

21. If Ken sued Steve for defamation, and Steve defended the action by alleging that it was true that Ken stole money from the cash register, Ken would:

(A) Be able to sue Steve in another defamation action because there is a new publication.

(B) Be able to sue Steve in another defamation action only if he can show that Steve did not believe the allegation to be true.

(C) Not be able to sue Steve in another defamation action because the accusation is absolutely privileged.

(D) Not be able to sue Steve in another defamation action because of the doctrine of collateral estoppel.

Questions 22-27 are based on the following fact situation:

One night when Dean and Alice had been drinking at a party, they decided they would take Dean's new four-wheel-drive vehicle for a test drive off the road. The nearest open area where they could drive the vehicle was in a large county park area near their home. A county ordinance, however, restricted the area for use by hikers, bike riders, and horse riders; vehicle traffic was totally prohibited on any of the riding or hiking trails.

In spite of the posted signs prohibiting vehicles on the bridle paths, Dean and Alice entered the county park by way of a narrow bridle path. A little while later, when trying to negotiate a sharp turn, the vehicle slipped and fell down a steep incline. As the vehicle fell, it turned over several times, landing on its tires when it reached the bottom of the incline. The vehicle was equipped with a roll bar, which was intended to protect the passengers in the event the vehicle turned over, but on the first or second turn-over the roll bar had collapsed. Dean was killed in the accident, and Alice suffered severe head and back injuries.

The vehicle was manufactured overseas by Musashi Motors and exported to the United States without the roll bar. When the vehicle arrived in the United States, a manufacturer of recreational safety equipment, Saf-T, installed the roll bars on Musashi's four-wheel-drive vehicles. Musashi had factory representatives at Saf-T to inspect samples of the manufactured roll bars and to conduct tests on a sample number of the vehicles after installation.

Alice sued both Musashi and Saf-T for her injuries. The jurisdiction follows traditional contributory negligence rules. Evidence at trial shows that Musashi had tested a sample of the roll bars in the same series as the one installed in Dean's vehicle, and had conducted its normal tests with regard to the installations. The particular roll bar installed on Dean's car, however, had a series of hairline cracks in the welded area of the brace that weakened the roll bar to the extent that it would collapse when the vehicle turned over.

22. In a negligence action by Alice against Musashi, Musashi cites as a defense the violation of the county ordinance by Dean. This violation of the ordinance will have the following effect:

(A) It bars recovery by Alice.

(B) It bars recovery by Alice only if it can be shown that she agreed with Dean to go driving in the county park.

(C) It will not bar recovery by Alice, because at the time she and Dean went into the park it was closed.

(D) It will not bar recovery by Alice.

23. Assume Musashi can show that Dean was negligent. Such proof would have the following effect on Alice's claim against Musashi:

(A) It would totally bar recovery by Alice.

(B) It would bar recovery by Alice if it is shown that Dean was the sole legal cause of Alice's injuries.

(C) It would bar recovery by Alice if it is shown that there is a direct connection between Dean's negligence and Alice's injuries.

(D) It would have no effect if Musashi had failed to test the roll bar.

24. In a suit for negligence, Alice must at least be able to show the following facts to establish a case against Musashi:

    (A) Musashi failed to inspect the roll bar on Dean's vehicle.

    (B) The roll bar on Dean's vehicle was defective.

    (C) The roll bar on Dean's vehicle was defective, and Musashi inspected the roll bar but failed to discover the defect.

    (D) The roll bar on Dean's vehicle was defective, and Musashi could have discovered the defect if it had inspected the vehicle properly.

25. Of the following, the best defense Musashi could assert against Alice in her negligence action is that:

    (A) Saf-T had guaranteed the reliability of its product, and, therefore, Musashi was under no obligation to inspect.

    (B) The roll bar was not designed to withstand the type of stress it suffered in the accident.

    (C) Musashi's inspection procedures were reasonable under the circumstances.

    (D) Saf-T manufactured the roll bar, and, therefore, it must be held solely liable for any defects.

26. To establish a showing of strict liability against Saf-T, Alice must:

    (A) Show that the roll bar was defective and failed to work in the proper manner, causing her injuries.

    (B) Show that her head and back injuries occurred as a result of the accident.

    (C) Show that she was wearing a seat belt at the time of the accident.

    (D) Rely on the doctrine of res ipsa loquitur.

27. In the negligence suit by Alice, Saf-T asserts that it is not liable for the accident because the defect could have been found if Musashi had properly inspected. As against Alice, this defense would:

    (A) Protect Saf-T from liability, because it no longer had a "duty" to Alice.

    (B) Protect Saf-T from liability, because under the reasonable person test, it was justified in relying on Musashi's testing.

    (C) Not protect Saf-T from liability, because Musashi had no obligation to test every roll bar.

    (D) Not protect Saf-T from liability, because Saf-T could be liable for negligence regardless of Musashi's inspection.

Questions 28-29 are based on the following fact situation:

Eb was driving his car negligently along a mountain road. He lost control of his car and careened over the side of a cliff. Tom, a passing motorist, saw Eb's car go off the road and stopped to see if he could help. Tom started to climb down the cliff to render aid to Eb. In doing so, Tom slipped and broke his leg.

28. If Tom sues Eb to recover damages for his broken leg:

    (A) Tom's best chance of recovery would be on the basis of an intentional tort.

    (B) Tom would have to show that Eb breached a duty to Tom not to place himself in a position of danger that might invite a rescue.

    (C) Tom could recover under the Andrews view of duty.

    (D) Tom could not recover under the Cardozo view of duty.

29. Regarding any defenses Eb might raise, which of the following statements is correct?

    (A) A rescuer acts at his own peril.

    (B) The excitement of the accident and the speedy response of the rescuer would be considered in a case such as this.

    (C) Assumption of the risk cannot be invoked against rescuers.

    (D) Eb would not have a valid defense.

Questions 30-31 are based on the following fact situation:

Fred was rushed from work to the Charity Hospital emergency room with excruciating pain in his lower left side. The emergency room doctor on duty quickly diagnosed the problem as a ruptured spleen. Fred was immediately taken to the operating room, and Doctor operated on Fred. Fred recovered from the operation and was released. Nine years later, Fred was promoted to a classified job that required a complete physical. One of the x-rays detected foreign metallic matter in his left side. Upon further examination and x-rays, it was determined that Fred had a small surgeon's clamp lodged in his left side. Recovery for negligence in the jurisdiction is limited to two years.

30. Fred brings an action joining Charity Hospital and Doctor as defendants, alleging negligence. In his complaint, he alleges that he does not know which of the defendants is responsible for the damages. Which of the following theories of law would be most helpful to Fred's suit?

    (A) Respondeat superior.

    (B) Res ipsa loquitur.

    (C) Contribution.

    (D) Indemnity.

31. Charity Hospital and Doctor file a general denial and a special affirmative defense alleging that the statute of limitations is a bar to the action. Fred's attorney makes a motion to strike the special affirmative defense. The motion should be:

    (A) Granted, because the statute of limitations is tolled under the circumstances.

    (B) Granted, because of the common law rule that one must know of a wrong in order to have a remedy.

    (C) Denied, because the facts do not present an exception to the statute of limitations.

    (D) Denied as to Doctor, but granted as to Charity Hospital.

Questions 32-33 are based on the following fact situation:

Michael asked Oscar if he could borrow the latter's pickup truck to use for hauling some firewood, and Oscar agreed. Michael drove his car to Oscar's house, parked it, and left in Oscar's truck. While Michael was driving back to his home to pick up his wife, Sally, Oscar remembered that the linkage in the truck's steering had been damaged in a recent off-road excursion, so he telephoned Sally and told her to warn Michael that the steering might fail in any violent maneuvering. Michael arrived home about 20 minutes later, and he and Sally prepared to drive to the mountains to cut wood. Sally, in the bustle of packing a picnic lunch and loading tools into the pickup, forgot to tell Michael about the steering. As Michael and his wife approached a gas station near their home, intending to refuel the pickup for the wood cutting trip, Inez, driving her car, made a left turn directly in front of Michael without looking to see if any cars were approaching. Michael jerked the pickup's wheel sharply to the left, and the steering gave way. The truck smashed into the rear of the car, and Michael suffered injuries. If the steering of the pickup had not been defective because of the damaged linkage, Michael could have swerved around the car, avoiding a collision.

32. If Michael asserts a claim for personal injuries against Oscar, who will prevail?

    (A) Oscar, because the failure of Sally to tell Michael about the steering on the pickup was the cause in fact of Michael's injuries.

    (B) Oscar, because as a gratuitous lender, his duty of care to Michael was very slight.

    (C) Michael, because Oscar was strictly liable for any damages caused by the defective steering in his truck.

    (D) Michael, because Oscar failed to tell him that the steering on the pickup was defective.

33. Assume for purposes of this question only that Inez had borrowed her friend Trudy's car to go on a job interview, and the accident occurred while Inez was rushing to the interview. If Michael asserts a claim against Trudy for personal injuries, he will probably:

    (A) Not recover, because the immediate cause of the collision was the failure of the pickup's steering.

    (B) Not recover, because Sally's negligence in not telling him about the steering defect will be imputed to him.

    (C) Recover, because a car owner is vicariously liable for the tortious acts of the driver.

    (D) Recover, if the jurisdiction has enacted a permissive use statute.

Questions 34-35 are based upon the following fact situation:

Homer was very proud of the spacious and superbly maintained landscaping around his home in a suburban neighborhood. But as he grew older, walking behind the mower during his frequent lawn cutting sessions gradually became an unbearable ordeal. When he saw a three-by-five card on the bulletin board at the senior citizens' center advertising a "practically new" riding mower at about half the price of a similar machine from a dealer, Homer immediately contacted the seller, who he discovered lived just two blocks away in the same neighborhood, and bought the mower for cash.

Unknown to Homer, although the mower was in good mechanical condition and suffered from no structural problems, it contained a design defect that caused it to topple over if the steering wheel were turned too sharply while the machine was in motion. One day, as Homer was using the riding mower to cut the grass in front of his residence, a group of college students, one of whom lived nearby, came roller blading down the sidewalk bordering Homer's front lawn. All of the students had been drinking, and Biff, something of a showoff, was quite intoxicated. Just as the group passed near Homer, mowing near the sidewalk, Biff shouted, "Look, I'm Dorothy Hamill!" and attempted to do a double axel. Flailing about in the air, Biff tumbled onto Homer's lawn directly in the path of the mower. Homer attempted to swerve violently to the left to avoid him, but the mower toppled forward, dumping Homer and itself over and giving Homer a concussion.

34. Homer brings an appropriate action against Biff for damages in state court. Will Homer recover for his injuries?

    (A) No, if Biff can show that the manufacturer of the mower is strictly liable for Homer's injuries.

    (B) No, if Biff can prove that Homer would not have been injured but for the existence of the design defect in the mower.

(C) Yes, because Homer was injured as a result of trying to avoid running over Biff.

(D) Yes, because Biff was negligent in trying to do the difficult skating maneuver while intoxicated.

35. Assume for the purposes of this question only that Homer had also named the private seller of the mower as a defendant in his action for personal injuries. Will Homer recover against the seller?

(A) No, unless the seller knew of the design defect when he sold the mower to Homer.

(B) No, because the mower worked properly in ordinary use.

(C) Yes, because the mower contained the design defect when the seller transferred ownership to Homer.

(D) Yes, if the seller had warranted to Homer that the mower had been well-maintained.

TORTS ANSWERS

Answer to Question 1

(C) Nancy will prevail because Marisa's negligence increased the risk of criminal conduct by a third party. Criminal acts and intentional torts of third persons are foreseeable independent intervening forces if the defendant's negligence created a foreseeable risk that they would occur. Here, Marisa's failure to lock the door created a risk of burglary; hence, the burglary does not cut off the agency's liability for Marisa's negligence. (A) is wrong because there is nothing in the facts to indicate that Nancy waived her right to bring tort claims against the agency. (B) is wrong because the burglary was not a superseding cause of the loss; it was within the increased risk caused by Marisa's negligence. (D) is incorrect because she reentered for purposes related to her employment and therefore was not a trespasser.

Answer to Question 2

(C) For Russell to prevail in a claim against Ashton, Russell is going to have to show some fault on Ashton's part. Generally, a person would not be deemed at fault if he had a surprise heart attack while driving, which, of course, opens the issue of whether that person should have known of the possibility that he might have a heart attack. If Ashton had no prior history of heart problems, it is hardly likely that he would have any reason to believe that he might have a heart attack while driving, so (C) is the proper answer. None of the other answers deals with the threshold problem of whether Ashton is at fault in the first place since he had a heart attack; therefore, they are wrong.

Answer to Question 3

(A) In a suit for strict liability, a plaintiff will win if he shows that the latch was defective and it was that defect that made the product unreasonably dangerous. Plaintiff can show that the design of the latch was defective by showing that a less dangerous modification or alternative was economically feasible. (B) is wrong; the mere fact that the latch came open does not satisfy the test. (C) is wrong because reasonably foreseeable misuse is not a defense to strict liability. While the car may not have been used in the normal manner, it was certainly being used in a reasonably foreseeable manner and that is all that is required. (D) is wrong because Simpson's actions are irrelevant to Modo's strict liability in tort.

Answer to Question 4

(A) Department Store could be liable to Martha for assault if its employees caused Martha to be in apprehension of an immediate battery. (C) is incorrect because there need be no actual injury for Martha to recover for assault. She is entitled at least to nominal damages, and depending on the nature of the defendant's conduct, she might be entitled to punitive damages. (B) is completely wrong. Deadly force is never permitted in making a misdemeanor arrest, and so there would be no privilege to the assault in this case. (D) is wrong because intent to injure is not an element of the tort of assault.

Answer to Question 5

(B) The facts satisfy the requirements of false imprisonment. (A) is wrong because reasonable belief is not sufficient by itself to establish a shopkeeper's privilege to detain a suspected shoplifter; the means of restraint must be reasonable and deadly force may not be used. (C) is wrong because the period of confinement, no matter how short, is irrelevant to the tort of false imprisonment. (D) is wrong because "harm" is not required.

Answer to Question 6

(A) Since Martha was falsely imprisoned, she can recover damages for the humiliation she suffered. (C) is incorrect on that point. (D) is an incorrect statement because while Department Store's outrageous conduct might be important with regard to Martha's right to recover for intentional infliction of emotional distress, she can recover humiliation damages because of the false imprisonment even without that showing. (B) is not quite an accurate statement. The fact that Martha was falsely imprisoned may be attributable to the fact that Department Store was negligent in identifying her, but her cause of action arises out of the fact that she was falsely imprisoned regardless of how it came about that she was.

Answer to Question 7

(B) Most jurisdictions follow the rule that a child's conduct is judged by the standard of care applicable to a child of similar age, experience, and intelligence in similar circumstances. Thus, (A) is wrong. Formerly, many jurisdictions would conclusively presume that a very young child was incapable of negligence, and that an older child was rebuttably presumed not to have acted negligently. Most courts today, however, do not fix these presumptions at an arbitrary age. Thus, (D) is a misstatement of law. (C) is wrong because the question refers to the negligence cause of action.

Answer to Question 8

(A) In a contributory negligence jurisdiction, Joseph's negligence would be a complete defense to his recovery, and any derivative action based on his injuries would also be barred. A parent's action for his or her child's medical expenses is a derivative action; hence, (C) is wrong. (B) is irrelevant. (D) is a misstatement of the law (*see* discussion in previous question).

Answer to Question 9

(A) Rider's negligence was not a substantial factor in causing his injuries since it did not create a foreseeable risk of being shot by Rancher (*i.e.,* a sober, careful Rider arriving at the same place at the same time would still have been shot). Therefore, none of Rider's damages would be attributable to his negligence, and his recovery from Rancher would be total. Thus, (B) and (C) are wrong. (D) is wrong because Rancher owes Rider a duty of reasonable care in his activities, because Rider is a "discovered trespasser."

Answer to Question 10

(A) Because the damage resulting from medical malpractice was a foreseeable result of Rancher's negligence, he is liable for such damage even though the negligent doctor contributed to Rider's damages; *i.e.,* Rancher does not escape liability because of the malpractice. Therefore, (C) is wrong. Rider would not be permitted to recover in full from both Rancher and the doctor, but could maintain an action for all his damages directly against Rancher with no need to join the doctor. Thus, (B) and (D) are wrong.

Answer to Question 11

(C) A product manufacturer is not strictly liable for defects that were not present when the product left the manufacturer's control. (A) is therefore wrong. (B) is wrong because Fixit altered the use of the bolt by attaching a nonconforming blade. (D) is wrong because the majority of courts do not require privity of contract in a strict liability in tort action.

Answer to Question 12

(C) Most courts have refused to extend strict products liability to cases in which plaintiffs suffer only economic loss when not accompanied by physical harm to the plaintiff. (A) is therefore wrong. (B) is wrong because it would have no bearing on a strict liability in tort action. (D) is wrong because strict liability extends to retailers.

Answer to Question 13

(D) A product manufacturer is not liable if the injury results from an unintended and unforeseeable misuse of the product. (A) is wrong since strict liability extends to foreseeable users. (B) is wrong because the facts do not indicate that Worker knew about the lightweight blade, and, in any case, states retaining traditional contributory negligence rules hold that ordinary contributory negligence is not a defense to strict products liability. (C) is wrong since the care exercised by the manufacturer is irrelevant in a strict liability action.

Answer to Question 14

(B) Mental incompetency does not preclude a showing that a defendant "intended" to inflict or to cause apprehension of a harmful touching. Hence, (C) is wrong. (D) is wrong because it makes no difference who Myron thought he was; it is only relevant that he intended to do what he did. (A) is irrelevant.

Answer to Question 15

(A) Consent to an intentional tort is ineffective if procured by fraud. Linda thought Myron was a doctor, and that is the only reason why she allowed him to treat her. (B) is arguable, but the facts really do not show Myron to have given her a shot and the facts only stated that Linda preferred to have pills instead of a shot. (C) is wrong because there is no need to show injury to prove battery. (D) is inconsistent with the facts; Linda was capable of giving consent.

Answer to Question 16

(D) Linda was in the room willingly and no facts show that she was there against her will. (A) is wrong because although a plaintiff need not risk harm by trying to escape, Linda was not trying to escape. (B) is incorrect, because whatever the reason for her conduct, there are no facts that tend to show Myron intended to falsely imprison her. (C) is not as good a choice as (D) because, while it is unlikely that Myron would have attempted to keep her locked in the room, the facts do not establish what his state of mind was.

Answer to Question 17

(C) Of all the defenses, the best defense is that Hospital acted reasonably under the circumstances and had no reason to know of Myron's conduct. (A) is incorrect; it goes only to the issue of

Linda's conduct, not whether Hospital was negligent. (B) is wrong, because Myron's conduct is not "intervening" but is the circumstance upon which Hospital's breach of its duty to Linda may be shown. (D) is contrary to the facts—Linda suffered at least some discomfort.

Answer to Question 18

(D) Steve's statement imputing dishonesty in a person's profession or business is slander per se and hence requires no proof of special damages. Thus, (A) and (B) are incorrect. (C) is irrelevant in an action against Steve.

Answer to Question 19

(C) As long as it is understood in its defamatory sense, an accusation need not be believed to be actionable. Hence, (A) is wrong. (D) is wrong because the fact that Jose does not believe the statement does not prove lack of basis for Steve to have made it. (B) is wrong because damages are presumed to exist if it is slander per se.

Answer to Question 20

(C) Defamation requires a publication to third persons; hence (A) and (B) are incorrect. (D) is incorrect because negligent infliction of emotional distress requires a showing by the plaintiff that defendant created a foreseeable risk of physical injury to plaintiff, typically by causing a threat of physical impact that leads to emotional distress. No such risk was present here. In contrast, the scope of intentional infliction of emotional distress is broad enough to allow recovery for emotional distress caused by defendant's intentional insults and indignities. While it is by no means certain that Ken would prevail, it is the only theory that offers Ken a chance of recovering.

Answer to Question 21

(C) Since Steve's allegation is relevant to a lawsuit, it is absolutely privileged regardless of its truth or falsity. Thus, (A) and (B) are wrong. (D) makes no sense; a different statement would be involved in the second action.

Answer to Question 22

(D) Violation of the ordinance will not bar recovery by Alice. When an applicable statute establishes a duty of care, a tortfeasor's conduct will be governed by that statutory duty of care. However, in order for Musashi to be able to assert the statute as a defense (to establish contributory negligence of the plaintiff), it will have to show that plaintiff was one of the class of persons who were intended to be protected by the statute. In all likelihood, the statute was intended to protect the hikers, horseback riders, and bicyclists who use the trails, not the occupants of vehicles. Furthermore, it was Dean, not Alice, who violated the statute, and there is no basis for imputing Dean's negligence to Alice. Hence, the violation of the statute would not bar recovery by Alice. Thus, (A) is wrong. (B) is wrong. Even if it were shown that she had agreed with Dean, it would not bar recovery. (C) is wrong because there are no facts that show the prohibition against vehicular traffic was limited to the hours the park was open.

Answer to Question 23

(B) Dean's negligence is relevant in determining the cause of Alice's injuries. Hence, (D) is wrong.

However, only if Dean's negligence is the sole proximate cause of Alice's injuries would it preclude Alice's suit against Musashi. Thus, (A) and (C) are incorrect.

Answer to Question 24

(D) The standard of care in a negligence action is reasonable care, and the plaintiff must show that the defendant has failed to exercise such care. (A) is wrong because it does not refer to the standard of care. (C) is wrong because it does not show that Musashi's standard of conduct was unreasonable. (B) is wrong because it does not refer to Musashi's conduct at all, which is critical to an action based on negligence.

Answer to Question 25

(C) Defendant's exercise of due care in the performance of a duty owing to plaintiff is a good defense in a negligence action. The fact that Saf-T guaranteed the product is irrelevant to Musashi's liability; thus (A) is wrong. (B) is not supported by the facts, which suggest that this roll bar collapsed because it was weakened by hairline cracks. (D) is a misstatement of the law in products liability cases.

Answer to Question 26

(A) Strict liability requires proof only that an unreasonably dangerous defective condition in defendant's product caused plaintiff's injury. (D) is wrong because res ipsa loquitur is applicable only in a negligence action. (B) is wrong because it only shows that Alice was injured, not that the bar was defective. (C) is wrong because whether Alice wore a seat belt is not part of her prima facie case; at most, her failure to wear a seat belt would be admissible in some states as evidence of contributory negligence.

Answer to Question 27

(D) The suit against Saf-T is for negligent manufacturing and installation of the roll bar. This negligence would not be superseded by any negligent conduct by Musashi, and there is no indication that Musashi discovered the defect but sold the vehicle anyway. (A) is wrong because the contract between Musashi and Saf-T cannot extinguish Saf-T's liability to third persons. (B) is wrong because the negligence of an intermediary does not relieve the manufacturer of liability for negligence. (C) is irrelevant.

Answer to Question 28

(B) This is a correct statement of the rescuer rule of duty. If Tom could show a breach of that duty, then he could recover from Eb on a negligence theory. (A) is therefore wrong. (C) and (D) are wrong because these theories apply to the unforeseeable plaintiff problem, which is not the case here because a rescuer is foreseeable.

Answer to Question 29

(B) All of the circumstances will be considered when evaluating the conduct of the rescuer. Thus, (A) and (D) are wrong. (C) is an incorrect statement of law; assumption of risk may be applicable, depending on the circumstances.

Answer to Question 30

(B) Res ipsa loquitur means the thing speaks for itself. It is appropriate in situations where an injury does not usually occur unless someone was negligent and plaintiff does not know which of the defendants caused the injury. While res ipsa loquitur is not always available where more than one person may have been in control of the instrumentality causing the injury, it is available in a case where a particular defendant had the power of control over the site of the injury. Even if Fred does not know who left the clamp in his body, Doctor, as the surgeon in charge, would be responsible and res ipsa loquitur could be used. (B) is thus the correct answer.

Answer to Question 31

(A) The general rule in malpractice actions is that the patient must know of the injury before the statute of limitations begins to run. Here, the subsequent examination for the promotion he received is the first indication of the negligence. The statute would begin to run from the time of that examination and would be tolled until that point in time.

Answer to Question 32

(D) Oscar's failure to ensure that Michael was made aware of the steering defect was negligent. In a gratuitous bailment, the bailor has a duty to inform the bailee of known dangerous defects. This duty is neither slight care nor strict liability. Thus, (C) and (B) are wrong. Sally's negligence in not telling Michael of the steering defect was a cause in fact, but would not supersede Oscar's negligence so as to relieve him of liability, because such negligence would not be so unforeseeable as to be a superseding cause. Thus, (A) is also incorrect.

Answer to Question 33

(D) The general rule is that an automobile owner is not liable for torts committed by another person driving the automobile. (C) is therefore incorrect. A permissive use statute, however, imposes liability for damage caused by anyone driving with the car owner's consent. (A) is wrong because Inez's negligence was also a causal factor. (B) is wrong because Sally's negligence will not be imputed to Michael.

Answer to Question 34

(D) Homer will recover because Biff's conduct created an unreasonable risk of harm to a foreseeable victim, and such harm proximately occurred. (A) is incorrect because the existence of a concurrent tortfeasor who is also liable for a plaintiff's injuries does not relieve another tortfeasor of liability. (B) is incorrect for a similar reason—Biff's actions were a concurrent cause of Homer's injuries, so he is liable even though the design defect was also a cause. (C) is wrong because it does not include the element of Biff's negligence—if Biff had been acting prudently or was operating under some privilege, the fact that Homer was injured while trying to avoid hitting him would not create liability. Thus, (D) is the best answer.

Answer to Question 35

(A) While a casual seller of personal property is not strictly liable for injuries caused by the defect, a seller who knows that the property has a dangerous defect has a duty to warn the buyer of the defect, and will be liable in a negligence action for failing to do so. (C) is wrong because it does not mention the necessary element that the seller knew of the design defect when he sold the mower to Homer. (D) is not correct because good maintenance had nothing to do with the accident that injured Homer. (B) is wrong because it was foreseeable that a user might have to turn sharply while riding the mower.

barbri®

BAR REVIEW

Mixed Subject Practice Questions and Analytical Answers

MIXED SUBJECT SET 1
ANSWER SHEET

1. Ⓐ Ⓑ Ⓒ Ⓓ
2. Ⓐ Ⓑ Ⓒ Ⓓ
3. Ⓐ Ⓑ Ⓒ Ⓓ
4. Ⓐ Ⓑ Ⓒ Ⓓ
5. Ⓐ Ⓑ Ⓒ Ⓓ

6. Ⓐ Ⓑ Ⓒ Ⓓ
7. Ⓐ Ⓑ Ⓒ Ⓓ
8. Ⓐ Ⓑ Ⓒ Ⓓ
9. Ⓐ Ⓑ Ⓒ Ⓓ
10. Ⓐ Ⓑ Ⓒ Ⓓ

11. Ⓐ Ⓑ Ⓒ Ⓓ
12. Ⓐ Ⓑ Ⓒ Ⓓ
13. Ⓐ Ⓑ Ⓒ Ⓓ
14. Ⓐ Ⓑ Ⓒ Ⓓ
15. Ⓐ Ⓑ Ⓒ Ⓓ

16. Ⓐ Ⓑ Ⓒ Ⓓ
17. Ⓐ Ⓑ Ⓒ Ⓓ
18. Ⓐ Ⓑ Ⓒ Ⓓ

19. Ⓐ Ⓑ Ⓒ Ⓓ
20. Ⓐ Ⓑ Ⓒ Ⓓ
21. Ⓐ Ⓑ Ⓒ Ⓓ
22. Ⓐ Ⓑ Ⓒ Ⓓ
23. Ⓐ Ⓑ Ⓒ Ⓓ

24. Ⓐ Ⓑ Ⓒ Ⓓ
25. Ⓐ Ⓑ Ⓒ Ⓓ
26. Ⓐ Ⓑ Ⓒ Ⓓ
27. Ⓐ Ⓑ Ⓒ Ⓓ
28. Ⓐ Ⓑ Ⓒ Ⓓ

29. Ⓐ Ⓑ Ⓒ Ⓓ
30. Ⓐ Ⓑ Ⓒ Ⓓ
31. Ⓐ Ⓑ Ⓒ Ⓓ
32. Ⓐ Ⓑ Ⓒ Ⓓ
33. Ⓐ Ⓑ Ⓒ Ⓓ

34. Ⓐ Ⓑ Ⓒ Ⓓ
35. Ⓐ Ⓑ Ⓒ Ⓓ
36. Ⓐ Ⓑ Ⓒ Ⓓ

MIXED SUBJECT QUESTIONS - SET 1

Question 1

Ken, John, and Sally were good friends. Ken knew that John and Sally cared deeply for each other and encouraged John to ask Sally to marry him. Unbeknownst to Ken, John was already married to a woman who lived in another state. Finally, after continued encouragement by Ken, John went through a marriage ceremony with Sally, and Ken was John's best man at the ceremony.

If Ken is charged with being an accessory to bigamy, he should be found:

(A) Guilty, because he encouraged John, and his mistake as to the existence of a prior marriage is no defense to a charge of bigamy.

(B) Guilty, because he was present when the crime occurred and is thus a principal in the second degree.

(C) Not guilty, because he did not have the mental state required for aiding and abetting.

(D) Not guilty, because his encouragement and assistance was not the legal cause of the crime.

Question 2

Trucko was driving a dump truck containing gravel at a safe speed. From the other direction Crasher drove his big semitrailer truck. Crasher came around a curve and was confronted with a very slow-moving steamroller just in front of him. To avoid colliding with the steamroller, Crasher pulled his wheel to the left and crossed the center lane, where he bore down on Trucko, who was coming from the other direction. Crasher showed no propensity to yield, and there were other vehicles to Trucko's left. Trucko's only option was to turn his truck to the right, onto the land of Paget. The truck caused damage to Paget's lawn.

Which of the following best describes Trucko's liability to Paget?

(A) Trucko is liable for the damage to the lawn.

(B) Trucko is liable for private nuisance, because he has interfered with Paget's use and enjoyment of the land.

(C) Trucko is liable for both trespass and public nuisance.

(D) Trucko is liable for nothing, because the incident was not his fault, and he acted in a reasonable and responsible manner.

Question 3

The police in Metropolis set up an undercover "sting" operation in which they posed as fences of stolen property and bought and sold such property to anyone who came into their down-town warehouse. Mike is being prosecuted for receiving stolen property in connection with his arrest by the undercover operatives, and the prosecution attempts to introduce a videotape showing Mike offering to sell a television set to one of the police officers.

If this evidence is held to be inadmissible, the most likely reason is that:

(A) It is hearsay not within any exception.

(B) It violates Mike's privilege against self-incrimination.

(C) A proper foundation was not established for its introduction into evidence.

(D) Criminality may not be proven by specific instances of misconduct.

Questions 4-5 are based on the following fact situation:

Bev and Nate had lived together for several years, but had never married because Nate was still married to another woman. During this time, Bev was not employed, but she took care of their home, did housekeeping and other chores, and acted as Nate's companion. Nate, however, informed her one day that he did not want to live with her anymore and told her to move out of the residence.

During the time Nate and Bev lived together, they had accumulated property. The state in which they lived recognized in general the validity of property agreements entered into by nonmarried couples who lived together, but there was a statute that provided that such agreements were void as being against public policy when one of the parties living together was married to another. Bev brought suit against Nate, alleging that they had an agreement to share equally all property accumulated by them during the time they lived together, and challenging the constitutionality of the statute. The state intervened to defend the statute.

4. Will Bev prevail in her challenge to the statute?

(A) Yes, if the state fails to prove that the statute is rationally related to a legitimate state purpose.

(B) Yes, if Bev can prove that the statute is not necessary to effectuate a compelling state interest.

(C) No, if Bev fails to prove that the statute is not rationally related to a legitimate government purpose.

(D) No, if the government proves that the statute was necessary and proper.

5. The state's strongest defense of the statute would be that:

(A) The Constitution of the United States does not affect the state's authority over marital and quasi-marital relationships.

(B) The state's interest in the promotion of family life and the preservation of marital property rights gives the law a rational basis.

(C) The statute does not proscribe all suits of this nature; thus there is no showing of invidious discrimination.

(D) The Constitution does not affect a state's inherent police powers.

Question 6

Michelle and her son Benji were walking through a park where dog owners frequently exercised their dogs and sometimes unleashed them so they could frolic unhindered by restraints. Without provocation or warning, a large black dog attacked Michelle, seriously injuring her. Benji suffered minor injuries when he tried to drive the dog away from his mother. Michelle and Benji filed a personal injury suit against William, named as the dog's owner by several witnesses to the attack. William denies the attacking animal was his dog. At trial, Benji is called as a witness to testify that he was looking directly at William when he unleashed the dog, which immediately ran up to them and attacked his mother.

Should this testimony be admitted over William's objection that Benji is not competent to testify?

(A) No, as a close relative of a party, Benji may not testify on that party's behalf.

(B) No, since he is a party-plaintiff, Benji may not testify as to the facts of the accident.

(C) Yes, but only if Benji is age 12 or over.

(D) Yes, there is nothing to indicate that Benji is incompetent to testify.

Question 7

Acting on an anonymous telephone call, police went to Della's apartment, pounded on the door, and demanded to search it for possible stolen property. Della refused. The police then kicked open the door and placed Della under arrest. As they were escorting Della out of her home, she offered to give the officers some inside information in exchange for her release. Before she could say anything else, Della was given *Miranda* warnings by the police. Thereafter, she told the police that she knew of a large supply of stolen property stored at a nearby warehouse leased by a friend of hers, and said that she and her friend had been selling the stolen property out of the warehouse for years. The police raided the warehouse and recovered the stolen property. Della was charged with conspiracy to sell stolen property and for possession of stolen property. At her trial, Della moved to suppress the statements.

Which of the following is Della's best argument in support of the motion to suppress?

(A) Della was intimidated by the forced entry into her home and since her statements were involuntary and coerced, their use against her would violate due process of law.

(B) Della is entitled to know the identity of her accuser, and the state cannot supply this information.

(C) The statements were fruits of an unlawful arrest, and though the *Miranda* warnings may have been sufficient to protect her right against self-incrimination, they were not sufficient to purge the taint of the illegal arrest.

(D) The police should have given Della *Miranda* warnings prior to entry into her home and the warnings were ineffectual once Della offered to give the police information.

Question 8

James was a geologist studying the land formations in and around a mountain that had undergone a volcanic eruption several years earlier.

When he came to town one day, he opened up a copy of the *National Newspaper* to find that he was in an ad for Mountain Cigarettes. The ad headline "quoted" James as saying, "They make you feel like you're in the mountains."

James is certain that it is his picture, but he never posed for the ad for Mountain Cigarettes.

James brings an action to recover damages against Mountain Cigarettes. Most likely his best cause of action is:

(A) Defamation.

(B) Invasion of privacy.

(C) Intentional infliction of emotional distress.

(D) Negligent infliction of emotional distress.

Questions 9-11 are based on the following fact situation:

In 1975, Leland purchased Whiteacre, a vacant tract of land, from Mabel, by warranty deed. Unknown to Leland, Mabel did not own Whiteacre. Whiteacre was owned in fee simple by Norris. Shortly after the purchase, Leland built a house on the northwest corner of Whiteacre. Other than that portion, Whiteacre remained vacant. In 1980, Leland decided to build a barn. He placed the barn on five acres of land that he believed to be a part of Whiteacre. The five acres actually belonged to Otis, an adjoining landowner. Otis did not live within the state, and so he was unaware that Leland had built the barn on his property. In 1990, Otis died, still without knowledge that Leland had built a barn on his land. His will left all of his property to his 5-year-old son, Pierre. In 2000, Norris died and left all her property to Quigley. The relevant statutory period for adverse possession is 20 years.

9. Leland brings suit to quiet title to Whiteacre. The court should decide that:

(A) Leland is the owner of Whiteacre.

(B) Quigley is the owner of Whiteacre, because as to him, adverse possession began in 2000.

(C) Quigley is the owner of Whiteacre, because Leland only occupied a part of Whiteacre.

(D) Quigley is the owner of Whiteacre, if Leland did not pay the property taxes on Whiteacre.

10. Assume that in 2002 Leland discovered that the five acres on which he built his barn were not part of Whiteacre. Leland brings a quiet title action against Pierre. Who will prevail?

(A) Pierre, because Leland did not pay the property taxes on the five acres.

(B) Pierre, because his status as a minor would toll the adverse possession statute until he reached his majority.

(C) Leland, because he honestly believed that the five acres were part of White-acre.

(D) Leland, because he was in continuous possession of the five acres for the statutory period.

11. Assume for purposes of this question only that in 1977 Norris learned of Mabel's transaction with Leland and prevented Leland from entering Whiteacre thereafter. This led to a costly court battle. When Leland notified Mabel and told her that he thought it was her duty to straighten this out, she told him to "get lost." Leland would succeed in a suit for damages against Mabel for breach of which of the following covenants of title?

(A) The covenant of quiet enjoyment only.

(B) The covenants of seisin, right to convey, quiet enjoyment, warranty, further assurances, and the covenant against encumbrances.

(C) The covenants of seisin, right to convey, quiet enjoyment, warranty, and further assurances.

(D) The covenants of seisin and right to convey only.

Question 12

Officer Taylor saw Elmer grab a coat off the rack of a store and run. As Taylor gave chase, Elmer ducked into an alley. When Taylor came to the alley, she saw movement behind some boxes. She yelled for Elmer to come out or she would shoot. When Elmer did not, Taylor shot at the boxes. Polly, a bag lady, had been asleep behind them, and she was killed. Taylor is charged with homicide.

A jury should find Taylor:

(A) Not guilty of homicide, because she was attempting to catch Elmer, who was fleeing from a crime, and Taylor had the right to use deadly force.

(B) Not guilty of homicide, because she saw Elmer commit a misdemeanor, and there-fore she had the right to use deadly force if necessary to arrest him.

(C) Guilty of homicide, unless she had reason to believe that Elmer was a felon.

(D) Guilty of homicide, because she was not entitled to use deadly force.

Question 13

Parker has brought an action against David-son for breach of contract. The existence and terms of the contract are in dispute. Parker's counsel calls him to the witness stand and seeks to elicit testimony that Parker and Davidson met in a restaurant on a certain date and reached an agreement that was reduced to a writing. Parker then intends to testify, "The writing, which was subsequently inadvertently destroyed, provided that Davidson would purchase 300 widgets from me at a price of $1,000."

The quoted testimony is admissible only if:

(A) The judge finds that the writing is unavail-able.

(B) The judge finds that Parker is accurately relating the contents of the writing.

(C) The jury finds that the writing is unavailable.

(D) The jury finds that Parker is accurately relating the contents of the writing.

Question 14

Congress determined that there should be a uniform law for handgun registration throughout the United States, and enacted the Federal Firearms Act.

Which of the following constitutional provisions could most easily be considered the basis of such enactment?

(A) The Equal Protection Clause of the Fourteenth Amendment.

(B) The Second Amendment.

(C) The Commerce Clause.

(D) The Necessary and Proper Clause.

Questions 15-18 are based on the following fact situation:

Ace Business Supplies sold office equipment and supplies to various companies in the area. Ace entered into a written agreement with Typitrite, Inc. to purchase from Typitrite all of Ace's monthly requirements of printers for a period of five years at a specified unit price. The agreement also provided that:

1. The parties covenant not to assign this contract.

2. Payments coming due hereunder for the first six months shall be made directly by Ace Business Supplies to Commercial Bank, a creditor of Typitrite, Inc.

Shortly thereafter, Typitrite, Inc. made an "assignment of the contract" to Equitable Loan Co., as security for a $50,000 loan. Ace Business

Supplies subsequently ordered the delivery of and paid Typitrite the agreed price of $10,000 for Ace's requirement of printers for the first month of the agreement.

15. Which of the following accurately states the legal effect of the covenant not to assign the contract?

(A) The covenant as properly interpreted was not breached, and the assignment was effective.

(B) The covenant made the assignment to Equitable Loan Co. ineffective.

(C) Typitrite's assignment was a breach of its contract with Ace Business Supplies, but was nevertheless effective to transfer to Equitable Loan Co. Typitrite's rights against Ace Business Supplies.

(D) The covenant is effective if the parties can establish a rational reason for including the covenant into their agreement.

16. Assume for this question only that the assignment from Typitrite to Equitable Loan was effective and that Ace Business Supplies was unaware of the assignment when it paid Typitrite the $10,000. Which of the following is correct?

(A) Ace Business Supplies and Typitrite are each liable to Equitable Loan for $5,000.

(B) Typitrite is liable to Equitable Loan for $10,000.

(C) Ace Business Supplies is liable to Equitable Loan for $10,000.

(D) Neither Ace Business Supplies nor Typitrite is liable to Equitable Loan for any amount.

17. Assume for this question only that the assignment from Typitrite to Equitable Loan was effective and that Commercial Bank did not become aware of the original agreement between Ace Business Supplies and Typitrite until after Typitrite accepted the $10,000 payment from Ace Business Supplies. Which of the following, if any, is (are) correct?

    I. Commercial Bank has a prior right to Ace Business Supplies's $10,000 payment as against either Typitrite or Equitable Loan.

    II. Commercial Bank was an incidental beneficiary of the Ace Business Supplies-Typitrite agreement.

    (A) I. only.

    (B) II. only.

    (C) Both I. and II.

    (D) Neither I. nor II.

18. Assume for this question only that two weeks after making the $10,000 payment to Typitrite, Ace Business Supplies, by written notice to Typitrite, terminated the agreement for purchase of printers, because the demand upon Ace Business Supplies for office supplies was so great that Ace decided to no longer carry office equipment. If Equitable Loan brings suit against Ace Business Supplies for total breach, which of the following would be useful for Ace Business Supplies's defense?

    (A) Ace Business Supplies ceased in good faith to have any further requirement for printers.

    (B) Typitrite's "assignment of the contract" to Equitable Loan to secure a loan would normally be interpreted as a delegation of Typitrite duties under the contract as well as an assignment of its rights, and its duties owed to

Ace Business Supplies were personal and therefore nondelegable.

    (C) Typitrite's rights under its agreement with Ace Business Supplies were personal and therefore nonassignable.

    (D) The original contract between Ace Business Supplies and Typitrite was unenforceable by either party for want of a legally sufficient consideration for Typitrite's promise to supply Ace Business Supplies's requirements of printers.

Questions 19-20 are based on the following fact situation:

Aerodrome, Inc., operates a private airfield for general aviation aircraft. In connection with an expansion of its facilities, extensive excavation work was being done next to the landing field, resulting in large mounds of earth next to the excavations. The chain link fence surrounding the airfield had been removed in one location to permit entry of very large earth-moving equipment, and a makeshift barrier was erected of wooden traffic barricades. Several children from a nearby residential area, ranging in age from seven to nine, discovered that the wooden barricades were easily bypassed and began playing "king of the mountain" and other games on the huge mounds of earth after the airfield was closed in the evening.

One evening, Luke was flying his small, single-engine airplane on a cross-country flight and passed near the Aerodrome airfield. Due to a defect in the electrical system of the aircraft, which was not discovered by professional aircraft mechanics at Luke's home field when they inspected the plane and certified it operable, Luke was forced to seek an emergency landing area, and glided toward the Aerodrome field. The electrical system defect rendered the aircraft very difficult to control, and as Luke made his landing he was unable to avoid striking and injuring Sally, who had been pushed onto the landing field during a game of "king of the mountain" on the mounds. If the electrical system defect had been discovered and remedied, in addition to probably not having to have made an emergency landing, Luke would have been able to avoid Sally.

19. If Sally brings an action for personal injuries against Luke, what is Luke's best defense?

    (A) He did not act willfully and wantonly.

    (B) He could not reasonably foresee that he would have to make an emergency landing.

    (C) He used reasonable care in the maintenance of his aircraft.

    (D) His conduct was not the cause in fact of the injury to Sally.

20. If Sally brings an action against the aircraft mechanics who certified Luke's plane as operable, what will be the probable outcome?

    (A) Judgment for the mechanics, because Sally was legally a bystander.

    (B) Judgment for the mechanics, because Aerodrome's negligence was an independent, superseding cause.

    (C) Judgment for Sally if the mechanics were negligent in inspecting the airplane.

    (D) Judgment for Sally, because the mechanics were strictly liable in tort.

Question 21

Alan was arrested by a police officer when he was found carrying an ice pick concealed in his pants. Alan stated that he carried the ice pick only for protection. Alan was convicted of violating a state statute prohibiting the carrying of a concealed "knife or dagger." Alan appeals his conviction on the basis that an ice pick does not fall within the purview of the statute under which he was convicted.

The appellate court will hold that:

    (A) Alan's conviction should be upheld if the appellate court finds that the statute sought to outlaw the classic instruments of violence and their homemade equivalents, such as an ice pick.

    (B) Alan's conviction should be upheld, because an ice pick is a weapon, by Alan's own admission.

    (C) Alan's conviction should be overturned, because he was carrying the ice pick for protection only.

    (D) Alan's conviction should be overturned, because he harbored no malicious intent.

Question 22

Oona owned Big Acre, a large tract of undeveloped land. Big Acre had a stream, which was not navigable, running across it in an east to west direction that eventually flowed into the Blue River. Beatrix was interested in buying the northern one-half of Big Acre to use as a cattle ranch. Oona and Beatrix eventually agreed upon the price, and in a cash transaction, Oona conveyed by deed to Beatrix according to the following description: "The upper portion of Big Acre from the northern boundary to the stream."

In determining the exact boundaries of the portion of Big Acre purchased by Beatrix, which of the following would be the most accurate?

    (A) Oona retained all of the stream as part of her portion of Big Acre.

    (B) Oona and Beatrix each own one-half of the stream bed.

    (C) Beatrix owns all of the stream because of the rule interpreting the words of a deed most stringently against the grantor.

    (D) Because the description is invalid, the ownership interest of Oona and Beatrix in the stream cannot be determined.

Question 23

Trudi's car was stolen when it was parked in a grocery store parking lot. The car was never recovered. Following all required procedures, Trudi filed a claim with her insurer, Trusty Insurance Company ("Trusty"). Trusty refused to pay, claiming that the loss was not covered because Trudi had not locked her car as required by her policy. In a declaratory judgment action, Trudi seeks to testify that she always locks her car when she gets out of it.

The judge should find the offer to testify:

(A) Objectionable, as calling for a self-serving declaration.

(B) Objectionable, because it is not relevant.

(C) Unobjectionable, as calling for evidence of habit.

(D) Unobjectionable, if it is offered as impeachment evidence.

Questions 24-25 are based on the following fact situation:

The President of the United States and the Prime Minister of Canada, recognizing a growing problem involving the killing of baby harp seals, agreed that each should appoint three members to a special commission to look into the problem. The commission was instructed to make a comprehensive study of the baby harp seal problem and to draft regulations that would provide for the preservation of the seal population while still allowing fur traders to take a certain number of furs each year. After studying the problem, the commission drafted proposed regulations and submitted them to the President and the Prime Minister. The President of the United States, acting in concert with the Prime Minister of Canada, named the commission as a permanent enforcement agency for the regulations that were adopted by both nations. The President, acting with prior congressional authorization, then entered into an executive agreement with the Prime Minister whereby the joint commission was granted adjudicative as well as enforcement powers with respect to the regulation of baby harp seals.

24. The executive agreement by the President is:

(A) Valid, because the President has unlimited powers in entering into executive agreements.

(B) Valid, because the President has plenary powers in the area of foreign affairs.

(C) Invalid, unless the Senate ratified the executive agreement by a two-thirds vote.

(D) Invalid, because conservation of wildlife is not an area left solely to Presidential discretion.

25. Assume that the joint commission adopted a regulation whereby all baby harp seal hunters were restricted to taking furs between December 1 and April 30 of each year, and that each hunter could take no more than one baby harp seal fur per day. Assume further that the state of Maine adopted a statute requiring baby harp seal hunters to register with the state and obtain a special hunting license that allowed year-round hunting of baby harp seals, for the price of $5,000. The joint commission filed an action in federal district court seeking to enjoin Maine from enforcing the statute. The district court most likely would declare the state statute to be:

(A) Constitutional, because the conservation of wildlife is an issue best left to the states in which the wildlife are located.

(B) Constitutional, because a state statute takes precedence over any executive agreement.

(C) Unconstitutional, because an executive agreement is the law of the land, and any acts by a state inconsistent therewith are null and void.

(D) Unconstitutional, because the state statute discriminates against baby harp seal hunters from the state of Maine.

Question 26

While in a department store, Defendant picked up a $400 imported cashmere sweater and slipped it under his shirt. Defendant then started for the door. Customer, who also was shopping in the store, saw Defendant take the sweater. Customer grabbed a baseball bat from the sporting goods aisle and chased Defendant into the parking lot. Customer began swinging the bat at Defendant's head, hoping to knock him out and thus prevent the theft. Defendant pulled a knife from his pocket and stabbed Customer, killing him. Defendant was arrested and charged with murder.

At trial, Defendant will most likely be found:

(A) Guilty, because the evidence shows that Defendant provoked the assault on himself by his criminal misconduct.

(B) Guilty, because the evidence shows that Defendant intended to kill or cause serious bodily harm.

(C) Not guilty, because the jury could find that Defendant acted recklessly and not with the intent to cause death or serious bodily harm.

(D) Not guilty, because Defendant was acting in self-defense.

Question 27

Tammy is on trial for the murder of her husband. She is accused of pushing him from the window of their 12th-floor apartment; she claims he committed suicide. Tammy called Barbara, an operator for a suicide-prevention clinic, to testify that Tammy's husband had called the clinic on more than one occasion threatening to "end it all."

The judge should rule the testimony:

(A) Admissible, because the statement was made in "contemplation" of death.

(B) Admissible, because it tends to show that Tammy's husband intended to commit suicide.

(C) Inadmissible, because it violates the psychiatrist-patient privilege.

(D) Inadmissible, because no phone calls were made to the clinic by Tammy's husband on the day he died.

Questions 28-29 are based on the following fact situation:

Elmo owns a large tract of undeveloped land near Mountainview. The jurisdiction in which the land is located has adopted the following statute:

> No conveyance or mortgage of an interest in land is valid against a subsequent purchaser for value without notice thereof whose conveyance is first recorded.

The following sequence of events occurred in the following order:

1990: Elmo owed money to Stanley, and in satisfaction of this debt, Elmo conveyed the Mountainview property to him. Although Stanley intended to have the deed recorded, he mistakenly failed to do so.

May 1992: Elmo borrowed $40,000 from First Central Bank and, to secure the loan, executed a mortgage deed on the Mountainview property. First Central promptly recorded this mortgage.

September 1992: Elmo, just before he died, donated the property to his son, Tom, who did not know about the prior events, by a general warranty deed. Tom recorded the deed and entered into a contract with Becky to sell her the Mountainview property.

November 1992: Stanley discovered that the deed in his safe was not recorded, and so without notice of any of the prior transactions, Stanley recorded the deed.

December 1992: Becky paid Tom full value for the property, and without actual knowledge of any of the other transactions regarding the Mountainview property, Becky had the deed duly recorded.

28. By late 1993, Becky had expended substantial sums of money to prepare for a subdivision she intended to build on the Mountainview property. However, when she put up the property as security for a loan from the bank for construction costs, she learned for the first time of Stanley's claim. In a suit between Becky and Stanley, which of the following statements most accurately describes the probable outcome?

(A) Becky would prevail, because the money she paid for the property and to prepare for its subdivision was far in excess of what Stanley paid, and under equity, Becky would be deemed the owner; however, she would have to reimburse Stanley for what he paid for the property.

(B) Becky would prevail, because under the doctrine of equitable conversion, her "right" to the property preceded Stanley's recordation, and thus whatever right he may have had would have been terminated before he could record.

(C) Becky would prevail because she purchased from Tom, whose deed was recorded before Stanley's deed.

(D) Stanley would prevail, because he recorded first.

29. First Central Bank intervened in the suit between Stanley and Becky to assert its claim with regard to the $40,000 mortgage. With regard to Stanley's claim to the property, First Central Bank most likely will:

(A) Not prevail, because Elmo conveyed his entire interest to Stanley, and therefore had no property left that he could have mortgaged.

(B) Not prevail, because to enforce First Central Bank's claim would aid Elmo to work a fraud on Stanley, and the law will not aid someone to commit an unlawful act.

(C) Prevail, because it loaned Elmo the money without notice of Stanley's interest, and it recorded first.

(D) Prevail, because the instrument that is recorded first under this type of statute always prevails over the unrecorded or subsequently recorded instrument.

Question 30

Gregory Richards, a well-known author, speaker, and civil rights activist, was addressing a community group on the disparate treatment afforded non-whites by the police as compared to their treatment of whites. In the course of his remarks, he said, "I'll bet that two kids, one white and one black, could do exactly the same thing at some suburban shopping center, and the cops would bust the black kid and not even bother the white one."

A group of teenagers of various races who were attending the address and who were friends decided to test Richards's theory at a nearby shopping mall. In pairs of varying racial composition, they approached shoppers and asked if they could carry their packages for a nominal fee. Many shoppers simply declined, some agreed, some thought the teenagers were soliciting for charity, and others thought they were panhandlers.

One elderly woman who had recently been the victim of a purse snatching in which she had received rather severe but noncrippling injuries was so frightened by the approach of two teenagers that she dropped her packages and screamed for assistance. Although immediately reassured by the teenagers and security personnel that nothing was amiss, she was so distraught that she had to be taken home by ambulance.

If the shopper seeks recovery from Gregory Richards, is she likely to prevail?

(A) No, because the teenagers were not employees of Richards.

(B) No, because Richards did not authorize the teenagers' acts.

(C) Yes, if the teenagers would not have acted as they did but for hearing Richards's comments.

(D) Yes, if her claim against the teenagers prevails on a theory of negligence.

Question 31

Bernie is on trial for aggravated assault after he allegedly injured another patron in a bar fight. Bernie claims that he was merely a bystander and that another patron was the actual aggressor. Bernie called Anne to testify that Bernie had a reputation for being a "good and loving person who would never hurt anyone."

The trial judge should rule the testimony:

(A) Admissible, because it is not hearsay.

(B) Admissible, because this is a criminal matter, and it tends to show relevant good character.

(C) Inadmissible, because the prosecution has not introduced evidence concerning Bernie's reputation.

(D) Inadmissible, because character evidence is not permissible to show that an accused has acted in conformity with the character.

Question 32

Fred did not like Joe, his daughter Lisa's boyfriend. In spite of the fact that Fred had told Lisa never to see Joe, Lisa continued to do so. One night when Lisa's parents went to a movie, Joe came over to the house. Lisa and he were in the den with the lights out when Fred and his wife came home unexpectedly. When Fred found Lisa and Joe together, he grabbed Joe and told him to get out of the house. Joe tried to explain to Fred why he was there, but Fred would not listen, and he threatened to beat Joe up if he did not leave immediately. When Joe attempted again to protest, Fred grabbed a poker from the den fireplace and raised it above his head in a threatening manner. Joe threw a heavy ashtray at Fred, hitting him in the side of the head and killing him. Joe was charged with murder.

The jury should find Joe:

(A) Guilty, because he had refused to immediately leave the house.

(B) Guilty, because his presence in Fred's home with Lisa provoked Fred to attack him.

(C) Not guilty, because a poker is a dangerous weapon.

(D) Not guilty, because it was Lisa's home also, and she invited Joe into it.

Question 33

The city of Kingco amended its ordinance to require that "adult theaters" (defined in the ordinance) could not be located either within 100 feet of each other or within 500 feet of any residential area. This zoning requirement was passed to protect the residential character of neighborhoods from destruction. American Red-White-and-Blue Movies, Inc., is the owner of two adult theaters. One is a regular theater building located about 1,000 feet from another adult theater. The second theater is a converted gas station which is near another adult theater and adjacent to a residential area, in violation of the zoning ordinance. American has filed this action to have the zoning requirement declared unconstitutional.

The court should hold that:

(A) The zoning ordinance is in violation of the protections afforded by the First Amendment of the Constitution.

(B) The zoning ordinance is invalid because it is a form of spot zoning.

(C) The zoning ordinance is valid in that it covers the whole city of Kingco.

(D) The zoning ordinance is valid because material protected by the First Amendment is subject to zoning and licensing requirements.

Questions 34-35 are based on the following fact situation:

When Nancy was jogging along a road by the beach, she came to a bike path that passed under a pier. A city code provided that only bicycles were to be used on this path and that pedestrians were prohibited. However, if Nancy were to continue her run along the road, she would have to detour around the pier; so her usual procedure when she jogged in the morning was to cut under the pier on the bike path and get back on the road on the other side. After she reached the road on the other side, she had gone about 15 feet when Al pulled out of the alley and hit her with his car, injuring her. There was a stop sign at the end of the alley, but Al had failed to see it and stop. Nancy sued Al.

34. On the basis of which standard of care will Al be judged?

   (A) Strict liability, because an automobile is an inherently dangerous instrument.

(B) That of a reasonable and prudent person under the facts of this situation.

(C) The standard set by the traffic ordinance, unless Al is excused from following its requirements.

(D) The doctrine of res ipsa loquitur, because it can be presumed that nobody would fail to stop at a stop sign in the absence of negligence.

35. Nancy's violation of the statute would not affect her claim against Al because:

(A) Al's negligence occurred after Nancy's.

(B) Al should have known that joggers frequently used the bicycle path in spite of the ordinance.

(C) Accidents that occurred after the pedestrian left the bicycle path were not within the risk that the statute was designed to prevent.

(D) There is a greater chance of causing injury when a car driver violates a statute than when a pedestrian does.

Question 36

Daniel was infuriated because he found out that Wallace was having an affair with his wife. Daniel saw a person whom he believed to be Wallace walking down the street ahead of him. This person was actually Victor, a first cousin of Wallace, who strongly resembled Wallace. Daniel struck Victor with a staggering blow. Daniel was arrested and charged with battery upon Victor.

Which of the following best states the rule to be applied?

(A) Daniel is not guilty of battery if a reasonable person would have mistaken Victor for Wallace.

(B) Daniel is not guilty of battery if a reasonable person would have mistaken Victor for Wallace, and also would have been so provoked under the circumstances as to strike him.

(C) Daniel is guilty of battery even if he honestly and reasonably believed that Victor was Wallace.

(D) Daniel is guilty of battery only if he realized that it was Victor whom he was striking.

MIXED SUBJECT SET 1 SUBJECT GUIDE

1. Criminal Law
2. Torts
3. Evidence
4. Constitutional Law
5. Constitutional Law
6. Evidence
7. Criminal Law
8. Torts
9. Real Property
10. Real Property
11. Real Property
12. Criminal Law
13. Evidence
14. Constitutional Law
15. Contracts
16. Contracts
17. Contracts
18. Contracts
19. Torts
20. Torts
21. Criminal Law
22. Real Property
23. Evidence
24. Constitutional Law
25. Constitutional Law
26. Criminal Law
27. Evidence
28. Real Property
29. Real Property
30. Torts
31. Evidence
32. Criminal Law
33. Constitutional Law
34. Torts
35. Torts
36. Criminal Law

MIXED SUBJECT ANSWERS - SET 1

Answer to Question 1

(C)   To hold Ken liable as an accessory, the state must show that his assistance or encouragement was given with intent that the crime be committed or knowing that he was aiding a crime. The facts indicate neither state of mind was present on Ken's part. (A) is wrong because it involves a mistaken legal premise insofar as liability as an accessory is concerned. (B) is accurate in part, but ignores the requirement of a mental state. (D) is wrong because the accessory can be liable even if he did not "cause" the crime.

Answer to Question 2

(A)   Even if Trucko can assert the defense of private necessity, he would still be liable for the damage to Paget's lawn. Trucko's entrance onto Paget's land constituted a prima facie case of trespass to land. The following elements must be proved for trespass to land: (i) an act of physical invasion of plaintiff's real property by defendant; (ii) intent on defendant's part to bring about a physical invasion of the plaintiff's real property; and (iii) causation. Intent to trespass is not required—intent to enter onto the land is sufficient. Thus, even though Trucko did not intend to trespass onto Paget's land, he did intend to drive onto it to avoid hitting Crasher. Under the defense of private necessity, however, a person may interfere with the property of another where it is reasonably and apparently necessary to avoid threatened injury and where the threatened injury is substantially more serious than the invasion that is undertaken to avert it. Where the act is solely to benefit any person or protect any property from destruction or serious injury (rather than to benefit the public as a whole), the defense is qualified; *i.e.,* the actor must pay for any injury he causes. Here, Trucko was acting to avoid serious injury. However, he must pay for the damage to the lawn. (D) is therefore incorrect because negligence concepts are irrelevant to an action based on trespass to land. (B) is incorrect because a private nuisance is a substantial and unreasonable interference with another private individual's use and enjoyment of his land. Even if Trucko interfered with Paget's use of his lawn, the interference was neither substantial nor unreasonable. (C) is incorrect because there is no public nuisance in this case. A public nuisance unreasonably interferes with the health, safety, or property rights of the community. Trucko's actions affected one individual rather than the community.

Answer to Question 3

(C)   Videotape evidence is treated the same as photographic and tape-recorded evidence. If it is properly authenticated, it is admissible, but it may not be properly admitted without the proper foundation first being established. (A) is wrong because the tape constitutes an admission and, therefore, is not hearsay. (B) is wrong because the privilege against self-incrimination applies only to testimonial evidence. (D) is nonsensical.

Answer to Question 4

(C)   Since the statute neither burdens a fundamental right nor creates a suspect or quasi-suspect classification, the rationality test is proper. Thus, (B) is wrong because it uses the wrong standard. Furthermore, the burden is on the challenger to show that a statute passes constitutional muster under the rational basis test. Thus, (A) is incorrect because it misallocates the burden. (D) is incorrect; the Necessary and Proper Clause has nothing to do with state statutes.

Answer to Question 5

(B) The right to enter into agreements is not a fundamental right; therefore, the state need only show that there is a rational basis for the statute. (A) is wrong because there are many instances when the Constitution may affect the state's authority over marital and quasi-marital relationships. Hence, (D) is also wrong. (C) makes no sense; if anything, the fact that other persons similarly situated can bring suits in this circumstance, but Bev cannot, tends to show some kind of discrimination, albeit not invidious.

Answer to Question 6

(D) All witnesses are competent unless physically or mentally impaired in some fashion not applicable here, or unless they are too young to understand the oath and the need to testify truthfully. Therefore, (A) and (B) are incorrect. (C) is wrong because there is no precise age at which an infant is deemed competent to testify; it depends on the capacity and intelligence of the particular child.

Answer to Question 7

(C) The entry into Della's apartment and her arrest without a warrant, probable cause, or circumstances permitting an exception from these requirements were illegal. The statements she made thereafter were fruits of the original illegality and are to be suppressed unless the taint is purged. The giving of *Miranda* warnings is not sufficient. (A) is wrong because the facts indicate that the statements were voluntarily made. (B) is an incorrect statement of law. (D) is wrong because *Miranda* warnings are only required prior to custodial interrogation.

Answer to Question 8

(B) James's best cause of action is for invasion of privacy. The facts do not show that James was defamed, nor do the facts indicate that he suffered any type of severe emotional harm. Thus, (A), (C), and (D) are wrong. The only cause of action would be for an invasion of privacy, specifically for commercial appropriation, because the defendant made unauthorized use of his picture for its commercial advantage.

Answer to Question 9

(A) Leland would be declared the owner of Whiteacre on the basis of the application of the rule of constructive adverse possession. The rule states that where the claimant goes into actual possession of some portion of the property under color of title, he will be deemed in adverse possession of the entire property described in the instrument on the basis that his adverse possession is constructive possession of the extended parts of the property not actually occupied. Thus, (C) is incorrect. (B) is incorrect because a transfer in ownership does not interrupt the statutory period for adverse possession. (D) is incorrect because only a minority of states require the adverse possessor to pay taxes on the property.

Answer to Question 10

(D) Since Leland was in continuous possession for the statutory period and has met all of the other requirements of adverse possession, he would be declared the owner of the five acres. (A) is incorrect because only a minority of states require the adverse possessor to pay property taxes. (B) is incorrect because the disability of Otis's successor in the interest will not toll the running of the statute. For a disability to stop the clock, the disability must have been in existence on the day the adverse possession began in 1980. (C) is incorrect because Leland's state of mind is irrelevant under the majority view. Even if he had possessed the land knowing he was trespassing, he could still claim it by adverse possession.

Answer to Question 11

(C) Since Mabel neither owned Whiteacre nor was acting as Norris's agent, she breached the covenants of seisin and right to convey at the time of the conveyance to Leland. Thus, (A) is incorrect. There is nothing in the facts to suggest the property is encumbered; thus, she did not breach the covenant against encumbrances. (B) is therefore incorrect. Under the covenants of quiet enjoyment, warranty, and further assurances, Mabel promised that (i) Leland would not be disturbed in his possession of Whiteacre; (ii) she would defend Leland's title against lawful claims; and (iii) she would perform whatever acts are necessary to perfect Leland's title. Mabel has obviously breached these covenants. Thus, (D) is incorrect.

Answer to Question 12

(D) The Supreme Court has held that it is unconstitutional for an officer to use deadly force to effectuate an arrest of an unarmed escaping felon unless the officer has probable cause to believe that the suspect poses a significant threat of death or serious physical injury to the officer or others. In jurisdictions following this approach, the use of deadly force to apprehend a fleeing felon is reasonable only where it is necessary to prevent the felon's escape *and* where the felon threatens death or serious bodily harm. Other jurisdictions allow use of deadly force whenever necessary to prevent a fleeing felon's escape. Regardless of the approach used, here it does not appear that shooting at Elmer was necessary to prevent his escape or that Elmer threatened serious bodily injury. Thus, (A), (B), and (C) are incorrect. (D) is a correct statement of the law because Taylor had the requisite intent for homicide.

Answer to Question 13

(A) The contents of a document are sought to be proven and the document is not collateral; thus, the judge must find that the document itself is not available for testimony on the issue to be admissible. (B) is wrong because, as stated, the document itself must be produced unless it is not available. (C) and (D) are wrong because the judge, not the jury, makes these types of determinations.

Answer to Question 14

(C) This statute deals with activities that have an effect on interstate commerce and, therefore, is within the commerce power. (B) is wrong because the Second Amendment is prohibitory; therefore, it could not be the basis of enactment, but could only prohibit some types of enactments. (A) is wrong because the Fourteenth Amendment Equal Protection Clause, which applies only to the states, cannot be the basis for federal powers by itself. Congress must rather invoke its powers pursuant to Section 5 of the Fourteenth Amendment when it acts to guarantee the equal protection of the laws. (D) is wrong because the Necessary and Proper Clause only broadens congressional power authorized under some other provision; it does not itself create the power to act.

Answer to Question 15

(A) Under U.C.C. section 2-210(3), which governs this sale-of-goods case, "unless the circumstances indicate the contrary, a prohibition of assignment of 'the contract' is to be construed as barring only the delegation to the assignee of the assignor's performance." In other words, the covenant "not to assign this contract" would be interpreted as barring *only* the delegation of Ace's ***duty to pay*** to some other party, not the assignment of the right to receive Ace's payment. Therefore, when Typitrite "assigns the contract" to Equitable, since Typitrite has assigned only the right to payments, it has not breached its contract with Ace. (B) and (C) are therefore wrong. (D) is wrong because the covenant would not stand or fall on its rationale.

Answer to Question 16

(B) When an assignment has been made, but the obligor on the contract has not been informed of the assignment, he is still obligated to pay the party with whom he originally dealt—the assignor. Therefore, Ace Business Supplies would not be liable to Equitable Loan, and (C) is therefore wrong. However, it appears that Typitrite is responsible to Equitable Loan for the $10,000 payment that it has received, at least in the event of default in their financing arrangement if the agreement so provides.

Answer to Question 17

(D) Neither of these factors is correct. I. is wrong, because Commercial Bank would be claiming as a third-party beneficiary, and Typitrite's subsequent acceptance of the payment indicates that it is modifying its original intent that Commercial Bank be paid. A contract with respect to which there is a third-party beneficiary can be modified to affect the third-party beneficiary's rights provided that the third-party beneficiary has not justifiably relied upon its status. Here the key is that Commercial Bank did not know of the original agreement until the modification occurred. II. is wrong, because Commercial Bank could not be described as an incidental beneficiary. It was a directly named intended beneficiary of the contract. Therefore (D) is the correct answer.

Answer to Question 18

(A) The obligation of a buyer under a requirements contract is to act in good faith. This is the U.C.C. rule. (B) and (C) are wrong, because the rights involved here are clearly assignable since the payment of money does not involve personal responsibilities. (D) is wrong because the U.C.C. regards requirements contracts as being supported by sufficient consideration.

Answer to Question 19

(C) Luke's best defense is that he was not negligent. A forced landing is foreseeable, and Luke need not have foreseen the presence of anyone in particular on the ground. Thus, (B) is wrong. (A) is wrong because Luke need not have acted willfully or wantonly to be liable. (D) is wrong because Luke's conduct was the cause in fact of Sally's injury; *i.e.*, Sally would not have been injured but for Luke's landing of the plane. Causation alone is not enough to impose liability; there must also be a breach of duty, and Luke did not breach his duty of reasonable care.

Answer to Question 20

(C) Sally will prevail if the mechanics were negligent. There is no strict liability in service transactions, so (D) is wrong. Privity of contract is not required to find liability for negligence, and Sally's presence on the landing field makes her a foreseeable plaintiff, so (A) is wrong. (B) is incorrect because this is not a superseding cause situation; the mechanics' potential negligence would not be cut off by Aerodrome's negligence.

Answer to Question 21

(A) The question here is one of statutory interpretation. The status of Alan's conviction will rest on how the appellate court interprets the statute. If the court interprets the statute to include the ice pick, Alan's conviction is proper. Thus, (A) is correct. (B) is wrong because it does not reach the issue of statutory interpretation; the statute prohibits a concealed "knife or dagger," not merely a concealed "weapon." Thus, Alan's "admission" is not enough to convict him under this statute. (C) and (D) are wrong because Alan's motive or intent is irrelevant; the statute makes carrying a concealed knife or dagger a crime regardless of the intent.

Answer to Question 22

(B) Each party owns one-half of the stream bed. The general rule is that where a stream is a boundary, abutting owners each own one-half of the bed. Thus, (C) and (A) are wrong. (D) is incorrect; the description is not invalid.

Answer to Question 23

(C) If Trudi "always" locks her car upon exiting it, the evidence is offered as habit and is admissible. (D) is wrong, because the evidence is admissible to establish habit even if it is not offered for impeachment. (B) is wrong because the evidence may tend to show that Trusty is required to cover Trudi's loss. (A) is wrong because "self-serving" is not a valid objection.

Answer to Question 24

(B) The Supreme Court has stated that in the field of foreign affairs, the President has "plenary" powers. Coupled with the President's power to enter into executive agreements, his power is almost unlimited in the area of foreign affairs. (A) is wrong because there are some limits on the President's powers to enter into executive agreements. (C) is wrong because a two-thirds vote is not required for an executive agreement. (D) is a correct statement, since Congress has authority to act to preserve wildlife. That authority does not, however, deprive the President of the power to enter agreements of this sort.

Answer to Question 25

(C) The Supreme Court has held that executive agreements are the law of the land until Congress enacts a statute that is inconsistent with the executive agreement. Since this is a state statute, it must be declared unconstitutional because it is in conflict with the executive agreement. Thus, (B) is incorrect. (A) is incorrect. The issue is not whether the question is "best" left to the states, but rather whether the President has the authority to enter into the agreement. (D) states the right conclusion, but the logic is not as good as in alternative (C).

Answer to Question 26

(D) A person is privileged to use deadly force to prevent a crime only if it is a ***dangerous*** felony. Shoplifting is not a dangerous felony; thus, Customer's use of deadly force was not privileged. Therefore, Defendant was entitled to defend himself against Customer's improper use of deadly force by using deadly force himself. (A) is wrong because Defendant did not initiate an assault. (B) is wrong because even if Defendant intended to kill Customer, his action was justified. (C) is a misstatement of the law and of the facts.

Answer to Question 27

(B) The testimony is hearsay, but admissible within the state-of-mind exception as circumstantial evidence that the declarant acted in accordance with his intention. (A) is incorrect because a "dying declaration" must be made while in fear of "impending" death. (C) is incorrect because Barbara is not a psychiatrist, and there is no evidence that Tammy's husband assumed her to be one. (D) is wrong because the state of mind need not be as of the time of the incident to be relevant.

Answer to Question 28

(D) Stanley would prevail because he recorded his deed before Becky recorded her deed. The jurisdiction in this question has a race-notice statute, under which a subsequent bona fide purchaser is protected only if she records before the prior grantee. While Becky was a bona fide purchaser, she did not record her interest in the property before Stanley did; thus Stanley will prevail. (A) is incorrect because priority under a race-notice recording act, such as the one in this question, is determined by the subsequent purchaser's status as a bona fide purchaser and on the basis of who records first. Courts do not determine ownership by balancing the equities on the basis of who spent the most money. (B) is wrong because the doctrine of equitable conversion, wherein equity regards the purchaser in a land sale contract as the owner of the real property, does not change the result under the recording statute. Stanley will prevail because he recorded first. (C) is incorrect because Becky cannot rely on Tom's recording of his deed; Stanley recorded his interest before Becky recorded hers. Furthermore, even if the issue were whether Becky had actual notice of Stanley's interest, Becky could not rely on the "shelter rule" that protects transferees from a bona fide purchaser, because Tom was not a purchaser for value and therefore not protected by the recording statute.

Answer to Question 29

(C) First Central Bank will prevail under the recording statute. The jurisdiction in this question has a race-notice statute, under which a subsequent bona fide purchaser is protected only if she records before the prior grantee or mortgagee. Here, First Central Bank recorded its mortgage prior to Stanley's recording of his deed; thus, Stanley will take Mountainview subject to the bank's mortgage. (A) is incorrect because even though at common law Elmo would not have had any title to mortgage to the bank after the conveyance to Stanley, the race-notice statute nullifies that priority as to the subsequent bona fide purchaser who first records. (B) is wrong because the court is not aiding Elmo, but protecting his innocent creditor, First Central Bank. (D) is incorrect because it more accurately describes a pure race jurisdiction. In a race-notice jurisdiction, only the bona fide purchaser for value will prevail over a prior unrecorded deed or mortgage interest; hence, a purchaser who records first under this statute would not prevail if he had actual notice of a prior unrecorded interest.

Answer to Question 30

(B) The shopper will not likely prevail because Richards did not authorize the teenagers' conduct. Cause in fact is not a sufficient basis for Richards's liability on these facts, nor would he be liable vicariously for the teenagers' negligence. Thus, (C) and (D) are wrong. (A) is not as good a choice as (B) because the mere fact that they were not his employees does not alone insulate Richards from liability.

Answer to Question 31

(B) This is a criminal matter, and the accused is permitted to introduce evidence of his good character for the trait involved in the case in support of the probability that he did not commit the crime alleged. Thus, (C) and (D) are wrong as misstatements of the law. (A) is wrong because just the fact that evidence is not hearsay is no reason to admit it.

Answer to Question 32

(C) Clearly Joe was acting in self-defense, and even if throwing a heavy ashtray could be deemed to be deadly force, Joe had the right to defend himself against the unprivileged attack with the use of deadly force. (A) and (B) are incorrect because Joe's presence in the house and failure to leave immediately did not give Fred a privilege to use deadly force against him. (D) is irrelevant.

Answer to Question 33

(D) In *Young v. American Mini Theaters* (1986), the Court held that the mere fact that the commercial exploitation of certain material was protected by the First Amendment does not prevent the city from zoning or imposing other licensing requirements, as long as the businesses are not totally banned. The Court has upheld zoning ordinances such as the one here as reasonable regulations of the secondary effects of the speech involved. [*See* City of Renton v. Playtime Theaters (1986)]

Answer to Question 34

(C) When an applicable statute establishes the due care, the defendant's conduct is governed by the special statutory standard rather than the usual "reasonable person" standard. The statute is applicable because Nancy appears to be within the class of persons to be protected and the type of harm that occurred is what the statute was intended to prevent. Thus, (B) is wrong. (A) is wrong because an automobile is not an inherently dangerous instrument. (D) is a misstatement of law.

Answer to Question 35

(C) Nancy's accident was not within the risk that the statute was designed to prevent, which is one of the requirements for a statutory standard to apply. Hence, (C) is the best answer because it precludes applicability of the statute altogether. (A) and (B) incorrectly assume that the statute imposes a special duty on Nancy (a breach of which may constitute contributory negligence) but state reasons why breach of the statute did not cause Nancy's injuries. (D) does not state a legally recognized basis for this result.

Answer to Question 36

(C) Daniel is guilty of battery regardless of his belief. Battery is an unlawful application of force to the person of another resulting in either bodily injury or an offensive touching. Here, Daniel made a mistake as to the identity of the person whom he struck, but there was no mistake as to the intention of Daniel to strike this person. Mistake of fact affects criminal guilt only if it shows that the defendant did not have the state of mind required for the crime. Although battery need not be intentional (*i.e.,* it can result from criminal negligence), it is clear from the facts that Daniel intended to strike Victor. Thus, the mistake made by Daniel (who apparently believed that he was striking Wallace) does not show the absence of the state of mind required for battery, and will therefore not affect Daniel's guilt. (A) is incorrect because, even if a reasonable person would have mistaken Victor for Wallace, the fact remains that Daniel committed a battery against

Victor. A case of mistaken identity provides no defense to the battery that was committed. (B) is incorrect for the same reason as (A), and also because it implies that a battery against Wallace would be excused by adequate provocation (presumably resulting from Wallace's affair with Daniel's wife). It is true that an intentional killing will be reduced from murder to voluntary manslaughter if the defendant acted under a legally adequate provocation, and finding one's spouse in the act of adultery is deemed to be adequate provocation. However, there is no rule of law that excuses a battery on the ground that the victim committed adultery with the defendant's wife. (D) is incorrect because it also is based on the premise that Daniel is not guilty if he thought that he was striking Wallace. As explained previously, regardless of who Daniel thought he was striking, the significant point is that he unlawfully struck Victor, and this constitutes a battery.

MIXED SUBJECT SET 2
ANSWER SHEET

1. Ⓐ Ⓑ Ⓒ Ⓓ
2. Ⓐ Ⓑ Ⓒ Ⓓ
3. Ⓐ Ⓑ Ⓒ Ⓓ
4. Ⓐ Ⓑ Ⓒ Ⓓ
5. Ⓐ Ⓑ Ⓒ Ⓓ

6. Ⓐ Ⓑ Ⓒ Ⓓ
7. Ⓐ Ⓑ Ⓒ Ⓓ
8. Ⓐ Ⓑ Ⓒ Ⓓ
9. Ⓐ Ⓑ Ⓒ Ⓓ
10. Ⓐ Ⓑ Ⓒ Ⓓ

11. Ⓐ Ⓑ Ⓒ Ⓓ
12. Ⓐ Ⓑ Ⓒ Ⓓ
13. Ⓐ Ⓑ Ⓒ Ⓓ
14. Ⓐ Ⓑ Ⓒ Ⓓ
15. Ⓐ Ⓑ Ⓒ Ⓓ

16. Ⓐ Ⓑ Ⓒ Ⓓ
17. Ⓐ Ⓑ Ⓒ Ⓓ
18. Ⓐ Ⓑ Ⓒ Ⓓ

19. Ⓐ Ⓑ Ⓒ Ⓓ
20. Ⓐ Ⓑ Ⓒ Ⓓ
21. Ⓐ Ⓑ Ⓒ Ⓓ
22. Ⓐ Ⓑ Ⓒ Ⓓ
23. Ⓐ Ⓑ Ⓒ Ⓓ

24. Ⓐ Ⓑ Ⓒ Ⓓ
25. Ⓐ Ⓑ Ⓒ Ⓓ
26. Ⓐ Ⓑ Ⓒ Ⓓ
27. Ⓐ Ⓑ Ⓒ Ⓓ
28. Ⓐ Ⓑ Ⓒ Ⓓ

29. Ⓐ Ⓑ Ⓒ Ⓓ
30. Ⓐ Ⓑ Ⓒ Ⓓ
31. Ⓐ Ⓑ Ⓒ Ⓓ
32. Ⓐ Ⓑ Ⓒ Ⓓ
33. Ⓐ Ⓑ Ⓒ Ⓓ

34. Ⓐ Ⓑ Ⓒ Ⓓ
35. Ⓐ Ⓑ Ⓒ Ⓓ
36. Ⓐ Ⓑ Ⓒ Ⓓ

MIXED SUBJECT QUESTIONS - SET 2

Question 1

As Bob walked out of a store, he saw his friend Rick under the hood of a car trying to get it started. When Bob asked what was wrong, Rick told him that he had lost the keys to his car and was trying to "hot wire" it. Bob told Rick to get behind the steering wheel, and when Rick was ready, Bob started the car by "hot wiring" it. In fact, Rick did not own the car, and Bob is charged with being an accessory to larceny.

Bob should be found:

(A) Guilty, because his actions enabled Rick to steal the car.

(B) Guilty, because he had no reason to believe that the car was really Rick's.

(C) Not guilty, because he did not intend to aid Rick in stealing a car.

(D) Not guilty, because Rick would have probably stolen the car without his help.

Questions 2-3 are based on the following fact situation:

Ham operates a shortwave radio in his home. Ham maintains a large radio antenna on the rear part of his lot. One day Ham noticed that the guide wires holding the antenna in place were frayed. Ham hired Fixer to replace the guide wires with new, stronger wire. Fixer replaced all of the guide wires as per his agreement with Ham. Four days after Fixer finished his work and Ham had paid him, the antenna fell over onto Neighbor's house, causing severe damage.

2. If Neighbor brings suit against Ham for damages to his home, Neighbor is most likely to prevail against Ham because:

   (A) Of respondeat superior.

   (B) He assumed responsibility when he paid Fixer for the repair.

   (C) He was in possession of the property from which the antenna fell.

   (D) Fixer was engaged in an inherently dangerous activity.

3. If Neighbor brings suit against Fixer for damage to his home, the best defense for Fixer is that:

   (A) He was relieved of liability when Ham paid for the repair.

   (B) He could not reasonably foresee that the antenna would fall.

   (C) He did all the work under the direction of Ham.

   (D) The antenna was on the property of Ham.

Question 4

Bob was helping his neighbor Ray clean out his garage. As he and Ray were moving some boards out of the garage, Ray ran into the overhead door's hinge, causing it to fall and hit Bob on his head, killing him. Bob's wife, Linda, sued Ray for the wrongful death of her husband, seeking damages of $100,000. Linda, who was present when the accident occurred, is called to testify that at the time of the accident, Bob was carrying the boards on his shoulder, and he therefore was unable to see that Ray had hit the door hinges.

As a witness, Linda is:

(A) Competent, if she is testifying as the personal representative of her husband's estate.

(B) Competent, in spite of the fact she is the plaintiff.

(C) Incompetent, because she is unqualified to give opinion evidence.

(D) Incompetent, because she cannot testify for her husband in a civil case.

Questions 5-7 are based on the following fact situation:

Congress enacted legislation that was intended to open up federal lands to private industry to explore for, and extract, oil and coal deposits. The act established the Federal Lands Exploitation Commission to supervise the exploration and extraction of fossil fuels from federal lands, and empowered the Commission to enter into contracts on behalf of the federal government with the private companies that wish to mine for coal and drill for oil. The Commission members were also required to investigate safe and sound methods of exploiting the oil and coal deposits without doing unnecessary harm to the environment and to make recommendations to Congress for new laws that would govern the exploitation of federal lands. Further, the commissioners were given the power to make the rules and regulations concerning the contracts with the companies and to appoint administrative law judges to conduct hearings regarding violation of the Commission's rules and disputes concerning the contracts.

The Commission's chairperson was designated as an Undersecretary of the Interior; the President appointed two commissioners from environmental groups; and the oil and coal companies selected one commissioner each, who were then appointed by Congress to the Commission.

5. The authority for the establishment of the Federal Lands Exploitation Commission is most likely:

(A) The Commerce Clause.

(B) The taxing and spending power.

(C) Congress's authority to regulate federal land.

(D) The war and defense power.

6. For its violation of the Commission's rules with regard to pollution of water resulting from drilling operations, AmOil was fined $5,000. AmOil files suit in the federal court to enjoin the Commission's enforcement of this rule. AmOil's best argument in support of its contention that the rule was illegal is:

(A) Regulations concerning criminal conduct cannot be made by agency rules, but must be made by federal statute.

(B) The appointment of the commissioners was illegal; therefore, the rules promulgated by the Commission are invalid.

(C) Since the fine was potentially $5,000 for violation of the rule, AmOil had a right to a trial by jury, which was denied when the matter was heard by the administrative law judge.

(D) The proceeding before the administrative law judge violated AmOil's rights of equal protection as guaranteed by the Fourteenth Amendment.

7. Administrative Law Judge May had been appointed to his position by a former Undersecretary of the Interior who was the Commission chairperson. When the new administration came into office, the new Commission chairperson removed May from his position as the ALJ, but offered May a position as an attorney in the enforcement division. May brought suit in the federal court to enjoin the Commission chairperson from removing him from his position. May should:

(A) Prevail, because a judge cannot be removed from office after appointment.

(B) Prevail, if it is shown that at all times he maintained good behavior.

(C) Not prevail, because he was not a judge within the meaning of Article III.

(D) Not prevail, because the appointing authority had changed.

Questions 8-9 are based on the following fact situation:

Able, Baker, Charlie, and Dick were on their way to Pasadena to the Rose Bowl when they were injured as their car was sideswiped and driven off the road by a large truck belonging to D-Liver-Co. Dick was driving the car at the time. Rev and Relief were the alternate drivers of the truck. Rev was driving and Relief was asleep in the sleeping cab portion of the truck at the time of the accident. Able, Baker, Charlie, and Dick brought an action against Rev and D-Liver-Co., alleging negligence by Rev in driving too fast. D-Liver-Co. answered and asserted the affirmative defense that Dick had been on quaaludes and cocaine and was intoxicated at the time of the accident.

8. D-Liver-Co.'s counsel seeks to have the highway patrolman who investigated the accident state that he overheard Dick tell Able, Baker, and Charlie, "This was probably all our fault; we shouldn't have been on 'ludes and snow." Assuming the trial judge takes judicial notice that "'ludes" means "quaaludes" and "snow" means "cocaine," the judge should rule that the tender of evidence is:

(A) Admissible, as an admission of a party.

(B) Admissible, to save time because the same statement could be admitted by way of the accident report.

(C) Inadmissible, because if he had been intoxicated, he would not be capable of making a rational decision as to fault.

(D) Inadmissible, because it is hearsay not within any exception.

9. Counsel for the plaintiffs seeks to introduce the statement of Relief, no longer in the employ of D-Liver-Co., that just before the accident he had stated to Rev, "You had better slow down. You have been warned by D-Liver-Co. many times not to go this fast." The judge should rule the statement admissible only if:

(A) The statement was made immediately after the accident, and was made under oath.

(B) Relief is unavailable to testify to the matters in the statement.

(C) Plaintiffs' attorney produces a record of three citations that Rev received in the last year for speeding, driving the same truck.

(D) Plaintiffs' attorney first proves as a preliminary question of fact that during the trip Relief was an agent of D-Liver-Co. and that the statement concerned the scope of his employment.

Question 10

Joe, who had been Bubba's roommate and lover for several years, decided to leave Bubba and move in with Roger. On the day that Joe was to move into Roger's condominium, Bubba shot Joe in the neck, intending to kill him. Joe was not severely wounded, but he was hospitalized for several days. During his stay at the hospital, it was discovered that Joe had developed a form of cancer that was invariably fatal. Three weeks after being shot, Joe died of pneumonia caused by an infection resulting from the bullet wound in his neck. Roger had been killed when his condo burned down as he slept. The fire occurred two days after Bubba shot Joe.

Is Bubba guilty of a criminal homicide?

(A) No, because his actions merely constituted attempt.

(B) No, because Joe was already suffering from an incurable disease.

(C) No, because Bubba actually prolonged Joe's life because he prevented his probable death in the fire that destroyed Roger's condo.

(D) Yes, because Bubba's act was the proximate cause of Joe's death.

Questions 11-14 are based on the following fact situation:

Martha needed a new pair of shoes. She went to her local Skysheim shop and told the salesperson that she worked in the city's downtown area and had to walk eight blocks to get from her house to her commuter train and then six blocks from her train to her office. During the workday, she had to climb up and down stairs several times. She wanted shoes that were suitable for walking on concrete, had gripping power for stairs, and were comfortable. The salesperson went into his stockroom and brought out four different styles of Skysheim's "Clouds," reputably the most comfortable shoe on the market, designed for the type of use that Martha had in mind. Martha tried on each of the four pairs but did not like the way any of them looked. While walking around the store, however, Martha saw a shoe she did like—"Hobblers," Skysheim's high-fashion shoe. She told the salesperson to bring her a pair to try. He did so and explained to Martha that Hobblers were completely made of the finest leather and would probably last for years. Martha tried on the shoes and told the salesperson that she would take them.

11. Assume for this question only that the salesperson took the shoes back to the register with him and collected Martha's money. As he was putting the shoes into a bag, a person brandishing a gun entered the store, forced the salesperson to put all of the money in the register into the bag with Martha's shoes, and fled with the bag, the money, and the shoes. After the police had come, Martha asked the salesperson to get her another pair of shoes. He told Martha that she would have to pay for them again.

Martha refused. If Martha sues Skysheim for another pair of shoes, who will prevail?

(A) Martha, because she did not yet have possession of the shoes.

(B) Martha, because the purpose of the contract had been made impossible by an unforeseen event.

(C) Skysheim, because title to the shoes had already passed to Martha.

(D) Skysheim, because the contract goods had already been identified.

12. Assume for this question only that Martha bought the shoes and wore them twice. She decided that they were too uncomfortable for her daily commute. She took the shoes back to the Skysheim shop and demanded her money back. Skysheim refused. If Martha sues to get her money back, under which theory would she most likely prevail?

I.   Breach of the implied warranty of fitness for particular purpose.

II. Breach of the implied warranty of merchantability.

III. Breach of express warranty.

(A) I. and II., but not III.

(B) I. and III., but not II.

(C) II. and III., but not I.

(D) None of the above.

13. Assume for this question only that Martha bought the shoes. She wore them to work regularly, but after a week she wore a hole through one shoe's sole. She took it to a shoe repair shop and was told that the sole was vinyl. If Martha sues Skysheim for a refund, under which theory would she most likely prevail?

I. Breach of an express warranty that the shoes were leather.

II. Breach of an express warranty that the shoes would last for years.

III. Breach of the implied warranty of merchantability.

(A) I. and II., but not III.

(B) I. and III., but not II.

(C) II. and III., but not I.

(D) I., II., and III.

14. Assume for this question only that Martha paid for the shoes and walked out of the store. A few moments later, she sat down to look at her new shoes in the sunlight. On close inspection, she noticed a small nick in the leather of one of the shoes. She immediately went back to Skysheim and demanded a refund. The salesperson refused. If Martha sues for a refund, who will prevail?

(A) Martha, because there was a breach of contract.

(B) Martha, because she had a reasonable time after purchase in which to inspect.

(C) Skysheim, because Martha accepted the goods.

(D) Skysheim, because Martha did not give written notice of the breach.

Question 15

Chuck recently moved to Hangtown and discovered an old friend, Roy, was living there. Chuck asked Roy to introduce him to the town's banker so that Chuck could apply for a loan to set up a hardware business. Roy, also a friend of the banker, arranged a meeting and later gave Chuck a glowing recommendation based upon their long and deep friendship. When the banker

approved a $25,000 loan, Roy was present at the signing of the loan papers and co-signed on Chuck's behalf. Unknown to Roy, Chuck intentionally misrepresented his intentions as to the proceeds of the loan and his financial status, forging some documents used to verify his solvency. Chuck has been tried and convicted of obtaining money by false pretenses (a felony) and sentenced to state prison.

If Roy is charged as an accessory to obtaining money by false pretenses, he should be found:

(A) Guilty, because he was present when the crime was committed and was thus a principal in the second degree.

(B) Guilty, because he encouraged and aided Chuck, and his ignorance of Chuck's insolvency is no defense to the charged crime.

(C) Not guilty, because he lacked the requisite mental state to be an aider and abettor.

(D) Not guilty, because his encouragement and aid was not the legal cause of the offense.

Questions 16-20 are based on the following fact situation:

Randy, having suffered a recent heart attack, asked his old friend Hilda to come by to visit him. When she got there, Randy told her that he was in very poor health and that, because he knew that she had wanted for a long time to start a riding school, he wanted to give her some property on which she could build the school. He then gave Hilda an envelope containing two grant deeds purchased in a stationery store and filled in and signed by Randy in ink. The first deed purported to give to Hilda "My property known as Twelve Oaks, with its five acres of land and the stable and dressage course located thereon." The second gave to Hilda "four acres of wooded land on the northwest section of my property located at Forest Knoll, adjacent to Twelve Oaks for use by Hilda in connection with her proposed riding school." Both deeds contained standard warranties, including a covenant against encumbrances, the right to convey, and the right of quiet enjoyment. Randy told Hilda that he was giving the property to her, but since he did not have a better description, he wanted to keep the deeds until his attorney could review them. Hilda agreed and gave them back to him.

Unfortunately, Randy suffered another heart attack the next day and died without seeing his attorney. However, when Hilda spoke with the administrator of Randy's estate, she learned that Randy had, as part of another deed 12 years before, sold that part of Twelve Oaks on which was located the stable and dressage course. The purchaser, Ruth, was also given an easement to cross over Randy's property to get to the property she purchased, although there is no evidence that Ruth had ever used this "right of way" since she preferred to reach her property by riding cross-country on her horse. Thus, there was no trail or road ever made across Randy's property.

16. Randy's heirs bring an action for declaratory relief against Hilda, asserting that the deed to Twelve Oaks is void because it contained an inaccurate and ambiguous description. A trial court would enter judgment:

   (A) Against Hilda, because the deed failed to give an accurate description of the property owned by Randy at the time of his death.

   (B) Against Hilda, because Randy informed Hilda that he did not know the description of his property and he wanted his attorney to prepare the deeds.

   (C) Against Hilda, because the deed purports to transfer more property than Randy owned and thus is void as a matter of law.

   (D) For Hilda, because the error in description was not sufficient to put in doubt what Randy intended to convey to her.

17. If, in the suit for declaratory relief, Randy's heirs attempt to void the deed to the Forest Knoll land, Hilda will:

   (A) Prevail, because Randy intended for Hilda to choose the appropriate acreage, and she can therefore select the four acres that satisfy her needs.

   (B) Prevail, because the deed clearly states what property Randy intended to grant to Hilda.

   (C) Not prevail, because the phrase "wooded land" is too uncertain.

   (D) Not prevail, because the description is too vague.

18. Assuming that a court finds the descriptions in both deeds to be sufficient, with regard to Hilda's interest in the property, which of the following findings is a court likely to make?

   (A) An interest was transferred to Hilda, because even though there was no actual delivery, the deeds can be treated as wills.

   (B) An interest was transferred to Hilda because there were valid deeds and a valid delivery.

   (C) No interest was transferred to Hilda because Randy kept both the deeds; thus, there was no delivery.

   (D) No interest was transferred to Hilda, because Randy did not have the chance to have his attorney review the deeds.

19. If Ruth has the right of way over the property Randy gave to Hilda, it is possible that Randy's estate would be liable for breach of the covenant:

   (A) Against encumbrances.

(B) Of quiet enjoyment, if such a right of way exists whether or not Ruth is using it.

(C) Of right to convey, because Randy, by not mentioning the right of way in Hilda's deed, implied that there were no easements.

(D) Of right to convey, because the existence of the right of way by Ruth is inconsistent with Randy's alleged title.

20. Randy's son Phil introduces evidence that Randy had promised him in writing that, if he was ever going to get rid of Twelve Oaks, Phil would have the right to purchase it first. The trial court will:

(A) Void the deed to Hilda.

(B) Require Hilda to convey to Phil if he tenders market price for the property.

(C) Not affect Hilda's deed, but Phil may have a cause of action against Randy's estate.

(D) Not affect Hilda's deed because Phil has no claim against either her or Randy's estate.

Question 21

Don was tried for the aggravated assault of Victor. Don called Xact to the witness stand. Xact was to testify that the night before the alleged crime, Don stated to Xact that he was going to visit his mother in a distant city some 1,000 miles away. The testimony is:

(A) Admissible, because it is a declaration of intent to do a future act.

(B) Admissible, because of the verbal acts exception.

(C) Inadmissible, because it is not relevant.

(D) Inadmissible, because it is hearsay not within any exception.

Question 22

Foley was a permanent resident alien of the United States who was awaiting an opportunity to become a citizen. Foley filed an application to become an instructor in the local public high school but was denied the position solely on the ground that he was not a citizen. Foley now brings suit, alleging that his status as a resident alien was not a proper ground for denying him a position as an instructor.

May the state deny a permanent resident alien employment as an instructor in the public high school?

(A) Yes, because employment by the state is a privilege, not a right.

(B) Yes, because citizenship bears some rational relationship to the interest that is being protected.

(C) No, to do so would be a denial of equal protection.

(D) No, because the evidence presented was uncontroverted that he was awaiting the opportunity to become a citizen.

Question 23

Midtown Bank was robbed on Thursday afternoon. The perpetrator was short (under 5' 5") and was wearing a purple jumpsuit with a red hood and green gloves. On Friday, the police received a tip from a neighbor of Digby that Digby treated the entire apartment complex to breakfast, boasted about coming into some money, and flashed a huge roll of bills. The police went to Digby's apartment. Digby, a man no taller than 5' 2", answered the door. Digby explained that a friend had paid off an old debt that Digby had long ago written off. After a few more questions, the police left. Late Friday afternoon, the police were summoned back to the building by sanitation workers who had found a purple jumpsuit and green gloves in the building's dumpster. The police arrested Digby and executed a search warrant for his apartment, which turned up nothing. At Digby's trial for bank robbery, the prosecution seeks to introduce into evidence the clothing recovered from the dumpster.

The clothing is:

(A) Admissible, as circumstantial evidence that Digby committed the robbery.

(B) Admissible, as direct evidence that Digby committed the robbery.

(C) Inadmissible, because it is irrelevant.

(D) Inadmissible, unless the prosecution proves beyond a reasonable doubt that it is the same clothing the robber wore.

Question 24

Ralph was recently divorced. In the property settlement, Alice was awarded all personal property that had been accumulated during the marriage, including Ralph's classic 19-inch black-and-white TV set. In order to get his prized TV set back, Ralph lied to Ed, telling him that Alice took the TV set in violation of the property settlement. Ed remembered that Alice gave Ed's wife a key to her new home, and he volunteered to go with Ralph to get the TV back while Alice was at work. Ralph and Ed went to Alice's house, but, unknown to them, Alice had taken the day off work. After Ed noisily opened the back door with his wife's key, Alice called the police, who quickly arrived and arrested Ralph and Ed.

As to a charge of common law conspiracy to commit larceny, Ed should be found:

(A) Not guilty, because he did not intend to steal.

(B) Not guilty, because he did not have a corrupt motive.

(C) Guilty, because there was an agreement, and the opening of the locked door was sufficient for the overt act.

(D) Guilty, because good motives are not a defense to criminal liability.

Question 25

The state of New York passed a statute that provided for direct reimbursement from public funds to nonpublic schools of the cost of performing various testing and reporting services required of all schools by state law. The three state-prepared tests involved consisted of a student evaluation test, a comprehensive achievement test, and scholarship and college qualification tests. The law also provided for payment to the nonpublic schools for the grading of the tests.

On review by the Supreme Court, the statute should be held:

(A) Constitutional, if objective grading standards are used and reimbursement covers only secular services.

(B) Constitutional, if the state interest is great enough to justify the burden on religion, and no alternative means are available.

(C) Unconstitutional, because direct payment to nonpublic schools is a violation of the Establishment Clause of the First Amendment.

(D) Unconstitutional, because the statewide administration of the test for nonpublic as well as public schools entangles the state with religious schools.

Question 26

Deanna purchased a wardrobe closet at an antique auction. The sale of all merchandise was specifically designated "as is." Three days later, while cleaning the inside of the closet, Deanna discovered a small quantity of a white powder inside a box. She showed the box to her boyfriend, a paralegal. He identified the powder as driscamine, a controlled substance. He told her that it was illegal to buy driscamine, but that since she did not know that it was in the closet when she purchased it, it was okay to keep it, which she did. A state statute prohibits "willful and unlawful possession of a controlled substance."

If Deanna is charged with violating this statute, she should be found:

(A) Guilty, because she knowingly possessed the driscamine.

(B) Guilty, because she acquired the driscamine when she intentionally purchased the wardrobe closet and, in doing so, committed the requisite unlawful act.

(C) Not guilty, because she thought she was acting lawfully.

(D) Not guilty, because she did not willfully acquire the driscamine and, hence, committed no unlawful act.

Question 27

Paul is suing Dan for injuries he suffered when their cars collided at an intersection controlled by stoplights. Paul called Whit, a witness to the accident, to testify that he saw Dan drive through a red light. On cross-examination, Dan's attorney asks Whit, "Isn't it true that Dan's ex-wife is paying $500 for your testimony today?" Paul's attorney objects.

The objection should be:

(A) Overruled, because the question gives Whit an opportunity to explain or deny the allegation.

(B) Overruled, because the question is a proper form of impeachment.

(C) Sustained, because the question addresses a collateral issue.

(D) Sustained, because it is a leading question.

Questions 28-30 are based on the following fact situation:

Nicholas owned a tract of land in Red Valley that he leased to Realty Corp. for 99 years.

Realty Corp. built a 60-story office complex on the property. Realty Corp. then sold the building to Rasputin, Inc., assigning the lease with Nicholas's approval. Ten years into the lease, Nicholas conveyed the property in joint tenancy to his twin sons, Alexander and Vladimir, as a birthday present. Unfortunately, a few years after the conveyance, Nicholas and his sons had a serious falling out over how to run the family business. Nicholas no longer wished the sons to control valuable commercial property, and so he demanded that they return the deed with which he conveyed the Red Valley property to them. The sons returned the deed, and Nicholas destroyed it. A few months later, Vladimir learned that he was seriously ill and not likely to live much longer. He executed a quitclaim deed conveying "any interest I have in the Red Valley property" to his daughter, Anastasia. Vladimir subsequently died.

28. Who owns the reversion in the Red Valley property?

(A) Alexander.

(B) Nicholas.

(C) Alexander and Anastasia as tenants in common.

(D) Alexander and Anastasia as joint tenants.

29. Assume for the purposes of this question only that Rasputin, Inc. has failed to make a rent payment for several months and has also failed to build the road that Realty Corp. agreed to build in the original lease. The landlord of the Red Valley property has a cause of action against:

(A) Rasputin for the rent only, because the rent covenant runs with the land.

(B) Rasputin for the rent and the road, but only if Rasputin expressly assumed performance of all covenants.

(C) Rasputin and Realty Corp. for both the rent and the road.

(D) Rasputin for the rent only, and Realty Corp. for the road only.

30. Assume for purposes of this question only that, after Vladimir died, Nicholas sold and conveyed the Red Valley property to Olga. Assume also that the deed from Nicholas to Alexander and Vladimir was never recorded and that the jurisdiction's recording act states the following: "No conveyance or mortgage of an interest in land is valid against any subsequent purchaser for value without notice thereof whose conveyance is first recorded." If Olga brings a quiet title action and is successful, which of the following best explains this result?

(A) As owner of the property, Nicholas was entitled to convey it to Olga.

(B) Alexander and Vladimir failed to record the deed they took from Nicholas.

(C) Alexander and Vladimir failed to record their deed, and Olga was unaware of their interest when she paid Nicholas market value for the property.

(D) Alexander and Vladimir failed to record their deed, Olga was unaware of their interest when she purchased the property, and Olga recorded her deed.

Questions 31-32 are based on the following fact situation:

Danny is a 10-year-old, and although his parents make sure he is home by 10 p.m. during the school week, they do not really enforce any sort of curfew on their son during the weekend. One Saturday night, when Danny's parents went to bed at midnight, Danny was still out. About 2 a.m., Danny and two other children were arrested by the police for breaking the windows and causing other damage to Bernadette's antique Cord automobile.

31. In a suit by Bernadette against Danny for the damages he caused to her automobile, Bernadette should:

(A) Prevail, because Danny, at the age of 10, should have been aware of the consequences of his action.

(B) Prevail, because Danny deliberately damaged her car.

(C) Not prevail, because Danny is presumed to be under the care of his parents and, therefore, is not legally responsible for his tortious conduct.

(D) Not prevail, unless she can show that Danny was mature enough to be aware of the consequences of his action.

32. Assume that the jurisdiction has no statute regarding parental liability. In a suit by Bernadette against Danny's parents for the damages caused to her automobile, Bernadette should:

(A) Prevail, because a minor's parents are vicariously liable any time the minor commits a tortious act.

(B) Prevail, because Danny's parents did not ensure that Danny was home at a reasonable hour.

(C) Not prevail, unless she can show that Danny's parents were aware that Danny has done this sort of act before.

(D) Not prevail, because there is no reason to assume that Danny's parents could know that Danny might damage Bernadette's automobile.

Questions 33-36 are based on the following fact situation:

Indegas wanted to ensure that it had sufficient stocks of gasoline and oil for its independent dealerships; it therefore entered into contracts with various refineries to purchase the gasoline they produced. One such agreement was with Cal-Tex, whereby Indegas was given the right to purchase all gasoline refined by Cal-Tex for the next five years at a price set at 95% of the domestic market price at the time of delivery. Indegas agreed to purchase no less than 5,000 gallons a week and to use its own tankers to transport the gasoline from Cal-Tex's refinery to its storage facilities. At the time this contract was signed, Indegas gave written notice to Cal-Tex that it intended to buy all gasoline produced by Cal-Tex until further notice.

For the first year, Indegas continued to purchase all gasoline produced by Cal-Tex. However, at the end of that year Cal-Tex purchased an out-of-state refinery that refined all its gasoline from domestic shale oil. As a result of this merger and of more efficient plant methods, Cal-Tex doubled its production of gasoline by the next year. At a meeting between Cal-Tex and Indegas, Cal-Tex's president noted that Indegas was getting as much gasoline as it needed, and that Cal-Tex intended to sell the extra gasoline it was producing on foreign markets at a higher price than Indegas was paying. Indegas agreed with this proposal and signed an addendum to the original agreement reflecting this change.

Thereafter, Indegas continued to purchase one-half of Cal-Tex's total capacity until the following year when, as a result of a foreign oil boycott, Cal-Tex was unable to purchase sufficient foreign oil to operate its local refinery profitably. Cal-Tex, by letter, notified Indegas that it could no longer deliver gasoline to it in accordance with their agreement. Nevertheless, Cal-Tex's other refinery was able to increase its production by 25% and continue to sell to foreign markets.

33. The original agreement between Cal-Tex and Indegas was:

(A) Unenforceable because of the failure to set a specific price for the gasoline.

(B) Unenforceable because it was for an unreasonable period of time.

(C) Enforceable as to price, but not as to the amount of gasoline Cal-Tex agreed to sell.

(D) Enforceable in all respects.

34. Assuming that Indegas had an enforceable agreement, the modification of this contract made by the addendum was:

(A) Enforceable to the extent that Indegas purchased the gasoline.

(B) Enforceable in all respects.

(C) Unenforceable, because there was no consideration for Indegas's agreement to take only one-half of the gasoline produced.

(D) Unenforceable, because the contract did not state the amount of gasoline produced by each refinery.

35. Assume that a contract existed between Indegas and Cal-Tex. Cal-Tex's refusal to deliver gasoline to Indegas is:

(A) Justifiable, because it was refining no gasoline at the local refinery.

(B) Justifiable, because its performance was excused because of the foreign boycott of oil.

(C) Justifiable, because Indegas was aware of the possibility of an oil boycott when it entered into the agreement.

(D) Not justifiable and a breach of contract.

36. Assume that the oil boycott ended, but that Cal-Tex sold both its refineries to a large oil company. What is the effect of this sale on Cal-Tex's obligation to Indegas?

(A) The sale discharges its obligation to Indegas because there has been a full performance.

(B) Cal-Tex is liable for damages if the other oil company fails to deliver gasoline to Indegas.

(C) Cal-Tex is excused from further performance because it has no more refineries to produce gasoline.

(D) Cal-Tex breached its contract with Indegas.

MIXED SUBJECT SET 2 SUBJECT GUIDE

1.	Criminal Law	19.	Real Property
2.	Torts	20.	Real Property
3.	Torts	21.	Evidence
4.	Evidence	22.	Constitutional Law
5.	Constitutional Law	23.	Evidence
6.	Constitutional Law	24.	Criminal Law
7.	Constitutional Law	25.	Constitutional Law
8.	Evidence	26.	Criminal Law
9.	Evidence	27.	Evidence
10.	Criminal Law	28.	Real Property
11.	Contracts	29.	Real Property
12.	Contracts	30.	Real Property
13.	Contracts	31.	Torts
14.	Contracts	32.	Torts
15.	Criminal Law	33.	Contracts
16.	Real Property	34.	Contracts
17.	Real Property	35.	Contracts
18.	Real Property	36.	Contracts

MIXED SUBJECT ANSWERS - SET 2

Answer to Question 1

(C) To hold a person liable under the theory of accessory or accomplice liability, the prosecution must show that the defendant helped with the crime with the intent to see the crime committed. Unless the prosecution can establish the unlawful mental state, there can be no criminal liability. Since Bob did not have the intent to see a larceny committed, he cannot be guilty. (A) is wrong because he did not have the necessary mental state. (B) is wrong; the issue is not whether he had reason to believe the car was Rick's, but whether he intended a larceny to take place. (D) is wrong because the fact that Rick would probably have stolen the car anyway will not relieve the defendant from liability if he helped with the necessary intent.

Answer to Question 2

(C) Ham's duty as possessor of land makes him liable to Neighbor for the damage from the antenna. The fact that an independent contractor may have negligently created the danger does not relieve the duty Ham owes to adjoining landowners. [*See* Restatement (Second) §422] (A) is not correct because respondeat superior refers to an employer-employee relationship; Fixer was an independent contractor. (B) is wrong because no shifting of responsibility was created by the payment under these facts. (D) is wrong because there are not enough facts to establish that Fixer's work was an inherently dangerous activity.

Answer to Question 3

(B) If Fixer could not reasonably foresee that the antenna would fall, then he was not negligent. (A) is wrong because payment does not relieve an independent contractor from liability. (C) is wrong because even if Fixer did do the work under the direction of Ham, he would then be liable along with Ham. (D) is wrong because the location of the antenna would not affect Fixer's liability.

Answer to Question 4

(B) Linda is competent to testify. Persons interested in a lawsuit are not disqualified as witnesses. (A) is wrong because Linda need not be the personal representative of Bob's estate to testify. (C) is incorrect because she is testifying as to what she saw, not as to her opinion. In any event, a lay witness may testify as to an opinion if she is a percipient witness. (D) is wrong because the common law spousal incapacity has been abolished.

Answer to Question 5

(C) Congress is specifically given the power to regulate federal lands in Article IV. Since there is no other authority that can regulate the use of federal lands but Congress, this is all the authority Congress would need to enact this type of statute. Thus, (B) and (D) are wrong. (A) is wrong because although Congress has broad powers under the Commerce Clause, this is not a matter falling under that clause.

Answer to Question 6

(B) The Appointment Clause of the Constitution permits Congress to vest appointments of inferior officers only in the President, the courts, or the heads of departments. Enforcement is an executive act; therefore, Congress cannot appoint its own members to the Commission to exercise enforcement powers. A duly appointed commission does have the power to make rules and regulations governing the subject matter for which it is appointed. Those rules are not "criminal" statutes in this case. Thus, (A) is wrong. (C) is wrong because Congress may establish new public rights and actions that may be adjudicated by agencies, without juries. (D) is wrong because there is no discrimination.

Answer to Question 7

(C) May is not a judge within the sense of Article III, and only such judges are protected by the provisions of that article. Thus, (A) and (B) are incorrect. (D) makes no sense. The statutory authority for appointments remains the same, and only the person holding the office has changed.

Answer to Question 8

(A) An admission by a party-opponent is the party's own statement offered against him by the opposing side, and under the Federal Rules, it is not hearsay. Thus, (D) is incorrect. (B) does not state a proper basis for admissibility; besides, the only way the statement could be admitted by way of the report is as an admission. (C) is wrong. If the statement qualifies as an admission—made by a party, offered by the opponent and relevant—it will be admissible even if the admitting party had no rational basis for the statement.

Answer to Question 9

(D) Under Federal Rule 801(d)(2), an out-of-court statement of an agent or an employee can be introduced as an admission against the principal or employer if it concerns a matter within the scope of the agency or employment, made during the existence of the relationship. Relief's statement constitutes an admission by a party-opponent and is not hearsay. (A) and (C) state requirements for admissibility that have no basis in law. Admissibility of an admission is not conditioned on the availability of the declarant; (B) is therefore incorrect.

Answer to Question 10

(D) Bubba shot Joe, intending to kill him, and Joe died. The only issue is whether Bubba's act was the proximate cause of Joe's death. Proximate cause is found when the results are the natural and foreseeable results of the defendant's acts. Infections and negligent medical treatment are deemed to be a foreseeable risk in homicide cases; since Joe died of pneumonia that resulted from the bullet, most courts would conclude that proximate cause has been established. (A) would be correct if proximate cause could not be established. (B) and (C) are wrong. The fact that Joe already had an incurable disease or would likely have died from another cause will not negate proximate cause.

Answer to Question 11

(A) Where the seller is a merchant, the risk of loss does not pass to the buyer until the buyer takes physical possession of the goods. (B) is wrong because performance was not impossible; Martha had already performed and Skysheim could perform by tendering another pair of shoes. (C) is wrong because passage of title does not shift the risk of loss in this case. (D) is wrong because while a buyer gains some rights once the goods are identified, identification does not shift the risk of loss.

Answer to Question 12

(D) An implied warranty of fitness for particular purpose arises where a seller knows that the buyer is relying on the seller to pick suitable goods for the buyer and the buyer relies on the seller's expertise. Here, Martha asked the seller to pick suitable goods, but declined the seller's advice and picked out her own shoes. Therefore, this warranty did not arise. The implied warranty of merchantability arose but was not broken. This warranty arises in every sale of goods by a merchant and ensures, generally, that goods shall be fit for ordinary purposes. Nothing in the facts indicates that the shoes here are not fit for ordinary purposes. The only express warranties here arose from the statement that the shoes were leather and, perhaps, from the sample shoe on the sales floor. However, nothing in the facts indicates that there has been a breach of either of these express warranties. Therefore, (D) is the correct answer.

Answer to Question 13

(B) An express warranty will arise from any statement of fact or promise. Here, the salesperson said that the shoes were completely made of leather and would last for years. The former is a statement of fact that will give rise to a warranty; thus, I. is a good theory. The latter is not a statement of fact, but a prediction of the future. Moreover, it is not specific—how long is "years"? This statement amounts to mere puffery and will not give rise to a warranty. Therefore, II. is not a good theory. An implied warranty of merchantability will arise in every sale by a merchant unless disclaimed. To be merchantable, goods must be fit for ordinary purposes, and arguably shoes that wear out in a week are not fit for ordinary purposes. Therefore, III. is a good theory.

Answer to Question 14

(C) Once a buyer has accepted goods, her right to reject for nonconformance generally lapses and her only remedy is a suit for damages. Acceptance usually occurs when the buyer takes possession of the goods. In some cases, the buyer can revoke acceptance, but the breach must be substantial and the buyer must have a good reason for accepting the goods (*i.e.*, something more than not taking the time to carefully inspect). Here, Martha accepted the goods and the breach appears minor. (A) entitles Martha only to damages, not a full refund. (B) is a misstatement of the law. (D) is wrong because written notice is not required; oral notice is acceptable.

Answer to Question 15

(C) To be liable as an aider and abettor (*i.e.*, an accomplice), the defendant must encourage or aid in commission of the underlying crime with intent that the crime be committed or, in certain cases, with knowledge that it was to be committed. Since Roy had no knowledge of the crime, he could not be an aider and abettor. (A) is wrong because mere presence at the scene of the crime is not enough to make Roy a principal in the second degree. (B) is wrong because, as stated, there must be intent or knowledge to be an aider and abettor. (D) is wrong because if the requisite intent is present, the defendant can be liable even though he did not "cause" the crime.

Answer to Question 16

(D) A description in a deed is sufficient if it furnishes a good lead as to the identity of the property. Hence, (A) is wrong. (C) is incorrect because a deed purporting to convey more land than the grantor owns does not invalidate the deed. (B) fails to conform to the facts.

Answer to Question 17

(D) The description is too vague in its entirety; there may be difficulty determining *which* four acres in the northwest section are meant. Thus, (B) is wrong. (C) is wrong because the "wooded land" language is not the only vague part; which four acres in the northwest section is a problem. (A) is wrong because whatever Randy's actual intent, he failed to accomplish it with this deed.

Answer to Question 18

(B) (A) is wrong because an undelivered deed cannot be sustained as a valid testamentary disposition under the Statute of Wills. (C) is wrong because the original giving of the deeds to Hilda constituted "delivery" and she accepted; the fact that she returned the deeds to Randy to hold does not change the fact that a delivery was made. (D) is irrelevant.

Answer to Question 19

(A) The existence of the easement breaches the covenant against encumbrances and Randy's estate is in breach of this covenant. (B), (C), and (D) are incorrect because the existence of an easement burdening the land does not breach the covenant of quiet enjoyment or right to convey, respectively. The covenant of quiet enjoyment is breached when the grantee is evicted by a third party with *paramount* title, *i.e.,* title or ownership of the estate conveyed that is superior to the grantor's title. The covenant of right to convey is breached if the grantor lacks title, *i.e.,* ownership of the estate conveyed, at the time of the grant.

Answer to Question 20

(C) If a "right of first purchase" is found to be valid, the agreement is merely a promissory restraint, the breach of which may give Phil a cause of action against Randy's estate, but will not affect Hilda's interest unless she had knowledge of the agreement at the time she acquired her deed from Randy. Thus, alternatives (A), (B), and (D) are incorrect.

Answer to Question 21

(A) The testimony would be hearsay, but it would be admissible under the exception of a declaration of an intent to do a future act, sometimes referred to as a declaration of present mental state. [Fed. R. Evid. 803(3)] (D) is therefore incorrect. The trip provides an alibi defense and is therefore relevant; so (C) is thus incorrect. (B) is wrong because this is not a verbal act; verbal acts are out-of-court statements that when spoken have legal significance, *e.g.,* words of contract or defamation.

Answer to Question 22

(B) Although state classifications based on alienage are generally suspect, a state may reserve a government position for citizens if it is related to self-governance, involves policymaking, or requires exercise of important discretionary power over citizens. In these cases, only a rationality test is used. A public school teacher performs an important governmental function (*e.g.,* he influences students' attitudes about government, the political process, citizenship, etc.), and therefore the exclusion of aliens is rationally related to the state's interest in furthering educational goals. [Ambach v. Norwick (1979)] (C) is, accordingly, incorrect. The principle articulated in (A) is correct, but has no bearing here, where the question is whether a distinction based on alienage is permissible. (D) is true, but irrelevant; the state may deny Foley's application regardless of his ultimate intentions, so long as he remains an alien.

Answer to Question 23

(A) The clothing is circumstantial evidence because the trier of fact is being asked to draw an inference that the clothes are Digby's based on the proven fact that the clothes were found in a dumpster at Digby's building. Direct evidence is evidence that, if believed, will by itself establish one of the propositions in the case; no inference will be necessary. Thus, (B) is incorrect. (C) is incorrect because finding the clothing matching the description of the robber's clothes near Digby's apartment tends to make it more probable that Digby committed the robbery than it would be without the clothing. (D) is incorrect because it states the standard for proving guilt, not for the admissibility of evidence.

Answer to Question 24

(A) Ed should be found not guilty because he did not intend to steal. Ed did not intend to achieve the objective of the conspiracy—to permanently deprive the owner of her property—since Ed thought Ralph was the true owner of the TV. (C) is incorrect because there must be an agreement to reach an *unlawful* objective. Because Ed thought he was achieving a *lawful* objective, he did not have the intent required for conspiracy. (B) is incorrect because a "corrupt motive" is not an element of a crime. A person could be found guilty of a crime even if he did not have a corrupt motive, assuming all required elements for a crime are present. (D) is incorrect for a similar reason. "Good motive" is largely irrelevant; the intent, or lack thereof, is what is important.

Answer to Question 25

(A) The nature of the aid provided by the statute has a secular purpose, is of legitimate interest to the state, and does not present any risk of being used to aid the transmission of religious views. (B) misstates the test; this is a test that was used for the Free Exercise Clause, and this is an Establishment Clause case. (C) is incorrect because not all aid to religious schools violates the Establishment Clause. (D) has no basis in the facts given.

Answer to Question 26

(A) As soon as Deanna's boyfriend informed her that driscamine was a controlled substance and she decided to keep it, she violated the statute, since she willfully possessed a controlled substance. (B) is incorrect because the statute does not punish mere possession; the possession must be "willful." (C) is incorrect because ignorance of the law is generally no excuse. It clearly does not negate the mental state required for this statutory crime. (D) is incorrect because the statute does not punish willful acquisition but willful possession.

Answer to Question 27

(B) The objection should be overruled. It is proper to impeach a witness by showing that the witness has a possible bias. Evidence that the witness is being paid to testify would be proper impeachment through bias. (A) states the requirement for introduction of a prior inconsistent statement; this is obviously inapplicable here. The credibility of a witness is not collateral, and so (C) is incorrect. Leading questions are proper on cross-examination; thus (D) is incorrect.

Answer to Question 28

(C) A conveyance of a co-tenant's interest in joint tenancy property severs the joint tenancy, and that interest is subsequently held as a tenancy in common with the other co-tenants. Thus, (D) is incorrect. Since the joint tenancy with right of survivorship was severed before Vladimir's death, (A) is incorrect. Returning the deed to Nicholas did not return ownership of the property to him; that would require a reconveyance. Thus, (B) is incorrect.

Answer to Question 29

(C) An assignment does not release the tenant from his contractual obligations to the landlord; thus, Realty Corp. is still liable for all of the lease provisions. Thus, (D) is incorrect. An assignee is in privity of estate with the landlord and is liable on all covenants in the lease that run with the land. His assumption of these duties is implied; it need not be expressed in the assignment. Covenants to pay money run with the land, as do covenants to perform physical acts on the property. Therefore, Rasputin, Inc. is liable for both the rent and the road even if it did not expressly assume performance of the covenants. Thus, (A) and (B) are incorrect.

Answer to Question 30

(D) Nicholas had no interest in the property that he conveyed to Olga; thus, (A) is wrong. However, if Olga is a bona fide purchaser for value who records first, the deed to Alexander and Vladimir (now to Alexander and Anastasia) would not be good against Olga's. (B) and (C) are incorrect because they do not contain every element necessary for Olga to prevail.

Answer to Question 31

(B) Bernadette is likely to prevail because Danny deliberately damaged her car. A minor child will be held liable for the consequences of his intentional tortious conduct whether or not he is "aware" of the consequences of that conduct. Hence, (A) and (D) are wrong. (C) is a misstatement of the law. Danny may be liable even though he is under the care of his parents.

Answer to Question 32

(C) The only basis on which to hold the parents liable here is if they had notice of their child's dangerous tendencies. (C) is a better answer than (D) because it holds out the possibility, not negated by the facts, that Danny's parents were on notice of Danny's tendency to misbehave. (A) misstates the law; in the absence of a statute, parents are not vicariously liable for the torts of their minor children. (B) is wrong because the mere failure to keep Danny in would not by itself amount to negligence with respect to Bernadette.

Answer to Question 33

(D) This is an output contract. (A) is wrong because there is a price term, although it is dependent on future events. (B) is wrong because there are no facts that show the five years to be "unreasonable" and even if there were, parties are free to enter into unreasonable contracts. (C) is wrong because Indegas agreed to buy at least 5,000 gallons a week by the original agreement, and all the gasoline by its notice. Such output contracts are enforceable.

Answer to Question 34

(B) Although there was no consideration for Indegas to take only one-half of the bargained-for production, none is required because this is a contract for the sale of goods, and subject to U.C.C. section 2-609 (which provides that good-faith modification is enforceable regardless of lack of consideration). (C) is therefore wrong. (A) and (D) make no sense.

Answer to Question 35

(D) The lack of foreign oil did not constitute an objective impossibility of performance, since Cal-Tex's other refinery was producing gasoline. (B) is therefore wrong. The contract did not contemplate a particular refinery producing the gasoline, and therefore (A) is wrong. (C) is wrong because Indegas's knowledge was not a condition of the contract, but the purpose for entering into it.

Answer to Question 36

(B) Since delivery of gas is not personal in nature, that duty can be assigned. The quantity will be measured by Cal-Tex's original output. However, when a duty is delegated to a delegate, the delegator remains liable should the delegate fail to perform. (A) is incorrect because the contract was for five years, and five years have not yet elapsed. (C) would be correct only if Cal-Tex went out of business without delegating its duties to another by selling the other the business, not the case here. (D) is wrong because, as indicated above, such a delegation is proper.

MIXED SUBJECT SET 3
ANSWER SHEET

1. Ⓐ Ⓑ Ⓒ Ⓓ	26. Ⓐ Ⓑ Ⓒ Ⓓ
2. Ⓐ Ⓑ Ⓒ Ⓓ	27. Ⓐ Ⓑ Ⓒ Ⓓ
3. Ⓐ Ⓑ Ⓒ Ⓓ	28. Ⓐ Ⓑ Ⓒ Ⓓ
4. Ⓐ Ⓑ Ⓒ Ⓓ	29. Ⓐ Ⓑ Ⓒ Ⓓ
5. Ⓐ Ⓑ Ⓒ Ⓓ	30. Ⓐ Ⓑ Ⓒ Ⓓ
6. Ⓐ Ⓑ Ⓒ Ⓓ	31. Ⓐ Ⓑ Ⓒ Ⓓ
7. Ⓐ Ⓑ Ⓒ Ⓓ	32. Ⓐ Ⓑ Ⓒ Ⓓ
8. Ⓐ Ⓑ Ⓒ Ⓓ	33. Ⓐ Ⓑ Ⓒ Ⓓ
9. Ⓐ Ⓑ Ⓒ Ⓓ	34. Ⓐ Ⓑ Ⓒ Ⓓ
10. Ⓐ Ⓑ Ⓒ Ⓓ	35. Ⓐ Ⓑ Ⓒ Ⓓ
11. Ⓐ Ⓑ Ⓒ Ⓓ	36. Ⓐ Ⓑ Ⓒ Ⓓ
12. Ⓐ Ⓑ Ⓒ Ⓓ	37. Ⓐ Ⓑ Ⓒ Ⓓ
13. Ⓐ Ⓑ Ⓒ Ⓓ	38. Ⓐ Ⓑ Ⓒ Ⓓ
14. Ⓐ Ⓑ Ⓒ Ⓓ	39. Ⓐ Ⓑ Ⓒ Ⓓ
15. Ⓐ Ⓑ Ⓒ Ⓓ	40. Ⓐ Ⓑ Ⓒ Ⓓ
16. Ⓐ Ⓑ Ⓒ Ⓓ	41. Ⓐ Ⓑ Ⓒ Ⓓ
17. Ⓐ Ⓑ Ⓒ Ⓓ	42. Ⓐ Ⓑ Ⓒ Ⓓ
18. Ⓐ Ⓑ Ⓒ Ⓓ	43. Ⓐ Ⓑ Ⓒ Ⓓ
19. Ⓐ Ⓑ Ⓒ Ⓓ	44. Ⓐ Ⓑ Ⓒ Ⓓ
20. Ⓐ Ⓑ Ⓒ Ⓓ	45. Ⓐ Ⓑ Ⓒ Ⓓ
21. Ⓐ Ⓑ Ⓒ Ⓓ	46. Ⓐ Ⓑ Ⓒ Ⓓ
22. Ⓐ Ⓑ Ⓒ Ⓓ	47. Ⓐ Ⓑ Ⓒ Ⓓ
23. Ⓐ Ⓑ Ⓒ Ⓓ	48. Ⓐ Ⓑ Ⓒ Ⓓ
24. Ⓐ Ⓑ Ⓒ Ⓓ	49. Ⓐ Ⓑ Ⓒ Ⓓ
25. Ⓐ Ⓑ Ⓒ Ⓓ	50. Ⓐ Ⓑ Ⓒ Ⓓ

MIXED SUBJECT QUESTIONS - SET 3

Question 1

Which of the following would provide the best constitutional underpinning for federal legislation requiring that state and local police departments receiving financial assistance from the Federal Law Enforcement Assistance Agency devote a specified amount of those resources to combatting "white-collar" crimes?

(A) The power to enforce the penal statutes of the United States.

(B) The police power.

(C) The war and defense power.

(D) The power to tax and spend for the general welfare.

Question 2

Pauline sought psychiatric treatment from Donald, a psychiatrist. During his treatment, which consisted of hour-long analysis sessions twice a week, Donald, unknown to Pauline, videotaped her. No sound recording was made of the sessions, but Donald was conducting a study on "body language" and planned to use the videotapes in those experiments. Pauline learned that Donald had been videotaping their analysis sessions and brought an action against him for battery.

If Pauline does not prevail as to this theory, it will probably be because:

(A) She did not suffer any injury as the result of Donald's actions.

(B) Donald had an implied consent to take the actions he did as part of the patient-physician privilege.

(C) She did not suffer an offensive touching.

(D) Donald intended that his actions would foster medical research.

Questions 3-6 are based on the following fact situation:

Frank, doing business as Cleveland Business Machines, agreed with Herbert, an accountant, to lease to Herbert a small business computer system, provide software and support, and maintain the system. Their oral agreement included that the lease would be for a term of three years, and that Herbert would pay a monthly charge of $500 for all services. Frank and Herbert further agreed that $100 of the monthly charge would be paid by Herbert directly to Noel, in satisfaction of a debt Frank owed him.

Frank prepared a written copy of the agreement on his own word processor, but accidentally printed the monthly rental and service charge as $400 rather than $500. He did not include the agreement that called for the direct payment to Noel in the written copy. Frank sent the copy of the written agreement, signed by him, to Herbert, who also signed it without discovering the error in the amount of the monthly rental and service charge.

3.   If Herbert refused to make any payments to Noel, and the latter brings an action against Herbert for damages as a consequence, which of the following, if true, would be most harmful to Noel?

(A) The obligation of Frank to Noel was subject to a statute of limitations which had run prior to the date the agreement between Frank and Herbert was first discussed.

(B) Noel never notified Frank or Herbert that he accepted their agreement to have Herbert make payments to him.

(C) No consideration supported the obligation owed by Frank to Noel.

(D) Before Noel learned of the agreement between Frank and Herbert, they agreed that Herbert would pay the entire $500 directly to Frank.

4.   In Noel's action against Herbert, which of the following, if any, are correct?

   I.   Enforcement of the agreement for Herbert to pay $100 per month is precluded by the Statute of Frauds because the agreement was to answer for the debt of another.

   II.   Herbert could successfully raise the Statute of Frauds because his agreement with Frank could not by its terms be performed within one year.

   (A) I. only.

   (B) II. only.

   (C) Both I. and II.

   (D) Neither I. nor II.

5.   If Noel brings an action against Herbert, which of the following will have the greatest effect on the outcome?

   (A) Whether Noel was a party to the agreement between Frank and Herbert.

   (B) Whether the agreement between Frank and Herbert was completely integrated.

   (C) Whether Frank was negligent in not discovering that the agreement omitted mention of the payment of money directly to Noel.

   (D) Whether Herbert was negligent in not discovering that the agreement omitted mention of the payment of money directly to Noel.

6.   Herbert refused to pay more than $400 per month for rental of the computer system and ancillary services. If Frank brings an action for the difference between the payment as orally agreed and as memorialized in the contract, which of the following, if proven, would most benefit Frank?

   (A) The parties made a mistake in integration.

   (B) The writing was only a partial integration.

   (C) The writing was intended as a sham.

   (D) Frank or Herbert misunderstood the amount the rental and service payment was to be.

Questions 7-8 are based on the following fact situation:

   Blackwood and Redwood were two adjoining undeveloped tracts of land. Art owned Blackwood, and Baker owned Redwood. Art decided to develop a recreational facility that would be open to the public on Blackwood. He prepared a development plan outlining the areas on Blackwood designated for recreational use. The plan provided for main access to the facility to be by way of a road to be constructed around the perimeter of Blackwood and to be known as Circle Drive. The plan was fully approved by all necessary governmental agencies and duly recorded. However, construction of the facility and of Circle Drive has not yet begun, and according to a local ordinance, Circle Drive cannot be opened as a public way until construction is finished on the recreational facility. Baker for many years had attempted to sell Redwood. However, since Redwood had no access to any public roadway except a narrow gravel road that was in very poor condition, its market value was minimal. Baker knew that he could sell Redwood for a higher price if he improved the access road, but to do so would cost a great deal of money.

   Shortly after Art's plans for development of Blackwood were announced, Baker sold Redwood to Carl. The description used in the deed from Baker to Carl was the same as that used in prior deeds except that the portion of the description that formerly said, "thence by land of Art South Easternly at a distance of 250 feet more or less" was changed to "thence by Circle Drive as laid out on the plan of Blackwood,

South 10 degrees East 254 feet," with full reference to the plan and recording data. Carl now seeks a building permit that would allow him to construct access from Redwood to Circle Drive. Art objects to the granting of the building permit on the grounds that he never granted any rights to Baker or Carl to use Circle Drive. There are no applicable statutes dealing with this situation. Carl brings an appropriate action to determine his rights to build an access connecting Redwood and Circle Drive.

7.   The best argument for Art in this action is that:

(A)   The Statute of Frauds prevents the introduction of evidence that might prove the necessity for Carl to use Circle Drive.

(B)   Carl would be unjustly enriched if he were permitted to use Circle Drive.

(C)   Carl's right must await the action of appropriate public authorities to open Circle Drive as a public street since no private easement arose by implication.

(D)   Carl's right to use Circle Drive is restricted to the assertion of a way by necessity, and the facts preclude the success of such a claim.

8.   The best argument for Carl in this action is that:

(A)   The deed from Baker to Carl referred to the recorded plan and therefore created rights to use this street delineated on the plan.

(B)   The recording of the plan is a dedication of the street shown on the plan to public use.

(C)   There is a way by necessity over Blackwood to gain access to a public road.

(D)   The fact that Carl could only gain access to Redwood by expending a large amount of money to repair and improve the one-lane gravel road creates a sufficient need for an easement across Blackwood to gain access to a public road.

Question 9

Joseph, angered because a rival gang member had twice beaten him up after school, obtained a heavy length of lead pipe and waited in a deserted alleyway which he knew the rival took as a route home every day after school. When his enemy came walking down the alley, Joseph leapt out behind him and smashed the pipe into the victim's head, knocking him to the ground. Joseph then rolled the victim over and pounded his face with 15 to 20 heavy blows with the lead pipe, killing him. The jurisdiction defines first degree murder as murder committed with premeditation and deliberation. All other murders are defined as second degree murders.

If Joseph is convicted of first degree murder (as opposed to second degree murder), it will be because:

(A)   The nature of the acts causing death distinguishes Joseph's action as first degree murder.

(B)   The degree of causative relationship between Joseph's acts and the death of the victim renders it murder of the first degree.

(C)   The relationship between Joseph and the victim requires that a finding of first degree murder be made.

(D)   Joseph's mental state up to and including the moment of the attack determines that the act is first degree murder.

Question 10

Louise is on trial for arson of the restaurant owned by her sister. Chemical tests by the fire department indicate that gasoline was used as the igniting agent of the fire. The prosecution calls to the stand Shari, a waitress who works at an all-night diner near the burned restaurant. She will testify that on the night of the fire, Louise came into the diner and ordered a cup of coffee, and that Louise smelled like gasoline.

Should the court admit this testimony over Louise's objection?

(A) No, it is inadmissible as the opinion of a nonexpert witness.

(B) No, it is inadmissible because the best evidence is the result of the chemical tests.

(C) Yes, it is admissible lay opinion testimony.

(D) Yes, it is admissible expert testimony because everyone who drives a car is an expert as to the smell of gasoline.

Questions 11-14 are based on the following fact situation:

In certain parts of the state of Pacifica, a single-family residence had become so expensive that the vast majority of families could no longer afford to buy a home of any kind, even with both husband and wife working. To alleviate this problem, the legislature enacted statutes creating a State Housing Development Corporation. This agency, organized along the lines of a private corporation, was authorized to act as general contractor and build homes in counties where the average cost of a new home exceeded by 50% the national average cost of a new home, then to sell the homes at the cost of materials and labor to first-time homebuyers. The national average cost of a new home at all relevant times was $74,000. In Midvalleyville, a medium-sized city in the middle of Pacifica, the average cost of a new home was $84,000. In Metropolis, a large city on the coast of Pacifica, the average cost of a new home was $135,000. The State Housing Development Corporation began building and selling homes in Metropolis, but did not operate in Midvalleyville.

11. About 35% of the population of Midvalleyville is of Armenian ethnicity. Sassoonian, of Armenian heritage, brings a class action

against the state seeking to have the State Housing Development Corporation's failure to operate in Midvalleyville declared a violation of the right to equal protection of the Armenian citizens of that city. What fact would be most helpful for Sassoonian in challenging the statute?

(A) The state could have permitted the housing corporation to build and sell homes in all areas of the state.

(B) Armenian citizens experience difficulty in affording single-family residences.

(C) The legislation setting up the housing corporation was intended to discriminate against Armenian citizens.

(D) The percentage of Armenian citizens is much higher in Midvalleyville than in Metropolis.

12. Rocky, a general contractor who builds and sells homes in Metropolis, discovers that his business has fallen off about 30% since the State Housing Development Corporation started doing business in Metropolis. He brings an action seeking to enjoin the operation of the State Housing Development Corporation. What will be the probable outcome of this litigation?

(A) Rocky will win, because operation of a state agency in competition with a private business violates the Due Process Clause of the Fourteenth Amendment.

(B) Rocky will win, because permitting some citizens to purchase from a state corporation while others purchase from private businesses violates the Equal Protection Clause of the Fourteenth Amendment.

(C) Rocky will lose, because he lacks standing to challenge the legislation, having suffered no direct injury.

(D) Rocky will lose, because the State Housing Development Corporation is a valid exercise of the state's powers.

13. Citizens for Fair Housing, a group of Midvalleyville residents, brings an action in federal court seeking to compel the State Housing Development Corporation to begin operations in Midvalleyville. What will be the probable outcome of this litigation?

(A) The action will be dismissed, because the state is immune from litigation under the Eleventh Amendment.

(B) The action will be dismissed, because the housing corporation is organized as a private business and thus does not engage in any state action.

(C) The state will prevail, because it has a rational basis for not operating in Midvalleyville.

(D) The citizens will prevail, because the state cannot show a compelling state interest in not operating in Mid-valleyville.

14. Assume for the purposes of this question only that the federal government has enacted legislation operative for the relevant period that regulates the manner in which building contractors conduct business. Is the State Housing Development Corporation subject to these federal regulations?

(A) No, because its activities take place entirely within the state.

(B) No, because as an agency of state government, it is immune from federal regulation.

(C) No, because the federal government is not empowered to enact legislation regulating state governments or their agencies.

(D) Yes.

Question 15

A city ordinance required that all dogs be leashed when taken outside of an enclosed area. Bee often allowed her dog, Bop, to run loose in front of Bee's house. One day, when Bop was running loose, Dina was driving her car up the street in front of Bee's house. The day was clear and sunny and Dina was driving carefully at a speed somewhat below the posted limit. Bop dashed out into the street from between two parked cars. Dina alertly applied her brakes, but could not avoid striking Bop. Pris, driving another vehicle behind Dina, promptly applied her brakes as soon as she saw the red lights glow on the rear of Dina's vehicle. However, Pris's vehicle struck the rear of Dina's vehicle. Both of the vehicles suffered damage and both drivers suffered minor injuries which required x-rays and other medical attention.

If Pris sues Dina for her vehicle damage and personal injuries, Pris will:

(A) Prevail, because the ordinance was designed to prevent dogs from being hit by cars.

(B) Prevail, because Dina was a proximate cause of the accident.

(C) Not prevail, because Dina obeyed the traffic laws.

(D) Not prevail, unless Dina herself was negligent.

Questions 16-19 are based on the following fact situation:

Joann entered into a written lease-option to purchase Norm's house. Under the terms of the agreement, Joann was to pay a fixed monthly rent plus all taxes and reasonable maintenance charges for the upkeep of the house. The option to purchase the home could be exercised at any time during the five-year term of the lease by giving Norm a written 30-day notice of the intent to exercise the option.

About three years after Norm entered into the lease, he died, leaving his entire estate to his late wife's sister, Sara. Several days before Norm's death, Joann had assigned her lease-option to Al by written agreement. Although Joann properly set forth the terms concerning the option, she failed to properly state that Al was liable to pay the real property taxes on the residence during the period of the lease.

16. Sara was informed that there was a tax lien on the residence. She paid the lien and brought suit against Al for the amount. Judgment for:

    (A) Al, because under the terms of his assignment with Joann he is not liable for the taxes.

    (B) Al, because the agreement to pay taxes was collateral, and thus is not a covenant running with the land.

    (C) Al, because in order for the agreement to be a covenant running with the land it must be expressly stated in the original agreement.

    (D) Sara, because payment of property taxes touches and concerns the land.

17. Al became very upset because Sara brought suit against him for the taxes, and he abandoned the residence. Can Sara bring a suit against Joann for this breach of the lease?

    (A) No, because Joann is no longer a tenant.

    (B) No, because Joann was not a tenant at the time Sara gained her interest in the property.

    (C) Yes, because Joann's assignment to Al did not terminate her obligations.

    (D) Yes, because Joann had caused the problem by failing to include the tax payment provisions in her assignment.

18. If Al had fully performed under the lease, including paying the taxes, could Al exercise the option to purchase that was given to Joann?

    (A) Yes, because both the burden and benefit of the covenant to convey run with the land.

    (B) No, because the covenant to convey does not touch or concern the land.

    (C) No, because the option to purchase was personal to Joann.

    (D) No, because the burden of the covenant to convey given in a lease does not run with the land.

19. Assume that instead of abandoning the premises, Al assigned the lease to Howard. If Howard fails to pay the rent, including payment of taxes, can Sara bring suit against Al to recover this money?

    (A) Yes, because Al remains in privity of estate with Sara.

    (B) Yes, because Al remains in privity of contract with Sara.

    (C) No, because Al is no longer in privity of estate with Sara.

    (D) No, because the fact that Joann was allowed to assign the lease means that Al is allowed to assign it also.

Question 20

Boss operated his own consulting firm from an office in his home. Dexter was one of several people Boss employed at his office. Dexter asked if he could stay late one night and type on Boss's computer a short story he had written. Boss replied, "Sure. I hate that machine. Consider it yours. I am getting a new one tomorrow." Dexter mistakenly believed that Boss was giving Dexter the computer. Dexter waited to take it home until he could borrow a car because it was too unwieldy to carry on the bus.

The next week, Boss's business took a dramatic turn for the worse, and Boss was forced to lay off all of his employees, effective immediately.

Since he no longer had a job, Dexter spent all of his time finishing his novel. He finished the novel late one night and thought he would get started typing it up right away. He borrowed his roommate's car and went to Boss's house to pick up the computer. Not wishing to wake anyone up at the late hour, Dexter went to the door leading directly to the office. It was unlocked, so he let himself in and took the computer.

The next day, Boss reported the computer as stolen, and the police arrested Dexter. Dexter can be convicted of:

(A) Burglary.

(B) Attempted burglary.

(C) Larceny.

(D) None of the above.

Question 21

In a civil action for personal injuries, Paul asserts that he was injured when Dawn negligently operated her motor vehicle and caused it to strike Paul's vehicle when both cars were being driven along Main Street, the principal north-south arterial street in Humberton. The accident occurred the previous July 15.

Concerning the following facts that arise during the trial, to which is it most appropriate for the judge trying the case to apply the doctrine of judicial notice?

(A) On July 15, the pavement on Main Street was wet, based on the judge's recollection that he had to cancel a golfing engagement on July 15 because it was raining heavily.

(B) Main Street runs in a north-south direction, based on information generally known by residents of Humberton.

(C) The brakes on Dawn's car were faulty, based on the uncontroverted testimony of Dawn's auto mechanic and an automotive engineer testifying as an expert for the plaintiff.

(D) Dawn was exceeding the speed limit when the accident occurred, based upon the testimony of Paul, two credible eyewitnesses, and the police officer who examined the skid marks, controverted by the testimony of Dawn and the nervous and rather unsure testimony of Walt, who was a passenger in Dawn's car.

Question 22

State A's penal statutes contain the following: "Any person who commits a battery upon a state official knowing that the victim is a state official shall be punished by imprisonment in the county jail for not more than one year or fined not more than $5,000, or both." While picking up his unemployment check at the state office building, Rod got into an argument with a man wearing a brown suit and angrily shoved the man against the wall, causing him no injuries. The man Rod shoved was the director of the state department of unemployment, and Rod is prosecuted under the penal statute quoted.

Rod admits that he shoved the victim intentionally, but denies that he knew the man was a state official. The jury should return a verdict of:

(A) Not guilty, if they find that the state should have warned Rod that the victim was an official, even though they do not believe Rod's testimony.

(B) Guilty, even if they believe Rod, because this is a public welfare offense.

(C) Not guilty, if they believe Rod's testimony.

(D) Guilty, regardless of whether they believe Rod or not, because he admitted that he intentionally shoved the victim.

Question 23

In Amy's civil suit for personal injuries against her stepfather, arising from acts of sexual abuse allegedly committed by him against her when she was a minor, Amy calls as a witness a police officer who will testify that, 11 years ago, the stepfather confessed to the witness that he had committed the acts complained of by Amy.

Should the trial court admit the police officer's testimony over the stepfather's objection?

(A) Yes, because past instances of misconduct may be used to impeach a witness.

(B) Yes, because the stepfather's confession is an admission of a party-opponent.

(C) No, because the best evidence of a conviction is the judgment of the court that convicted him.

(D) No, because the sexual assault that is the subject of the evidence is more than 10 years old.

Question 24

During the Miss Metropolis competition, the judges announced that Wilma was first runner-up and that Kerry was the winner. As the auditorium quieted for Kerry's acceptance remarks, Wilma said loudly, "You only won because you slept with all of the judges, you slut!" Kerry immediately slapped Wilma forcefully in the face.

Wilma brings an action for battery against Kerry. Who will prevail?

(A) Kerry, because she was provoked by Wilma's comment.

(B) Kerry, because a reasonable person would have slapped Wilma under the circumstances.

(C) Wilma, unless Kerry's slap was totally spontaneous.

(D) Wilma, because Kerry intentionally caused an offensive touching.

Questions 25-26 are based on the following fact situation:

Producer hired Fiddler to play in an orchestra that was to leave on a 10-week tour of the United States. Fiddler, a musician, turned down another job opportunity in order to accept Producer's job offer. One week after the start of the tour, Fiddler was hospitalized with a bad back and was unable to perform. Producer hired Player to take Fiddler's part in the orchestra. Four days later, Fiddler recovered but Producer refused to allow Fiddler to rejoin the orchestra or to complete the tour. Fiddler then sued Producer for breach of contract.

25. Which of the following is Fiddler's best legal theory?

(A) His reliance on the job offered by Producer by declining another job opportunity created an estoppel against Producer.

(B) His failure to perform with the orchestra for four days was not a material failure so as to discharge Producer's duty to perform.

(C) His performance with the orchestra for the four-day period was physically impossible.

(D) Fiddler was never told that an injury might jeopardize his continued employment with the orchestra.

26. Which of the following, if true, would adversely affect Fiddler's rights in his action against Producer?

(A) Most of the orchestra members felt that Player was a better addition to the orchestra than Fiddler.

(B) Producer had offered Fiddler a job in the ticket office at a higher salary but Fiddler had declined.

(C) Producer could not find any substitute except Player, who demanded a contract for a minimum of 10 weeks if he was to perform at all.

(D) Fiddler was not pleased about his continued employment by Producer because he did not like to travel.

Question 27

Hagler owned Greenacre, a 30-acre tract of land divided into three 10-acre segments. Hagler built a home on one of the segments and used the middle segment to raise crops. The third 10-acre segment remained undeveloped. The undeveloped 10-acre segment was covered by a number of small trees. Hagler decided to subdivide the undeveloped 10-acre segment into seven lots suitable for single-family residences. The first step in the development was the removal of the trees. Neighbor, who lived next to Hagler, knew that Hagler intended to remove the trees from his property. Because he needed firewood, Neighbor decided to cut down several of the trees on Hagler's property. The day before development was to start on Hagler's property, Neighbor went onto Hagler's land, cut down a number of trees, cut the wood into fireplace-sized pieces, and moved them onto his property. Hagler brought an appropriate action against Neighbor for damages.

Hagler most likely will:

(A) Recover only nominal damages, because the value of the land was not diminished.

(B) Recover nominal damages and the value of the trees removed.

(C) Not recover, because removal of the trees saved Hagler money in the development of the land.

(D) Not recover, because the value of the land was not diminished by the removal of the trees.

Question 28

Jack has brought an action for personal injuries against Store, in connection with an incident in which Jack slipped and fell after Store's linoleum floors had been mopped. A major issue at trial is the degree of moisture that remained on the floor, since it had been mopped 45 minutes before Jack walked on it. Store offers the testimony of Edgar, who will tell about an experiment he conducted measuring the amount of time necessary for a linoleum floor to dry completely after having been mopped.

Should the court admit this testimony?

(A) Yes, if a representative of Jack was present when the experiment was conducted.

(B) Yes, if it is shown that the conditions of Edgar's experiment were substantially similar to the conditions of Store's floor when Jack slipped.

(C) Yes, if Jack was given an opportunity to conduct his own experiment with the same type of linoleum used by Edgar.

(D) Yes, if it is shown that Edgar is not an employee or otherwise related in interest to Store.

Question 29

Two days before the junior prom, Brenda was horrified to discover that her cat had clawed the back of her taffeta prom dress. She hurried to Zelda's Tailoring Shop where she explained her predicament to Zelda. Zelda assured her she could make the gown as good as new for $175. Brenda knew she could not pay Zelda $175 but asked her to do the work anyway. Zelda worked furiously and phoned Brenda at 4:30 the following afternoon to let her know the dress was ready. Brenda told Zelda she would be by the next morning to pick the dress up and pay for the work. After talking to Zelda, Brenda telephoned her best friend Cheryl and promised Cheryl that if she would stop by Zelda's shop after 5 p.m. and pick up Brenda's gown, Cheryl could dance with Brenda's boyfriend Newt at the prom. (Brenda knew that Zelda would be gone by that time and that Milt, the always intoxicated janitor, would hand the gown over with no questions asked.) Brenda forged a claim ticket and gave it to Cheryl to show to Milt. Cheryl did as Brenda asked and picked up the gown from Milt and gave it to Brenda.

Cheryl will be found not guilty of taking the gown from Zelda's shop because:

(A) Brenda was the principal in the conspiracy to obtain the gown without payment.

(B) She was acting under Brenda's direction.

(C) Milt, whom Cheryl knew was intoxicated, handed over the gown without asking questions.

(D) She sincerely believed that Zelda was expecting the gown to be picked up without money changing hands.

Question 30

Donamae lived alone except for her large Persian cat, "Fluffkins," in a single-family home in a fine subdivision in prosperous Lime County. Although Donamae had never had any problems with crime in the area, she bought a handgun to protect herself.

One night at about 11 p.m., Donamae heard a strange noise. She put on a robe, took the gun from her nightstand, and proceeded down her stairs, as her bedroom was located on the second floor of her house.

At about the same time, Donamae's next-door neighbor, Nathaniel, also heard a strange noise. He walked out of his house and onto Donamae's lawn, because he thought the sound came from the direction of Donamae's abode. He stood silently on Donamae's lawn, listening.

As Donamae reached the last step, Fluffkins playfully charged down the stairs. The 15-pound cat struck the back of Donamae's legs, causing her to lose her balance. Although Donamae did not fall, her loss of balance caused her to drop the gun. The gun hit the floor and discharged. The bullet went through Donamae's front window and struck Nathaniel in the shoulder.

If Nathaniel sues Donamae on a battery theory, he will:

(A) Prevail, because handguns are highly dangerous instrumentalities.

(B) Prevail, because the cat's actions are imputed to Donamae.

(C) Lose, because the firing of the gun was a nonvolitional act.

(D) Lose, because Nathaniel was a trespasser.

Question 31

Darrell was out for his daily morning walk. While walking, Darrell noticed that Tim, a long-lost friend he had not seen in years, was walking in the opposite direction. Darrell started waving his arms in a desperate attempt to get Tim's attention. Unfortunately, Darrell did not notice Violet, who was walking past him, and negligently struck Violet with his elbow with sufficient force to cause her to stumble to the pavement. The fall did not, however, cause Violet any major injury.

If Darrell is prosecuted for criminal battery, he will probably be found:

(A) Not guilty, because Darrell's act did not cause serious bodily injury.

(B) Not guilty, because Darrell did not have the mental state required for criminal battery.

(C) Guilty, because Darrell failed to exercise due care in flailing his arms about near a public sidewalk.

(D) Guilty, because Darrell caused an offensive touching.

Question 32

Office Building, Inc. contracted to build a large, multistory building for a client and began construction through various subcontractors. Mid-State Excavators, Inc. dug the excavation for the foundation and basement levels as called for by the plans, and Acme Engineering, a partnership, began work on the foundation. Just after the foundation was completed, Jed, an employee of the subcontractor doing structural work, was killed when one of the walls of the excavation collapsed, burying him under tons of soil.

Jed's survivors brought an appropriate action against all of the involved parties, and each defendant cross-complained for indemnity against each of the other defendants. At trial, Acme Engineering calls Willis, a civil engineer licensed by the state, who is prepared to testify that he examined the geologist's reports of the soil conditions surrounding the construction site, plus a report by the engineer who retrieved Jed's body and examined the site of the collapse, and that it is his (Willis's) opinion that the collapse of the wall of the excavation was caused by Mid-State Excavators' failure to take into consideration the composition of the soil being excavated, rather than any defects in the shoring constructed by Acme.

Is Willis's testimony admissible?

(A) Yes, if civil engineers in his field rely upon such materials as plans and reports by geologists and others in reaching conclusions such as his.

(B) Yes, if he was not professionally negligent in his analysis.

(C) No, because his opinion relates to an ultimate issue that must be determined in the case.

(D) No, because his opinion was based upon facts not personally within his knowledge.

Question 33

Congress created by statute the Small Business Administration Appeals Tribunal, which was empowered to review claims made by clients of the SBA and make recommendations to the agency regarding their merits. Agnew was properly appointed to the Tribunal. Six years later, the Tribunal was abolished by repeal of the authorizing legislation, and Agnew was offered an administrative position in the Department of Transportation at a lower salary. Agnew has now brought an action against the federal government on the grounds that Congress may not remove a federal judge from office during good behavior nor decrease his salary during continuance in office. Counsel for the government has made a motion to dismiss.

The trial court should rule:

(A) For the government, because Agnew was not an Article III judge and is not entitled to life tenure.

(B) For the government, because Agnew lacked standing to raise the question.

(C) For Agnew, because he has established a property right to his position on the Tribunal.

(D) For Agnew, because of the independence of the federal judiciary constitutionally guaranteed by Article III.

Questions 34-37 are based on the following fact situation:

Shortly after a series of rapes took place within Big City, the city council of Big City approved the offering of a $25,000 reward for the arrest and conviction of anyone guilty of the rapes. Information concerning the reward was broadcast by Big City's sole radio station once daily for one week. Shortly thereafter, Karen, a victim of one of the rape attacks, hired Stevens, a private detective, to find the person responsible for perpetrating the rapes. Karen had agreed to pay Stevens $100 for each day spent investigating the rapes. The next year, the city council of

Big City passed a resolution repealing its reward offer. The city council caused this resolution to be telecast once daily for a week over Big City's local television station, the local radio station, meanwhile, having ceased operations. One month later, Philip voluntarily confessed to Stevens to having committed all of the earlier rapes. Philip was arrested and ultimately convicted of all the rapes. Karen thereupon paid Stevens at the agreed-on rate and suggested also that Stevens claim the city's $25,000 reward, of which Stevens had been previously unaware. Stevens immediately made the claim. The city refused to pay Stevens anything, although he swears that he never heard of the city's repeal of the reward offer before claiming the reward. Assume that Big City has no immunity to suit.

34. In which of the following ways could Big City's reward offer be effectively accepted?

(A) Only by an offeree's making the arrest and assisting in the successful conviction of a rapist within the scope of the offer.

(B) Only by an offeree's return promise to make a reasonable effort to bring about the arrest and conviction of a rapist within the scope of the offer.

(C) By an offeree's communication of assent through the same medium (radio) used by the city in making its offer.

(D) By an offeree's supplying information leading to arrest and conviction of a rapist within the scope of the offer.

35. If Big City's reward offer was revocable, revocation could be effectively accomplished only:

(A) In the same manner as made or by a comparable medium and frequency of publicity.

(B) In the same manner as made only.

(C) By simply passing the resolution, since the events that transpired at the city council meeting are considered to be of public notice.

(D) By notice mailed to all residents of the city and all other reasonably identifiable potential offerees.

36. If Stevens sues Big City to recover the $25,000 reward, which of the following would be most helpful to Stevens?

(A) Big City was benefited by Stevens's services.

(B) The attempted revocation of the reward was against public policy.

(C) Big City's offer was in the nature of a bounty so that the elements of contract are not essential to the city's liability.

(D) Big City is estopped from denying the reward to Stevens because he acted in the public interest.

37. If Stevens sues Big City to recover the $25,000 reward, which of the following would be least helpful to Big City?

(A) The consideration furnished by Stevens, if any, for the city's reward promise, was legally insufficient under the preexisting duty rule.

(B) Stevens was already compensated by Karen for his investigative services.

(C) Big City's offer had effectively been revoked prior to Stevens's attempted acceptance.

(D) Stevens failed to communicate his acceptance of the offer to Big City.

Questions 38-39 are based on the following fact situation:

Gardner purchased a new riding lawn mower, manufactured by Lawn Co., from Garden Center.

Gardner decided to use the lawn mower that afternoon to mow her lawn. Although the instructions recommended against it, Gardner ran the mower at full throttle around her yard because she was in a hurry to finish. As she was nearing the edge of her property, she attempted to turn the mower. However, the steering wheel locked and she was unable to turn. Unable to stop in time, she hit her neighbor, Bystrom, who was watching from his property. The collision caused the mower to overturn. Both Bystrom and Gardner were injured. Assume that the jurisdiction follows traditional contributory negligence rules.

38. If Gardner asserts a claim against Garden Center based on strict liability in tort, will Gardner prevail?

   (A) Yes, because the steering locked while Gardner was riding the mower.

   (B) Yes, if the steering locked because of a defect present when the mower left the factory at Lawn Co.

   (C) No, if Gardner contributed to her own injury by running the mower at full throttle.

   (D) No, if Garden Center carefully inspected the mower before selling it.

39. If Bystrom asserts a claim based on negligence against Lawn Co., and if it is established that the locking of the steering wheel resulted from a manufacturing defect in the mower, will Bystrom prevail?

   (A) Yes, because Lawn Co. placed a defective product into the stream of commerce.

   (B) Yes, if the defect could have been discovered through the exercise of reasonable care by Lawn Co.

   (C) No, because Bystrom was not a purchaser of the mower.

   (D) No, if Gardner was negligent in running the mower at full throttle.

Question 40

Deft drove his automobile into the intersection and struck Plain, a pedestrian. Deft immediately left his car and ran to Plain. Before the ambulance arrived, Deft said to Plain, "It was all my fault; I'm sorry I ran the red light." (Statement 1) "I'll pay for all your medical expenses." (Statement 2)

Plain sued Deft for his injuries and, at the resulting trial, Plain wished to testify to the two statements made by Deft. The defense objected.

The court should rule:

(A) Both Statement 1 and Statement 2 are admissible.

(B) Statement 1 is admissible; Statement 2 is inadmissible.

(C) Statement 1 is inadmissible; Statement 2 is admissible.

(D) Neither Statement 1 nor Statement 2 is admissible.

Question 41

Shortly before their wedding, Harvey and Winona bought Pinkacre, taking title in both names. They had intended to build a summer cottage there, but many years after their marriage Pinkacre was still a vacant lot. Harvey decided that their introverted son, Sampson, would have more confidence if he were a landowner; thus, Harvey drew up a deed conveying a one-quarter interest in Pinkacre to Sampson. Not wanting to show favoritism, two weeks later, Harvey drew up a deed conveying a one-quarter interest in Pinkacre to their daughter, Delilah.

Who owns Pinkacre?

(A) Harvey and Winona share ownership of Pinkacre with rights of survivorship, and Sampson and Delilah have no interests.

(B) Sampson has a one-quarter interest, Delilah has a one-quarter interest, and Winona has a one-half interest.

(C) Sampson has a one-quarter interest, Delilah has a one-quarter interest, and Winona has a one-half interest, with rights of survivorship.

(D) Winona owns Pinkacre.

Question 42

As Velma was walking home on a dark cloudy night, a man came upon her from behind and stole her purse. Dirk was arrested nearby shortly thereafter. After Dirk had been booked, the police took his photograph. They then showed Dirk's photograph, along with the photographs of four people who had the same general features as Dirk, to Velma. Velma identified Dirk as the culprit. At trial, after Velma had identified Dirk as the person who stole her purse, Dirk's attorney objects to the prosecution's introduction into evidence of the photograph identification.

The objection will most likely be:

(A) Denied.

(B) Sustained, because Dirk's right to counsel was violated at the showing of the photograph to Velma.

(C) Sustained, because Velma did not have a good opportunity to observe the culprit.

(D) Sustained, because a photograph identification must be considered a critical stage of the proceeding.

Question 43

The state of New Calexico requires all businesses engaged in any form of retail sales to be licensed. The state legislature amended the statutes governing licensing so that any business seeking a license to engage in retail sales must establish that at least 40% of the items sold will be manufactured or produced within the state.

Which of the following constitutional provisions will provide the best basis upon which to attack the validity of the state licensing provision requiring a minimum percentage of local goods?

(A) The Privileges and Immunities Clause of the Fourteenth Amendment.

(B) The Commerce Clause.

(C) The Equal Protection Clause.

(D) The Due Process Clause of the Fourteenth Amendment.

Question 44

While on routine patrol late one night, Officer Heart noticed that a car, driven by Daniels, was weaving recklessly across several lanes of traffic. Officer Heart stopped Daniels, believing that he was driving while intoxicated. By state law, Officer Heart was empowered to arrest Daniels and take him to the nearest police station for booking. Officer Heart arrested Daniels and then searched Daniels's vehicle looking for evidence of alcohol consumption. In the glove compartment, Officer Heart discovered a vial containing a small amount of cocaine. Daniels was charged with possession of cocaine. At trial, Daniels's attorney moves to prevent introduction of the cocaine into evidence on the grounds that the search violated his client's federal constitutional rights.

This motion will most likely be:

(A) Denied, because Officer Heart was acting under a fear for his own personal safety.

(B) Denied, because the search was incident to a valid custodial arrest.

(C) Granted, because Officer Heart needed a warrant to search the glove compartment.

(D) Granted, because there was no reasonable or proper basis on which to justify conducting the search.

Question 45

Carla was injured when the car she was driving was struck by a truck driven by Elwood and owned by Art's Freight Lines. Carla brings an action for personal injuries against Art's. The complaint alleges that Elwood was drunk at the time of the accident and that Art's was negligent in hiring him and permitting him to drive knowing that he had a drinking problem and convictions for drunk driving.

Elwood is called as a witness by Art's and is expected to testify that he was not drunk at the time of the accident. Instead, Elwood states on direct examination that he had had several beers as he drove his truck that evening and was "really high" when his truck struck Carla's car. The counsel for Art's wants to confront Elwood with his deposition testimony that he was "stone cold sober" at the time of the accident.

Will this be permitted?

(A) No, the statement is hearsay not within any recognized exception.

(B) No, Art's cannot impeach its own witness.

(C) Yes, but it may be used only to refresh Elwood's recollection.

(D) Yes, it can be used to impeach and as substantive evidence that Elwood was sober.

Question 46

A federal statute was enacted that provided federal funds to open child health care centers in inner-city areas. The strongest constitutional basis for this enactment is the:

(A) Commerce Clause.

(B) Equal Protection Clause.

(C) Taxing and Spending Clause.

(D) General federal police powers.

Question 47

Art had been hospitalized for several weeks suffering from a very rare blood disorder, which had proven to be fatal in most cases. It was determined that Art's life could be saved only by undergoing a new treatment developed by Doctor. However, Doctor was the only person capable of administering the treatment. It was, therefore, arranged that Art would fly to the city where Doctor would perform the treatment. The day before Art was to leave, Sarah, who was Art's sole heir and stood to inherit from him, poisoned him. The poison produced a reaction that required postponement of the journey. The plane on which Art was to have flown crashed and all aboard were killed. The next day Art died from the combined effects of the poison and the blood disorder. Sarah was arrested and charged with criminal homicide.

Sarah should be found:

(A) Not guilty, because the poison was not the sole cause of death.

(B) Not guilty, because Art would have died anyway if Sarah had not poisoned him.

(C) Not guilty, because her actions resulted in postponing Art's death by one day.

(D) Guilty.

Question 48

Ellen is suing Burger Pub for injuries she suffered when she fell after slipping on a wet spot on the floor of the restaurant. At trial, Ellen introduced evidence that someone had spilled a drink on the floor and that an employee had just finished mopping up the spill before Ellen walked over the wet spot and fell, injuring her back. Ellen then calls Paul, Burger Pub's manager, as a hostile witness, and attempts to elicit testimony that, after her fall, Burger Pub instituted a policy requiring that bright yellow signs with red letters stating "CAUTION, WET FLOOR" be placed on wet spots after mopping the floor.

Will this be permitted?

(A) Yes, to establish that Burger Pub was negligent in not warning customers that the floor was wet.

(B) Yes, to show that Burger Pub was aware that a wet floor creates a hazardous condition.

(C) No, because its admission would discourage other tortfeasors from taking remedial measures.

(D) No, because it is not a proper form of impeachment.

Question 49

In an effort to preserve the family farm, Grey willed his farm to his daughter Gwendolyn. The will stated that the property would go to Gwendolyn for her life with a remainder to each of her children living at the time of Grey's death. The will further provided that "The interest of any child who attempts to mortgage or sell his or her interest shall immediately terminate and shall pass to and become the property of the remaining children of Gwendolyn who are alive at the time of my death, in equal shares."

Several weeks later Grey died. Geoffrey, one of Gwendolyn's three children, wants to sell his interest in the farm. Gwendolyn and the two other children object to the sale.

In an action for declaratory relief by Geoffrey that the stated restriction on the sale is void, what would be the probable result?

(A) The suit would be dismissed, because Geoffrey has no interest in the property.

(B) The gift to Gwendolyn's children is void in its entirety, because it violates the Rule Against Perpetuities.

(C) The restriction would be stricken, because it unlawfully restricts the alienation of real property.

(D) The restriction is proper, because all Geoffrey has is a defeasible estate.

Question 50

In response to a number of accidents involving pedestrians in the local business district, City enacted a statute making it illegal for a pedestrian to walk through City's central business district anywhere other than on the sidewalk. City also enacted a statute making it illegal for any business to obstruct the sidewalk in front of its establishment. As Turner was walking along the sidewalk in the central business district on his way to lunch, he discovered that Loader had stacked a pile of boxes in front of his establishment in such a way that it totally obstructed the sidewalk. Turner stepped into the street to walk around the obstruction of boxes. While in the street, Turner was struck by a taxicab, negligently driven by Cabbie. The jurisdiction follows traditional contributory negligence rules.

If Turner asserts a claim against Cabbie, Turner's act of leaving the sidewalk and walking into the street will have which of the following effects?

(A) It will bar Turner's recovery as a matter of law.

(B) It will bar Turner's recovery unless Cabbie saw Turner in time to avoid the impact.

(C) It may be considered by the trier of fact on the issue of Cabbie's liability.

(D) It is not relevant in determining the rights of Turner.

MIXED SUBJECT SET 3 SUBJECT GUIDE

1. Constitutional Law
2. Torts
3. Contracts
4. Contracts
5. Contracts
6. Contracts
7. Real Property
8. Real Property
9. Criminal Law
10. Evidence
11. Constitutional Law
12. Constitutional Law
13. Constitutional Law
14. Constitutional Law
15. Torts
16. Real Property
17. Real Property
18. Real Property
19. Real Property
20. Criminal Law
21. Evidence
22. Criminal Law
23. Evidence
24. Torts
25. Contracts

26. Contracts
27. Torts
28. Evidence
29. Criminal Law
30. Torts
31. Criminal Law
32. Evidence
33. Constitutional Law
34. Contracts
35. Contracts
36. Contracts
37. Contracts
38. Torts
39. Torts
40. Evidence
41. Real Property
42. Criminal Law
43. Constitutional Law
44. Criminal Law
45. Evidence
46. Constitutional Law
47. Criminal Law
48. Evidence
49. Real Property
50. Torts

MIXED SUBJECT ANSWERS - SET 3

Answer to Question 1

(D) Prior to disbursement, the federal government may attach any reasonable condition to expenditures under the general welfare power. (A) is not a power of Congress enumerated in the Constitution. There is no general federal police power, the federal government being one of limited, enumerated powers. Thus, (B) is incorrect. (C) is incorrect because the war and defense power does not apply to the facts presented.

Answer to Question 2

(C) Pauline cannot make out a case for battery because she did not experience an offensive touching. To make out a prima facie case for battery, the plaintiff must show an intentional act by the defendant that caused harmful or offensive contact to the plaintiff's person. Here, nothing indicates that Pauline was touched in any way; thus, (C) is correct. (A) is incorrect because injury is not an element of battery; battery can be established even absent a showing of injury or damages. (B) is incorrect because if the elements of battery were present, the physician-patient privilege would not protect Donald here because Pauline did not impliedly consent to the taping. When a patient consents to a doctor's treatment, she impliedly consents to all necessary touching that goes along with the treatment. However, when the doctor goes beyond the scope of the acts consented to and does something substantially different, the defense of consent is no longer available. Here, Pauline consented to talk with Donald, but that is substantially different from agreeing to be the subject of an experiment. Thus, if taping Pauline were a battery, Donald could not rely on implied consent to relieve him of liability. (D) is incorrect because a benevolent motive is not a defense to a battery. If the other elements of battery were present, the fact that the battery occurred to foster medical research would not be a defense—that would allow psychiatrists to physically strike their patients merely to study their reactions!

Answer to Question 3

(D) The parties to a contract that benefits a third party may validly modify the contract before the beneficiary learns of the contract and relies upon it to his detriment. (A) and (C) are incorrect because, if Frank intended to confer a benefit on Noel by entering into the contract with Herbert, Noel could enforce the agreement as a donee third-party beneficiary whether or not an enforceable obligation existed between Frank and Noel. (B) is incorrect because a third-party beneficiary is not obligated to notify the parties that he accepts the benefit of their agreement, especially when the agreement merely calls for the payment of money to him.

Answer to Question 4

(B) The portion of the Statute of Frauds requiring that a contract to answer for the debt of another be in writing applies only to sureties or guarantors—Herbert is not guaranteeing any debt of Frank; he is promising to pay a portion of what he will owe Frank to Noel. As to the requirement that contracts not performable by their terms within one year be in writing, the agreement to pay money to Noel could be seen as collateral to the main agreement, but since it calls for payments over the same three-year period, it is not performable within one year either.

Answer to Question 5

(B) The effect of a completely integrated agreement, meaning that the writing embodies the entire agreement of the parties, is that evidence could not be introduced to show a prior or collateral oral agreement. (A) is incorrect since Noel need not be a party to the contract since he has rights as a third-party beneficiary. (C) and (D) are incorrect since the negligence of either of the parties has no bearing on whether the collateral oral agreement can be proved or enforced.

Answer to Question 6

(A) Where the parties make a mistake in integrating their agreement into a writing, the courts will permit the error to be corrected. (B) is wrong because, while it is conceivable that the additional term ($100 to Noel) was left out, the correction of the mistake in price ($500 instead of $400) would *most* benefit Frank. If the writing was a sham, no rights would arise from it; hence, (C) is wrong. (D) is wrong because if one of the parties made a mistake as to the payment amount, he would not necessarily be entitled to relief.

Answer to Question 7

(C) Carl's rights clearly depend on the existence of a public street. (A) is wrong because no issue of the Statute of Frauds is present. There has been no purported conveyance to Carl of rights in the street by anyone who owns such rights. (B) is wrong since there is no legal objection to the enrichment that results if persons other than the dedicator are permitted to use a public street. (D) is wrong since, if a public street exists, Carl need not assert a way by necessity.

Answer to Question 8

(B) Generally, a city accepts a dedication when it approves the plans. (A) is wrong because a simple referral to a recorded plan does not automatically create rights. (C) is wrong because Carl does not need a way of necessity since he has other access to his land. (D) is wrong because the alternative access exists, and the amount of money required to improve the access does not determine need for an easement by necessity.

Answer to Question 9

(D) The degree of murder under the statute is determined by the defendant's mental state—whether the killing was intentional and accomplished after premeditation and deliberation. The defendant's relationship with the victim and the manner of killing may have evidentiary significance with regard to the defendant's mental state, but do not themselves distinguish first from second degree murder. Thus, (A) and (C) are incorrect. The causal relationship between the defendant's act and the death of the victim may determine whether the act is murder, but once that analytical hurdle has been passed, it has no further significance as to the degree of murder. Therefore, (B) is incorrect.

Answer to Question 10

(C) Shari should be allowed to testify as to what she perceived. To be admissible under the Federal Rules, evidence must be probative of a material issue in the case and must be competent (*i.e.*, not otherwise excludable). Evidence is material if it relates to an issue in the case, and it is probative if it tends to prove the fact for which it is offered. Evidence is competent if it does not violate a specific exclusionary rule. At issue here is whether Louise started the restaurant fire. If gasoline was used to start the fire, the fact that Louise was seen near the fire and smelled like gasoline makes it more likely that she started the fire; so the proffered evidence is material and relevant. It is also competent: under the Federal Rules, opinion testimony by lay witnesses is admissible when (i) it is rationally based on the perception of the witness, and (ii) it is helpful to a clear understanding of her testimony or to the determination of a fact in issue. Matters involving sense recognition, such as what something smelled like, are common subjects of opinion testimony. Here, Shari's testimony satisfies both elements of the test and should be admitted. Thus, (C) is correct and (A) is incorrect. (D) is incorrect because to testify as an expert one must have special knowledge, skill, experience, or education as to the subject of her testimony, and if everyone who drives a car knows the smell of gasoline, there is nothing special about that knowledge. (B) is incorrect because the best evidence rule requires that the original document be produced only when the terms of the document are material and sought to be proved. The fact to be proved— that gasoline was used—exists independently of any written record of the chemical tests; therefore, the best evidence rule does not apply.

Answer to Question 11

(C) State action that is facially neutral will nevertheless be struck down if it can be shown that it was intended to discriminate on the basis of race or national origin and does in fact have that effect. Sassoonian must show that the legislature selected the specific cost guidelines with full knowledge of the population characteristics in Midvalleyville and with the specific intent to disqualify that city from participation in the program because of its high concentration of Armenians. If he proves that intent, he will prevail, and (C) is accordingly his best argument. (A) would not be as helpful because the state could show a rational basis for not operating in Midvalleyville—that housing costs were not high enough to warrant state intervention—which would suffice to justify different treatment not based upon purposeful discrimination. (B) is not a good answer because the difficulty experienced by Armenian citizens in obtaining housing may have nothing to do with state action and may be experienced by other groups as well. (D) is not the best answer because, while it is arguably some evidence of purposeful discrimination, it does not state it as clearly as (C).

Answer to Question 12

(D) Providing housing for its citizens is clearly within the reserved police powers of the state. Since this is facially neutral economic and social legislation, the state simply needs a rational basis for its actions, and that is present. (A) and (B) are, accordingly, wrong. A state may undertake traditionally private business activities, and the analysis for both due process and equal protection purposes is rational basis review, under which the state will prevail. (C) is not a good answer because Rocky has suffered a direct injury (lost business) caused by the state government action. He has standing to challenge the legislation, but standing has nothing to do with the merits of his claim and he will lose.

Answer to Question 13

(C) Because this is economic legislation not involving fundamental rights or suspect classifications, it will be upheld if it has a rational basis. The higher housing costs justify intervention in areas like Metropolis rather than in Midvalleyville, and so the legislation would probably be valid. (A) is wrong because while the Eleventh Amendment immunizes states from suit in federal courts, that immunity does not authorize a state to violate the Constitution; a suit alleging such a violation may be filed against the responsible officials. (B) is an incorrect statement of law; as an agency of the state, the corporation's operations are state action. (D) is wrong because it applies the wrong standard of review.

Answer to Question 14

(D) In theory, the Tenth Amendment prohibits federal regulation of state activities if the regulation would virtually eliminate the state's local functions. As a practical matter, the Court's holding in *Garcia v. San Antonio Metropolitan Transit Authority* (1985) gives Congress broad authority when it acts pursuant to its enumerated powers. Accordingly, a federal regulation that controls the states as well as private persons is valid. Thus, the housing corporation would have to follow the federal regulations which control due to the Supremacy Clause. Thus, (D) is correct, and (B) and (C) are wrong. (A) is wrong because even intrastate activities are subject to Federal Commerce Clause regulation if they substantially affect interstate commerce.

Answer to Question 15

(D) Even though Dina may have been a cause of the accident, she is liable only if she was negligent. Thus, (B) is incorrect, and (D) is correct. (A) is incorrect because Dina did not violate the applicable statute. (C) is incorrect because obeying a law does not preclude negligent conduct; *i.e.*, even though she obeyed the traffic laws, she would be liable if she had been negligent in some way (*e.g.*, driving within the speed limit but going too fast on a day when the streets were icy).

Answer to Question 16

(D) An assignee is in privity of estate with the lessor, and is liable for those covenants in the original lease that run with the land. Hence, (A) is wrong. (B) and (C) are wrong because an agreement to pay taxes touches and concerns the land, and thus runs with the land.

Answer to Question 17

(C) The tenant-assignor remains in privity of contract with the lessor and is liable for the rent reserved in the lease. (A) and (B) are incorrect because Joann's status as a tenant is immaterial. (D) is incorrect because Joann's failure to include the tax payment provision in her assignment to Al does not affect her liability as the assignor under privity of contract.

Answer to Question 18

(A) A covenant to convey touches and concerns both the leasehold and reversion, and therefore runs with those respective interests in the land. Thus, (B) is incorrect. (C) is incorrect because there is nothing about the option in the facts that shows it to be personal. (D) is incorrect because, as explained above, the burden of the covenant to convey does run with the land.

Answer to Question 19

(C) Absent an express assumption, an assignee is not liable on the original covenants once he reassigns. Hence, (A) is wrong. (B) is wrong because an assignee is not in privity of contract with the lessor unless the assignee expressly assumes the lease obligations. (D) is incorrect because Al's ability to subsequently assign the lease is unrelated to the issue of liability. Al, as an assignee of Joann, is liable for covenants running with the land on the basis of privity of estate. Once Al assigns the lease to Howard, privity of estate ends and Al's liability is terminated.

Answer to Question 20

(D) To be guilty of burglary, a person must have the intent to commit a felony in the structure at the time of entry. Attempted burglary requires the same specific intent. Since Dexter merely intended to retrieve what he believed was his own property, he did not intend to commit a felony. Thus, (A) and (B) are wrong. Likewise, (C) is wrong because, since Dexter believed the computer was his own, he lacked the intent to permanently deprive Boss of his interest, which would be necessary for his act to constitute larceny. Thus, (D) is correct.

Answer to Question 21

(B) The fact that Main Street runs in a north-south direction is the most appropriate item for the judge to apply the doctrine of judicial notice to because it is a matter of common knowledge in the community. The Federal Rules conform to the existing state rules governing judicial notice. Federal Rule 201(b) defines a fact that may be noticed as "one not subject to reasonable dispute in that it is either (i) generally known within the territorial jurisdiction of the trial court, or (ii) capable of accurate and ready determination by resort to sources whose accuracy cannot reasonably be questioned." To be considered generally known within the community, the fact must be something that well-informed people generally know and accept. Although usually facts of common knowledge are known everywhere, it is sufficient for judicial notice if they are known in the community where the court is sitting. Because the fact that Main Street runs in a north-south direction is generally known by the community in which the courts sits, judicial notice may be taken of it. (A) is incorrect because judicial notice may not be taken of a fact solely because it is personally known by the judge. A judge may have to ignore facts that he knows as a private person if those facts are neither commonly known in the community nor capable of certain verification by resort to easily accessible sources of indisputable accuracy. Therefore, the judge may not take judicial notice of the wet pavement based solely on his recollection. (C) is incorrect because the fact that the brakes were faulty is subject to reasonable dispute. As discussed above, judicial notice may only be taken of matters of common knowledge in the community where the court sits or facts capable of certain verification. Here, the fact that Dawn's brakes were faulty was not a matter of common knowledge in Humberton. They were only faulty in the opinion of two witnesses. Also, the condition of the brakes is not easily verified by resorting to well-established sources. Even though their testimony was uncontroverted, the auto mechanic and engineer would not be considered such sources because their conclusions could be reasonably questioned. Therefore, the condition of the brakes would be considered to be subject to reasonable dispute and not appropriate for judicial notice. (D) is also incorrect because Dawn's speed at the time of the accident was subject to reasonable dispute. As discussed above, judicial notice may only be taken of facts not subject to reasonable dispute—*i.e.,* matters of common knowledge in the community or facts capable of certain verification. Whether Dawn exceeded the speed limit is not a matter of common knowledge in the community. In fact, there was conflicting testimony concerning Dawn's speed. The speed also was not a fact capable of certain verification from well-established sources. The skid marks would not be considered certain enough to be such a source.

Answer to Question 22

(C) The statute punishes a battery committed against a victim the defendant *knows* is a state official. Therefore, if the jury believes Rod's testimony that he did not know the man was a state official, they must find him not guilty of the charged violation. This is not a public welfare offense, but a particular form of battery. Thus, (B) is incorrect. (D) is incorrect because the statute requires knowledge of the status of the victim. (A) is wrong. There is no duty on the part of the state to warn Rod. If Rod knew, he will be guilty; if Rod did not know, he will not be guilty.

Answer to Question 23

(B) The officer's testimony should be admitted because it is an admission by a party-opponent. Generally, evidence is admissible if it is relevant, *i.e.,* if it has a tendency to prove any fact of consequence to the action. The testimony here is relevant because it makes it more likely that the defendant committed the acts complained of. It is also competent because its admission does not violate any exclusionary rule of evidence. Evidence law generally prohibits admission of hearsay—out-of-court statements offered to prove the truth of the matter asserted—but the rule does not apply to admissions by party-opponents—they are treated as nonhearsay under the Federal Rules. Thus, the testimony is admissible and (B) is correct. (A) may be a true statement—past instances of misconduct may be used to impeach a witness, at least if they are probative as to whether he is worthy of belief—but it is an incorrect answer because it focuses on impeachment, and Amy's father is not being impeached here. (C) is incorrect because the best evidence rule is not applicable here. The rule requires that when the contents of a writing are sought to be proved, the writing itself should be admitted if it is available. Here, however, the witness is not trying to prove that the defendant has been convicted, but rather that he made the admission. (D) is incorrect for reasons similar to why (C) is incorrect. It is true under the Federal Rules that convictions generally are not admissible for impeachment of a witness if more than 10 years old, but the officer is not trying to admit the defendant's conviction here (and is not trying to impeach the defendant, who may not even have testified). Rather, Amy is seeking to admit the defendant's confession. The confession is an admission by a party-opponent and is admissible as substantive evidence.

Answer to Question 24

(D) Wilma will prevail because Kerry intentionally caused an offensive touching. To make out a prima facie case for battery, Wilma need only show an act by Kerry that brings about harmful or offensive contact, intent by Kerry to bring about the contact, and causation. These elements are present here, and no defense is available (provocation is not a defense—insulting words do not give one the privilege to strike another). Therefore, (D) is correct. (A) and (B) are incorrect because, as indicated above, neither actual provocation nor reasonable provocation is a defense to battery. (C) is incorrect because even spontaneous acts are volitional movements, and that is all that is required to meet the "act" requirement. As long as the act is triggered by the conscious mind, it will be considered a volitional movement.

Answer to Question 25

(B) The contract extended for a 10-week period. Missing only four days of a performance to run for 10 weeks would not be considered a total material breach of the contract. (A) is wrong because this would tend to go more to a formation problem. Here the contract has already been validly formed. (C) is wrong because a claim of impossibility could conceivably discharge the entire contract, and, therefore, Fiddler would have no claim. (D) is wrong because Fiddler need not be warned of the consequences of a breach.

Answer to Question 26

(C) Producer is entitled to find a substitute to perform in Fiddler's absence. If this was the only way Producer could acquire a substitute, then Producer's actions would be proper. (A) is wrong because this would not relieve Producer from liability to Fiddler. (B) is wrong because Fiddler does not have to accept any job under the contract, only the job that was the subject of the contract or a similar job to mitigate damages. (D) is wrong because this factor would not excuse Fiddler from his liability under the contract.

Answer to Question 27

(B) Neighbor trespassed onto Hagler's land and took the trees, which belonged to Hagler. However, Hagler is entitled to receive only nominal damages for the act of trespass, since the trespass caused no damage. Hagler is also entitled to receive the value of the trees removed by Neighbor since this amounted to a taking of Hagler's property. (A) and (D) are therefore incorrect. (C) is incorrect because the fact that Neighbor's actions benefited Hagler would not diminish Hagler's right of recovery.

Answer to Question 28

(B) Edgar's testimony is only relevant if the conditions of the experiment were substantially similar to the conditions at the time and place of the accident. Evidence of pretrial experiments that does not require expert testimony is treated no differently under the Federal Rules from other evidence. It will be admissible if it is relevant (*i.e.*, if it has any tendency to prove or disprove a fact that is of consequence to the action) and if it is not barred by a specific exclusionary rule or the general balancing test of Rule 403. To the extent that the conditions of Edgar's experiment replicated the conditions of the accident, the experiment is relevant because whether Edgar's linoleum was wet after 45 minutes tends to establish whether Store's floor was wet when Jack walked on it, and this fact is of major consequence to Jack's personal injury action. To the extent that the conditions of Edgar's experiment are not similar, the minimal probative value of his testimony probably would be outweighed under Rule 403 by considerations of unfair prejudice or waste of time. (A) is incorrect because the Federal Rules do not require a representative of the adverse party to be present at the experiment; Jack's attorney can subject the conditions of the experiment to scrutiny through cross-examination of Edgar. (C) is incorrect for the same reason: Jack's attorney can effectively cross-examine Edgar even without having conducted his own experiments. (D) is incorrect because the person conducting the experiment need not be an independent observer. If Edgar is an employee, his potential bias can be elicited on cross-examination.

Answer to Question 29

(D) The crime of larceny requires an intent to steal. Cheryl was operating under an honest mistake of fact. (A) is incorrect because there was no conspiracy; if there were a conspiracy, Cheryl would be guilty. (B) is incorrect because a person can be guilty of a crime even though someone else directs her to do it. (B) does not state the reason why Cheryl would not be guilty. (C) is incorrect because the fact that Milt handed it over would not absolve Cheryl of liability.

Answer to Question 30

(C) To prevail in an action for battery, Nathaniel must show that Donamae engaged in volitional conduct with knowledge or desire to cause a battery. Here, the gun discharged without any volitional act, and so Nathaniel will lose. (A) is incorrect because even if a gun is considered to be a dangerous instrumentality, that fact is not relevant to a battery action, which is based on intent rather than strict liability. A cat's actions are not imputed to its owner; thus, (B) is incorrect. (D) is incorrect because Nathaniel's status as a trespasser would not necessarily prevent him from prevailing in an action for battery; Donamae did not have a right to use deadly force to protect her property here.

Answer to Question 31

(B) Darrell will probably be found not guilty. The mental state necessary for criminal battery is either intentional or reckless conduct. Clearly, Darrell did not intend to have bodily contact with Violet, and in light of the circumstances it will be unlikely that Darrell's conduct will be considered such an extreme deviation from ordinary behavior as to establish recklessness. (A) is wrong; a serious injury is not required for battery. (C) is wrong because recklessness requires a much greater deviation from ordinary behavior than simply a "failure to exercise due care." (D) is not as accurate as (B). It does not address the critical issue in the case—the mental state of Darrell.

Answer to Question 32

(A) Willis's testimony is admissible as relevant opinion testimony by an expert witness. The Federal Rules permit witnesses qualified as experts to testify in the form of an opinion if the subject matter is one where scientific, technical, or other specialized knowledge will assist the jury in understanding the evidence or determining a fact in issue. [Fed. R. Evid. 702] Under Federal Rule 703, the expert may base his opinion on facts not known personally but supplied to him outside the courtroom (*e.g.*, reports of other experts). Such facts need not be admissible in evidence as long as the facts are of a kind reasonably relied on by experts in the particular field. Here, Willis, as a state-licensed engineer, probably qualifies as an expert on the subject of his testimony and therefore can state his opinion as to the cause of the collapse of the excavation wall. As choice (A) states, he may base his opinion on the building plans, the geologist's report, and the engineer's report if civil engineers in his field rely on this type of data in reaching conclusions such as his. Thus, choice (D) is incorrect. Choice (B) is incorrect because whether this analysis is negligent is irrelevant to its admissibility; this fact can be brought out by cross-examination. A prudent analysis will still be inadmissible if it was based on materials that experts in his field did not reasonably rely on. Choice (C) is incorrect; Federal Rule 704(a) provides that otherwise admissible opinion testimony is not objectionable because it embraces the ultimate issue to be decided by the trier of fact.

Answer to Question 33

(A) Only Article III judges enjoy the constitutional grant of life tenure, and Agnew is not an Article III judge. The Tribunal is an administrative agency with limited jurisdiction, and while Agnew exercises some adjudicatory powers, all persons with some adjudicatory functions are not judges within the meaning of Article III. (A) is thus correct and (D) is wrong. (C) is also wrong, since the Constitution does not recognize property rights in employment. Agnew could show some kind of wrongful discharge only if he could claim that he was deprived of something "in the nature of a property right." (B) is incorrect because Agnew clearly has standing; he alleges a specific injury to himself and brings the claim in his own right, alleging the violation of a constitutional right.

Answer to Question 34

(D) The language of the reward offer should not be read with total literalness, but rather in the context of what Big City was seeking to obtain and the normal duties required to accept an offer of this kind. Therefore, (A), which would require that the offeree actually participate in the arrest, can be eliminated. Offers of this type normally require only that the offerees supply information leading to the arrest and conviction of the culprit. (B) and (C) can be ruled out without difficulty because they would envision a bilateral contract under which the offeree would be promising or assenting to Big City's proposal. In this kind of word context the offer is obviously the unilateral proposal that can be accepted only by performance.

Answer to Question 35

(A) This kind of reward offer can be revoked by comparable publicity as to the revocation by the offeror. (B) is wrong because the facts make it impossible to use the same manner to revoke the offer. (C) does not go far enough in communicating the revocation effectively to anyone who heard the offer originally. (D) would be too onerous a task.

Answer to Question 36

(C) Stevens cannot successfully recover on a contract theory because he was unaware of the offer. An offeree must be aware of the offer before he can, by his actions, accept it. Big City, therefore, would not be liable on a contract theory. The bounty idea has sometimes been used in reward cases when the offeror is a governmental agency. Therefore, (C) is the best answer. (A) does not go far enough because a party will not be liable for benefits gratuitously lavished upon it. (B) is wrong because public policy cannot limit a party's right to revoke an offer. (D) is incorrect because estoppel requires detrimental reliance on the other party's conduct, and here Stevens could not rely on the offer since he was unaware of it.

Answer to Question 37

(D) (D) is least helpful because the contract with Big City was unilateral and did not require a notice of acceptance; rather, performance was sufficient. (A) is helpful because the fact that Stevens was already under contract might have impact with respect to the preexisting duty rule. (B) is helpful because the fact that Stevens had been compensated already would not have a bearing on a contract theory but might on a quasi-contractual theory. (C) is helpful because the broadcast of the revocation on the television station would most likely have effectively revoked Big City's offer.

Answer to Question 38

(B) Gardner will prevail if the steering locked because of a defect present when the mower left the manufacturer. A retailer is strictly liable for injuries caused by a defect in a product sold by that retailer. This is true even if the retailer carefully inspects the product before selling it. (D) is therefore incorrect. (A) is incorrect because the fact that the steering locked is not enough to create liability without evidence that it was the result of a defect in the mower. (C) is incorrect because contributory negligence is not a good defense to strict liability in tort in jurisdictions retaining traditional contributory negligence rules.

Answer to Question 39

(B) Bystrom will prevail if Lawn Co. should have discovered the defect. The key is realizing that Bystrom is basing his claim on negligence. To recover, he must show that Lawn Co. failed to act reasonably with respect to the mower. (A) is incorrect because it speaks to strict liability in tort, not negligence. (C) is incorrect because there is no privity requirement in a negligence action. (D) is incorrect because Gardner's contributory negligence, assuming it was a cause in fact of the accident, was foreseeable and therefore not a superseding cause. Thus, it would have no bearing on Bystrom's potential recovery. (B) is the only alternative that speaks to the negligence of Lawn Co.

Answer to Question 40

(B)   The court should rule Statement 1 admissible and Statement 2 inadmissible. Statement 1 is admissible as an admission by a party-opponent, while Statement 2 is inadmissible as an offer to pay medical expenses. An admission is a statement made or act done that amounts to a prior acknowledgment by one of the parties to an action of one of the relevant facts. The Federal Rules treat such statements as nonhearsay. [Fed. R. Evid. 801(d)(2)] In Statement 1, Deft acknowledges that he ran the red light, and that the incident resulting in Plain's injuries was his fault. This statement clearly amounts to an acknowledgment of relevant facts (*i.e.,* that Deft was at fault) and qualifies as an admission by a party-opponent. Evidence that a party paid (or offered to pay) an injured party's medical bill is not admissible to prove liability for the injuries. [Fed. R. Evid. 409] Such payment (or offer to pay) might be prompted solely by humanitarian motives. Statement 2 is clearly an offer by Deft to pay the medical bills of Plain, an injured party. Thus, the statement is not admissible to prove liability for Plain's injuries (and proving liability appears to be the only reason Plain has for attempting to introduce the statement into evidence). Note that had this been a single statement, the outcome would have been the same since an admission of fact accompanying offers to pay medical expenses is admissible. (A) is wrong because, as explained above, Statement 2 is inadmissible. (C) is wrong as to both statements because Statement 1 is admissible and Statement 2 is inadmissible. (D) is wrong because Statement 1 is admissible.

Answer to Question 41

(B)   There is a presumption that Harvey and Winona are tenants in common. For a joint tenancy to exist, there must be an express creation of such tenancy; thus, there is a presumption of tenancy in common unless the conveyance is to a husband and wife in a state that recognizes tenancy by the entirety. Here, Harvey and Winona were not married when they took title to Pinkacre. Each tenant in common has an undivided interest, which may be conveyed by inter vivos transfer. Harvey started with an undivided one-half interest, one-half of which he conveyed to Sampson and the other half of which he conveyed to Delilah. Harvey has thus conveyed all of his interest in Pinkacre, and so (A) is incorrect. There is no right of survivorship in a tenancy in common; therefore, (C) is incorrect. (D) is not supported by the facts.

Answer to Question 42

(A)   Under Federal Rule of Evidence 801, after a witness has testified, statements of prior identification are admissible to prove their truth unless the defendant can show that the circumstances of the identification were unnecessarily suggestive and likely to result in irreparable misidentification. There is no evidence of that in the facts. (B) is wrong since there is no right to counsel at a photo display. (C) is wrong because it goes to the weight to be given the evidence rather than its admissibility. (D) is wrong because the photograph identification would not be considered a critical stage.

Answer to Question 43

(B)   The statute burdens interstate commerce by diverting purchase of items from interstate to intrastate commerce, discriminating against the former. (A) is incorrect because the Privileges and Immunities Clause does not apply: the sale of products does not fall within the limited number of "privileges" the Court has recognized under the Fourteenth Amendment. Since the statute applies to all businesses, it does not create the sort of classification that triggers equal protection analysis and so (C) is incorrect. Since the license requirement is well within the traditional state police powers, and would be reasonable except for the Commerce Clause problems, (D) is incorrect.

Answer to Question 44

(B) A search incident to a full custodial arrest can be made without a warrant or probable cause to believe that evidence or weapons will be found. Thus, (B) is correct and (D) is wrong. (A) is wrong because the police officer need not fear for his safety to make a valid search incident to a lawful arrest. (C) is wrong because, incident to a lawful arrest, the police may conduct a warrantless search of the area within the defendant's "wingspan." This includes the glove compartment.

Answer to Question 45

(D) Under the Federal Rules, this prior inconsistent statement may be used to impeach and as substantive evidence. A prior inconsistent statement made while under oath and subject to penalty of perjury in a deposition or prior hearing is not hearsay under Federal Rule 801. (A) is therefore incorrect. (B) is incorrect because the Federal Rules permit a party to impeach its own witness, even if not "surprised." (C) is incorrect because it is too narrow.

Answer to Question 46

(C) The federal government has the power to tax and spend funds for the general welfare of the citizens of the United States. (A) is arguable since, under the Commerce Clause, Congress has enacted a wide variety of social legislation. However, since this legislation is strictly dealing with welfare, the act would most probably be based on the Taxing and Spending Clause. (B) is incorrect because the facts do not indicate that any citizen is being deprived of any federal right. There is no general federal police power, so (D) is wrong.

Answer to Question 47

(D) Sarah's act was not only the "but for" cause, but also, since the death was the natural foreseeable result, the "proximate" cause. The fact that other preexisting conditions contributed to the death does not absolve Sarah. (A) is wrong; there is no requirement that the defendant's acts be the sole cause of the result. Most results have more than one cause. (B) is wrong; we all will die at some point.

Answer to Question 48

(C) Federal Rule 407 makes evidence of subsequent remedial measures inadmissible to show negligence. Rule 407 is based on the public policy of safety. The law wants to encourage people to make repairs or take other remedial measures after an accident. Thus, (A) and (B) are incorrect. (D) is wrong because Ellen is not trying to impeach Paul or anyone else.

Answer to Question 49

(C) There are two gifts to Gwendolyn's children. The first is a vested remainder that follows Gwendolyn's life estate, and the second is the executory interest that is given to the other children if one purports to sell or mortgage his or her interest. This second restriction is an attempt to absolutely restrain the alienation (sale) of property, which is void. Thus, (D) is incorrect. (A) is incorrect because Geoffrey and the other children have interests that are vested at Grey's death. (B) is incorrect for the same reason. The children's interests vested and their class closed at the time of Grey's death and thus are not subject to the Rule Against Perpetuities.

Answer to Question 50

(C) Since Turner was not where Cabbie might have expected him to be, it would be relevant in judging the reasonableness of Cabbie's conduct. For this reason, (D) is wrong. (A) and (B) are wrong since Turner's violation would probably be excused under the circumstances. While (B) raises the issue of last clear chance, which would negate a contributory negligence defense, the facts do not establish that Turner was contributorily negligent.

MIXED SUBJECT SET 4
ANSWER SHEET

1. Ⓐ Ⓑ Ⓒ Ⓓ		26. Ⓐ Ⓑ Ⓒ Ⓓ	
2. Ⓐ Ⓑ Ⓒ Ⓓ		27. Ⓐ Ⓑ Ⓒ Ⓓ	
3. Ⓐ Ⓑ Ⓒ Ⓓ		28. Ⓐ Ⓑ Ⓒ Ⓓ	
4. Ⓐ Ⓑ Ⓒ Ⓓ		29. Ⓐ Ⓑ Ⓒ Ⓓ	
5. Ⓐ Ⓑ Ⓒ Ⓓ		30. Ⓐ Ⓑ Ⓒ Ⓓ	

6. Ⓐ Ⓑ Ⓒ Ⓓ		31. Ⓐ Ⓑ Ⓒ Ⓓ	
7. Ⓐ Ⓑ Ⓒ Ⓓ		32. Ⓐ Ⓑ Ⓒ Ⓓ	
8. Ⓐ Ⓑ Ⓒ Ⓓ		33. Ⓐ Ⓑ Ⓒ Ⓓ	
9. Ⓐ Ⓑ Ⓒ Ⓓ		34. Ⓐ Ⓑ Ⓒ Ⓓ	
10. Ⓐ Ⓑ Ⓒ Ⓓ		35. Ⓐ Ⓑ Ⓒ Ⓓ	

11. Ⓐ Ⓑ Ⓒ Ⓓ		36. Ⓐ Ⓑ Ⓒ Ⓓ	
12. Ⓐ Ⓑ Ⓒ Ⓓ		37. Ⓐ Ⓑ Ⓒ Ⓓ	
13. Ⓐ Ⓑ Ⓒ Ⓓ		38. Ⓐ Ⓑ Ⓒ Ⓓ	
14. Ⓐ Ⓑ Ⓒ Ⓓ		39. Ⓐ Ⓑ Ⓒ Ⓓ	
15. Ⓐ Ⓑ Ⓒ Ⓓ		40. Ⓐ Ⓑ Ⓒ Ⓓ	

16. Ⓐ Ⓑ Ⓒ Ⓓ		41. Ⓐ Ⓑ Ⓒ Ⓓ	
17. Ⓐ Ⓑ Ⓒ Ⓓ		42. Ⓐ Ⓑ Ⓒ Ⓓ	
18. Ⓐ Ⓑ Ⓒ Ⓓ		43. Ⓐ Ⓑ Ⓒ Ⓓ	
19. Ⓐ Ⓑ Ⓒ Ⓓ		44. Ⓐ Ⓑ Ⓒ Ⓓ	
20. Ⓐ Ⓑ Ⓒ Ⓓ		45. Ⓐ Ⓑ Ⓒ Ⓓ	

21. Ⓐ Ⓑ Ⓒ Ⓓ		46. Ⓐ Ⓑ Ⓒ Ⓓ	
22. Ⓐ Ⓑ Ⓒ Ⓓ		47. Ⓐ Ⓑ Ⓒ Ⓓ	
23. Ⓐ Ⓑ Ⓒ Ⓓ		48. Ⓐ Ⓑ Ⓒ Ⓓ	
24. Ⓐ Ⓑ Ⓒ Ⓓ		49. Ⓐ Ⓑ Ⓒ Ⓓ	
25. Ⓐ Ⓑ Ⓒ Ⓓ		50. Ⓐ Ⓑ Ⓒ Ⓓ	

MIXED SUBJECT QUESTIONS - SET 4

Question 1

The state of North Pacific contains major deposits of natural gas. In an effort to support this industry, and at the same time save its citizens substantial sums for the cost of heating their homes and businesses, the legislature enacted a substantial tax on out-of-state suppliers of natural gas. In addition, the state required state licensed public utilities to buy no less than 75% of their natural gas needs from sources within the state as long as their needs could be met. Muni-Power, an out-of-state supplier, brought suit against North Pacific challenging this statute.

The best constitutional argument Muni-Power could make is that the statute violates:

(A) The Due Process Clause of the Fourteenth Amendment.

(B) The Equal Protection Clause of the Fourteenth Amendment.

(C) The Privileges and Immunities Clause of Article IV.

(D) The Commerce Clause.

Question 2

Paul sues Daniel for personal injuries that Paul suffered as a result of a battery committed on Paul by Daniel. Daniel's defense is that it is all a case of mistaken identity. Daniel admits that Paul was beaten up, but claims he had nothing to do with Paul's injuries. At trial, Daniel testified in his own behalf that on the date that Paul suffered his injuries, Daniel was on an extended vacation in England, 2,000 miles away from the place where the battery occurred. Paul's attorney did not cross-examine Daniel regarding that testimony. In rebuttal, Paul's attorney calls Walter, who is willing to testify that one week after Paul suffered his injuries, Daniel said to Walter, "I haven't been out of the country in five years."

Walter's testimony is:

(A) Admissible as a statement against interest by Daniel.

(B) Admissible as a prior inconsistent statement of Daniel.

(C) Admissible as an admission by Daniel.

(D) Inadmissible, because Daniel was not given an opportunity to comment on the statement prior to Walter's testimony.

Question 3

In which of the following circumstances would Defendant most likely be guilty of common law murder?

(A) Defendant and Nate are having an argument, and Nate punches Defendant. Mistakenly believing that Nate intends to stab him, Defendant shoots him.

(B) At a Fourth of July celebration, Defendant fires a pistol, and the ricocheting bullet hits and kills Al.

(C) While hunting, Defendant sees a movement. Although he cannot see what moved, he believes it to be a deer and fires into the bush. In fact, the movement was caused by George, and George is killed by the bullet fired by Defendant.

(D) During a robbery, Defendant accidentally drops a grenade. It goes off and a customer is killed.

Questions 4-5 are based on the following fact situation:

Pitts purchased a new Stratton Spitfire sports-car manufactured by the Stratton Corporation from a local dealership. While Pitts was driving home from the dealership, she stopped at a red light. She was struck from behind by a truck driven by Drago, who had negligently failed to stop. On impact, the door on the driver's side of the car flew open because of a defective latch. Pitts fell out the open door and was injured. Pitts fell even though she was wearing a seat belt at the time of the impact because the seat belt buckle was also defective and failed to hold Pitts. Assume that a local ordinance requires all automobiles to be equipped with door latches that will not open on impact, and that the jurisdiction follows traditional contributory negligence rules.

4.   If Pitts asserts a claim against Drago, Pitts will:

(A)   Prevail, unless Stratton was negligent in the manufacture of the car that Pitts was driving.

(B)   Prevail, because Drago's negligent driving was a cause in fact of the collision.

(C)   Not prevail, because the door latch on Pitts's car violated a local ordinance.

(D)   Not prevail if Pitts would not have been injured but for the failure of the seat belt buckle.

5.   If Pitts asserts a claim against Stratton, will Pitts prevail?

(A)   Yes, unless Pitts could have discovered either of the defects.

(B)   Yes, because the car she was driving was dangerously defective.

(C)   No, because Drago's negligent driving was the cause of Pitts's injuries.

(D)   No, unless Stratton knew or had reason to know of either of the defects.

Question 6

State B's legislature passed a statute that required every used car sold in the state to be tested prior to sale to determine whether it was in compliance with a set of strict exhaust emission standards that were also included in the legislation. Used cars would have to be brought up to standard and pass the emissions test prior to sale. Certain persons in the state object to the legislation because one of its results will be to raise the average price of used cars in State B. Only cars to be sold for junk are exempt from the statute.

Among the following, who would be most likely to have standing to raise a constitutional challenge to the legislation?

(A)   A State B resident who was thinking about selling used cars in State B.

(B)   A State B resident who was thinking about buying a used car in State B.

(C)   An out-of-state dealer in used cars who had a contract to sell cars to a large dealer in State B.

(D)   An out-of-state manufacturer who might be required to indemnify its dealers in State B for costs arising from the statute.

Question 7

The state of North Freedonia has long had a reputation for growing the biggest and tastiest potatoes in the country. Growers of potatoes in North Freedonia recently began spraying Bugoff onto their crops to prevent the spread of the Potato Maggot, an insect that can destroy young potato plants. Bugoff is manufactured exclusively by Growit, Inc., at its plant in South Freedonia. When the plant is producing Bugoff it emits a fine, sticky, harmless mist as a byproduct. The mist drifts over Clampett's property which is adjacent to Growit's plant. Although Growit uses the best technology available, it is unable to prevent the release of the mist. Clampett brings suit against Growit on the theory of private nuisance to enjoin the production of Bugoff at the South Freedonia plant.

Which of the following facts, if established, will be most helpful to Growit's defense?

(A)   Growit commenced the manufacture of Bugoff at the South Freedonia plant three years before Clampett acquired the land adjacent to the plant.

(B) Federal, state, and local agencies approved the design of the plant and equipment used to produce Bugoff.

(C) The principal users of Bugoff are State and Federal Departments of Agriculture.

(D) Bugoff is the only pesticide that can safely and effectively kill the Potato Maggot, which, if not controlled, would destroy North Freedonia's potato crop, its principal product.

Questions 8-9 are based on the following fact situation:

While Doug was driving Olivia's car, he hit Peter in a pedestrian right-of-way. Peter sued both Doug and Olivia, alleging that Doug had negligently driven the car and that Olivia had negligently permitted an unfit driver to use her car.

8. Peter calls Walter as his first witness. Walter testifies that within the last several months he is aware of three instances in which Doug has engaged in reckless driving. Both Doug and Olivia object to the admission of this evidence. The objection should be:

(A) Sustained, because Doug's character is not in issue.

(B) Sustained, because specific evidence of misconduct is not admissible to establish evidence of character.

(C) Overruled as to the case against Olivia, but sustained as to the case against Doug.

(D) Overruled, because the evidence goes to the issue of Doug's criminal negligence.

9. As part of her defense, Olivia calls her husband, Harry, to testify for her. Harry offers testimony that Olivia rarely loans her automobile to anybody, but that when she does loan it, Olivia invariably checks to see

whether the driver is careful and law abiding. Peter objects to the admission of this evidence. His objection should be:

(A) Sustained, because there is no evidence to corroborate Harry's testimony.

(B) Sustained, because it seeks to prove conduct in conformity with the character evidence.

(C) Overruled, because Olivia's character is in issue.

(D) Overruled, because it tends to establish Olivia's habit.

Questions 10-13 are based on the following fact situation:

Owner and Builder executed a contract providing that Builder was to construct a residence on a specified location according to plans and specifications drawn up by Architect. The total contract price was $500,000. The lot on which the residence was to be built was located on the seashore in Palm Beach, Florida and there was an existing woodframe structure that had to be demolished before the residence could be built. Owner contracted with Designer to furnish the interior of the residence after Builder completed construction, but no date was included in either contract for completion of the home. The contract between Owner and Builder stated that construction would begin within two weeks after the existing structure was demolished and the rubble removed from the lot. The contract between Owner and Builder was signed November 12, and the contract between Owner and Designer was signed November 11.

10. Assume for the purposes of this question only that the day after the preexisting structure is demolished and the rubble removed, a severe storm causes gigantic waves that erode the seashore so that Owner's lot is now under water. Must Builder still perform the contract?

(A) No, the contract is void because the subject of the contract was destroyed through no fault of the parties.

(B) No, Builder is discharged of his obligation because of impossibility of performance.

(C) Yes, if Owner obtains an alternative lot within a reasonable period of time.

(D) No, the contract is void because of mutual mistake.

11. Assume for the purposes of this question only that after Builder has completed 5% of the residence, a severe storm causes gigantic waves that demolish the construction but leave the lot undamaged. Must Builder still perform the contract?

(A) No, the contract is void because the subject of the contract was destroyed through no fault of the parties.

(B) No, Builder is discharged of his obligation because of impossibility of performance.

(C) Yes, but he is entitled to a quantum meruit recovery for the work done prior to the destruction of the construction.

(D) Yes, Builder must perform the original contract without any compensation for the destruction of the construction.

12. Assume for the purposes of this question only that after Builder has completed 60% of the residence, a severe storm causes gigantic waves that partially erode the lot but leave the construction undamaged. Builder determines that it will cost an additional $1.2 million to repair the lot by shoring and construction of a seawall so that the residence can be constructed according to the plans of Architect. Without the additional lot repair work, the residence cannot be constructed at all. Must Builder perform the contract?

(A) No, if the increased costs of construction would bankrupt him.

(B) No, the contract is void because of mutual mistake.

(C) No, Builder is discharged of his obligation because of impracticability of performance.

(D) Yes, but he may bring an action against Owner for the increased costs of construction.

13. Assume for the purposes of this question only that after the contract was signed by the parties and after the preexisting structure has been demolished but before the rubble has been removed, the Florida Coastal Commission declares the land including Owner's lot part of a natural wilderness area, requiring that all residences constructed therein be single story and have plans approved by the Coastal Commission. The original plans called for a three-story, castle-like structure totally incompatible with the Commission's guidelines for residences in a wilderness area. Must Builder perform the contract?

(A) No, the contract is void because of mutual mistake.

(B) No, and he may recover his lost profits in an action against Owner.

(C) No, Builder is discharged of his obligation because of supervening illegality.

(D) Yes, if Owner and Architect supply new plans approved by the Coastal Commission.

Question 14

In 1951, Owner conveyed Blackacre to Brian for "so long as Blackacre is used solely for residential purposes. Should Brian ever use Blackacre for any other purpose, the interest in Blackacre shall revert to Owner and his heirs."

Brian used Blackacre as his personal residence for 20 years, but in 1971, he began operating a bar on Blackacre. Owner knew that Brian was operating a bar on Blackacre, but he took no action.

In 2000, the aged Brian decided to get out of the saloon business. Brian closed his business and once again began to use Blackacre solely as his personal residence. Also in 2000, Owner died, survived by his son and only heir, Stephen. In 2002, Stephen laid claim to Blackacre.

The jurisdiction in which Blackacre is located has a seven-year adverse possession statute and another statute that bars enforcement of possibilities of reverter 55 years after their creation.

May Stephen validly claim title to Blackacre?

(A) Yes, because less than 55 years has elapsed since the creation of the possibility of reverter.

(B) Yes, because the adverse possession period began to run when Brian returned the property to residential status, and Brian has not held for the requisite seven years.

(C) No, because the adverse possession period began to run in 1971, and Brian has held the property for more than the requisite seven years.

(D) No, because Owner did not assert his possibility of reverter; thus, no cause of action arose in Owner or his heirs.

Question 15

One night when Bob was very drunk, he took one of his rifles, loaded it, and fired a bullet through his front door. Unknown to him, at the time he fired the rifle, someone was driving by the house. The bullet went through the front door, through the window of the car, and killed the driver.

Bob was convicted of murder and appeals. He contends that there was insufficient evidence to support a finding of murder.

The court of appeals should rule that the evidence is:

(A) Sufficient to prove that the killing was intentional.

(B) Sufficient to prove that the killing was done with malice aforethought.

(C) Insufficient, because Bob did not know that the driver was driving by his house and therefore he could not have acted intentionally.

(D) Insufficient, because at most Bob's conduct constituted gross negligence and involuntary manslaughter.

Questions 16-17 are based on the following fact situation:

Commercial fishing, primarily for salmon and tuna, in the waters of the Pacific Ocean along the state's western boundary, has long been one of Washington's major industries. To protect the fishing industry, which was being harmed by the too rapid depletion of the fish in the waters of the state's coast, and to promote the general welfare of the state's citizens, the state legislature enacted statutes for the first time requiring licenses for commercial fishing. To receive a license, the applicant must pay a $500 fee and establish by acceptable evidence that he has been engaged in commercial fishing in the waters of the state of Washington (including ocean waters within three miles of its coastline) since January 1, 1995. A limited number of special licenses are available for those who do not meet the requirements of the regular licenses, and these special licenses are expressly reserved for citizens who have resided in Washington for at least three years prior to the date of the application.

16. Ng, a legally admitted alien who has been residing in the state of Washington for 10 years, brings suit in federal court to enjoin enforcement of the licensing statute as to himself and all other similarly situated noncitizen legal residents of the state of

Washington. Which of the following doctrines will probably be determinative of his claims?

(A) The powers reserved to the states by the Tenth Amendment to the Federal Constitution.

(B) The Equal Protection Clause of the Fourteenth Amendment.

(C) The Due Process Clause of the Fifth Amendment to the Federal Constitution.

(D) The Privileges and Immunities Clause of Article IV.

17. Limpett is a commercial fisherman residing in northern California. He frequently takes his fishing boat up the coast. His favorite spot is approximately two miles off the coast of Washington. If Limpett challenges the constitutionality of the Washington statutes, the court should find the statutes:

(A) Constitutional, because Congress has not enacted legislation regarding the subject matter of the statutes.

(B) Constitutional, because economic and social regulations are presumed valid.

(C) Unconstitutional, because less restrictive means are available.

(D) Unconstitutional, because Congress has exclusive power to regulate foreign commerce, which includes commercial ocean fishing.

Question 18

Oliver, who owned the Rocking O Ranch in fee simple, died and left the property to his daughter, "Melinda, her heirs and assigns; but if my son, Oliver Jr., is living 25 years from the date of my death, then to Oliver Jr., his heirs and assigns." At the time of Oliver's death, Oliver Jr. was one year old. The common law Rule Against Perpetuities is unmodified in the jurisdiction.

The grant in the will to Oliver Jr. is:

(A) Valid, because the interest vests, if at all, within a life in being.

(B) Valid, because it grants Oliver Jr. a reversionary interest.

(C) Invalid, because the will grants Melinda the complete interest in the property, so there is nothing to be left to Oliver Jr.

(D) Invalid, if this jurisdiction does not recognize a testator's ability to convey a possibility of reverter by will.

Questions 19-21 are based on the following fact situation:

Fred is arrested and charged with the burglary of Sam's warehouse.

19. At trial, prosecution offers evidence that when Fred was arrested, shortly after the crime had been committed, he had a large amount of cocaine hidden in the trunk of his car. This evidence should be:

(A) Admitted to prove Fred's propensity to commit crimes.

(B) Admitted to prove Fred's general bad character.

(C) Excluded because such evidence may be offered only to rebut evidence of good character offered by the defendant.

(D) Excluded because its probative value is substantially outweighed by the danger of unfair prejudice.

20. At the request of the police investigating the burglary, the night watchman at Sam's Warehouse who had seen the thief leaving the premises wrote out a description of a person who bore a strong likeness to Fred. However, the night watchman died of a heart attack before Fred was arrested and brought to trial. The prosecution attempts

to offer the description written out by the night watchman into evidence. The description is:

(A) Admissible as a past recollection recorded.

(B) Admissible as an identification of a person the night watchman knew committed the crime in question.

(C) Inadmissible as hearsay not within an exception.

(D) Inadmissible as an opinion of a nonexpert.

21. On cross-examination of Fred, the prosecution asked Fred whether he had been convicted of fraudulent business practices six months earlier. This question is:

(A) Proper to show that Fred is a bad character.

(B) Proper to show that Fred is inclined to lie.

(C) Improper because the probative value of the evidence is outweighed by the danger of unfair prejudice.

(D) Improper because the conviction has insufficient similarity to the crime charged.

Question 22

Dennis was charged with larceny. His principal defense was that he had no intent to permanently deprive the victim of her property. The judge instructed the jury that the State had to prove beyond a reasonable doubt that Dennis was guilty of larceny and that the evidence tended to show that Dennis had taken some jewels belonging to the victim; but if they believed that Dennis had proven by a fair preponderance of the evidence that he did not intend to keep the jewels, but to return them, they should find him not guilty. Dennis was

convicted of larceny. He appeals the conviction, contending that the judge erred in his instructions to the jury.

Dennis's conviction will probably be:

(A) Affirmed, because the jury has the power to ignore Dennis's testimony if they do not believe him.

(B) Affirmed, because Dennis had failed to rebut the State's evidence tending to show that he intended to keep the jewels.

(C) Reversed, because the judge cannot comment at all on the evidence.

(D) Reversed, because the instructions put some of the burden of proof on Dennis.

Question 23

At the intersection of First and Main Streets, a large truck owned by Ace Meat Packing Co. collided with a car driven by Sam. At the time of the accident, Wilber, the driver of the truck, said to Sam, "The accident was my fault; I wasn't paying any attention. Don't worry, my company will make it right." The subsequent investigation of the accident by Ace revealed that Wilber had been drinking on the day of the accident. Wilber was fired.

Sam brings an appropriate action against Ace for damages resulting from the accident. Wilber has disappeared. Sam seeks to testify as to what Wilber said at the time of the accident.

The evidence is:

(A) Admissible, as an admission by an employee of the defendant.

(B) Admissible, as an excited utterance.

(C) Inadmissible, because Wilber is no longer employed by Ace.

(D) Inadmissible, unless Ace authorized Wilber to speak on its behalf.

Question 24

Alice owned Lot A, and Barry owned the adjacent Lot B. Both lots were located in State Red, which has a 20-year adverse possession statute. In 1970, Alice married and left State Red to reside in State Blue. Alice did not return to view the property during her period of residence in State Blue. In 1971, Barry built a driveway on Lot B. The driveway extended three feet over onto Lot A. Barry mistakenly believed that this three-foot strip of land was his property. Barry regularly used the driveway and continued to use it when Alice, having been widowed, returned to State Red in 2002. Alice discovered the encroachment upon her return.

If Alice consults you as to her rights against Barry, how should you advise her?

(A) Alice has no action against Barry, because Barry's title to the three-foot strip has been established by adverse possession.

(B) Alice has no action against Barry, because her prolonged absence from State Red establishes a presumption of abandonment of her rights in the property.

(C) Alice has an action against Barry, because Alice had no knowledge of Barry's encroachment.

(D) Alice has an action against Barry, because Barry mistakenly thought the three-foot strip was his.

Question 25

Carter, a nonunion carpenter, went to work on a construction project that was involved in a labor dispute. Every morning when he arrived at work, he would be accosted by the picketers who would try to persuade him not to continue to work. One morning while Carter was trying to get to work, one of the union workers, John, stopped Carter at the gate and told him that he shouldn't go to work. When Carter insisted that John get out of the way, John said, "Try to make me, scab!" Carter, intending to frighten John,

swung his hammer at him. The head on the hammer, however, was defective and it flew off, hitting John in the face.

John sues Carter for battery. Most likely he will:

(A) Prevail, because he was struck by the hammer head.

(B) Prevail, unless he intended to provoke Carter.

(C) Not prevail, because the negligence of the manufacturer of the hammer was the direct cause of the injury.

(D) Not prevail, if a reasonable person would have been angered by what John had said.

Question 26

Dr. Wally, a local physician who was prominent in the community and beloved by his patients, died suddenly of a heart attack. Wally was only 46 years old at the time of his death, and so the local newspaper, *The Daily Bleat,* had never prepared a "pre-obituary," as it did for many prominent figures. Snoops, a reporter with *The Daily Bleat,* was assigned to write an obituary before the next day's edition went to press. Snoops talked briefly with Mary, Wally's widow, and then called State Medical School, from which Wally had always said he had graduated. As it was late in the afternoon, all the professors were out on the golf course; thus, Snoops spoke with Nina, a secretary in the office of the dean of the medical school. When asked about Wally, Nina replied, "I don't think Wally ever graduated."

In Snoops's obituary, which appeared in the next morning's *Daily Bleat,* Snoops had written that Wally had never actually received a medical degree from State Medical School. Upon reading the obituary, Mary broke into tears and then became very angry, for she had worked hard to help put Wally through State Medical School, from which Wally had, in fact, graduated with high honors. Wally's executor, Eddie, was equally incensed. Both Eddie and Mary called *The Daily Bleat,* demanding a retraction. The next day, on the front page, *The Daily Bleat* admitted its error and stated that Wally graduated with high honors from State Medical School. They also fired Snoops. Nonetheless, both Eddie and Mary sued *The Daily Bleat* for defamation.

What is *The Daily Bleat's* best defense?

(A) There was no malice on the part of the defendant.

(B) The newspaper's retraction negated any harm.

(C) Snoops got his information from a secretary at the Medical School.

(D) Wally is dead.

Questions 27-28 are based on the following fact situation:

Christine and her friend Zelda were going away to college and had quite a few personal belongings to transport. Christine's father offered to drive them in his van, but when the van was loaded they discovered there was only room for two people, so Christine asked her boyfriend Harry to drive her in his car while Christine's father and Zelda rode in the van.

About halfway to the college, while the van and Harry's car were driving down the freeway, the van in front, the van suddenly swerved out of control and ran off the highway, ending up on its side in the center divider. When Harry stopped his car and Christine ran to the van, she discovered to her horror that her father was dead. Zelda appeared to be injured, but not severely. Because her father previously had heart trouble, Christine assumed that he had had a heart attack while driving, although a later investigation would reveal that the accident was caused solely by a defect in the steering mechanism of the van. Filled with remorse, Christine told Zelda, "I'm so sorry about this. I'll make good any losses you suffer because of this accident." Later, when

Christine learned that Zelda was going to seek treatment from Dr. Winston, she wrote the doctor a letter stating that she would be responsible for all of Zelda's medical expenses; Dr. Winston received the letter the next day.

27. Assume for purposes of this question only that several months after the accident, but within the applicable statute of limitations, Zelda discovered that she had suffered an injury to her spinal column that would prevent her from ever playing basketball again. Zelda had been a scholarship athlete in basketball at the college and was considered to be a certain high draft selection for the newly formed women's professional basketball league when she graduated. She brought an action against Christine for several million dollars in damages. Which of the following is the best defense Christine could assert against Zelda's claim?

(A) There was no consideration supporting her promise to Zelda to make good any losses.

(B) She did not intend to offer to pay Zelda for the loss of her professional career when she said she would make good any losses.

(C) She was in error when she assumed that her father's heart attack was the cause of the accident.

(D) She did not know that Zelda would not be able to play basketball when she offered to make good any losses.

28. Assume for purposes of this question only that, after treating Zelda for her injuries until she recovered, Dr. Winston sent Christine a bill for services rendered. When Christine refused to pay, Dr. Winston brought an action to recover the amount of her bill. Who will prevail?

(A) Dr. Winston, because she gave medical treatment to Zelda after receiving Christine's letter.

(B) Dr. Winston, because Christine's promise to pay Zelda's medical expenses was in writing.

(C) Christine, because there was no consideration for her promise to Dr. Winston.

(D) Christine, because she derived no benefit from the medical services rendered to Zelda.

Questions 29-30 are based on the following fact situation:

Ben and Sandy, brother and sister, received a $50,000 inheritance from their deceased father. By mutual agreement, they used the money to purchase a 10-acre parcel of land. Ben and Sandy took title as joint tenants. Three years after the purchase, Ben suggested to Sandy that they build an apartment house on the property. Sandy rejected this idea. Ben then asked if he could build an apartment house on his half of the property; Sandy agreed. Ben then built an apartment house on the eastern five acres of the property. Six months later, Sandy gave permission to the Boy Scouts of America to use the western half of the property as a site for weekend camping trips. Two years later, Ben died, leaving his entire estate to his son, Steven.

29. In an appropriate action to determine the respective interests of Sandy and Steven in the property, if Steven is judged to be the owner of the eastern five acres of the property, the most likely reason for the judgment will be that:

(A) Sandy's conduct during Ben's lifetime estopped her from asserting title to the eastern half of the property.

(B) The taking of title as joint tenants does not conclusively presume that the property is held as joint tenants.

(C) The joint tenancy was terminated by the oral agreement of Ben and Sandy at the time it was made.

(D) A joint tenant may will away his interest in property, provided it is passed on to a lineal descendant.

30. In an appropriate action to determine the respective interests of Sandy and Steven in the property, if Sandy is adjudged to be the owner of all of the property, the most likely reason for the judgment will be that:

(A) The Statute of Frauds prevents the enforcement of Sandy's oral agreement.

(B) The record title of the property as joint tenancy can be changed only by a duly recorded instrument.

(C) Ben could not unilaterally sever the joint tenancy.

(D) Ben's expenditure of funds in building the apartment house in reliance on Sandy's oral promise estops her from denying the oral permission.

Question 31

The state legislature of Nevada enacted legislation prohibiting the use of tractor-trailer rigs weighing more than 100,000 pounds gross, after lengthy hearings demonstrated to the legislators' satisfaction that superheavy trucks rapidly degrade the state's roadways and pose a greater safety danger than smaller trucks. Western States Freight, a trucking firm that frequently uses Nevada highways for trips between Colorado and California, has recently purchased several tractor-trailer rigs weighing over 100,000 pounds when loaded. Most of its equipment may still be legally used in Nevada, but the firm does not want to have to exclude the superheavies from the California runs and plans to gradually replace its older trucks with larger models. Western brings an action for declaratory relief in federal court in Colorado, seeking to have the Nevada legislation declared unconstitutional. The state of Nevada asserts that the legislation is justified as an exercise of the state's police power based upon safety considerations, and that the court may not second-guess the state legislators as to this subject. None of the evidence presented at the legislative hearings is produced in court. Western presents expert testimony that the heavier trucks are no less safe than smaller models.

The trial court should rule:

(A) That the legislation is an unconstitutional violation of Western's Fourteenth Amendment rights to due process of law.

(B) That the legislation is unconstitutional because it violates the Commerce Clause.

(C) That the legislation is a valid exercise of the state's police power to regulate highway safety.

(D) That the evidence of the damage done to the state's highways by the superheavy trucks is sufficient to uphold the legislation independently of the safety argument.

Questions 32-33 are based on the following fact situation:

Baxter was heavily in debt and was concerned that his home was about to be repossessed. To try to generate money to satisfy his creditors, Baxter promised to pay his friend Dunn $100 if Dunn would enter Baxter's house that evening and take his expensive color television and stereo. Baxter explained that he would then report the items as being stolen to the insurance company and collect a settlement from them. Baxter gave Dunn directions to his home, which was one of several tract houses in a fairly new development. Baxter told Dunn to arrive at approximately 9 p.m. and to enter through a window at the rear of the house that Baxter would leave ajar. Dunn knew that since Baxter lived alone, there was no possibility that he might find someone within the house when he arrived at the appointed time. Dunn arrived at the location at approximately 9 p.m., but due to the darkness of the evening and the fact that all of the homes in the development looked the same, he mistakenly entered the house belonging to Baxter's neighbor. He found a window ajar at the rear of the neighbor's home and pushed it

open. He entered and took the neighbor's television set and stereo. When he returned to the bar where Baxter was waiting for him, both men were arrested by the police.

32. If Baxter and Dunn are tried for conspiracy, the court will most likely find them:

(A) Not guilty, because Dunn failed to take Baxter's property.

(B) Not guilty, because Dunn, being in the wrong house, could not take Baxter's property.

(C) Guilty, because they actually took the neighbor's property.

(D) Guilty, because they intentionally agreed to defraud the insurance company.

33. If Dunn is charged with burglary, his best argument for acquittal would be that:

(A) He acted under a mistake of law.

(B) There was no breaking.

(C) There was no entry.

(D) He reasonably thought that he was in Baxter's home.

Questions 34-35 are based on the following fact situation:

Allan invited all of his neighbors to a July 4th party in his backyard. Practically the entire neighborhood showed up, except for Clem, who lived next door. Clem was an elderly man with a known heart condition who chose not to participate in neighborhood social functions. That evening, after a full day of festivities and much beer drinking, someone at the party suggested, "We ought to set off some fireworks!" Bob, another guest, thereupon produced a large skyrocket, which he lit. However, the skyrocket failed to climb properly and crashed into Clem's garage, starting a fire. Clem rushed out of his house and attempted to put out the flames, but he suffered a heart attack and was rendered unconscious. The garage burned to the ground before the fire department arrived. Fortunately, however, the firefighters were able to revive Clem, and he has since recovered from the heart attack. A local ordinance made it a misdemeanor to sell fireworks within the city limits.

34. If Clem sues Allan for the damage to his garage, the theory on which he is most likely to prevail is that:

(A)   Allan failed to exercise due care to control the acts of his guests.

(B)   Allan is strictly liable for harm resulting from ultrahazardous activities performed on his land.

(C)   Clem had been invited to Allan's party; as an invitee, Allan owed him a duty to discover and guard against activities on his land involving an unreasonable risk of harm.

(D)   Allan is liable on a negligence per se theory because of the local ordinance banning the sale of fireworks within the city.

35. If Clem sues Bob for the damage to his garage on a theory of negligence, which of the following arguments, if sustained by the facts, would be most helpful for Bob to avoid liability?

(A)   The setting off of skyrockets on July 4th is an accepted custom in the community.

(B)   The skyrocket was aimed by Bob to avoid crashing into Clem's garage.

(C)   The fire that started would have burned itself out but for the fact that Clem's garage was built out of substandard, highly flammable material.

(D)   Bob was a guest on Allan's property and entitled to the same restricted scope of liability as Allan.

Question 36

Vincent, who operated a local neighborhood liquor store, was robbed by a man wielding an unusual knife with a pearl-studded handle. Davis was arrested and charged with armed robbery of Vincent. At trial the prosecution calls Wilma to testify that, three days after the robbery of Vincent, she was robbed by Davis with a knife that had a pearl-studded handle.

The court will most likely hold that Wilma's testimony is:

(A)   Admissible, as showing habit.

(B)   Admissible, as establishing an identifying circumstance.

(C)   Inadmissible, because it is improper character evidence.

(D)   Inadmissible, because its probative value is substantially outweighed by the danger of unfair prejudice.

Question 37

A state penal statute makes it a misdemeanor to "willfully shut off the gas, electricity, or any other form of power for cooking, heating, or illumination to an inhabited dwelling" unless strictly outlined procedures for notice and hearing are met. Shelley owned several small, single-family residences in City, which she rented to various student groups and families. One such rental, a small, furnished two-bedroom house located in one of the poorer sections of City, had been rented to a young married couple for several months when Shelley failed to receive the monthly rent check. She drove by the house several times for two weeks and received no answer to her knocks. Neighbors told her that they had not seen the couple for at least three weeks. Finally, Shelley used her keys to enter the house. She discovered that the old set of dishware and utensils she had permitted the couple to use was still in the kitchen, but that there was no food in the house and all but a few old items of clothing had been removed from the closets. Concluding that the couple had abandoned the rental without paying the last month's rent, Shelley called the power company and had the electricity and gas shut off until she could find another tenant.

A week later, the couple returned from an extended visit to the young wife's sick mother in Mexico. When they found that their power had been turned off, they reported this to the authorities and Shelley was prosecuted under the misdemeanor statute. At trial, it was established that the couple had inadvertently failed to place the proper postage on the rent check, which they had mailed from Mexico, and it had eventually been returned by Mexican postal authorities to the wife's mother's residence.

Shelley will probably be:

(A) Convicted, because the charged crime is violation of a public safety statute, and she is strictly liable for her action in turning off the power.

(B) Convicted, because she did not undertake a more thorough inquiry or wait a more reasonable length of time before concluding that the house had been abandoned.

(C) Acquitted, if the trier of fact concludes that Shelley was reasonable in believing that the house had been abandoned.

(D) Acquitted, if the trier of fact concludes that the young couple was negligent in not placing proper postage on the rent check mailed from Mexico.

Question 38

When Sandra graduated from high school, her elderly Aunt Mildred asked her to come and live with her in the large, three-story brownstone owned by Mildred in Manhattan. Mildred had recently had hip replacement surgery and could no longer attend to even minor household activities, and needed assistance in caring for the several thousand orchids she cultivated in her rooftop greenhouse. Mildred said to Sandra, "I probably have about five years left, so if you will live here and take care of me and my

flowers for the rest of my life, this house and the flowers will be yours." Sandra agreed, and moved from her parents' home in Yonkers to the brownstone in Manhattan.

Mildred lived for eight years after Sandra came to live with her. Sandra attended to Mildred's personal needs, an increasing necessity as Mildred grew more frail. Sandra also maintained the household, did the shopping, cooking, etc., and cared, with less and less assistance from Mildred, for the numerous orchids. Mildred's moderate income from her investments provided the money necessary to support the household.

No further discussion was ever had between Mildred and Sandra regarding conveyance of the brownstone and its contents. Shortly after Mildred died, Sandra was contacted by a Mr. Cramer, who identified himself as Mildred's lawyer and stated that he was in possession of Mildred's last will and testament and would seek to have it admitted to probate. In the subsequent proceedings, it was revealed that Mildred had devised her orchids to a Nero Wolfe, also residing in Manhattan, and her investments, the house, and the remainder of her estate to her daughter who lived in California and whom Mildred had not seen or heard from in over 15 years. When Sandra refused to vacate the brownstone or surrender the orchids, Cramer, now representing Mildred's daughter, brought action for possession of the house.

If Sandra prevails in the action brought by Mildred's daughter, it will be because:

(A) She can successfully assert the doctrine of "unclean hands" to prevent Mildred's daughter from pressing her claim under the will.

(B) The Statute of Frauds need not be satisfied as between family members.

(C) The Statute of Frauds will not bar enforcement of Mildred's promise because her promise induced Sandra to perform, and injustice can be avoided only by enforcement.

(D) The Statute of Frauds will not be applied where there has been part performance and where that performance is such as can be explained by the existence of the asserted contract and in no other way.

Question 39

Hines and West had been dating for many years. They decided to live together and some day, should things work out, get married. Since each earned a sizable income, they decided to invest some of their money in real estate. They purchased Blackacre for $100,000, each contributing half the purchase price from savings. They took title as joint tenants with right of survivorship. Two years later, Hines and West were married. One year after that, the parties separated. Hines then quitclaimed all of his interest in Blackacre to his brother, Brown, who duly recorded the deed. The jurisdiction has no applicable statute.

Blackacre is now held by:

(A) West and Brown, as joint tenants with right of survivorship.

(B) West and Brown, as tenants in common.

(C) Hines and West, as tenants by the entirety.

(D) Hines and West, as joint tenants with right of survivorship.

Question 40

Sonny was arrested for shoplifting. As Sonny was being booked at the police station, Sonny's mother, Betty, arrived at the station. As she was talking with Sonny, Photog, a reporter for the *Daily News*, took Betty's picture. The photograph of Betty appeared on the front page of the next day's edition of the *Daily News*. The story of Sonny's arrest appeared just below it. A caption to the photograph identified Betty as Sonny's mother. Later that week, Betty lost her job as a result of the story in the *Daily News*.

If Betty asserts a claim against the *Daily News* for invasion of privacy, Betty most likely will:

(A) Recover, if she was not involved in the events that led to Sonny's arrest.

(B) Recover, because the photograph and news story caused Betty to be discharged from her employment.

(C) Not recover, since Betty's photograph was taken in a public place.

(D) Not recover, because the caption was accurate.

Question 41

In which of the following situations is Defendant most likely to be guilty of common law murder?

(A) As a joke, Defendant trips Tom as he walks by. As a result of the fall, Tom hits his head on the corner of a desk and dies immediately.

(B) During a heated argument, Ed punches Defendant in the stomach. Angered, Defendant responds by stabbing Ed with a knife and killing him instantly.

(C) While driving home from work late one night, Defendant falls asleep behind the wheel of his automobile. His car drifts across the middle of the road, strikes a car, and the other driver is killed instantly in the collision.

(D) Angered because his neighbor is playing his stereo at a very high volume, Defendant fires a gun into the neighbor's house. The bullet strikes and kills neighbor's wife.

Question 42

The United States General Accounting Office issued a call for competitive bids for a contract to supply the National Park Service with 3,000 four-wheel drive utility vehicles; the detailed specifications for the vehicles were included in the announcement. Auto Modifiers, Inc., of the state of Midwest won the contract as low bidder and began manufacture of the vehicles. Midwest statutes require that automobiles manufactured in that state be equipped with certain antipollution devices and have a maximum displacement of 2,500 cubic centimeters. The specifications of the federal contract require Auto Modifiers to manufacture the utility vehicles without the antipollution devices and with engines with a displacement of 4,000 cubic centimeters. When the president of Auto Modifiers learns that the Midwest Attorney General's office is investigating the manufacture of the government vehicles, he instructs his legal department to take affirmative action to protect the company. Auto Modifiers then files suit in state court for declaratory relief, seeking a judicial declaration that the state statute prescribing antipollution devices and engine size may not be enforced as to it.

The court should rule:

(A) The statute may not constitutionally be applied to Auto Modifiers in this instance because to do so would violate the Supremacy Clause.

(B) The statute may not constitutionally be applied to Auto Modifiers because to do so would violate the Contracts Clause.

(C) The statute may not constitutionally be applied to Auto Modifiers because to do so would violate the Commerce Clause.

(D) All of the above.

Questions 43-44 are based on the following fact situation:

Driver knew that children frequently played in the street along Elm Street. As Driver was operating his vehicle along Elm Street, he saw a ball roll into the street. A few seconds later, Child darted out into the street after the ball. Pedestrian, a passerby, saw Driver's vehicle bearing down on Child. Concerned that Child would be hurt, Pedestrian rushed into the street to try to save Child. Just as Pedestrian reached Child, Pedestrian tripped and fell down in the street. Driver's car struck both Pedestrian and Child, and both were injured. The jurisdiction follows traditional contributory negligence rules.

43. Assuming that Child is four years old, will Child prevail in a personal injury suit against Driver?

(A) Yes, because Driver knew that children played in Elm Street.

(B) Yes, unless Driver was going no faster than the posted speed limit.

(C) No, because Child negligently darted into the street.

(D) No, because Child's parents were negligent in not properly supervising Child.

44. If Pedestrian sues Driver for personal injuries, who will prevail?

(A) Driver, because Driver could not have expected an adult to run into the street.

(B) Driver, if he was traveling no faster than the posted speed limit.

(C) Driver, because Pedestrian was unrelated to Child.

(D) Pedestrian, if Driver had the last clear chance to avoid the accident.

Question 45

Howard and Wendy were engaged and looking for a lovely lot on which to build their dream house. They fell in love with Blueacre at first sight and purchased it, taking title as joint tenants with right of survivorship. Before construction of the dream house could begin, Howard discovered that Wendy was having an affair with Claude, and the engagement was called off. Wanting to obtain the money to run off with Claude, Wendy wanted to sell Blueacre. Howard refused to sell. Wendy put Blueacre up for sale anyway, and when Tim agreed to purchase it, Wendy forged Howard's signature on the deed conveying Blueacre to Tim.

Who owns Blueacre?

(A) Howard only.

(B) Tim only.

(C) Howard and Tim as tenants in common.

(D) Howard, Wendy, and Tim as tenants in common.

Question 46

The large metropolitan areas of East Rabbit's Foot and West Rabbit's Foot, Wyoming, lie adjacent to each other on the county line separating, respectively, Pecos and Tuscaloosa Counties, each city being entirely within its respective county. Wyoming state law grants each county great autonomy in setting the health standards governing the preparation, packaging, transportation, and sale of foodstuffs. The Pecos County council recently enacted an ordinance, valid under the constitution and statutes of Wyoming, prohibiting the packaging and sale of any food item in any nonbiodegradable material; the ordinance defines nonbiodegradable and specifically lists as prohibited all forms of plastics, cellophane, or similar materials. The ordinance specifically exempts from its terms sales of food to public institutions such as hospitals, jails, and schools.

Snak-Mart, a retail food seller in East Rabbit's Foot, files an appropriate court action attacking the Pecos County ordinance on the grounds that it violates the Equal Protection Clause of the Fourteenth Amendment. The court should rule:

(A) For Snak-Mart, because the state's interests could be effectuated by alternative methods less intrusive upon Snak-Mart's constitutional rights.

(B) For Snak-Mart, because no compelling state interest is served by the challenged ordinance.

(C) For Pecos County, because the state may regulate in this area as Congress has not entered the field.

(D) For Pecos County, because the ordinance is rationally related to a legitimate state interest—the health and safety of its citizens.

Questions 47-48 are based on the following fact situation:

On January 1, Fred executed and delivered a deed to his daughter, Diane, conveying his avocado ranch as follows: "To Diane for life, but if Diane dies survived by her spouse and children, then to Diane's spouse for life, with the remainder in fee simple to Diane's children; but if Diane dies survived by her spouse and no children, then to my son Sam in fee simple."

On June 15, Diane married George and as a wedding gift Fred quitclaimed his interest in the avocado ranch to George. Assume that the jurisdiction does not follow the doctrine of destructibility of contingent remainders.

47. On December 1, Diane died without children and without a will. The applicable law of intestate succession provides that George is Diane's only heir. Sam claims that George has no interest in the land. Title to the avocado ranch is held by whom?

(A) George, because of the doctrine of merger.

(B) George, because Diane died intestate and her fee simple passed to him as her intestate heir.

(C) Sam, because the interest granted to Diane's spouse is void under the Rule Against Perpetuities.

(D) Sam, because Diane, although survived by her spouse, died without children.

48. Assume for the purposes of this question only that Diane died survived by George and two children, Ann and Bradley. Bradley dies intestate two days after Diane, leaving one child, Curtis, as his only heir. What are the respective interests of George, Ann, and Curtis in the avocado ranch?

(A) George has a life estate, Ann has an absolutely vested remainder, and Curtis has nothing.

(B) George has fee simple ownership of the ranch, and Ann and Curtis have nothing.

(C) George has a life estate, and Ann and Curtis have absolutely vested remainders.

(D) George has a life estate, and Ann has a vested remainder subject to open.

Question 49

Nimrod, who held a hunting license issued by the state of West, was hunting deer and elk in that state. After two days of fruitless hunting, Nimrod spied an elk. Nimrod was hunting on private land, but the elk was 200 yards away, inside a fence that surrounded a federal military base. Nimrod shot the elk from where he was standing, but entered the military base to retrieve the carcass. Nimrod took the carcass away and had it dressed and frozen for Nimrod's meals through the winter. A federal statute prohibits the removal of wild animals or the carcasses thereof from United States military bases. Nimrod is prosecuted under the statute.

The best argument in favor of upholding the statute as constitutional would be based on:

(A) The Supremacy Clause.

(B) The Army and Navy Clause.

(C) The Commerce Clause.

(D) The Privileges and Immunities Clause of the Fourteenth Amendment.

Question 50

Thomas wanted to give his home to his brother Ben. In 1995, Thomas executed a warranty deed conveying the home to Ben. Thomas then wrote a letter to Ben saying, "Dear Ben, My home is now yours." He put the letter and deed in an envelope and wrote the following on the outside of the envelope: "Kenneth, you are to give this deed to my brother Ben when I die. Until then, you should safeguard this envelope and the documents inside. Signed Thomas." Thomas delivered these items to his cousin Kenneth and continued to live in his home by himself.

In 1997, Thomas executed a will leaving all of his property to his sister Sally.

Thomas died in January 2004. Shortly thereafter, Kenneth delivered the envelope containing the deed to Ben, who promptly recorded the deed.

Thomas's will has been admitted to probate and Xavier is the executor. Xavier has brought an appropriate action against Ben to determine the title to Thomas's home.

The court should rule:

(A) For Sally, because the deed was not effectively delivered before Thomas died.

(B) For Sally, because the deed was not recorded before the grantor died.

(C) For Ben, because the deed effectively conveyed title when it was executed.

(D) For Ben, because Thomas no longer owned his home when he died.

MIXED SUBJECT SET 4 SUBJECT GUIDE

1. Constitutional Law	26. Torts
2. Evidence	27. Contracts
3. Criminal Law	28. Contracts
4. Torts	29. Real Property
5. Torts	30. Real Property
6. Constitutional Law	31. Constitutional Law
7. Torts	32. Criminal Law
8. Evidence	33. Criminal Law
9. Evidence	34. Torts
10. Contracts	35. Torts
11. Contracts	36. Evidence
12. Contracts	37. Criminal Law
13. Contracts	38. Contracts
14. Real Property	39. Real Property
15. Criminal Law	40. Torts
16. Constitutional Law	41. Criminal Law
17. Constitutional Law	42. Constitutional Law
18. Real Property	43. Torts
19. Evidence	44. Torts
20. Evidence	45. Real Property
21. Evidence	46. Constitutional Law
22. Criminal Law/Procedure	47. Real Property
23. Evidence	48. Real Property
24. Real Property	49. Constitutional Law
25. Torts	50. Evidence

MIXED SUBJECT ANSWERS - SET 4

Answer to Question 1

(D) Clearly this statute burdens interstate commerce by diverting purchases which would otherwise be made from interstate businesses to intrastate suppliers and by imposing a tax on interstate suppliers. Both requirements have the purpose and effect of imposing a direct burden on interstate commerce and, especially in the case of the tax, do so in a facially discriminatory manner. As such, they would be subjected to strict scrutiny, and would fail. (D) is therefore the best answer. (A) is incorrect because the measures involve economic and social matters and would, under the usual due process analysis, be subjected to rational basis scrutiny, which they would survive. (B) is wrong because there is a rational basis for the classification and no suspect classification or fundamental right is involved. (C) is wrong because, while a corporation as a legal entity may be considered a person for some purposes, corporations are not citizens for the purposes of the Article IV Privileges and Immunities Clause.

Answer to Question 2

(C) Daniel's statement is an admission—an out-of-court statement by a party being offered into evidence by an opposing party. [Fed. R. Evid. 801(d)(2)] Since it is not considered hearsay evidence and is obviously relevant to the underlying question of who committed the battery against Paul, it would be admissible. (A) is incorrect because the "statement against interest" exception to the hearsay rule provides that a declarant's out-of-court statement is admissible *if it is against the declarant's interest when made*. [Fed. R. Evid. 804(b)(3)] Daniel's out-of-court statement ("I haven't been out of the country in five years") was not clearly against his interest when it was made. It is vastly different, for example, than if Daniel had confided to Walter that he had beaten Paul; that would be a statement against interest at the time the statement was made. That Daniel's actual statement to Walter was ultimately used against Daniel does not qualify it as a statement against interest. Also, and equally important, (A) is incorrect because the "statement against interest" exception to the hearsay rule comes into play only *if the declarant is unavailable to testify* (*e.g.*, because the declarant is dead or cannot be found). [Fed. R. Evid. 804(a)] The question makes clear that Daniel not only is available to testify, but he actually does testify. Hence, the "unavailability" requirement of the "statement against interest" exception has not been satisfied. (B) is a plausible answer, but not as good as (C) because it contains several ambiguities. The answer is ambiguous as to the purpose for which Daniel's prior inconsistent statement is offered into evidence. If offered for the purpose of proving the truth of the matter asserted in the statement, it would be inadmissible hearsay evidence; it would not meet the specific requirements of Rule 801(d)(1)(A) to qualify as nonhearsay evidence: Daniel's prior inconsistent statement was not made *under oath* at *another proceeding*. If offered for the purpose of impeaching Daniel's testimony, however, the prior inconsistent statement might be admissible. Proving the prior inconsistent statement of a witness is a well-accepted method for impeaching the testimony of that witness. In this case, though, *extrinsic evidence* (the testimony of another witness, Walter) is being offered to prove Daniel's prior inconsistent statement. Extrinsic evidence can be used to show a prior inconsistent statement of a witness, for purposes of impeachment, only if the inconsistency goes to a *material* issue in the case. It would, at best, be a judgment call as to whether Daniel's not having left the country in five years is a material issue in Paul's suit against Daniel for battery. Thus, (C) is a better answer than (B). (D) is incorrect because, since Daniel's statement is an admission, its admissibility is not dependent on Daniel's having the opportunity to comment on it. Moreover, even if Daniel's statement were analyzed solely from the standpoint of being a prior inconsistent statement offered to impeach, (D) would be incorrect.

The Federal Rules have abolished the common law requirement that a witness be given an opportunity to explain a prior inconsistent statement *before* extrinsic evidence of the statement can be admitted; the opportunity may be provided after introduction of the statement.

Answer to Question 3

(D) (A) is not the most likely answer, because the facts indicate that Defendant believed himself to be in danger. Even if it is found that his belief was unreasonable, at most he would be guilty of voluntary manslaughter. (B) is not the most likely answer either, because there is no showing that Defendant intended to kill anyone, or that when he fired the pistol it was likely that he would kill anyone. The fact that the bullet which killed Al ricocheted appears to make this killing a result of, at most, gross negligence. Thus, under this fact situation, Defendant most likely would be guilty of involuntary manslaughter. The facts in (C) do not indicate that Defendant would be charged with a crime at all since he did not intend to shoot at George and had no real reason to believe that George would be endangered by his conduct. At most, Defendant could be charged with negligent homicide if he were charged with a crime at all. In (D), Defendant would probably be charged with murder because, although it is arguable that the death of the customer was "accidental," it occurred during the commission of a dangerous felony, and under common law, would be subject to the felony murder rule.

Answer to Question 4

(B) But for Drago's negligent act of colliding with Pitts's car, Pitts would not have been injured. Drago is thus a cause in fact of Pitts's injuries. (A) is incorrect because Stratton's negligence would not qualify as an intervening act since it occurred earlier in time than Drago's. (C) is incorrect because the failure of the latch is not the type of intervening force that would relieve Drago from liability. (D) is incorrect because the "but for" test is used to establish liability in concurrent cause cases, not limit another's liability.

Answer to Question 5

(B) Pitts's claim against Stratton would be based on strict liability in tort. As such, she would only need to establish that the car was dangerously defective in order to recover. (A) is incorrect because Pitts's failure to discover the defect would be, at best, contributory negligence, which is not a defense to strict liability in tort in jurisdictions retaining traditional contributory negligence rules. (C) is incorrect because Drago's negligence would qualify as a foreseeable intervening force which would not relieve Stratton from liability. (D) is incorrect because Stratton is strictly liable even if it did not know or have reason to know of the defect.

Answer to Question 6

(C) Standing requires an allegation of such a personal stake in the outcome of the controversy as to assure that concrete adverseness which sharpens the presentation of issues. Abstract injury is not enough; the plaintiff must show that he has sustained or is immediately in danger of sustaining some direct injury as the result of the challenged official conduct. The injury or threat of injury must be real and immediate, not conjectural or hypothetical. Here, the potential plaintiffs in (A) and (B) are merely thinking about selling or buying used cars in State B. Thus, any injury or threat of injury to them is strictly hypothetical and abstract. Consequently, the potential plaintiffs in (A) and (B) are unlikely to have standing. Likewise, the out-of-state manufacturer in (D), who *might* be required to indemnify its dealers in State B, is at this point able to assert merely a hypothetical injury, not one that is real and immediate. On the other hand, the potential plaintiff in (C), who already has a contract to sell used cars to a State B dealer, is immediately in danger of sustaining a direct economic injury as a result of the statute—*i.e.*, costs associated with testing each car and bringing up to standard those cars found to be deficient.

Answer to Question 7

(D)   A private nuisance action requires a showing that defendant's interference with the use and enjoyment of plaintiff's property was unreasonable. To be characterized as unreasonable, the severity of the inflicted injury must outweigh the utility of defendant's conduct. Here, the fact that the pesticide is the only means of preventing destruction of the state's principal agricultural product would be the most persuasive additional fact for Growit's defense. (A) is incorrect because coming to the nuisance is generally not a good defense to a nuisance action. (B) and (C) are incorrect even though they state factors which may be considered by a court in determining whether an injunction should be issued. The main question is whether the severity of the injury outweighs the utility of defendant's conduct, and these two factors do not speak as well to this point as (D).

Answer to Question 8

(C)   Walter's testimony of three instances of reckless driving by Doug would be considered character evidence. Character evidence is not admissible in a civil case if offered to show that a party probably acted in conformity with that character. Character evidence is admissible in a civil case when the character of a person is an issue in the case. Peter is suing Olivia on a negligent entrustment theory, and thus Doug's character as a safe driver is in issue in the case against Olivia, but not in the case against Doug himself. (A) is wrong; as stated, Doug's character is in issue in determining whether Olivia was negligent. (B) is wrong because specific instances of conduct may be used to prove character when character is an issue in the case. [Fed. R. Evid. 405(B)] (D) is wrong because this is not a criminal case.

Answer to Question 9

(D)   Peter's objection should be overruled. Harry's testimony is a classic example of evidence regarding habit, and Olivia's habit is relevant to the issue of negligent entrustment. (A) is wrong because neither the Federal Rules nor the prevailing common law requires the corroboration of habit evidence. (B) and (C) are wrong because the testimony is evidence of habit, not character.

Answer to Question 10

(B)   Prevention of performance by an irresistible, superhuman cause is an excuse for nonperformance of a contract, unless the parties stipulate to the contrary. The destruction of the lot by the forces of nature rendered performance impossible, so Builder need not perform. (A) is wrong because destruction of the property does not make the contract void; it merely discharges Builder. (C) is a misstatement of law. (D) is wrong because there was no mutual mistake.

Answer to Question 11

(D)   The general rule is that a contractor is responsible for destruction of the premises under construction prior to completion. Once the residence is completed, risk of loss shifts to the owner. Builder must perform the original contract without compensation for the work that was destroyed by the storm. Thus, (D) is correct and (C) is wrong. (A) is wrong because the subject matter was not destroyed; and even if it were, the contract would not be void. (B) is wrong because performance is not impossible; he can rebuild the residence.

Answer to Question 12

(C) Modern courts recognize that impracticability due to excessive and unreasonable difficulty or expense is a defense to breach of contract for nonperformance. Since the cost to Builder to perform under the original contract would exceed more than double what he would be paid, under the modern view, he would be excused from performance by commercial impracticability. Unlike destruction of the building itself before completion, which will not discharge a contractor's duty, the erosion of the lot, which destroys the means of performing the contract, will generally not be one of the risks that a contractor will be deemed to have assumed. Thus, (D) is wrong. (A) is wrong because Builder's bankruptcy is irrelevant for this purpose. (B) is wrong because there is no mutual mistake here.

Answer to Question 13

(C) Performance is excused where prevented by operation of law, despite any stipulation to the contrary. Because governmental interference made performance of the contract as contemplated illegal, Builder is excused from performance, even though some performance is possible. Thus, (C) is correct, and (D) is incorrect. (A) is incorrect because there was no mutual mistake when the contract was formed. (B) is wrong because Owner did not breach the contract.

Answer to Question 14

(C) On the happening of the prohibited event (using Blackacre for other than residential purposes), Brian's fee simple determinable automatically came to an end, and Owner was entitled to present possession. Not having claimed possession within the applicable seven-year period, and with Brian's possession being open, notorious, continuous, and adverse, any action by Owner or his heirs is now barred by adverse possession. Thus, (A) and (B) are incorrect. (D) is incorrect because a possibility of reverter becomes possessory automatically upon termination of the prior determinable estate. Unlike a right of entry, a grantor does not have to assert a possibility of reverter in order for a cause of action to arise.

Answer to Question 15

(B) Under the facts of this case, to support a finding of murder, the trial court would have to find that Bob acted either intentionally or with malice aforethought. The facts clearly indicate that Bob did not know of the car, so it cannot be said that he shot at it intentionally, and therefore (A) is not correct. "Malice aforethought" has several definitions, one of which is that the defendant is acting in a "wanton" state of mind. There is little question that shooting a rifle through a front door can be considered "wanton." Thus, the question is whether Bob's intoxication was sufficient to negate this state of mind. If a defendant's lack of awareness results from *voluntary intoxication*, his conduct will nevertheless be deemed wanton. (C) is not a correct analysis of the issue, because his intentional act was firing the rifle, not shooting at the car. (D) is not the best answer, because although there is the possibility that Bob might have been able to show only gross negligence, there is sufficient evidence to support a finding of malice aforethought and murder.

Answer to Question 16

(B) This situation presents a possible violation of the Equal Protection Clause. A state may not favor established residents over new residents. To do so in an area that affects a person's ability to engage in his livelihood impedes migration from state to state. Interstate travel is a fundamental right, and a classification that burdens it would trigger a strict scrutiny analysis. In any case, the classification would be subjected to something more than the mere rationality test. (A) is incorrect because this is not an area reserved to the states, and even if it were, the United States Constitution would take precedence over state law. (C) is wrong because the Fifth Amendment applies only to federal, not state, government action. (D) is wrong because the Privileges and Immunities Clause does not apply to aliens.

Answer to Question 17

(C) The statutes violate the Privileges and Immunities Clause of Article IV, which prohibits discrimination against nonresidents with respect to essential activities (*e.g.*, pursuing a livelihood) unless (i) the discrimination is closely related to a substantial state purpose, *and* (ii) less restrictive means are not available. Here, other controls could be placed on fishing without discriminating against out-of-state fishermen. (A) is wrong because, even though Congress has not acted in this area, the statutes would still be unconstitutional in light of the negative implications of the "dormant" Commerce Clause. Congressional silence is, therefore, irrelevant. (B) states a due process test which, even if applicable, would not preclude a finding of unconstitutionality on other grounds. (D) is wrong because the activity here does not involve foreign commerce—this is a dispute between one state and a citizen of another state.

Answer to Question 18

(A) The grant is valid because Oliver Jr. was a life in being when the interest was created. (B) is incorrect because a reversionary interest is an interest remaining in the grantor. (D) is incorrect because a possibility of reverter is the interest left in the grantor after a conveyance of a fee simple determinable. Here, Oliver Sr. did not create such an estate. (C) is obviously incorrect, since the language of the deed clearly shows that Oliver Sr. was not giving Melinda the complete interest in this property; she received a fee simple subject to divestment by Oliver Jr.'s executory interest.

Answer to Question 19

(D) In a criminal case, other crimes and wrongs of the defendant may be admissible even though they are not charged, but they are not automatically admissible. There are two basic ideas: other crimes or wrongs are not admissible to show that the defendant is a bad person, nor are they admissible to show the defendant is a person of the type likely to commit this crime. Other crimes or wrongs may be admissible if they are relevant to show proof of motive, opportunity, intent, preparation, plan, knowledge, identity, or absence of mistake or accident, unless the judge determines that the probative value is substantially outweighed by prejudice. (A) and (B) are therefore wrong. (C) is wrong because extrinsic evidence of specific crimes is not admissible to rebut evidence of good character. While (D) calls for a judgment on the part of the trial judge and could be debated, it is the best answer because (A), (B), and (C) are incorrect statements of the law.

Answer to Question 20

(C) (B) is wrong. Under Federal Rule 801, prior identification can be admissible. The description is in the nature of prior testimony or prior identification. To be admissible, however, the declarant must testify at the trial and be subject to cross-examination. Since the night watchman died, this requirement cannot be satisfied. On these facts, there are no exceptions to the hearsay rule that would make the description admissible. (A) is wrong because before a document can be admitted as a past recollection recorded, the person whose statement appears in the document must be on the witness stand. (D) would have no bearing on the admissibility of the description.

Answer to Question 21

(B)   Since the question involves a crime of dishonesty, and the conviction is less than 10 years old, the question is proper on cross-examination because it goes to Fred's credibility. Evidence is not admissible to show general bad character or propensity to commit crimes; (A) is therefore wrong. (C) is wrong because this crime has plenty of probative value on the issue of credibility and because most courts hold that impeachment with a crime requiring proof or admission of an act of dishonesty or false statement cannot be excluded as too prejudicial. (D) is wrong because similarity to the crime charged is not required by the federal rules.

Answer to Question 22

(D)   The prosecutor is required by the Due Process Clause to prove each and every element of a crime beyond a reasonable doubt. One of the elements of larceny is an intent to permanently deprive a victim of his or her property, and the instructions in this case put the burden of proof on Dennis to show that there was no such intent. This relieves the prosecution of its burden because it implies that there is a presumption that Dennis intended to permanently deprive her of her jewels. (A) is wrong. The jury does have the power to ignore Dennis's testimony, but the conviction will be reversed because of the unconstitutional instruction on burden of proof. (B) is wrong. Dennis is not required to rebut the state's evidence; the state must prove each element beyond a reasonable doubt. (C) is not the best answer. While it is true that in some jurisdictions the judge cannot comment on the evidence in a criminal case, that prohibition would not be violated by an appropriate instruction on burden of proof.

Answer to Question 23

(A)   This question raises the issue of whether an employee's out-of-court statement ("The accident was my fault; I wasn't paying any attention") will be attributed to the employer, and thus considered an admission when the employer is a party. The answer is yes, provided the statement was made **while the person was employed by the employer** (not before or after the period of employment) **and** provided the statement **related to the employment**. [Fed. R. Evid. 801(d)(2)(D)] (A) is correct. Wilber's statement was made while he was employed by Ace Meat Packing Co., and it related to his employment in that it pertained to an accident that occurred when he was driving an Ace truck, presumably in the course of employment. Conversely, (C) is incorrect. That Wilber is no longer employed by Ace does not bear on the admissibility of his statement; what counts is that he was employed by Ace at the time he made the statement. (D) is also incorrect. That Ace may not have authorized Wilber to make the statement does not preclude it from being admissible; what counts is that the statement was made by an employee and related to his employment. Although one basis for attributing an employee's statement to the employer is the employer's authorization for the employee to speak on its behalf about the matter [Fed. R. Evid. 801(d)(2)(C)], that is not the only basis for treating the employee's statement in such a manner. (B) is incorrect because there is little reason to conclude that Wilber's statement was an "excited utterance" within the meaning of that hearsay exception. [Fed. R. Evid. 803(2)] The question does not indicate that Wilber spoke in an excited manner. The words in the statement itself do not suggest that the statement was made while Wilber was agitated. That Wilber spoke shortly after the accident would not alone be sufficient to make his statement an "excited utterance."

Answer to Question 24

(A) Barry had exclusive, continuous possession of the three-foot strip for the requisite statutory period. This possession was open and notorious; *i.e.*, it was possession as an owner would make of the land, and it put the true owner and the community on notice of the fact of possession. This possession was also hostile and under claim of right. Under the majority view, Barry's mistake as to the ownership of the three-foot strip is not determinative. Barry has held under claim of right because his actions appear to the community to be a claim of ownership and he is not holding with permission of the owner. Thus, (D) is incorrect. (C) is incorrect because the open and notorious nature of Barry's possession was sufficient to put the true owner on notice that a possession adverse to the owner's title had been taken. (B) is simply an incorrect statement of the law; there is no such presumption.

Answer to Question 25

(A) The facts state that Carter swung the hammer at John "intending to frighten" him. Thus, Carter did an act with the intent of causing the apprehension of immediate harmful or offensive contact, *i.e.*, an "assault." Because John was actually hit by the hammer head, the trial court would utilize the ***transferred intent doctrine*** to supply the necessary intent for battery. It makes no difference that Carter may not have known that the hammer was defective, because he set in motion the force that injured John; hence, (C) is an improper answer. (B) and (D) are not correct answers because they both go to the issue of a defense, and a person is not privileged to use deadly force against another no matter how provoking the other's mere statements may have been. Clearly, being hit with a hammer would be considered deadly force.

Answer to Question 26

(D) *The Daily Bleat's* best defense is that Dr. Wally is dead. Only living persons can be defamed; defamation of a deceased person is not an actionable tort. Thus, because Dr. Wally is dead, *The Daily Bleat* can obtain dismissal of the defamation action without having to establish any defamation defenses. Therefore, (D) is correct. (A) is not as good a defense as (D) because, in order to use the defense of absence of malice, the newspaper would have to establish that Dr. Wally was a public figure, which would be more difficult than showing that the doctor is dead. Moreover, it is not conclusive from the facts that Dr. Wally is a public figure as defined by the *Gertz* case (someone of pervasive fame or who is involved in a particular public controversy), since the facts merely state that he was prominent in the community. (B) is incorrect because a retraction, while it may show lack of actual malice in mitigation of damages, would not necessarily eliminate all of the harm to Dr. Wally's reputation. The fact that the retraction ran the next day on the front page gives the newspaper a better case, but it is not as good a defense as the fact that Wally is dead. (C) is incorrect because the fact that Snoops got his information from a secretary at the Medical School does not preclude liability for defamation. At most, that fact may be asserted to disprove malice if Dr. Wally was a public figure or negligence if the doctor's death was a matter of public concern. However, even assuming that one of these standards applies, Snoops may still be at fault for not having obtained a more authoritative statement from someone at the Medical School.

Answer to Question 27

(A) Zelda did not promise to do anything she was not otherwise obligated to do in bargained-for exchange for Christine's promise, so no consideration supported the latter's promise. If the agreement were otherwise enforceable, none of the other facts offered by the answers would prevent it from being carried out. (B) is incorrect because a court will not examine the promisor's subjective intent when making a promise. (C) is incorrect because mistake as to a fact that motivated the contract is not a defense under these circumstances; Christine had assumed the risk of mistake by making the promise without being certain of the cause of the accident. (D) is similarly incorrect. Mistake as to the value of the promise is generally a risk assumed by the parties.

Answer to Question 28

(A)   Christine offered to pay Dr. Winston if Dr. Winston treated Zelda. Dr. Winston accepted by treating Zelda; this treatment was also her consideration for the contract. Thus, Christine was contractually bound to pay for the medical expenses and (A) is correct. (B) is incorrect because Christine's promise need not have been in writing to be enforceable. The requirement of a writing under the Statute of Frauds for promises to pay the debt of another is not applicable here. Christine's promise was not a suretyship promise that was collateral to a promise of Zelda's; it was an independent promise by Christine to be primarily liable for Zelda's medical expenses, and therefore need not be in writing to be enforceable. (C) is incorrect because Dr. Winston's treatment is the consideration for Christine's promise to pay. There is nothing in the facts to suggest that Dr. Winston had incurred a preexisting duty to treat Zelda until she recovered; even if Dr. Winston had already agreed to begin treating Zelda, Dr. Winston received Christine's letter and then proceeded to treat Zelda until she recovered, sending Christine the bill in reliance on her promise. Hence, a court will find sufficient consideration here to avoid a preexisting duty problem. (D) is incorrect because Dr. Winston's treatment was the benefit that Christine sought to derive from her bargain. Remember that the benefit need not have economic value. Christine's benefit here is her peace of mind.

Answer to Question 29

(A)   Since Sandy informed Ben that he could develop the eastern five acres of the land, and since he reasonably relied on her statement to his detriment, she probably will be estopped to deny its effect. (B) is incorrect. Where the language of the grant is clear and a joint tenancy is created, no presumption is needed or applies. The joint tenancy cannot later be changed by subsequent informal action. (C) is wrong because an oral agreement is not effective to terminate a joint tenancy. (D) is an incorrect statement of the law. A joint tenant may not pass an interest to anyone at death, due to the right of survivorship.

Answer to Question 30

(A)   The Statute of Frauds prevents the enforcement of an oral agreement concerning an interest in land. (B) is wrong because there is no issue as to the record title to the land. The agreement between Ben and Sandy, if it had been reduced to writing, would have been perfectly valid as between them. (C) is wrong because a joint tenancy can be unilaterally severed. (D) is wrong because this would not support Sandy's ownership of the entire piece of land.

Answer to Question 31

(B)   As a general matter, a state may regulate in ways that impact on interstate commerce as long as the regulation does so only indirectly and the benefits outweigh the burdens imposed by compliance with the regulation. [Kassel v. Consolidated Freightways Corp. (1981)] When, as here, only a bare assertion that the regulation would increase safety is involved, a court will generally find that the regulation is invalid. This does not mean that a state could not prevail if it proved that the benefits of the regulation do in fact outweigh the burdens. Indeed, the Court intimated that such would be the case in *Bibb v. Navajo Freight Lines, Inc.* (1959). But Nevada has not made a sufficient showing here, and Western has presented colorable "expert" evidence to the contrary. (A) is incorrect because economic and social regulations are tested at the rational basis level for due process purposes, and even the minimal showing here would suffice for the state. (C) states a correct premise (*i.e.,* that the state is regulating for highway safety), but an incorrect result, and is wrong. (D) is wrong because the state has in fact made no such showing before the court. Thus, while there is a normal presumption of constitutionality, the state here has not met its burden in defending the measure in the face of contrary, expert evidence.

Answer to Question 32

(D) A conspiracy requires an agreement between two or more people to accomplish an unlawful act or objective. The parties must intend to enter into the agreement and intend to achieve the objective of the agreement. Baxter and Dunn agreed to defraud the insurance company and had the requisite intent. They also committed an overt act in furtherance of that intent. Thus, they can be convicted of conspiracy. (A) is wrong because the crime is complete upon agreement with the requisite intent; the objective does not have to be accomplished. (B) is wrong because impossibility is not a defense to conspiracy. (C) is wrong. Taking the neighbor's property could make them guilty of some other crime, but it is not necessary to convict them of conspiracy.

Answer to Question 33

(D) Common law burglary is the breaking and entering of the dwelling house of another in the nighttime with the intent to commit a felony or larceny inside the house. However, in addition to the specific intent to commit a felony (for which insurance fraud might qualify), the defendant also must have intended to break and enter the dwelling. If Dunn reasonably believed it was Baxter's home, he would not have the intent to break and enter, as he would believe he was invited to enter the house the way he did. (A) is wrong because mistake of law generally is not a defense. (B) is wrong; opening the window, even though it was ajar, would be considered a breaking under the better view. (C) is wrong; there clearly was an entry.

Answer to Question 34

(A) Clem's best theory is that Allan negligently failed to control the conduct of his guests. A landowner has a duty to exercise reasonable care with respect to his own activities on the land and to control the conduct of others on his property so as to avoid unreasonable risk of harm to those outside the property. It was reasonably foreseeable that a large skyrocket might malfunction and cause injury or damage to the person or property of someone outside Allan's land, especially to an adjoining landowner. By failing to prevent his guest from lighting the skyrocket, Allan breached his duty to control the conduct of persons on his property so as to avoid an unreasonable risk of harm to those outside the property. This breach actually and proximately caused the damage to Clem's garage. Therefore, Clem would prevail under the theory set forth in (A). Regarding (B), it is questionable whether the setting off of fireworks constitutes an ultrahazardous activity. However, even if this is deemed to be an ultrahazardous activity, simply failing to control Bob's activities will not render Allan strictly liable for harm that results. Allan would owe an absolute duty to make safe an ultrahazardous activity in which he was actually engaged (*e.g.,* if Allan himself was setting off the fireworks or if he had organized the party with a purpose of having his guests shoot fireworks out of his backyard). However, Allan was not so engaged. At most, Allan failed to prevent someone else from shooting fireworks. For this, Allan can be held liable on a negligence basis, but not in strict liability. (C) is incorrect for two reasons. First, Clem's being invited to Allan's party does not make Clem an "invitee." A social guest is deemed to be a licensee, *i.e.,* one who enters on land with the permission of the owner or possessor for his own purpose rather than for the benefit of the owner or possessor. Second, at the time of the damage to the garage, Clem was not even on the land of Allan. Thus, Clem is neither a licensee nor an invitee; Allan's duty toward him is one of ordinary care because he is an adjoining property owner. (D) is incorrect because Allan did not violate the ordinance. The precise standard of care in a common law negligence case may be established by proving the applicability to the case of a statute providing for a criminal penalty. Where the plaintiff is in the class intended to be protected by the statute and the statute was designed to prevent the type of harm suffered by the plaintiff, violation of the statute is negligence per se in most jurisdictions, *i.e.,* plaintiff will have established a conclusive presumption of duty and breach of duty. The ordinance here at issue proscribes the sale of fireworks within the city. Allan did not engage in any transaction involving fireworks. Thus, Allan did not violate the ordinance, and negligence per se is inapplicable.

Answer to Question 35

(B) Bob probably will be able to avoid liability if he can establish that he aimed the skyrocket to avoid crashing into Clem's garage. The element of breach of duty in a negligence case requires a showing that the defendant acted unreasonably, which is a question for the trier of fact. Assuming that Bob owed a duty to avoid harm to Clem's garage, Bob will be able to argue that he did not breach that duty because he aimed the skyrocket to avoid crashing it into Clem's garage. If the facts support this argument, Bob probably will be able to avoid liability to Clem. (A) is incorrect because customary methods of conduct do not conclusively establish the standard for determining whether a defendant's conduct amounted to negligence. Although it may have been an "accepted custom" in the community to set off skyrockets on the Fourth of July, this custom may in fact present an unreasonable risk of injury to persons in the position of Clem. Thus, the argument in (A) does not enable Bob to avoid liability. (C) is incorrect because all of the direct consequences of a negligent act are viewed as proximately caused by that act. If it was reasonably foreseeable that firing the skyrocket would cause damage to Clem's garage, then Bob's conduct was negligent. If some damage to the garage from the skyrocket was foreseeable, Bob is liable for the total destruction that occurred, despite the fact that the garage would not have burned down if it were not built of highly flammable material (*i.e.,* Bob must "take his plaintiff as he finds him"). (D) is incorrect because there really is no restricted scope of liability for Allan with respect to persons outside his property. A landowner has a duty to exercise reasonable care with respect to his own activities on the land so as to avoid unreasonable risk of harm to others outside the property. Thus, Allan would be liable to Clem if Allan had fired the skyrocket and thereby created an unreasonable risk of harm to Clem's garage, resulting in damage to the garage. Bob's status as a guest on Allan's property does not excuse Bob from the duty to refrain from creating an unreasonable risk of harm to the person or property of a foreseeable plaintiff, such as Clem. Therefore, (D) presents nothing that will enable Bob to avoid liability.

Answer to Question 36

(B) Other crimes and wrongs are generally not admissible to prove that a person acted in conformity with his bad character. They are sometimes admissible to establish the identity of the accused. Other crimes are admissible on identity when they are committed in a very unique way that shows what amounts to a "signature" of the perpetrator. Theoretically, even signature crimes can be excluded if the judge determines that the probative value is substantially outweighed by prejudice. However, a crime qualifying as a signature crime is highly probative and would rarely be excluded under that theory. Therefore (B) is the most likely result. (C) and (D) are not wrong but, given the highly unique weapon, they are not as likely as (B). (A) is wrong. One other crime could not establish habit.

Answer to Question 37

(C) Shelley would be acquitted if the jury found that she was reasonable in believing that the house was abandoned. Under the terms of the statute, the actor must "willfully shut off the gas . . . to an inhabited dwelling." The requirement of an inhabited dwelling is a material element of the crime. A reasonable mistake about a material element will negate criminal liability for all crimes except strict liability offenses. This is not a strict liability offense since a mental state of willfulness is required. Thus, if Shelley reasonably believed that the house was abandoned, she made a reasonable mistake about whether it was an "inhabited dwelling," and she should be found not guilty. (A) is wrong because, as mentioned, this is not a strict liability offense; willfulness is required. (B) is not as good an answer as (C) because there is no specific amount of time that she must wait before reasonably concluding that the house has been abandoned. (B) assumes that the jury will find her actions unreasonable, but it is also possible that they will find her actions reasonable. (D) is wrong because if all the elements of the statute were present, Shelley would not be excused from criminal liability simply because the couple had been negligent in mailing the rent check.

Answer to Question 38

(C) If Sandra prevails, it will be because the court has applied the promissory estoppel exception to the Statute of Frauds. [*See* Restatement (Second) of Contracts §§129, 139] Because Sandra relied on Mildred's promise by moving in with her and caring for her, and because the monetary value of her services is difficult to determine, specific enforcement of Mildred's promise is necessary to avoid injustice. [*See* Restatement (Second) of Contracts §129, illus. 10] (D) is wrong because Sandra's performance of the oral agreement is not such as could be explained only by the existence of an oral agreement to convey the brownstone. Mildred's daughter has done nothing but assert her legal rights, and a familial relationship does not obviate the Statute of Frauds. Thus, (A) and (B) are incorrect.

Answer to Question 39

(B) An inter vivos conveyance by one joint tenant of his interest in the property severs the joint tenancy and changes it to a tenancy in common. (A) is wrong because, as discussed above, severance results in a tenancy in common. West and Brown could not hold as joint tenants because the unity of time is lacking. (C) is incorrect because a tenancy by the entirety can be created only in a husband and wife. Hines and West were not married until after the creation of the tenancy, and their marriage does not change the nature of their title to Blackacre. (D) is wrong because Hines's conveyance to Brown severed the joint tenancy.

Answer to Question 40

(C) The facts do not make out a claim for invasion of privacy in any of the four forms that invasion of privacy takes. The photograph was not an appropriation for commercial purposes because it was incidental to a legitimate news story and was not used in an advertisement. The photograph did not involve intrusion because it was taken in a public place. The news feature did not involve false light because the caption correctly identified Betty as Sonny's mother and the facts do not indicate anything else to suggest that the photograph conveyed a false impression. Finally, Betty's appearance at the police station simply was not a private fact, because it is generally agreed that anything visible in a public place may be recorded and given circulation by means of a photograph. (A) and (B) are therefore incorrect. (D) is incorrect because truth is not a defense to most invasion of privacy actions. Even for false light invasion of privacy, the fact that the caption was true does not preclude recovery if the photograph otherwise conveyed a false impression. Thus, (C) is a better choice than (D).

Answer to Question 41

(D) At common law, murder was the unlawful killing of a human being with malice aforethought. Malice aforethought could be established with any one of the following states of mind: intent to kill; intent to cause serious bodily harm; the depraved heart killing (a reckless indifference to an unjustifiably high risk to human life); or the commission of a felony. It is unlikely the defendant in (A) would be found guilty of murder. The defendant's action does not indicate the depraved heart mental state. There clearly was no intent to kill, intent to cause bodily harm, or commission of a felony. In (B), the defendant's crime would most likely be classified as voluntary manslaughter in light of the provoking event and subsequent heat of passion. It is unlikely the defendant in (C) would be guilty of murder. While the defendant's action might be classified as negligent or even reckless, it would not represent a depraved heart—reckless indifference to life state of mind. (D) represents the fact pattern where the defendant is most likely guilty of murder. Firing a gun into a house would demonstrate a reckless indifference to a high risk to human life.

Answer to Question 42

(A) Since the state statute conflicts with the terms of the federal contract, the federal contract must take precedence, pursuant to the Supremacy Clause and principles of federal immunity from state regulation. (B) is not a good answer because there are no facts indicating that the statute was enacted after the contract was formed; in fact, the problem implies that the reverse is true. (C) is not the best answer because, although it is possible that a state's regulation of the manufacture of goods might affect interstate commerce so as to invoke the commerce power, the facts of this problem do not indicate any likelihood of such a circumstance and are insufficient to be conclusive anyway. Thus, (A) is the only correct answer.

Answer to Question 43

(A) Child will prevail because a jury easily could find that a reasonable person, knowing that children frequently played in Elm Street and observing a ball roll into the street, would take reasonable care to avoid the foreseeable risk of hitting a child darting into the street. (B) is wrong because reasonable care in the circumstances could require driving at less than the speed limit. (C) raises the possibility of a contributory negligence defense. A child, however, is usually held to the standard of a reasonable child of like age, intelligence, and maturity. The facts tell us nothing about Child's intelligence and maturity, but a jury is likely to find that most children four years of age are unlikely to watch out for traffic. (C) thus is wrong because Child probably would not be considered negligent under a child standard of care. (D) is wrong because the parents' potential negligence, even if it gave rise to a contribution claim by Driver against them, would not cut off Child's claim against Driver because Driver's negligence would remain both an actual and a proximate cause of the accident—even if parental negligence was also a cause. A parent's negligence ordinarily is not imputed to a child, and no other basis appears from the fact pattern for doing so.

Answer to Question 44

(D) Pedestrian had fallen and was in "helpless peril" when Driver's car struck him. If Driver had the "last clear chance" to avoid the accident, that would override any contributory negligence on Pedestrian's part. (A) is incorrect because "danger invites rescue," and it is foreseeable that an adult would rush out to aid a child in danger. (B) is incorrect because one may be negligent even if speed limits are observed. (C) is incorrect because relatives are not the only people who may be expected to be rescuers, even though Pedestrian did not have a **duty** to rescue Child.

Answer to Question 45

(C) Because Blueacre was held in joint tenancy, all of the interest in Blueacre could only be conveyed by both of the joint tenants. The forgery of Howard's signature on the deed is ineffective to convey his interest in the property. Thus, (B) is incorrect. However, Wendy's signature on the deed will serve to convey her interest in Blueacre. (D) is therefore incorrect. This conveyance of Wendy's interest in the property terminates the joint tenancy, leaving Howard and Tim holding their interests as tenants in common. Thus, (A) is incorrect.

Answer to Question 46

(D) Where no suspect or quasi-suspect classification or fundamental rights are involved, the equal protection analysis uses the rational basis test: if the statute is rationally related to a legitimate state interest, it is valid. Since there appears to be a rational basis for the challenged legislation—protecting the environment and the citizenry from the effects of potentially permanent artificial materials—the law is valid. (A) is incorrect because it assumes that the state must use the least restrictive alternative, but that is not required except when strict scrutiny is used. There is no basis for such review under the facts of this question because there is neither a suspect classification nor a fundamental right. (B) is wrong for the same reason: under equal protection analysis, a "compelling purpose" is required only when strict scrutiny is used. Challenges to economic regulations are subjected only to a rational basis test. (C) is incorrect because whether Congress has entered the field is irrelevant to an equal protection analysis. The call of the question specifically asks for the determination of the equal protection challenge; federal preemption issues are irrelevant here.

Answer to Question 47

(D) The ranch will pass exactly as expressed by Fred in the deed. Since Diane died without children, George does not have a life estate. (A) is wrong because, absent applicability of the doctrine of destructibility of contingent remainders, merger occurs when a life estate and a vested remainder or reversion is held by the same person—not the case here because George has no life estate. Diane's interest is a life estate; thus, she has no interest to pass to George by intestate succession. (B) is therefore wrong. (C) is wrong because the Rule Against Perpetuities is not violated; the spouse's interest will vest, if at all, within a life in being plus 21 years, since Diane's spouse will be identifiable at her death.

Answer to Question 48

(C) George has a life estate, Ann has an absolutely vested remainder, and Curtis, by intestate succession, will inherit Bradley's absolutely vested remainder. The remainder to Diane's children was vested subject to open upon the birth of her first child. Since Diane cannot have any more children after her death, all members of the class are ascertained at that time and the remainder becomes indefeasibly vested. Since the grant was to Diane's "children" rather than "issue" or "descendants," there is no unborn spouse problem. (A) is wrong because Bradley's vested remainder is inheritable by Curtis. (B) is wrong because George has only a life estate—not a fee simple absolute—and Ann and Curtis have absolutely vested remainders. (D) is wrong because the class gift in the limitation "to the remainder in fee simple to Diane's children" closes upon Diane's death; no children thereafter can be born to her, which precludes the remainder's being "subject to open."

Answer to Question 49

(A) Absent consent or cession, a state retains jurisdiction over federal lands within its territory. However, Congress also retains the power to enact legislation respecting such lands, pursuant to the Property Clause. When Congress so acts, the federal legislation necessarily overrides conflicting state laws under the Supremacy Clause. Here, the laws of the state of West permit Nimrod to hunt in the state. However, under the Supremacy Clause, the federal statute overrides West's law with respect to matters involving the federal military base which is located in West. The power to raise and maintain an army and navy does not necessarily include the right to regulate certain property. Thus, (B) is wrong. The Commerce Clause could possibly be a proper basis for upholding the statute, but there is nothing in the facts indicating that Congress has exercised the commerce power in this manner. (A) is therefore a better answer. (D) is wrong because the Privileges and Immunities Clause applies to state action.

Answer to Question 50

(D) Since Thomas did not retain a right to revoke the escrow, his delivery of the deed to Kenneth completes the conveyance. Title passes to Ben automatically on Thomas's death and "relates back" to the date of delivery to Kenneth. Thus, Thomas's home was not his property at his death, and it cannot pass to Sally. Thus, (A) is incorrect. (B) is incorrect because recording is a form of protection; it is not required to convey property. (C) is incorrect because execution of the deed alone is not enough to convey title; delivery is also required for a valid conveyance.

MIXED SUBJECT SET 5
ANSWER SHEET

1. Ⓐ Ⓑ Ⓒ Ⓓ		26. Ⓐ Ⓑ Ⓒ Ⓓ	
2. Ⓐ Ⓑ Ⓒ Ⓓ		27. Ⓐ Ⓑ Ⓒ Ⓓ	
3. Ⓐ Ⓑ Ⓒ Ⓓ		28. Ⓐ Ⓑ Ⓒ Ⓓ	
4. Ⓐ Ⓑ Ⓒ Ⓓ		29. Ⓐ Ⓑ Ⓒ Ⓓ	
5. Ⓐ Ⓑ Ⓒ Ⓓ		30. Ⓐ Ⓑ Ⓒ Ⓓ	

6. Ⓐ Ⓑ Ⓒ Ⓓ		31. Ⓐ Ⓑ Ⓒ Ⓓ	
7. Ⓐ Ⓑ Ⓒ Ⓓ		32. Ⓐ Ⓑ Ⓒ Ⓓ	
8. Ⓐ Ⓑ Ⓒ Ⓓ		33. Ⓐ Ⓑ Ⓒ Ⓓ	
9. Ⓐ Ⓑ Ⓒ Ⓓ		34. Ⓐ Ⓑ Ⓒ Ⓓ	
10. Ⓐ Ⓑ Ⓒ Ⓓ		35. Ⓐ Ⓑ Ⓒ Ⓓ	

11. Ⓐ Ⓑ Ⓒ Ⓓ		36. Ⓐ Ⓑ Ⓒ Ⓓ	
12. Ⓐ Ⓑ Ⓒ Ⓓ		37. Ⓐ Ⓑ Ⓒ Ⓓ	
13. Ⓐ Ⓑ Ⓒ Ⓓ		38. Ⓐ Ⓑ Ⓒ Ⓓ	
14. Ⓐ Ⓑ Ⓒ Ⓓ		39. Ⓐ Ⓑ Ⓒ Ⓓ	
15. Ⓐ Ⓑ Ⓒ Ⓓ		40. Ⓐ Ⓑ Ⓒ Ⓓ	

16. Ⓐ Ⓑ Ⓒ Ⓓ		41. Ⓐ Ⓑ Ⓒ Ⓓ	
17. Ⓐ Ⓑ Ⓒ Ⓓ		42. Ⓐ Ⓑ Ⓒ Ⓓ	
18. Ⓐ Ⓑ Ⓒ Ⓓ		43. Ⓐ Ⓑ Ⓒ Ⓓ	
19. Ⓐ Ⓑ Ⓒ Ⓓ		44. Ⓐ Ⓑ Ⓒ Ⓓ	
20. Ⓐ Ⓑ Ⓒ Ⓓ		45. Ⓐ Ⓑ Ⓒ Ⓓ	

21. Ⓐ Ⓑ Ⓒ Ⓓ		46. Ⓐ Ⓑ Ⓒ Ⓓ	
22. Ⓐ Ⓑ Ⓒ Ⓓ		47. Ⓐ Ⓑ Ⓒ Ⓓ	
23. Ⓐ Ⓑ Ⓒ Ⓓ		48. Ⓐ Ⓑ Ⓒ Ⓓ	
24. Ⓐ Ⓑ Ⓒ Ⓓ		49. Ⓐ Ⓑ Ⓒ Ⓓ	
25. Ⓐ Ⓑ Ⓒ Ⓓ		50. Ⓐ Ⓑ Ⓒ Ⓓ	

MIXED SUBJECT QUESTIONS - SET 5

Questions 1-2 are based on the following fact situation:

Cheryl is on trial for fraud, it having been alleged that she participated in an illegal scheme in which her victims were invited to become local distributors for a supposed cosmetics manufacturer. The victims were given bonus payments, after they had made a large initial "investment," for additional distributors who they would bring to the manufacturer. Cheryl's defense is that she knew nothing of the scheme. She claims she was brought into the scheme by the purported head of the manufacturer's sales department and was just following instructions to bring additional distributors into the sales force.

1. The prosecution intends to call Darryl, who will testify that Cheryl had talked him into making an investment in a similar scheme involving household products, rather than cosmetics, five years ago. Should the trial court admit this evidence over Cheryl's objection?

   (A) No, because evidence of other acts or wrongs is not admissible to prove character and action in conformity therewith.

   (B) No, because it is irrelevant.

   (C) Yes, because it is evidence of Cheryl's character for dishonesty.

   (D) Yes, because it is evidence of Cheryl's state of mind.

2. The prosecution calls Zeke as a witness. Zeke is a former business associate of Cheryl's, and he testifies that her reputation in the community is for frequently participating in very questionable transactions, usually resulting in heavy losses for her investors. He testifies further that he thinks she is dishonest. Should the trial court admit this evidence over Cheryl's objection?

   (A) No, because the prosecution cannot initiate evidence of the accused's character.

   (B) No, because use of Zeke's opinion is improper.

   (C) Yes, because it is evidence of Cheryl's character for dishonesty.

   (D) Yes, because it is evidence of habit.

Questions 3-8 are based on the following fact situation:

In early January 2004, representatives of MacDougall Corporation, makers of the famous "MacDougall Dog" hot dog and related convenience foods sold through thousands of owned and franchised "MacDougall's" restaurants, met with representatives of Time Management, Inc. ("TM"), a firm specializing in time-and-motion studies of labor intensive industries. After extensive negotiations, it was orally agreed that TM would redesign the food production area of MacDougall's restaurants, including modification of cooking equipment, if necessary, so that, using existing MacDougall's food products, savings in labor costs through reduction in restaurant cooking staffs would result. Lawyers for MacDougall's subsequently drafted a written agreement, sent it to TM, whose lawyers modified the draft, and returned the modified draft to MacDougall's. This modified writing, signed by both parties, stated in its entirety:

> Provided that at least 2,000 work-hours per restaurant are eliminated, MacDougall Corporation will pay to TM within 90 days of installation of new food production systems at MacDougall's restaurants in Richmond a first installment of $1 million. Upon installation of new food processing systems nationwide, MacDougall Corporation will pay to TM a second and final installment of $1.5 million. Nationwide installation must be completed by January 15, 2005. Any amendments to this agreement must be in writing signed by both parties.

TM immediately began work on the restructuring of MacDougall's food processing methods. On September 5, 2004, a radical change in the layout of MacDougall's kitchen area and new personnel assignments had been designed, and TM demanded payment of the first installment payment of $1 million. MacDougall Corporation refused, but negotiations conducted between the parties resulted in an oral agreement that MacDougall's would pay $750,000 immediately and then the $1.5 million second installment as originally agreed, after nationwide installation of the new system.

The restructured food production system was installed and in operation in all Richmond MacDougall's restaurants on October 1, 2004. Subsequent audits revealed that the new system enabled MacDougall Corporation to eliminate 1,500 work-hours per restaurant, saving the corporation $90,000 in labor costs for all Richmond restaurants. The new system required that MacDougall's increase the length of the famous "MacDougall Dog" by three centimeters and that the "Mother MacDougall Hot Apple Fritters" be made in a rectangular shape rather than the traditional round form. Nationwide installation of the new system in all MacDougall's restaurants was completed on January 30, 2005. The 1,500 work-hours per restaurant savings to MacDougall Corporation was projected at $1.8 million per year. TM sent a certified letter to the chief executive officer of MacDougall Corporation requesting his certification that the new food production system was in place and operating as promised, and demanding the $1.5 million second installment. The CEO refused to so certify and refused to make any payment, noting in his reply letter that the system had not been installed by January 15, 2005, and that it did not use existing MacDougall's food products, as promised by TM.

3. Was TM entitled to payment of the first installment when it completed design work on the new system on September 5, 2004?

   (A) No, because substantial completion of installation of the system in Richmond restaurants would be a constructive condition precedent to MacDougall's duty to pay.

   (B) No, because the phrase "within 90 days of installation" would be interpreted to mean within 90 days *after* installation.

   (C) Yes, because September 5 was "within 90 days of installation" of the food processing system on October 1, 2004.

   (D) Yes, because TM had completed work on designing the new system and could expect to install it within 90 days.

4. Assume for the purposes of this question only that TM brings an action for breach of contract against MacDougall Corporation seeking as damages $1.5 million. MacDougall's attempts to introduce the testimony of its chief negotiator describing the oral agreement with TM representatives that the new food processing system would use existing MacDougall's food products. TM objects, arguing that the parol evidence rule bars admission of this testimony. Which of the following is the best argument supporting admission of the testimony?

   (A) The memorandum signed by the parties was not a complete integration of their agreement.

   (B) The parol evidence rule does not bar evidence interpreting a written agreement.

   (C) MacDougall Corporation detrimentally relied on the oral agreement in signing the memorandum.

   (D) The parol evidence rule does not exclude misrepresentations.

5. Assume for the purpose of this question only that the new food processing system

had eliminated 2,000 work-hours per restaurant when installed. Does the fact that nationwide installation was not completed until January 30, 2005, justify MacDougall Corporation's refusal to pay the second installment?

(A) No, because the agreement did not contain a liquidated damage clause providing for delay in completion.

(B) No, because neither party manifested an understanding that time was of the essence in the agreement.

(C) Yes, because nationwide installation by January 15, 2005, was an express condition of the agreement.

(D) Yes, because the doctrine of substantial performance does not apply to commercial contracts.

6. Was the oral agreement that MacDougall Corporation pay $750,000 to TM after September 5, 2004, a valid modification of the original agreement?

(A) Yes, because the Statute of Frauds does not bar subsequent oral modification of a written agreement to which it is applicable.

(B) Yes, because contracts for services may be orally modified, if consideration is present, despite the existence of a no-oral-modification clause.

(C) No, because it was not in writing.

(D) No, because it was not supported by consideration.

7. Assume for the purpose of this question only that the delay in completion of nationwide installation was not a breach by TM, that MacDougall Corporation could not rescind, and that the agreement that resulted in payment of $750,000 to TM was a valid modification of the original agreement. If TM brings an action against MacDougall Corporation for breach of contract, what will be the likely outcome?

(A) TM will recover on the contract, because it substantially performed under the agreement.

(B) TM will recover on the contract, because its services saved MacDougall's $1.8 million per year in labor costs.

(C) TM will not recover on the contract, because savings of 2,000 work-hours was an express condition that was not fulfilled.

(D) TM will not recover on the contract, because MacDougall's CEO would not certify that the new system was operating as promised.

8. Assume for the purpose of this question only that an express condition of MacDougall Corporation's duty to pay the contract price failed and that TM was in breach because it failed to complete nationwide installation of the food processing system by January 15, 2005. If TM brings an action to recover the *reasonable value* of its services, will it likely succeed?

(A) No, because failure of an express condition precedent would excuse MacDougall Corporation of its duty to pay TM.

(B) No, because a claim for reasonable value of services would be inconsistent with a claim by MacDougall Corporation against TM for breach of contract.

(C) Yes, because MacDougall Corporation continued to use the new food processing system and was aware that TM expected to be paid for its services.

(D) Yes, because MacDougall Corporation continued to use the new food processing system and would realize $1.8 million per year as a consequence of the contractual relationship between the parties.

Question 9

A federal statute provided for federal grants to cities that desired to reclaim and rebuild inner-city areas for multi-family residential housing. The city of Owenoak applied for funding to build housing and received a grant of $2.5 million. After the area was prepared for construction, however, the city council decided it would greatly benefit the inner-city dwellers if, in addition to housing, commercial property was built. Thus, the Council decided to use $1.5 million for housing and to "borrow" the remaining $1 million from the housing fund to build a commercial mall. The city resolution provided that 30% of the rental from the mall each year would go to a fund for maintenance of the housing and for funds to build additional housing. Construction had started on two high-rise residential buildings and the commercial mall when the federal court, at the request of the federal government, froze the construction accounts containing the proceeds from the grant.

In a motion by the city to release the funds, the court would most likely:

(A) Grant the motion, because the city's plan for a fund to build more residential housing substantially complies with the terms of the grant.

(B) Grant the motion, because the doctrine of preservation of state sovereignty prevents the federal government from interfering with the state's discretion in this situation.

(C) Deny the motion, because the federal government can control the expenditure of the funds since it provided the funds.

(D) Deny the motion, since the doctrine of state sovereignty has no application in this situation since the action was by the city council and not the state legislature.

Questions 10-11 are based on the following fact situation:

Jesse was a member of an extreme right-wing, paramilitary organization. While out drinking with several fellow members one evening, Jesse got into an argument with a soldier from the nearby Army base and was bested in a brief exchange of punches. Feeling humiliated, he went to a different bar and drank a considerable amount of liquor. Vowing revenge on the soldier who had beaten him, Jesse and his friends drove out to the Army base. Using infiltration tactics practiced on weekends, they surreptitiously approached what they believed to be the barracks where the soldier slept. As Jesse was climbing through the window he had jimmied, a military police officer happened by and challenged him. In a tussle with the MP, Jessie struck the MP with his own baton, killing him. Still extremely intoxicated, Jesse abandoned the idea of finding and severely beating the soldier, and staggered to a nearby armored vehicle park. Since he was a heavy equipment operator, Jesse was familiar with the operation of such vehicles, and soon was driving an armored personnel carrier through the streets of the base and then out into the city. A curious police officer followed the armored vehicle for a few blocks, then pulled alongside in an attempt to determine whether it was on official Army business. At that moment, Jesse swerved the armored personnel carrier to the left, crushing the police car as it ground to a halt. The police officer inside was killed.

The jurisdiction's statutes define murder as "the premeditated and intentional killing of another or the killing of another in the commission of robbery, rape, burglary, or arson." Manslaughter is defined as "the killing of a human being in a criminally reckless manner." Criminal recklessness is "consciously disregarding a substantial and unjustifiable risk resulting from the actor's conduct." The statutory definition of burglary is identical to the common law except that the prohibited conduct need not occur in the nighttime. The jurisdiction's statutes provide that intoxication is not a defense to a crime unless it negates an element of the offense.

10. Jesse is charged with the murder of the military police officer. At his trial on this charge, the court should instruct the jury on the issue of the defense of intoxication that:

(A) Voluntary intoxication is a defense to the crime of murder if Jesse would not have killed the MP but for the intoxication.

(B) Jesse is guilty of murder despite his intoxication only if the prosecution proves by clear and convincing evidence that Jesse acted with premeditation and intentionally.

(C) Voluntary intoxication is no defense to the crime of murder.

(D) Intoxication is a defense to the crime of burglary if it prevented Jesse from forming the intent to commit a crime inside the barracks, in which case he could only be convicted of murder upon the requisite showing of intentional action and premeditation.

11. In a separate proceeding, Jesse is tried for manslaughter in connection with the death of the city police officer. The prosecution's best reply to Jesse's defense of intoxication in the charged manslaughter is that:

(A) Whether Jesse was intoxicated is not the crucial issue; whether the manner in which he was operating the armored personnel carrier was criminally reckless is determinative.

(B) Conscious risk taking refers to Jesse's entire course of conduct, including drinking with the knowledge that he might become intoxicated and perform an act that might severely injure or kill someone.

(C) Intoxication is a defense to a crime only if the intoxication is involuntary.

(D) Intoxication is not a defense to the crime charged, because at common law manslaughter is a general intent crime.

Questions 12-13 are based on the following fact situation:

Jack, a 17-year-old high school student living at home with his parents, decided one day to try the old practical joke he had seen so many times on television and in movies where a bucket of water is balanced on a partially open door so that the next person to enter the room through that door is drenched. Knowing that his parents were giving a dinner party that evening, Jack obtained a bucket from the tool shed, filled it with ice water, and balanced it on the partially open door of the guest bedroom, knowing that his father would take the guests' coats and wraps in there and toss them on the bed. Later that evening, Walt, an invited guest of Jack's parents, mistakenly wandered into the guest bedroom in search of the bathroom. Jack's father had decided to keep all the guests' coats in the hall closet, since there were only three couples coming to dinner. As Walt opened the door to the guest bedroom, the bucket of ice water plunged down upon him, opening a four-inch cut in his scalp. Walt was rushed to the hospital, where 12 stitches were required to close the head wound.

12. In an action by Walt against Jack and his parents for personal injuries, the court should determine Jack's culpability according to:

(A) The presumption against negligence afforded to all minors.

(B) The age, experience, and intelligence of an ordinarily prudent minor in circumstances similar to Jack's.

(C) The standard applicable to adults, since Jack is nearly grown.

(D) Strict liability, since the practical joke turned out to be so dangerous.

13. Assume for the purposes of this question only that the jury believes Jack's testimony that he did not mean to hurt anyone, and did not expect anyone other than his father to enter the room where the bucket trap was set. Jack may be held liable for:

(A) Negligence only.

(B) Negligence and recklessness only.

(C) Negligence, recklessness, and battery.

(D) Battery only.

Question 14

Opal owned a large tract of land in fee simple and subdivided 100 acres into 250 lots. She obtained all the necessary governmental approvals, and between 1991 and 2003 sold 175 of the lots.

Preston, who purchased one of the lots to build a house, received a deed containing the following provision, which was in all the deeds to these 175 lots:

> It is agreed and covenanted by Opal that the property conveyed herein shall be used for a single-family dwelling only and that no structure, other than a single-family dwelling, shall be erected or maintained; further, that occupancy in any dwelling built on this property shall be by a single family for residential purposes only. This agreement is specifically made binding on the grantee and grantee's heirs, their assigns and successors.

In 2004, Opal contracted with Fun Spa to sell an additional 100 acres that she owned contiguous to these lots. As part of this agreement, Opal conveyed to Fun Spa the 75 lots she had not previously sold. Nothing in the deeds for these 75 lots restricted their use to single-family residences, and in fact, Fun Spa was planning to use all the property purchased from Opal for a resort and for multi-family dwellings.

If Preston brought suit against Opal to establish that all the original 250 lots, including the 75 she had agreed to sell to Fun Spa, had to be used only for single-family dwellings in a proper proceeding, what would be the most likely result?

(A) Opal will prevail, because the provision in the deed only binds the grantee.

(B) Opal will prevail, because the remaining 75 deeds did not contain this provision.

(C) Preston will prevail, if he can show that a common development scheme had been established for the entire subdivision.

(D) Preston will prevail, unless the evidence shows that Fun Spa was not aware of this provision at the time of its agreement with Opal.

Question 15

The Bedford City Council enacted an ordinance regarding the right to parade in the streets of Bedford. The ordinance provided that city officials should automatically issue a parade permit to any group filing the proper papers with city authorities, except in situations where a prior group had already received permission to parade on the same street at the same time on the same day. Another city ordinance prescribed fines for persons conducting a parade in the city of Bedford without a permit.

The Reverend Jim, leader of the Poor People's Association ("PPA"), filed appropriate papers with city officials to parade down Main Street in the city of Bedford at 1 p.m. on July 15. City officials checked their records and noted that they had already issued a parade permit to the Little League Baseball Supporters to conduct a parade on Main Street at 1 p.m. on July 15. The officials told Jim that he could not have a parade permit for the time and place requested and suggested that Jim select another day and/or location. Jim refused and told the city officials, "This is yet another insult to the poor from this administration. We poor people *will* march on Main Street any time we please, with or without your permits!" On July 15 at 1 p.m. both Little League and PPA assembled on Main Street and began to parade. There was much confusion. City officials asked Jim and his followers to desist, but they refused. Jim and other PPA supporters were arrested, convicted, and fined under the city ordinance.

If Jim and other convicted PPA members seek to have their convictions overturned by the federal courts, they will:

(A) Lose, because Jim should have gone to federal court to secure PPA's rights before violating the ordinance.

(B) Lose, because the Bedford ordinances are a reasonable restriction on time, place, and manner of speech and were not applied in a discriminatory manner.

(C) Lose, because the Bedford ordinances represented the will of the people as expressed through the city council.

(D) Win, because the Bedford ordinances, on their face, violate the free speech guarantees of the First Amendment.

Question 16

Which of the following would the court be *least likely* to take judicial notice of?

(A) The birthdate of the plaintiff's son is June 14, 1974.

(B) The defendant has filed 25 frivolous lawsuits in the same court in which the case is being tried.

(C) It rained in the city in which the parties reside on March 28, 1987.

(D) Independence Day is July 4, and it is a state holiday.

Question 17

Prentiss was a salesman and assistant manager of Pretty Petals, a retail florist. He was employed by Lilac, the owner of Pretty Petals. Lilac owned the land and building. A large wholesale nursery was located directly across the street from Pretty Petals. Although other effective fertilizers were available at comparable prices, Doreen, the owner of the nursery, liked to use "Chemgrow," a brand-name artificial fertilizer, to nourish her young plants and trees. She stored a large quantity of Chemgrow granules in a mountainous heap on an empty lot adjacent to the nursery office. The Chemgrow gave off fumes that caused Prentiss to suffer eye, lung, and sinus irritation. Occasionally, Prentiss's irritations became so bad that he had to take off from work and seek medical attention. After losing a few hundred dollars in wages and amassing a few hundred dollars in medical expenses, Prentiss sued Doreen for damages.

The court is likely to rule in favor of:

(A) Prentiss, because Doreen had equally effective fertilizers available at comparable prices to Chemgrow.

(B) Prentiss, because Doreen is strictly liable for injuries caused by emissions from her property.

(C) Doreen, if the selection of Chemgrow was reasonable and it was stored in a reasonable manner.

(D) Doreen, because Prentiss is merely an employee of Pretty Petals and does not own the property upon which the shop is located.

Question 18

Bruno is on trial in federal court, charged with having sold cocaine to an undercover agent. Bruno calls Flossie to the stand, and Flossie testifies that she was with Bruno in another state on the date of the alleged drug sale. Following Flossie's testimony, the prosecution seeks to introduce the record of judgment of Flossie's seven-year-old embezzlement conviction. Bruno's attorney objects.

The court should rule the record of judgment:

(A) Admissible, as going to Flossie's credibility.

(B) Admissible, provided no appeal is pending.

(C) Inadmissible, because the record is inadmissible hearsay.

(D) Inadmissible, because, for impeachment, a specific act of misconduct cannot be shown by extrinsic evidence.

Question 19

The United States entered into a treaty with Mexico whereby both countries agreed to ban hunting of the red tailed raccoon, a species of raccoon indigenous to both the United States and Mexico. The red tailed raccoon had been placed on the endangered species list of the International Wildlife Federation and other conservation groups. The raccoons tend to roam in small family groups in the semidesert lands of the western United States and northern Mexico. The raccoons freely crossed state lines and the international boundary. Laws in Texas, Arizona, and New Mexico permitted hunting of the red tailed raccoons.

After the treaty was fully ratified by the United States and Mexico, a federal court would most likely hold that the state laws permitting hunting of the raccoons are:

(A) Unconstitutional, because a treaty is the supreme law of the land.

(B) Unconstitutional, because free roaming wildlife is federal property.

(C) Constitutional, because wild animals are natural inhabitants of the state, and the federal government may not take state property without consent of the state.

(D) Constitutional, under the rights reserved to the states by the Tenth Amendment.

Question 20

Asa was an old man who had few friends and most of whose relatives had died. One day, while Asa was studying a chess problem at the senior citizens center, a young woman asked him if he would care to play a game. The woman had accompanied her grandmother to the center.

Soon the woman, whose name was Stephanie, was visiting the center regularly to play chess with Asa. They became close friends and often visited each other's homes.

Asa decided that he would like Stephanie to have his only real asset, Oldacre, the single-family residence in which he lived. He wrote a note to Stephanie dated December 25, 2003, stating, "Because you have been such a good friend to a lonely old man, I want you to have this house and land." He then went to Lawyer and had Lawyer draft a deed conveying Oldacre to Stephanie. Asa validly executed the deed and gave both the note and the executed deed to the director of the senior citizens center telling him to give them to Stephanie upon his death.

Asa continued to live at Oldacre until his death in July of 2004. A will Asa had executed in 1987 was admitted to probate shortly thereafter; the will left all of Asa's property to a cousin in another state. When Stephanie received the note and deed from the lawyer prior to the probate of Asa's estate, she promptly recorded the deed, and after probate, she brought an appropriate action to quiet her title to the property conveyed by the deed.

In that action, the court should find for:

(A) Stephanie, because the deed as delivered constituted a valid conveyance of Oldacre.

(B) Stephanie, because Asa's note to her constituted a valid conveyance of Oldacre.

(C) The cousin, because the deed conveying Oldacre to Stephanie was not recorded and thus was not effective until after Asa's death.

(D) The cousin, because the fact that Asa remained in possession of Oldacre rendered the conveyance in the deed to Stephanie ineffective.

Question 21

Under which of the following circumstances would the named defendant be *least likely* to be convicted of the charged offense?

(A) Walter, a chemical engineer, painstakingly constructs an explosive device from readily available materials and secretes it beneath the house where his ex-wife and her boyfriend are living. He waits until he is sure both have had time to get home from their jobs, and then detonates the device by remote control, totally demolishing the house. Unknown to Walter, his ex-wife and her boyfriend had impulsively decided to spend the evening at a motel downtown. Walter is charged with attempted murder.

(B) Yvette attempts to charge an expensive leather coat using a credit card that her boyfriend obtained when he stole a woman's purse. The store's electronic credit reporting system indicates the account is defunct, and the store clerk refuses to complete the transaction. Yvette is charged with attempting to obtain property by false pretenses.

(C) Hazel, seeing a well-heeled couple cross the park, decides to rob them and use the money for groceries. Hazel approaches the couple, pulls out a gun, and tells them to hand over all of their money and valuables. The couple was having an unusually bad day: they had just been mugged five minutes before and were on their way to notify the police when Hazel approached them. Consequently, they had no money or valuables. Hazel is charged with attempted robbery.

(D) Farley, a married man who believes adultery to be a felony, begins a torrid affair with Edna, his best friend's wife. Unknown to either of them, the jurisdiction they reside in has a statute that expressly makes noncriminal any sexual act between consenting adults in private. Farley is charged with attempted adultery.

Question 22

To protect the minor children living in the area, the Rock Creek Town Council enacted an ordinance that prohibited advertisements that include "a depiction of a nude person, whether male or female." Sylvester Screen owns and operates Rock Creek Video, a videotape rental shop. Screen often posts large posters to advertise movies he has available for rent. A substantial part of his business consists of the rental of "X-rated" movies. These adult tapes are kept in a separate part of the shop. In the adult tape room he hangs movie advertisements, many of them depicting nude or partially nude people. Screen does not allow minors to enter the adult tape room.

If Screen challenges the ordinance, and assuming that he has standing to sue, how will the court most likely rule?

(A) For the town, because the ordinance is a valid exercise of the town's power to protect the morals of its minor citizens.

(B) For Screen, because prohibiting the posting of the movie advertisements violates his First Amendment rights.

(C) For the town, because the posters may appeal to a minor's prurient interest in sex.

(D) For Screen, because not all nudity is obscene.

Question 23

Penelope was injured when the car she was driving was struck by a truck owned by Deeco and driven by Deeco's employee, Albert. Albert was just finishing his deliveries for Deeco when the accident occurred. At the scene of the accident, Walter, a bystander, heard Albert say, "I can't believe it . . . I shouldn't have had all those beers." Penelope sued Deeco for her injuries and asked Walter to testify at trial as to Albert's statement.

Walter's testimony should be ruled:

(A) Admissible, as a statement against interest.

(B) Admissible, as an admission of a party-opponent.

(C) Admissible, as an excited utterance.

(D) Inadmissible, as hearsay.

Question 24

Photog, a freelance professional photographer, went to Department Store to purchase some film. As he was leaving the store, he noticed that Actress, a well-known Hollywood starlet, was browsing through the women's clothing department in Department Store. Photog took a picture of Actress in the clothing department without Actress's knowledge. Several days later, Photog took the photograph to the manager of Department Store and sold him the picture, explaining that Actress had agreed that Department Store could use the photograph in an advertising campaign. The manager enlarged the photograph and hung it above the main entrance to Department Store with a caption that read, "The store where Actress shops." One month earlier, Actress had entered into a contract with Hardware Store, the terms of which provided that Hardware Store had the exclusive right to use Actress's name and likeness for advertising purposes. As a result of the photograph's appearing at Department Store, Hardware Store canceled its contract with Actress.

If Actress asserts a claim based on invasion of privacy against Department Store, will Actress prevail?

(A) Yes, because Department Store, without Actress's permission, used Actress's picture for profit.

(B) Yes, because Photog had no right to take Actress's picture.

(C) No, because Department Store believed it had permission to display Actress's picture.

(D) No, because Actress would clearly qualify as a public figure.

Questions 25-26 are based on the following fact situation:

Alice owned Red Acre, a tract of land with a one-story house on it. Alice leased Red Acre to Betty for a term of three years. Betty and her teenage son, Norm, planned to live in the house for this period. Norm was a star baseball player for the local high school team. To provide Norm with an adequate place to practice, Betty installed a fully operational batting cage in the backyard located on Red Acre. In addition to the batting cage, Betty installed an automatic pitching machine and electric lights so that Norm could practice at night. Six months after Alice leased the premises to Betty, Alice mortgaged Red Acre to State Bank to secure a loan. Betty was not notified directly of the mortgage but the mortgage was recorded. Six months before the three-year term was to end, Alice defaulted on her mortgage payments, and State Bank began foreclosure proceedings, as it was entitled to do on the terms of the mortgage. Although unaware of the mortgage proceedings, Betty knew that her lease with Alice was about to end; she therefore began to remove all of the equipment she had installed in the backyard. State Bank brought an action to enjoin the removal of the equipment, naming both Betty and Alice as defendants in the suit.

25. If the court refuses the injunction, it would be because:

(A) The circumstances reveal that the equipment was installed for Betty's (Norm's) exclusive benefit.

(B) The Statute of Frauds precludes the bank from claiming any interest in the equipment.

(C) Betty was never given direct notice of the mortgage.

(D) In the absence of a contrary agreement, a residential tenant is entitled to remove any personal property she voluntarily brings upon the premises.

26. If the equipment concerned had been installed by Alice, but the facts were otherwise unchanged, the effect of State Bank's prayer for an injunction would be that the:

(A) Likelihood of State Bank's succeeding would be lessened.

(B) Likelihood of State Bank's succeeding would be improved.

(C) Likelihood of State Bank's succeeding would be unaffected.

(D) Outcome of the litigation would depend on whether the mortgage expressly mentioned personal property located on the premises.

Questions 27-28 are based on the following fact situation:

Civil service rules, which have been on the books in the city of Charlesville for many years, provide that any member of the police department must serve a one-year probationary period before he or she will be considered a permanent employee. In fact, this rule was enacted before Charlesville had a police academy, and now a prospective police officer spends six months in the academy before being hired by the city. Ruby, a graduate of the police academy, was with the city police department for eight months when she was terminated. There were no city ordinances or state laws that required that Ruby be given a reason for the termination or a hearing, and she was given neither.

27. Ruby brought suit against the city in the state court because of the termination of her employment. Which of the following would most likely give Ruby a constitutional basis to force the city to give her a statement of reasons for the termination of her employment and an opportunity for a hearing?

(A) No police officer had ever been terminated during probation except where there was actual cause.

(B) The six months she spent in the academy must be considered as part of her probation period.

(C) The budget of the police department was recently increased to allow for the hiring of additional officers.

(D) She was the only female police officer on probation and the only officer not given permanent employment.

28. Which of the following facts, if shown, gives the city of Charlesville the strongest argument for refusing to give Ruby a statement of reasons why her employment was terminated and for denying her the opportunity to contest the termination?

(A) Ruby, as a female, did not perform as a police officer as well as her male counterparts.

(B) Ruby had failed to include in her application the fact that during college she was a member of a radical student organization.

(C) Ruby had not been granted permanent employment status.

(D) Ruby had graduated in last place in her class at the police academy.

Questions 29-30 are based on the following fact situation:

While it was parked on a side street, Driver's car was severely damaged by a hit-and-run accident. While the car was being repaired, Driver arranged to borrow a car from his friend, Lender, to drive until Driver's car was finished. Lender had an extra car that had not been driven for some time, which he gladly allowed Driver to use. However, when Driver picked up the car, Lender forgot to warn Driver that the brake fluid had a tendency to leak out of the brake system and needed to be replaced regularly. Lender telephoned Driver's wife, Rider, and warned her about the brake fluid problem. Rider, however, forgot to tell Driver. Shortly thereafter, Driver was driving Rider to work in the borrowed car. Driver was proceeding along at a reasonable rate of speed and within the posted speed limit. As he approached an intersection, another car, driven by Reckless, ran through the red light and into the intersection. Driver, upon seeing Reckless's car, stepped on the brakes, but the brakes failed and the two cars collided. If the proper amount of brake fluid had been in the brake system, Driver could have stopped in time to avoid the collision. Driver and Rider were injured. The jurisdiction has adopted "pure" comparative negligence.

29. If Driver asserts a claim against Reckless, Driver will:

   (A) Recover only a portion of his damages, because Rider was also at fault.

   (B) Recover the full amount of his damages, because Driver himself was not at fault.

   (C) Not recover, because Driver had the last clear chance to avoid the accident.

   (D) Not recover, because Rider was negligent in not telling Driver about the defective brake condition, and Rider's negligence would be imputed to driver.

30. If Rider asserts a claim against Reckless, Rider will:

   (A) Recover in full for her injury, because Driver, who was driving the car in which she was riding, was not himself at fault.

   (B) Recover a portion of her damages, based on the respective degrees of her negligence and that of Reckless.

   (C) Not recover, because Driver had the last clear chance to avoid the accident.

   (D) Not recover, because Rider was primarily at fault for the collision.

Questions 31-33 are based on the following fact situation:

Joey escaped from prison and stole a car. He picked up a young woman hitchhiker, Jenny, and told her what he had done. Jenny was emotionally disturbed and of borderline mental retardation, but understood that the police were after Joey, and because she hated the police, she told Joey she would do anything she could to help him. To avoid the police, they drove to the mountains with Jenny doing much of the driving.

The following day, they were both very hungry. Toward evening, Joey saw Fisher camped by a stream nearby, and told Jenny, "Go down there and steal some food from his ice chest; he'll never even see you, but if he does, hit him with something heavy." When she hesitated, Joey became angry and said, "Go on, or I'll just leave you here to starve!" Jenny went down to Fisher's campsite, and had just grabbed a sandwich out of his ice chest and taken a bite out of it, when Fisher, who was 6'6" tall and weighed 250 pounds, ran back from the stream and grabbed her arm. Jenny was terrified and picked up a heavy frying pan and hit Fisher on the head; he slumped to the ground apparently dead. Joey then ran up and said, "He's dead. We'd better put him in the stream so it will look like he drowned after slipping and falling." They thereupon put Fisher in the stream without attempting to determine if he was alive or dead. Later, a medical examination showed conclusively that the blow only knocked Fisher out; he died of suffocation due to water in the lungs.

31. With respect to the stolen car, at common law, Jenny is:

   (A) Liable as a co-conspirator to car theft.

   (B) Liable as an accessory after the fact to car theft.

   (C) Liable for compounding a felony.

   (D) Not liable for any common law crime.

32. If Jenny is charged with petit theft of Fisher's food, a misdemeanor, the court should rule that:

   (A) Jenny is not guilty because she was acting under the direction of Joey.

(B) Jenny is guilty because an otherwise criminal act cannot be justified by threats of starvation.

(C) Jenny is not guilty because there was no "carrying away" of Fisher's food, and hence no completed theft crime was committed.

(D) Jenny is not guilty if a reasonable person would have regarded the theft as essential to avoid starvation.

33. Assume for purposes of this question only that Joey is charged with causing the death of Fisher. If the jury believes his story that he thought Fisher was already dead before he and Jenny put the body in the stream, although he had made no effort to determine if Fisher was alive, the killing was:

(A) Excusable homicide.

(B) Voluntary manslaughter.

(C) Involuntary manslaughter.

(D) Murder, if the jury finds that a reasonable person would have determined whether Fisher was alive.

Question 34

In which of the following situations would Defendant's claim of intoxication most likely result in a finding of not guilty?

(A) Defendant is charged with battery after wounding Hal by shooting him. Defendant claims that he was too drunk to realize that anyone was in the house into which he shot.

(B) Defendant is charged with manslaughter when he hit and killed a child while riding his motorcycle. Defendant claims that he was so drunk he did not see the child in time to avoid hitting her.

(C) Defendant is charged with larceny. Defendant claims that when he took the car he was too drunk to realize that it was not his.

(D) Defendant is charged with involuntary manslaughter after her unsupervised four-year-old child was killed in a fire at their home. Defendant claims that she was at the corner bar, drunk, when the fire occurred.

Question 35

Mom, a wealthy woman, wished to buy her son Sylvester an expensive Rolls-Royce for a wedding present. She visited Dealership, a Rolls-Royce dealer, several times, looked at many cars, and discussed possible sales prices with Huck, a salesman. On May 15, after much discussion, Huck and Mom signed a writing that stated, "If we can agree on price on or before June 1, Mom agrees to buy and Huck, for Dealership, agrees to sell one yellow Rolls-Royce Silver Streak, serial number XO857623." On May 20, Mom dispatched a letter to Huck stating, "I will buy the Rolls-Royce for $150,000." On the same day, Huck dispatched a letter to Mom, stating, "I will sell the Rolls-Royce for $150,000."

Has a valid contract been formed between Dealership and Mom?

(A) Yes, because the May 15 writing constitutes a contract with a missing price term, and that term was filled by the crossing offers.

(B) Yes, because when two crossing offers are identical in import, one will be treated as an offer and the other as an acceptance.

(C) No, because there were two crossing offers and no acceptance; hence there was no mutual assent.

(D) No, but the result would be different if Mom were a merchant.

Question 36

The legislature of State Yellow passed a "Fairness in Elections" statute. A major provision of the statute stated that "no newspaper in this state shall publish a political endorsement or an editorial favoring one political candidate or party over another on either the day of election or the day preceding the day of election." The stated purpose for the legislation was to prevent unfair attacks on candidates and to ensure that they would have time to respond to or rebut any published article prior to the election. The *Yellow Press* was the leading newspaper published in State Yellow. It had a high reputation regionally and was also distributed in states bordering on Yellow. The *Yellow Press* filed suit in federal court seeking to enjoin enforcement of the statute.

The newspaper's best argument for the invalidity of the statute is which of the following?

(A) The statute unduly burdens interstate commerce, because the *Yellow Press* is circulated in other states.

(B) The statute unduly interferes with the *Yellow Press*'s property interest in distributing newspapers.

(C) The statute unduly restricts the *Yellow Press*'s freedom of speech.

(D) The statute violates the Equal Protection Clause, because restrictions are imposed merely on the basis of the day the newspaper is printed, while the same material can be printed on other days.

Question 37

Moms operated a corner drugstore. One afternoon she heard a screeching of brakes and Moms immediately rushed out of the store. She saw a car speeding off into the distance and found a badly injured Victor lying in the street. Victor gasped to Moms, "I'm going to die. The car that hit me had license number DD666!" Victor then lapsed into unconsciousness. Moms gave her information to the police, including a description of the car and Victor's comment on the license plate. Police traced the registration to Dick Devilish. Victor recovered from his injuries but now suffers permanent disabilities. Victor filed suit against Devilish for his injuries. At the trial, Victor wants to have Moms testify as to Victor's statement regarding Devilish's license number.

The court should rule that such testimony by Moms is:

(A) Inadmissible, because it is more prejudicial than probative.

(B) Inadmissible, because it is hearsay not within any recognized exception to the hearsay rule.

(C) Admissible, as a declaration made in belief of impending death.

(D) Admissible, as an excited utterance.

Question 38

Mary boarded a city bus. The bus prominently displayed a sign stating "No Smoking. Violators Will Be Prosecuted." Mary was tired after a long day at work, and deciding that she could not wait until she got home, she lit a cigarette. The bus driver shouted, "Read the sign, lady; put that out or get off my bus!" Mary told the bus driver, "I've had a rough day; you can go to hell," and walked to the back of the bus and took a seat. The bus driver flagged down a passing police officer and told him that Mary was smoking on the bus (which was the misdemeanor of "disorderly conduct"). Mary, meanwhile, quickly extinguished the cigarette and put the butt in her purse so that by the time the police officer had boarded the bus, she was sitting there innocently chewing a breath mint. The officer told Mary that she was charged with disorderly conduct, and then he searched her purse and the coat that she was carrying. The officer found not only the recently extinguished cigarette butt, but also a marijuana cigarette in the coat pocket. Mary was then charged with possession of a controlled substance.

At Mary's trial for possession, should the marijuana cigarette be admitted over Mary's objection?

(A) Yes, because it was obtained in a search incident to a valid arrest.

(B) Yes, because the coat was within Mary's "wingspan" or reach.

(C) No, because the arrest was invalid.

(D) No, because the police officer did not give Mary *Miranda* warnings.

Question 39

Shelley and Herman decided to get married. Both were in their final year of high school; Shelley was one month short of her 18th birthday, and Herman was 19. They went to a local jeweler and looked at gold wedding bands, but saw nothing that appealed to them. When they discovered that the jeweler was himself a goldsmith and could make rings to order, they described what they were interested in and signed a purchase order for two rings; a woman's band for $500 and a man's for $650.

Three weeks later, the jeweler called Shelley and informed her that the rings were ready. In the meantime, she and Herman had broken up and Herman had enlisted in the Marines and been sent to another state for training. The day after her 18th birthday, Shelley went to the jeweler and told him that they would not be needing the rings. When he protested that they were custom-made and would probably not sell to anyone else, Shelley said, "All right, I've got $400 in my savings account. I'll take my ring, but you'll have to find Herman about the other one." The jeweler had Shelley sign another purchase order for the woman's band at $400, payment to be made by the end of the month.

When the jeweler did not hear from Shelley after another month, he brought an action for breach of contract against her. Evidence produced at trial established that the market value of the rings was $500 and $650 for the woman's and man's, respectively, and that the age of majority in the jurisdiction was 18.

Is the jeweler entitled to recover against Shelley?

(A) Yes, in the amount of $1,150.

(B) Yes, in the amount of $500.

(C) Yes, in the amount of $400.

(D) No.

Question 40

Lynn entered into an enforceable written agreement to sell her home to Werner for $150,000. The agreement provided that escrow would close on March 31, and on that date Lynn would provide good and marketable title to the house, free and clear of all encumbrances. On March 10, Lynn was notified by her insurance company that she had to renew her insurance policy by March 15. Lynn immediately notified the company that she did not want the insurance renewed at that time. Consequently, when the house was destroyed by fire on March 25, it was uninsured.

On March 31, Werner refused to close and Lynn immediately brought an action against him for specific performance. In this jurisdiction, which has no applicable statute to govern this situation, the most probable result of this action would be:

(A) Werner prevails, because an implied term of all conveyances is that the property at the time of closing will be in substantially the same condition as it was at the time the contract was entered into.

(B) Werner prevails, because as the house was destroyed, Lynn would have nothing to "sell" and, therefore, could not convey marketable title.

(C) Lynn prevails, because under the doctrine of equitable conversion, the risk of loss was on Werner.

(D) Lynn prevails, but since the house was destroyed, she is only entitled to recover the fair market value of the land itself.

Questions 41-42 are based on the following fact situation:

Donald is being tried for the murder of Vincent, which occurred during the burglary of Vincent's house.

41. In its case-in-chief, the prosecution seeks to offer evidence that Donald, who was arrested several days after the crime, had been caught with 50 grams of cocaine in his car. This evidence will most likely be:

    (A) Inadmissible, because Donald has not offered evidence of good character.

    (B) Inadmissible, because it has limited probative value and is unduly prejudicial.

    (C) Admissible, because it tends to show what Donald did with the money he stole.

    (D) Admissible, because it tends to show that Donald is capable of committing serious crimes.

42. Wilson, who knew Donald, is called to testify that on the day after the robbery he saw Donald buying some groceries, and when Donald removed a large roll of money, Wilson had asked, "You didn't steal that from someone, did you?" Donald nodded. This evidence is:

    (A) Admissible, as an excited utterance.

    (B) Admissible, because it is not hearsay.

    (C) Inadmissible, because it is hearsay not within any exception.

    (D) Inadmissible, because Donald had no reason to respond to this statement.

Question 43

The state police of New Lancashire wished to infiltrate the Aryan Consciousness Movement ("ACM"), a racist organization devoted to the goal of creating an "All White America." The New Lancashire police decided to create a new undercover position for the person who would infiltrate the ACM. The pay was substantially better than the salary of ordinary officers. Dimer, the chief personnel officer of the New Lancashire State Police, put out a memo inviting all white New Lancashire police officers to apply for the undercover position. Pendergrass had been a New Lancashire State Police officer for eight years and had received many citations for efficiency, bravery, and public service. However, Pendergrass is black, and Dimer refused to even accept his application for the undercover position, even though Pendergrass told Dimer that he was very desirous of obtaining the position.

If Pendergrass sues to require Dimer to give serious consideration to his application, should the court rule that Dimer has acted in a manner in accordance with the principles of the United States Constitution?

(A) Yes, because the state has a rational basis for using race as a qualification for the job.

(B) Yes, because the state has a compelling interest in infiltrating ACM, to promote the general welfare of its citizens.

(C) No, because Dimer's actions were discriminatory per se.

(D) No, if there is a chance that Pendergrass might be able to win the confidence of ACM leaders.

Questions 44-45 are based on the following fact situation:

Baker had a contract with City to supply City with five computers a month for seven months. At the start of the fourth month, Baker realized that his supply of computers had dwindled to one. Baker called his normal supplier of computers but was informed that the supplier was out of computers. Baker immediately sent a fax to Stevens explaining the situation and asking for "a price quote for 20 computers to be delivered before the first of next month." Stevens responded by fax: "I can deliver 20 computers from my present stock at a cost of $2,000 per computer." Baker responded the next day with a fax that stated: "I will buy 20 computers at a cost of $2,000 per computer."

44. Assume no further communications between the parties. At this point has a contract been formed?

   (A) Yes, because Baker's fax ordering the computers was an acceptance of Stevens's offer.

   (B) Yes, because Stevens's fax was an acceptance of the offer in Baker's first fax.

   (C) No, because the fax sent by Baker was an offer that was never accepted by Stevens.

   (D) No, because none of the communications were worded in such a way as to be definite and certain enough to be offers.

45. Assume for the purpose of this question only that a contract exists between the parties for the sale of the 20 computers. The payment provisions are $20,000 upon acceptance of the contract, $10,000 upon delivery of the computers, and $10,000 when Baker receives his last payment from City. City defaults on its payments to Baker. Is Baker liable for the last payment of $10,000 to Stevens?

   (A) Yes, because the provisions only set a reasonable time for payment.

   (B) Yes, because a buyer may not delegate the duty of payment.

   (C) No, because an express condition for payment to Stevens has not occurred.

   (D) No, because Baker has not received sufficient funds to make the payment to Stevens.

Question 46

On January 1, 2000, Red leased Whiteacre from Blue for a period of 10 years. On January 1, 2005, the state took title to Whiteacre under proper eminent domain proceedings. Which of the following statements are correct concerning the rights of Red?

I. Red may continue to occupy Whiteacre, as eminent domain proceedings will not affect lessees.

II. Red may not continue to occupy Whiteacre, is relieved from his obligation to pay rent to Blue, and will not share in the condemnation award.

III. Red may not continue to occupy Whiteacre and is entitled to share in the condemnation award based on the value of the remaining five years, less rent that would have been paid during that period.

   (A) Only I. is correct.

   (B) Only II. is correct.

   (C) Only III. is correct.

   (D) None of the above are correct.

Question 47

The Social Security Act provided that surviving spouses and stepchildren would be denied benefits unless the decedent wage-earner spouse had been married at least nine months prior to death. Sal married her husband, who was in apparent good health, five months before his death. Sal was denied survivor benefits by the Social Security Administration. She now brings an action to compel the Social Security Administration to award her benefits.

The decision of the court should be that:

   (A) Sal should be awarded benefits, because the nine-month period is arbitrary, capricious, and without any rational justification.

   (B) Sal should be awarded benefits, because the classification is an invidious scheme and violates her rights to equal protection.

(C) Sal should not be given benefits, because the nine-month period in question is reasonably calculated to achieve a permissible governmental end.

(D) Sal should not be awarded benefits, because it would be an undue burden on the public treasury to allow all wives survivor benefits.

Question 48

Pops, owner of a street corner candy store, heard several gunshots and rushed out in the street. He found Velma lying on the sidewalk, bleeding profusely. She gasped to Pops, "I'm going to die. Danny Deft shot me." Velma lapsed into unconsciousness and died on the way to the hospital without uttering another word. Danny Deft was arrested and charged with the murder of Velma. At Deft's trial, the prosecution seeks to have Pops testify as to Velma's statement.

Such testimony should be ruled:

(A) Inadmissible, because it is more prejudicial than probative.

(B) Inadmissible, because it is hearsay not within any recognized exception to the hearsay rule.

(C) Admissible, as a declaration made in belief of impending death.

(D) Admissible, as an excited utterance.

Question 49

A construction crew for the Municipal Telephone Company was sent out to install new fiberoptic cables at a downtown intersection on a vacant lot where an old building that had been demolished had stood. The telephone workers had to dig out the old copper cables, install new sheathing, and then connect and insert the new cables. Because they ran into some portions of the old sidewalk that had been in front of the old building and that had been buried over the years, the excavating took much longer than planned,

and by the end of the day they had just finished removing the old copper cables. The foreman of the crew put up a couple of wooden barriers around the trench, which was about 12 feet deep, 6 feet wide, and 30 feet long, and posted signs on each of the barriers reading, "Open trench, do not approach."

Marcus and a few friends had been playing basketball after they got out of their seventh grade classes and passed by the excavation on their way home. Marcus could not quite make out what the signs on the barriers said in the deepening dusk, so he walked over to the nearest one and read it. His friends, who had continued walking, called for him to hurry along, and as he ran toward where they had moved ahead on the street, the soft edge of the excavation gave way and Marcus fell into the trench, severely injuring himself.

If Marcus's mother brings an action against the telephone company, what will be the probable outcome of her litigation? Assume that the jurisdiction follows traditional contributory negligence and assumption of risk rules.

(A) She will lose, because the construction foreman posted a warning notice that Marcus read and understood.

(B) She will lose, because Marcus assumed the risk of injury when, after reading the warning notice, he carelessly ran along the trench after his friends.

(C) She will win, if the trier of fact concludes that the construction crew was negligent in leaving the open trench without additional protection for passersby.

(D) She will win, because the telephone company is strictly liable for the injuries to Marcus.

Question 50

Breeze was arrested for carrying a concealed weapon in violation of his parole. The police had reason to believe that Breeze was part of a group that had been stripping automobiles and selling the stolen parts. The police interrogated Breeze continually for 10 hours. Finally, the police threatened to have Breeze's parole revoked if he did not cooperate. Fatigued from the lengthy interrogation and afraid of going back to jail, Breeze confessed to being a member of the group involved in the theft of automobile parts. Breeze gave the police the location of a friend's garage where the stolen parts were located. Based on this confession, the police obtained a search warrant to search the garage, where they discovered a large quantity of stolen automobile parts. Breeze was prosecuted for conspiracy to sell stolen automobile parts. Before trial, he moved to prevent use of the stolen parts as evidence.

The court will most likely rule that the evidence should be:

(A) Admitted, because it was obtained pursuant to a warrant.

(B) Admitted, because Breeze had no standing to object to the search of the garage.

(C) Suppressed, because the uncorroborated statements of a criminal suspect are not a sufficient basis for a warrant.

(D) Suppressed, because it is the fruit of Breeze's involuntary statements.

MIXED SUBJECT SET 5 SUBJECT GUIDE

1.	Evidence	26.	Real Property
2.	Contracts	27.	Constitutional Law
3.	Contracts	28.	Constitutional Law
4.	Contracts	29.	Torts
5.	Contracts	30.	Torts
6.	Contracts	31.	Criminal Law
7.	Contracts	32.	Criminal Law
8.	Constitutional Law	33.	Criminal Law
9.	Real Property	34.	Criminal Law
10.	Criminal Law	35.	Contracts
11.	Criminal Law	36.	Constitutional Law
12.	Torts	37.	Evidence
13.	Torts	38.	Criminal Law/Procedure
14.	Real Property	39.	Contracts
15.	Constitutional Law	40.	Real Property
16.	Evidence	41.	Evidence
17.	Torts	42.	Evidence
18.	Evidence	43.	Constitutional Law
19.	Constitutional Law	44.	Contracts
20.	Real Property	45.	Contracts
21.	Criminal Law	46.	Real Property
22.	Constitutional Law	47.	Constitutional Law
23.	Evidence	48.	Evidence
24.	Torts	49.	Torts
25.	Real Property	50.	Criminal Law/Procedure

Answer to Question 1

(D) Although evidence of other crimes, wrongs, or bad acts is not admissible to prove character and conformity therewith, it may be admissible if it is relevant to some issue other than the defendant's character or disposition to commit the crime. Here, the testimony is relevant to counter Cheryl's assertion that she lacked knowledge. (A) is therefore incorrect. (B) is incorrect because the testimony tends to make the fact that Cheryl knew about the scheme more probably true than it would have been without the testimony. (C) is incorrect because Cheryl has neither taken the stand nor introduced evidence of her good character.

Answer to Question 2

(A) The prosecution cannot initiate evidence of the defendant's bad character. The prosecution may offer such evidence only after the accused has put her character in issue by either taking the stand (placing credibility in issue) or offering evidence of her good character. Thus, (C) is incorrect. (B) is incorrect because, under the Federal Rules, character may be proven by opinion evidence. (D) is incorrect because this does not constitute a regular response to a specific set of circumstances; it is merely reputation and opinion evidence.

Answer to Question 3

(B) Within 90 days after installation is the most reasonable interpretation of the relevant contract language. The agreement is express, not constructive, on this point, and the normal situation would be that the parties expected payment to occur after installation, since a contrary interpretation would require a prediction as to when installation would be completed. Thus, (B) is correct, and (C) and (D) are incorrect. (A) is incorrect because it does not take into account the 90 days.

Answer to Question 4

(A) The memorandum does not cover the entire agreement between the parties and was thus not a complete integration. Since the writing contains no mention of the oral agreement to use existing food products, the testimony would not "interpret" it in any way. Thus, (B) is incorrect. (C) and (D) are wrong because there is no evidence that MacDougall Corporation detrimentally relied upon the oral agreement in signing the memorandum, or that TM's promise constituted a misrepresentation at the time it was made.

Answer to Question 5

(B) Generally, late performance of a contract is treated as a minor breach that gives the nonbreaching party a right to damages but does not relieve him of his duty to perform. Late performance will be considered to be material only if the nature of the contract requires timely performance (such as in "goods" contracts within the U.C.C.) or if the contract provides that time is of the essence. Nothing in the contract here states that time is of the essence, and the contract does not by its nature require timely performance (it is a "services" contract rather than a "goods" contract under the U.C.C.). (A) is incorrect because absence of a liquidated damage clause does not have a bearing on whether delay in performance is a material breach. (C) is incorrect because the completion date is stated in terms of a promise rather than as an express condition. (D) is an untrue statement; the doctrine applies to commercial contracts for services.

Answer to Question 6

(B) The parties may orally waive the contract provision limiting amendment to a writing; thus (B) is correct and (C) is incorrect. (D) is incorrect because the compromise itself is consideration for the oral agreement. (A) is incorrect because the Statute of Frauds may bar subsequent oral modification of contracts to which it is applicable, but it is not applicable to the services contract here.

Answer to Question 7

(C) The circumstances show that the requirement that MacDougall Corporation realize a savings of 2,000 work-hours per restaurant was an express condition of the contract, and TM explicitly assumed the risk of meeting this condition. Therefore, substantial performance of the contract is not sufficient, nor is the actual savings achieved, which was less than promised. Thus, (A) and (B) are wrong. (D) is wrong because certification by MacDougall's CEO was never made a condition of the contract.

Answer to Question 8

(D) TM will likely succeed because MacDougall will otherwise be unjustly enriched by getting the system without having to pay the second installment. A party who has breached a contract (and therefore cannot enforce it) can recover restitution under the modern view to prevent unjust enrichment of the other party. Hence, neither the failure of the express condition (A) nor the breach of contract claim (B) would preclude TM from recovering restitution for the reasonable value of its services. (C) is not as good a choice as (D) because all that is necessary to recover in a breached contract situation is that the other party would otherwise be unjustly enriched. Where there is no contractual relationship between the parties, the party seeking restitution in a quasi-contract action must specifically show that his expectation of being compensated is reasonable and that the benefits were conferred at the express or implied request of the defendant, but those elements are assumed when the unjust enrichment occurs in a breached contract situation. Hence, (D) states the rule in this situation more accurately than (C).

Answer to Question 9

(C) The court will likely deny the motion because Congress generally has the power to condition federal spending if Congress reasonably finds that the spending program is for the general welfare. (A) is incorrect because the federal government determines how the funds are to be expended, not the recipient. Thus, while it may be arguable that the city's plan is a better way to use the money, the fact remains that the money was given for one purpose only and it must be expended for that purpose. Hence, (B) is wrong because the federal government in this situation does have the authority to control the spending of its funds and it is not an interference with the state's sovereign powers. (D) is wrong because the doctrine of sovereignty does not just extend to the state's executive or legislative branch, but to all governmental activities and entities within the state.

Answer to Question 10

(D) Burglary requires a specific intent to commit a crime and intoxication might negate the existence of that intent. In the circumstances of the problem, Jesse could argue with some force that he did not intend to kill the MP or act with premeditation, but must account for the fact that the killing occurred in what could be characterized as a burglary, which would be murder under the statutes of the jurisdiction. Thus, if Jesse did not have the requisite intent, he did not commit burglary and so the killing does not fall under the felony murder part of the statute. Jesse can therefore be convicted only if he acted intentionally or with premeditation. (A) is incorrect because voluntary intoxication is not a defense unless it negates *intent*; (A) concerns the issue of causation. (B) is wrong because it states the wrong standard of proof—the prosecution must prove all elements of the crime beyond a reasonable doubt. (C) is wrong because voluntary intoxication may be a defense to the felony murder definition of murder.

Answer to Question 11

(B) Voluntary intoxication has historically been treated as the equivalent of recklessness for the reasons outlined in (B). (A) is wrong because intoxication *is* the crucial issue; drinking was a major part of Jesse's conscious risk taking. (C) is wrong because voluntary intoxication is a defense to some crimes. (D) is wrong; it is irrelevant what the common law definition of manslaughter is because here there is a statute defining the crime.

Answer to Question 12

(B) The general rule is that a minor's conduct is judged by the standard applicable to an ordinarily prudent minor of the same age, experience, and intelligence in similar circumstances. Thus, (A) is wrong. The fact that Jack is almost an adult does not make this rule inapplicable, but would affect the level of care to which he would be held. Therefore, (C) is wrong. (D) is a misstatement of law; strict liability does not apply.

Answer to Question 13

(C) Whether Jack possessed the requisite intent for battery is determined by the substantial certainty that a harmful or offensive contact would result from his intentional action. Even if Jack did not mean to hurt anyone, he knew that at least an offensive contact would result from putting the bucket on the door. Under the circumstances, such contact was practically inevitable, even though Jack's plans were not carried out exactly as he intended, since the "wrong" victim was struck. Under the transferred intent doctrine, Jack's intent is transferred from his father to Walt. If liable for an intentional tort, Jack would also be liable for the "lesser" torts of negligence and reckless conduct.

Answer to Question 14

(C) Since Opal had a scheme for an exclusively residential subdivision that included these lots when the sales began, a court will imply a reciprocal negative servitude limiting the remaining lots to the same use. (A) is incorrect because Opal also covenanted to restrict the lots to single-family use. (B) is incorrect, because if there is a reciprocal negative covenant, it would apply whether or not the deeds specifically contained the provision. Fun Spa's actual knowledge is not the issue; Fun Spa must have had actual notice, record notice, or, as is likely here, inquiry notice (*e.g.*, neighborhood appears to conform to common restriction). Thus, (D) is not the best answer.

Answer to Question 15

(B) The government can place reasonable restrictions on time, place, and manner of speech in public forums. It would be difficult to envision more reasonable ordinances than the ones involved here.

Therefore (B) is correct, since it states the appropriate rule. (D) is wrong, since a facial challenge requires that there be no conceivable circumstances under which the ordinance could be constitutionally applied, and that is clearly not the case here. (A) is wrong; the unconstitutionality of the ordinance could be raised for the first time as a defense in the criminal case. Under accepted principles of comity, Jim does not have to go to federal court to litigate federal constitutional claims. (C) is wrong because even if the law represents the "will of the people," it could still be unconstitutional. The Supreme Court has emphasized repeatedly that constitutional rights are neither subject to, nor can be compromised by, a "vote of the people."

Answer to Question 16

(A) A birthdate (other than that of a famous person such as George Washington) is not the type of fact that a court will recognize as true without formal presentation of evidence (*e.g.*, presentation of a certified copy of a birth certificate). Under the Federal Rules, courts may judicially notice a fact that is (i) generally known within the territorial jurisdiction of the court or (ii) capable of accurate and ready determination by resort to sources whose accuracy cannot reasonably be questioned. Records of any state or federal court may be judicially noticed; they are easily verifiable. Thus, (B) is incorrect. (C) can be determined by consulting an almanac. It is therefore a manifest fact and can properly be noticed. The grounds for judicial notice of (D) are several: it is common knowledge, it is easily verifiable by reference to a calendar, and the state holiday is subject to judicial notice as a state law.

Answer to Question 17

(C) The only basis of liability that Prentiss could use in his suit is negligence—*i.e.,* that Doreen negligently selected and stored the fertilizer. If Doreen acted reasonably in selecting and storing the fertilizer, she will prevail. (A) is wrong because Doreen would not be liable simply because other fertilizers were available. (B) is wrong because property owners are not strictly liable for all emissions from their property. There is no suggestion that the storage of the fertilizer was an ultrahazardous activity that would allow Prentiss to bring a strict liability action. (D) is wrong despite the fact that Prentiss's lack of property rights in the land would preclude him from maintaining a nuisance action; he could still maintain a negligence action as a foreseeable victim of negligent conduct. (C) is the best answer because it precludes this result.

Answer to Question 18

(A) A witness other than the accused may be impeached by (i) any felony conviction (unless the judge determines that its probative value is substantially outweighed by Rule 403 considerations) and (ii) conviction of any other crime requiring proof or admission of an act of dishonesty or false statement. [Fed. R. Evid. 609(a)] Embezzlement is both. The fact that an appeal is pending does not affect the admissibility of the conviction; thus, (B) is incorrect. The official record of judgment is always admissible proof that the judgment was entered; (C) is therefore incorrect. While the proposition in (D) is correct, it does not apply to proof of prior convictions. A prior conviction may be shown either by cross-examination of the witness or introducing a record of judgment.

Answer to Question 19

(A) A treaty is the supreme law of the land, and state statutes that conflict with ratified treaties are invalid. (B) and (C) state incorrect rules of law. The federal government may exercise its property powers to acquire control of free roaming animals on public land. The federal government does not, however, have inherent authority over or ownership of all "free roaming wildlife." A state may, in turn, assert some rights over animals within its borders. That power must, nevertheless, give way in the face of a valid exercise of federal power. (D) is wrong because a treaty, being the supreme law of the land, takes precedence over the rights reserved to the state under the Tenth Amendment.

Answer to Question 20

(A) A grantor may deliver a deed to an escrowee with instructions that it be delivered to the grantee when certain conditions (*e.g.*, death of the grantor) are met. When the conditions occur, title passes automatically to the grantee and relates back to the date of delivery to the escrowee. Thus, (D) is incorrect. (B) is not as good an answer because the facts given are insufficient to conclude that the note is a valid conveyance. To work a conveyance, the note would have to include the names of the grantor and grantee, operative words of conveyance (questionable here), a description of the land, and the grantor's signature. (C) and (D) are wrong because deeds may be effective to convey property although recorded after the grantor's death or although the grantor remains in possession after executing the deed.

Answer to Question 21

(D) To convict for attempt, the prosecutor must establish that the defendant (i) had the specific intent to commit the crime; and (ii) engaged in behavior that constituted a substantial step toward commission of the crime and was strongly corroborative of the defendant's criminal purpose. In (A), Walter could be found guilty of attempted murder. He had the specific intent to kill, and the jury could find he took a substantial step toward commission of the crime. In (B), Yvette could be found guilty of attempting to obtain property by false pretenses. She had the specific intent to commit the crime, and the jury could find she took a substantial step toward commission of it. In (C), Hazel could be found guilty of attempted robbery; she had the specific intent, and the jury could find the necessary act. In (D), Farley could not be guilty of attempt. Since the activity he was engaging in, and intending to engage in, is not illegal, he cannot be found guilty of attempt even if he thought he was engaging in criminal conduct. This is the doctrine of legal impossibility.

Answer to Question 22

(D) This ordinance is too broad. The Supreme Court has defined obscenity as a description or depiction of sexual conduct that taken as a whole, by the average person, applying contemporary community standards, appeals to the prurient interest in sex, portrays sex in a patently offensive way, and using a reasonable person standard, does not have serious literary, artistic, political, or scientific value. Thus, under this definition, not all nudity is obscene. (A) is incorrect because although the town may try to protect its minors, that purpose does not allow it to prohibit all such advertisements. The ordinance is too broad to be valid and its purpose will not save it. (B) is incorrect because if the posters fall within the Court's definition of obscenity, they could be prohibited because obscenity is not protected by the First Amendment. (C) is incorrect because the "average person" in the above definition does not include children.

Answer to Question 23

(B) Albert's statement is a vicarious admission by a party-opponent. The statement acknowledges significant consumption of alcohol, which could have contributed to the accident. Under the Federal Rules, statements by an agent concerning a matter within the scope of his agency, made during the existence of the relationship, is nonhearsay. Thus, Albert's admission of drinking is admissible against his employer, and (D) is therefore incorrect. (A) is incorrect because the statement against interest exception requires that the declarant be unavailable as a witness. The facts do not indicate that Albert is unavailable. (C) is incorrect because the excited utterance exception requires that the statement concern the immediate facts of the startling occurrence. Albert's admission of drinking does not concern the immediate facts of the accident. Moreover, (A) and (C) are hearsay exceptions, and the Federal Rules do not recognize Albert's statement as hearsay.

Answer to Question 24

(A) Where plaintiff is well-known, so that her name and likeness have commercial value, using plaintiff's name or likeness for commercial purposes without permission is an invasion of privacy. (B) is wrong. There is generally no violation of one's right of privacy when her picture is taken in a public place. (C) is wrong. In the absence of actual consent or some other recognized privilege, the appropriation is actionable. Department Store's good faith belief that consent was obtained is no defense. (D) is wrong because Actress's status as a public figure bolsters this type of invasion of privacy charge (commercial appropriation) rather than diminishes it.

Answer to Question 25

(A) Since Betty installed the equipment without any intention to benefit her landlord, the chattels have not become fixtures, and she is entitled to remove them at the end of the lease term if she repairs any damage done by the removal. (B) is wrong because the Statute of Frauds does not preclude the bank from claiming an interest in chattels that have become fixtures and thus part of the real estate, and are nonremovable. (C) is wrong since Betty's notice of the mortgage is immaterial. The mortgagee's rights are no greater than those of the landlord herself, so the same issue could arise even without any mortgage being involved in the question. (D) is wrong because personal property that a tenant attaches to the real property may become a fixture (and thus part of the real property) if the tenant intended to improve the realty.

Answer to Question 26

(B) If Alice had installed the chattels herself, clearly Betty would have no right to remove them upon termination of a lease. The bank acting under its mortgage would be entitled to treat the items as part of the real estate since it is reasonable to assume that chattels attached to realty by the owner of the real property were intended to be a permanent part of the property as fixtures. Thus, (A) and (C) are incorrect. (D) is wrong because the mortgage need not expressly mention personal property in the event that the personal property in question had been so attached to the real estate as to become fixtures.

Answer to Question 27

(A) The fact that no police officer has been terminated during probation except for cause may be enough for Ruby to show that she has a right to a hearing. Continued public employment may be a protected property interest if there is a clear practice or mutual understanding that an employee can be terminated only for "cause." If Ruby can establish this, she will be able to force the city to give her a reason for her termination and a hearing. (C) is incorrect because a general increase in police officer positions does not establish a specific right to employment for Ruby. (B) is wrong because there is nothing in the Constitution that requires that a city follow any particular method of employment practice, as long as the method chosen by a city does not violate some constitutional prohibition. The fact that the city's civil service law was not changed to reflect the additional period of time a police officer spends in the police academy does not create a right protected by the Fourteenth Amendment. (D) also states facts that could give rise to an equal protection, rather than due process, claim.

Answer to Question 28

(C) While on probation, Ruby was subject to being fired at any time. Thus, she had no right in the nature of a property right and, constitutionally, would not be entitled to a hearing. (A), (B), and (D) are all arguable reasons for terminating Ruby's employment. However, just because the city might have had a valid reason for firing her, it does not follow that, if she were otherwise entitled to a hearing, the city could forgo it. (A), in addition, is not a good argument if the standard by which Ruby was tested was an artificial standard based solely on the physical differences between men and women, having no rational relationship to the needs of the job of a police officer.

Answer to Question 29

(B) There is no evidence that Driver was negligent. Thus, he can recover the full amount of his damages regardless of the jurisdiction's adoption of comparative negligence. (A) and (D) are wrong since one spouse's negligence is ordinarily not imputed to the other. (C) is wrong because this is not the proper use of the last clear chance doctrine, which is used by plaintiffs to rebut a contributory negligence defense, not by defendants to defend a negligence claim, and is not applicable in comparative negligence jurisdictions.

Answer to Question 30

(B) Rider's negligence will proportionately reduce her recovery (even if greater than that of Reckless). (A) is incorrect because Rider's damages will be reduced by the amount of her own fault, regardless of whether Driver was negligent. (C) is incorrect because the last clear chance doctrine is used by plaintiffs to counter a contributory negligence defense, not by defendants to defend a negligence claim, and is not applicable in comparative negligence jurisdictions. (D) is incorrect because pure comparative fault allocates liability based on the percentage of a tortfeasor's fault, not on the basis of who is "primarily" at fault.

Answer to Question 31

(B) Jenny is liable as an accessory after the fact because she helped Joey to escape arrest. An accessory after the fact is one who receives, relieves, comforts, or assists another knowing that he has committed a felony, in order to help the felon escape arrest, trial, or conviction. The felony must be completed at the time the aid is rendered. Joey committed the felony of car theft. Although Jenny was emotionally disturbed and of borderline mental retardation, she understood what Joey had done and that the police were after him. Knowing these things, Jenny decided to help Joey escape the police, and she actively assisted him by doing much of the driving to the mountains to avoid the police. Thus, Jenny knowingly assisted a felon in an effort to help him escape apprehension. This conduct renders Jenny liable as an accessory after the fact. Because Jenny is liable for the common law crime of being an accessory after the fact, (D) is incorrect. (A) is incorrect because Jenny and Joey did not enter into an agreement to commit car theft. A conspiracy is a combination or agreement between two or more persons to accomplish some unlawful purpose, or to accomplish a lawful purpose by unlawful means. Conspiracy requires: (i) an agreement between two or more persons; (ii) an intent to enter into an agreement; and (iii) an intent to achieve the objective of the agreement. Each conspirator is liable for the crimes of all other conspirators if: (i) the crimes were committed in furtherance of the objectives of the conspiracy; and (ii) the crimes were a natural and probable consequence of the conspiracy. Here, there was no agreement between Jenny and Joey to accomplish the theft of the car by mutual action. Jenny did not even meet Joey until after he had stolen the car, at which time she agreed to help him escape capture. Helping Joey escape capture after the completion of the car theft does not make Jenny a co-conspirator with regard to the theft itself. (C) is incorrect because compounding a felony consists of entering into an agreement for valuable consideration not to prosecute another for a felony or to conceal the commission of a felony or the whereabouts of a felon. Although Jenny helped to conceal the whereabouts of Joey, she did so simply because of her dislike for the police. Jenny did not agree to conceal Joey's whereabouts in exchange for valuable consideration. Therefore, Jenny is not guilty of compounding a felony.

Answer to Question 32

(D) If a reasonable person would have regarded the theft as essential to avoid starvation, Jenny will be deemed to have acted under the defense of necessity. Conduct otherwise criminal is justifiable if, as a result of pressure from natural forces, the defendant reasonably believes that the conduct is necessary to avoid harm to society exceeding the harm caused by the conduct. The defense of necessity is to be contrasted with the excuse of duress, under which a person is not guilty of an offense, other than homicide, if she performs an otherwise criminal act under the threat of imminent infliction of death or great bodily harm, provided that she reasonably believes death or great bodily harm will be inflicted on herself or on a member of her immediate family if she does not perform such conduct. Here, Joey threatened to drive off and leave Jenny to starve in the mountains. Although this threat came directly from a human source, rather than from natural forces, the actual harm with which Jenny was faced emanated from the physical need for food. Because the defense of necessity requires an objective test, it is necessary that Jenny have had a reasonable belief that she had to steal the food to avoid starvation, which would have been a greater societal harm than the theft. If Jenny had such a belief, and it was reasonable, she has a valid defense of necessity and is not guilty. (B) is incorrect because an otherwise criminal act can be justified if there is a reasonable belief that such an act is necessary to avoid an even greater harm to society. Certainly, a threat of starvation would present a greater harm than that posed by the theft of Fisher's food. Consequently, a threat of starvation can justify an act that is otherwise criminal. (A) is incorrect because it implies that Jenny's conduct is excused by duress. As noted previously, Joey did not threaten Jenny with imminent death if she failed to steal the food. The threat with which Jenny was faced was one of eventual starvation if Joey left her in the mountains. Thus, it cannot be said that Joey's "direction" actually exerted any coercion or duress over Jenny. (C) is incorrect because larceny (of which petit theft is a variety) requires for asportation that the property be moved (even if only slightly) and that such movement be part of a carrying away process. Jenny moved the sandwich from Fisher's ice chest to her mouth and took a bite out of it. Although this movement may have been slight, it was certainly part of a carrying away process.

Answer to Question 33

(C) Joey's failure to determine whether Fisher was dead or alive when Joey and Jenny threw Fisher into the stream constitutes criminal negligence, and when a death is caused by criminal negligence, it is involuntary manslaughter. Criminal negligence requires a greater deviation from the reasonable person standard than is required for civil liability. The defendant must have taken a very unreasonable risk in light of the utility of his conduct, knowledge of the facts, and the nature and extent of the harm that may be caused. Joey's conduct in throwing Fisher into the stream was designed merely to disguise the fact that Fisher had been hit on the head and apparently killed by Jenny. Such conduct has no social utility. In addition, Joey was certainly aware that, if Fisher was not actually dead, throwing him into the stream would most likely result in his death by drowning. Thus, Joey acted with a sufficiently high degree of deviation from the reasonable person standard of care as to constitute criminal negligence. This negligence caused the death of Fisher. Therefore, the killing is involuntary manslaughter. (A) is incorrect because an excusable homicide is one for which there is a defense to criminal liability. Joey's commission of involuntary manslaughter means that the death of Fisher is the result of criminal homicide rather than excusable homicide. (B) is incorrect because the killing of Fisher was not intentional. An intentional killing is reduced from murder to voluntary manslaughter if the defendant committed the killing under a provocation that would arouse sudden and intense passion in an ordinary person such as to cause him to lose self-control, and there was insufficient time between the provocation and the killing for the passions of a reasonable person to cool. As noted above, Joey's act resulting in the death of Fisher was not intentional, but was rather committed as a consequence of criminal negligence. In addition, Joey was not acting under any provocation that would have reduced an intentional killing to voluntary manslaughter. For these reasons, the killing is not voluntary manslaughter. (D) is incorrect because Joey did not act with malice aforethought. Murder is the unlawful killing of a human being with malice aforethought. Malice aforethought exists if the defendant: (i) intends to kill; (ii) intends to inflict great bodily injury; (iii) is aware of an unjustifiably high risk to human life; or (iv) intends to commit a felony. It is theoretically possible that Joey could be convicted of murder based on awareness of an unjustifiably high risk to human life (depraved heart). However, a finding that Joey acted unreasonably would not establish this state of mind. When Joey threw Fisher into the stream, he was most likely acting with criminal negligence rather than with any of the states of mind that would constitute malice aforethought. Therefore, Joey is not guilty of murder.

Answer to Question 34

(C) Larceny is a specific intent crime that requires that the defendant intend to permanently deprive the owner of his property. If Defendant can show that he really believed the car to be his own, there is no intent to deprive the owner of his property, and, therefore, Defendant is not guilty of larceny. (A) is wrong because battery is a general intent crime that can arise out of a showing of gross negligence. Shooting at a residence is gross negligence and can support a finding of battery even if the defendant does not know that anyone is home. (B) is obviously wrong because the defendant's criminal act does not lie in the fact that he did not see the child in time, but in the fact that he was driving while intoxicated, and it was his intoxication (grossly negligent conduct) that caused him to be unable to see the child in time. (D) is an interesting problem. The defendant in this case was drunk at the corner bar when the child was killed, so it cannot be determined whether this defendant was the cause of the fire. However, a parent has an obligation at common law to supervise and protect her children. Since the defendant left this child alone and unsupervised, it is possible that the defendant could be charged with involuntary manslaughter when the child was accidentally killed. The fact that she was intoxicated at the time would not be a defense to a charge of involuntary manslaughter arising out of the fact that this child was left alone.

Answer to Question 35

(C) If offers stating precisely the same terms cross in the mail, they do not give rise to a contract. An offer cannot be accepted if there is no knowledge of it. The letters sent by Mom and Huck constitute crossing offers, of which there was no acceptance. Thus, there is no contract. (B) is incorrect; it is a misstatement of the law. (A) is incorrect because, under the U.C.C., a reasonable price will be supplied by the court unless the parties have shown that they do not want a contract until they have agreed on price. Here, the May 15 writing indicates that Mom and Huck did not intend to be contractually bound until they agreed on a price. As explained above, the crossing letters do not indicate an agreement on price. (D) is an incorrect statement of the law.

Answer to Question 36

(C) The validity of a law that regulates elections is determined by a balancing test. If the law regulates "core political speech," rather than the process surrounding elections, strict scrutiny is applied (*i.e.,* the law must be narrowly tailored to achieve a compelling interest). The Supreme Court has held that a state law prohibiting campaigning on election day is invalid as applied to a newspaper editorial urging voters to vote a certain way, because the right to comment on political issues is an essential element of free speech. The State Yellow statute here at issue is similar to the law that was held invalid by the Court; thus, its enforcement should be enjoined on free speech grounds. (A) does not offer a very good argument for the paper. It is true that the regulation affects interstate commerce because the newspaper is circulated in other states. However, because the regulation does not directly burden interstate commerce (*i.e.,* it does not discriminate against interstate commerce by favoring local economic interests), the newspaper must argue that the burden on interstate commerce outweighs the promotion of legitimate local interests. Here, the local interest of promoting fair elections is quite strong, and the burden on interstate commerce is very weak. Therefore, the Commerce Clause argument is not very strong. (B) is incorrect because the statute in fact does not affect the newspaper's right to distribute the paper; it merely prohibits the paper from containing certain material on certain days. (D) would not be a good argument because the Equal Protection Clause only prohibits setting up classes to treat similar persons or groups in a dissimilar manner. Here, all similar entities (newspapers) are treated alike—none is allowed to publish political editorials the day before and the day of an election. The fact that the same material can be printed on other days does not create an equal protection problem.

Answer to Question 37

(D) Moms's proposed testimony about Victor's statement ("I'm going to die. The car that hit me had license number DD666!") is hearsay evidence. Hearsay is an out-of-court statement offered in evidence to prove the truth of the matter asserted in the statement. [Fed. R. Evid. 801(c)] Since it appears that Victor's statement is being offered to establish that the car that hit him had license number DD666, it is hearsay. Nevertheless, it is admissible under the "excited utterance" exception to the hearsay rule. Hence, (D) is correct. At first glance it might seem that the "dying declaration" exception to the hearsay rule applies as well. [*See* Fed. R. Evid. 804(b)(2)] There is no indication, however, that the declarant (Victor) is *unavailable* to testify, a prerequisite for admitting evidence under the dying declaration exception. [Fed. R. Evid. 804(a)] Victor is a party and thus would seem to be available to testify. If Victor were to testify that he had no memory as to the license number, he would be considered unavailable [Fed. R. Evid. 804(a)(3)], but there is no indication that Victor has so testified. Therefore, the dying declaration exception does not apply, and (C) is incorrect. (B) is incorrect because Moms's proposed testimony is admissible under the hearsay exception for "excited utterances." [Fed. R. Evid. 803(2)] This hearsay exception, like most, does *not* require the declarant to be unavailable as a condition for the admission of hearsay evidence. It merely requires that the hearsay statement relate to a *startling event or condition*, made while the declarant was under the *stress of excitement* caused by the event or condition. Victor's statement relates to a startling event (the car crash) that prompted the statement. Because the statement was made so soon after the crash, while Victor was badly injured, it probably constitutes an excited utterance. Moms's testimony is highly probative in establishing that Dick Devilish was driving the car that struck Victor. (A) is incorrect in asserting that Moms's testimony is inadmissible because it is more prejudicial than probative. Moms's testimony is in no sense *unfairly* prejudicial to Devilish.

Answer to Question 38

(C) There are six exceptions to the warrant requirement. The only exception applicable to this case is a search incident to a lawful arrest. However, if an arrest is unlawful, then any search incident to that arrest is also unlawful. At common law a police officer could not make a warrantless arrest for a misdemeanor unless it was committed in his presence. While it is unclear whether a warrantless arrest for a misdemeanor not committed in the officer's presence would violate the Fourth Amendment, practically all states follow the common law rule. Because Mary did not commit the misdemeanor of disorderly conduct in the presence of the officer, his arrest and accompanying search were invalid. It follows that (A) is incorrect. (B) is incorrect because it simply states the geographic scope of a search incident to a lawful arrest. (D) is incorrect because *Miranda* warnings, which protect a person's Fifth Amendment right against self-incrimination, do not generally affect seizure of evidence, and would not affect the seizure in this case.

Answer to Question 39

(C) The jeweler is entitled to recover $400 because, upon attaining the age of majority, Shelley affirmed the contract as to her ring at that price. Infants generally lack legal capacity to incur binding contractual obligations. Contracts entered into by infants are voidable at this election unless the contract is for a "necessity." On reaching majority, an infant may affirm; *i.e.,* choose to be bound by her contract. Here, at the time of entering into the contract for the two rings, Shelley was not yet 18 years old (the applicable age of majority). Because a wedding ring is not a necessity, Shelley's contract was voidable at her option. However, when Shelley went back to see the jeweler, she had reached the age of 18. At that time, she chose to be bound by the contract, although her affirmation was limited to her ring (instead of both rings), and to a lower price for her ring than that which was originally agreed upon. When a voidable promise is reaffirmed, the promise will be enforced according to the terms of the reaffirmation rather than the original obligation. Thus, Shelley is now bound by her contract, but only for the purchase of ***her*** ring at a price of $400. (D) is incorrect because it ignores the fact that, having affirmed the contract (albeit at different terms), Shelley, who is no longer an infant, is bound to the terms of the reaffirmed contract. (A) is incorrect because $1,150 reflects the purchase price of both rings as contained in the original contract. Upon reaching majority, Shelley chose not to be bound by the original contract. Similarly, (B) is incorrect because $500 reflects the purchase price of Shelley's ring as contained in the original agreement (as well as the market value of the ring). Upon reaching majority, Shelley could have refused to pay anything. She is now bound only to the contract as affirmed by her, which is for $400.

Answer to Question 40

(C) The doctrine of equitable conversion places the risk of loss on the purchaser as soon as the enforceable contract is entered into. (B) is wrong because "marketable" title does not refer to whether Lynn would be able to sell a destroyed home or not. It refers to a deed free of any possible dispute as to who is the owner of the property. (A) is wrong because the doctrine of equitable conversion applies to the risk of loss and, thus, there is no such implied term in the conveyance or contract. (D) is wrong because equitable conversion puts the risk of loss on Werner, and Lynn is entitled to receive the contract price in the specific performance action.

Answer to Question 41

(B) Other crimes and wrongdoings of a defendant are sometimes admissible to prove motive, opportunity, intent, preparation, plans, knowledge, identity, or absence of mistake [Fed. R. Evid. 404(b)], provided, however, that the probative value of the evidence is not substantially outweighed by prejudice or other Rule 403 considerations. On these facts, the probative value of possession of cocaine seems very slight and is highly prejudicial. Therefore, the evidence will probably be inadmissible. (A) is wrong. Other crime evidence is sometimes admissible to show motive, opportunity, etc., even if the defendant does not place his character in issue. Also, if the defendant offers evidence of good character, the prosecutor cannot for that reason alone offer extrinsic evidence of specific crimes. (C) is wrong. The issue is whether Donald murdered Vincent during a burglary, not what he did with the money. It is true that the evidence tends to show that Donald had money, but the probative value that he committed the crime charged would be very slight and clearly outweighed by prejudice. (D) is wrong. If the evidence were offered to prove that Donald is capable of committing serious crimes, it would be inadmissible character evidence.

Answer to Question 42

(B) The nod constitutes nonverbal conduct intended as an assertion and would thus be considered a "statement" for purposes of the hearsay rule. However, this statement constitutes an admission and hence is not hearsay under Federal Rule 801. (C) is therefore incorrect. Likewise, (A) is incorrect, because (i) an excited utterance is an exception to the hearsay rule and this is not hearsay, and (ii) even if it were hearsay, this does not constitute an excited utterance since the statement was not made during or soon after the startling event and under the stress of that event. (D) is incorrect. Donald responded to the question with a nod. If Donald had failed to respond and the prosecutor wished to introduce his silence as an adoptive admission, then it would be necessary to determine whether there was a reason to respond.

Answer to Question 43

(B) This is one of the very rare situations in which a distinction on race is likely to be upheld. The government, based on the facts, has a compelling interest in infiltrating the racist group. Due to the nature of the group, a white police officer is obviously necessary for this task. This means the action meets both elements of the strict scrutiny test: the interest is compelling and the means selected are narrowly tailored since no other nondiscriminatory action would work. The increased salary likely reflects the danger of the undercover task, and so is justifiable. (A) is incorrect because the rational basis test is never used for racial discrimination. Strict scrutiny always is employed. (C) is incorrect because even discriminatory conduct is permissible if it is necessary to achieve a compelling government interest and the means selected are narrowly tailored. (D) is incorrect because, based on the facts of the question, the group prohibits association with black persons. Thus, it is highly improbable that a black person could win the confidence of the group.

Answer to Question 44

(A) Stevens's fax will be considered an offer and Baker's second fax will be considered an acceptance of the offer. Although Baker merely asked for a price quote, Stevens's fax in response will be construed as an offer because the language and surrounding circumstances make it reasonable for Baker to expect that Stevens was willing to enter into a contract. "I can deliver 20 computers . . . [for] $2,000 per computer" coupled with the fact that Stevens knew that Baker wanted to buy 20 computers makes it reasonable for Baker to assume that Stevens was manifesting a promise, undertaking, or commitment to enter into a contract, especially since the terms were so specific here as to quantity, price, and delivery date. Baker's response was an acceptance of Stevens's offer to sell the computers. (B) is wrong because Stevens's fax was the offer, not the acceptance. Baker's initial fax could not be construed as an offer because it did not manifest present contractual intent and was not definite as to the terms. Therefore, (C) is also wrong. (D) is wrong because Stevens's fax was definite enough to be an offer. The U.C.C. does not require the same degree of formality as the common law, and so a contract was clearly formed when Baker responded with the fax.

Answer to Question 45

(A) The fact that Baker was to pay the $10,000 when he received his last payment from City would be interpreted as a provision setting the time for payment rather than the source from which the payment was to come, because the price was clearly set at $40,000 and was not expressly made conditional on City's paying Baker. Therefore, Baker could not claim that since he had not received payment from City he did not have to pay Stevens. Thus, (C) and (D) are incorrect. (B) is incorrect because it misstates the law.

Answer to Question 46

(C) I. is incorrect. The taking of land through eminent domain results in the taking of all interests in the land. II. is incorrect. It is true that Red may not continue to occupy the land and that he is free of his rent obligation, but he will share in the condemnation award. III. is correct. Since the leasehold interest is a property interest, Red has a constitutional right to compensation for the property interest taken through eminent domain. Compensation will be determined by the value of the estate, less the rent Red no longer is required to pay. Thus, (C) is correct, and (A), (B), and (D) are wrong.

Answer to Question 47

(C) Sal should not be given benefits. The Supreme Court in *Weinberger v. Salfi* (1975) held that the government does not have to show a compelling reason for denying noncontractual benefits. Sal's rights were noncontractual, and the only obligation of the government was to show that the classification of nine months served some proper governmental purpose. The Court stated that the purpose behind the requirement is to prevent sham marriages (*i.e.,* those solely to qualify for benefits). Thus, (A) and (B) are wrong. (D) is wrong. It implies that distinctions predicated on gender are appropriate in the face of a claim that more women than men would qualify for the benefits, a proposition the Court has rejected on numerous occasions.

Answer to Question 48

(C) Pops's proposed testimony about Velma's statement ("I'm going to die. Danny Deft shot me.") is hearsay evidence. Hearsay is an out-of-court statement offered in evidence to prove the truth of the matter asserted in the statement. [Fed. R. Evid. 801(c)] Since it appears that Velma's statement is being offered to establish that Danny did the shooting, it is hearsay. Nevertheless, it is admissible under the "dying declaration" exception to the hearsay rule. For a dying declaration to be admissible, two prerequisites must be met: (i) The declarant must be *unavailable* to testify. [Fed. R. Evid. 804(a)] Velma, being dead, obviously is unavailable to testify. (ii) A dying declaration can only be admitted *in certain kinds of cases*—homicide prosecutions and civil cases. [Fed. R. Evid. 804(b)(2)] This is an appropriate case, a murder prosecution. This hearsay exception further requires that the declarant's statement be made while believing her death to be *imminent*, and that the statement concern the *cause or circumstances* of what the declarant believed to be impending death. [Fed. R. Evid. 804(b)(2)] Velma believed her death was imminent. She was bleeding profusely from being shot and gasped, "I'm going to die." In addition, her statement ("Danny Deft shot me") pertained to the cause or circumstances of her death. Pops's proposed testimony might also be admissible under the hearsay exception for "excited utterances." Rule 803(2) makes admissible a hearsay statement relating to a *startling event or condition*, made while the declarant was under the stress of excitement caused by the event or condition. Certainly one could argue that Velma's statement was an excited utterance. But the question does not make clear that her statement was made while under the stress of excitement. Thus, while (D) is a plausible answer, (C) is better because Velma's statement fits so precisely within the dying declaration exception to the hearsay rule. (B) is clearly wrong because it asserts that the statement does not fit within any recognized exception to the hearsay rule. (A) is wrong. Pops's testimony obviously would be highly probative in establishing that Danny murdered Velma. (A) nonetheless asserts that the testimony should be inadmissible because it is more prejudicial than probative. This answer is incorrect because it fundamentally misconceives the concept of prejudice in the context of the Rule 403 probative value/prejudicial impact balancing test. The only kind of prejudice that can properly be balanced under this test is *unfair* prejudice. The "prejudice" surrounding the admission of Pops's testimony is not in any sense unfair; it is merely the natural result of any evidence having such *persuasive* force. In other words, it is prejudicial only in the sense that it will harm Danny's defense because it is highly probative of the fact that Danny killed Velma.

Answer to Question 49

(C) If the telephone company is found to be negligent, it will be liable despite the posting of warning notices. A finding of negligence establishes the prima facie elements of duty and breach in a negligence action. The other elements of actual cause, proximate cause, and damages are indicated by the facts. As discussed below, the telephone company's defenses to negligence will not be successful; hence, Marcus's mother will win. (A) is incorrect because Marcus appears to have been attracted to the trench by the warning sign, which was not readable from the street, and he was injured only while attempting to leave the site of the excavation. Therefore, his conduct in walking up to the sign was not contributorily negligent, nor did he knowingly and voluntarily assume any risk by reading the sign. (B) is wrong because assumption of risk requires that plaintiff know of the risk as well as voluntarily assume it. Marcus cannot be said to have known of a risk that the edge of the excavation would give way. Although knowledge may be implied where the risk is one that the average person would clearly appreciate, the court will take into account the plaintiff's age and any other relevant circumstances. It is unlikely that a court would find that an average seventh-grader would appreciate the unstable nature of the edge of the trench in the dusk. (D) is incorrect because strict liability would only be imposed if excavations were considered ultrahazardous or abnormally dangerous activities. For an activity to be ultrahazardous, it (i) must involve a risk of serious harm to persons or property, (ii) must not be capable of being performed with complete safety no matter how much care is taken, and (iii) must not be a commonly engaged-in activity in the community. Although involving a risk of serious harm, an excavation generally is not classified as an ultrahazardous activity because it can be done safely and is a fairly common activity. (Note that even if you were not sure whether courts treated excavations as ultrahazardous activities, (C) would be the better choice because the only difficult issue in a negligence action under these facts is breach of duty, and that is resolved by the additional facts in the choice.)

Answer to Question 50

(D) A statement is only considered to be voluntary if it is the product of a free and rational choice. If from the surrounding circumstances it appears that the statement was produced by either physical or mental coercion, it will not be considered to be voluntary. While it is a judgment for the court as to whether the confession would be voluntary or involuntary, the lengthy interrogation would probably result in a finding that the confession was involuntary. If the confession is determined to be involuntary, the evidence obtained as a direct result of the confession will probably be suppressed as the fruit of the poisonous tree. (A) is incorrect because evidence obtained pursuant to a warrant is inadmissible if the warrant was improperly issued. (B) is incorrect because Breeze is not basing his motion to suppress on the search of the garage but on the illegally obtained statement. (C) is incorrect because a warrant may be issued on the basis of such uncorroborated statements.